Input-Output Economics: Theory and Applications

Featuring Asian Economies

Input-Output Economics: Theory and Applications

Featuring Asian Economies

Thijs ten Raa

Tilburg University, The Netherlands

World Scientific

NEW JERSEY • LONDON • SINGAPORE • BEIJING • SHANGHAI • HONG KONG • TAIPEI • CHENNAI

Published by

World Scientific Publishing Co. Pte. Ltd.
5 Toh Tuck Link, Singapore 596224
USA office: 27 Warren Street, Suite 401-402, Hackensack, NJ 07601
UK office: 57 Shelton Street, Covent Garden, London WC2H 9HE

British Library Cataloguing-in-Publication Data
A catalogue record for this book is available from the British Library.

INPUT-OUTPUT ECONOMICS: THEORY AND APPLICATIONS
Featuring Asian Economies

ISBN-13 978-981-283-366-2
ISBN-10 981-283-366-8

Typeset by Stallion Press
Email: enquiries@stallionpress.com

Printed by FuIsland Offset Printing (S) Pte Ltd. Singapore

Contents

Part VII The Canadian Economy

Chapter 24 Competitive Pressures on Chinese ... and Migration

Chapter 25 Bilateral Trade between India and Bangladesh: A General Equilibrium Approach

Chapter 26 Competitive Pressure on the Indian Households: A General Equilibrium Approach ... 519

Index ... 529

Acknowledgments

We would like to thank the publishers and publications who granted the reprint permissions for the following papers:

PART I NATIONAL ACCOUNTS

1. Reprinted from *Nieuw Archief voor Wiskunde* 8(3), National Accounts, Planning and Prices, 375–85 (1990), with kind permission from Wiskundig Genootschap.
2. Reprinted from *Annali di Statistica*, Serie X(6), Commodity and Sector Classifications in Linked Systems of National Accounts. In: E. Giovarmini (ed.), *Social Statistics, National Accounts and Economic Analysis*, 31–6 (1995), with kind permission from ISTAT.
3. Reprinted from *Handbook of National Accounting: Use of Macro Accounts in Policy Analysis*, Studies in Methods, Series F, No. 81, Input–Output Requirements of National Accounts, 65–82, United Nations (2002), with kind permission from United Nations.

PART II ACCOUNTING OR TECHNICAL COEFFICIENTS?

4. Reprinted from *International Economic Review* 31(1), The Choice of Model in the Construction of Input–Output Coefficients Matrices, with Pieter Kop Jansen, 2, 13–27 (1990), with kind permission from Blackwell.

5. Reprinted from *Review of Economics and Statistics* 70(3), An Alternative Treatment of Secondary Products in Input–Output Analysis: Frustration, 535–38 (1988), with kind permission from MIT Press.
6. Reprinted from *Economic Systems Research* 15(4), The Construction of Input–Output Coefficients Matrices in an Axiomatic Context: Some Further Considerations, with José Rueda-Cantuche, 439–55 (2003), with kind permission from International Input–Output Association.
7. Reprinted from *Economic Systems Research* 19(1), A Generalized Expression for the Commodity and the Industry Technology Models in Input–Output Analysis, with José Rueda-Cantuche, 99–104 (2007), with kind permission from International Input–Output Association.
8. Reprinted from *Economic Systems Research* 19(4), The Extraction of Technical Coefficients from Input and Output Data, 453–59 (2007), with kind permission from International Input–Output Association.

PART III NEOCLASSICAL AND CLASSICAL CONNECTIONS

9. Reprinted from *Regional Science and Urban Economics* 24(1), On the Methodology of Input–Output Analysis, 3–25 (1994), with kind permission from Elsevier.
10. Reprinted from *Regional Science and Urban Economics* 24(1), Neoclassical Input–Output Analysis, with Pierre Mohnen, 135–58 (1994), with kind permission from Elsevier.
11. Reprinted from *Journal of Economic Theory* 66(2), The Substitution Theorem, 632–36 (1995), with kind permission from Elsevier.
12. Reprinted from *Prices, Growth and Cycles*, Bródy's capital, A. Simonovits and A. Steenge (eds.), 218–23 (1997), with kind permission from Palgrave Macmillan.

PART IV DYNAMIC INPUT–OUTPUT ANALYSIS

13. Reprinted from *Review of Economics and Statistics* 68(2), Dynamic Input–Output Analysis with Distributed Activities, 300–10 (1986), with kind permission from MIT Press.
14. Reprinted from *European Economic Review* 30(4), Applied Dynamic Input–Output with Distributed Activities, 805–31 (1986), with kind permission from Elsevier.

15. Reprinted from *Economic Systems Research* 1(1), Working Capital in an Input–Output Model, with Debesh Chakraborty and Tuhin Das, 53–68 (1989), with kind permission from International Input–Output Association.

PART V STOCHASTIC INPUT–OUTPUT ANALYSIS

16. Reprinted from *Review of Income and Wealth* 43(4), Primary Versus Secondary Production Techniques in U.S. Manufacturing, with Joe Mattey, 449–64 (1997), with kind permission from Blackwell.
17. Reprinted from *Review of Income and Wealth* 53(2), Stochastic Analysis of Input–Output Multipliers on the Basis of Use and Make Tables, with José Rueda-Cantuche, 318–34 (2007), with kind permission from Blackwell.

PART VI PERFORMANCE ANALYSIS

18. Reprinted (slightly revised) from *Essays in Honor of Wassily Leontief* E. Dietzenbacher and M. Lahr (eds.), A Neoclassical Analysis of TFP Using Input–Output Prices, (2003), with kind permission from Cambridge University Press.
19. Reprinted from *Journal of Productivity Analysis* 18(2), Neoclassical Growth Accounting and Frontier Analysis: A Synthesis, with Pierre Mohnen, 111–28 (2002), with kind permission from Kluwer Academic Plenum Publishers.
20. Reprinted from *Journal of Economic Behavior and Organization* 65(3–4), Competition and Performance: The Different Roles of Capital and Labor, with Pierre Mohnen, 573–84 (2008), with kind permission from Elsevier.

PART VII THE CANADIAN ECONOMY

21. Reprinted from *Structural Change and Economic Dynamics* 11(4), A General Equilibrium Analysis of the Evolution of Canadian Service Productivity, with Pierre Mohnen, 491–506 (2000), with kind permission from Elsevier.
22. Reprinted from *The Growth of Service Industries, The Paradox of Exploding Costs and Persistent Demand*, Th. ten Raa and R. Schettkat

(eds.), Productivity Trends and Employment Across Industries in Canada, with Pierre Mohnen, 105–18 (2001), with kind permission from Edward Elgar.

23. Reprinted from *Economic Systems Research* 13(1), The Location of Comparative Advantages on the Basis of Fundamentals Only, with Pierre Mohnen, 93–108 (2001), with kind permission from International Input–Output Association.

PART VIII ASIAN ECONOMIES

24. Reprinted from *Regional Science and Urban Economics* 35(6), Competitive Pressures on China: Income Inequality and Migration, with Haoran Pan, 671–99 (2005), with kind permission from Elsevier.
25. Reprinted from *Economic Systems Research* 18(3), Bilateral Trade between India and Bangladesh: A General Equilibrium Approach, with Chandrima Sikdar, Pierre Mohnen and Debesh Chakraborty, 257–79 (2006), with kind permission from International Input–Output Association.
26. Reprinted from *Economic Systems Research* 19(1), Competitive Pressure on the Indian Households: A General Equilibrium Approach, with Amar Sahoo, 57–71 (2007), with kind permission from International Input–Output Association.

Introduction

Input–output analysis is an important quantitative economic technique that shows the interdependencies between the various branches of a national economy and even between the various branches of different, possibly competing economies. It has been invented by Wassily Leontief, who received the Nobel Prize for this contribution. Perhaps the main contribution of input–output analysis is that it facilitates a consistent picture of the economic system. The input–output accounts of an economy are the core of the national accounts. The so-called System of National Accounts has been designed by Richard Stone and is now the world-wide standard, authorized by the United Nations. Stone was a keen student of input–output analysis and used it as point of departure. In the old days, students of economics had to learn national accounting, but it went out of fashion, and nowadays many economists feel uncomfortable when confronted with national economies. Imagine that you are dispatched on a mission to a developing economy with the task to report on its performance and to suggest policies for improvement. It would be extremely useful, if not necessary, to comprehend the System of National Accounts, particularly its input–output core, and its connection with applied economic models.

Much like the length of ladies skirts, economic fashion changes in a cyclical manner. Like the miniskirt, input–output analysis is back. I can think of an array of reasons to explain this resurgence. First and foremost, unlike mainstream Western economic models, input–output analysis transcends free market economies. In fact, many economists think input–output is a tool for planned economies, but it transcends that as well. One of the fascinating recent applications of input–output analysis is the measurement of market power, the distance from the free market competitive benchmark, and the investigation if such a departure is good or bad. Ultimately, these are empirical issues and their resolution demands a solid quantitative framework. This book provides it. A second, related reason of the resurgence of input–output analysis is globalization, including international trade and environmental impacts. The traditional approach to international trade is that economies specialize according to their comparative advantages and that the latter are determined by the relative abundance of their resources. Nowadays, at least as much prominence is ascribed to technological advantages and it takes input–output analysis to expose that driver of international trade. A third reason of the recent popularity of input–output analysis is a practical one. The OECD in Paris has organized and maintained a consistent international input–output database which facilitates worldwide use.

Most people get hooked on input–output economics when they see it in action. In my case, that happened in the late 70s, when I was a research assistant to Wassily Leontief at New York University and we analyzed the foreign dependence of the Unites States economy on mineral resources, which is still a hot issue. I studied the use of those inputs in steel plants with different modes of production and outputs, and had the task to construct sensible input coefficients which were subsequently used to project future import requirements. I must confess that my preference has been to probe theory and therefore, I changed my focus to an economy with better organized national accounts. The System of National Accounts was (and still is) much better organized in Canada, under the leadership of input–output economist Kishori Lal. This explains why I have studied extensively the Canadian economy independently, and with my friend and co-author Pierre Mohnen, who then worked in Montreal. The center of gravity has shifted to the Pacific Ocean and very exciting developments are taking place in Asia, particularly China and India. This is also true academically, and recently, I have been fortunate to supervise bright students from there, who were keen to analyze the transition of their economies from planning to openness and competition. Input–output is a great tool to analyze the reallocations that prompted competitive pressure. I am proud to expose these studies to a broad public. Roughly speaking, globalization is good for the standard of living, but bad for the distribution of the latter.

Since this book is fairly advanced, you may wish to consult my textbook, *The Economics of Input–Output Analysis*, published by Cambridge University Press (2005).

This book consists of eight parts. In Part I, I analyze the relationship between national accounts and economic analysis. In the first chapter, I present the textbook case of an economy with industries which produce their own specific products. This serves as an easy introduction, but in reality, industries produce overlapping varieties of products and we distinguish industry and product classifications in the second chapter. I close this part with my views on the relationship between input–output and national accounting, published by the United Nations.

In Part II, I analyze the derivation of input–output coefficients from national accounts. A key problem is how to sweep secondary products under the carpet. The first three chapters show that one procedure, the so-called commodity technology model, is attractive, but not trouble-free. The fourth chapter provides a more general framework that encompasses the main competition, the so-called industry technology model. The last chapter is very new and returns to Leontief's idea that input–output coefficients represent the production function of an industry or an economy, in which case, minimum proportions seem more relevant than the accounting based average proportions.

Part III connects input–output accounts with economic models. Perhaps surprisingly, I show that there is a close connection with mainstream economic analysis, including the substitutability of inputs in neoclassical models and the relationship between time and capital in a classical model.

Dynamic input–output models are analyzed in Part IV. The first chapter shows that the basic idea of input–output analysis still applies when an input coefficient is distributed over time. They are still multiplied with outputs to determine requirements, but the multiplication must now be the so-called convolution product. Some technical problems are resolved. The first chapter shows that although capital matrices are not invertible, the input–output model can be solved nonetheless. The second chapter applies it to the Polish economy and the third analyzes working capital.

Stochastic input–output analysis is the subject of Part V. The first chapter shows that input–output coefficients can be considered regression coefficients and tested to see if they are the same for different production units. The second chapter shows how firm data can be used to assess the precision of input–output coefficients.

Part VI is important. It shows how input–output analysis can be used to measure the performance of an economy. The concept of productivity is the key link. This should not come as a surprise, because an input–output coefficient measures input per output and productivity output per input. It all has to be connected across industries and products. The first chapter does so in a neoclassical framework. The second chapter connects neoclassical growth accounting with frontier analysis (data envelopment analysis). The third chapter investigates the difference between observed market prices and marginal productivities to get a handle on market power — the main departure from perfect competition — and to assess if it is good or bad. Input–output analysis throws light on the debate between neoclassical and Schumpeterian economists.

Part VII analyzes the Canadian economy further. The first two chapters investigate if services suffer from the Baumol productivity disease, but find them in good health. The last chapter is a much applied trade model, that shows how one can pinpoint the comparative advantage of an economy and decompose it in resource advantages and technology differences.

Part VIII is the climax of the book, addressing the difficult problem of the transition of Asian economies to competitive market economies. In this part, a firm connection between input–output analysis and income distribution measurement is established. In the first paper, Haoran Pan develops a huge input–output data base for the Chinese provinces and we use it to track the pressure of free competition on income differences, consequent migration pressures, and development. In the second paper, the impact of free trade between India and Bangladesh is projected. The last paper extends the input–output model to a Social Accounting Matrix for India and shows that globalization has a positive effect on efficiency, productivity and poverty, but an adverse effect on income distribution. All these are seemingly slippery economic issues, but this book shows how input–output analysis puts numbers on them.

There is no way I could have achieved this by myself and I am grateful to my co-authors. First and foremost, I thank Pierre Mohnen, who co-authored a quarter of the chapters. Our prolific collaboration dates back to the period when we were Ph.D. students at New York University, and is a constant source of satisfaction. José Rueda-Cantuche, whose Ph.D. work I supervised at Universidad Pablo de Olavide, Seville, has become one of the movers and shakers in the input–output world, and I enjoy our collaboration. I am grateful to my Tilburg students, Pieter Kop Jansen, Haoran Pan and Amar Sahoo, for the beautiful joint work. I thank Joe Mattey for our early work in stochastic input–output analysis. I am grateful to Jan van Tongeren for input, particularly on chapter 3. Last, but not least, I thank co-authors Debesh Chakraborty, Tuhin Das and Chandrima Sikdar, who were all with Jadavpur University. I dedicate this book to the memory of Wassily Leontief. His total independence of thinking is an enduring flame.

[illegible] Ph.D. [illegible] Tianjin [illegible] Chen [illegible] students [illegible] for discussions [illegible] this book to the memory of [illegible] for independence in thinking [illegible] father.

Part I

National Accounts

Chapter 1

National Accounts, Planning and Prices

Thijs ten Raa

Abstract: Input–output analysis is the study of quantitative relations between the output levels of the various sectors of an economy, a practical tool for national accounting and planning. Neoclassical economics focusses on the pure theory of the price mechanism, equilibrating supply and demand in free market economies. This paper consolidates the two approaches. The mathematical theory of linear programming is used to establish price relations in an input–output model which match neoclassical results.

1. Introduction

Input–output analysis was invented by Wassily Leontief, who received the Nobel Prize for this achievement in 1973. Rudimentary ideas came about when Leontief (1925) thought through the problem of setting up national accounts in the Soviet Union. Input–output analysis orders national accounts in a suggestive way, which is useful for planning. Professor Leontief has contributed to the planning of the United States war economy of 1940–1945. During the cold war, input–output analysis was surrounded

The research has been made possible by a Senior Fellowship of the Royal Netherlands Academy of Arts and Sciences. I have benefited from suggestions by a referee.

with suspicion, because of its use in central planning, and became out of fashion. Neoclassical economics, the analysis of utility maximizing individuals and profit maximizing firms, whose actions are coordinated by the invisible hand of the price mechanism, became predominant and its results about the optimality of the free market have a wide impact to date.

Input–output analysis is thought to specialize in quantity relations between levels of outputs of the various sectors of an economy. It may also account for cost components, but is thought to do so in a mechanical way, independent of the levels of outputs. I refer to Leontief (1966, chapter 7). Conversely, neoclassical economics is thought to focus on the price system, with limited capability to explain or prescribe levels of outputs, particularly when production is characterized by so-called constant returns to scale.

Samuelson (1961) has shown that in a neoclassical model, input–output proportions will be fixed, if there is only one factor of production (labor, say). If there are more factors of production (labor and capital, for example), input–output analysis and neoclassical economics can still be considered two sides of one coin. Perhaps I should add a personal note to explain how I came to ponder about the connection. When I was a Ph.D. student, I was research assistant to Wassily Leontief, but my thesis advisor was William Baumol, who is notorious for his neoclassical views. However separate the two schools of thought operated, even within one and the same Department of Economics, I considered it a challenge to reconcile the two approaches. This paper attempts to render an account of my thinking. To bridge input–output analysis and neoclassical economics, I will use the mathematical theory of linear programming.

Neoclassical economics, particularly generally equilibrium analysis, is relatively close to mathematics and, therefore, determines by and large the perception of economics by mathematicians. Most other papers in this issue exemplify this approach. It is my hope that this paper narrows the gap with applied economics. The paper proceeds from the practical to the theoretical, in an admittedly uneven manner. Section 1 introduces national accounts and their use in planning. Section 2 is an excursion into some dynamic aspects. I include it to draw the attention of interested mathematicians to some matrix issues. It may be skipped. Not so Section 3, which is central. It develops an essentially competitive price theory in an input–output model of an open economy. Section 4 discusses further links with neoclassical economics.

2. National Accounts and Planning in One Lesson

Input–output analysis puts order and structure in national accounts. Historically, the order component came first. When the Soviet accounts were organized, Leontief detected some double counting. To get a feel for this, consider the following production of consumption goods from raw materials. Mining yields iron ore; it is processed by the steel industry; and manufacturing makes the final product. Now, if you would add the outputs of the three sectors to the national product, you would be accused of double counting. To understand why, stick in an imaginary sector between the steel industry and manufacturing that wraps steel. The wrapping sector purchases steel and sells wrapped steel. In the process, it would contribute the same amount to the national product as the steel industry. The problem of eliminating double counting from national accounts is nontrivial, because production is not directed as in our example, but roundabout. All sectors purchase from and sell to each other. Input–output analysis disentangles this. Moreover, it can be used to add structure to national production. By assuming that input–output ratios are constant in sectors, one can analyze the production requirements of sustaining alternative bills of final goods, such as a war effort. When the United States participated in World War II, it was so late that the government did not want to rely exclusively on the price mechanism to sustain the defense industry. Production was planned, using input–output analysis as a tool.

I need notation. Divide the economy into n production sectors, including the ones mentioned in the example. (Here n is an integer.) The first sector, mining, say, sells, per unit of time, amounts $x_{11}, \ldots, x_{1n}$ to sectors 1 through n, and y_1 to final demand, that is households, government, net exports and for investment. Table 1 organizes these data in rows and adds a row $V_1, \ldots, V_n$ which will be explained below.

Now consider a column, say the first one: $x_{11}, \ldots, x_{n1}$ are the amounts purchased by sector 1 from sectors 1 through n. Thus, sector 1 receives

Table 1: Input–Output Table.

Sales of sector 1	$x_{11} \ldots x_{1n}\ y_1$
Sales of sector n	$x_{n1} \ldots x_{nn}\ y_n$
	$V_1 \ldots V_n$

$x_{11} + \cdots + x_{1n} + y_1$ and spends $x_{11} + \cdots + x_{n1}$ on material inputs. The difference defines V_1, value added. It consists of wages, capital returns, profits and taxes. Note that if we do so for all sectors, i, and sum, we obtain

$$\sum_{i=1}^{n}[x_{i1} + \cdots + x_{in} + y_i - (x_{1i} + \cdots + x_{ni})] = \sum_{i=1}^{n} V_i.$$

On the left-hand side, all x terms cancel out, hence

$$\sum_{i=1}^{n} y_i = \sum_{i=1}^{n} V_i. \tag{1}$$

This is the well-known macro-economic identity of national product and national income. By definition, national product includes only final demand items, and national income only outlays on nonmaterial input. Double counting is avoided by the exclusion of all intermediate flows. Note, however, that the interaction between all sectors invalidates a sectoral breakdown of the equality of national product and national income. In other words, (1) does not necessarily hold term by term.

Sector 1 has material inputs $x_{11}, \ldots, x_{n1}$ and output $x_{11} + \cdots + x_{1n} + y_1$, x_1 is common shorthand for the latter sum. Dividing the inputs by the output, we obtain technical coefficients, the so-called input–output coefficients, $a_{11} = x_{11}/x_1, \ldots, a_{n1} = x_{n1}/x_1$. They constitute the recipe for the production of commodity 1. Turn to planning. We consider an alternative n-dimensional vector of final demand, $\tilde{y}$, with a greater airplane component, say. The question to be addressed is which sectoral outputs and distributions sustain the new vector of final demand. The assertion of input–output analysis is that technical coefficients are constant, constituting the structure of the economy. As Samuelson (1961) shows, constant coefficients may be an implication rather than an assumption. The new sales figure of sector i to sector j fulfills

$$\tilde{x}_{ij} = a_{ij}\tilde{x}_j, \tag{2}$$

where $\tilde{x}_j$ is the new output of sector j. It is more convenient to define the latter for sector i. Hence

$$\tilde{x}_i = \tilde{x}_{i1} + \cdots + \tilde{x}_{in} + \tilde{y}_i. \tag{3}$$

Substitution of (2) into (3) and obvious matrix notation (n-vectors $\tilde{x}$ and $\tilde{y}$ and $n \times n$-matrix A) yields

$$\tilde{x} = A\tilde{x} + \tilde{y}. \tag{4}$$

The answer to the planning problem is obtained by solving (4). Thus, the new output levels that sustain final demand $\tilde{y}$ are given by

$$\tilde{x} = (I - A)^{-1}\tilde{y} \tag{5}$$

The matrix on the right hand side is the so-called Leontief inverse of A. If in Table 1 all data are nonnegative and at least one sector is strictly 'productive', meaning that sales exceed material costs, making value added positive, then the Leontief inverse can be shown to exist and to be nonnegative. The most general conditions on A that insure existence and nonnegativity of the Leontief inverse are due to Hawkins and Simon (1949); basically they give a very explicit account of the spectral radius of A being less than unity. The distribution of outputs across sectors is given by $A\hat{\tilde{x}}$, where $\tilde{x}$ is given by (5) and $\wedge$ places it in a diagonal matrix.

Once the matrix of input–output coefficients is constructed, notation x and y need no longer be reserved for the data, and the planning problem can be summarized as follows. For any bill of final goods, y, find the vector of sectoral outputs, x, through the so-called material balance equation,

$$x = Ax + y. \tag{4'}$$

3. An Investment Aspect

There are limits to the national product. Increases of final demand, y, yield increases of sectoral outputs, x, but the latter are constrained by capacities. Consider sector 1. Define $b_{11}, \ldots, b_{n1}$ as the stocks of commodities 1 through n that must be present to accommodate the production of one unit of output, without being absorbed though. These are the so-called capital stock coefficients representing building, machinery, equipment requirements, and so on. The classification of these capital goods can be the same as that of the material inputs in sector 1, albeit that most components of $(b_{11}, \ldots, b_{n1})$ will be zero. Taking into account the other sectors, we obtain the so-called matrix of capital coefficients, B. Typically, only a few rows are nonzero. Thus, to sustain production x, the economy needs capital stocks Bx. These are quantities that must be present without being absorbed. Introduce time. From now on, let x and y be functions of time. Assuming full capacity and constant capital stock coefficients, changes of output, $\dot{x}$ (dot denoting time derivative), induce changes of capital stock requirements, $B\dot{x}$. Changes of capital stocks are called investment. So, if we limit final demand to household and government consumption, and net exports, separating out investment, the material balance becomes

$$x = Ax + B\dot{x} + y. \tag{6}$$

The dynamic planning problem consists of solving these ordinary differential equations with respect to the path of sectoral outputs, x, given a final demand path, y. Since the matrix of capital coefficients, B, is singular, some special attention must be paid. Recently, ten Raa (1986) showed that a generalized inverse of B can be used to establish a closed form solution. It is a member of the Rao class of generalized inverses, but not the Moore-Penrose one.

Definition. Let B be a square matrix of which the zero eigenvalue has a complete system of eigenvectors. A generalized inverse of B is a square matrix B^- such that $B^-B^2 = B$.

Proposition. *Let A fulfill the Hawkins-Simon (1949) conditions (amounting to nonnegativity and spectral radius less than one). Let B's zero eigenvalues have a complete system of eigenvectors. Then for every y the solution to equation (6) is*

$$x = \{\check{H}\exp[B^-(I-A)t]\} * B^-(I-A)B^-B\sum_0^\infty A^k y + (I - B^-B)\sum_0^\infty A^k y, \tag{7}$$

where $\check{H}$ is the Heavyside function on the negatives defined by $\check{H}(t) = 1$ for $t < 0$ and zero elsewhere and $*$ is the convolution product.

The operator on the right hand side is the so-called dynamic inverse of (A, B). It was first computed in a special case by Leontief (1970). The assumption on B can be dropped, see ten Raa (1986) or Chapter 13.

So far it is implicitly assumed that production is instantaneous, whereas in real life, planning involves the timing of inputs and outputs. Now time consumption in production can be modelled by replacing A and B by distributions over time and convoluting them through with x and $\dot{x}$, respectively, as ten Raa's (1986) account of the material balance shows. He also solves the consequent convolution differential equation for final demands fulfilling a so-called convolution condition.

4. Price Theory

Unfortunately, capital matrices are rarely available. Statistical offices document sales and purchases, but seldom stocks. For reasons like this, limits to the national product are usually modelled by caps on output without dynamic adjustments. Returning to the static model of Section 1, let an economy be endowed with a stock of capital K, a nonnegative scalar. For simplicity I assume that there is only one capital good, malleable across sectors. There may be other restraining factors, for example a labor force, L. Let k and l be the row vectors of capital and labor coefficients, that is the stocks of each of these factors of production employed in the various sectors per unit of the respective outputs. Then the constraints on output are

$$kx \leq K, \quad lx \leq L. \tag{8}$$

In economics, factors of production are priced according to their so-called marginal productivities. Imagine some objective function values alternative national products, y. Then the marginal product of capital is the rate of change of the constrained maximum value of the objective function with respect to the level of the stock of capital in (8). Similarly, the marginal product of labor is the rate of change of the maximum value with respect to the size of the labor force. In other words, factor prices are Lagrange multipliers. The same can be observed of commodity prices. It is convenient to rewrite the constraints on the commodities as

$$x \geq Ax + y. \tag{9}$$

In other words, industrial plus final demand cannot exceed supply. Typically, the objective function is an increasing function of final demand, y, and, therefore, the material balance constraint, (9), will be binding. This justifies the use of the supply-demand constraint, (9), instead of the material balance. (4′). The last inequality we impose is a nonnegativity constraint,

$$x \geq 0. \tag{10}$$

Final demand, y, may be negative for open economies. (Recall that final demand consists of households consumption, government spending, investment and net exports. The latter item is negative for commodities that are imported).

Open economies have access to common or world markets and may swap any surplus with another bundle of goods of the same value. Let the common market or world prices be denoted by a positive row vector, p. Then, if y is feasible, fulfilling constraints (8), (9) and (10), any y' with $py' = py$ is attainable through trade. It is in the interest of an open economy to select surplus y, such that its value at world prices, py, is maximized. To appreciate this fact, suppose, to the contrary, that some surplus vector, y^0, is selected with suboptimal value at world prices. Then there exists feasible y^1 with $py^0 < py^1$. Now define $y^2 = \frac{py^1}{py^0}y^0$. If the objective function of the economy is increasing in surplus, y^2 is superior to y^0. On the other hand, y^2 is attainable by producing y^1 and swapping it with y^2, which has the same value as y^1 as can be seen by the premultiplication of the expression defining y^2 by p. This completes the argument by which we may assume that the value of final demand at world prices is maximized. Thus, we face the linear program,

$$\text{maximize } py \text{ subject to } (8, 9, 10) \tag{11}$$

Denote the Lagrange multiplier by $r, w, \tilde{p}$ and s. r and w are the rental rate of capital and the wage rate, associated with constraint (8). $\tilde{p}$ is the commodity price row vector, associated with constraint (9). s is a slack row vector, associated with constraint (10). These prices fulfill a linear program which is dual to the primal program, (11). The connection is established by the main theorem of linear programming.

Duality Theorem of Linear Programming. Let C be a matrix, and let b and c be column and row vectors, respectively. Then

$$\max\{cz \mid Cz \leq b\} = \min\{\lambda b \mid \lambda \geq 0,\ \lambda C = c\},$$

provided that both sets are nonempty.

This formulation is by Schrijver (1986, p. 90), who also provides a proof. (I changed his notation to avoid confusion).

It is easy to cast our problem in the mold of the duality theorem. For this purpose, specify the symbols in the theorem as follows:

$$z = \begin{pmatrix} x \\ y \end{pmatrix}, \quad C = \begin{pmatrix} k & 0 \\ l & 0 \\ A-I & I \\ -I & 0 \end{pmatrix}, \quad b = \begin{pmatrix} K \\ L \\ 0 \\ 0 \end{pmatrix} \quad \text{and} \quad c = (0\, p).$$

Then the maximization problem in the theorem specializes to (10). Turn to the minimization problem in the theorem. Spell out $\lambda = (r\, w\, \tilde{p}\, s)$, as introduced before. Hence the minimization problem reduces to

$$\text{minimize } rK + wL \text{ subject to}$$

$$(r\, w\, \tilde{p}\, s) \begin{pmatrix} k & 0 \\ l & 0 \\ A-I & I \\ -I & 0 \end{pmatrix} = (0\, p) \text{ and nonnegativity of all prices.}$$

The second component of the equality reads $\tilde{p} = p$. Hence the Lagrange multipliers of the commodity constraints, called shadow prices by economists, of an open economy match world prices. An efficient, open economy, where everything is priced by its marginal productivity, admits no wedge between domestic and foreign prices. The competitive notion underlying this is revealed by the first component of the equality, where we substitute $\tilde{p} = p$ and $s \geq 0$,

$$rk + wl \geq p(I - A). \tag{12}$$

Summarizing, the dual program reads

$$\text{minimize } rK + wL \text{ subject to } p \leq pA + rk + wl; \quad r, w \geq 0. \tag{13}$$

The nonemptiness condition of the duality theorem is fulfilled by $z = 0$ for the primal program. For the dual program, some (r, w) must fulfill (12). The right hand side of this constraint is a row vector of which the i-th entry represents value added per unit of output i. The left hand side can exceed it, if k_i or l_i, is strictly positive, by a sufficiently large choice of r or w, respectively. We assume this holds for all sectors. In practice, both factor coefficients are positive for each sector, so that this assumption is fulfilled. Note that (13) corresponds with the value relations of Leontief (1966, chapter 7), apart from the inequality signs. Leontief, however, set these independently of the quantity system, a practice that persisted in the later literature.

Now, by the duality theorem, solutions (x, y) and (r, w) fulfill

$$py = rK + wL. \tag{14}$$

This is the value of surplus to the factors of production, according to their marginal productivities. This equality is a special case of macro-economic accounting identity (1). Micro-economists call it Walras' Law. It is a sort of budget constraint for the entire economy. The left hand side is the value of a basket of final demand items, the right hand side is available income to purchase it. Walras' Law is usually derived from individual budget constraints. It is illuminating to push it back to a disaggregated level. An appropriate vehicle is a result of linear programming which is subsidiary to the duality theorem. By definition, z_0 and λ_0 are feasible solutions, if they fulfill the constraints of the maximum and the minimum problems, respectively. The phenomenon is as follows.

Complementary Slackness. Assume both optima of the duality theorem are finite, and let z_0 and λ_0 be feasible solutions. Then the following are equivalent:

(i) z_0 and λ_0 are optimum solutions,
(ii) $\lambda_0(b - Cz_0) = 0$.

This formulation is by Schrijver (1986, p. 95), who also provides proof.

Recall that we assumed that for each sector, i, k_i or l_i is strictly positive. By primal constraints (8) and (9), x, y and py are finite. Recall that the assumption yielded feasible r and w for the dual program, (13), providing an upper bound for the optimum. Since the optimum value to (13) is also nonnegative, it must be finite. Hence our assumption insures applicability of the principle of complementary slackness. Note that since each vector in (ii) is nonnegative, their inner product must be zero term by term. It is interesting to push back properties (i) and (ii) to the economic variable of linear programs (11) and (13). The result is as follows.

Let (x_0, y_0) and (r_0, w_0) be feasible solutions to (11) and (13). Then they are optimal if and only if the following holds:

(a) $r_0(K - kx_0) = 0$,
(b) $w_0(L - lx_0) = 0$,
(c) $y_0 = x_0 - Ax_0$,
(d) $(pA + r_0k + w_0l - p)x_0 = 0$,

By (a), capital gets a rate of return only if it is operated at full capacity. By (b), workers get wages only at full employment. By (c), no net output is wasted. (d) is the crux of the complementary slackness phenomenon. A sector is operated only if the price of output equals unit costs, including the return on capital. The prices in dual program (13) are knife edge. They are less than or equal to unit costs, $pA + rk + wl$. Production is unprofitable or breaks even. In the former case, output must be zero. In the latter case, output must be positive to equilibrate the capital and labor markets in the sense of (a) and (b). These complementary slackness conditions describe precisely how profit-maximizing entrepreneurs would behave in perfect competitive equilibrium.

The structure of the solution to the linear programs is given by the following result.

Corollary to Carathéodory's theorem. If the optimum in the duality theorem is finite, then the minimum is attained by a vector $\lambda \geq 0$ such that positive components index linearly independent rows of C.

This formulation is by Schrijver (1986, p. 96), who also provides proof.

The finiteness conditions has been seen to hold. Recall $C = \begin{bmatrix} k & 0 \\ l & 0 \\ A-I & I \\ -I & 0 \end{bmatrix}$ and $\lambda = (r\, w\, \tilde{p}\, s)$ with $\tilde{p} = p$ and s the slack in (12). $\tilde{p} = p > 0$ corresponds to $[A - I \quad I]$, Consider the remaining rows of C and entries of λ. The rank of $\begin{bmatrix} k \\ l \\ -I \end{bmatrix}$ is the number of sectors, n. Hence the solution is attained by λ with at most n components of $n + 2$-dimensional vector $(r\, w\, s)$ positive. Typically, the positive components are: r, w and $n - 2$ elements of s. This is true if and only if (K, L) is in the so-called cone of diversification of (k, l, A), given p (see Chipman, 1966). Note that these coefficients need not be fixed. If they are elements of a 'menu', the optimum one (in the sense of the linear program) will fulfill the property reported here. Since s is the slack in (12), complementary slackness condition (d) yields that the outputs of $n-2$ sectors are zero. (If r or w is zero, the outputs of $n-1$ sectors are zero).

5. Relation to Mainstream Economics

The two active sectors constitute the comparative advantage of the economy, the hallmark of the theory of international trade. Their unit costs, elements of the right hand side of the inequality in the dual program, (13), match world prices. Other sectors' unit costs exceed them. Since all these unit costs are evaluated at shadow prices associated with the factor-constrained primal program, (11), they are called direct resource costs, one of the hallmarks of the theory of development economics.

The net output of the economy, y, has maximum value at world prices and is the best starting point for international trade. We may add any net trade, Δy, which is budgetarily neutral, $p\Delta y = 0$. The choice of Δy will reflect the preferences of the consumers in the economy. Clearly, efficient net output, y, and net trade, Δy, will depend on the parametrically given world prices, p. If we apply our model to all other economies in the world as well, we get a number of net trades, all functions of p. The world markets clear if these net trades cancel out. The world price vector for which net trades sum to zero is called the equilibrium price system, the hallmark of general equilibrium analysis. See Talman's (1990) paper in this issue.

The input–output model and its associated competitive prices are classical in the sense that allocations and prices are determined using only technological constraints. It is possible, however, to complicate the basic model in various directions: dynamics, taxation, rationing, etc. See van der Laan's (1990) paper in this issue. Just to give the flavor of how one proceeds in addressing economic problems, let us consider the economic development issue of self-sufficiency. Ignoring non-technological constraints, the basic model yields the most efficient allocation of activity in an open economy. It is efficient to specialize in a number of sectors, where the number is equal to the number of factor constraints, two in our prototype model. This is, indeed, the success story of the Pacific Rim economies. The risks are great, however. For example, if world prices change, the comparative advantage may shift to other sectors and adjustment costs may be high.

On the other extreme of the spectrum of development policies is the case of autarky. This is modelled by imposing a nonnegativity constraint on net output in the linear program, (11). Autarky has four consequences. First and foremost, the value of the objective function will drop. In other words, purchasing power reduces and so does, by duality result (14), national income. Second, for an economy with an indecomposable matrix of technical coefficients, A, as is common, all sectors will be activated, even when they do not contribute to final demand. Third, the price inequalities will be binding, completing the correspondence with the value relations of Leontief (1966, Chapter 7). Fourth, domestic prices no longer match world prices. Except for the commodities in which the economy has a comparative advantage, prices will be increased by the Lagrange multipliers of the autarky constraints. This is the price of self-sufficiency paid by an economy like Albania.

6. Conclusion

If the quantity relations of input–output analysis are used to constrain the efficiency problem of an open economy, the associated Lagrange multipliers constitute a competitive price system and, by the duality theorem of linear programming, they fulfill the value relations of input–output analysis. The phenomenon of complementary slackness and a corollary to Carathéodory's theorem identify the comparative advantage of the economy.

References

Chipman, J.S. (1966) A survey of the theory of international trade: Pt. III, The Modern Theory, *Econometrica*, 34(1), pp. 18–76.

Hawkins, D. and H.A. Simon (1949) Some conditions of macro-economic stability, *Econometrica*, 17, pp. 245–48.

van der Laan, G. this issue (1990).

Leontief, W. (1925) Balans narodnogo khoziaistva SSSR — metodologi cheskii razbor rabotii TSSU, *Planovoe Khoziaistvo*, 12, pp. 254–258.

Leontief, W. (1966) *Input–Output Economics*, Oxford University Press, New York.

Leontief, W. (1970) *The dynamic inverse*, in: A.P. Carter and A. Bródy (eds.), *Contributions to Input–Output Analysis*, North-Holland Publishing Company, Amsterdam, pp. 17–46.

ten Raa, Th. (1986) Dynamic input–output analysis with distributed activities, *The Review of Economics and Statistics*, 68(2), pp. 300–310.

Samuelson, P.A. (1961) *A Theory of Endogenous Technological Change*, in: H.E. Hegeland (ed.), Money, Growth, and Methodology and Other Essays in Economics in Honor of Johan Akerman. Lund: CWK Gleerup.

Schrijver, A. (1986) *Theory of Linear and Integer Programming*. Chichester: John Wiley & Sons.

Talman, A. (1990) General equilibrium programming, *Nieuw Archief roor Wiskunde*, 8(3), pp. 387–398.

Chapter 2

Commodity and Sector Classifications in Linked Systems of National Accounts

Thijs ten Raa

1. Introduction

Professor Stone conceived 'A System of National Accounts', which was authorized by the United Nations in 1968. Traditional accounting is by means of so-called T-tables, one for each account. Professor Stone's device of matrix accounting is ingenious. Instead of a T-table, an account is a pair of a row and a column (with the same index). With T-tables, it is cumbersome to locate the debit and the credit entries of a single transaction; with a matrix of accounts, it is automatic. Matrix accounting employs the consistency of a system of accounts: a transaction has the same debit and credit values. T-tables need not be consistent. A seller and a buyer may report a transaction differently. In matrix accounting, one must decide on a common value. This problem emerges in a well-known form: matrix accounts must be balanced. Professor Stone has not only recognized the consistency requirements of a matrix system of accounts, but also offered a scientific resolution (Stone 1984 and the references given there).

Professor Stone's contributions are relatively timeless. It is only now that his system of national accounts has been revised. The revised System of National Accounts (see United Nations 1992) will be published by the United Nations in December 1993. Even more striking is the substance of the revision. The first paragraph of Annex II ('Changes from the 1968 SNA') speaks for itself:

> The revised System of National Accounts, (revised SNA), retains the basic theoretical framework of its predecessor A System of National Accounts (1968 SNA). However, in line with the mandate of the United Nationals Statistical Commission, it contains clarifications and justifications of the concepts presented, it is harmonized with other related statistical systems and it introduces a number of features that reflect new analytical and policy concerns of countries and international organizations.

The System of National Accounts is so stable because of its flexibility. Classification problems can be accommodated by introducing separate accounts. The prime example of this flexibility is Professor Stone's resolution of classification problems called for by input–output (I–O) analysis. Professor Leontief's transactions table of the sectors of the American economy and his inversion constitute the first application of general equilibrium analysis. The power of his analysis has a price: it is rigid. The concept of a sector consolidates a commodity and an activity. In practice, it is difficult to classify enterprises in this sectoral framework. The US Bureau of Economic Analysis juggles with the so-called transfer method in order to produce a transactions table. Professor Stone simply enters separate accounts for separate items, such as commodities and activities. A clean collection and organization of statistics is facilitated and manipulations are relegated to where they belong: the economic analysis.

The revised System of National Accounts (United Nations 1992, ch. II, pp. 11 and 12) proposes that commodities and activities are classified according to the Central Product Classification and the International Standard Industrial Classification of All Economic Activities, respectively.

Classification problems persist. Modern establishments engage in a multitude of activities. Moreover, the specification of the latter hinges on primary output which cannot always be identified. In this chapter, I wish to point out that Professor Stone's system is so flexible that a standard classification is not required. I will investigate some traditional economic problems, the determination of productivity, competitiveness and comparative advantages, and show how they can be analyzed in the framework of a System of National Accounts with different establishment classifications across countries.

2. The Measurement of Sectoral Productivity Rates

Productivity is the ratio of output to input. For a national economy, output comprises commodities and input comprises capital and labor. We need prices to measure output and input. The appropriate numerical values will be determined in the next section. As regards notation, commodity prices are listed in a row vector, p, and the prices of capital and labor are denoted r, and w, respectively. Then productivity is $py/(rM + wN)$ where y is the net output commodity vector of the economy, and M and N are capital and labor inputs. If the commodity prices coincide with production costs, then productivity equals one by the equality of the national product (py) and income ($rM + wN$). The formula becomes more interesting when it is used to account for the growth of productivity. The weights are held constant and factor productivity growth becomes the growth rate of the numerator, $p\,\mathrm{d}y/(py)$, minus the growth rate of the denominator, $(r\,\mathrm{d}M + w\,\mathrm{d}N)/(rM + wN)$. In short, total factor productivity growth equals

$$\rho = \frac{p\,\mathrm{d}y - r\,\mathrm{d}M - w\,\mathrm{d}N}{py}$$

where we invoked the national income identity.

A sectoral decompostion of total factor productivity growth using the System of National Accounts is as follows. Let the use and make tables be U and V. The commodity inputs and outputs of sector j are in column j and row j of U and V, respectively. $(V^{\mathrm{T}} - U)$ is the net output vector of sector j. Let the sectoral employment row vectors be K and L, respectively. Then $y = (V^{\mathrm{T}} - U)e$, $M = Ke$ and $N = Le$, where e is the summation vector (all entries are equal to one). Substitution yields

$$\rho = \frac{[p\,\mathrm{d}(V^{\mathrm{T}} - U) - r\,\mathrm{d}K - w\,\mathrm{d}L]e}{py}$$
$$= \sum_j \frac{p\,\mathrm{d}(V^{\mathrm{T}} - U)e_j - r\,\mathrm{d}K_j - w\,\mathrm{d}L_j}{py}$$

The numerator is a sum of sectoral terms and each term denotes the growth of real value added per factor input. (The weights are still p, r and w.) Note that this decomposition of total factor productivity growth does not require that the number of sectors is equal to the number of commodities.

Intuitively, a great sectoral contribution to total factor productivity growth signals greater strength of the sector, a greater likelihood that a comparative advantage resides in this sector. Comparative advantages can be determined by a model of free trade between at least two economies. For a number of reasons, such a model requires that there is a unique classification of commodities common to both economies. First and foremost, total net exports are zero for each commodity and this fact can be used to balance the accounts and to specify a model of trade with sensible feasibility constraints only if net exports can be summed on a commodity-by-commodity basis. The United Nations Statistical Commission recommends the Central Product Classification (CPC). The aggregation level can be selected by choice of digit level (1–5).

A sector is a segment of the economy where factor and commodity inputs are transformed into outputs. The statistical unit is the establishment. Ideally a unit engages in only one productive activity at a single location. A number of complications seems to plague the System of National Accounts. First, reporting units may be large and, therefore, engage in more activities. The System of National Accounts distinguishes primary and secondary activities and recommends the separation of the latter. Second, productive activities may include more than a single product. The System of National Accounts notes that in practice, by-products are treated in the same way as secondary products, the products of secondary activities. Third, how to group statistical units? The System of National Accounts recommends identifying a principal activity on the basis of value added and to group establishments that have the same principal activity in industries according to the International Standard Industrial Classification (United Nations 1992, ch. XI, p. 4 and ch. II, p. II). It acknowledges that this procedure does not eliminate secondary activities, but outlines in great detail how the use and make tables can be converted into product-by-product I–O tables (ch. XV, pp. 33–45).

In many cases, there is no need to relate the sectoral classification to the product classification. An example is the above-mentioned decomposition of total factor productive growth. The decomposition is by direct application to the use and make tables, without invoking the usual I–O coefficients table. Not only is there no need to reconcile sectoral classification with the CPC, but it is not even necessary to have a unique classification of sectors. International comparisons and trade studies are perfectly feasible when reporting units accomodate country-specific sectors. The need to classify statistical units by primary activity and the practice to separate secondary activities stem from the imposition of the International Standard Industrial Classification. If productive activities are not only specified by their inputs and outputs, but also by location, why group them according to primary activities by ISIC? It is in the spirit of I–O analysis where commodities, activities and industries are conveniently identified by means of the concept of a sector, but there are no analytical requirements on the international comparability of industries.

3. The Location of Comparative Advantages

The extension of productivity analysis to the location of comparative advantages may illustrate my point. **U** and **V** are the use and make tables of the home country. **K** and **L** are the sectoral factor employment row vectors with totals **M** and **N**. Introduce a foreign country, with accounts given by U, V, K and L (and totals M and N). The commodity classification is the same, but the sectoral classification may be different. **U** and U have the same row dimensions, but the column dimensions differ. For **V** and V, it is the other way round. **K** and K have different dimensions as do **L** and L. The net output vectors $\mathbf{y} = (\mathbf{V}^T - \mathbf{U})\mathbf{e}$ and $y = (V^{\mathrm{T}} - U)e$ reside in the common commodity space (**e** and e have all entries equal to one, but are of different dimensions). Net output consists of domestic final demand, **f**, and net exports, $\mathbf{g} : \mathbf{y} = \mathbf{f} + \mathbf{g}$ and $y = f + g$. In a two-country model, $\mathbf{g} + g = 0$, since the net exports of one country are the net imports of the other. If **p** is the row vector of terms of trade, the **pg** is the trade surplus of the home country or the deficit of the foreign. To locate the comparative advantages, let us determine the re-allocation of activity prompted by competitive markets, including free trade. I make the conservative assumption that the economic agents want to stick to the observed domestic final demand proportions. If this assumption is dropped, further reallocations would take place. In other words, we will condition the comparative advantages on the observed patterns of domestic final demand. I also make the conservative assumption that no substitution takes place within sectors. (I consider them ideal statistical units in the sense of the System of National Accounts (United Nations 1992, ch. II, p. 11). It is consistent with the country-specific classification of activities. If the assumption is not fulfilled, further reallocation effects are to be expected.)

Invoking the relationship between general equilibrium and Pareto optimality, the allocation of acitivity under free trade can be determined by the maximization of the domestic final demand level subject to a foreign final demand level, the material balance for the commodities and the factor input constraints:

$$\max_{\mathbf{s},\mathbf{c},s} \mathbf{c} \text{ subject to}$$

$$(\mathbf{V}^{\mathrm{T}} - \mathbf{U})\mathbf{s} + (V^{\mathrm{T}} - U)s \geq \mathbf{fc} + fc$$

$$\mathbf{Ks} \leq \mathbf{M}, \quad Ks \leq M, \quad \mathbf{Ls} \leq \mathbf{N}, \quad Ls \leq N, \quad \mathbf{s} \geq 0, \quad s \geq 0.$$

The commodity accounts are pooled and the factor input accounts are separate, assuming mobility of the former and immobility of the latter. These specifications can be altered in accordance with the facts. In general, mobile inputs have pooled balances and immobile inputs have separate balances. Now let us consider the distribution of final demand. The bigger the foreign level of final demand, c, the smaller the domestic level of final demand, $\mathbf{c}$. The allocations of activity under free trade are determined by $\mathbf{s}$ and s. Net exports are the difference between net output and domestic final demand: $(\mathbf{V}^{\mathrm{T}} - \mathbf{U})\mathbf{s} - \mathbf{fc}$ for the home country and $(V^{\mathrm{T}} - U)s - fc$ for the foreign country. In the solution, the material balance will be binding and the net exports vectors are opposite. Its value is the deficit. The deficit of the home economy is a monotonic function of parameter c, the foreign consumption level. The equation with the observed deficit fixes the value of this parameter. The consequent net exports vector determines the pattern of free trade and locates the comparative advantages on a commodity basis. The underlying activity vectors, $\mathbf{s}$ and s, identify the competitive sectors. If a sectoral component exceeds unity, that sector would expand under competitive conditions.

The relationship with factor productivities is established by the shadow prices to the constraint of the maximization program. Active sectors break even and inactive sectors are unprofitable. Consequently the ratios of value added and factor costs are one and smaller than one, respectively. For the national economies, factor productivities are $\mathbf{r}$ per unit of capital and $\mathbf{w}$ per worker and their rates of change $\dot{\mathbf{r}}$ and $\dot{\mathbf{w}}$. Total factor productivity growth is obtained by the weighting of the factor input stocks and the result coincides with the traditional total factor productivity growth expression, ρ, by the differentiation of the main theorem of linear programming. It is the values of these shadow prices that ought to be used in the total factor productivity growth measure.

Hallmarks of economic analysis, measurement of productivity, allocation of comparative advantages and the identification of competitive sectors can be based on a System of National Accounts without a standard industrial classification. International sectoral comparisons can be made in terms of productivity, but do not hinge on a common classification scheme. Consider, for example, the question if agriculture is more efficient at home than abroad. Typically, agriculture is classified as the first sector. One might compare $\mathbf{s}_1$ and s_1 in the solutions to the above-mentioned program. One might also evaluate the value added/factor costs ratios of the sectors. But strictly speaking, the issue of efficient agriculture boils down to the question of which sector produces those commodities and there is no reason to limit the candidate sectors to the first ones of the respective economics. It is conceivable that the products will be produced as secondary output of some other sectors. The very industrial organization or products, as determined by the make table, may in one country be different and possibly more efficient than in another.

Once it is fully recognized that activities are location-specific, the identification of sectors across countries becomes redundant. A more formal approach is given by a simple rewrite of the constraints of this model.

The material balance reads

$$\left(\begin{bmatrix}\mathbf{V}\\ V\end{bmatrix}^{\mathrm{T}} - (\mathbf{U}\ U)\right)\begin{pmatrix}\mathbf{s}\\ s\end{pmatrix} \leq \mathbf{fc} + fc$$

and the factor constraints are

$$\begin{pmatrix}\mathbf{K} & 0\\ 0 & K\\ \mathbf{L} & 0\\ 0 & L\end{pmatrix}\begin{pmatrix}\mathbf{s}\\ s\end{pmatrix} \leq \begin{pmatrix}\mathbf{M}\\ M\\ \mathbf{N}\\ N\end{pmatrix}.$$

The tables can be conceived as a system of world accounts in which activities remain reported separately when they take place at different locations. For example, the world-use table, $(\mathbf{U}\ U)$, has a row for each commodity and a column for each national sector. The sectors are simply stacked next to each other and there is no need to have equal numbers of them in the different countries, let alone a standard classification.

4. Conclusion

A standard industrial classification is of course a useful device to organize enterprise data in a system of national accounts. But, unlike the classification of commodities, there is no economic analytical requirement for uniformity across national economies. Moreover, since the industrial classification is independent of the commodity classification anyway, it may be refined to accommodate enterprise data which otherwise are difficult to classify. In other words, the national sectoral classification may reflect the industrial organization of its economic activities. The classification of commodities must be as disaggregated as possible, uniformly across national accounts.

References

Stone, R. (1984) Balancing the national accounts: The adjustment of initial estimates — a neglected stage in measurement. In: A. Ingham and A. M. Ulph (eds), *Demand, Equilibrium and Trade* (Macmillan, London),

United Nations (1992) Revised System of National Accounts, *Provisional Document*, ST/ESA/STAT/SER.F/2/ Rev.4, New York.

Chapter 3

Input–Output Requirements of National Accounts

Thijs ten Raa

The input–output (I–O) framework has transcended its role as a tool for economic analysis and is now an important organizing principle for national accounts and a statistical instrument to balance supply and use of products in considerable detail. Many statisticians and economists feel uncomfortable using the supply and use tables (SUT), when the latter include make and use matrices that are rectangular, or even squarish, but with different classifications for the rows and the columns. A first purpose of the present chapter is to demonstrate that there is no need for this concern. Supply and use tables are fine from a modern I–O analytic perspective.

A second purpose is to discuss the role of data reliability in economic analysis. There is much need for information on this to enable economists to produce confidence intervals for their results. Conversely, the need to know some scenario results relatively precisely identifies the data for which the quality must be enhanced.

Reliability is a large issue for the services industries. The measurement of output (net versus gross) and the eventual way to analyze it — the determination of stocks by industry — is discussed in this chapter.

Some of the theoretical and practical consequences of SUTs developed by national accountants, and how I–O analysis can be adapted to the use of the SUT, instead of the square I–O table, are reviewed here.

1. The SUT Framework of the 1993 SNA

The SUT framework is presented in Figure 3.1 as part of the comprehensive SNA framework (for a brief description, see *Handbook of National Accounting*, section 11. A).[1] It consists of two separate segments of the SNA, that is, the SUT proper and the CCIS (Cross Classification of Industries and Sectors). Details of the two data segments are described in the United Nations (1994) *1993 SNA*[2] — chapters II (Overview) and XV (Supply and use tables and input–output) — and also in the United Nations *Handbook on Input–Output Table Compilation and Analysis* — chapter 2 (SNA framework of supply and use tables).[3] The main features, which are relevant for the analytical issues addressed, are summarized in the following paragraphs.

The SUT proper includes two matrices, that is, an output and an intermediate consumption or input matrix, instead of a square I–O matrix used in traditional I–O analysis. The first one classifies output by CPC[4] categories of goods and services (products) produced in rows and ISIC[5] categories of producing industries in columns. The input matrix classifies intermediate consumption by CPC categories of products used and the same ISIC categories of industries, which are using the products in their intermediate consumption. The number of CPC product categories is typically much larger than the number of ISIC categories, so that output and input matrices are generally rectangular. This rectangular feature of the two matrices derives directly from differences in the detail and structure of ISIC and CPC, and also from the definition of the establishment unit used in classifying industries, as defined in the SNA (for further details, see *1993 SNA*, paras 15.13–15.18).

[1] Handbook of National Accounting: Use of Macro Accounts in Policy Analyses, Studies in Methods, Series F, No. 81, pp. 65–82, United Nations (2002).

[2] United Nations (1994), *System of National Accounts, 1993*, Sales No. E.94.XVI1.4.

[3] *Handbook of Input–Output Table Compilation and Analysis,* Handbook of National Accounting, United Nations, Series F, No. 74 (United Nations publication, sales no. E.99.XVI1.9).

[4] *Central Product Classification*, Statistical Papers, Series M. 77, ver. 1.0 (United Nations publication, sales no. E.98.XV11.5).

[5] *International Standard Industrial Classification of All Economic Activities*, Statistical Papers, Series M, No. 4, Rev. 3 (United Nations publication, sales no. E.90.XVII.11).

			Outlays						
			Our economy					Rest of the world	Totals
			Institutions		Production				
Incomes			Current	Capital	Factors	Products	Activities		
Our economy	Institutions	Current	Current transfers		Factor income	Taxes on products	Taxes on activities	Current transfers from abroad	Current disposable income
		Capital	Savings	Capital transfers				Capital transfers from abroad	Available funds
	Production	Factors					Payments for factors services	Factor incomes received from abroad	Factor incomes
		Products	Consumption expenditure	Investment expenditure			Intermediate demand for products	Exports of products	Demand for products
		Activities				Sales of products			Revenue
Rest of the world			Current transfers to abroad	Captial transfers to abroad	Factor income paid to abroad	Imports of products			Use of foreign exchange
Totals			Use of income	Use of funds	Allocation of factor incomes	Supply of products	Allocation of revenue	Available foreign exchange	

Fig. 3.1: A Basic Social Accounting Matrix.

Input–output analysis has traditionally been applied to data that are organized by industries, where the data are limited to output, intermediate consumption and value added. The output and intermediate consumption data may be broken down by products, and value added by compensation of employees and other value-added components, in order to serve I–O analysis. The *1993 SNA* has extended the traditional industry vector to allow for the inclusion of other elements that can be observed for establishments, such as information on employment, capital formation, capital stock used in production and so forth. In principle, the industry vector could be extended to any other data set that can be observed for industries, such as environmental data that are compiled for the purpose of environmental-economic accounts.

Furthermore, in addition to the separate SUTs, the *1993 SNA* introduced another new feature, namely, the CCIS of data related to production. This matrix serves to link production analyses, which are based on establishments, products and units of classification, with mainly income and financial analyses that use enterprises and other institutions (government, households, non-profit institutions) as units of classification and analysis. The CCIS regroups the data on output, intermediate consumption, value added, employment, capital formation, capital stock and other production-related data, which have traditionally been analyzed by industries, to sector groupings. Thus, it is possible to determine to what extent manufacturing activities are managed by large corporations (non-financial corporations sector), by households as small household production units, and/or are managed by private or public agencies. The CCIS is thus an important instrument to determine the institutional organization of production. It can show, for instance, how, over time, production is moving from public to private management or from small household to large corporate units.

The type of valuations used in recording the flows in the SUT proper is another feature that I–O analysts should take into account. The SNA recommends using two different valuations for recording supply and use in the table. The supply, that is, output and imports, of products is valued at basic prices[6] and the use of products in intermediate consumption and final demand is valued at market (purchasers') prices. The basic prices

[6]The SNA also allows for the use of producers' prices, if countries are not able to separate out all product taxes from the output flows (for more details see *1993 SNA*, paras 15.33 and 6.205–6.221).

exclude trade and transport margins as well as product taxes, such as value-added tax, sales tax and the like. As a consequence, value added for each industry, which is derived as the difference between output at basic prices and intermediate consumption at market prices, is recorded at basic prices, excluding the product taxes. As a consequence, the valuation at basic prices in the first row of the table is not the same as the value at market prices of uses in the second row of the table. The difference consists of trade and transport margins and product taxes less subsidies. Those are recorded in separate columns of the table with a classification by product, which is in line with the product detail in which supply and use matrices are recorded in the SUT proper.

Imputations and valuations of output at cost are other features that may impact on the I–O analysis (for more details, see *1993 SNA*, paras 6.90–6.146). Analysts in general are familiar with the inclusion of imputations such as subsistence farming for own final consumption, own-account use of dwelling services by owners of dwellings, and own-account construction of dwellings, other buildings and roads by the same establishments that add those assets to their capital formation. However, there are other imputations that may exert an impact on the analysis. One group includes the services produced by the government and non-profit institutions, which are not marketed. In the SNA, they are assumed to have a value equal to their cost and are allocated to the final consumption of the government and NPIs. The cost used to calculate the output includes intermediate consumption elements, compensation of employees and also consumption of fixed capital, but excluding any operating surplus. Then, finally, there are the imputed insurance and financial intermediate services, and their allocation to uses, which are approximated with the help of imputations. For banks, the output is estimated as the difference between interest received and paid, and the allocation may be done on the basis of the difference between actual interest rates and a reference rate. Insurance output is estimated as the difference between claims and premiums, plus interest on actuarial and other reserves, and the allocation to users is based on premiums as an allocation key.

Capital formation and capital stock concepts are important for dynamic I–O analysis. They refer to fixed assets and inventories. The further development of this information is essential for the application of the I–O analysis to services, where the main components of such analysis are labor and capital. When considering this, however, one should take into account the many changes in the scope and treatment of capital assets that have been incorporated in the *1993 SNA*. The main changes are briefly reviewed here. For a more extensive review, the reader should refer to annex V of the *1993 SNA*.

The inventory concept has been extended (see *1993 SNA*, paras 10.96–10.115) to reflect the growth of natural resources managed by man, including the growth of agricultural crops and livestock (for meat production), the growth of trees planted for use in industrial production and the growth of fish stock in fishing ponds, Also included in changes in inventories is the work-in-progress on large projects such as ships, as well as bridges and other parts of the infrastructure that cannot be used until they are finalized. On the other hand, the work-in-progress on buildings, roads and so on, are treated as gross fixed capital formation under the assumption that unfinished works can already be used in production. Also treated as gross fixed capital formation is the growth of natural assets, such as orchard trees producing fruits, or the growth of livestock for the production of milk or used for reproduction. Gross fixed capital formation, furthermore, includes the production or acquisition of intangible assets, including literary-artistic originals, expenses on the exploration of minerals, software development and so forth. The growth of research and development (R&D) is not treated as gross fixed capital formation, however. The stock of non-financial assets in the SNA refers to produced as well as non-produced assets. The non-produced assets mainly include natural assets, such as mineral resources, forest resources and water resources, and also assets such as patents, which are considered non-produced assets, as the output of R&D activities is not considered as capital formation. Growth and other changes in non-produced assets are not treated as gross capital formation.

Capital formation, changes in non-produced assets and the stock of produced and non-produced assets are recorded in the so-called asset accounts of the *1993 SNA* (paras 2.161–2.162, 10.15–10.19, 13.1–13.7). The asset accounts cover only economic assets, that is, produced and non-produced assets over which a property right can be established and which provide economic benefits to their owner. The asset accounts do not cover wild forests, fish in the ocean, unproved mineral reserves, water in the ocean, rivers and lakes, or air. However, for purposes of environmental accounts, the scope of asset accounts can be extended (see United Nations 2002,

Handbook of National Accounting sec. IV.D). Also excluded is human capital, but selected aspects of human resources can be incorporated for satellite accounts analysis (see United Nations 2002, Handbook of National Accounting sec. IV.A). When asset accounts are restricted to economic assets, stocks and changes in stocks are recorded in market value terms, but when extending the scope of natural assets or human capital, the stocks and changes therein may be in physical terms.

The asset accounts record the opening and closing stock of assets and all changes that take place during the accounting period, and that explain the difference between the opening and the closing stock. The main changes are gross capital formation and depreciation, which exclusively refer to produced assets, re-evaluation of assets and other volume changes of assets. So-called other volume changes include, in the case of produced assets, obsolescence, destruction of assets owing to other than economic causes, transfer of assets between sectors as a consequence of, for instance, the privatization or nationalization of assets, and also changes in assets because produced assets that previously did not appear in the balance sheet of a country (e.g. historical buildings) are brought within the realm of produced assets used in production (e.g. tourism services). In the case of non-produced assets, other volume changes include the depletion of mineral and other natural resources and the degradation of assets owing to industrial pollution and other emissions. Also included as other volume changes is the discovery of new mineral resources. What is important to note here is that capital formation is not the only reason for a change in the stock of assets, as is generally assumed in I–O analysis, but other volume changes and revaluation may also play an important role in explaining changes in the stock of assets used in production.

2. SUT Features Determined by Analytical Uses

With the help of selected analytical I–O examples, it is shown below that the I–O analysis may be adapted to the new features of the I–O framework of the *1993 SNA*, while other features, currently incorporated in the SUT of the *1993 SNA*, may be given less emphasis as they are not needed for all types of I–O analyses.

2.1. *Input and Output Matrices*

The traditional I–O matrix makes use of the square I–O table, with either industries or products in both the rows and columns. It is shown here, with the help of some analytical examples, that there is theoretically no need to force the separate I–O matrices included in the SUT framework of the *1993 SNA* into the traditional I–O straitjacket. The SUT can be directly used in the analysis.

If the use and make matrices are denoted by U and V, respectively, where the former represents dimension products by industries and the latter dimension industries by products, the V^{T} (transposed) is also dimension products by industries, and the summation over industries by post-multiplication with the unit vector, e (all entries equal to one), yields the gross output of the economy, $x^{\mathrm{o}} = V^{\mathrm{T}}e$. Here, the superscript (o) stands for 'observed'. If it is dropped, gross output is obtained as a variable, the main one in I–O analysis. It is best to think of this by the replacement of e by activity vector s; $x = V^{\mathrm{T}}s$ is the gross output of the economy when the activity level of industry 1 is inflated by a factor s and so forth. Instead of using x as a variable, it is equally acceptable to work with activity vectors. This is merely a change of variable. For example, the net output of the economy is

$$y = (V^{\mathrm{T}} - U)s = x - UV^{-\mathrm{T}}V^{\mathrm{T}}s = x - Ax,$$

provided that I–O coefficients are defined according to the commodity model,

$$A = UV^{-\mathrm{T}}.$$

where $-\mathrm{T}$ represents the combined operations of inversion and transposition.

Even when a symmetrical I–O coefficients table is wanted, for the purpose of cost decompositions or standard impact analysis, it is preferable to have raw use and make matrices without purified or otherwise manipulated industries. Input–output coefficients postulate proportionality between inputs, collected in use table U, and output, collected in make table V, to be transposed, according to

$$U = AV^{\mathrm{T}}.$$

This equation requires no commonality of product and industry classifications. U and V may be rectangular. If there are more activities than products (U has more columns than rows), then this system of equations will be overdetermined. In this case, an error term must be added and the equation becomes a regression equation. Indeed, I–O coefficients can be estimated as regression coefficients. This approach enables the analyst to determine their accuracies (variances) and to test hypotheses such as 'input–output coefficients are constant'. The latter hypothesis has been confirmed for the United States economy by Mattey and ten Raa.[7]

Thus, instead of working with fixed I–O coefficients A and variable x, one may just as well work with the SUTs directly in an activity model, without the need to compute I–O coefficients. To make this point, recall the investigation of some classical economic problems, namely the determination of productivity, competitiveness and comparative advantages, in Chapter 2 (Sections 2 and 3).

2.2. *Impact Analysis*

An important application of I–O tables is impact analysis. What are the effects of domestic final expenditures on input, output, employment and income? Domestic final expenditures are paid by households, the government, corporations (gross capital formation) and possibly, the non-profit institutions serving households (most of the demand is not final, but intermediate). Net exports are not included.

2.3. *Imports and Impact Analysis*

The analysis of the impact of domestic final expenditures on input, and particularly on imports, is given by the Leontief inverse of the full I–O coefficients matrix. An assessment of this impact can be made following the corresponding presentations in the United Nations, *Handbook* on I–O tables. The *Handbook* uses the terms 'input' and 'output multipliers'.[8] An input multiplier translates final demand into total demand. To determine the

---

[7] Mattcy, J. and Th. ten Raa (1997) Primary versus secondary production techniques in US manufacturing, *Review of Income and Wealth*, 43(4), 449–64; see Chapter 16.

[8] See note 3, p. 250.

effect on output, employment and income, one must model the division of input between domestic and foreign sources, that is, trade. Output multipliers are defined in the *Handbook* as the Leontief inverse of the domestic I–O coefficients matrix. Its typical elements are the coefficients representing the amount of domestically-produced product i needed per unit output of product j. The relationship between I–O multipliers is determined by the model of trade that is implicit in the presentation of the *Handbook*. It may be made explicit as follows: the product balance (see *Handbook* equation (13.3)), reads

$$x = Ax + s + e - n,$$

where x is the vector of outputs, A the matrix of I–O coefficients, s the vector of domestic final expenditures, and e and m the vectors of exports and imports, all classified by products. (The meanings of the symbols s and e differ from that of the section discussed earlier.) The impact analysis is concern with the effects of changes of s on x. Employment and income effects are obtained by pre-multiplying the changes of x by the labor and value-added coefficients (i.e. per unit of output). The *Handbook* input multipliers are obtained by imposing:

Assumption 1. *Assume net trade*: $e - m =$ constant.

When imposing the constraint of the product balance, the change in output is given by the Leontief inverse of A times the postulated change in s. The *Handbook* output multipliers are obtained by imposing:

Assumption 2. *Assume* e $=$ constant, *but let imports be linearly dependent on output, that is,* $M = M^{\mathrm{id}}x +$ constant.

Here, $M^{\mathrm{id}}x$ is the matrix of intermediate import coefficients and the constant is the vector of final demand products imported.[9] Now, the product balance yields that the change in output is given by the Leontief inverse of $(A - M^{\mathrm{id}}x)$ times the postulated change in s. The output multipliers are smaller than the aforementioned input multipliers because imports are

[9] Ibid., p. 161.

assumed to increase and exports are not, so that a part of the activity output is 'leaked' abroad. Matrix $A - M^{id}x$ is called the matrix of domestic I–O coefficients (A^{d}) in the *Handbook*.[10]

Assumption 2 is justified if domestic and foreign input components are in fixed proportions, like different products. Strictly speaking, however, this assumption is only appropriate for non-competitive imports. Competitive imports are defined in the *Handbook* to 'include imported products that are also being produced by the domestic economy', as distinct from 'non-competitive imports [which] include products that are either not producible or not yet produced in the country'.[11] By applying the assumption to all imports included in the product balance, that is, to competitive as well as non-competitive imports, an increase in imports m results in a parallel increase in output x. Competitive imports, however, are perfect substitutes for domestically-produced inputs, yielding straight isoquants in input space, rather than the L-shaped curves underlying Assumption 2. Thus, Assumption 2 is inappropriate for impact analysis based on the product balance. Indeed, import coefficients do not show the same stability over time as input coefficients.

The conclusion is that for competitive imports it is irrelevant what their distribution across industries is. The very concept of an import coefficient is ill-conceived for competitive imports. For instance, in New York State, industries may consume Quebec electricity as well as New York electricity. One wants to know the total import of Quebec electricity; its allocation by the consuming industry is irrelevant. On the other hand, there is no need to know explicitly imports by the industry for non-competitive imports, as they are automatically identified in a product classification of the supply and use table.

Another way of appreciating the complications surrounding Assumption 2 is by considering the balance of payments. When trade is modelled by Assumption 2, any final expenditure program causes the deterioration of the balance of payments. This is not realistic. It is more common to assume that additional imports must be paid for. A simple way is Assumption 1,

---

[10]Ibid.

[11]Ibid., p. 155.

where neither exports nor imports need to be fixed, but only net exports. A more flexible way is to use a balance of payments constraint in the model.

2.4. Household Consumption and Impact Analysis

Another candidate for economizing statistical effort, at least from the viewpoint of impact analysis, is personal consumption expenditures. Again using the presentation in the *Handbook*,[12] it shows how household final consumption can be 'endogenized' to assess the impact of the government's final consumption expenditures, exports, changes in inventories, and gross capital formation, not only through inter-industry multipliers, but also through the household consumption multiplier effect. It argues that such an analysis requires the assumption of constant consumption behavior, fixed expenditure shares and statistics on household final consumption expenditures. However, this is not strictly true. It is true that household consumption reinforces inter-industry multipliers and yields greater income and employment multipliers. Theoretically, I–O coefficients a_{ij} are augmented $a_i v_j$, where a_i is the household consumption coefficient on commodity i and v_j is the value-added coefficient for industry j. To produce one unit of j, not only a_{ij} of i in production is needed, but also a_i times the additional income v_j in household consumption. As before, income multipliers are obtained by pre-multiplying changes in output by the row vector of value-added coefficients. The changes in output (for final expenditure changes in the respective products) are determined by (the columns of) the Leonlief inverse. Now, the replacement of a_{ij} by $a_{ij} + a_j v_j$ has a special structure (the added matrix has rank one), in fact so special that all income multipliers are inflated by the same amount, namely, the Keynesian multiplier. The latter is the inverse of the propensity to save, which is a macroeconomic entity, independent of the microeconomics of consumption, such as expenditure shares. For proof of this result, reference is made to theorem 3.1 of ten Raa[13] The analysis for employment multipliers is somewhat different, but has the same implication: production I–O statistics suffice for the impact analysis.

---

[12] Ibid., pp. 252–3.

[13] ten Raa, Th. (1995) *Linear Analysis of Competitive Economics* (Hemel Hempstead, UK, Prentice Hall-Harvester Wheatsheaf).

3. Requirements of Detail and Compilation

3.1. *ISIC and CPC Classifications*

The United Nations' objective is to harmonize national accounts across countries in order to facilitate international comparisons and linkages of national models. The *Handbook* is quite explicit in promoting ISIC:[14]

> Countries and groups of countries may develop their own industrial classification to meet their specific requirements, but they should be able to link with ISIC.
>
> Similar to industries, countries and groups of countries may develop their own product classification to meet their specific requirements, but they should be able to link with ISIC.[15]

In view of the previous arguments, there is agreement on the use of a common product classification, but not strictly on a common industrial classification.

A common product classification, at least for tradable products, is required to link models by trade relations and to make international price comparisons. For the type of analysis discussed, a standard classification is not required for industries, let alone a common classification for industries and products. In the absence of this, it may be hard to compute I–O coefficients, but one should realize that the latter are only tools for solving economic problems. It is not too difficult to replace these tools by others, which keep the supply and use tables intact, without the need to force them into a traditional I–O straightjacket.

Unlike the classification of products, there is no economic analytical requirement for uniformity across national economies. Moreover, since the industrial classification is independent of the commodity classification anyway, it may be refined to accommodate enterprise data that are otherwise difficult to classify. In other words, the national industry classification may reflect the industrial organization of its economic activities. The classification of products must be as disaggregated as possible, and be uniform across national accounts.

---

[14]See note 3, paras 2.5 and 2.6.

[15]The *Handbook* assumes in the paragraphs quoted that there is correspondence between ISIC and CPC categories.

There is no need to have a correspondence between ISIC and CPC.[16] By the same token, the European Union's use of the Classification of Products according to Activities (CPA) and the detailed classification of products for community surveys on manufacturing industries (PRODCOM) as national classifications since 1993, in order to build a better correspondence between product and activity classifications, is also not crucial.[17]

While it has been argued here that there is no strict need for a standard use of ISIC across countries, ISIC is a useful device for organizing enterprise data in a system of national accounts.

3.2. *Reliability of Data and Coefficients*

Not all I–O statistics are reliable. While manufacturing statistics tend to be accurate, services industries are notoriously not. This may suggest that more accurate studies are feasible in manufacturing, but it is not that simple. Industries feed each other in terms of inputs and outputs and, therefore, cannot be compartmentalized, For example, business services are often a link between manufacturing industries. It is important to trace the effect of data reliabilities on model outcomes. The question here is how data reliabilities influence multipliers, that is, the elements of the Leontief inverse.

Ideally, industry reliabilities are calculated by taking variances of establishment data. As noted in the section 'Input and output matrices', this ambitious approach has been pursued recently by Mattey and ten Raa.[18] They accessed the census of manufactures tapes, which are confidential. In practice, one must deal with subjective reliability data. Barker *et al.*[19] balanced the national accounts for the United Kingdom. The underlying reliabilities are published in ten Raa and van der Ploeg[20] and are reproduced in Table 1.

Given the accuracy reflected by standard deviations in the table, it is easy to find the variances. The variance of the first I–O coefficient, a_{11}, is

---

[16]See note 3, p. 43.

[17]Ibid.

[18]See note 7.

[19]Barker, T. F., R. van der Ploeg and M. Weale (1984) A balanced system of national accounts for the United Kingdom, *Review of Income and Wealth*, series 30, no. 4, 461–85.

[20]ten Raa, Th. and R. van der Ploeg (1989) A statistical approach to the problem of negatives in I–O analysis. *Economic Modelling*, 6(1), 2–20.

Table 1: Reliability of Industry Data.

Index	Industry	Accuracy (Percentage)	Index	Industry	Accuracy (Percentage)
1	Agriculture, etc.	5	21	Textiles	5
2	Coal mining	5	22	Leather, clothing, etc.	5
3	Mining	10	23	Bricks	5
4	Petroleum and natural gas	5	24	Timber and furniture	5
5	Food manufacturing	5	25	Paper and board	5
6	Drink	5	26	Printing and publishing	5
7	Tobacco	5	27	Other manufacturing	5
8	Coal products	5	28	Construction	15
9	Petroleum products	5	29	Gas	5
10	Chemicals	5	30	Electricity	5
11	Iron and steel	5	31	Water	15
12	Non-ferrous metals	5	32	Rail	5
13	Mechanical engineering	5	33	Road	40
14	Instrument engineering	5	34	Other transport	40
15	Electrical engineering	5	35	Communication	5
16	Ship building	5	36	Distribution	50
17	Motor vehicles	5	37	Business services	60
18	Aerospace equipment	5	38	Professional services	60
19	Other vehicles	5	39	Miscellaneous services	60
20	Metal goods	5			

$\sigma_{11}^2 = (5 \text{ per cent of } a_{11})^2 = 0.0025 * a_{11}^2$. The variance of a_{21} is similar, as the reliability of the data of the second industry is also 5 per cent. However, the third coefficient is more complex, since a_{31} is not confined to industry data with the same reliability. Its accuracy is neither 5 nor 10 per cent, but some average. The reporting of errors as percentages suggests that mixed data have geometric mean accuracy. Hence, it is natural to set the variance of a_{31} equal to $\sigma_{31}^2 = (\surd(0.05 * 0.10 a_{31}))^2 = 0.0050 * a_{31}^2$. The variances of the other coefficients can be determined in the same way.

Statistical effort will reduce the variances and the question arises as to how to target the effort. This raises the issue of the importance of coefficients. A simple, direct approach would be to declare a_{hk} important if the policy is to boost the final demand for commodity k and the industry of interest is h, but this would neglect the indirect inter-industry effects. The total requirements imposed on industry h by a unit increase of final demand for commodity k is given by the (h, k)th element of the Leontief inverse;

hence, it is necessary to investigate the variance of the latter. The transmission of errors through the Leontief inverse is not easy, as the operation is non-linear. Fortunately, a useful formula for the variance of the elements of $B = (I - A)^{-1}$ is given by ten Raa:[21]

$$V(b_{hk}) = \sum_{i,j} (b_{hi}b_{jk})^2 \sigma_{ij}^2.$$

The variance of a_{ij} has a large influence on the variance of the Leontief inverse element b_{hk} if $b_{hi}b_{jk}$ is large. If the policy focuses on multiplier b_{hk}, more precision is obtained by sharpening the estimate of a_{ij}, for which $b_{hi}b_{jk}$ is large. In other words, if the issue is the multiplier effect of k on h, then one must look for the industries that use h and produce k, in the sense of both high total multipliers b_{hi} and b_{jk}, and enhance the quality of the data at their interface (a_{ij}).

This application of the importance/sensitivity analysis to I–O multipliers is, but one example. For a general analysis, reference is made to ten Raa and Kop Jansen.[22]

Measurement issues in particular affect services. Services are intangible and, therefore, hard to measure in current as well as in constant prices. It is thus difficult to measure the output of services and also their contribution to productivity.

The output of some service industries, such as retail and wholesale trade, as well as transport services, is measured by margins. Since margins are the difference between the values of two product flows (known here as gross output and inputs), the measurement of the 'net output' of trade and transport services differs from the measurement of (gross) output of goods. This in itself is no cause for concern, as there is a clear-cut translation from gross to net I–O coefficients. Thus, if the gross output of these services is assumed to be of a single type, say $\tilde{v}_{jj}$, and the inputs are $\tilde{u}_{ij}$, as usual, then net output becomes $v_{jj} = \tilde{v}_{jj} - \tilde{u}_{jj}$ and the corresponding inputs remain $u_{ij} = \tilde{u}_{ij}$ for $i \neq j$, while $u_{jj} = 0$. In gross terms, I–O coefficients are $a_{ij} = \tilde{u}_{ij}/\tilde{v}_{jj}$, and in net terms $a_{ij} = u_{ij}/v_{jj} = \tilde{u}_{ij}/(\tilde{v}_{jj} - \tilde{u}_{jj})$. The division of the numerator and denominator by $\tilde{v}_{jj}$ yields $a_{ij} = \tilde{a}_{ij}/(1 - \tilde{a}_{ij})$. This holds for $i \neq j$; a_{jj} is simply zero.

[21] See note 16, p. 178.

[22] ten Raa, Th. and P. Kop Jansen (1998) Bias and sensitivity of multipliers, *Economic Systems Research*, 10(3), 275–83.

The use of margins, however, causes the additional problem of negative values for output, and this does not only apply to trade and transport services, but also to other services, such as banking and insurance services, for which services output is imputed also as the difference between, respectively, the values of interest and insurance-related flows (see *1993 SNA*, paras 6.120–6.141). In the case of trade and transport, the margins may become negative when prices are marked down, the output of banking services may become negative if interest payments exceed interest receipts under certain circumstances or during certain periods, and output of insurance services may be negative when claims exceed premiums plus interest on reserves during periods of extensive disasters. In the case of trade and transport margins, the occurrence of negative values reflects the inability to separate volume from price effects. Using gross output measurements would eliminate those negatives, but would not, however, solve the underlying measurement problem. Different solutions for the negatives would need to be found in the case of banking and insurance services, as imputations for these services are not based on calculating the difference between product flows in an I–O table.

Ultimately, services are rendered by labor or capital, or other factor inputs, and this observation suggests how they should be measured in the long run. In research and development, the bulk of expenses is on workers with particular skills. If it were fully accounted for, the rate of return to R&D would be the skill premium of these workers, at least in perfectly competitive markets (for non-competitive markets, the shadow price of the skill would have to be calculated). The implication for statistical work is to link types of labor and capital with activities, such as in R&D activities or in the distributional activities of trade.

The most difficult issue is the measurement of software services. These are important quantitatively, as computerization is a widespread phenomenon and accounts for a high share of expenditure. Here, too, the point is to measure the capital stock and to link it to activities. The Netherlands Central Bureau of Statistics shows that the approach is doable. Reference is made here to the study by Pomme and Baris.[23]

[23] Pomme, M. and W. Baris (1996) Balance sheet valuation: produced intangible assets and non-produced assets, *Links between Business Accounting and National Accounting* (United Nations publication, sales no. E.00.XVII.13), ch. 9.

4. Theoretical and Practical Considerations for Future I–O Work

In the section 'Theoretical considerations', a number of theoretical conclusions with regard to I–O requirements are discussed. These hold under ideal circumstances when there are no data constraints. In the section 'Practical considerations', there is a discussion of the data constraints and institutional conditions that are encountered when coordinating the compilation and analysis of I–O tables in practice.

4.1. *Theoretical Considerations*

The main conclusion of this section is that the use of SUTs can replace the use of square I–O tables in the analysis. There is no analytical need to merge products and industries in a common classification. Moreover, the industry classification may vary across countries. Only tradable products must be classified in a harmonized way to pursue international productivity and trade studies. There is no need to identify competitive imports separately, as import coefficients cannot be used as stable coefficients in the type of analyses presented earlier.

Also, a more refined industry classification is preferable, ideally all the way down to the level of plants, as it would make it easier to estimate the confidence intervals of technical coefficients and their equivalents in social accounting matrices. When such data are not available from the SNA compilation, it is useful to gather subject confidence percentages, as these can be used to determine variances of data and model coefficients, including multipliers.

In impact analysis, the largest gain in precision is obtained by enhancing the quality of the data of the industry that has the strongest links to policy instruments and the industry of concern. The influence of policy instrument k on industry of concern h is measured by the multiplier b_{hk}, which is an element of the Leontief inverse. The largest gain in precision of this multiplier is obtained by enhancing the quality of the data of industry j that have the strongest links to policy instrument k (a high value of b_{jk}) and industry of concern h (a high value of b_{hj}). Thus, efforts should be concentrated on input i of industry j, which corresponds to a high value of $b_{hi}b_{jk}$.

Even more important is the collection of labor force and capital stock data by industry, preferably by skill and type, respectively. Such data are highly desired in order to determine the productivity of not only the traditional factors, labor and capital, but also that of R&D, and information and communication technology (ICT). Moreover, they are the key to the measurement of services output.

4.2. *Practical Considerations*

Input–output analysis is generally based on theoretical considerations, which do not take into account data deficiencies that limit the application of I–O techniques. One such limitation is that countries are rarely able to collect, through statistical surveys and other sources, detailed information on products produced by every establishment. Similar products are classified roughly into the same category and, not uncommonly, products produced by one establishment are lumped together in one single product identified by the characteristic of the establishment. If product detail is not available, it is useful for analysts to have production data that are at least classified by a standard industry classification. Furthermore, when carrying out cross-country productivity studies or other comparisons of production structures across countries, data need to be classified by a standard industrial classification based on ISIC.

Another consideration implicit in the analytical examples presented in this section is that it is theoretically advantageous that statisticians leave to economists the merger of separate supply and use tables into a square I–O table, while using assumptions they deem appropriate for the type of analysis pursued. This is theoretically correct. However, few economists may be capable or have the resources to do this type of work in practice, and statisticians often know more about the data to do the job more effectively. An intermediate strategy may be that statisticians provide the supply and use tables in addition to the merged square I–O table, thus providing analysts with information to experiment with alternative solutions.

In conclusion, for the purpose of using technical coefficients of I–O analysis, there is no need to make a distinction between imported and domestically-produced products, as import coefficients of competitive imports cannot be assumed to be stable over time. In practice, however, the assumption of stable import coefficients is widely used as a simple analytical tool that is not too unreliable, particularly at an aggregate level. However, when more detail is used, this rough technique needs to be replaced by more sophisticated modelling techniques that are related to the analyses presented here.

Part II

Accounting or Technical Coefficients

Chapter 4

The Choice of Model in the Construction of Input–Output Coefficients Matrices

Pieter Kop Jansen and Thijs ten Raa[1]

Abstract: The construction of input–output coefficients on the basis of flow data is complicated by the presence of secondary outputs. Seven methods to deal with this problem coexist. For example, U.S. input–output requirement tables are based on the so-called industry technology model; Japan adopts the so-called Stone method, while West German tables are based on the so-called commodity technology model. This paper settles the issue on the ground of theory.

It postulates invariance and balance axioms, and proceeds to characterize one of the methods to construct input–output coefficients. The commodity technology model is singled out.

1. Introduction

Many applied economic models are built around a so-called *input–output matrix*, $A = (a_{ij})_{i,j=1,\ldots,n}$, of technical coefficients, a_{ij}, representing the

[1] Fred Muller, Ed Wolff, Aart de Zeeuw and two referees kindly provided suggestions. The Netherlands Organization for the Advancement of Pure Research (Z. W. O. grant R 46-177) and the C. V. Starr Center for Applied Economics supported the research. The research of the second author has been made possible by a senior fellowship of the Royal Netherlands Academy of Arts and Sciences.

direct requirements of commodity i needed for the production of one physical unit of commodity j. Here n is the total number of commodities. Now, if sectors consume an arbitrary number of inputs, but produce only a single output, then the construction of their technical coefficients is standard. One simply takes input i of sector j and divides by output of sector j to obtain the unit requirement, a_{ij}. In practice, however, the situation is more complicated. Sectors do not only consume many inputs, but also produce a multitude of outputs. Although output flow tables reported by statistical offices are heavily diagonal, meaning that sectors' own or *primary* output is dominant, there are also some other or *secondary* outputs on the off-diagonal parts of the tables. Thus, we have an input or "use" table $U = (u_{ij})_{i,j=1,\ldots,n}$ of commodities i consumed by industries j and also an output or "make" table $V = (v_{ij})_{i,j=1,\ldots,n}$ of industries i producing commodities j (U.N. 1967; or ten Raa, Chakraborty and Small, 1984). Note that, for simplicity, we assume the same number of industries as of commodities. The problem, then, is to derive input–output coefficients or "requirements" table $A = (a_{ij})_{i,j=1,\ldots,n}$ of commodities i needed for commodities j. (Industry tables and mixed tables are not considered.) Since values of input–output coefficients clearly depend on the data, we write $A(U, V)$.

In the just mentioned textbook case, V is diagonal and one simply puts $a_{ij}(U, V) = u_{ij}/v_{jj}, i, j = 1, \ldots, n$. Otherwise we must somehow deal with the off-diagonal entries of V. There are many established methods which will be reviewed in the next section. Each method is known to have advantages and disadvantages. The choice of construct seems a matter of judgment or taste. Different statistical offices employ different methods. As far as we know, a systematic theoretical investigation of the alternatives has not been carried out in the literature. Although ten Raa, Chakraborty and Small (1984) criticize some methods on theoretical grounds, and present and implement an alternative, it is not clear if their construct is, in some sense, the best solution to the problem. Fukui and Seneta (1985) approach alternative treatments of joint products theoretically, but only to the extent of a quantitative comparison. More precisely, they demonstrate that total output requirement vectors based on alternative input–output coefficients matrices can be ordered, if a certain condition holds. This paper undertakes a qualitative comparison of input–output coefficients constructs. Models will be sorted out axiomatically. The purpose is to single out one method through characterization.

2. The Established Constructs

There are many methods to construct an input–output coefficients matrix, $A(U, V)$, from input and output data, U and V, respectively. We will index A by method. For example, A_L is the construction of *a* requirements table based on the lump-sum method (L), to be defined below.

In what follows, e denotes the column vector with all entries equal to one. T denotes transposition and -1 inversion. Since the latter two operations commute, their composition may be denoted $-$T without confusion. $\hat{}$ denotes diagonalization either by the suppression of the off-diagonal entries of a square matrix or by the placement of the entries of a vector. $\check{}$ denotes off-diagonalization by the suppression of the diagonal elements of a square matrix. (For example, $V = \hat{V} + \check{V}$.)

It is standard to derive input–output constructs from alternative assumptions. However, since we will subject them to an axiomatic analysis anyway, we present the formulas directly, referring the reader to sources for motivation and derivations. A good general overview is obtained by consulting ten Raa, Chakraborty and Small (1984) and Viet (1986). Altogether, there are seven methods.

Three methods are basically statistical tricks designed to remove secondary products from the make table. Thus, the problem of constructing input–output coefficients is reduced to the standard case mentioned in the introduction.

Model (L). The *lump-sum* method (Office of Statistical Standards 1974, p. 116; or Fukui and Seneta 1985, p. 177) specifies

$$A_L(U, V) = U\widehat{Ve}^{-1}.$$

Model (E). The *European System of Integrated Economic Accounts* (EUROSTAT 1979; or Viet 1986, pp. 18–19) recommends

$$A_E(U, V) = U\widehat{V^T e}^{-1}.$$

Model (T). The *transfer* method (Stone 1961, pp. 39–41; Fukui and Seneta 1985, p. 178; or Viet 1986, pp. 16–18) specifies

$$A_T(U, V) = (U + \check{V})(\widehat{Ve} + \widehat{V^T e} - \hat{V})^{-1}.$$

The four remaining methods for the construction of input–output coefficients are based on economic assumptions given in the references. Since we will subject the constructs to an axiomatic analysis anyway, we are not interested in the plausibility or even the specification of the assumptions.

Model (C). The *commodity technology* model (U.N. 1967; van Rijckeghem 1967; ten Raa, Chakraborty and Small 1984, p. 88; or Viet 1986, p. 20) yields

$$A_C(U,V) = UV^{-T}.$$

Model (B). The *Stone* method or *by-product technology* model (Stone 1961, pp. 39–41; ten Raa, Chakraborty and Small 1984, p. 88; Fukui and Seneta 1985, p. 178; or Viet 1986, pp. 15–16) yields

$$A_B(U,V) = (U - \check{V}^T)\hat{V}^{-1}.$$

Model (I). The *industry technology* model (U.N. 1967; or ten Raa, Chakraborty and Small 1984, pp. 88–89) yields

$$A_I(U,V) = U\widehat{Ve}^{-1}V\widehat{V^Te}^{-1}.$$

Fukui and Seneta's (1985, p. 178) reference to A_I by the "redefinition" method is confusing since the common denotation of that term is broader and, in particular, meant to cover empirical methods for the removal of secondary outputs and the associated inputs (Viet 1986, pp. 19–20).

Model (CB). The *mixed technology* model was originally presented implicitly by Gigantes (1970) as a mixture of the industry technology and commodity technology models. Ten Raa, Chakraborty and Small (1984, Sections III and IV) replaced the industry technology component by the by-product technology model and derived a closed form expression:

$$A_{CB}(U,V) = (U - V_2^T)V_1^{-T}$$

where "make table V is split into a table V_1 of primary products and ordinary secondary products and a table V_2 of by-products" and the classification is done empirically. This mixed technology model does generalize others, namely the commodity and by-product technology models, (C) and (B), respectively, as can be verified by appropriate choices of V_1 and V_2. If $V_1 = V$ and $V_2 = 0$, then $A_{CB}(U, V) = UV^{-T} = A_C(U, V)$. While if $V_1 = \hat{V}$ and $V_2 = \check{V}$, the $A_{CB}(U, V) = (U - \check{V}^T)\hat{V}^{-1} = A_B(U, V)$.

Different countries employ different methods of the just completed list. For example, the Federal Republic of Germany uses the commodity technology model (C); Japan adopts the Stone method (B), whereas the U.S. uses the industry technology model (I). See Stahmer (1982), Office of Statistical Standards (1974) and U.S. Department of Commerce (1980). Viet (1986) surveys more comprehensively. In practice, statisticians and economists fish after each other's recommendations. This paper aims to provide a way out of the dilemma.

3. Desirable Properties

So far, methods of constructing input–output requirements tables have been judged on the basis of the plausibility of the assumptions from which they are derived. This approach is not very fruitful. We hope to turn around conventional thinking about the subject by starting at the other end. What are desirable properties of $A(U, V)$? Which construct do they pin down? We hope that our deduction will be a fresh substitute for the more inductive inquiries which have been carried out so far.

Some desirable properties are implicit in the literature. For example, input–output matrices are typically used in the Leontief equations, "total output $=$ input–output coefficients $*$ total output $+$ final demand." So, the fulfillment of this material balance by the data and the derived input–output coefficients constitutes a practical axiom. Also, ten Raa, Chakraborty and Small (1984, section II) have rejected the industry technology model on the ground that the choice of base year prices affects the results in more than a scaling fashion. This suggests an axiom of base year price invariance.

We will now list reasonable properties of input–output coefficients and deduce their axiomatic context in terms of construct A which maps data (U, V) to square matrices of coefficients.

Axiom (M). Leontief's material balance is familiar in the form

$$x = ax + y$$

where x is commodity output, a matrix of input–output coefficients and y surplus. Formally, in terms of our data-construct framework, they are defined by

$$x = V^T e,$$
$$a = A(U, V),$$
$$y = V^T e - Ue.$$

By substitution, the material balance is reduced to

$$A(U, V)V^T e = Ue. \tag{M}$$

In words, the input requirements of total output must match observed total input. This is the axiomatic content of Leontief's material balance in terms of mapping A.

Axiom (F). Dual to the material balance is the financial balance. It is familiar in the form

$$p^T = p^T a + v^T$$

where p is the price vector, containing the revenues for each unit of the various commodities, a the matrix of input–output coefficients and v value added by commodity. $p^T a$ is the *cost* row vector; the i-th component is the material cost of a unit of commodity i. Thus, the financial balance states that for each commodity unit, revenue equals material cost plus value added. The reduction of the financial balance into our data-construct framework is a bit more delicate than that of the material balance, since, unlike surplus, value added is reported by sector rather than commodity, as we shall see now. The account of sector j is obtained by considering an arbitrary output of this sector, v_{jk}. Revenues are $p_k v_{jk}$. Costs are $(p^T a + v^T)_k v_{jk}$. Summing up commodities, we obtain the total revenue of sector j, $\Sigma_k p_k v_{jk} = p^T V_{j.}$, and the total cost of sector j, $\Sigma_k (p^T a + v^T)_k v_{jk} = (p^T a + v^T)V_{j.}$. The equation of these two financial items yields the account of sector j,

$$p^T V_{j.} = p^T a V_{j.} + v^T V_{.j}.$$

In words, revenue equals material costs plus value added by sector. Formally, in terms of our data-construct framework, the constituent parts of the account of sector j are defined by

$$p = e,$$
$$a = A(U, V),$$
$$v^T V_{j.} = e^T V_{j.} - e^T U_{.j}.$$

The second relationship is as before, the other two are classified now. Without loss of generality, in a sense that will be made precise below, data are assumed to be reported in current prices, so that the physical unit of any commodity is the amount that costs one dollar and therefore, the price vector is e, which explains the first relationship. Consequently, the value of the net output of the sector j is $e^T(V_{j.} - U_{.j})$, which explains the third relationship. By substituting into the account of sector j and subtracting $e^T V_{j.}$ from the left- and right-hand sides, we obtain

$$e^T A(U, V) V_{j.} = e^T U_{.j}.$$

In words, the input cost of output must match the observed value of input. Since this must hold for all sectors j, we can line up the accounts in the row vector equation,

$$e^T A(U, V) V^T = e^T U. \tag{F}$$

This completes the reduction of the financial balance to the axiomatic content in terms of mapping A. Note that the financial balance (F) is dual to the material balance (M), in accordance with Leontief's (1966, chapter 7) price and quantity equations.

Axiom (P). The above assumption that data are reported in current prices was claimed not to inflict generality. This is made precise as follows. In the general case, data are reported in some arbitrary base year money terms. If the base year is pegged at the current year, we are in the situation considered so far, with prices equal to e. Otherwise p remains the vector of price levels relative to the base year. For example, if $p_i = 2$, then good i has become twice as expensive and, therefore, the current money-based physical unit is one half of the base year physical unit. Revalued at the new prices, flows of good i are doubled. For example, input i of sector j revalued at the new prices is $p_i u_{ij}$. All inputs revalued at the new prices are given by $\hat{p}U$. Similarly, the primary output of sector j becomes $v_{jj} p_j$

and all output data revalued at the new prices are given by $V\hat{p}$. Thus, in the textbook case mentioned in the introduction, where V is diagonal and $a_{ij}(U,V) = u_{ij}/v_{jj}$, we want the new input–output coefficient to be $a_{ij}(\hat{p}U, V\hat{p}) = (p_i u_{ij})/(v_{jj}p_j) = p_i a_{ij}(U,V)/p_j$. Letting i and j run through all sectors, Stone (1961, formula VIII.37) obtains

$$A(\hat{p}U, V\hat{p}) = \hat{p}A(U,V)\hat{p}^{-1} \quad \text{for all } p > 0. \tag{P}$$

Here, positivity is defined in the strict way, that is for each and every component. The price invariance is equally desirable for the general case where V is not necessarily diagonal. So we postulate (P) for all U and V.

Axiom (S). Dual to the price invariance axiom is a scale axiom in the sense of activity analysis. The price invariance axiom considers the multiplication of commodities by factors. Now we consider the multiplication of sectors by factors. So we multiply all inputs and outputs of sector 1 by a common factor, say s_1, and similarly for the other sectors. In other words, we imagine constant returns to scale economy. Then we expect input–output coefficients to remain the same. Formally,

$$A(U\hat{s}, \hat{s}V) = A(U,V) \quad \text{for all } s > 0. \tag{S}$$

This axiom is not a constant returns to scale assumption. It merely postulates that *if* input–output proportions are constant for each sector, *then* input–output coefficients must be fixed. The logical negation of this implication is that input–output coefficient changes must be ascribable to technical change in some sectors.

Mathematically, the four axioms are independent in a sense that will be made precise in Section 5. Economically however, we wish to postulate the financial balance axiom in conjunction with price invariance, as has been motivated above.

4. Performance

Now that we have listed all the established input–output constructs in Section 2 and the desirable properties in Section 3, it is interesting to test how well the various methods perform. Table 1 summarizes the results. Proofs are relegated to the Appendix, except for the commodity technology model.

Table 1: Input–Output Coefficient Constructs and the Properties They Fulfill.

Model Axiom	Material Balance	Financial Balance	Scale Invariance	Price Invariance
Lump-sum			√	
European System	√			√
Transfer				
Commodity Technology	√	√	√	√
By-product Technology			√	√
Industry Technology	√			
CB-mixed Technology			√	√

Let us discuss the results. The statistical methods, (L), (E) and (T), are crude from the theorist's point of view. Each of them violates both a balance and an invariance axiom, although the European System model does not perform too badly.

Of the economic methods, the commodity technology model fulfills all properties.

Theorem 1. *The commodity technology model fulfills all axioms: material balance, financial balance, scale invariance and price invariance.*

Proof. Under the commodity technology model, the left-hand side of the material balance, (M), becomes

$$A(U,V)V^Te = A_C(U,V)V^Te = UV^{-T}V^Te = Ue$$

which is the right-hand side. The left-hand side of the financial balance, (F), becomes

$$e^TA(U,V)V^T = e^TA_C(U,V)V^T = e^TUV^{-T}V^T = e^TU$$

which is the right-hand side. The left-hand side of the scale invariance axiom, (S), becomes

$$\begin{aligned} A(U\hat{s},\hat{s}V) &= A_C(U\hat{s},\hat{s}V) = (U\hat{s})(\hat{s}V)^{-T} = (U\hat{s})(V^T\hat{s})^{-1} \\ &= U\hat{s}\hat{s}^{-1}V^{-T} = UV^{-T} = A_C(U,V) = A(U,V) \end{aligned}$$

which is the right-hand side. The left-hand side of the price invariance axiom, (P), becomes

$$\begin{aligned} A(\hat{p}U,V\hat{p}) &= A_C(\hat{p}U,V\hat{p}) = (\hat{p}U)(V\hat{p})^{-T} = (\hat{p}U)(\hat{p}V^T)^{-1} = \hat{p}UV^{-T}\hat{p}^{-1} \\ &= \hat{p}A_C(U,V)\hat{p}^{-1} = \hat{p}A(U,V)\hat{p}^{-1} \end{aligned}$$

which is the right-hand side. □

The industry technology model is not price invariant (ten Raa, Chakraborty and Small, 1984 section II). Table 1 reveals that it is of scale invariant. This defect is due to the fixed market share property of the industry technology model. When some sector is blown up more than others, its market shares increase and, therefore, the structure of such a sector has more impact on the input–output coefficients. Thus industry technology coefficients may vary without change in technique. Ten Raa, Chakraborty and Small's (1984) alternative constitutes an improvement in both respects. However, slightly to the dismay of at least one of the present authors, it violates the balance axioms. This observation, due to Fred Muller, motivated our theoretical inquiry. The source of the complication is the by-product or the Stone component of the ten Raa, Chakraborty and Small construct. Implications will be discussed later on.

5. Characterization

True, the results of the preceding section favor the commodity technology model over all other established constructs. However, this is not enough. The construction of input–output matrices has become a sort of an industry and, at least a *priori*, some establishment may turn out yet another construct that performs as well as the commodity technology model in the above aspects, but better in unforeseen ones. Our objective is to settle the issue more definitely. This will be done by starting with some desirable properties and deriving the commodity technology model. To understand the definitive nature of this approach, it is illuminating to address two questions. First, what about other performance criteria? Second, do similar characterization results not hold for the other models? As regards other performance criteria, we ourselves have considered a bunch of them. For example, it is natural to require that the standard model with no secondary products is generalized. Another criterion is that nonnegative data yield nonnegative coefficients, and so on. We have applied Ockham's razor however, to obtain a minimal set of properties that characterizes the method that fulfills most properties. The minimal set contains weak properties which are generally accepted. Since they characterize, other performance criteria are either implied by the properties we have identified, or inconsistent with them. Now we see the full sway of an axiomatic approach. The next theorems and remarks demonstrate that other performance criteria, which constitute axioms independent of the ones we have considered so far, do not exist. For example, the requirement that the standard model is generalized can be seen to be implied by our desirable properties and the nonnegativity property is inconsistent with our properties. This brings us to the second question, the possibility of similar characterization results for the other models. In principle, this is possible. However, our results continue to have an enormous impact. For example, the industry technology model fulfills the nonnegativity property and it is conceivable that yet another property yields a characterization result. By our settlement, however, it cannot be a balance and invariance property.

As far as we know, this is the first paper that provides a characterization result pertaining to the construction of input–output coefficients. This amounts to a more definite debate settlement than the previous literature which is confined to a partial comparison of alternative methods.

This section presents the main results. They imply that the commodity technology model is the only construct that fulfills the desirable properties listed in Section 3. In fact, two axioms are redundant. If we accept one balance and one invariance axiom, either both in the real sphere or both in the nominal one, then we *must* impose the commodity technology model.

The first theorem concerns the real sphere.

Theorem 2. (*Real sphere.*) *The material balance and scale invariance axioms characterize the commodity technology model.*

Proof. The commodity technology model implies that the material balance and scale invariance are met by Theorem 1.

Conversely, let the material balance (M) and scale invariance (S) axioms hold. By (M),

$$A(U, V)V^T e = Ue$$

for all (U, V). Substitute $(U\hat{s}, \hat{s}V)$. Then

$$A(U\hat{s}, \hat{s}V)(\hat{s}V)^T e = U\hat{s}e.$$

By (S) and the fact $\hat{s}e = s$,

$$A(U, V)V^T s = Us.$$

Since this is true for all $s > 0$ and hence for a basis, the matrices acting on them must be equal:

$$A(U, V)V^T = U.$$

Hence

$$A(U, V) = UV^{-T}$$

or

$$A = A_C. \qquad \square$$

The next theorem concerns the nominal sphere. It neatly combines the two axioms that have been introduced in conjunction with each other in Section 3.

Theorem 3. (*Nominal sphere.*) *The financial balance and price invariance axioms characterize the commodity technology model.*

Proof. Necessity has been proved in Theorem 1. Sufficiency is proved as follows. By the financial balance (F),

$$e^T A(U, V)V^T = e^T U$$

for all (U, V). Substitute $(\hat{p}U, V\hat{p})$. Then

$$e^T A(\hat{p}U, V\hat{p})(V\hat{p})^T = e^T \hat{p}U.$$

By price invariance (P) and the fact $e^T\hat{p} = p^T$,

$$p^T A(U, V)V^T = p^T U.$$

Since this is true for all $p > 0$, we may proceed as in the proof of Theorem 2 to obtain

$$A = A_C. \qquad \square$$

Remarks. 1. Singularity of the make table, V, renders the commodity technology model nonexistent and voids the statements and proofs of the theorems. In practice, V is heavily diagonal so that this problem does not occur.

2. Theorems 2 and 3 are as sharp as possible. Table 1 demonstrates this for Theorem 2. Scale invariance cannot be dispensed with, since it may lead us to the European System or industry technology models, and neither can the material balance, since it may lead us to the lump-sum,

by-product technology or mixed technology model. It also shows that in Theorem 3, the financial balance cannot be dispensed with. (Check the European System, by-product technology or mixed technology model in Table 1.) That price invariance is necessary is shown by the counterexample $A(U,V) = \widehat{e^T U} V^{-T}$. This construct is easily seen to fulfill the financial balance, but it is not price invariant. For example, if $V = I$, then $A(\hat{p}U, V\hat{p}) = \widehat{p^T U}\hat{p}^{-1}$ and $\hat{p}A(U,V)\hat{p}^{-1} = \hat{p}\widehat{e^T U}\hat{p}^{-1}$. If p tends to the first unit vector, then we get u_{11} and $u_{11} + \cdots + u_{n1}$, respectively, which are clearly different. This remark demonstrates that the axioms are independent, both in Theorem 2 and in Theorem 3.

3. Theorem 2 uses the real balance and invariance axioms and Theorem 3 the nominal balance and invariance axioms. It is natural to ponder other combinations. In other words, can we combine the material balance with price invariance, or the financial balance with scale invariance, to characterize the commodity technology model? The answer is no. The material balance and price invariance axioms are fulfilled not only by the commodity technology model, but also by the European System model A_E, as Table 1 reveals. As regards to the other combination, the financial balance and scale invariance axioms are fulfilled not only by the commodity technology model, but also by the counterexample presented in the previous remark. (The fulfillment of the financial balance was noted there, while scale invariance is trivial too.) In short, it is not possible to cross the balance and invariance axioms of Theorems 2 and 3.

As a corollary, note that it is no coincidence that none of the established constructs is second best in that three axioms of Table 1 are fulfilled. In such a second best case, either Theorem 2 or Theorem 3 must apply and; therefore, the construct must be the commodity technology model and hence fulfill the remaining axiom as well.

6. Conclusion

Either of the characterizations (Theorem 2 or Theorem 3) constitutes a pure theoretical solution to the model selection problem in the input–output analysis, leading to the commodity technology model. Yet we do not expect applied economists to be convinced fully, as we will discuss now.

In the environmental repercussion analysis, pollution should be treated as a by-product, no matter the fine points of pure theory. The inclusion of by-products in the commodity technology model, yields the mixed technology model of ten Raa, Chakraborty and Small (1984), instead of the commodity technology model itself. So? Well, the theorems remain valid. By Theorem 2, the material balance or scale invariance must be violated and, by Table 1, we know it is the former. Consequently, the Leontief equation may not be used to calculate, for example, the total output requirements of a given bill of final goods. It must be modified. In fact, it can be shown that the Leontief equation remains valid not in the sense of outputs, but of Koopman's (1951) activity levels. The calculated "total output" levels are valid sectoral activity levels where the activity level is measured by primary output or independent secondary output in the sense of ten Raa, Chakraborty and Small (1984). This is implicit in Fukui and Seneta (1985).

Another example is the productivity decomposition analysis. Wolff (1985) employs standard U.S. Bureau of Economic Analysis input–output matrices to study the slowdown. But, by Theorem 3, the financial balance or price invariance must be violated and, by Table 1, we know both are. The violation of price invariance does not cause much trouble, since macro productivity measures have this defect anyway. However, the financial balance is a standard tool in relating the national product to national income and the factor composition of the latter. The Leontief equation of this balance must be modified. In fact, productivity decompositions as of Wolff are biased and the bias can be determined along the lines of this paper.

A final problem of the commodity technology model is that in practice, some technical coefficients turn out as negatives. In another paper, we have tested the hypothesis that this problem is due to errors in measurement, see ten Raa and van der Ploeg (1989).

The intricacies of the modifications of the applied input–output analysis fall, however, outside the scope of the present paper. If one does not want to deal with delicate modifications of the basic input–output model, but prefers to stick to the textbook Leontief equations, then theory forces the commodity technology model. For example the use of the mixed technology model requires a tedious modification of Leontief's material balance equation and the use of the industry technology model requires a similar adjustment of the value equations. If one does not want to bother, then one *must* use the commodity technology model. Convenience limits the choice of model in the input–output analysis.

References

EUROSTAT (1979) *European System of Integrated Economic Accounts* (*ESA*), 2nd ed. (Brussels and Luxemburg: Office of the Official Publications of the European Communities).

Fukui, Y. and E. Seneta (1985) A theoretical approach to the conventional treatment of joint product in input–output tables, *Economics Letters*, 18, pp. 175–179.

Gigantes, T. (1970) The representation of technology in input–output systems, in A. P. Carter and A. Brody (eds.), *Contributions to Input–Output Analysis* (Amsterdam: North-Holland Publishing Company).

Koopmans, T. C., ed. (1951) *Activity Analysis of Production and Allocation*, Cowles Commission Monograph No. 13 (New York: Wiley).

Leontief, W. (1966) *Input–Output Economics* (New York: Oxford University Press).

Office of Statistical Standards (1974) *Input–Output Tables for 1970* (Tokyo: Institute for Dissemination of Government Data).

Stone, R. (1961) *Input–Output and National Accounts* (Paris: O.E.C.D.).

Stahmer, C. (1982) Connecting National Accounts and Input–Output Tables in the Federal Republic of Germany, in J. Skolka, ed., *Compilation of Input–Output Tables* (Heidelberg: Springer Verlag).

ten Raa, Th., D. Chakraborty and J. A. Small (1984) An alternative treatment of secondary products in input–output analysis, *Review of Economics and Statistics*, 66, pp. 88–97.

— and R. van der Ploeg (1989) A statistical approach to the problem of negatives in input–output analysis, *Economic Modelling*, 6, pp. 2–19.

van Rijckeghem, W. (1967) An exact method for determining the technology matrix in a situation with secondary products, *Review of Economics and Statistics*, 49, pp. 607–608.

U.N. Statistical Commission (1967) *Proposals for the Revision of SNA, 1952,* Document E/CN.3/356.

U.S. Department of Commerce (1980) Philip M. Ritz, *Definitions and Conventions of the 1972 Input–Output Study*, BEA Staff Paper 34.

Viet, V. Q. (1986) Study of Input–Output Tables: 1970–1980, U.N. Statistical Office.

Wolff, E. N. (1985) Industrial composition, interindustry effects, and the U.S. productivity slowdown, *Review of Economics and Statistics*, 67, pp. 268–277.

Appendix

The Appendix proves that the established input–output constructs fulfill the properties as indicated in Table 1 of Section 4. It also provides counterexamples to the fulfillment of properties that are not checked in

Table 1. The commodity technology model is not treated here, but in Section 4. To generate counterexamples, define

$$U_0 = \begin{pmatrix} 1/2 & 0 \\ 1 & 1/2 \end{pmatrix}, \quad V_0 = \begin{pmatrix} 1 & 1 \\ 0 & 1 \end{pmatrix} \quad \text{and} \quad p_0 = s_0 = \begin{pmatrix} 2 \\ 1 \end{pmatrix}.$$

A straightforward computation now shows:

$$U_0 e = \begin{pmatrix} 1/2 \\ 3/2 \end{pmatrix}, \quad e^T U_0 = (3/2 \quad 1/2),$$

$$\hat{p}_0 U_0 = \begin{pmatrix} 1 & 0 \\ 1 & 1/2 \end{pmatrix}, \quad U_0 \hat{s}_0 = \begin{pmatrix} 1 & 0 \\ 2 & 1/2 \end{pmatrix},$$

$$V_0 \hat{p}_0 = \begin{pmatrix} 2 & 1 \\ 0 & 1 \end{pmatrix} \quad \text{and} \quad \hat{s}_0 V_0 = \begin{pmatrix} 2 & 2 \\ 0 & 1 \end{pmatrix}.$$

Model (*L*).

$$\begin{aligned} A_0 &= A_L(U_0, V_0) \\ &= U_0 \widehat{V_0 e}^{-1} = \begin{pmatrix} 1/2 & 0 \\ 1 & 1/2 \end{pmatrix} \begin{pmatrix} 1/2 & 0 \\ 0 & 1 \end{pmatrix} = \begin{pmatrix} 1/4 & 0 \\ 1/2 & 1/2 \end{pmatrix} \end{aligned}$$

and, therefore,

$$A_0 V_0^T = A_L(U_0, V_0) V_0^T = \begin{pmatrix} 1/4 & 0 \\ 1/2 & 1/2 \end{pmatrix} \begin{pmatrix} 1 & 0 \\ 1 & 1 \end{pmatrix} = \begin{pmatrix} 1/4 & 0 \\ 1 & 1/2 \end{pmatrix}.$$

Now

$$A_0 V_0^T e \neq \begin{pmatrix} 1/2 \\ 3/2 \end{pmatrix}$$

and

$$e^T A_0 V_0^T \neq (3/2 \quad 1/2),$$

so axioms (M) and (F) do not hold. Axiom (S) is easily verified:

$$A_L(U\hat{s}, \hat{s}V) = (U\hat{s})(\widehat{\hat{s}Ve}^{-1}) = U\hat{s}\widehat{Ve}^{-1}\hat{s}^{-1} = U\hat{s}\hat{s}^{-1}\widehat{Ve}^{-1} = A_L(U, V).$$

Axiom (P) is violated as

$$A_L(\hat{p}_0 U_0, V_0 \hat{p}_0) = \begin{pmatrix} 1 & 0 \\ 1 & 1/2 \end{pmatrix} \begin{pmatrix} 1/3 & 0 \\ 0 & 1 \end{pmatrix} = \begin{pmatrix} 1/3 & 0 \\ 1/3 & 1/3 \end{pmatrix},$$

but

$$\hat{p}_0 A_0 \hat{p}_0^{-1} = \begin{pmatrix} 2 & 0 \\ 0 & 1 \end{pmatrix} \begin{pmatrix} 1/4 & 0 \\ 1/2 & 1/2 \end{pmatrix} = \begin{pmatrix} 1/2 & 0 \\ 0 & 1 \end{pmatrix}$$
$$= \begin{pmatrix} 1/4 & 0 \\ 1/4 & 1/2 \end{pmatrix}.$$

Model (*E*). Axiom (M) is easily verified:

$$A(U,V)V^T e = U\widehat{V^T e}^{-1} V^T e = Ue.$$

Axiom (F) is not fulfilled, since

$$A_0 = A_E(U_0, V_0)$$
$$= U_0 \widehat{V_0^T e}^{-1} = \begin{pmatrix} 1/2 & 0 \\ 1 & 1/2 \end{pmatrix} \begin{pmatrix} 1 & 0 \\ 0 & 1/2 \end{pmatrix} = \begin{pmatrix} 1/2 & 0 \\ 1 & 1/4 \end{pmatrix}$$

and, therefore,

$$A_0 V_0^T = \begin{pmatrix} 1/2 & 0 \\ 1 & 1/4 \end{pmatrix} \begin{pmatrix} 1 & 0 \\ 1 & 1 \end{pmatrix} = \begin{pmatrix} 1/2 & 0 \\ 5/4 & 1/4 \end{pmatrix}$$

Axiom (P) is easily verified:

$$A_E(\hat{p}U, V\hat{p}) = \hat{p}U\widehat{(V\hat{p})^T e}^{-1}$$
$$= \hat{p}U\widehat{\hat{p}V^T e}^{-1} = \hat{p}U\widehat{V^T e}^{-1}\hat{p}^{-1} = \hat{p}A(U,V)\hat{p}^{-1}.$$

Axiom (S) is violated by

$$A_E(U_0\hat{s}_0, \hat{s}_0 V_0) = \begin{pmatrix} 1 & 0 \\ 2 & 1/2 \end{pmatrix} \begin{pmatrix} 1/2 & 0 \\ 0 & 1/3 \end{pmatrix} = \begin{pmatrix} 1/2 & 0 \\ 1 & 1/6 \end{pmatrix} \neq A_0.$$

Model (*T*). Neither axiom (M) nor axiom (F) is fulfilled, since

$$A_0 = A_T(U_0, V_0) = (U_0 + \check{V}_0)(\widehat{V_0 e} + \widehat{V_0^T e} - \hat{V}_0)^{-1}$$
$$= \begin{pmatrix} 1/2 & 1 \\ 1 & 1/2 \end{pmatrix} \begin{pmatrix} 1/2 & 0 \\ 0 & 1/2 \end{pmatrix} = \begin{pmatrix} 1/4 & 1/2 \\ 1/2 & 1/4 \end{pmatrix},$$

and, therefore,

$$A_0 V_0^T = \begin{pmatrix} 1/4 & 1/2 \\ 1/2 & 1/4 \end{pmatrix} \begin{pmatrix} 1 & 0 \\ 1 & 1 \end{pmatrix} = \begin{pmatrix} 3/4 & 1/2 \\ 3/2 & 1/4 \end{pmatrix},$$

which yields the same inequalities as in model (L).

Axiom (S) is violated because

$$A_T(U_0\hat{s}, \hat{s}V_0) = \begin{pmatrix} 1 & 2 \\ 2 & 1/2 \end{pmatrix}\begin{pmatrix} 1/4 & 0 \\ 0 & 1/3 \end{pmatrix} = \begin{pmatrix} 1/4 & 2/3 \\ 1/2 & 1/6 \end{pmatrix} \neq A_0.$$

Axiom (P) is violated, as

$$A_T(\hat{p}_0 U_0, V_0\hat{p}_0) = \begin{pmatrix} 1 & 1 \\ 1 & 1/2 \end{pmatrix}\begin{pmatrix} 1/3 & 0 \\ 0 & 1/2 \end{pmatrix} = \begin{pmatrix} 1/3 & 1/2 \\ 1/3 & 1/4 \end{pmatrix},$$

whereas

$$\hat{p}_0 A_0 \hat{p}_0^{-1} = \begin{pmatrix} 2 & 0 \\ 0 & 1 \end{pmatrix}\begin{pmatrix} 1/4 & 1/2 \\ 1/2 & 1/4 \end{pmatrix}\begin{pmatrix} 1/2 & 0 \\ 0 & 1 \end{pmatrix} = \begin{pmatrix} 1/4 & 1 \\ 1/4 & 1/4 \end{pmatrix}.$$

Model (*B*). Axioms (M) and (F) are violated, since

$$A_0 = A_B(U_0, V_0) = (U_0 - \check{V}_0^T)\hat{V}_0^{-1} = \left(\begin{pmatrix} 1/2 & 0 \\ 1 & 1/2 \end{pmatrix} - \begin{pmatrix} 0 & 0 \\ 1 & 0 \end{pmatrix}\right)$$

$$= \begin{pmatrix} 1/2 & 0 \\ 0 & 1/2 \end{pmatrix}$$

and, therefore,

$$A_0 V_0^T = 1/2\begin{pmatrix} 1 & 0 \\ 1 & 1 \end{pmatrix},$$

which yields the same inequalities as in model (L).

See the more general model (CB) for proof of fulfillment of axioms (S) and (P).

Model (*I*). Axiom (M) is easily verified:

$$A_I(U, V)V^T e = U\widehat{Ve}^{-1} V\widehat{V^T e}^{-1} V^T e = U\widehat{Ve}^{-1} Ve = Ue.$$

Axiom (F) is violated, since

$$A_0 = A_I(U_0, V_0)$$

$$= U_0 \widehat{V_0 e}^{-1} \widehat{V_0^T e}^{-1} = \begin{pmatrix} 1/2 & 0 \\ 1 & 1/2 \end{pmatrix}\begin{pmatrix} 1/2 & 0 \\ 0 & 1 \end{pmatrix}\begin{pmatrix} 1 & 1 \\ 0 & 1 \end{pmatrix}\begin{pmatrix} 1 & 0 \\ 0 & 1/2 \end{pmatrix}$$

$$= \begin{pmatrix} 1/4 & 0 \\ 1/2 & 1/2 \end{pmatrix}\begin{pmatrix} 1 & 1/2 \\ 0 & 1/2 \end{pmatrix} = \begin{pmatrix} 1/4 & 1/8 \\ 1/2 & 1/2 \end{pmatrix}$$

and, therefore,

$$A_0 V_0^T = A_0 \begin{pmatrix} 1 & 0 \\ 1 & 1 \end{pmatrix} = \begin{pmatrix} 3/8 & 1/8 \\ 1 & 1/2 \end{pmatrix},$$

so that

$$e^T A_0 V_0^T = (11/8 \quad 5/8) \neq (3/2 \quad 1/2).$$

Axiom (S) is violated because

$$\begin{aligned} A_I(U_0\hat{s}_0, \hat{s}_0 V_0) &= \begin{pmatrix} 1 & 0 \\ 2 & 1/2 \end{pmatrix} \begin{pmatrix} 1/4 & 0 \\ 0 & 1 \end{pmatrix} \begin{pmatrix} 2 & 2 \\ 0 & 1 \end{pmatrix} \begin{pmatrix} 1/2 & 0 \\ 0 & 1/3 \end{pmatrix} \\ &= \begin{pmatrix} 1/4 & 0 \\ 1/2 & 1/2 \end{pmatrix} \begin{pmatrix} 1 & 2/3 \\ 0 & 1/3 \end{pmatrix} = \begin{pmatrix} 1/4 & 1/6 \\ 1/2 & 1/2 \end{pmatrix} \neq A_0. \end{aligned}$$

Axiom (P) is disproved by ten Raa, Chakraborty and Small (1984, section II).

Model (*CB*). First we demonstrate that each of axioms (M) and (F) holds if and only if model (CB) reduces to model (C).

As for axiom (M):

$$\begin{aligned} (U - V_2^T)V_1^{-T} V^T e &= (U - V_2^T)V_1^{-T}(V_1^T + V_2^T)e \\ &= (U - V_2^T)e - (U - V_2^T)V_1^{-T} V_2^T e = Ue \end{aligned}$$

if and only if $(UV_1^{-T}V_2^T - V_2^T - V_2^T V_1^{-T} V_2^T)e = 0$ for all U.

This implies $V_1^{-T}V_2^T e = 0$, so $V_2^T e = 0$, so (because $V \geq 0$) $V_2 = 0$, which reduces the model to model (C).

Similarly, for axiom (F):

$$\begin{aligned} &e^T AV^T = e^T U \text{ if and only if} \\ &\qquad e^T(UV_1^{-T}V_2^T - V_2^T - V_2^T V_1^{-T} V_2^T) = 0 \quad \text{for all } U. \end{aligned}$$

This holds if and only if $V_2 = 0$, that is, model (CB) reduces to model (C) again. Axiom (S) is easily verified:

$$\begin{aligned} A_{CB}(U\hat{s}, \hat{s}V) &= (U\hat{s} - (\hat{s}V_2)^T)(\hat{s}V_1)^{-T} = (U - V_2^T)\hat{s}\hat{s}^{-T} V_1^{-T} \\ &= (U - V_2^T)V_1^{-T} = A_{CB}(U, V). \end{aligned}$$

Axiom (P) is demonstrated analogously:

$$\begin{aligned} A_{CB}(\hat{p}U, V\hat{p}) &= (\hat{p}U - (V_2\hat{p})^T)(V_1\hat{p})^{-T} \\ &= \hat{p}(U - V_2^T)V_1^{-T}\hat{p}^{-T} = \hat{p}A_{CB}(U, V)\hat{p}^{-1}. \end{aligned}$$

Chapter 5

An Alternative Treatment of Secondary Products in Input–Output Analysis: Frustration[1]

Thijs ten Raa

Abstract: ten Raa, Chakraborty and Small (1984) rule out industry technology based input–output coefficients in favor of a construct based on the commodity technology model. The latter, however, produces negative coefficients. This note shows that the negatives cannot be ascribed to errors of measurement. The very framework of deriving unique technical coefficients matrices from the black-box of a single pair of input and output flows must be abandoned.

[1] Received for publication September 8, 1987. Revision accepted for publication December 16, 1987. Rick van der Ploeg contributed heavily to this note. Anton Markink programmed the statistical adjustment procedure extremely well. A referee provided illuminating comments which actuated the inclusion of a discussion. The research has been made possible by a Senior Fellowship of the Royal Netherlands Academy of Arts and Sciences and a grant (R 46–177) of the Netherlands Organization for the Advancement of Pure Research (Z.W.O.).

1. Introduction

ten Raa, Chakraborty and Small (1984) derived and implemented a mixed technology model to deal with secondary products in the construction of input–output coefficients matrices. Secondary products were classified as by-products or independent secondary outputs and the former were treated as negative inputs, while the latter were subjected to the so-called commodity technology model. Some of the input–output coefficients turned out negative. In case this was due to the byproduct modeling, the negatives were to be expected and admitted a natural interpretation. Many negatives, however, were a consequence of the commodity technology model.

This problem is assessed statistically in the present note. The mixing of technology is ignored in the interest of clarity and brevity. Our main finding is negative. The negative coefficients are tiny in magnitude and it is common to sweep them under the carpet, but the underlying adjustments of the data which generate non-negativity of the coefficients are surprisingly large and, in fact, unlikely. Hence the commodity technology model and, therefore, the mixed technology model of ten Raa, Chakraborty and Small (1984) is rejected.

2. The Model and Its Reestimation

The set-up is as in ten Raa, Chakraborty and Small (1984). $U = (u_{ij})$ is the "use" table of commodities i consumed by industries j. $V = (v_{jk})$ is the "make" table of industries j producing commodities k. The commodity technology model postulates technical coefficients a_{ik} no matter the sector of fabrication, j. ten Raa, Chakraborty and Small (1984) derive that the matrix of coefficients is $A = UV^{-T}$ where T denotes transposition and -1 inversion. (Since the latter two operations commute, their composition may be denoted $-T$ without confusion.)

u_{ij} and V_{jk} are now considered true values. Attached are error terms δ_{ij} and ϵ_{jk}. Summing up, we get the observed data, u_{ij}^0 and v_{jk}^0:

$$u_{ij}^0 = u_{ij} + \delta_{ij}$$
$$v_{jk}^0 = v_{jk} + \epsilon_{jk}.$$

Following ten Raa and van der Ploeg (1988), δ_{ij} and ϵ_{jk} are independent, normally distributed with zero means and standard deviations σ_{ij} and τ_{jk},

Table 1: Aggregated U, Accuracies, and Reestimates.

	agricult	mining	fd dr tb	mingaspr	metals	heav man	lght man	construc	services
agricult	1420.20	0.00	2947.20	36.00	2.40	0.20	310.30	4.10	174.40
	5.0%	—	4.5%	5.0%	3.7%	3.5%	2.6%	8.7%	15.7%
	1420.00	0.00	6753.00	37.08	2.10	0.24	269.90	4.15	0.11
mining	3.60	59.30	13.90	3369.30	494.00	17.10	152.30	294.40	1319.10
	6.9%	4.5%	4.9%	4.6%	3.8%	3.3%	4.9%	12.2%	4.2%
	3.60	61.20	14.65	3292.00	494.00	17.10	152.30	292.70	1288.00
fd dr tb	936.70	0.00	2794.60	136.30	0.10	1.70	28.30	2.90	919.70
	4.9%	—	4.4%	4.8%	5.0%	4.4%	2.3%	8.7%	12.3%
	936.70	0.00	2884.00	10.55	0.10	1.77	28.24	2.88	601.30
mingaspr	392.80	128.80	461.20	3775.70	1007.00	392.30	1709.60	340.70	2385.40
	4.5%	4.5%	2.9%	3.4%	2.1%	2.1%	2.0%	6.5%	5.9%
	392.80	128.80	461.20	3776.00	1007.00	392.30	1710.00	340.70	2385.40
metals	45.40	231.60	111.30	142.90	6239.10	3023.50	336.30	1478.00	893.00
	4.6%	2.7%	2.6%	2.8%	1.7%	2.0%	1.5%	5.0%	4.5%
	45.40	231.60	111.30	142.90	6239.00	3023.00	336.30	1478.00	893.00
heav man	55.40	34.20	311.80	237.60	1266.40	2973.70	401.70	408.20	1210.90
	2.7%	2.9%	3.5%	4.2%	2.6%	2.2%	2.1%	7.9%	7.0%
	55.40	34.20	311.80	237.60	1266.00	2974.00	401.70	408.20	1211.00

(*Continued*)

Table 1: (*Continued*)

	agricult	mining	fd dr tb	mingaspr	metals	heav man	lght man	construc	services
lght man	97.10	51.80	771.60	378.40	813.10	715.80	6314.40	2328.00	2629.50
	2.2%	2.5%	2.2%	2.5%	1.4%	2.1%	1.7%	5.6%	4.4%
	97.10	51.80	771.60	378.40	813.10	715.80	6314.00	2328.00	2630.00
construc	129.60	106.00	18.00	8.40	128.10	28.30	46.30	2836.30	707.20
	8.7%	7.3%	6.0%	7.8%	7.3%	4.4%	3.4%	15.0%	14.5%
	129.60	106.00	18.00	8.76	128.00	28.30	46.29	2421.00	683.20
services	592.40	593.70	2148.30	2025.70	3397.00	1615.40	3059.60	1151.80	14390.30
	7.5%	5.2%	6.2%	5.2%	3.6%	3.6%	2.6%	13.0%	12.2%
	592.40	593.70	2148.00	2026.00	3397.00	1615.00	3060.00	1152.00	14390.00

Note: agricult = Agriculture etc.
mining = Mining & Gas
fd dr tb = Food, Drink & Tobacco
mingaspr = Mining & Gas Products
metals = Metals
heav man = Heavy Manufacturing
lght man = Light Manufacturing
construc = Construction
services = Services.

Table 2: Aggregated V, Accuracies, and Reestimates.

	agricult	mining	fd dr tb	mingaspr	metals	heav man	lght man	construc	services
agricult	5616.90	0.00	0.00	0.00	0.00	0.00	0.00	30.20	0.20
	5.0%	—	—	—	—	—	—	8.7%	17.3%
	5617.00	0.00	0.00	0.00	0.00	0.00	0.00	30.20	0.20
mining	0.00	2622.40	0.00	0.80	0.00	0.00	36.00	12.10	69.60
	—	4.0%	—	5.0%	—	—	7.1%	8.4%	14.8%
	0.00	2622.00	0.00	0.00	0.00	0.00	0.00	0.00	0.00
fd dr tb	0.00	0.00	11844.30	24.80	0.00	0.00	5.60	19.10	731.00
	—	—	4.1%	3.7%	—	—	4.0%	5.9%	8.3%
	0.00	0.00	11540.00	24.43	0.00	0.00	5.60	19.07	657.80
mingaspr	0.00	0.00	21.80	12413.20	31.20	3.60	48.90	56.10	277.90
	—	—	5.0%	3.5%	3.2%	5.0%	3.2%	8.2%	10.7%
	0.00	0.00	22.58	12560.00	31.20	3.60	48.89	53.87	288.40
metals	0.00	0.00	0.00	272.20	20450.00	401.50	21.40	55.50	554.80
	—	—	—	4.6%	2.6%	1.7%	2.5%	5.6%	6.3%
	0.00	0.00	0.00	273.80	20780.00	401.50	21.42	55.35	0.00
heav man	0.00	0.00	0.00	1.10	457.10	12582.00	47.20	32.50	363.40
	—	—	—	5.0%	2.0%	2.7%	3.6%	5.4%	8.0%
	0.00	0.00	0.00	1.09	452.60	12580.00	15.73	31.95	307.50

(*Continued*)

Table 2: (*Continued*)

	agricult	mining	fd dr tb	mingaspr	metals	heav man	lght man	construc	services
lght man	0.00	33.90	0.10	53.60	23.80	40.40	19482.90	32.90	657.70
	—	7.1%	5.0%	4.4%	3.5%	3.9%	1.9%	4.3%	4.3%
	0.00	33.90	0.10	53.61	23.80	40.40	20650.00	32.90	658.40
construc	0.00	0.00	0.00	0.00	0.00	0.00	0.00	15669.70	21.90
	—	—	—	—	—	—	—	15.0%	27.4%
	0.00	0.00	0.00	0.00	0.00	0.00	0.00	19230.00	21.98
services	0.00	0.00	0.00	0.00	36.20	0.00	0.00	507.40	61567.30
	—	—	—	—	5.0%	—	—	6.2%	20.6%
	0.00	0.00	0.00	0.00	36.20	0.00	0.00	507.90	106100.00

Note: See Table 1.

based on subjective information regarding 1975 U.K. statistics and reported in Tables 1 and 2. Minus twice the log-likelihood of real values (U, V) is

$$f(U, V) = \sum_{i,j} \sigma_{ij}^{-2}\left(u_{ij} - u_{ij}^{0}\right)^2 + \sum_{j,k} \tau_{jk}^{-2}\left(v_{jk} - v_{jk}^{0}\right)^2.$$

Maximum likelihood reestimation is equivalent to

$$\text{minimize } f(U, V) \text{ subject to } UV^{-T} \geq 0.$$

Data $(U_0, V_0) = \left(\left(u_{ij}^0\right), \left(v_{jk}^0\right)\right)$ and reestimates (U, V) are also reported in Tables 1 and 2, where the unit is million pounds. The input–output coefficients matrix $U_0 V_0^{-T}$ and the adjusted $A = UV^{-T}$ are presented in Table 3, multiplied by a factor of 100, so that the unit is pennies per pound.

Table 2 shows that to render input–output coefficients nonnegative, some secondary outputs are set to zero. These adjustment steps involve many standard deviations and are very unlikely. One way of obtaining insight into this question is the use of the likelihood-ratio test. Since the variances are assumed to be known, $f(U, V)$ is the test statistic. It is distributed as a $\chi^2(r)$ variate, where r is the number of binding nonnegativity constraints. In our case, $r = 9$ and the test statistic is 1914.2. Since the critical value of $\chi^2(9)$ at the 5% significance level is 16.92, the nonnegativity constraints are violated at the 5% level. This leaves no room other than for an empirical rejection of the commodity technology model.

3. Discussion

At least in principle, two considerations may muffle the rejection of the commodity technology based input–output coefficients construct. Firstly, the above minimization problem presents one approach to incorporating the nonnegativity constraint — it uses subjective information on data uncertainties to "reallocate" excessive errors to other flows and checks to see if that *particular* reallocation scheme is consistent with all the *subjective* error estimates. Perhaps, there are other reallocation schemes or less stringent evaluation criteria. Clearly, the subjective error estimates could themselves be wrong. Secondly, the requirement of the nonnegativity of input–output coefficients may be *inadequate* ground for the rejection of an input–output

Table 3: Technical Coefficients and Their Reestimates.

	agricult	mining	fd dr tb	mingaspr	metals	heav man	lght man	construc	services
agricult	25.28	−0.03	24.86	0.23	−0.00	−0.01	1.58	0.03	0.28
	25.28	0.00	58.50	0.18	0.01	0.00	1.31	0.02	0.00
mining	0.05	2.18	−0.07	27.08	1.99	−0.01	0.63	1.88	2.13
	0.06	2.33	0.00	26.17	2.03	0.03	0.62	1.52	1.21
fd dr tb	16.68	−0.04	23.50	1.02	−0.05	−0.03	0.09	0.02	1.49
	16.68	0.00	24.94	0.03	0.00	0.00	0.12	0.01	0.57
mingaspr	6.98	4.67	3.59	30.27	4.35	2.81	8.54	2.17	3.85
	6.98	4.91	3.80	29.96	4.38	2.89	8.11	1.77	2.24
metals	0.76	8.73	0.84	0.99	29.98	22.87	1.56	9.43	1.36
	0.77	8.83	0.90	1.00	29.55	22.93	1.49	7.68	0.79
heav man	0.97	1.21	2.50	1.83	5.65	23.36	1.93	2.60	1.94
	0.97	1.30	2.63	1.83	5.61	23.40	1.85	2.12	1.13
lght man	1.65	1.35	6.21	2.74	3.65	5.28	32.22	14.85	4.15
	1.66	1.98	6.51	2.77	3.71	5.43	30.46	12.10	2.42
construc	2.21	3.93	0.06	−0.04	0.55	0.13	0.17	18.10	1.00
	2.24	4.04	0.10	0.00	0.58	0.16	0.18	12.59	0.58
services	10.51	21.78	16.65	15.63	15.51	11.53	14.78	7.32	23.30
	10.51	22.64	17.79	15.67	15.88	11.90	14.26	5.97	13.53

Note: See Table 1.

model. The strict application of this criterion may return the industry technology model to the limelight. The errors of that model are forced to reside under the camouflage of positive coefficients, but are probably larger. I shall take up the two points in turn.

With regards to the alternative reallocation schemes, it is instructive to view the reestimation procedure as an analogon to the balancing of flows. Basically, the re-estimation procedure is obtained by substituting the non-negativity constraints for the balance constraints in the Stone, Champernowne and Meade (1942) balancing mechanism. Clearly, alternative reallocation schemes are obtained by departing from other balancing mechanisms, such as linear or quadratic programming (Matuszewski, Pitts and Sawyer 1964 and Harrigan and Buchanan 1984, respectively) and RAS or entropy methods (Bacharach 1970 and Theil 1967, respectively). The main reason that I do not adapt any of these methods is that they do not admit a statistical interpretation, let alone testing. In other words, it is impossible to assess the acceptability of adjustments. A further reason is that the error estimates will not be affected significantly. As is long known to input–output practitioners, a negative coefficient typically emerges when some secondary output has an own input structure of which a component is not used by the sector under consideration. To render such a coefficient non-negative, the secondary output or the associated input component *must* be set to zero, irrespective the objective function. This observation is the key to my rejection of the commodity technology model and it is robust with respect to the reallocation scheme or evaluation criterion.

Turning to the adequacy issue, I can be brief. The requirement of nonnegativity yields a sufficient likelihood criterion for the rejection of an input–output model, but not a necessary one. Indeed, the industry technology model passes the test, but this does *not* imply that it is better. Other theoretical considerations must be taken into account (see ten Raa, Chakraborty and Small 1984). In fact, I reject both models, for different reasons though. That is why I am frustrated.

4. Conclusion

Theoretical considerations of ten Raa, Chakraborty and Small (1984) rule out industry technology based input–output coefficients matrices in favor of a construct based on the commodity technology model. The latter, however, produces negative coefficients. Either the underlying model is wrong or errors in the data produce negatives. This note renders the latter hypothesis unlikely and, therefore, rejects the commodity technology model and the derived construct of ten Raa, Chakraborty and Small (1984). In conclusion, we must abandon the very framework of deriving unique technical unit coefficients (A) from the black-box of a single pair of input and output flows (U, V). We must accept that technical coefficients vary within and across industries, and need more data to model them.

References

Bacharach, M. (1970) *Biproportional Matrices and Input–Output Change* (Cambridge: Cambridge University Press).

Harrigan, Frank J. and I.T. Buchanan (1984) A quadratic programming approach to input–output estimation and simulation, *Journal of Regional Science*, 24(3), pp. 339–358.

Matuszewski, T.I., P.R. Pitts and I.A. Sawyer (1964) Linear programming estimates of changes in input coefficients, *Canadian Journal of Economics and Political Science*, 30(2), pp. 203–210.

Stone, J., N. Richard, D.G. Champemowne and James E. Meade (1942) The precision of national income estimates, *Review of Economic Studies*, 9(2), pp. 111–125.

ten Raa, Th., D. Chakraborty and J.A. Small (1984) An alternative treatment of secondary products in input–output analysis, *The Review of Economics and Statistics*, 66(1), pp. 88–97.

ten Raa, Th. and R. van der Ploeg (1988) A statistical approach to the problem of negatives in input–output analysis, *Economic Modelling*, 5(4).

Theil, H. (1967) *Economics and Information Theory* (Amsterdam: North-Holland).

Chapter 6

The Construction of Input–Output Coefficients Matrices in an Axiomatic Context: Some Further Considerations

Thijs ten Raa and José Manuel Rueda-Cantuche

Abstract: Kop Jansen and ten Raa (1990) established a purely theoretical solution to the problem of selecting a model for the construction of coefficients on the basis of make and use tables. In an axiomatic context, they singled out the so-called commodity technology model as the best one according to some desirable properties. The aim of this paper is to delineate the restrictions on the relevant data sets that ensure the fulfillment of the desirable properties by other models used by statistical offices.

Keywords: Input–output analysis; technical coefficients.

1. Introduction

An input–output matrix of technical coefficients, $\mathbf{A} = (a_{ij})_{i,j=1,\ldots,n}$ (where n is the number of commodities), represents the direct requirements of commodity i needed to produce a physical unit of commodity j. For instance, if industry 1 corresponds to agriculture and industry 2 corresponds to chemicals, then a_{21} will be the amount of chemical products consumed by agriculture per physical unit of peach, apple and so on. In more general terms, the standard reference is Leontief (1986).

The matrix of technical coefficients **A** has been used for economic analysis by means of the so-called quantity equation or material balance (supply and demand) and the value equation or financial balance (costs and revenues),

$$\mathbf{x} = \mathbf{A}\mathbf{x} + \mathbf{y}$$

$$\mathbf{p} = \mathbf{p}\mathbf{A} + \mathbf{v}$$

Here, **x** is a column vector of gross outputs; **y** is another column vector of final demand; **p** is a row vector of prices; and lastly, **v** is a row vector of value-added coefficients.

The quantity equation is used for national or regional economic planning; for instance, the output requirements to satisfy a certain final demand level could be analyzed. Final demand could be influenced by an exports or investments policy. Thus, there will be a direct effect over the output levels, which will depend on the final demand variations ($\Delta\mathbf{y}$) and additional indirect effects that will be determined by the **A**-matrix, in accordance with the material balance equation. The value equation can be used to assess the price effects resulting from an energy shock, which surely will bring about variations in the value-added shares of a product, to mention an example.

National and regional statistical offices have concentrated almost exclusively on industry input–output tables, instead of commodity tables and set up so-called transactions tables $\mathbf{T} = (t_{ij})_{i,j=1,\ldots,n+1}$ (where n is the number of sectors or industries) (ten Raa, 1994). In such a table, each element displays the input requirements of sector i per unit of sector j's production, as well as the final demand compartments (household and government consumption, investment and net exports).

ten Raa (1994) noted that an input–output transactions table **T** reduces the construction of a matrix of technical coefficients **A** to a matter of divisions:

$$a_{ij} = \frac{t_{ij}}{\sum_{s=1}^{n+1} t_{js}}$$

However, there are three problems. Firstly, commodities and sectors cannot always be classified in the same way. Secondly, in addition to a multitude of inputs, sectors may also have a multitude of outputs. In other words, secondary products must be accommodated. Thirdly, commodities contained in each row and column of an industry-by-industry table are not homogeneous in terms of production (see Rainer 1989; Braibant 2002).

To address these complications, the System of National Accounts proposed by the United Nations (1967, 1993) first established the concepts of use and make matrices within an input–output framework.[1] The demand and supply of commodities are described by industries. Thus, let us define a use table, $\mathbf{U} = (u_{ij})_{i,j=1,\ldots,n}$ of commodities i consumed by sector j, and a make table $\mathbf{V} = (v_{ij})_{i,j=1,\ldots,n}$ where sector i will produce commodity j (UN 1967; ten Raa, Chakraborty and Small 1984; Kop Jansen and ten Raa 1990). Notice that, though several attempts have been made to deal with rectangular use and make matrices (see Konijn 1994), the numbers of commodities and of industries are presumed equal. Following Kop Jansen and ten Raa (1990), industry tables and mixed tables are not considered either.

This new framework provided a more accurate description of commodity flows and at the same time, made economists face a new problem of constructing technical coefficients matrices, according to some mathematical method based on use and make matrices and which did not always make sense economically (Viet, 1994).

Basically, the construction of a technical coefficients matrix **A** is a matter of treatment of secondary products. Many establishments produce only one group of commodities, which are the primary products of the industry in which they are classified. However, some establishments produce commodities that are not among the primary products of the industry to which they belong. As a result, non-zero off-diagonal elements appear in the make matrix. Alternative treatments of secondary products rest upon the separation of outputs and inputs associated with secondary products so that they can be added to the outputs and inputs of the industry in which the secondary product is a characteristic output. Assumptions on these inputs structures imply an **A**-matrix of technical coefficients as a function of the use and make matrices.

---

[1]The derivation of use and make matrices was first given by van Rijckeghem (1967) and a noteworthy precursor is Edmonston (1952).

Table 1: General Input–Output Accounting Framework.

	Commodities	Industries	Final demand	Total
Commodities		$\mathbf{U}$	$\mathbf{Y}$	$\mathbf{q} = \mathbf{e}^{\mathrm{T}}\mathbf{V}$
Industries	$\mathbf{V}$			$\mathbf{g} = \mathbf{Ve}$
Primary inputs		$\mathbf{W}^{\mathrm{T}}$		
Total	$\mathbf{V}^{\mathrm{T}}\mathbf{e}$	$\mathbf{e}^{\mathrm{T}}\mathbf{V}^{\mathrm{T}}$		

In what follows, $\mathbf{e}$ will denote a column vector with all entries equal to one, ^{T} will denote transposition and -1 inversion of a matrix. Since the latter two operations commute, their composition may be denoted $-\mathrm{T}$. Also, $^\wedge$ will denote diagonalization, whether by the suppression of the off-diagonal elements of a square matrix, or by the placement of the elements of a vector. $^\sim$ will denote a matrix with all the diagonal elements set null. Table 1 shows the general input–output accounting framework from the SNA (see UN 1967; Gigantes 1970; UN 1973; Armstrong 1975).

Section 2 reviews the literature on the different methods for the treatment of secondary products. In Section 3, we show the theoretical solution given by Kop Jansen and ten Raa (1990) in order to select the best method for constructing a technical coefficients matrix $\mathbf{A} = (a_{ij})_{i,j=1,\ldots,n}$ (of commodities i needed for the production of one physical unit of commodity j). Further considerations will be taken into account with respect to hybrid models. The aim of this paper is to analyze how bad or good are the alternative methods of constructing technical coefficients $\mathbf{A}$-matrices in the presence of data restrictions; this is done in Section 4. Lastly, Section 5 draws some conclusions.

2. Description of the Models

Table 2 describes the literature on the treatment of secondary products. The methods can be divided into two groups: those, which transfer outputs only and those, which transfer both inputs and outputs.

2.1. *Methods Based on the Transfer of Outputs Only*

Methods based on the transfer of outputs only are not based on economic assumptions, but are mainly statistical devices to remove secondary

Table 2: Treatment of Secondary Products.

Review of approaches to the treatment of secondary products
1. TRANSFER OF OUTPUTS ALONE: (a) *Transfer method* (Stone 1961, pp. 39–41; UN 1973, p. 25; Fukui and Seneta 1985, p. 178; Viet 1986, pp. 16–18; Kop Jansen and ten Raa 1990, p. 215; or Viet 1994, pp. 36–38). (b) *Stone method or by-product technology model* (Stone 1961, pp. 39–41; UN 1973, p. 26; ten Raa Chakraborty and Small 1984, p. 88; Fukui and Seneta 1985, p. 178; Viet 1986, pp. 15–16; Kop Jansen and ten Raa 1990, p. 215; or Viet 1994, p. 38). (c) *European System of Integrated Economic Accounts (ESA) method* (EUROSTAT 1979; Viet 1986, pp. 18–19; Kop Jansen and ten Raa 1990, p. 214; or Viet 1994, pp. 38–40).
2. TRANSFER OF INPUTS AND OUTPUTS: 2.1. *Lump-sum or aggregation method* (Office of Statistical Standards 1974, p. 116; Fukui and Seneta 1985, p. 177; Kop Jansen and ten Raa 1990, p. 214; or Viet 1994, pp. 42–43). 2.2. *One technology assumption methods* (a) *Commodity technology model* (UN 1967, 1973 pp. 26–32; van Rijckeghem 1967; Gigantes 1970, pp. 280–284; Armstrong 1975, pp. 71–72; ten Raa, Chakraborty and Small 1984, p. 88; Viet 1986, p. 20; Kop Jansen and ten Raa 1990, p. 215; or Viet 1994, p. 41). (b) *Industry technology model* (UN 1967, 1973 pp. 26–32; Gigantes 1970, pp. 272–280; Armstrong 1975, pp. 71–72; ten Raa, Chakraborty and Small 1984, pp. 88–89; Fukui and Seneta 1985, p. 178; Viet 1986, p. 21; Kop Jansen and ten Raa 1990, p. 215; or Viet 1994, pp. 40–41). (c) *Activity technology model* (Konijn 1994; Konijn and Steenge 1995). 2.3. *Hybrid technology assumptions methods* (a) *Mixed commodity and industry technology assumptions* (UN 1968, 1973, pp. 33–34; Gigantes 1970, pp. 284–290; Armstrong 1975, pp. 72–76). (b) *ten Raa, Chakraborty and Small 1984* (Commodity technology assumption and by-product technology method).

products from the make table. Viet (1994) suggests that the Stone and ESA methods should be used only for by-products.[2]

2.1.1. *Transfer method*

The transfer method treats a secondary product as if it is sold by the industry in which it is a primary product to the industry that actually produces

[2]For a more detailed explanation of the consequences of each one of these methods on the construction of input–output tables, see also Viet (1994).

it. Mathematically, the technical coefficients matrix **A** is derived by the following formula, where $\mathbf{g} = \mathbf{Ve}$ and $\mathbf{q} = \mathbf{e}^T\mathbf{V}$ (see Table 1):

$$\mathbf{A}_\mathrm{T}(\mathbf{U}, \mathbf{V}) = (\mathbf{U} + \widetilde{\mathbf{V}})(\hat{\mathbf{g}} + \hat{\mathbf{q}} - \widehat{\mathbf{V}})^{-1}$$

The input structure of the industry in which the secondary products are primary outputs is distorted by the inclusion of the transfer. As a result, an increase in the final demand of those secondary products would lead to an increase in the demand for the primary outputs of the industry that actually produce them, which need not be true. Besides, the input structures of industries that produce secondary products can be altered if the proportion in which they are produced changes. Lastly, sectors outputs can either be industry or commodity outputs.

2.1.2. *Stone method (or by-product method)*

By the Stone method, all secondary products are considered by-products. Therefore, they can be treated as a negative input in the industry where it is actually produced. Mathematically, we can obtain the technical coefficients matrix **A** by the following formula:

$$a_{ij}^B(\mathbf{U}, \mathbf{V}) = \begin{cases} \dfrac{u_{jj}}{v_{jj}} & \text{if } i = j \\ \dfrac{u_{ij} - v_{ji}}{v_{jj}} & \text{if } i \neq j \end{cases}$$

or, in matrix notation,

$$\mathbf{A}_\mathrm{B}(\mathbf{U}, \mathbf{V}) = (\mathbf{U} - \widetilde{\mathbf{V}}^\mathrm{T})\widehat{\mathbf{V}}^{-1}$$

Negative values of technical coefficients are obtained as a result of applying the Stone method. They appear when the actual use of a commodity i by an industry j is smaller than its secondary output of commodity i. Industry j would need a net amount $u_{ij} - v_{ji}$ of commodity i, which is actually a secondary product of industry j, for the production of v_{jj} units of its primary output. Note that, necessarily $i \neq j$. Besides, the input structure of the industry that produces the secondary product is distorted according to this method for the treatment of secondary outputs.

2.1.3. *ESA Method*

The European System of Integrated Economic Accounts (ESA) published in 1979 recommends that secondary products should be treated as if they were produced by the industry for which these secondary outputs are primary products. Mathematically, the technical coefficients matrix **A** is calculated as follows:

$$a_{ij}^{E}(\mathbf{U},\mathbf{V}) = \frac{u_{ij}}{\sum_{j=1}^{n} v_{ji}} \qquad i,j = 1,2,\ldots,n$$

or, in matrix notation,

$$\mathbf{A}_{\mathrm{E}}(\mathbf{U},\mathbf{V}) = \mathbf{U}\hat{\mathbf{q}}^{-1}$$

The technical coefficients are constructed by division of all the entries of the use table by the total output of the commodity corresponding to the column in the make table. This total output is not necessarily produced by a single sector.

The shortcoming of this treatment is the distortion of the input structures of industries with no secondary products, but with primary products, which are also produced by other industries. Input structures of industries with secondary production are distorted similarly. Moreover, the sum of intermediate uses of industry j can be larger than the total output of commodity j due to the subtraction of their secondary outputs. This will lead to sums of input coefficients greater than one, and therefore, to the non-existence of the Leontief inverse or the negativity of some of its cells.

2.2. *Methods Based on the Transfer of Inputs and Outputs*

Other methods transfer secondary products and their inputs to the outputs and inputs of the industries where the secondary products constitute a primary output. Since data on inputs associated with secondary products are rarely available, assumptions are made, such as the commodity technology hypothesis, by which the input structure of a secondary commodity is independent of the sector of production, or the industry technology hypothesis, by which the input structure of a secondary output is the same as that of the industry in which it is a primary output. In other terms, production processes substitute commodities when the activity technology model is applied (Konijn 1994). In fact, this model borrows the mathematical structure of the commodity technology model. Also, we will present hybrid methods based on mixed technology assumptions.

2.2.1. *Lump-sum or aggregation method*

This method treats a secondary product as if it were actually produced as a primary output. Mathematically, the matrix of technical coefficients **A** is given by:

$$a_{ij}^{L}(\mathrm{U},\mathrm{V}) = \frac{u_{ij}}{\sum_{i=1}^{n} v_{ji}} \qquad i,j = 1,2,\ldots,n$$

or, in matrix notation,

$$\mathbf{A}_{\mathrm{L}}(\mathbf{U},\mathbf{V}) = \mathbf{U}\hat{\mathbf{g}}^{-1}$$

Technical coefficients are obtained by dividing all the entries of each of the columns from the use table by the total output of industry j, specified in row j of the make table. This total output includes not only primary products, but also secondary products and by-products.

2.2.2. *Methods with a single technology assumption*

Three methods rely on a single technology assumption, namely the commodity, industry and activity technology models.

The commodity technology model assumes that each commodity has its own input structure, irrespective the industry of production.[3] Hence, if a_{ik} represents the direct requirements of commodity i needed by industry j for the production of one physical unit of commodity k and also v_{jk} stands for the total secondary output of commodity k produced by industry j, it can be derived that the amount $a_{ik}v_{jk}$ is the total inputs requirements of commodity i needed for the production of v_{jk} units of output k. Then, if we also assume that industry j has multiple outputs and all different from

[3] Actually, under the commodity technology model, not only are input structures of industries proportional to their outputs, but also the output structures of the commodities they produce.

commodity k, we finally could sum over outputs to obtain industry j's total demand for input i. Thus, u_{ij} can be written as:

$$u_{ij} = \sum_{k=1}^{n} a_{ik} v_{jk} \quad i,j = 1,\ldots,n$$

If industry j produces v_{jk} outputs of commodity k, a_{ik} inputs of commodity i per physical unit of output k will be required. Furthermore, another industry t produces v_{tk} outputs of commodity k, the direct requirements of input i per physical unit of output k, results again in a_{ik}. In matrix terms, the commodity technology assumption is given by:

$$\mathbf{U} = \mathbf{A}_{\mathrm{C}}(\mathbf{U}, \mathbf{V})\mathbf{V}^{\mathrm{T}}$$

And therefore,

$$\mathbf{A}_{\mathrm{C}}(\mathbf{U}, \mathbf{V}) = \mathbf{U}\,\mathbf{V}^{-\mathrm{T}}$$

This method requires the same number of commodities as industries due to the inverse of the make table. However, its main shortcoming is the negativity of some technical coefficients. According to Viet (1994), negative elements arise when the input structure of the secondary output is not the same as that of the primary product produced elsewhere, and the input, which is transferred, is greater than the input that is actually consumed. Negative values in the **A**-matrix have prompted a huge literature on the possible solutions to overcome this shortcoming (Armstrong 1975; Almon 1972; ten Raa, Chakraborty and Small 1984; ten Raa 1988; ten Raa and van der Ploeg 1989; Rainer 1989; Steenge 1990; Rainer and Richter 1992; Mattey 1993; Konijn 1994; Konijn and Steenge 1995; Mattey and ten Raa 1997; Avonds and Gilot 2002).

By the industry technology assumption, each industry has the same inputs requirements for any unit of output (this time, measured in values). This implies that every commodity has different technologies depending on what industry produces it. Actually, the industry technology model assumes that:

(1) Input structures of industries are proportional to their outputs (as the commodity technology model does).

(2) Market shares of industries are fixed and independent of the level of commodity or industry outputs.

Mathematically, the **A**-matrix of technical coefficients is given by:

$$a_{ij}^{I}(\mathbf{U},\mathbf{V}) = \sum_{k=1}^{n}\left(\frac{u_{ik}}{v_k}\right)\left(\frac{v_{kj}}{v'_j}\right)$$

where v_k is the total output of industry k and v'_j is the total output of commodity j. In matrix notation,

$$\mathbf{A}_{\mathrm{I}}(\mathbf{U},\mathbf{V}) = \mathbf{U}\hat{\mathbf{g}}^{-1}\mathbf{V}\hat{\mathbf{q}}^{-1}$$

Let us examine in more detail the above expression in order to cast light on the economic foundations of the industry technology model. u_{ik}/v_k represents the direct requirements of commodity i needed for the production of one physical unit of commodity k. On the contrary, v_{kj}/v'_j denotes the proportion of the commodity j output produced by industry k to the total output of such commodity. In short, the result is called market share. Hence, according to this model, technical coefficients result from a (market share) weighted average over industries k.

Though this assumption has been widely used in many countries, its popularity stemming from the non-negativity of the resulting technical coefficients matrix, as well as the fact that the number of commodities need not be equal to the number of industries, is economically unacceptable. As Viet (1994) pointed out, the resulting **A**-matrix is obtained, assuming that costs associated with either primary or secondary products are the same, while prices of these products are obviously different. Since the financial balance in the input–output analysis states that for each commodity unit, revenue equals to material cost plus value added, applying the industry technology model implies that this meaningful input–output economics assumption does not hold. Moreover, a change in the base year prices and also proportional variations in input requirements and outputs alone will affect the internal structure of technical coefficients.

With respect to the activity technology model, Konijn (1994) redefine the use and make matrices in such a way that the application of the commodity technology formula prompts no negatives. Instead of the commodity unit, Konijn assumes that industries can produce commodities according to several production processes and that the same production process can be used by other industries. Moreover, one commodity can be produced by several production processes just as one production process can generate different goods. Unfortunately, the resulting activity-by-activity input–output table does not get rid of the negatives. Konijn (1994), and Konijn and Steenge (1995) argue that remaining negatives indicate that some classification adjustments must be made, or some further research on errors data must be developed. Although the need for further information on the use and make system is required to apply this activity technology model, Statistics Netherlands adopts this way of removing negatives. In conclusion, Konijn (1994) proposes that we explicitly look at production processes, instead of commodities, and that we consider the commodity classification of use and make matrices an instrument, instead of an exogenous scheme.

2.2.3. *Mixed technology assumptions methods*

Following Armstrong (1975), hybrid technology methods assume that subsidiary production fits either the commodity technology or the industry technology assumptions. That is, one would expect that most commodities have the same input structure wherever they are produced, but when secondary products are obtained as a result of industrial processes (i.e. by-products), the assumption of an industry technology assumption may be more appropriate. Hybrid methods require that the make matrix is split in two matrices, $\mathbf{V}_1$ and $\mathbf{V}_2$, where the first one includes outputs for which the commodity technology assumption is made and the second includes those, which are to be treated on an industry technology assumption.

The hybrid technology methods suggested by Gigantes (1970), and incorporated in the United Nations System of National Accounts (SNA 1968), are based on the following assumptions over the use and make matrices.

Firstly, industries' outputs of commodities for which a commodity technology assumption is made are proportional to the output of each industry. This is implicitly assumed when the commodity technology model is applied. It is denoted as:

$$\mathbf{V}_1^{\mathrm{T}} = \mathbf{C}_1\hat{\mathbf{g}}_1 \tag{1}$$

where $\mathbf{g}_1 = \mathbf{V}_1\mathbf{e}$.

Secondly, industries' outputs of commodities for which an industry technology assumption is made are proportional to these commodity outputs. The proportions are the market shares of each industry's products in the total output of each one of these kind of commodities. This is implicitly assumed when the industry technology model is applied:

$$\mathbf{V}_2 = \mathbf{D}_2^*\hat{\mathbf{q}}_2 \tag{2}$$

where $\mathbf{q}_2 = \mathbf{V}_2^{\mathrm{T}}\mathbf{e}$.

Thirdly, the production of commodities for which an industry technology assumption is made follows fixed market shares. That is, industries' commodity outputs for which an industry technology assumption is made are proportional to the total commodity outputs produced in the economy. It is denoted as:

$$\mathbf{g}_2 = \mathbf{D}_2\mathbf{q} \tag{3}$$

where $\mathbf{g}_2 = \mathbf{V}_2\mathbf{e}$.

Following Armstrong (1975), after some transformations, the resulting matrix of technical coefficients is given by:

$$\mathbf{A}_{\mathrm{H}}(\mathbf{U},\mathbf{V}) = \mathbf{U}\hat{\mathbf{g}}^{-1}(\hat{\mathbf{g}}_1\mathbf{V}_1^{-\mathrm{T}}(\mathbf{I} - \hat{\mathbf{q}}^{-1}\hat{\mathbf{q}}_2) + \mathbf{V}_2\hat{\mathbf{q}}^{-1})$$

It can be seen that if $\mathbf{V}_2 = 0$ then $\mathbf{V} = \mathbf{V}_1$, $\mathbf{g}_1 = \mathbf{g}$ and $\mathbf{q}_2 = 0$; hence, the solution is given by:

$$\mathbf{A}_{\mathrm{H}}(\mathbf{U},\mathbf{V}) = \mathbf{U}\mathbf{V}^{-\mathrm{T}} = \mathbf{A}_{\mathrm{C}}(\mathbf{U},\mathbf{V})$$

which is the commodity technology model. Analogously, if $\mathbf{V}_1 = 0$, then $\mathbf{V} = \mathbf{V}_2$, $\mathbf{q}_2 = \mathbf{q}$ and $\mathbf{q}_1 = 0$; hence the solution is given by:

$$\mathbf{A}_{\mathrm{H}}(\mathbf{U},\mathbf{V}) = \mathbf{U}\hat{\mathbf{g}}^{-1}\mathbf{V}\hat{\mathbf{q}}^{-1} = \mathbf{A}_{\mathrm{I}}(\mathbf{U},\mathbf{V})$$

which is the industry technology model.

The hybrid technology model generates negative values of technical coefficients, just like the commodity technology model. A different solution can be obtained if we assume that the outputs of the products for which an industry technology assumption is made, are proportional to the outputs of the producing industries, instead of to the outputs of each commodity, whatever industry produce them. A more detailed explanation is shown in Armstrong (1975, pp. 74–76). The resulting **A**-matrix is given by:

$$\mathbf{A}_{\mathrm{Y}}(\mathbf{U}, \mathbf{V}) = \mathbf{U}\hat{\mathbf{g}}^{-1}(\hat{\mathbf{g}}_1\mathbf{V}_1^{-\mathrm{T}}(\mathbf{I} - \mathbf{V}_2^{\mathrm{T}}\hat{\mathbf{g}}^{-1}\mathbf{H}) + \mathbf{V}_2\hat{\mathbf{q}}^{-1})$$

with **H** such that $\mathbf{g} = \mathbf{Hq}$.

ten Raa, Chakraborty and Small (1984) elaborated a new hybrid technology model where the industry technology assumption was replaced by the Stone (or by-product) method. In this case, the make table is split into two matrices, $\mathbf{V}_1$ and $\mathbf{V}_2$. $\mathbf{V}_1$ includes those outputs for which a commodity technology assumption is made (primary and ordinary secondary outputs) and $\mathbf{V}_2$ includes those, which are to be treated on a by-product technology assumption (by-products). Since by-products are treated as negative inputs, the total requirements of commodity *i* by industry *j* for the production of all primary and ordinary secondary products of industry *j* are given by a net amount of requirements. Mathematically,

$$\mathbf{A}_{\mathrm{CB}}(\mathbf{U}, \mathbf{V}) = (\mathbf{U} - \mathbf{V}_2^{\mathrm{T}})\mathbf{V}_1^{-\mathrm{T}}$$

Notice that if all secondary products are ordinary ($\mathbf{V}_1 = \mathbf{V}$), we will have the commodity technology model and that if all secondary products are by-products ($\mathbf{V}_1 = \widehat{\mathbf{V}}, \mathbf{V}_2 = \widetilde{\mathbf{V}}$), we will have the Stone method (or the by-product technology model). As discussed in ten Raa, Chakraborty and Small (1984), negative elements in the technical coefficients matrix also arise when this hybrid model is applied.

3. The Choice of Model

Kop Jansen and ten Raa (1990) developed and examined axiomatically how well various methods for the treatment of secondary products fulfill four desirable properties of input–output coefficients $\mathbf{A}(\mathbf{U}, \mathbf{V})$, namely:

(1) Axiom *M* refers to the material balance or the quantity equation and is denoted by

$$\mathbf{A}(\mathbf{U}, \mathbf{V})\mathbf{V}^{\mathrm{T}}\mathbf{e} = \mathbf{Ue}$$

Economically, this axiom implies that total supply must meet total demand (intermediate consumption plus final demand compartments).

In other words, the total input requirements must be equal to the observed total input.

(2) Axiom F refers to the financial balance, or the value equation, and is denoted by

$$\mathbf{e}^{\mathrm{T}}\mathbf{A}(\mathbf{U},\mathbf{V})\mathbf{V}^{\mathrm{T}} = \mathbf{e}^{\mathrm{T}}\mathbf{U}$$

That is to say, for each commodity unit, revenue equals to material cost plus value added. In words, the input cost of output must match the observed value of input.

(3) Axiom P refers to the invariance of the resulting **A**-matrix with respect to units of measurement or, in other terms, to prices. It is called the price invariance axiom and denoted by

$$\mathbf{A}(\hat{\mathbf{p}}\mathbf{U},\mathbf{V}\hat{\mathbf{p}}) = \hat{\mathbf{p}}\mathbf{A}(\mathbf{U},\mathbf{V})\hat{\mathbf{p}}^{-1} \quad \forall\, \mathbf{p} > 0$$

Evidently, this property tries to avoid the possibility that a change in the base year prices could affect technical coefficients. Variations in the internal structure of **A**(**U**, **V**) should be caused by real economic phenomena.

(4) Axiom S is the so-called scale invariance axiom:

$$\mathbf{A}(\mathbf{U}\hat{\mathbf{s}},\hat{\mathbf{s}}\mathbf{V}) = \mathbf{A}(\mathbf{U},\mathbf{V}) \quad \forall\, \mathbf{s} > 0$$

It stipulates that technical coefficients do not change when input requirements and outputs vary proportionally.

Kop Jansen and ten Raa (1990) developed and examined how well various methods for the treatment of secondary products fulfill axioms M, F, P and S. More precisely, the authors proved that the just described structure of input–output analysis, involving the four axioms, not only imposes restrictions on the choice of model of construction, but also determines it uniquely, namely the commodity technology model. Their theorem in the real sphere states that the combination of axioms M and S implies that the commodity technology model specifies the **A**-matrix and their theorem in the nominal sphere that the combination of axioms F and P has the same implication.

Table 3 illustrates how the other methods fare in the light of the axioms. In addition to the results obtained by Kop Jansen and ten Raa (1990), Table 3 includes the performance of the mixed commodity and industry technology

Table 3: Axioms Fulfillment of Input–Output Coefficients Constructs.

Model	Axiom *M*	Axiom *F*	Axiom *P*	Axiom *S*
Transfer				
Stone method			√	√
ESA method	√		√	
Lump-sum				√
Commodity technology	√	√	√	√
Industry technology	√			
ten Raa *et al.* method			√	√
United Nations hybrid model	√			

Source: Kop Jansen and ten Raa (1990) and own elaboration.

models (UN 1968; Gigantes 1970); the proofs are in the Appendix. Lastly, since the activity technology model (Konijn 1994) borrows the mathematical structure from the commodity technology model, it requires no separate performance report.

Our main result is a closer examination of Table 3, answering the question what restrictions on the data restore the desirable properties for the models. In other words, for each input–output construct, we delineate regions in the data space where axioms are fulfilled.

4. Equivalent Conditions for Axioms *M and F*

In this section, we will prove that under certain data limitations, some methods for the treatment of secondary products other than the commodity technology model fulfill the material and financial balance. Unfortunately, the price and scale invariance axioms admit no such results.

Two theorems express the material and financial balance axioms in terms of the commodity technology model.

Theorem 1. *A technical coefficients matrix* $\mathbf{A}(\mathbf{U}, \mathbf{V})$ *fulfills axiom M for all* $\mathbf{U}$ *and non-singular* $\mathbf{V}$ *if and only if,*

$$\sum_{j=1}^{n} a_{ij}q_j = \sum_{j=1}^{n} a_{ij}^{C}q_j \quad \forall\, i = 1, \dots, n$$

or, in matrix terms,

$$\mathbf{A}(\mathbf{U}, \mathbf{V})\mathbf{V}^{\mathrm{T}}\mathbf{e} = \mathbf{A}_{\mathrm{C}}(\mathbf{U}, \mathbf{V})\mathbf{V}^{\mathrm{T}}\mathbf{e}$$

Proof. By definition of $\mathbf{A}_\mathrm{C}$, the right hand side of axiom M reads

$$\mathbf{Ue} = \mathbf{UV}^{-\mathrm{T}}\mathbf{V}^\mathrm{T}\mathbf{e} = \mathbf{A}_\mathrm{C}(\mathbf{U},\mathbf{V})\mathbf{V}^\mathrm{T}\mathbf{e}$$ □

Theorem 2. *A technical coefficients matrix* $\mathbf{A}(\mathbf{U},\mathbf{V})$ *fulfills axiom F if and only if the sum of each column of* $\mathbf{A}(\mathbf{U},\mathbf{V})$ *matches the sum of the respective column of* $\mathbf{A}_\mathrm{C}(\mathbf{U},\mathbf{V})$ *for all* $\mathbf{U}$ *and non-singular* $\mathbf{V}$.

$$\sum_{i=1}^{n} a_{ij} = \sum_{i=1}^{n} a_{ij}^{C} \quad \forall j = 1, \ldots, n$$

or, in matrix terms,

$$\mathbf{e}^\mathrm{T}\mathbf{A}(\mathbf{U},\mathbf{V}) = \mathbf{e}^\mathrm{T}\mathbf{A}_\mathrm{C}(\mathbf{U},\mathbf{V})$$

Proof. Sufficiency is proved as follows. Suppose

$$\mathbf{e}^\mathrm{T}\mathbf{A}(\mathbf{U},\mathbf{V}) = \mathbf{e}^\mathrm{T}\mathbf{A}_\mathrm{C}(\mathbf{U},\mathbf{V}),$$

then, by definition of $\mathbf{A}_\mathrm{C}$,

$$\mathbf{e}^\mathrm{T}\mathbf{A}(\mathbf{U},\mathbf{V}) = \mathbf{e}^\mathrm{T}\mathbf{UV}^{-\mathrm{T}}$$

and, therefore,

$$\mathbf{e}^\mathrm{T}\mathbf{A}(\mathbf{U},\mathbf{V})\mathbf{V}^\mathrm{T} = \mathbf{e}^\mathrm{T}\mathbf{UV}^{-\mathrm{T}}\mathbf{V}^\mathrm{T}$$

or

$$\mathbf{e}^\mathrm{T}\mathbf{A}(\mathbf{U},\mathbf{V})\mathbf{V}^\mathrm{T} = \mathbf{e}^\mathrm{T}\mathbf{U}$$

which is axiom F indeed. All steps can be reversed, proving necessity. □

For the lump-sum (or aggregation) method, we have the following result.

Corollary 1. *The lump-sum method fulfills the material balance axiom if the total output of industry j matches the total output of commodity j, for all* $\mathbf{U}$ *and* $\mathbf{V}$ *with* $\mathbf{q}_j = \mathbf{g}_j, \forall j$.

Proof. Under the lump-sum method, the $\mathbf{A}$-matrix is defined as:

$$\mathbf{A}_\mathrm{L}(\mathbf{U},\mathbf{V}) = \mathbf{U}\,\hat{\mathbf{g}}^{-1}$$

and, therefore, if we assume that $\mathbf{Ve} = \mathbf{V}^\mathrm{T}\mathbf{e}$, that is all $\mathbf{g}_j = \mathbf{q}_j$, we obtain:

$$\mathbf{A}_\mathrm{L}(\mathbf{U},\mathbf{V})\mathbf{q} = \mathbf{U}\hat{\mathbf{g}}^{-1}\mathbf{q} = \mathbf{U}\hat{\mathbf{q}}^{-1}\mathbf{q} = \mathbf{U}\hat{\mathbf{q}}^{-1}\hat{\mathbf{q}}\mathbf{e} = \mathbf{Ue}$$

since $\mathbf{q} = \hat{\mathbf{q}}\mathbf{e}$. □

We conclude that the material balance axiom will be fulfilled in the lump-sum model if, for all j, total industry output is equal to total commodity output. The reverse does not hold; axiom M does not imply that $\mathbf{g}_j = \mathbf{q}_j$.

The Stone (or by-product) technology model also admits a specific result.

Corollary 2. *The Stone (or by-product) technology model fulfills the financial balance axiom for all* **U** *and* **V** *if and only if the value added is zero.*

$$\mathbf{e}^{\mathrm{T}}\mathbf{V}^{\mathrm{T}} = \mathbf{e}^{\mathrm{T}}\mathbf{U}$$

Proof. Under the financial balance axiom, the by-product technology model should verify,

$$\mathbf{e}^{\mathrm{T}}\mathbf{A}_{\mathrm{B}}(\mathbf{U},\mathbf{V})\mathbf{V}^{\mathrm{T}} = \mathbf{e}^{\mathrm{T}}\mathbf{U}$$

with the left-hand side of this equality such as,

$$\begin{aligned}\mathbf{e}^{\mathrm{T}}(\mathbf{U} - \widetilde{\mathbf{V}}^{\mathrm{T}})\widehat{\mathbf{V}}^{-1}\mathbf{V}^{\mathrm{T}} &= (\mathbf{e}^{\mathrm{T}}\mathbf{U} - \mathbf{e}^{\mathrm{T}}\widetilde{\mathbf{V}}^{\mathrm{T}})\widehat{\mathbf{V}}^{-1}\mathbf{V}^{\mathrm{T}}\\ &= \mathrm{e}^{\mathrm{T}}\mathbf{U}\widehat{\mathbf{V}}^{-1}\mathbf{V}^{\mathrm{T}} - \mathbf{e}^{\mathrm{T}}\widetilde{\mathbf{V}}^{\mathrm{T}}\widehat{\mathbf{V}}^{-1}\mathbf{V}^{\mathrm{T}}\end{aligned}$$

Moreover, since $\widetilde{\mathbf{V}}^{\mathrm{T}} = \mathbf{V}^{\mathrm{T}} - \widehat{\mathbf{V}}^{\mathrm{T}}$ and $\widehat{\mathbf{V}}^{\mathrm{T}} = \widehat{\mathbf{V}}$, it yields,

$$\begin{aligned}&\mathbf{e}^{\mathrm{T}}\mathbf{U}\widehat{\mathbf{V}}^{-1}\mathbf{V}^{\mathrm{T}} - \mathbf{e}^{\mathrm{T}}\widetilde{\mathbf{V}}^{\mathrm{T}}\widehat{\mathbf{V}}^{-1}\mathbf{V}^{\mathrm{T}}\\ &\quad = \mathbf{e}^{\mathrm{T}}\mathbf{U}\,\widehat{\mathbf{V}}^{-1}\mathbf{V}^{\mathrm{T}} - \mathbf{e}^{\mathrm{T}}\mathbf{V}^{\mathrm{T}}\widehat{\mathbf{V}}^{-1}\mathbf{V}^{\mathrm{T}} + \mathbf{e}^{\mathrm{T}}\widehat{\mathbf{V}}^{\mathrm{T}}\widehat{\mathbf{V}}^{-1}\mathbf{V}^{\mathrm{T}}\end{aligned}$$

which is the same as,

$$\mathbf{e}^{\mathrm{T}}\mathbf{A}_{\mathrm{B}}(\mathbf{U},\mathbf{V})\mathbf{V}^{\mathrm{T}} = (\mathbf{e}^{\mathrm{T}}\mathbf{U} - \mathbf{e}^{\mathrm{T}}\mathbf{V}^{\mathrm{T}})\widehat{\mathbf{V}}^{-1}\mathbf{V}^{\mathrm{T}} + \mathbf{e}^{\mathrm{T}}\mathbf{V}^{\mathrm{T}}$$

So, let us assume now that $\mathbf{e}^{\mathrm{T}}\mathbf{V}^{\mathrm{T}} = \mathbf{e}^{\mathrm{T}}\mathbf{U}$, then

$$\mathbf{e}^{\mathrm{T}}\mathbf{A}_{\mathrm{B}}(\mathbf{U},\mathbf{V})\mathbf{V}^{\mathrm{T}} = \mathbf{e}^{\mathrm{T}}\mathbf{V}^{\mathrm{T}} = \mathbf{e}^{\mathrm{T}}\mathbf{U}$$

All steps can be reversed, proving necessity. □

The last model we consider is the mixed technology model presented by ten Raa, Chakraborty and Small (1984), where the make matrix is split into a table $\mathbf{V}_1$ of primary products and ordinary secondary products, i.e. those products which involve an alternative activity and which are not being generated automatically by the primary productive process, and a table $\mathbf{V}_2$ of by-products.

Kop Jansen and ten Raa (1990) demonstrate that both axioms M and F hold if and only if the mixed technology model proposed by ten Raa, Chakraborty and Small (1984) reduces to the commodity technology model. In other words, both axioms hold only when the $\mathbf{V}_2$ table is null, i.e. when there are no by-products, since according to the authors, the so-called ordinary secondary products are included in table $\mathbf{V}_1$.

But what happens in the presence of by-products? Under what restrictions on the data, would the axioms M and F still hold? We will take some preliminary results from Kop Jansen and ten Raa (1990) as our point of departure in order to cast some light on this issue.

Corollary 3. *The CB-mixed* (*ten Raa, Chakraborty and Small 1984*) *technology model fulfills the material balance axiom for all* $\mathbf{U}$ *and non-singular* $\mathbf{V}_1$ *when* $\mathbf{U} = \mathbf{V}^{\mathrm{T}}$.

Proof. Under the CB-mixed technology model construct, the material balance axiom should verify that,

$$\mathbf{A}_{\mathrm{CB}}(\mathbf{U}, \mathbf{V})\mathbf{V}^{\mathrm{T}}\mathbf{e} = (\mathbf{U} - \mathbf{V}_2^{\mathrm{T}})\mathbf{V}_1^{-\mathrm{T}}\mathbf{V}^{\mathrm{T}}\mathbf{e} = \mathbf{U}\mathbf{e}$$

where $\mathbf{V}_1$ stands for the primary outputs and those secondary products considered as "ordinary" according to the ten Raa, Chakraborty and Small (1984) definition, and $\mathbf{V}_2$, for the by-products. Since we are assuming that $\mathbf{U} = \mathbf{V}^{\mathrm{T}} = \mathbf{V}_1^{\mathrm{T}} + \mathbf{V}_2^{\mathrm{T}}$, it can be shown that,

$$(\mathbf{U} - \mathbf{V}_2^{\mathrm{T}})\mathbf{V}_1^{-\mathrm{T}}\mathbf{V}^{\mathrm{T}}\mathbf{e} = \mathbf{V}_1^{\mathrm{T}}\mathbf{V}_1^{-\mathrm{T}}\mathbf{V}^{\mathrm{T}}\mathbf{e} = \mathbf{U}\mathbf{e} \qquad \square$$

Corollary 4. *The CB-mixed* (*ten Raa, Chakraborty and Small 1984*) *technology model fulfills the financial balance axiom if and only if the value added is zero.*

$$\mathbf{e}^{\mathrm{T}}\mathbf{V}^{\mathrm{T}} = \mathbf{e}^{\mathrm{T}}\mathbf{U}$$

Proof. As Kop Jansen and ten Raa (1990) demonstrate, under the CB-mixed technology model construct, the financial balance axiom should verify that,

$$\mathbf{e}^{\mathrm{T}}\mathbf{A}_{\mathrm{CB}}(\mathbf{U}, \mathbf{V})\mathbf{V}^{\mathrm{T}} = \mathbf{e}^{\mathrm{T}}(\mathbf{U} - \mathbf{V}_2^{\mathrm{T}})\mathbf{V}_1^{-\mathrm{T}}\mathbf{V}^{\mathrm{T}} = \mathbf{e}^{\mathrm{T}}\mathbf{U}$$

This can also be expressed as,

$$\mathbf{e}^{\mathrm{T}}\mathbf{A}_{\mathrm{CB}}(\mathbf{U},\mathbf{V})\mathbf{V}^{\mathrm{T}} = \mathbf{e}^{\mathrm{T}}(\mathbf{U} - \mathbf{V}_2^{\mathrm{T}})\mathbf{V}_1^{-\mathrm{T}}\mathbf{V}^{\mathrm{T}} = (\mathbf{e}^{\mathrm{T}}\mathbf{U} - \mathbf{e}^{\mathrm{T}}\mathbf{V}_2^{\mathrm{T}})\mathbf{V}_1^{-\mathrm{T}}\mathbf{V}^{\mathrm{T}}$$

and substituting $\mathbf{e}^{\mathrm{T}}\mathbf{V}^{\mathrm{T}} = \mathbf{e}^{\mathrm{T}}\mathbf{U}$, it yields,

$$\begin{aligned}\mathbf{e}^{\mathrm{T}}\mathbf{A}_{\mathrm{CB}}(\mathbf{U},\mathbf{V})\mathbf{V}^{\mathrm{T}} &= (\mathbf{e}^{\mathrm{T}}\mathbf{V}^{\mathrm{T}} - \mathbf{e}^{\mathrm{T}}\mathbf{V}_2^{\mathrm{T}})\mathbf{V}_1^{-\mathrm{T}}\mathbf{V}^{\mathrm{T}} = \mathbf{e}^{\mathrm{T}}(\mathbf{V}^{\mathrm{T}} - \mathbf{V}_2^{\mathrm{T}})\mathbf{V}_1^{-\mathrm{T}}\mathbf{V}^{\mathrm{T}} \\ &= \mathbf{e}^{\mathrm{T}}\mathbf{V}_1^{\mathrm{T}}\mathbf{V}_1^{-\mathrm{T}}\mathbf{V}^{\mathrm{T}} = \mathbf{e}^{\mathrm{T}}\mathbf{V}^{\mathrm{T}} = \mathbf{e}^{\mathrm{T}}\mathbf{U}\end{aligned}$$

All steps can be reversed, proving necessity. □

5. Summary and Conclusions

The most interesting conclusion is that the material and financial axioms will be fulfilled under some restrictions on the data (Theorems 1 and 2). For the lump-sum method, the material balance is fulfilled if the total commodity outputs match respective total industry outputs. A brief summary

Table 4: Additional Assumptions Over Axioms According to Models.

Model	Axiom *M*	Axiom *F*	Axiom *P*	Axiom *S*
Transfer	$A_T(U,V)V^Te = A_C(U,V)V^Te$	$e^TA_T(U,V) = e^TA_C(U,V)$	Never	Never
By-product technology	$A_B(U,V)V^Te = A_C(U,V)V^Te$	$e^TA_B(U,V) = e^TA_C(U,V)$ or $e^TV^T = e^TU$	√	√
European System	√	$e^TA_E(U,V) = e^TA_C(U,V)$	√	Never
Lump-Sum	$A_L(U,V)V^Te = A_C(U,V)V^Te$ or $Ve = V^Te$	$e^TA_L(U,V) = e^TA_C(U,V)$	Never	√
Commodity technology	√	√	√	√
Industry technology	√	$e^TA_I(U,V) = e^TA_C(U,V)$	Never	Never
ten Raa *et al.* method	$A_{CB}(U,V)V^Te = A_C(U,V)V^Te$ or $U = V^T$	$e^TA_{CB}(U,V) = e^TA_C(U,V)$ or $e^TV^T = e^TU$	√	√

of the main results is presented in Table 4. The transfer and the industry technology model need restrictive conditions in order to fulfill all axioms.

Acknowledgments

The authors thank F. M. Guerrero, E. Fedriani, E. Romero and two anonymous referees for valuable comments.

References

Almon, C. (1972) Investment in input–output models and the treatment of secondary products, in: A. P. Carter & A. Bródy (eds.), *Applications of Input–Output Analysis* (Amsterdam: North-Holland).

Armstrong, A.G. (1975) Technology assumptions in the construction of United Kingdom input–output tables, in: R. I. G. Allen & W. F. Gossling (eds.), *Estimating and Updating Input–Output Coefficients* (London: Input–Output Publishing Co).

Avonds, L. and A. Gilot (2002) The new Belgian Input–Output Table. General Principles, XIV*th International Conference on Input–Output Techniques*, Montreal, Canada.

Braibant, M. (2002) Transformation of supply and use tables to symmetric input–output tables, XIV*th International Conference on Input–Output Techniques*, Montreal, Canada.

Edmonston, J.H. (1952) A treatment of multiple-process industries, *Quarterly Journal of Economics*, pp. 557–571.

EUROSTAT (1979) *European System of Integrated Economic Accounts — ESA* (Luxembourg, EUROSTAT).

Fukui, Y. and E. Seneta (1985) A theoretical approach to the conventional treatment of joint product in input–output tables, *Economic Letters*, 18, pp. 175–179.

Gigantes, T. (1970) The representation of technology in input–output systems, in: A.P. Carter & A. Bródy (eds.), *Contributions to input–output analysis* (Amsterdam: North-Holland).

Konijn, P.J.A. (1994) The make and use of commodities by industries, PhD Thesis, University of Twente, The Netherlands.

Konijn, P.J.A. and A.E. Steenge (1995) Compilation of input–output data from the National Accounts, *Economic Systems Research*, 7, pp. 31–45.

Kop Jansen, P.S.M. and Th. ten Raa (1990) The choice of model in the construction of input–output coefficients matrices, *International Economic Review*, 31, pp. 213–227.

Leontief, W. (1986) *Input–Output Economics* (New York: Oxford University Press).

Mattey, J.P. (1993) Evidence on Input–Output technology assumptions from the Longitudinal Research Database, *Discussion Paper Center for Economic Studies,* 93–8, (Washington DC, US Bureau of the Census).

Mattey, J.P. and Th. ten Raa (1997) Primary versus secondary production techniques in US manufacturing, *Review of Income and Wealth*, 43, pp. 449–464.

Office of Statistical Standards (1974) *Input–Output tables for 1970* (Tokyo, Institute for Dissemination of Government Data).
Rainer, N. (1989) Descriptive versus analytical make-use systems: some Austrian experiences, in: R. Miller, K. Polenske & A. Z. Rose (eds.) *Frontiers of input–output analysis* (New York: Oxford University Press).
Rainer, N. and J. Richter (1992) Some aspects of the analytical use of descriptive make and absorption tables, *Economic Systems Research*, 4, pp. 159–172.
Steenge, A.E. (1990) The commodity technology revisited: theoretical basis and an application to error location in the make-use framework, *Economic Modelling*, 7, pp. 376–387.
Stone, R. (1961) *Input–Output and National Accounts* (Paris, OECD).
ten Raa, Th. (1988) An alternative treatment of secondary products in input–output analysis: frustration, *Review of Economics and Statistics*, 70, pp. 535–540.
ten Raa, Th. (1994) On the methodology of input–output analysis, *Regional Science and Urban Economics*, 24, pp. 3–27.
ten Raa, Th., D. Chakraborty, and J.A. Small (1984) An alternative treatment of secondary products in input–output analysis, *Review of Economics and Statistics*, 66, pp. 88–97.
ten Raa, Th. and R. van der Ploeg (1989) A statistical approach to the problem of negatives in input–output analysis, *Economic Modelling*, 6, pp. 2–19.
United Nations (1968) *A system of national accounts,* Studies in Methods Series F, no. 2, rev. 3 (New York: United Nations).
United Nations (1973) *Input–Output tables and analysis*, Studies in Methods Series F, no. 14, rev. 1 (New York: United Nations).
United Nations (1993) *Revised system of national accounts,* Studies in Methods Series F, no. 2, rev. 4 (New York: United Nations).
United Nations Statistical Commission (1967) *Proposals for the revision of SNA*, 1952, Document E/CN.3/356 (New York: United Nations).
van Rijckeghem, W. (1967) An exact method for determining the technology matrix in a situation with secondary products, *Review of Economics and Statistics*, 49, pp. 607–608.
Viet, V.Q. (1986) *Study of Input–Output Tables:* 1970–1980 (New York: UN Statistical Office).
Viet, V.Q. (1994) Practices in input–output table compilation, *Regional Science and Urban Economics*, 24, pp. 27–54.

Appendix

This Appendix proves that the established hybrid constructs on the basis of commodity and industry technology assumptions fulfill only the material balance. As in Kop Jansen and ten Raa (1990), and using their same imaginary use and make matrices, it also presents counterexamples that violate the financial balance, price or scale invariance axioms. Let us define the following use and make matrices to generate counter-examples:

$$\mathbf{U} = \begin{pmatrix} \frac{1}{2} & 0 \\ 1 & \frac{1}{2} \end{pmatrix}, \quad \mathbf{V} = \begin{pmatrix} 1 & 1 \\ 0 & 1 \end{pmatrix} \quad \text{and} \quad \mathbf{p} = \mathbf{s} = \begin{pmatrix} 2 \\ 1 \end{pmatrix}$$

Also, the make table is split into the following $\mathbf{V}_1$ and $\mathbf{V}_2$ matrices,

$$\mathbf{V}_1 = \begin{pmatrix} 1 & 0 \\ 0 & 1 \end{pmatrix} = \mathbf{I}, \quad \mathbf{V}_2 = \begin{pmatrix} 0 & 1 \\ 0 & 0 \end{pmatrix}$$

A straightforward computation shows that,

$$\mathbf{g} = \mathbf{Ve} = \begin{pmatrix} 2 \\ 1 \end{pmatrix}, \quad \mathbf{g}_1 = \mathbf{V}_1\mathbf{e} = \begin{pmatrix} 1 \\ 1 \end{pmatrix},$$

$$\mathbf{q} = \mathbf{V}^{\mathrm{T}}\mathbf{e} = \begin{pmatrix} 1 \\ 2 \end{pmatrix}, \quad \mathbf{q}_2 = \mathbf{V}_2^{\mathrm{T}}\mathbf{e} = \begin{pmatrix} 0 \\ 1 \end{pmatrix}$$

and therefore,

$$\mathbf{A}_{\mathrm{H}}(\mathbf{U},\mathbf{V}) = \begin{pmatrix} \frac{1}{4} & \frac{1}{8} \\ \frac{1}{2} & \frac{1}{2} \end{pmatrix} \quad \text{and} \quad \mathbf{A}_{\mathrm{Y}}(\mathbf{U},\mathbf{V}) = \begin{pmatrix} \frac{1}{4} & \frac{1}{8} \\ 0 & \frac{3}{4} \end{pmatrix}$$

with $\mathbf{H} = \begin{pmatrix} 2 & 0 \\ -1 & 1 \end{pmatrix}$.

Material balance (*Axiom* M)

The material balance equation for $\mathbf{A}_{\mathrm{H}}$ is verified as follows:

$$\begin{aligned} \mathbf{A}_{\mathrm{H}}(\mathbf{U},\mathbf{V})\mathbf{V}^{\mathrm{T}}\mathbf{e} &= \mathbf{A}_{\mathrm{H}}(\mathbf{U},\mathbf{V})\mathbf{q} \\ &= \mathbf{U}\hat{\mathbf{g}}^{-1}(\hat{\mathbf{g}}_1\mathbf{V}_1^{-\mathrm{T}}(\mathbf{I} - \hat{\mathbf{q}}^{-1}\hat{\mathbf{q}}_2) + \mathbf{V}_2\hat{\mathbf{q}}^{-1})\mathbf{q} \qquad (4) \end{aligned}$$

Since it is true that $\hat{\mathbf{q}}^{-1}\mathbf{q} = \mathbf{e}$, $\mathbf{g}_2 = \mathbf{V}_2\mathbf{e}$ and $\hat{\mathbf{q}}^{-1}\hat{\mathbf{q}}_2\mathbf{q} = \mathbf{q}_2$ equation (4) can be written as:

$$\begin{aligned} \mathbf{A}_{\mathrm{H}}(\mathbf{U},\mathbf{V})\mathbf{V}^{\mathrm{T}}\mathbf{e} &= \mathbf{U}\hat{\mathbf{g}}^{-1}(\hat{\mathbf{g}}_1\mathbf{V}_1^{-\mathrm{T}}\mathbf{q} - \hat{\mathbf{g}}_1\mathbf{V}_1^{-\mathrm{T}}\mathbf{q}_2 + \mathbf{g}_2) \\ &= \mathbf{U}\hat{\mathbf{g}}^{-1}(\hat{\mathbf{g}}_1\mathbf{V}_1^{-\mathrm{T}}(\mathbf{q} - \mathbf{q}_2) + \mathbf{g}_2) \\ &= \mathbf{U}\hat{\mathbf{g}}^{-1}(\hat{\mathbf{g}}_1\mathbf{V}_1^{-\mathrm{T}}\mathbf{q}_1 + \mathbf{g}_2) \qquad (5) \end{aligned}$$

and if we substitute $\mathbf{q}_1 = \mathbf{V}_1^T\mathbf{e}$ in equation (5), bearing in mind that $\mathbf{g}_1 = \hat{\mathbf{g}}_1\mathbf{e}$,

$$\begin{aligned}\mathbf{A}_H(\mathbf{U},\mathbf{V})\mathbf{V}^T\mathbf{e} &= \mathbf{U}\hat{\mathbf{g}}^{-1}(\hat{\mathbf{g}}_1\mathbf{V}_1^{-T}\mathbf{q}_1 + \mathbf{g}_2) = \mathbf{U}\hat{\mathbf{g}}^{-1}(\hat{\mathbf{g}}_1\mathbf{e} + \mathbf{g}_2)\\ &= \mathbf{U}\hat{\mathbf{g}}^{-1}(\mathbf{g}_1 + \mathbf{g}_2) = \mathbf{U}\hat{\mathbf{g}}^{-1}\mathbf{g} = \mathbf{U}\mathbf{e}\end{aligned}$$

For $\mathbf{A}_Y$, axiom M is verified as follows:

$$\begin{aligned}\mathbf{A}_Y(\mathbf{U},\mathbf{V})\mathbf{V}^T\mathbf{e} = \mathbf{A}_Y(\mathbf{U},\mathbf{V})\mathbf{q} &= \mathbf{U}\hat{\mathbf{g}}^{-1}(\hat{\mathbf{g}}_1\mathbf{V}_1^{-T}(\mathbf{I} - \mathbf{V}_2^T\hat{\mathbf{g}}^{-1}\mathbf{H}) + \mathbf{V}_2\hat{\mathbf{q}}^{-1})\mathbf{q}\\ &= \mathbf{U}\hat{\mathbf{g}}^{-1}(\hat{\mathbf{g}}_1\mathbf{V}_1^{-T}\mathbf{q} - \hat{\mathbf{g}}_1\mathbf{V}_1^{-T}\mathbf{V}_2^T\hat{\mathbf{g}}^{-1}\mathbf{H}\mathbf{q} + \mathbf{V}_2\hat{\mathbf{q}}^{-1}\mathbf{q}) \qquad (6)\end{aligned}$$

Since $\hat{\mathbf{q}}^{-1}\mathbf{q} = \hat{\mathbf{g}}^{-1}\mathbf{g} = \mathbf{e}$, $\mathbf{g}_2 = \mathbf{V}_2\mathbf{e}$ and $\mathbf{g} = \mathbf{H}\mathbf{q}$ (see Armstrong 1975, p. 75), equation (6) can be written as:

$$\begin{aligned}\mathbf{A}_Y(\mathbf{U},\mathbf{V})\mathbf{V}^T\mathbf{e} &= \mathbf{U}\hat{\mathbf{g}}^{-1}(\hat{\mathbf{g}}_1\mathbf{V}_1^{-T}\mathbf{q} - \hat{\mathbf{g}}_1\mathbf{V}_1^{-T}\mathbf{V}_2^T\mathbf{e} + \mathbf{g}_2)\\ &= \mathbf{U}\hat{\mathbf{g}}^{-1}(\hat{\mathbf{g}}_1\mathbf{V}_1^{-T}(\mathbf{q} - \mathbf{q}_2) + \mathbf{g}_2)\\ &= \mathbf{U}\hat{\mathbf{g}}^{-1}(\hat{\mathbf{g}}_1\mathbf{V}_1^{-T}\mathbf{q}_1 + \mathbf{g}_2) \qquad (7)\end{aligned}$$

for $\mathbf{V}_2^T\mathbf{e} = \mathbf{q}_2$.

If we substitute $\mathbf{q}_1 = \mathbf{V}_1^T\mathbf{e}$ in equation (7), bearing in mind that $\mathbf{g}_1 = \hat{\mathbf{g}}_1\mathbf{e}$,

$$\begin{aligned}\mathbf{A}_Y(\mathbf{U},\mathbf{V})\mathbf{V}^T\mathbf{e} &= \mathbf{U}\hat{\mathbf{g}}^{-1}(\hat{\mathbf{g}}_1\mathbf{V}_1^{-T}\mathbf{q}_1 + \mathbf{g}_2) = \mathbf{U}\hat{\mathbf{g}}^{-1}(\hat{\mathbf{g}}_1\mathbf{e} + \mathbf{g}_2)\\ &= \mathbf{U}\hat{\mathbf{g}}^{-1}(\mathbf{g}_1 + \mathbf{g}_2) = \mathbf{U}\hat{\mathbf{g}}^{-1}\mathbf{g} = \mathbf{U}\mathbf{e}\end{aligned}$$

Financial balance (*Axiom* F)

For both hybrid technology assumptions, the financial balance equation is not fulfilled since,

$$\mathbf{e}^T\mathbf{A}_H(\mathbf{U},\mathbf{V})\mathbf{V}^T = \begin{pmatrix}1 & 1\end{pmatrix}\begin{pmatrix}\frac{1}{4} & \frac{1}{8}\\ \frac{1}{2} & \frac{1}{2}\end{pmatrix}\begin{pmatrix}1 & 0\\ 1 & 1\end{pmatrix} = \begin{pmatrix}\frac{11}{8} & \frac{5}{8}\end{pmatrix},$$

$$\mathbf{e}^T\mathbf{A}_Y(\mathbf{U},\mathbf{V})\mathbf{V}^T = \begin{pmatrix}1 & 1\end{pmatrix}\begin{pmatrix}\frac{1}{4} & \frac{1}{8}\\ 0 & \frac{3}{4}\end{pmatrix}\begin{pmatrix}1 & 0\\ 1 & 1\end{pmatrix} = \begin{pmatrix}\frac{9}{8} & \frac{7}{8}\end{pmatrix}$$

and

$$\mathbf{e}^{\mathrm{T}}\mathbf{U} = \begin{pmatrix} 1 & 1 \end{pmatrix} \begin{pmatrix} \frac{1}{2} & 0 \\ 1 & \frac{1}{2} \end{pmatrix} = \begin{pmatrix} \frac{3}{2} & \frac{1}{2} \end{pmatrix}.$$

Price invariance (*Axiom* P)

The price invariance axiom is violated since,

$$\mathbf{A}_{\mathrm{H}}(\hat{\mathbf{p}}\mathbf{U}, \mathbf{V}\hat{\mathbf{p}}) = \begin{pmatrix} \frac{1}{3} & 0 \\ \frac{1}{3} & \frac{1}{2} \end{pmatrix} \left[\begin{pmatrix} 1 & 0 \\ 0 & 1 \end{pmatrix} \begin{pmatrix} 1 & 0 \\ 0 & \frac{1}{2} \end{pmatrix} + \begin{pmatrix} 0 & \frac{1}{2} \\ 0 & 0 \end{pmatrix} \right]$$

$$= \begin{pmatrix} \frac{1}{3} & \frac{1}{6} \\ \frac{1}{3} & \frac{5}{12} \end{pmatrix},$$

$$\mathbf{A}_{\mathrm{Y}}(\hat{\mathbf{p}}\mathbf{U}, \mathbf{V}\hat{\mathbf{p}}) = \begin{pmatrix} \frac{1}{3} & 0 \\ \frac{1}{3} & \frac{1}{2} \end{pmatrix} \left[\begin{pmatrix} 1 & 0 \\ 0 & 1 \end{pmatrix} \begin{pmatrix} 1 & -1 \\ 0 & 1 \end{pmatrix} + \begin{pmatrix} 0 & \frac{1}{2} \\ 0 & 0 \end{pmatrix} \right]$$

$$= \begin{pmatrix} \frac{1}{3} & \frac{-1}{6} \\ \frac{1}{3} & \frac{1}{3} \end{pmatrix}$$

but

$$\hat{\mathbf{p}}\mathbf{A}_{\mathrm{H}}(\mathbf{U}, \mathbf{V})\hat{\mathbf{p}}^{-1} = \begin{pmatrix} 2 & 0 \\ 0 & 1 \end{pmatrix} \begin{pmatrix} \frac{1}{4} & \frac{1}{8} \\ \frac{1}{2} & \frac{1}{2} \end{pmatrix} \begin{pmatrix} \frac{1}{2} & 0 \\ 0 & 1 \end{pmatrix} = \begin{pmatrix} \frac{1}{4} & \frac{1}{4} \\ \frac{1}{4} & \frac{1}{2} \end{pmatrix}$$

and

$$\hat{\mathbf{p}}\mathbf{A}_{\mathrm{Y}}(\mathbf{U}, \mathbf{V})\hat{\mathbf{p}}^{-1} = \begin{pmatrix} 2 & 0 \\ 0 & 1 \end{pmatrix} \begin{pmatrix} \frac{1}{4} & \frac{1}{8} \\ 0 & \frac{3}{4} \end{pmatrix} \begin{pmatrix} \frac{1}{2} & 0 \\ 0 & 1 \end{pmatrix} = \begin{pmatrix} \frac{1}{4} & \frac{1}{4} \\ 0 & \frac{3}{4} \end{pmatrix}$$

Scale invariance (*Axiom* S)

According to the real sphere theorem in Kop Jansen and ten Raa (1990), the material balance and scale invariance axioms characterize the commodity technology model. Hence, if it has been proved that the material balance holds under hybrid technology assumptions, scale invariance axioms need not necessarily hold. Otherwise, the commodity technology model must be imposed. Actually, scale invariance axiom holds when the hybrid technology model is reduced to the commodity technology model.

Chapter 7

A Generalized Expression for the Commodity and the Industry Technology Models in Input–Output Analysis

Thijs ten Raa and José Manuel Rueda-Cantuche

Abstract: Technical coefficients are usually constructed from commodity or industry technology models. Although these models are considered as competing, there is an encompassing framework which admits a clear comparison.

Keywords: Technical coefficients; commodity technology; industry technology; input–output analysis.

1. Introduction

Leontief's input–output model industries features a one-to-one correspondence between industries and products (Steenge, 1990). The matrix of inter-industry flows is a square and the resulting input–output table is homogeneous; it can be interpreted as a commodity-by-commodity or industry-by-industry table. A first complication comes with the presence of secondary products (by-products, joint products or subsidiary products). During the 1950s and 1960s, rapid industrial diversification caused further problems since input–output tables were being constructed on a single product industrial basis. To cope with these problems, the United Nations System of National Accounts (SNA) created two new tables: the so-called use and make tables (recently renamed as use and supply tables in the SNA-93). Although this new framework solved many problems, new problems arose, such as the construction of a technical coefficients matrix on the basis of use and supply matrices (Steenge 1990)[1]. A *use* matrix $\mathbf{U} = (u_{ij})_{i,j=1,\ldots,n}$ comprises commodities i consumed by sectors j, a *supply* matrix $\mathbf{V} = (v_{ij})_{i,j=1,\ldots,n}$ (formerly the transposed of a make matrix) shows the produce of commodities i in terms of industries j, and an issue is the estimation of the amount of commodity i needed per unit of commodity j.

We formalize the construction of a technical coefficients matrix within a supply-use framework and derive a general mathematical expression which encompasses the commodity and the industry technology models. We treat the compilation of product-by-product input–output tables; industry-by-industry input–output tables may be compiled by assuming fixed product or fixed industry sales structures. This task is on our agenda since industry-by-industry input–output tables are compiled by several statistical offices in countries including Denmark, the Netherlands, Norway, Canada and Finland.

2. Formalization of the Models

Since survey data are based on industry establishments rather than products, we will take as our point of departure the amount of commodity i used by industry j for making either their primary or their secondary outputs (u_{ij}). One must subtract from u_{ij} the consumption of commodity i used by industry j for its secondary products. Secondary outputs of industry j do not necessarily use the inputs structure of their corresponding commodities (as industries could have their own specific input structures). On the other

[1]Multipliers estimation is another problem mentioned in Steenge (1990) although it is proved in ten Raa and Rueda-Cantuche (2004) that employment and output multipliers can be estimated on the basis of use and supply matrices at a micro data level.

hand, the requirements of commodity i by other industries for making commodity j as secondary output must be added, if we want to determine the average input requirements of product j, a_{ij}. The total input requirements of commodity i for making commodity j (as a single product) by the economy is thus:

$$u_{ij} - \sum_{\substack{k=1 \\ k \neq j}}^{n} a_{ijk} v_{kj} + \sum_{\substack{k=1 \\ k \neq j}}^{n} a_{ikj} v_{jk},$$

where n is the number of industries as well as of commodities; u_{ij} is the amount of commodity i consumed by industry j, a_{ijk}; the amount of commodity i used by industry j for making each unit of commodity k, a_{ikj}; the amount of commodity i used by other industries k for making each unit of commodity j; and v_{kj} (or v_{jk}), the produce of industry j (or k), in terms of commodity k (or j). The first subindex of a_{ijk} denotes commodity inputs (i), the second industries (j), and the third commodity outputs (k).

Bearing in mind that a technical coefficient a_{ij} measures the amount of commodity i used per unit of commodity j, produced by industry j as primary output, we can write:

$$a_{ij} = \frac{u_{ij} - \sum_{\substack{k=1 \\ k \neq j}}^{n} a_{ijk} v_{kj} + \sum_{\substack{k=1 \\ k \neq j}}^{n} a_{ikj} v_{jk}}{\sum_{k=1}^{n} v_{jk}}. \tag{1}$$

The problem is that n^2 equations (one for each technical coefficient, a_{ij}) have n^3 unknowns (a_{ijk}, for all $i, j, k = 1, 2, \ldots, n$). To solve the equations system (1), assumptions are made, of which the commodity technology and the industry technology assumptions are best known.[2]

The commodity technology hypothesis assumes that all commodities have the same input structure irrespective of the industry that produces it. That is, for $j = 1, \ldots, n$

$$a_{ijk} = a_{ik}. \tag{2}$$

[2]See ten Raa and Rueda-Cantuche (2003) for a complete review.

Under equation (2), equation (1) becomes:

$$a_{ij} = \frac{u_{ij} - \sum\limits_{\substack{k=1 \\ k\neq j}}^{n} a_{ik}v_{kj} + \sum\limits_{\substack{k=1 \\ k\neq j}}^{n} a_{ij}v_{jk}}{\sum\limits_{k=1}^{n} v_{jk}}, \tag{3}$$

In matrix terms, equation (3) reads[3]:

$$\begin{aligned} \mathbf{A} &= (\mathbf{U} - \mathbf{A}\widetilde{\mathbf{V}} + \mathbf{A}(\widehat{\widetilde{\mathbf{V}}\mathbf{e}}))(\widehat{\mathbf{V}\mathbf{e}})^{-1} \\ &= (\mathbf{U} - \mathbf{A}\widetilde{\mathbf{V}} + \mathbf{A}(\widehat{\widetilde{\mathbf{V}}\mathbf{e}}))(\widehat{\mathbf{V}^{\mathbf{T}}\mathbf{e}} + (\widehat{\widetilde{\mathbf{V}}\mathbf{e}}) - \widehat{\widetilde{\mathbf{V}}^{\mathbf{T}}\mathbf{e}})^{-1}, \end{aligned} \tag{4}$$

Manipulating (4) yields:

$$\begin{aligned} &\mathbf{U} - \mathbf{A}\widetilde{\mathbf{V}} + \mathbf{A}(\widehat{\widetilde{\mathbf{V}}\mathbf{e}}) = \mathbf{A}(\widehat{\mathbf{V}\mathbf{e}}) = \\ &\quad = \mathbf{A}(\widehat{\mathbf{V}^{\mathbf{T}}\mathbf{e}} + (\widehat{\widetilde{\mathbf{V}}\mathbf{e}}) - \widehat{\widetilde{\mathbf{V}}^{\mathbf{T}}\mathbf{e}}) = \mathbf{A}\widehat{\mathbf{V}^{\mathbf{T}}\mathbf{e}} + \mathbf{A}(\widehat{\widetilde{\mathbf{V}}\mathbf{e}}) - \mathbf{A}(\widehat{\widetilde{\mathbf{V}}^{\mathbf{T}}\mathbf{e}}), \end{aligned}$$

which is the same as:

$$\begin{aligned} \mathbf{U} - \mathbf{A}\widetilde{\mathbf{V}} &= \mathbf{A}\widehat{\mathbf{V}^{\mathbf{T}}\mathbf{e}} - \mathbf{A}(\widehat{\widetilde{\mathbf{V}}^{\mathbf{T}}\mathbf{e}}) = \mathbf{A}(\widehat{\mathbf{V}^{\mathbf{T}}\mathbf{e}} - \widehat{\widetilde{\mathbf{V}}^{\mathbf{T}}\mathbf{e}}) \\ &= \mathbf{A}(\widehat{\mathbf{V}^{\mathbf{T}}\mathbf{e} - \widetilde{\mathbf{V}}^{\mathbf{T}}\mathbf{e}}) = \mathbf{A}(\widehat{\widehat{\mathbf{V}}^{\mathbf{T}}\mathbf{e}}) = \mathbf{A}\widehat{\mathbf{V}} \end{aligned}$$

or:

$$\mathbf{U} = \mathbf{A}\widetilde{\mathbf{V}} + \mathbf{A}\widehat{\mathbf{V}} = \mathbf{A}(\widetilde{\mathbf{V}} + \widehat{\mathbf{V}}) = \mathbf{A}\mathbf{V}.$$

Consequently,

$$\mathbf{A} = \mathbf{U}\mathbf{V}^{-1}. \tag{5}$$

The technical coefficients determined by equation (5) can be negative when the total consumption of input i for the making of secondary outputs of industry j, according to each one of these commodity technologies, exceeds

[3] In what follows, e will denote a column vector with all entries equal to one. ^{T} will denote transposition and -1 inversion of a matrix. Since the latter two operations commute, their composition may be denoted $^{-\mathrm{T}}$. Also, $\wedge$ will denote diagonalization, whether by the suppression of the off-diagonal elements of a square matrix, or by the placement of the elements of a vector. $\sim$ will denote a matrix with all the diagonal elements set at null.

the total use of commodity i by the industry j, either for its primary or secondary products.

The industry technology hypothesis assumes that all industries have the same input structure irrespective of the commodities they produce. This means that for all $k = 1, \ldots, n$

$$a_{ijk} = a_{ij}, \tag{6}$$

and that u_{ij} can be said to be proportional to total industries' outputs, that is,

$$u_{ij} = z_{ij} \sum_{k=1}^{n} v_{kj},$$

or in matrix terms,

$$\mathbf{U} = \mathbf{Z}(\widehat{\mathbf{V}^{\mathbf{T}}\mathbf{e}})$$

Hence, (1) becomes:

$$a_{ij} = \frac{u_{ij} - \sum\limits_{\substack{h=1 \\ h \neq j}}^{n} z_{ij} v_{hj} + \sum\limits_{\substack{h=1 \\ h \neq j}}^{n} z_{ih} v_{jh}}{\sum\limits_{h=1}^{n} v_{jh}},$$

which, in matrix terms, is:

$$\mathbf{A} = (\mathbf{U} - \mathbf{Z}(\widehat{\widetilde{\mathbf{V}}^{\mathbf{T}}\mathbf{e}}) + \mathbf{Z}\widetilde{\mathbf{V}}^{\mathbf{T}})(\widehat{\mathbf{V}\mathbf{e}})^{-1}, \tag{7}$$

or, manipulating (7),

$$\mathbf{A} = (\mathbf{U} - \mathbf{U}(\widehat{\mathbf{V}^{\mathbf{T}}\mathbf{e}})^{-1}(\widehat{\widetilde{\mathbf{V}}^{\mathbf{T}}\mathbf{e}}) + \mathbf{U}(\widehat{\mathbf{V}^{\mathbf{T}}\mathbf{e}})^{-1}\widetilde{\mathbf{V}}^{\mathbf{T}})(\widehat{\mathbf{V}\mathbf{e}})^{-1},$$

and,

$$\begin{aligned}
\mathbf{A} &= (\mathbf{U} - \mathbf{U}(\widehat{\mathbf{V}^{\mathbf{T}}\mathbf{e}})^{-1}((\widehat{\mathbf{V}^{\mathbf{T}}\mathbf{e}}) - (\widehat{\widehat{\mathbf{V}}^{\mathbf{T}}\mathbf{e}})) + \mathbf{U}(\widehat{\mathbf{V}^{\mathbf{T}}\mathbf{e}})^{-1}\widetilde{\mathbf{V}}^{\mathbf{T}})(\widehat{\mathbf{V}\mathbf{e}})^{-1} \\
&= (\mathbf{U} - \mathbf{U} + \mathbf{U}(\widehat{\mathbf{V}^{\mathbf{T}}\mathbf{e}})^{-1}\widehat{\mathbf{V}}^{\mathbf{T}} + \mathbf{U}(\widehat{\mathbf{V}^{\mathbf{T}}\mathbf{e}})^{-1}\widetilde{\mathbf{V}}^{\mathbf{T}})(\widehat{\mathbf{V}\mathbf{e}})^{-1} \\
&= (\mathbf{U}(\widehat{\mathbf{V}^{\mathbf{T}}\mathbf{e}})^{-1}(\widehat{\mathbf{V}}^{\mathbf{T}} + \widetilde{\mathbf{V}}^{\mathbf{T}}))(\widehat{\mathbf{V}\mathbf{e}})^{-1}
\end{aligned}$$

or, since $\widetilde{\mathbf{V}}^{\mathbf{T}} = \mathbf{V}^{\mathbf{T}} - \widehat{\mathbf{V}}^{\mathbf{T}}$,

$$\mathbf{A} = \mathbf{U}(\widehat{\mathbf{V}^{\mathbf{T}}\mathbf{e}})^{-1}\mathbf{V}^{\mathbf{T}}(\widehat{\mathbf{V}\mathbf{e}})^{-1}. \tag{8}$$

Under the industry technology assumption, technical coefficients are non-negative by equation (8).

3. An Empirical Comparison

The general concept of an input–output coefficient a_{ijk}, the amount of commodity i used by industry j for making each unit of commodity k, encompasses the commodity and industry technology models according to restrictions (2) and (6), respectively. The restriction that is most likely in the sense that it best fit the data identifies the more suitable model. Following Mattey and ten Raa (1997), input–output coefficients are considered input regression coefficients of outputs of firm data. Thus, let $l = 1, \ldots, n_j$ be the firms populating industry j. Regress each input i on industry j's outputs:

$$u_{ijl} = \sum_{k=1}^{n} a_{ijk} v_{kjl} + \varepsilon_{ijl} \tag{9}$$

where u_{ijl} and v_{kjl} are the input i and the outputs k of industry j's firm l. The commodity technology hypothesis (2), where the coefficients a_{ik} are given by equation (5), has a p-value, say p_C. For example, if $p_C = 0.2$, then the imposition of the commodity technology assumption pushes the error terms of (9) in the tail with a 20%-mass. Similarly, the industry technology assumption has a p-value, say p_I. For example, if $p_I = 0.3$, the imposition of the industry technology assumption pushes the error terms of (9) less, in the tail with a 30%-mass. In general, a greater p-value indicates a better fit of the technology assumption with the data. Since the input, i, has been fixed in this regression analysis, for some inputs, the commodity technology assumption may prove better and for other inputs, the industry technology model.

4. Conclusion

The two main methods to construct a technical coefficients matrix within a supply-use framework, the competing commodity and industry technology models, are encompassed by a single formula featuring input–output coefficients a_{ijk}, for the amounts of commodities i used by industries j for making units of commodities k. The two models are represented by alternative restrictions on these industry-specific input–output coefficients. This framework is capable of testing which model is more compatible with the data. Following a suggestion by one of the referees, it seems possible to apply the commodity and industry technology approaches to different inputs, thus providing a new form of a mixed technology model.

References

Mattey, J. and T. ten Raa (1997) Primary versus secondary production techniques in U.S. manufacturing, *Review of Income and Wealth*, 43(4), pp. 449–464.

ten Raa, T. and J.M. Rueda-Cantuche (2003) The construction of input–output coefficients matrices in an axiomatic context: Some further considerations, *Economic Systems Research*, 15, pp. 439–455.

ten Raa, T. and J.M. Rueda-Cantuche (2004) How to estimate unbiased and consistent input–output multipliers on the basis of use and make matrices, *Economic Working Papers Series* E14/2004, Foundation Center for Andalusian Studies: CentrA, Seville, Spain.

Rueda-Cantuche, J.M. (2004) *Stochastic Input–Output Analysis of the Andalusian Economy*, European PhD thesis, Pablo de Olavide University, Seville.

Steenge, A.E. (1990) Commodity technology revisited: Theoretical basis and an application to error location in the make-use framework, *Economic Modelling*, 7, pp. 376–387.

Chapter 8

The Extraction of Technical Coefficients from Input and Output Data

Thijs ten Raa

Abstract: Presumably, input–output coefficients reflect technology, and these coefficients measure the input requirements per unit of product. The concept has been extended to consumption theory, where it models expenditure shares. Input–output coefficients are extracted from the national accounts of an economy, by taking average proportions between inputs and outputs. Since the latter represent all sorts of inefficiencies, this practice blurs the measurement of technology. Input requirements are better measured by minimal proportions between inputs and outputs. This approach separates the measurement of technology from that of productive efficiency.

Keywords: Input–output coefficient.

1. Introduction

What is an input–output coefficient? Presumably, it measures some input requirement per unit of some output. The inventor of input–output coefficients, Wassily Leontief, thought of them as recipes. To bake a pie, you need so much flour, butter, sugar, etc. He thought the coefficients can be estimated by dividing the amount of consumed flour by the volume of produced pies and implemented this technique for the U.S. economy. To date, this is still the standard procedure. When applying thus constructed coefficients, the implicit assumption is that market shares between firms with different input–output proportions are constant. This assumption is not innocent. Not only may changes in the business climate favor more (or less) competitive firms, but the very concept of constant market shares is inconceivable in a world of multi-product firms with partially overlapping markets, particularly when the pattern of demand changes.[1]

There are two issues. One is the problem that requirements are measured by average input/output proportions. In my opinion, a requirement better be measured by a minimal proportion. The other is that the multi-product nature of firms complicates the assignment of inputs to outputs and the reference set over which the average or the minimum is taken.

To address the choice between average and minimal input–output coefficients, consider a single input/single output industry. Firm i transforms l_i units of labor into x_i units of the product. Industry input and output are $\sum l_i$ and $\sum x_i$, respectively, and the standard way to determine the input–output coefficient is by division: $a = \sum l_i / \sum x_i$. This procedure amounts to taking a weighted average of the well-defined firm input–output coefficients, $a_i = l_i/x_i$. An econometric variant of the procedure is to estimate the ratio between inputs and outputs by regressing the inputs on the outputs without a constant term: $a = \sum l_i x_i / \sum x_i^2$.[2] It can be argued, certainly under the customary assumption of constant returns to scale, that the number of workers *required* per unit of product is determined by the firm which uses the least labor per unit of output: $a = \min l_i/x_i$. I believe that this statistic measures the production function. After all, a production function determines the maximum amount of output that can be produced with given input.

Suppose, without loss of generality, that firm 1 uses the least labor per unit of output, then $a = a_1 = l_1/x_1$. The other firms underperform. Take firm 2. It produces x_2 units of output and uses $l_2 = a_2 x_2$ units of input, but if it would adopt the technique of firm 1, firm 2 would need only $l_2^* = a_1 x_2$

---

[1] See ten Raa and Rueda-Cantuche (2007a) for a recent review of the construction of input–output coefficients.

[2] Mattey and ten Raa (1997), and ten Raa and Rueda-Cantuche (2007b) construct confidence intervals for the coefficients and their Leontief inverse. In principle, this can also be done for the standard formula.

units of input. The inefficiency can also be measured on the output side. If we invert the input–output coefficients, we get output per unit of input, which is productivity. Firm 1 is the most productive firm: $1/a_1 = \max x_i/l_i$. Firm 2 uses l_2 units of input and produces $x_2 = (1/a_2)l_2$ units of output. If firm 2 would adopt the technique of firm 1, it could produce $x_2^* = (1/a_1)x_2$ units of output, which is more. Its output is x_2, but its *potential* output is x_2^*. The latter is the value of the production function. The slope of this function equals the productivity of firm 1 and the technical coefficient of firm 1 thus determines the production function.

We must bear in mind the aim of an input–output coefficient. One aim is to assess the employment impact of an increase in demand. Consider a raise in the total demand from $\sum x_i$ to $\sum x_i + \Delta x$. The additional labor requirement is $a\Delta x$. What is the relevant input–output coefficient? The answer is: it depends. It is determined by which firm(s) pick(s) up the additional production. If all firms pick up a proportionate share, the standard input–output coefficient is appropriate. If the most competitive firm picks up the additional production, the technology-based coefficient is relevant. I find that additional information is needed to answer this question. There is a range of answers. The technology-based coefficient sets the minimum employment impact. The maximum impact is attained if one employs the worst coefficient of the least productive firm. To me, the former seems more interesting. Ultimately, it is a matter of projecting efficiency. This requires a forecast of the distance to the production possibility frontier and the determination of the latter must be based on technology coefficients.

The analysis becomes more complicated when firms produce different (combinations of) outputs. Consider a single input/double output industry with three firms, each employing one worker. Firms 1 and 2 are specialized, each producing one unit of each output, respectively. Firm 3 produces $\frac{3}{4}$ unit of each product. What are the input–output coefficients for the two products? The standard procedure allocates the labor input of firm 3 equally to the two products, because their labor intensities are the same in view of the symmetry of the data. For each product, the input is 1.5 and the output 1.75. The standard coefficients are $1.5/1.75 = 0.86$ for both products. Now let us replicate the input requirement and potential output calculations. Firm 1 produces 1 unit of product 1. The only alternative to do so would be to adopt the technique of firm 3, but then it would require 4/3 units of labor to produce the unit of product 1, which is more. Hence firm 1 is efficient. Firm 2 is efficient for the same reason. Firm 3 could adopt the techniques of firms 1 and 2 to produce its respective outputs, but dividing its labor in the specialized activities would yield $\frac{1}{2}$ a unit of each product only, which is less than the $\frac{3}{4}$ unit of each product it produces. Hence firm 3 is also efficient! The input–output coefficients of firms 1 and 2 for products 1 and 2, respectively, are both 1, which is more than the standard value of 0.86. The reason is that firm 3 is more efficient than the combination of firms 1 and 2 in the production of the *bundle* of products 1 and 2. Its coefficients are $\frac{1}{2}/\frac{3}{4} = 0.67$, which is less than the standard value.

Not only firm inefficiencies, but also industrial organization inefficiencies blur the measurement of technology. Moreover, input–output coefficients differ by region in the input or output space. In the last example, the subset of firms 1 and 3 best produces both products if the demand for the first product is the greatest. Then firm 1 determines the input–output coefficient of product 1, namely 1, and firm 3 uses $1 - \frac{3}{4}$ units of labor for $\frac{3}{4}$ units of product 2; the input–output coefficient of the latter is therefore $\frac{1}{3}$. If the demand for the second product is the greatest, the input–output coefficients become $\frac{1}{3}$ and 1. When the demands are equal, they are $\frac{2}{3}$.

In the next section, I show how the best practice input–output coefficients can be extracted from use and supply data conditional on the proportions of final demand. In the section thereafter, I show how reductions in these coefficients measure technical change.

2. Inputs, Outputs, and the Production Function

The cumbersome variation of input–output coefficients with the proportions of the (net) outputs and the inputs of the economy leads me to work with the production function, instead of the input–output coefficients. There is a tight connection though. For example, if the input–output coefficients of some product are $a_1, \ldots, a_n$, then the underlying producion function is $\min(u_1/a_1, \ldots, u_n/a_n)$, where $u_1, \ldots, u_n$ are the inputs. The production function measures potential output, which typically exceeds actual output.

U and **V** are the use and supply tables of dimension products by industries and have more rows than columns: they are long. However, since I consider technical coefficients as representatives of best practices, it is essential not to aggregate firms' data into industries. The number of columns is *not* reduced to the number of industries, but remains the number of firms. The traditional use and supply tables — with columns aggregated to the level of industries — are not used in my analysis. The raw use and supply tables are rectangular as well, but the opposite way. They are of dimension products by firms and have more columns than rows: they are wide.[3] The factor inputs are given by a table **F** (dimension factors by firms).[4]

The vector of available factor inputs, **f**, comprises the employed factor inputs, **Fe**, plus possibly idle factor inputs. Here, unit vector **e** (of which all components are defined 1) sums across firms. The net output is $\mathbf{y} = (\mathbf{V} - \mathbf{U})\mathbf{e}$. Given the factor inputs, how much more net output can be produced? In other words, how close is the economy to its frontier? I will answer this question *keeping the proportions of final demand fixed*. This is a conservative approach that steers the best practice coefficients proposed in this paper close to the conventional ones. The procedure can be given a theoretical foundation. Elsewhere, I (2003) show that freeing Debreu's (1951) coefficient of resource utilization from individual household data requirements is equivalent to the imposition of Leontief preferences. Moreover, the rate of growth of the modified Debreu coefficient and the Solow residual are then shown to add up to TFP growth.

Let *potential* output be a factor $1/\varepsilon$ greater. Here ε is the *efficiency* of the economy. For example, if potential output exceeds actual output by 25%, the economy produces only 80% of its potential. Let us reallocate the factor inputs by running the firms at activity levels given by vector **s** (dimension number of firms). If the first component is 1.1, firm 1 is operated at 10% higher a level. The actual activity vector is represented by $\mathbf{s} = \mathbf{e}$. Potential output is determined by the following program:

$$\max_{\mathbf{s},\varepsilon\geq 0} \mathbf{e}^{\top}\mathbf{y}/\varepsilon : (\mathbf{V} - \mathbf{U})\mathbf{s} \geq \mathbf{y}/\varepsilon, \mathbf{Fs} \leq \mathbf{f} \tag{1}$$

[3]A referee notes that in Sweden, the number of enterprises is close to 1 million and that the number of products is less indeed. Products by enterprise supply and use tables are not balanced and should not.

Valuations should be in basic prices. ten Raa and Rueda-Cantuche (2007a) detail the procedure, including the assumed equality of margins and net commodity taxes between establishments in a given industry, consuming a given commodity.

[4]Normally, capital input is calculated by first using e.g. the perpetual inventory method to get the productive stock by asset type and then estimating the respective user costs in one way or other. This requires a long investment series hardly available for single enterprises and may require industry proxies.

I do *not* value net outputs at current prices. The inclusion of constant $\mathbf{e}^\top\mathbf{y}$ (which is Gross Domestic Product, $\top$ is transposition) in the objective function is as inessential as the inclusion of any positive constant. It merely constitutes a monotonic transformation and proves useful for price normalization. Indeed, the dual program associated with (1) is:

$$\min_{\mathbf{p}^\top,\mathbf{w}^\top\geq 0} \mathbf{w}^\top\mathbf{f} : \mathbf{p}^\top(\mathbf{V}-\mathbf{U}) \leq \mathbf{w}^\top\mathbf{F}, \quad \mathbf{p}^\top\mathbf{y} = \mathbf{e}^\top\mathbf{y} \tag{2}$$

The advantage of the dual program is its low dimension. The number of (price) variables is the number of inputs, or the number of products plus the number of factor inputs. The prices are competitive. For each firm, value added is less than or equal to factor costs. In the first case, firms are shut down, in the second case, firms are active.[5] Denote the lower dimensional use and make tables of the active firms by $\mathbf{U}^*$ and $\mathbf{V}^*$, respectively. Aggregate the factor input table, $\mathbf{F}$, using the factor input prices, $\mathbf{w}$, into row vector $\mathbf{w}^\top\mathbf{F}$.

The aggregated linear program

$$\max_{\mathbf{s},\varepsilon\geq 0} \mathbf{e}^\top\mathbf{y}/\varepsilon : (\mathbf{V}-\mathbf{U})\mathbf{s} \geq \mathbf{y}/\varepsilon, \quad \mathbf{w}^\top\mathbf{F}\mathbf{s} \leq \mathbf{w}^\top\mathbf{f} \tag{3}$$

has the same solution as (1). In (3), the number of variables is the number of firms plus 1 for the expansion factor, while the number of constraints is the number of products plus 1 for the factor inputs. Consequently, there need be only as many active firms as there are products; in this case, it follows that matrices

$$\mathbf{U}^* \text{ and } \mathbf{V}^* \text{ are square} \tag{4}$$

They represent the inputs and the outputs of the resource efficient providers of net output $\mathbf{y}$. The commodity technology input–output coefficients are given by:

$$\mathbf{A}^* = \mathbf{U}^*\mathbf{V}^{*-1}, \quad \mathbf{B}^* = \mathbf{F}^*\mathbf{V}^{*-1} \tag{5}$$

On average, these coefficients are smaller than the standard input–output coefficients, based on $\mathbf{U}$, $\mathbf{F}$ and $\mathbf{V}$. Two warnings are in order. First, matrices

[5] This is the phenomenon of complementary slackness. For the theory of linear programming, see Chapter 4 of my 2005 book.

$\mathbf{A}^*$ and $\mathbf{B}^*$ are contingent on final demand, y. Second, they imply neither material nor financial balance. For example, the implied requirements fall short of the observed ones. This casts some doubt on the balance axioms of Kop Jansen and ten Raa (1990).

3. Technical Change and Efficiency Change

Monitor the data over time. If the changes are small, linear analysis takes us back to input–output coefficients that are independent of the direction of the final demand changes. By the main theorem of linear programming, the primal and dual programs, (1) and (2), have equal values:

$$\mathbf{p}^\top \mathbf{y}/\varepsilon = \mathbf{w}^\top \mathbf{f} \tag{6}$$

Here, I used the price normalization constraint in program (2). Equation (6) is the macro-economic identity between the potential national product and income. Differentiating equation (6) with respect to time, using dots for time derivatives:

$$\dot{\mathbf{p}}^\top \mathbf{y}/\varepsilon + \mathbf{p}^\top \dot{\mathbf{y}}/\varepsilon - \mathbf{p}^\top \mathbf{y}\varepsilon^{-2}\dot{\varepsilon} = \dot{\mathbf{w}}^\top \mathbf{f} + \mathbf{w}^\top \dot{\mathbf{f}} \tag{7}$$

Assuming that program (1) is nondegenerate, the partition between the binding dual constraints, $\mathbf{p}^\top(\mathbf{V}-\mathbf{U})_{\cdot j} = \mathbf{w}^\top \mathbf{F}_{\cdot j}$ in (2), and the nonbinding, the other j columns, remains constant (ten Raa 2005, section 4.6). Hence $\dot{\mathbf{w}}^\top \mathbf{F}_{\cdot j} = \dot{\mathbf{p}}^\top(\mathbf{V}-\mathbf{U})_{\cdot j} + \mathbf{p}^\top(\dot{\mathbf{V}}-\dot{\mathbf{U}})_{\cdot j} - \mathbf{w}^\top \dot{\mathbf{F}}_{\cdot j}$. The post-multiplication by the positive components of $\mathbf{s}$ and the inclusion of the zero components yield $\dot{\mathbf{w}}^\top \mathbf{F}\mathbf{s} = \dot{\mathbf{p}}^\top(\mathbf{V}-\mathbf{U})\mathbf{s} + \mathbf{p}^\top(\dot{\mathbf{V}}-\dot{\mathbf{U}})\mathbf{s} - \mathbf{w}^\top \dot{\mathbf{F}}\mathbf{s}$. In fact, by the phenomenon of complementary slackness and the constant partition, we may write $\dot{\mathbf{w}}^\top \mathbf{f} = \dot{\mathbf{p}}^\top \mathbf{y}/\varepsilon + \mathbf{p}^\top(\dot{\mathbf{V}}-\dot{\mathbf{U}})\mathbf{s} - \mathbf{w}^\top \dot{\mathbf{F}}\mathbf{s}$. Substitution into equation (7) and rearrangement of terms yields:

$$\mathbf{p}^\top \dot{\mathbf{y}}^\top/\varepsilon - \mathbf{w}^\top \dot{\mathbf{f}} = \mathbf{p}^\top(\dot{\mathbf{V}}-\dot{\mathbf{U}})\mathbf{s} - \mathbf{w}^\top \dot{\mathbf{F}}\mathbf{s} + \mathbf{p}^\top \mathbf{y}\varepsilon^{-2}\dot{\varepsilon} \tag{8}$$

Division of equation (8) by equation (6) yields

$$\mathbf{p}^\top \dot{\mathbf{y}}/\mathbf{p}^\top \mathbf{y} - \mathbf{w}^\top \dot{\mathbf{f}}/\mathbf{w}^\top \mathbf{f} = [\mathbf{p}^\top(\dot{\mathbf{V}}-\dot{\mathbf{U}})\mathbf{s} - \mathbf{w}^\top \dot{\mathbf{F}}\mathbf{s}]/\mathbf{w}^\top \mathbf{f} + \dot{\varepsilon}/\varepsilon \tag{9}$$

On the left hand side is Solow's residual expression for total factor productivity growth. The first term on the right hand side is Domar's decomposition of technical change (Hulten 1978). The last term is efficiency change. It is well-known that productivity may grow as a result of technical change or efficiency improvements. The former effect represents the shift in technology and the latter a better allocation of the factor inputs. Only if we define input–output coefficients as best practice coefficients do we capture the efficiency effect.

The input–output coefficients were extracted by the active firms in program (1), denoted by the attachment of *'s to the input and output tables. Recall finding (4). Now substitute into the Domar term the first term on the right hand side of equation (9):

$$[\mathbf{p}^\top(\dot{\mathbf{V}} - \dot{\mathbf{U}})\mathbf{s} - \mathbf{w}^\top\dot{\mathbf{F}}\mathbf{s}]/\mathbf{w}^\top\mathbf{f} = [\mathbf{p}^\top(\dot{\mathbf{V}}^* - \dot{\mathbf{U}}^*)\mathbf{s}^* - \mathbf{w}^\top\dot{\mathbf{F}}^*\mathbf{s}^*]/\mathbf{w}^\top\mathbf{f} \quad (10)$$

Denote potential gross output by $\mathbf{x}^* = \mathbf{V}\mathbf{s} = \mathbf{V}^*\mathbf{s}^*$ and potential net output by $\mathbf{y}^* = \mathbf{y}/\varepsilon = (\mathbf{V} - \mathbf{U})\mathbf{s} = (\mathbf{V}^* - \mathbf{U}^*)\mathbf{s}^*$, where I use the first constraint in (1).[6] Now $\mathbf{p}^\top(\dot{\mathbf{V}}^* - \dot{\mathbf{U}}^*)\mathbf{s}^* = \mathbf{p}^\top[(\mathbf{V}^* - \mathbf{U}^*)\mathbf{s}^*]^{\cdot} - \mathbf{p}^\top(\mathbf{V}^* - \mathbf{U}^*)\dot{\mathbf{s}}^*$ and $\mathbf{w}^\top\dot{\mathbf{F}}^*\mathbf{s}^* = \mathbf{w}^\top(\mathbf{F}^*\mathbf{s}^*)^{\cdot} - \mathbf{w}^\top\mathbf{F}^*\dot{\mathbf{s}}^*$. The two respective last terms are equal by the dual constraint in (2) (which is binding for $\mathbf{s}^* > 0$). Substitution in (10) yields:

$$\begin{aligned}
&[\mathbf{p}^\top(\dot{\mathbf{V}} - \dot{\mathbf{U}})\mathbf{s} - \mathbf{w}^\top\dot{\mathbf{F}}\mathbf{s}]/\mathbf{w}^\top\mathbf{f} \\
&= [\mathbf{p}^\top[(\mathbf{V}^* - \mathbf{U}^*)\mathbf{s}^*]^{\cdot} - \mathbf{w}^\top(\mathbf{F}^*\mathbf{s}^*)^{\cdot}]/\mathbf{w}^\top\mathbf{f} \\
&= [\mathbf{p}^\top[(\mathbf{I} - \mathbf{A}^*)\mathbf{x}^*]^{\cdot} - \mathbf{w}^\top(\mathbf{B}^*\mathbf{x}^*)^{\cdot}]/\mathbf{w}^\top\mathbf{f} \\
&= [(-\mathbf{p}^\top\dot{\mathbf{A}}^* - \mathbf{w}^\top\dot{\mathbf{B}}^*)\mathbf{x}^* + [\mathbf{p}^\top(\mathbf{I} - \mathbf{A}^*) - \mathbf{w}^\top\mathbf{B}^*]\dot{\mathbf{x}}^*]/\mathbf{w}^\top\mathbf{f}
\end{aligned} \quad (11)$$

In the last term, $\mathbf{p}^\top(\mathbf{I} - \mathbf{A}^*) - \mathbf{w}^\top\mathbf{B}^* = \mathbf{p}^\top(\mathbf{I} - \mathbf{U}^*\mathbf{V}^{*-1}) - \mathbf{w}^\top\mathbf{F}^*\mathbf{V}^{*-1} = \mathbf{p}^\top(\mathbf{V}^* - \mathbf{U}^* - \mathbf{w}^\top\mathbf{F}^*)\mathbf{V}^{*-1} = 0$, again by the dual constraint in (2) (binding for $s^* > 0$). Consequently, the substitution of the Domar term (11) in equation (9) yields:

$$\mathbf{p}^\top\dot{\mathbf{y}}/\mathbf{p}^\top\mathbf{y} - \mathbf{w}^\top\dot{\mathbf{f}}/\mathbf{w}^\top\mathbf{f} = -(\mathbf{p}^\top\dot{\mathbf{A}}^* + \mathbf{w}^\top\dot{\mathbf{B}}^*)\mathbf{x}^*/\mathbf{w}^\top\mathbf{f} + \dot{\varepsilon}/\varepsilon \quad (12)$$

This is Wolff's (1985) technical coefficient reductions representation of productivity growth, but augmented with efficiency change.

---

[6] If it is nonbinding, the slack will be killed by the shadow prices in the Domar effect.

4. Conclusion

Technical coefficients control the input requirements of outputs, or the output producible with inputs, and therefore they need to be determined by the best-practice firms. A linear program that determines how much output can be produced given the intermediate and factor inputs identifies the best-practice firms. The final output/factor input ratio of the economy, i.e. productivity, can be increased by the reductions of these technical coefficients or by efficiency improvements.

A main contribution of my musings is the separation of the dual roles of input coefficients, describing technology and reflecting cost structures. The former role is best played by best-practice coefficients, the latter by average proportions. There are critical differences. Standard input–output table coefficients add to unity, even at constant prices, if the double deflation methodology is applied, but best-practice coefficients don't. Much of the fun is in the differences. In theory, they catch the inefficiencies.

The proof of the eating is in the pudding. I hope a reader will attempt to implement my proposal. There is also more theory to be done. A main complication I have foreshadowed is the role of balancing. Best practice coefficients are and should not be balanced. But it will be difficult to disentangle errors of measurement from true cost advantages or disadvantages. Stochastic frontier estimation has the potential to overcome this complication and I hope another reader spells it out.

Acknowledgement

I thank two anonymous referees and editor Erik Dietzenbacher for the extremely insightful feedback.

References

Debreu, G. (1951) The coefficient of resource utilization, *Econometrica*, 19, pp. 273–292.

Hulten, C.R. (1979) Growth accounting with intermediate inputs, *Review of Economic Studies*, 45, pp. 511–518.

Kop Jansen, P. and Th. ten Raa (1990) The choice of model in the construction of input–output coefficients matrices, *International Economic Review*, 31, pp. 213–227.

Mattey, J. and Th. ten Raa (1997) Primary versus secondary production techniques in U.S. manufacturing, *Review of Income and Wealth*, 43, pp. 449–464.
ten Raa, Th. (2003) Debreu's Coefficient of Resource Utilization, the Solow residual, and TFP: The Connection by Leontief Preferences, Center Discussion Paper 111.
ten Raa, Th. (2005) *The Economics of Input–Output Analysis*, (Cambridge: Cambridge University Press).
ten Raa, Th. and J.M. Rueda-Cantuche (2007a) A generalized expression for the commodity and the industry technology models in input–output analysis, *Economic Systems Research*, 19, pp. 99–104.
ten Raa, Th. and J.M. Rueda-Cantuche (2007b) Stochastic analysis of input–output multipliers on the basis of use and make matrices, *Review of Income and Wealth*, 53, pp. 318–334.
Wolff, E. (1985) Industrial composition, interindustry effects, and the U.S. productivity slowdown, *Review of Economics and Statistics*, 67, pp. 268–277.

Part III

Neoclassical and Classical Connections

Chapter 9

On the Methodology of Input–Output Analysis

Thijs ten Raa

Abstract: The basic elements of input–output analysis, notably technical coefficients, quantity and value equations, and a total factor productivity growth measure, are derived as intermediate constructs when the problem of national income or product determination is directly related to input and output flow data. By embedding input–output concepts in a neoclassical framework, specification issues are resolved, notably the problems of construction of coefficients and of determination of value. Conversely, neoclassical concepts of marginal productivities can be related to a consistent input–output framework of data. Sources of substitution are identified.

JEL classification: C67; D57

1. Introduction

Input–output analysis and neoclassical economics seem to part as schools of thought, with little appreciation of each others' contributions. Neoclassical economists criticize the rigidity of the input–output model, particularly its assumption of fixed coefficients and the failure to explain factor rewards. Input–output analysis is perceived as a mechanical manipulation

---

Final version received July 1993.

of data. On the other hand, the neoclassical concept of a smooth production function which maps factor inputs directly into some jelly output, and its associated marginal productivities, meets a cool reception in the world of input–output economists. Neoclassical economics is considered an elegant, but futile theory. I do not intend to contribute to the criticism, but will attempt to accommodate it. I take the neoclassical critique seriously and will rethink the methodology of input–output analysis. By relating input–output, including its statistical basis, to economic problems and applications, I hope to inject a theoretical stucture. Open issues, such as the choice of model in the construction of coefficients, the relationship with fixed proportions, the consolidation of the quantity and value systems in a unifying framework, and the foundation of productivity measurement, can be enlightened by an open-minded reconsideration of the relationship between data and economic objectives. The basic assumptions and equations of input–output analysis may emerge in the process, but possibly modified.

The core sections of the paper are the next two. In section 2, the construction of an input–output matrix is related to the quantity and value equations in which they are put to use. The equations, in turn, are derived in section 3 from the formulation of an economic problem, such as the determination of the national product. Section 4 introduces substitution. Section 5 discusses patterns of specialization that trouble solutions to economic models at the interface of neoclassical economics and input–output analysis. Section 6 resolves the trouble in a framework of intercountry substitution. An intertemporal version of substitution is reflected in productivity growth. Section 7 embeds the concept in the same economic problem that was used to generate the equations of input–output analysis.

2. Quantity and Value Equations: Construction Implications

The centerpiece of the input output analysis is a matrix,

$$A = \begin{bmatrix} a_{11} & \dots & a_{1n} \\ \vdots & & \vdots \\ a_{n1} & \dots & a_{nn} \end{bmatrix},$$

of technical coefficients, a_{ij}, which describe the commodity inputs per unit of commodity outputs. Here $(1, \ldots, n)$ classifies the commodities. For example, if 1 is iron and 2 is automobiles, then a_{12} is the quantity of iron needed in the production of an automobile. The standard reference is Leontief (1966). The simplicity of the framework has attracted both economists and statisticians to the field of input–output analysis. The matrix of coefficients, A, is thus used as the point of departure both for economic analysis and for national or regional accounting. In the economic analysis, two input–output equations are prominent, namely the following:

$$x = Ax + y, \tag{M}$$

$$p = pA + v. \tag{F}$$

Here, x is a vector of gross outputs; y is a vector of net outputs; p is a row vector of prices; and v is a row vector of value–added coefficients. The first equation equilibrates supply and demand and the second equation balances revenues and costs. They are the so-called quantity and value equations of input–output analysis, also called the material and financial balances. The latter terminology is reflected in the notation indexing the equations (M) and (F). A well-known application of the input–output equations is national planning, particularly the determination of output levels which are required to sustain a certain level of final demand. An example would be a study of the implications of an exports promotion program. The increase of exports would appear in the final demand vector, y, directly, and in the gross output vector, x, indirectly through equation (M). Another example would involve the tracing of price effects which result from an increase in the value-added coefficients associated with an energy shock. It is straightforward to assess the direct energy costs increase in the row vector of value-added coefficients, v, but the indirect price effects are determined through eq. (F). In either case, analysis amounts to the solution of the input–output equations. Mathematically, the inversion of the matrix $I - A$ is at stake, which defines the so-called Leontief inverse of the A-matrix.

Since input–output constitutes a more or less unified framework for an economy-wide analysis, statisticians use it for the organization of intersectoral data. If the above commodity classification, $(1, \ldots, n)$, can also be used for sectors, then it is natural to set up a so-called transactions table,

$$T = \begin{bmatrix} t_{11} \dots t_{1n} & t_{1n+1} \\ \vdots & \\ t_{n1} \dots t_{nn} & t_{nn+1} \end{bmatrix},$$

The first row of the table displays the sales receipts of sector 1 from sectors $1, \dots, n$, as well as the final demand compartments (household and government consumption, investment and net exports). Table T underlies matrix A, in the sense that by the appropriate divisions of transactions elements of T, one may calculate the technical coefficients of A. Thus, the input–output coefficients matrix bridges the gap between economic analysis and national accounts. However, one must be careful not to consider the input–output coefficients matrix as the point of departure for analysis. If all interaction between input–output statisticians and economists were channeled through the single concept of an input–output coefficients matrix, the two departments of investigation would have their own dynamics, with little cross fertilization. Moreover, by taking an input–output coefficients matrix as the point of departure, one risks imposing a framework of analysis that simply does not fit reality.

A prime illustration of an active interface between statistical and economic investigations is the construction of input–output matrices. If reality were to present itself through a simple input–output transactions table, T, the construction of a matrix of technical coefficients, A, would be a straightforward matter of divisions:

$$a_{ij} = t_{ij} \Big/ \sum_{k=1}^{n+1} t_{jk}.$$

This situation is too simplistic. For one, the very existence of a transactions table presumes that commodities and sectors can be classified in the same way. Moreover, it suggests that sectors have a multitude of inputs, but only single outputs. To accommodate the obvious implications, Professor Stone has suggested accounting for inputs and outputs separately. Hence input flows are tabulated in a use table, U, and output flows in a make table, V. In the System of National Accounts (S.N.A.) proposed by the United Nations (1967), the convention is that the dimensions of matrices U and V are commodities $\times$ sectors and sectors $\times$ commodities, respectively. The inputs of sector 1 are listed in the first column of matrix V and the outputs in the first row of matrix V, and so on. The framework is general. In particular, the traditional transactions model is recovered if sectors can be identified with their primary commodity outputs or, more precisely, if table V is made diagonal. Then the transactions table, T, coincides with the use table, U, augmented by a column. The last column of T makes the row totals add up to the gross outputs, as determined by the column totals of the make table, V. In this case, the matrix of technical coefficients is obtained by dividing the use part of the transactions matrix by the (diagonal) output matrix that is $A = UV^{-1}$. In general, however, the make table, V, features non-zero off-diagonal elements, since sectors produce mixtures of outputs. The problem of constructing an input–output matrix, be it T or A, is therefore non-trivial. Alternative methods to deal with it exist and are described by Viet (this issue). These are the industry technology model, the commodity technology model and many more. Alternative assumptions are made on the nature of the off-diagonal elements of make table V, also called secondary products, or on their input technologies. The choice of model is made on the basis of the reasonableness of the assumptions, as judged by the statisticians or the economists. Whatever model is employed, some matrix of technical coefficients, A, comes out of it and is used in the equations of input–output analysis, particularly (M) and (F).

Implications of input–output applications for the statistical construction of an input–output matrix can be introduced by reporting some of my own experience at the Institute for Economic Analysis at New York University, where I had to construct input–output coefficients for non-fuel minerals. The coefficients were to be part of an enlargement of the United States Bureau of Economic Analysis (BEA) input–output matrix. The BEA constructs the input–output matrix, A, according to the so-called industry technology model, on the assumption that each industry has a specific input technology which is independent of the commodity composition of its output vector [Viet (this issue)]. This methodology is problematic. The resulting A-matrix is not invariant with respect to units of measurement. Invariance with respect to units of measurement simply means that, for example, the quantity of iron per automobile (a_{12} in section 2) ought to double when metric pounds are used instead of kilograms (one metric pound is 500 grams). The reason that the industry technology model fails to meet this requirement, is that it employs a concept of 'industry output', which intermingles different commodities. In other words, apples and oranges are added up. Wassily Leontief urged me to think of an alternative method for the construction of input–output coefficients to comply with the requirements of invariance with respect to units of measurement. Now, if this were the only concern, one might propose setting all elements of the A-matrix to zero. This 'zero' method is well-defined and invariant with respect to units of measurement. Intuitively, however, putting $A = 0$ is nonsense. It is important to clarify this intuition. The 'zero' method is nonsensical in the context of the application because it invalidates the material balance equation, (M), or, for that matter, the financial balance equation, (F). The left-hand sides would no longer be equal, but exceed the right-hand sides. Hence (M) and (F) impose restrictions on the construction of the matrix A.

The moral of my thought experiment is that the economic structure of input–output analyisis has implications for the statistical construction of the matrix. Kop Jansen and ten Raa (1990) list the elements of the structure, namely the material balance and the financial balance, as well as base year price invariance and a scale property. The material and financial balances are essentially equations (M) and (F) presented above. Only when they are observed do input–output matrices balance material requirements and financial accounts. The element of base year price invariance, (P), is essentially the invariance with respect to units of measurement, since a price system is basically a system of measures. The scale property, (S), is a counterpart of the latter in the real sphere. It requires that *if* an economy must have constant returns to scale and fixed proportions, *then* it must have constant coefficients. This logical requirement makes no assumptions on the observation of economies, but restricts the method of construction of the coefficients. More precisely, Kop Jansen and ten Raa (1990) have proved that the just described structure of input–output analysis, involving (M), (F), (P) and (S), not only imposes restrictions on the choice of model of construction, but determines it uniquely. By one theorem, in the real sphere, the combination of (M) and (S) is shown to imply that the A-matrix must be constructed by the so-called commodity technology model. By another theorem, in the nominal sphere, the combination of (F) and (P) is shown to imply the same result. The theorems do not necessarily favor the commodity technology model over alternative constructs. If, however, an alternative method of constructing input–output matrices is used, then one must be prepared to revise the basic structure of input–output analysis, since at least one of the equations or properties must be violated. For example, if one uses the U.S. input–output coefficients, which are constructed according to the industry technology model, but continues to decompose productivity growth rates by standard input–output analysis without revision, then a bias creeps in. This bias has been analyzed and estimated by ten Raa and Wolff (1991).

As mentioned before, another risk of considering an A-matrix as the point of departure for statistical and economic work is that the frame need not fit reality. An input–output matrix, however constructed and however sensitive to the data, suggests economy-wide relations which need not hold. For the purpose of clarification, suppose we accept the basic structure of input–output analysis, say (M) and (S) and/or (F) and (F), and suppose we construct the input–output matrix accordingly. Then, following Kop Jansen and ten Raa (1990), the matrix A is constructed by the specifications of the commodity technology model. This model is defined by the assumption that each commodity has a unique input structure, irrespective of the sector of fabrication. Now it is well-known that the commodity technology model has the problem of negatives. If applied mechanically, the formula yields some negative coefficients. The negatives are very small and are usually suppressed one way or another. It is natural to hypothesize that the negatives are due to errors of measurement. To his own surprise, ten Raa (1988) has rejected the hypothesis. In other words, the construction of coefficients which is consistent with the basic structure of input–output analysis yields negatives which cannot be ascribed to errors of measurement.

One reason that might account for the rejection is that ten Raa (1988) assumes that the variances of the errors are known. If the variances have to be estimated from a sample, it is more difficult to reject and the requirement of non-negative coefficients may be salvaged. I shall detail this approach after the introduction of multiple observations in section 4. The nature of the problem of negatives is easy to understand. Imagine that sector 1 is pure, producing a single output, commodity 1, but that sector 2 produces not only commodity 2, but also commodity 1 as a secondary product. The input coefficients for commodity 1 are revealed by sector 1. The input coefficients for commodity 2 are obtained by the purification of sector 2. More precisely, the evaluation of the commodity technology model formula of the matrix of input–output coefficients involves the inversion of the output flow table, which in this example, amounts to the subtraction of the secondary product and the associated input requirements from sector 2. The input requirements associated with the secondary product (commodity 1) are given by the already computed input coefficients for this commodity. The problem of negatives emerges when sector 1 uses an input which is not used by sector 2. This input must be subtracted from sector 2 in the process of purification. The subtraction creates a negative input coefficient for this input in sector 2. Statistically, the problem can be ascribed to an error of measurement only by hypothesizing that either the entire input cell in sector 1 creating the negative in sector 2 or the zero entry in sector 2 is fake. I find this difficult to accept. A more reasonable approach of the problem seems to me to accept the possibility of coexisting technologies for the production of commodity 1 in sectors 1 and 2.

When this point of view is adopted, there is no point in constructing a single matrix of technical coefficients. The question of what remains to be done cannot be answered in general, but depends on the economic issue that is addressed, as well as data availability. A good example is the issue of profit maximization, which can be modeled in an input–output like framework, without technical coefficients. The relationship with input output coefficients matrices will be discussed, but is not essential to the model and certainly imposes no non-negativity requirements.

3. Quantity and Value Equations: Economic Origins

Optimization naturally is at the core of neoclassical economics. However, formulating an input–output problem in terms of a linear programming model does not necessarily introduce neoclassical elements in input output models. Since the 1960s, linear programming formulations of Leontief-type systems, in which real and price systems can be viewed as a set of constraints, are a normal part of standard texts. The Dorfman *et al.* (1958) model considers the maximization of the value of a given bill of final demands by choice of prices and the minimization of labor input by choice of gross outputs. As ten Raa and Mohnen (1994) argue, these combinations of objectives and instruments are not neoclassical. The problem is that the

Leontief-type systems have been taken for granted and that the linear programs have been chosen to make the systems dual to each other.

Instead of taking an input–output coefficients matrix as a point of departure, I propose to relate data directly to economic problems, without imposing a preconceived input–output structure. To illuminate, consider the problem of the maximization of the national product, y, valued at the world price vector, p subject to a constraint on resources, say a labor force, N. Here, y is a commodity vector, which lumps together the familiar categories of the national product, namely household and government demand, investment and net exports. In view of the last item, y may have negative components. Other items in the final demand may have negative elements as well. Investment, for example, comprises gross fixed capital formation and net inventory change. If inventory depletions exceed inventory additions and if the negative net inventory change exceeds new capital formation, as may well occur in severe recessions, elements of this component will also be negative. Individual elements of private consumption may also be negative if consumers sell used materials (cars, clothing, etc.). p is an exogenous row vector of given world prices. N is the exogenous number of workers. The input–output data comprise a use table, U_0, a make table, V_0, and a sectoral employment row vector, L_0. If we drop the subscripts, the data turn variables, namely U, V, and L. We now relate the subjects of the economic problem, the national product, y, and the labor force, N, to the variables, (U, V, L). Recalling the dimensions of U (commodity × sector) and V (sector × commodity), we see that $V^{\mathrm{T}} - U$ is the net output matrix (commodity × sector) and that the aggregation over sectors yields the net output vector. Hence $y = (V^{\mathrm{T}} - U)e$, where e is the vector with all entries equal to unity and T denotes transposition. Similarly, the resource constraint reads $Le \leqq N$. It remains to restrict the variables, (U, V, L), in agreement with the production possibility set. Certainly feasible are the observed values, (U_0, V_0, L_0). If we assume constant returns to scale, then $(U, V, L) = (U_0\hat{s}, \hat{s}V_0, L_0\hat{s})$ is also feasible for any non-negative vector of scales, s. (Here $\hat{s}$ is the associated diagonal matrix.) Thus, the problem is written as

$$\max_{s \geqq 0} py$$

subject to

$$y = (V^T - U)e,\ Le \leqq N,\ (U, V, L) = (U_0\hat{s}, \hat{s}V_0, L_0\hat{s}).$$

As far as I am concerned, we are done. We have related the economic problem directly to the data and economic analysis can be performed; see ten Raa and Mohnen (1994). Input–output analysis is implicit. To reveal it, consider the following change of variables:

$$x = V^{\mathrm{T}}e = (\hat{s}V_0)^{\mathrm{T}}e = V_0^{\mathrm{T}}\hat{s}e = V_0^{\mathrm{T}}s \quad \text{or} \quad s = V_0^{-\mathrm{T}}x = (V_0^{\mathrm{T}})^{-1}x.$$

The change of variables is one-to-one only if the make table, V_0, is invertable. In other words, the recognition of standard input–output analysis is possible only if there are equally many commodities and sectors. This condition is not needed for a head-on analysis of the above economic problem. I now invite the reader to go through a number of steps, which are mathematically trivial, but not so methodologically. The change of variables turns the problem into

$$\max_{x \in X} py$$

subject to

$$y = (V^{\mathrm{T}} - U)e,\ Le \leqq N,\ (U, V, L) = \left(U_0\widehat{V_0^{\mathrm{T}}x}, \widehat{V_0^{\mathrm{T}}x}V_0, L_0\widehat{V_0^{\mathrm{T}}x}\right).$$

where X is the cone spanned by the rows of V_0, because of $x = V_0^{\mathrm{T}}s$, $s \geqq 0$.

The elimination of (U, V, L) by the substitution of the last constraint yields

$$\max_{x \in X} py$$

subject to

$$y = \left[\left(\widehat{V_0^{-\mathrm{T}}x}V_0\right)^{\mathrm{T}} - U_0\widehat{V_0^{-\mathrm{T}}x}\right]e, \quad L_0\widehat{V_0^{-\mathrm{T}}x}e \leqq N.$$

This can be simplified to

$$\max_{x \in X} py$$

subject to

$$y = V_0^{\mathrm{T}}V_0^{-\mathrm{T}}x - U_0V_0^{-\mathrm{T}}x, \quad L_0V_0^{-\mathrm{T}}x \leqq N$$

or

$$\max_{x \in X} py$$

subject to

$$x = Ax + y, \quad lx \leqq N,$$

where we introduced the shorthand $A = U_0 V_0^{-T}$ and $l = L_0 V_0^{-T}$. This notation may be recognized as the formula for technical coefficients according to the commodity technology model. We see that standard input–output analysis *may* provide the correct formulation of an economic problem, but that it is by no means trivial. In particular, the method of construction of the input–output matrix is implicit in the formulation of the economic problem. The analysis involved a listing of the economic variables of the problem, (y, N), plus a relationship with the data, (U_0, V_0, L_0), and the associated variables, (U, V, L). In proceeding this way, technical coefficients merely fall out as values of mappings defined on the data. The mappings are determined by the formulation of the economic problem.

The material balance equation, (M), has emerged in the course of rewriting the economic problem. I shall now discuss the emergence of the financial balance equation, (F). Let us assume, in addition to constant returns to scale, free disposability and that output vectors span non-negative space. The problem becomes

$$\max_{x \geqq 0} py$$

subject to

$$x \geqq Ax + y, \quad lx \leqq N.$$

Although the material balance constraint set is widened by the replacement of the equality sign, this will not affect the solution, for it is easy to show that the constraint is binding. The latter problem, also called the primal program, lends itself to a more convenient formulation of the so-called dual program. Applying Schrijver (1986, p. 90), the dual program becomes

$$\min_{w \geqq 0} wN$$

subject to

$$p \leqq pA + wl.$$

Here, w is the Lagrange multiplier associated with the labor force constraint, or the marginal productivity of labor. An increase in N by one unit in the primal problem would increase the solution value of py. The latter increase is w, which, therefore, is also called the shadow wage rate. In contrast to standard input–output analysis, the wage rate is related to the quantity system through the concept of marginal productivity. This is the central place where a neoclassical framework provides structure to input–output analysis. The extension to other factor inputs, such as capital, is obvious. Although there is non-substitutability at the sectoral levels, changes in the composition of final demand allow for factor intensity variation and, therefore, full employment. The rewards are the marginal productivities with respect to the national product.

By the main theorem of linear programming, the solutions to the primal and dual programs yield equal values:

$$py = wN.$$

This is the equality between the national product and income in our single-factor economy with zero operating surplus. Now, by the two inequalities of the primal program,

$$(p - pA - wl)x \geqq py - wN = 0.$$

A last step to establish the value equations involves a new concept, Define active and sleeping sectors as follows. Sector $i \in I$ (the active sectors) if $x_i > 0$, and $i \in II$ (the sleeping sectors) if $x_i = 0$. Then I and II partition the sectors and

$$x = \begin{pmatrix} x_I \\ x_{II} \end{pmatrix},$$

with x_I strictly positive and x_{II} zero. The last inequality becomes

$$(p - pA - wl)_I x_I + 0 \geqq 0,$$

and by the constraint of the dual program,

$$(p - pA - wl)_I = 0$$

or

$$p_I = (pA)_I + wl_I$$

We have now arrived at the value equations of input–output analysis, previously indicated by (F), the financial balance. They are not standing by themselves, but follow from the same economic problem that was also used to establish the quantity equations or the material balance, (M). Once more, it is important to note the unification brought about by the neoclassical framework of profit maximization. The equations not only emerge as primal and dual constraints to a common problem, but the quantities and the value are determined jointly. In particular, the wage rate is the marginal productivity of labor and the prices are consistent with it through competitive cost equations. Only active sectors are relevant in the determination of value. This is a methodological point that would have been overlooked if the basic structure of input–output analyis had been taken for granted rather than derived.

The various assumptions that I made in the course of the derivation were introduced to reveal the implicit role of standard input–output analysis, but are not really necessary to the investigation of the economic problem. For example, the shadow prices of factor inputs are presented directly as the Lagrange multipliers to the program and are thus available without the necessity to set up value equations.

4. Substitution

Input–output economics was invented by Wassily Leontief and the so-called Leontief production function is defined by the absence of substitution. Many economists therefore think that in input–output analysis, there is no substitution. Substitution will be analyzed as an issue of changing coefficients, A. Let us investigate the thought that input–output analysis excludes substitution. As before, we have input and output matrices, U and V, and observations U_0 and V_0. We have seen that economic problems may be expressed in terms of U and V, and that in the course of analysis, an input–output matrix based on U_0 and V_0 may emerge. The latter dependence is denoted by writing $A(U_0, V_0)$. Taken as a mapping, A is a model of construction, a device that tells you how to manipulate the arguments. Whatever the model of construction, if we change the data, (U_0, V_0), then the coefficients, $A(U_0, V_0)$, change as well, except when the new observations, say U_1 and U_1, are collinear, with the collinearity given by the old coefficients: $U_1 = A(U_0, V_0)V_1$. This change involves the *substitution* of inputs if and only if components in the column of A move in opposite directions. In other words, the very fact that coefficients change with data changes indicates the presence of substitution in input–output analysis. This is not what is meant by the neoclassical critics. Instead, they refer to the use of coefficients based on one observation. In scenario analysis, the constructed coefficients matrix, $A(U_0, V_0)$, is applied to some hypothetical (U, V), and the feasibility of the latter reads

$$Ue = A(V_0, V_0)V^{\mathrm{T}}e.$$

This equation can be shown to be equivalent to the material balance, (M), using the change of variables, $x = V^{\mathrm{T}}e$. The equation holds trivially for $(U, V) = (U_0, V_0)$, at least when model A is an established one, For example, if A is the commodity technology model, then $A(U_0, V_0) = U_0V_0^{-\mathrm{T}}$ and the above feasibility equation reads $Ue = U_0V_0^{-\mathrm{T}}V^{\mathrm{T}}e$, which is true for $(U, V) = (U_0, V_0)$. If this equation is required for all feasible (U, V), including hypothetical ones, then inputs and outputs must be proportional (with coefficients $U_0V_0^{-\mathrm{T}}$) and therefore, substitution is assumed away indeed. This methodology may make sense if there is only one observation, (U_0, V_0), and even then merely reflects an extreme restriction of data availability. Otherwise the neoclassical critique becomes most relevant and substitution becomes unavoidable.

Consider a second observation, (U_1, V_1). It would be a coincidence if $A(U_1V_1) = A(U_0, V_0)$. If in the scenario analysis, some weighted average of $A(U_0, V_0)$ and $A(U_1, V_1)$, say $\bar{A}$, were applied to (U, V), then feasibility would read $Ue = \bar{A}V^{\mathrm{T}}e$ and substitution would still be absent. However common this approach seems inconsistent to me, at least in a non-stochastic world. For example, the observations $(U, V) = (U_0, V_0)$ and $(U, V) = (U_1, V_1)$ need not be feasible under $\bar{A}$, not even under standard technology assumptions like constant returns to scale and free disposability. A simple illustration is given by the following pair of observations,

$$(U_0, V_0) = \left(\begin{bmatrix} \frac{1}{3} & 0 \\ 0 & \frac{2}{3} \end{bmatrix}, I\right) \quad \text{and} \quad (U_1, V_1) = \left(\begin{bmatrix} \frac{2}{3} & 0 \\ 0 & \frac{1}{3} \end{bmatrix}, I\right)$$

Then

$$A(U_0, V_0) = \begin{bmatrix} \frac{1}{3} & 0 \\ 0 & \frac{2}{3} \end{bmatrix} \quad \text{and} \quad A(U_1, V_1) = \begin{bmatrix} \frac{2}{3} & 0 \\ 0 & \frac{1}{3} \end{bmatrix}$$

Hence

$$\bar{A} = \begin{bmatrix} a & 0 \\ 0 & b \end{bmatrix}$$

with $1/3 < a, b < 2/3$. (U_0, V_0) is feasible under $\bar{A}$ if and only if $U_0 e \geqq \bar{A} V_0^{\mathrm{T}} e$ (using the free disposability of inputs) or

$$\begin{bmatrix} \frac{1}{3} \\ \frac{2}{3} \end{bmatrix} \geqq \begin{bmatrix} a \\ b \end{bmatrix}.$$

(U_1, V_1) is feasible under $\bar{A}$ if and only if

$$\begin{bmatrix} \frac{2}{3} \\ \frac{1}{3} \end{bmatrix} \geqq \begin{bmatrix} a \\ b \end{bmatrix}.$$

These two conditions cannot be met by $a, b > 1/3$. This completes the demonstration that a weighted average of the coefficients is inconsistent with feasibility of the observed flows.

It seems more appropriate to declare (U, V) feasible if it can be decomposed into two terms, say $(U, V) = (U^0, V^0) + (U^1, V^1)$, with (U^0, V^0) feasible with respect to $A(U_0, V_0)$ and (U^1, V^1) feasible with respect to $A(U_1, V_1)$. In the input space, isoquants no longer have the familiar L-shape of a Leontief production function, but look like . Such an isoquant features an interval of perfect substitution.

A prime setting for this elementary type of substitution is a model of international trade between countries with different technologies, that is $A(U_0, V_0) \neq A(U_1, V_1)$, where 0 now represents the home country and 1 the foreign country. Although each country may be incapable of substituting inputs, reallocations of activity brings it about at a global level. Trade mitigates substitution and, when modeled properly, input–output thus loses its problematic features of excess supplies and zero prices for some inputs, at least when net output proportions are fixed, as we shall see in section 6. Neoclassical features are thus introduced without having to go all the way to the concept of a smooth production function. In my view, a Cobb-Douglas production function, or any other function with smooth isoquants, is generated only in a world with infinitely many observations. The above shape of an isoquant is modified further by more kinks, and eventually becomes smooth.

Bert Steenge has pointed out that my discussion of two (or more) observations is unambiguous only in a non-stochastic setting. He also suggested that if (U_0, V_0) and (U_1, V_1) are viewed as realizations of a random variable, $\bar{A}$ can be interpreted as an approximation of the 'true' input–output matrix, In this case, infeasibilities of observations under $\bar{A}$ could be ascribed to errors. A discussion of the implications of allowing for a stochastic approach may be as follows. Input observations would be related to output observations through the 'true' matrix, say $\mathcal{A}$ and discrepancies are collected in error terms, say ε:

$$(U_0, U_1) = \mathcal{A}(V_0^{\mathrm{T}}, V_1^{\mathrm{T}}) + (\varepsilon_0, \varepsilon_1).$$

(The extension to more than two observations is obvious.) A would be an estimator of $\mathcal{A}$, and hence a function of (U_0, U_1) and (V_0, V_1). It could be ordinary least squares, or restricted ordinary least squares, if the true matrix is non-negative. The framework is consistent with the axioms of Kop Jansen and ten Raa (1990), as well as non-negativity requirements. Non-negativity is less likely to be rejected as in ten Raa (1988), since the variance-covariance matrix is no longer known, but must be estimated from (U_0, U_1) and (V_0, V_1). If non-negativity continues to be rejected in the presence of many observations, my preferences would be to drop the notion of a common 'true' matrix by admitting different coefficients, that is substitution. Moreover, I would not enforce non-negativity on each realization. In fact, the explicit evaluation of the coefficients is not necessary in economic analysis, not even when proportions are assumed to be constant. I refer to the analysis of ten Raa and Mohnen (1994) for an illustration.

A multitude of observations and underlying techniques is one source of substitution between factor inputs. Another source is the commodity composition of final demand or more precisely, its variability. Neoclassical economists exploit this source of substitution as well, but in a rather implicit manner, through the concept of an aggregated commodity. It is illuminating to establish the relationship a bit more clearly. It suffices to consider one observation, (U_0, V_0, L_0, K_0), including sectoral labor and capital employment row vectors. Turning to variables by dropping the zero subscripts and introducing, as before, technical coefficients $A = U_0 V_0^{-\mathrm{T}}$, $l = L_0 V_0^{-\mathrm{T}}$ and $k = K_0 V_0^{\mathrm{T}}$, the factor requirements of a bill of final goods, y, becomes $l(I - A)^{-1}y$ and $k(I - A)^{-1}y$, which clearly vary with the composition of vector y. This simple source of substitution is sufficient to obtain full employment of resources (ten Raa and Mohnen, 1994).

Most neoclassical economists think of a combination of the two sources of substitution when modeling a national production function. The effects of choice of techniques, and hence alternative technical coefficients, on the relationship between net outputs and factor inputs are envisaged. It should now be clear that methodologically, this is a problem of the effects of coefficients variation on $(I - A)^{-1}$, the Leontief inverse of A. Thus, the input–output counterpart of neoclassical substitution is a variation of the Leontief inverse. This problem is analyzed in a stochastic setting by Kop Jansen and Steel (1994).

In a neoclassical framework, the substitutability of inputs is determined by their marginal productivities. For factor inputs, the commodity composition effect of final demand is, as mentioned, one source of substitution. If we denote the solution to the primal program, py, by Q, then, by the main theorem of linear programming, $Q = wL_0 + rK_0$, where w and r are the Lagrange multipliers of the labor and capital constraints which fulfill $w = \partial Q/\partial N$ and $r = \partial Q/\partial K$. So even though there may be no substitution of inputs within sectors, the possibility of varying components of the net output vector in solving the economic program yields the substitutability of factor inputs.

Conceptually, substitution is modeled by constructing the hybrid economy comprising all the observed techniques. The first application is in Carter (1970). In the solution, only one technique of the observed will be active and the others are worse as valued by the shadow prices of the material balance and factor input constraints, by the phenomenon of complimentary slackness. So all you know is such types of inequalities. When the techniques are not finite but constitute a continuum and can thus be parameterized, the superiority of the active techniques in terms of value can be assigned first-order conditions, yielding the equality between relative prices and marginal rates of substitution. However, I dislike this idealization and therefore, refrain from relating coefficients changes to the dual prices.

5. Specialization

When an economic problem is formulated mathematically as a linear program, bang-bang behavior is to be expected. Typically, the number of active variables is no more than the number of constraints. When the value of the national product is maximized subject to the material balance constraints and the primary factor constraints, the former are binding and can be used to express national product components in sectoral activity levels. This elimination procedure leaves only the primary factor constraints to bind the sectoral activity levels and therefore, the number of active sectors will match the number of primary factors. For example, in section 3, where only labor was considered, an extreme form of specialization in only one sector results.

The extreme behavior of input–output type models is believed to be caused by the assumption of the non-substitutability of inputs of a technique. This belief is false. In fact, substitution makes things worse. My elaboration comes in three folds. First, I shall reproduce the argument of non-substitutability as a source of extreme behavior. Second, I shall discuss the consequences of the introduction of substitution in the maximization problem of this paper. Third, I shall comment on a neoclassical approach to the problem of specialization.

A macro-economic production function relates the net output of a national economy directly to its factor inputs. Gross outputs and intermediate inputs are implicitly eliminated by the Leontief inversion. Although no one would argue that this procedure yields a Leontief production function for an aggregate measure of output, many applied input–output studies exhibit this behavior. Whenever the proportions of the final bill of goods are fixed by consumption and trade coefficients, the fixed primary input proportions can be associated with components of the vector of final goods and be weighted. In this case, the national economy is implicitly modeled by a Leontief macro-economic production function and bang-bang behavior emerges in the form of some zero shadow prices of factor inputs. These observations pertain to standard linear programming formulations of the input–output model, such as Dorfman *et al.* (1958), but not to our approach. The proportions of final goods many vary freely and therefore, the aggregate factor intensities also. Since the objective function is a linear valuation of net outputs, the latter are perfect substitutes and since factor intensities vary across net outputs, there is some degree of substitution between factor inputs as well. So the extreme behavior of our model is not the usual phenomenon of Leontief-type models. As a matter of fact, the introduction of substitution makes things worse. The best way to understand this is to go back to the very first formulation of the economic problem in section 3. As we have seen in section 4, the introduction of substitution merely increases the dimension of the activity space (or the vector of scales, s). The linear programming result that the active number of activities matches the number of primary inputs remains. The disaggregation of a sectoral activity into a number of activity vectors that comes with the introduction of substitution cannot increase the number of active sectors, but has the possibility of concentrating activities in fewer sectors. By going to the limit of neoclassical production functions, one cannot escape this logic. A fine example is Diewert and Morrison (1986). To avoid specialization, they impose a translog structure not on the production function or inputs of the economy, but on the national product function, or outputs of the economy. This procedure eliminates specialization, but it is brute force for four reasons. First, a peculiar jointness of net output is implicitly assumed. Second, since the signs of the components cannot flip when a translog function is imposed, the pattern of trade must be considered as given. Third, the estimation at the net output side of the economy requires the assumption that the observed flows are consistent with perfect competition. Fourth, even when the previous point is taken for granted, the required concavity assumptions are inconsistent at the output level, as admitted in a footnote by Diewert (1982, p. 576).

Specialization is a serous 'problem' that plagues input–output, as well as neoclassical models of national product determination. In applications, additional constraints are considered, such as the non-tradability of certain commodities, and the number of active sectors is increased accordingly. An intermediate device is to model imports as imperfect substitutes. Although such practices remedy the extreme nature of corner solutions, the economics of specialization must be accepted. The best objection against our linear programming approach is that the pattern of specialization is dependent on the coefficients of the objective functions, such as the world terms of trade, and that variations in the latter cannot be anticipated, so that diversification is a safe policy. However, without imposing a peculiar jointness on net outputs, Gilchrist and St. Louis (1994) are able to address diversification by taking into account the fluctuations in the terms of trade. Their study is regional economic. Patterns of specialization, as predicted by international trade theories, are best tested in regional economics since impediments to trade are less prevalent between regions than between nations.

6. Closing the Model

The possibility of importing commodities admits negative components to the net output vector of a national economy and therefore, the specialization in a number of sectors. Under conditions of national product maximization and free trade, the structure of an economy thus degenerates into a number of columns and the usual input–output multiplier effects evaporate from the national economy. It is only at the level of the world economy that the circularity of production and traditional input–output results re-emerge. The international division of labor is a vehicle for substitution. Commodities can be produced in different national economies with varying input proportions. As noted in section 4, substitution is modeled by constructing the hybrid economy comprising all the observed techniques. The commodity × sector use tables are stacked next to each other and the sector × commodity make tables are stacked under each other. In other words, sectors in different countries are treated as separate sectors. Since the system of National Accounts makes a distinction between commodities and sectors anyway, identifying the latter with pairs of input columns and output rows, there is no need to classify sectors across countries. Their numbers and order may vary; we only have to put them next to each other.

Thus let U_0, V_0, and L_0 be the use, make, and employment tables of the world, obtained by stacking the national ones. Let s be the column vector of sectoral activity levels. The number of components is the sum of the numbers of sectors in the various countries. The sign pattern of the economic variable s will reveal the pattern of specialization between countries in the different commodity markets. The net output of the world will be $(V_0^{\mathrm{T}} - U_0)s$, assuming constant returns to scale. The total labor requirements are L_0s.

For ease of exposition, I assume that labor is mobile, so that activities are constrained by $L_0s \leqq N$, the world labor force. The alternative assumption of immobile labor could be accommodated by treating workers of different countries as different factor inputs.

Unlike the national economic analysis expounded in section 3, it does not make sense to maximize world net output at given world prices. Components of net output would be negative. They might be forced to be positive by adding constraints, but those constraints would be binding and their specification would drive the allocation of activity in a direct, mechanical manner. The world economy is closed and all trades cancel out in its net output vector. The net output must be related to preferences rather than some exogenous price system. Thus, let the desired net output proportions be given by a vector a with non-negative shares for the commodities, adding to unity. There is no objection against declaring the status quo of net output proportions desirable. The level of the desired net output vector is variable in the economic analysis and in fact, constitutes the objective function:

$$\max_{s,c \geqq 0} c$$

subject to

$$(V_0^{\mathrm{T}} - U_0)s \geqq ac, \quad L_0 s \leqq N.$$

This program determines the pattern of specialization of countries. Net output is non-negative at the world level, by the constraint that imposes the desired proportions, but may have negative components for individual countries. Commodity prices are endogenous. In fact, they are the shadow prices associated with the net output constraints. The dual program reads

$$\min_{p,w \geqq 0} wN$$

subject to

$$pV_0^{\mathrm{T}} \leqq pU_0 + wL_0, \quad pa = 1.$$

Note that this dual program is basically the same as the dual program in the national product maximization program of section 3. The only essential difference is that the commodity price vector is now variable. The derivation of the value equations of input–output analysis is unaffected. As before, the solutions to the primal and dual programs yield equal values:

$$c = wN.$$

This is the equality between the world product and income. By the constraints of the primal program and the normalization of prices,

$$\left(pV_0^{\mathrm{T}} - pU_0 - wL_0\right)s \geqq pac - wN = 0.$$

As before, partition sectors in active ones ($s_i > 0$) and sleeping ones ($s_i = 0$) constitute index sets I and II, respectively. Then

$$\left(pV_0^{\mathrm{T}} - pU_0 - wL_0\right)_I s_I + 0 \geqq 0,$$

and by the constraint of the dual program,

$$\left(pV_0^{\mathrm{T}} - pU_0 - wL_0\right)_I = 0$$

or

$$pV_{0I}^{\mathrm{T}} = pU_{0I} + wL_{0I},$$

where I selects the active columns. It can be shown that the number of active comumns need not be greater than the number of commodities. Moreover, if the desired net output proportions (a) are not so extreme that some component can be supplied as a by-product, the number of active sectors must be at least equal to the number of commodities. Thus, V_{0I}^{T} will be a square matrix. Moreover, if primary output is dominant, it is invertible and we obtain

$$p = pA_I + wl_I,$$

where $A_I = U_{0I}V_{0I}^{-\mathrm{T}}$ and $l_I = L_{0I}V_{0I}^{-\mathrm{T}}$, the input coefficients according to the commodity technology model as applied to the active sectors. Consequently,

$$p = wl_I(I - A_I)^{-\mathrm{T}},$$

the Marxian labor values as determined by the coefficients of the active sectors. Note that this general equilibrium price does not depend on the assumed desired net output proportions, a. As a matter of fact, not even the selection of active sectors, I, depends on a. In the dual program, a only normalizes prices. It can be shown that the price vector that solves the dual program is independent of the normalization constants listed in the vector a. Consequently, a component of the dual constraint is binding or not binding, whatever a is. Thus, the classification of break-even and unprofitable sectors is independent of a. By the above analysis, the break-even sectors are precisely the active sectors, and the profitable sectors are the sleeping sectors. This shows that the classification of sectors as active and sleeping is independent of the preferences. The application of the theory of linear programming thus provides a simple proof of the substitution theorem of Samuelson (1951), by which an economy with a single factor input will not substitute techniques in response to changing demand conditions.

Note that the dual variables (prices) are positive. In the same way that the dual constraints were shown to be binding when the primal variables (activity levels) are positive, we can now conclude that the primal constraints are binding,

$$\left(V_0^{\mathrm{T}} - U_0\right) s = ac,$$

and therefore,

$$\left(V_0^{\mathrm{T}} - U_0\right)_I s_I = ac.$$

By a change of variable, $V_0^{\mathrm{T}} s_I = x$, we now have

$$x = A_I x + ac,$$

the traditional input–output equation, featuring the circularity of production and the consequent multiplier effects:

$$x = (I - A_I)^{-\mathrm{T}} ac.$$

The technical coefficients are not determined by the aggregation of sectors across countries and the submission of the world use and make tables to the standard formula, but by the best practice techniques selected by the linear program. While the selection is robust in our simple world model with one factor input, the situation becomes more complicated when more factor inputs are introduced. The input–output relations are maintained, but the set of active sectors may vary to accommodate factor scarcities.

Although the national product maximization program expounded in Section 3 and the desired consumption level program for the world economy of this section would make no sense in each other's contexts (the national program entails negative net outputs and the world program excludes them), they are consistent. The general equilibrium model of this section subsumes the partial equilibrium model of Section 3 if the prices which were considered there are the solution to the world model. Otherwise the extreme patterns of national net exports would yield excess supplies or demands in the world markets.

7. Productivity Growth

One might argue that neoclassical economics provides a reduced form of the input–output model. The Leontief inversion is presumed implicitly in neoclassical models and the value of the net output attainable for given levels of resources is written by a simple function in lieu of the solution to a linear program as in Section 3. Since the neoclassical production function is essentially the value function of a linear program, the marginal productivities of the resources are the Lagrange multipliers to the linear program. To introduce productivity more precisely, recall the data of an economy: use and make tables, labor and capital employment row vectors, as well as total endowment stocks. As before, the net output is $y = (V^{\mathrm{T}} - U)e$, while factor inputs are stocks N and K. Roughly speaking, productivity is net output divided by factor input; hence, profitability growth is the change of net output minus the change of factor input. The traditional measure of total factor productivity growth is

$$(p\,\mathrm{d}y - w\,\mathrm{d}N - r\,\mathrm{d}K)/(py),$$

where w is the wage rate and r the rental rate of capital. Input–output economists [Wolff (1994)] consider w and r as exogenous, and commodity prices p as endogenous, using the value equations of Section 2,

$$p = pA + wl + rk. \tag{F'}$$

The traditional measure of productivity growth is rather mechanical, but can provide a theoretical foundation by embedding the input–output relationships in the neoclassical framework of profit maximization. Productivity is properly defined only if there is a criterion, or objective function, to measure the contributions of factor endowments. In my view, factor productivity is w or r, the shadow prices or Lagrange multipliers to a maximization problem. After all, shadow prices measure the contributions of factor inputs. Consequently, since factor productivity growth ought to be the growth of factor productivity, it must be $\mathrm{d}w$ or $\mathrm{d}r$. Hence, factor productivity growth rates are changes in shadow prices resulting from changes in the data $(U_0, V_0, L_0, K_0, N, K)$. Since $\mathrm{d}w$ and $\mathrm{d}r$ are per unit of the factor input, total factor productivity growth is $N\,\mathrm{d}w + K\,\mathrm{d}r$, or relative to the national product or income,

$$(N\,\mathrm{d}w + K\,\mathrm{d}r)/(py).$$

This shadow-price-based measure of total factor productivity growth can be used as a foundation for the traditional measure through the main theorem of linear programmity of Section 3:

$$py = wN + rK.$$

Here, w and r are endogenous marginal productivities associated with unit increases in N and K, but p is the exogenous row vector specifying the criterion (the national product of world prices, for example). Hence, differentiation yields

$$p\,\mathrm{d}y = w\,\mathrm{d}N + N\,\mathrm{d}w + r\,\mathrm{d}K + K\,\mathrm{d}r.$$

Substituting into my direct definition of total factor productivity growth, $(N\,\mathrm{d}w+K\,\mathrm{d}r)/(py)$, yields the traditional measure outlined at the beginning of this section.

Note that in defining and deriving total factor productivity growth, I made no appeal to the traditional value equations, (F′). p is exogenous and w and r are the shadow prices associated with a maximization problem. It is an open question which value equations they fulfill. If there are no lower bounds to the net output, they fulfill the value equations restricted to the active sectors in the maximization problem, as defined in Section 3. Typically, their number is the number of constraints, which is only two. This case is relevant to the measurement of the productivity growth of an open economy under free trade. Under alternative regimes, commodity prices pick up tariffs and the consequent full prices observe a more complete system of traditional value equations. These tariffs are endogenous, see ten Raa and Mohnen (1994). Input–output economists, by using the full price vector in evaluating total factor productivity growth, implicitly take trade restrictions for granted. The precise relationship between trade regimes and the measurement of total factor productivity growth is an open issue and presently under investigation.

8. Conclusion

In this paper, we have used the neoclassical concept of profit maximization as a framework for the input and output data of an economy. The basic elements of input–output analysis, notably technical coefficients, and the quantity and value equations, emerged as intermediate constructs in the course of analysis. The technical coefficients construction methodology is forced by the quantity and value equations, and the latter are derived from the primal and dual constraints to the problem of profit maximization. Value-added coefficients are no longer exogenous, but related to the quantity system as shadow prices. Their rates of change can be used to define factor productivity growth rates, and the traditional input–output measure of total factor productivity growth has thus been provided with a neoclassical foundation.

Acknowledgements

I wish to acknowledge an intellectual debt to my teachers, William Baumol and Wassily Leontief. I thank Bert Steenge, an anonymous referee, and editor Konrad Stabl for stimulating remarks, and the Royal Netherlands Academy of Sciences for a senior fellowship. This paper was refereed under the editorial control of Konrad Stahl and John Quigley.

References

Carter, A.P. (1970) Structural change in the American economy (Harvard University Press. Cambridge, MA).

Diewert, W.E. (1982) Duality approaches to microeconomic theory, in: Arrow, K.J. and M.D. Intriligator (eds.), Handbook of mathematical economics, vol. 11 (North-Holland, Amsterdam).

Diewert, W.E. and O.J. Morrison (1986) Adjusting output and productivity indexes for changes in the terms of trade, *Economic Journal*, 96, pp. 659–679.

Dorfman, R., P.A. Samuelson and R.M. Solow (1958) Linear programming and economic analysis (McGraw-Hill, New York).

Gilchrist, D.A. and L.V. St. Louis (1994) An Equilibrium analysis of regional industrial diversification, *Regional Science and Urban Economics*, 24(1), pp. 115–133.

Kop Jansen, P. (1994) Analysis of multipliers in stochastic input–output models, *Regional Science and Urban Economics*, 24(1), pp. 55–74.

Kop Jansen, P. and Th. ten Raa (1990) The choice of model in the construction of input–output coefficients matrices, *International Economic Review*, 31(1), pp. 213–227.
Leontief, W. (1966) Input–output economics (Oxford University Press, New York).
ten Raa, Th. (1988) An alternative treatment of secondary products in input–output analysis: Frustration, *Review or Economics and Statistics*, 70(3), pp. 535–538.
ten Raa, Th. and P. Mohnen (1994) Neoclassical input–output analysis, *Regional Science and Urban Economics*, 24(1), pp. 135–158.
ten Raa, Th. and E. Wolff (1991) Secondary products and the measurement of productivity growth, *Regional Science and Urban Economics*, 21, pp. 581–615.
Samuelson, P.A. (1951) Abstract of a theorem concerning substitution in open Leontief mode's, in: Koopmans, T.C. (ed.), Activity analysis of production and allocation, Cowles Commission Monograph no. 13 (Wiley, New York).
Schrijver, A. (1986) Theory of linear and integer programming (Wiley, Chichester).
United Nations (1967), Proposals for the revision of SNA 1952, Document F/CN.3/356.
Wolff, E.N. (1994) Productivity measurement within an input–output framework, *Regional Science and Urban Economics*, 24(1), pp. 75–92.

Chapter 10

Neoclassical Input–Output Analysis

Thijs ten Raa and Pierre Mohnen

Abstract: The Canadian comparative advantage is determined by the maximization of foreign earnings, subject to 10 input–output relations between 29 industries and 92 commodities. Free trade would boost the mining, quarrying & oil wells, tobacco, and machinery sectors. The structure of the economy is not self-sufficient, as a necessary and sufficient price condition shows. When commodities are aggregated into the 29 sectors, the shadow prices of the programs fulfill the value equations of the input–output analysis and admit a decomposition of Canadian inefficiency in 5% X-inefficiency, 15% allocative inefficiency, and 80% international specialization mismatch.

JEL classification: F11; C67

1. Introduction

Neoclassical input–output analysis?! If neoclassical economists and input–output economists share a view at all, it is the agreement to disagree. The two schools differ in terms of subject as well as method. Neoclassical economists address the question of value (including allocation) and

Received August 1991, final version received September 1992.

relate it to the endowments and technology of an economy by the concept of marginal productivity. Input–output economists address the question of the transmission of effects (due to shocks, for example) and relate it to the structure of an economy by the concept of a technical coefficient. The marginal analysis of value seems particularly relevant in the short-to-medium run, while the structural analysis of transmissions seems relevant in the medium-to-long run. When the scopes differ, it is perfectly all right to have differences in methods.

A certain degree of complementarity can be considered a source of synthesis. In this paper, we instill a neoclassical ingredient in the input–output framework, such that prices and quantities can be determined simultaneously. The ingredient is the concept of profit maximization at the aggregate level. The intersectoral substitution of activity provides the economy with neoclassical features at the macro level, such as the pricing of labor and capital according to their marginal productivities. At the sectoral level, production functions remain of the standard input–output type.

In a classical input–output study, Leontief (1953) assessed the factor position of an economy. He concluded that the exports of the U.S. economy were labor-intensive relative to the imports. Factor contents of exports and imports were calculated with the aid of U.S. input–output coefficients. This so-called Leontief paradox casted doubt on the Heckscher-Ohlin theorem of international trade which predicts that exports are relatively factor-intensive in the abundant endowment. (Abundance is taken relative to the endowments in the rest of the world.) But Leontief did not explain the pattern of trade. To detect the sectors of comparative advantage or disadvantage of sectors, one needs a criterion. The criterion we take is profit or, in the context of international trade, foreign earnings. We follow Williams (1978), but endogenize the direction of trade.

In this paper, we make three contributions. First, the quantity and value equations of input–output analysis are unified in a neoclassical model of profit maximization. Second, we perform the analysis in a rectangular use make framework and relate it to traditional input–output analysis. Third, we identify the comparative advantage of an economy given only its factor endowments and technology, and reveal the inefficiencies present in the data.

Sectors will be characterized by the observed input and output proportions, and will be hypothetically scaled down, or up in accordance with profitability. The number of commodities may exceed the number of sectors. As far as we know, this is the first empirical application of von Neumann's (1945) activity model. The optimum levels of activity signal comparative advantages and will be compared with the observed ones and the increase of profits will be decomposed into three parts. The parts are associated with full capacities utilization, reallocations that increase all components of net exports, and respecialization, respectively. In this way, we make operational the neoclassical notions of X-efficiency, allocative efficiency, and gains to trade.

The paper is organized as follows. The rectangular commodity-sector model is presented in section 2. How the model can detect the comparative advantages is explained in section 3. The relationship with traditional input–output analysis follows in section 4. Section 5 explains the efficiency decomposition. The results of the traditional and the rectangular analyses are presented in sections 6 and 7, respectively.

2. The Model

We study the Canadian economy of 1980. The data comprise material inputs, U_0, outputs, V_0, labor employment by sector, L_0, capital stocks by sector, K_0, capacity utilization rates by sector, c, and a labor force, N. The economy is divided into 29 sectors and broken down further into 92 commodities, Therefore, U_0 and V_0 are rectangular matrices of dimension sources 92×29 and 29×92, respectively. L_0, K_0 and c are row vectors of dimension 1×29. N is a scalar. The total capital stock is obtained by summing the components of $K_0 : K_0e$, where e is the vector with all entries equal to unity. We also need world prices p for the tradable commodities. p is a commodity row vector with non-tradable components set at zero. These prices will be parametrically given to the Canadian economy. In view of the small size of the Canadian economy, this assumption seems reasonable. Note that $y_0 = (V_0^{\mathrm{T}} - U_0)e = f_0 + g_0$ is observed final demand, consisting of net exports, g_0, and all other components (consumption and investment) which may be referred to as domestic final demand, f_0. Net exports will be varied given the terms of trade and therefore, the analysis is relevant for small, open economies.

We wish to investigate the optimum pattern of trade. All other components of final demand, collected in commodity vector f_0, are considered exogenous. We thus determine trade improvements upon the status quo. Indirect improvements, through consumption and investment adjustments, are ignored. Variables are obtained by dropping subscripts. Since net exports are the only varying component, we may just as well optimize the entire final demand vector, $y = (V^{\mathrm{T}} - U)e$. Introducing industry activity levels (or scales) by the vector s, the maximization of foreign earnings subject to the input–output structure of the economy is (see ten Raa 1994)

$$\max_{s \geqq 0} py$$

subject to

$$y = (V^{\mathrm{T}} - U)e \geqq z, \quad Le \leqq N, \quad Ke \leqq K_0 e,$$
$$(U, V, L, K) = (U_0\hat{s}, \hat{s}V_0, L_0\hat{s}, K_0\hat{c}\hat{s})$$

Final demand, y, and hence net exports, is subject to alternative restrictions, z, reflecting different trade programs. Under *free trade*, net exports and hence y_i, are free for tradable commodities i. For non-tradable commodities j, final demand, y_j, consists of domestic final demand and may not drop below the observed level: In short, the free trade program is specified by

$$z_i = -\infty \text{ (} i \text{ tradable).} \quad z_j = y_{0j} \text{ (} j \text{ non-tradable).}$$

This restriction may also be written as follows. Let j be the 0 1 matrix which selects the non-tradable commodities. If commodity i is non-tradable, J has one 92-dimensional row with the ith entry one and all others zero. The number of rows of J equals the number of non-tradable commodities. The free trade constraint becomes

$$Jy \geqq Jy_0.$$

Under an *export promotion* program, net exports exceed prevailing levels, obtained by specifying

$$z = y_0.$$

Under an *import substitution* program, autarky is imposed by the self-sufficiency constraint that final demand exceeds domestic final demand,

$y \geqq f_0$, where the lower bound can also be written

$$z = y_0 - g_0.$$

The free trade constraint is wider than either the export promotion or the import substitution constraint. The latter are not comparable, since some components of y_0 exceed those of $y_0 - g_0$, while others fall short, depending on the sign of observed net exports, as indicated by the components of, g_0.

Substitution simplifies the canonical model to

$$\max_{s \geqq 0} p\left(V_0^{\mathrm{T}} - U_0\right)s$$

subject to

$$\left(V_0^{\mathrm{T}} - U_0\right)s \geqq z, \quad L_0 s \leqq N, \quad K_0 \hat{c} s \leqq K_0 e.$$

By the first constraint, production must meet a prescribed level of net demand, z. For example, in the export promotion program, production must meet the levels called forth by the requirements of the prevailing levels of final demand. This, however, constitutes no more than a lower bound on the effective sales, since the latter also include additions to net exports. Through variations of the latter, the whole pattern of net output may change. This liberty is neoclassical in spirit and constitutes a departure from the traditional input–output analysis and the closely-related linear program of Dorfman *et al.* (1958, p. 228) who choose gross outputs to minimize total labor costs of a *specified* bill of final goods.

3. Prices and Comparative Advantages

In neoclassical economics, factor and material inputs are priced according to their marginal productivities. In the input–output analysis, proportions are assumed to be fixed and an increase in a single input, however marginal, does not contribute to output or profit. When marginal productivity analysis is not applicable at the sectoral level, it may be relevant economy-wide. A marginal increase in a single factor input contributes to foreign earnings, provided the economy accommodates it by a shift towards sectors that are relatively intensive in the factor considered. Intersectoral substitution in the input–output model facilitates a marginal productivity analysis of value.

Formally, the wage and rental rates are the Lagrange multipliers associated with the labor and capital constraints. The determination of commodity prices is analogous.

The Lagrange multipliers to the three constraints of the above generic model, also called shadow prices, can be denoted by tariffs, t, wage rate, w, and rental rate, r, respectively. They solve the so-called dual program (Schrijver 1986, p. 90), which in the present context reads

$$\min_{t,w,r \geqq 0} \; wN + rK_0 e - tz$$

subject to

$$(p+t)\left(V_0^{\mathrm{T}} - U_0\right) \leqq wL_0 + rK_0\hat{c}.$$

Like the wage and rental rates, the tariffs are not the observed ones, but purely theoretical constructs. Their meaning will transpire after the presentation of the duality theory. The neoclassical primal objective of profit maximization naturally yields the above neoclassical dual of cost minimization. In Dorfman *et al.* (1958, p. 228), quantities were chosen to minimize the costs of a specified bill of final goods. The duality of this problem involves the maximization of the value of net output by choice of prices with quantities fixed. This combination of objective and instruments is not neoclassical.

I now return to the above linear program. By the so-called phenomenon of complementary slackness (Schrijver 1986, p. 95), a primal (commodity) constraint has slack only if the dual price (tariff) is zero:

$$t\left[\left(V_0^{\mathrm{T}} - U_0\right)s - z\right] = 0.$$

Commodities whose production exceeds minimum requirements contribute to the objective function of the primal program. They are signaled by a competitive domestic price (world price cum tariff) which is equal to just the world price. These are the comparative advantage commodities which can compete on the world market. However, not all commodities with a zero tariff are truly commodities of comparative advantage in a rectangular model. Some commodity production is unavoidable given the fixed net output proportions.

Another application of the phenomenon of complementary slackness yields that a sectoral activity level is positive only if the dual constraint is binding. Such sectors are active and break even at shadow prices $p + t$. In other words, the revenues of net outputs match the costs of the factor inputs. Since the shadow prices render sectors that are active in the solution just profitable, they constitute a competitive price system through which the optimum may be attained in a decentralized fashion. The competitive price system reflects the second welfare theorem of neoclassical economics. A warning is in order: positive activity need not signal a comparative advantage. It may merely be required to fulfill intermediate demand of other sectors through the trade regime constraints.

By the main theorem of linear programming (Schrijver 1986, p. 90), the solution values of the primal and dual programs match:

$$p\left(V_0^{\mathrm{T}} - U_0\right)s = wN + rK_0e - tz.$$

Substituting the last term by the complementary slackness equation, we obtain

$$wN + rK_0e = (p + t)\left(V_0^{\mathrm{T}} - U_0\right)s = (p + t)y.$$

This is the macro identity between national income and product. Note that the domestic final demand is valued at competitive domestic prices. The role of the tariffs is to fill the gap between factor costs and world prices of the commodities that must be produced due to restrictions on net exports. Note also that national income entails a valuation of fully-employed resources at flexible prices. The solutions to the programs involve full employment indeed. We do not claim free trade, export promotion or import substitution as simple recipes for full employment, but merely use the programs as analytical devices to associate hypothetical, competitive outcomes, featuring comparative advantages, with the input–output structure of the Canadian economy. In other words, competitive outcomes are an analytical device to link concepts as comparative advantages with the structure of an economy.

4. Traditional Input–Output Analysis

When commodities are aggregated up to the same classification as industries (see the columns of Table 1 for the correspondence), the use and make tables become square, and the latter may be inverted to define one-to-one

Table 1: Sector and Commodity Aggregations.

Statistics Canada (1990a, 1990b) 29 sectors[a]	Statistics Canada (1987) M-classification	
	50 sectors	92 commodities
1. Agricultural & related services	1	1–3
2. Fishing & trapping	2	5, 6
3. Logging and forestry	3	4
4. Mining, quarrying & oil wells	4–**7**	7–12, **13**
5. Food	8	14–22
6. Beverage	9	23, 24
7. Tobacco products	10	25, 26
8. Plastic products	12	29
9. Rubber & leather products	11, **13**	27, 28, 30
10. Textile & clothing	14, **15**	31–35
11. Wood	16	36–38
12. Furniture and fixtures	17	39
13. Paper & allied products	18	40–42
14. Printing, publishing & allied	19	43, **44**
15. Primary metals	20	45–49
16. Fabricated metal products	21	50–52
17. Machinery	22	53, 54
18. Transportation equipment	23	55–57
19. Electrical and electronic products	24	58, 59
20. Non-metal lie mineral products	25	60, 61
21. Refined petroleum & coal	26	62, 63
22. Chemical & chemical products	27	64, 67
23. Other manufacturing	28	68, 69
24. Construction	29	**70–72**
25. Transportation & communication	30–33	**73–77**
26. Electric power and gas	34	78, 79
27. Wholesale & retail trade	35,36	80, **81**
28. Finance, insurance and real estate	37–40	**82**, 83
29. Community, business, personal services	41–50	84–87, **88**, 89, 90, **91–92**

[a]The industry codes adopted here are slightly different from those in Statistics Canada (1990a, 1990b), where sector 26 is missing for reasons of confidentiality so that the last sector is indexed by no. 30. Non-tradable commodities and the sectors declared non-trable are set bold face.

changes of variables between sectoral activity levels, s, industry outputs, $q = Ve = \hat{s}V_0 e$ and commodity outputs, $x = V^{\mathrm{T}}e = (\hat{s}V_0)^{\mathrm{T}}e = V_0^{\mathrm{T}}s$. The variables in the canonical trade model concluding section 2 affect the objective function and the constraint through the final demand vector:

$$y = \left(V_0^{\mathrm{T}} - U_0\right)s.$$

The change of variables to industry outputs involves rescaling only. More precisely, $q = \hat{s}V_0e = \widehat{V_0e}s$, hence $s = \widehat{V_0e}^{-1}q$. The final demand becomes

$$y = \left(V_0^{\mathrm{T}}\widehat{V_0e}^{-1} - U_0\widehat{V_0e}^{-1}\right)q$$

and features the commodity-by-industry input–output matrix, $U_0\widehat{V_0e}^{-1}$. Industry outputs are not obtained by the Leontief inverse of the latter, since $V_0^{\mathrm{T}}\widehat{V_0e}^{-1} \neq 1$. The change of variables to commodity outputs involves a full inversion, $s = V_0^{\mathrm{T}}x$. Final demand becomes

$$y = \left(I - U_0V_0^{-\mathrm{T}}\right)x$$

and features the commodity-by-commodity input–output matrix, $U_0V_0^{-\mathrm{T}}$. No change in the sectoral activity variables can generate an industry-by-industry variant, because the left-hand side of the final demand equation has the commodity dimension. For sectoral analysis, it is more advisable to stick to the sectoral activity levels variables. Then there is no need to identify commodities and sectors. Such an analysis can just as well be performed in the rectangular framework (section 7 below).

We confine the discussion of traditional input–output to the commodity-by-commodity input–output model, $A = U_0V_0^{-\mathrm{T}}$, which was obtained by the change in variables, $x = V_0^{\mathrm{T}}s$. Any positive element of s yields a multitude of positive elements of x, due to the off-diagonal elements of V_0. In other words, the domain $s \geqq 0$ corresponds not to the entire non-negative orthant, $x \geqq 0$, but to only a subset, in fact a cone. Conversely, the non-negative orthant, $x \geqq 0$, corresponds to a larger subset of sectoral activity space than $s \geqq 0$. Hence, by admitting all $x \geqq 0$, traditional input–output economists implicitly extend the analysis to sectoral activity sectors with negative components. Some input–output coefficients are negative for this reason. On the suggestion of an anonymous referee, we have considered adjusting the negatives and the observed output vector to preserve feasibility, but it did not affect the results. In other words, the extension of the domain implied by the traditional input–output instead of the sectoral activity analysis is not pertinent to the solution of the trade programs.

The substitution of the change of variables, $s = V_0^{-\mathrm{T}}x$, transforms the canonical trade program of section 2 to

$$\max p(I - A)x$$

subject to

$$(I-A)x \geqq z, \quad lx \leqq N, \quad kx \leqq K_0 e,$$

where technical coefficients are defined by the so-called commodity technology model:

$$A = U_0 V_0^{-\mathrm{T}}, \quad l = L_0 V_0^{-\mathrm{T}} \quad \text{and} \quad k = K_0 \hat{c} V_0^{-\mathrm{T}}.$$

Maximizing over $x \geqq 0$, the dual program becomes

$$\min_{t,w,r \geqq 0} \; wN + rK_0 e - lz$$

subject to

$$(p+t)(I-A) \leqq wl + rk.$$

The slack in the (primal) commodity constraint or a zero (dual) tariff detects a comparative advantage. Strictly speaking, it belongs to commodities, but in this traditional input–output framework, they are identified with sectors. It is not difficult to see that in the export promotion and import substitution programs, the material balance constraints yield positive gross outputs. By the phenomenon of complementary slackness, the dual constraints are binding. Postmultiplication by the Leontief inverse yields

$$p + t = (wl + rk)(I-A)^{-1},$$

the traditional value equations of input–output analysis. Here, however, the value equations are constraints to the dual program which determines all shadow prices. It is interesting to note that in the traditional input–output framework, factor costs, $wl + rk$, cannot be equated with net revenues, $p(I-A)$, for exogenous prices p. The number of degrees of freedom (two, for w and r) is too low. The resolution is possible, however, if prices include tariffs.

In traditional input–output analysis (Leontief 1979), prices are determined by the value system and outputs by the quantity system. Although the systems are similar mathematically, prices and outputs are determined independently of each other. The introduction of the neoclassical principle of profit maximization pairs the systems and allows a simultaneous determination of value and output. The value system emerges as the dual to the quantity system in the sense of linear programming. It should be mentioned that it has been attempted before to consolidate the equations of the input–output analysis in this manner, but the attempt (Dorfman *et al.*

1958) has failed to explain quantities by the unfortunate combinations of objective functions and instruments. When profit is the criterion and activity levels are the instruments, the dual program can be used to calculate the tariffs necessary to sustain economic programs, such as export promotion or import substitution. The primal program can be used to compute the required activity levels which can be attained by pure competition under the shadow prices. In short, a neoclassical specification unifies the elements of the input–output analysis.

5. Efficiency Analysis

Consider the free trade program, the export promotion program, and a constrained export promotion program. The constraint defining the latter rules out the reallocations of labor and capital, and will be specified below. Let the solutions be attained by y_{ft}, y_{ep}, and y_{cep}. Let us compare them with the observed final demand. y_0, y_{ep} and y_{cep} are bigger, but not ordered among each other. y_{ft} is not ordered relative to any of the other vectors. In terms of value, py, the picture is clearer. Since the free trade program is least constrained, it yields the greatest value. The constrained export promotion program can generate no more value than the export promotion program. Since the observed vector is feasible in all programs, its value constitutes a lower bound. In short,

$$py_0 \leqq py_{\mathrm{cep}} \leqq py_{\mathrm{ep}} \leqq py_{\mathrm{ft}}.$$

The total potential efficiency gain, $py_{\mathrm{ft}} - py_0$, can be decomposed into three terms, associated with the above inequalities. The first term, $py_{\mathrm{cep}} - py_0$, is the efficiency gain that can be attained without labor or capital reallocation, and is called the X-inefficiency of the economy. It represents a distance towards the production possibility frontier. We do not allow for the temporary location in the interior of the production possibility set as a means to overcome a recession, while maximizing output in a boom, because we neglect adjustment costs of capital and labor. In this respect, our estimate of X-inefficiency will be an overstatement. The sum of X-inefficiency and allocative inefficiency amounts to $py_{\mathrm{ep}} - py_0$, and measures the gain that can be made without any reduction in the net output vector; it may be called domestic inefficiency. The third term, $py_{\mathrm{ft}} - py_{\mathrm{ep}}$, is the efficiency gain that can be obtained by reductions of the net output vector through imports. It constitutes the pure potential gain to trade and is called the international specialization mismatch. In sum, total inefficiency, $py_{ft} - py_0$, consists of X-inefficiency, allocative inefficiency and international specialization mismatch.

The X-efficiency gain in the export promotion program is isolated by ruling out reallocations of labor and capital between sectors. In the use make framework, the constraints

$$s \leqq c^1 \quad \text{and} \quad L_0 \max\{s, e\} \leqq N$$

(where c^{-1} is the column vector of inverse sectoral capital utilization rates and max operates on each component) limit activities to full capacity levels and confine labor recruits to the pool of the unemployed, without decreasing employment in other sectors. In the traditional framework, X-efficiency is isolated by the imposition of

$$k_i x_l \leqq K_i^c \text{ (all } i) \quad \text{and} \quad l \max\{x, x_0\} \leqq N,$$

where capital and labor are associated with commodities rather than sectors. K_i^c is the stock of capital available for the production of *commodity i*. It is inaccurate to substitute K_i, the stock of capital in sector i, since that is also used for the production of commodities other than i. In doing traditional input–output analysis, not only intermediate flows U_0 have to be purified in the construction of $A = U_0 V_0^{-T}$, but also the stocks. The construction of the capital stock vector, K^c, is explained in the appendix.

The import substitution program is included for the sake of theoretical comparison. The shadow prices associated with the commodity constraints $z = y_0 - g_0$ are essentially autarky prices. The Ricardian theory of trade uses them to predict the pattern of free trade.

6. Traditional Input–Output Analysis of the Canadian Economy

We report the traditional input–output results, obtained by aggregating commodities up to the sectoral classification according to Table 1, and by maximization with respect to gross output levels and subject to commodity

Table 2: Net Exports (Millions of Dollars[a]).

Sector	Actual	X-efficiency	Export promotion	Free trade	Import substitution
1	3,645.4	3, 645.4	3, 645.4	−258, 870.0	0.0
2	51.8	**220.8**	51.8	10.8	0.0
3	10.1	10.1	10.1	−126.9	0.0
4	−2,929.1	**1,343.0**	**16,340.7**	**26,732.8**	**32,499.0**
5	−847.4	−847.4	−847.4	−16, 040.0	0.0
6	12.1	12.1	12.1	−2, 703.7	0.0
7	10.3	10.3	10.3	**1,013,304.5**	0.0
8	−435.6	−435.6	−435.6	−5, 061.2	00
9	−818.0	−818.0	−818.0	−1, 758.6	0.0
10	−2,231.4	−2,231.4	−2, 231.4	−6, 554.7	0.0
11	3,568.0	3,568.0	3, 568.0	−2, 873.1	0.0
12	−90.5	−90.5	−90.5	−2, 363.5	0.0
13	7,218.4	7,218.4	7, 218.4	116, 050.8	0.0
14	−583.5	−583.5	−583.5	−583.5	0.0
15	2,934.2	2,934.2	2, 934.2	−2, 945.3	0.0
16	−1,554.5	−1,554.5	−1, 554.5	−10, 482.0	0.0
17	−6,743.5	6,743.5	**31,807.9**	−10, 496.3	**30,661.0**
18	−2,781.9	−2,781.9	−2, 781.9	12, 800.1	0.0
19	−3,158.6	−3,158.6	−3, 158.6	−8, 536.8	0.0
20	543.2	543.2	−543.2	−3, 271.0	0.0
21	1,597.2	1,597.2	1, 5972	−8, 253.3	0.0
22	−3,561.0	−3,561.0	−3, 561.0	−14, 195.0	0.0
23	2,102.3	−2,102.3	−2, 102.3	−4, 389.5	0.0
24	0.0	0.0	0.0	0.0	0.0
25	719.8	719.8	719.8	−15, 514.5	0.0
26	807.5	**1,764.4**	807.5	−9, 483.4	0.0
27	2,170.6	**10,876.2**	2, 170.6	−49, 245.3	0.0
28	−753.9	−753.9	−753.9	−753.9	0.0
29	1,982.8	1, 982.8	1,982.8	186, 026.5	0.0
Increase as % of GDP	0.0	6.0	23.7	121.0	27.7

[a]Figures in bold indicate improvements on actual levels, i.e sectors with comparative advantages.

technology constraints. See Tables 2 and 3 for net trades and prices, respectively, for all trade programs.

The comparative advantages are detected in sectors 4 (mining, quarrying and oil wells) and 7 (tobacco products) under free trade. Sector 4 persists under the export promotion and import substitution programs, but is then accompanied by sector 17 (machinery), in either case. In fact, table 3, reveals that the shadow prices under the export promotion and import substitution are equal. Woodland (1982) has shown that comparative advantages are locally constant with respect to endowment changes, even in the

Table 3: Tariffs.

Sector	*X*-efficiency	Export promotion	Free trade	Import substitution
1	0.15	1.33	0.00	1.33
2	0.00	0.83	0.00	0.83
3	0.74	0.23	0.00	0.23
4	0.00	0.00	0.00	0.00
5	1.09	0.72	0.00	0.72
6	2.41	0.31	0.00	0.31
7	1.42	0.35	0.00	0.35
8	1.65	0.49	0.00	0.44
9	0.98	0.41	0.00	0.41
10	0.57	0.36	0.00	0.36
11	0.80	0.32	0.00	0.32
12	0.51	0.30	0.00	0.30
13	0.82	0.53	0.00	0.53
14	153.25	1.19	1.35	1.19
15	0.59	0.38	0.00	0.38
16	0.28	0.15	0.00	0.15
17	0.12	0.00	0.00	0.00
18	1.23	0.26	0.00	0.26
19	0.27	0.06	0.00	0.06
20	0.99	0.42	0.00	0.42
21	0.45	0.39	0.00	0.39
22	1.70	0.62	0.00	0.62
23	1.31	0.31	0.00	0.31
24	1.56	1.02	1.12	1.02
25	0.58	0.88	0.00	0.88
26	0.00	2.25	0.00	2.56
27	0.00	0.25	0.00	0.25
28	0.87	0.57	0.66	0.57
29	8.35	0.46	0.00	0.46
Wage rale ($/hour)	0.00	10.8	21.0	10.8
Rental rate	147.3%	33.1%	31.4%	33.1%

presence of substitution. Apparently, the difference between the constraints characterizing export promotion and import substitution constitutes a small change in terms of factor intensities relative to the final demand vector, i.e. GDP. In other words, Canadian endowments are balanced with respect to domestic final demand.

The slack in the Canadian economy consists of 5% *X*-inefficiency, 15% allocative inefficiency, and 80% international specialization mismatch. These figures are obtained by taking the increments at the bottom line of Table 2 as percentages of the total figure of the free trade scenario (121.0). The procedure has been explained in section 5. The main problem is the international misdirection of the Canadian economy. The patterns of optimum and actual commodity net exports are very different.

Domestic production or *autarky* prices are obtained by adding the import substitution tariffs to the world prices (recall the derivation of the traditional value equations from the dual program). Table 3 shows that the lowest autarky prices are for sectors 4 and 17. The Ricardian theorem predicts that they signal the net exports under free trade. Table 2 confirms this result for sector 4, but not sector 17, in agreement with recent theoretical falsifications (Drabicki and Takayama 1979; Woodland 1982). A more detailed analysis, undertaken in the next section, will include sector 17 as an exporter in the free trade scenario and thus resurrect the Ricardian theorem.

We have also calculated the optimum activity levels under the various trade regimes by maximizing with respect to the activity vector, s, rather than the gross output vector, x. This model is in between traditional input–output and activity analysis, as commodities are aggregated into sectors, but sectors are not purified by change of variables (from s to x). Within the class of square input–output models (Kop Jansen and ten Raa 1990), the traditional input–output model is essentially the commodity technology model, while the intermediate model with its fixed output proportions is essentially the by-product model. The results of the intermediate model are qualitatively the same as the traditional model, and quantitatively, very close. We have decided, therefore, not to report them.

7. Rectangular Input–Output Analysis of the Canadian Economy

Returning to the full use-make framework, we maximize surplus with respect to activity levels and subject it to observed sectoral input and output proportions. When we use the observed or zero values, $s = e$ or 0, as initial points, the program got stuck. One reason for this might be that any increase at the activity levels sparks off a flurry of commodity net input increases and that the fulfilment of the detailed commodity constraints cannot be controlled by the relatively few activity variables. If so, the commodity constraints would imply that the value of the objective function cannot be increased in the admittedly rigid activity model with its fixed input and output proportions.

To investigate this possibility, we have utilized a result of Rockafellar (1970) on inequalities implied by a system of inequalities. His theorem 22.3 shows that if and only if the coefficients of a 'new' inequality are non-negative combinations of the coefficients of a system of 'old' inequalities and the right-hand side of the new inequality is a relaxation of the non-negative combination of the right-hand sides of the old inequalities would any solution to the system of old inequalities also fulfill the new inequality. Now our model comprises the system of inequalities

$$\begin{bmatrix} U_0 - V_0^{\mathrm{T}} \\ L_0 \\ K_0\hat{c} \\ -I \end{bmatrix} s \leqq \begin{bmatrix} -z \\ N \\ K_0 e \\ 0 \end{bmatrix}.$$

The model can provide no better than $s = e$ if and only if the system implies

$$p\left(V_0^{\mathrm{T}} - U_0\right)s \leqq p\left(V_0^{\mathrm{T}} - U_0\right)e.$$

By Rockafeller's theorem, the latter inequality is implied if and only if there exists $(t\ w\ r\ \sigma) \geqq 0$ such that

$$p(V_0^{\mathrm{T}} - U_0) = (t\ w\ r\ \sigma)\begin{bmatrix} U_0 - V_0^{\mathrm{T}} \\ L_0 \\ K_0\hat{c} \\ -I \end{bmatrix}$$

and

$$p\left(V_0^{\mathrm{T}} - U_0\right)e \geqq (t\ w\ r\ \sigma)\begin{bmatrix} -z \\ N \\ K_0 e \\ 0 \end{bmatrix}.$$

An alternative derivation of this result is by the application of the main theorem of linear programming (Schrijver 1986, p. 90). So we are stuck at $s = e$ if and only if there exists $(t\ w\ r) \geqq 0$ such that

$$(p + t)\left(V_0^{\mathrm{T}} - U_0\right) \leqq wL_0 + rK_0\hat{c}$$

and

$$p\left(V_0^{\mathrm{T}} - U_0\right)e + tz \geqq wN + rK_0 e.$$

We investigate the possibilities of being stuck at $s = e$ for three scenarios: the export promotion program, the import substitution program, and the free trade program, respectively. The scenarios differ only by specification of the constraints vector, z.

In the *export promotion* program,

$$z = y_0 = \left(V_0^{\mathrm{T}} - U_0\right)e.$$

Multiplying the first inequality by e and combining with the second inequality through $L_0 e < N$ and $K_0 \hat{c} e < K_0 e$, we obtain a string of inequalities with equal extreme left- and right-hand sides. Hence the middle sides are also equal:

$$wL_0 e + rK_0 \hat{c} e = wN + rK_0 e,$$

which is equivalent to $w = r = 0$. Thus, $s = e$ is optimum if and only if there exists $t \geqq 0$ such that

$$(p + t)\left(V_0^{\mathrm{T}} - U_0\right) \leqq 0$$

and

$$(p + t)\left(V_0^{\mathrm{T}} - U_0\right)e \geqq 0.$$

Since the first inquality is equivalent to the statement that for all non-negative s, $(p + t)(V_0^{\mathrm{T}} - U_0)s \leqq 0$, the observed levels of activities are optimum if and only if there exist competitive domestic prices under which profits are non-negative and any other combination of activities would yield non-positive profits. (This connection between optimality and competitive prices reflects the welfare theorems of neoclassical economics.) The pair of inequalities is equivalent to

$$(p + t)\left(V_0^{\mathrm{T}} - U_0\right) = 0$$

for some $t \geqq 0$. By homogeneity, it suffices to find $\pi \geqq \varepsilon \geqq 0$, with $\varepsilon_i > 0$ for tradables and $\pi e = 1$ (constituting a closed set), such that

$$\pi\left(V_0^{\mathrm{T}} - U_0\right) = 0.$$

For this purpose, consider the linear program,

$$\min_{\pi,\mu} \mu$$

subject to

$$\pi\left(V_0^{\mathrm{T}} - U_0\right) = \mu e^{\mathrm{T}}\left(V_0^{\mathrm{T}} - U_0\right).$$

where the scalar μ is non-negative. Then $\pi = e^{\mathrm{T}}/n$, $\mu = 1/n$, where n is the number of commodities, is feasible. If the solution is (π^*, μ^*) and $\mu^* = 0$, then π^* is as desired and $s = e$ is optimum in the export promotion program.

The analysis of the *import substitution* program is a corollary to the investigation of the export promotion program. In the import substitution program, net outputs may not decrease below domestic final demand. Since the latter is non-negative, net outputs must certainly be non-negative:

$$\left(V_0^{\mathrm{T}} - U_0\right)s \geqq 0.$$

Consider any $s \geqq 0$ consistent with this autarky constraint. Then $e + \varepsilon s$ is consistent with the export promotion constraints. [The labor and capital constraints are fulfilled for ε small enough. The commodity constraint,

$$\left(V_0^{\mathrm{T}} - U_0\right)(e + \varepsilon s) \geqq \left(V_0^{\mathrm{T}} - U_0\right)e = y_0 = z \text{ (export promotion)},$$

is equivalent to the above autarky constraint.] If e is optimum in the export promotion program, then

$$p\left(V_0^{\mathrm{T}} - U_0\right)(e + \varepsilon s) \leqq p\left(V_0^{\mathrm{T}} - U_0\right)e,$$

and therefore

$$p\left(V_0^{\mathrm{T}} - U_0\right)s \leqq 0,$$

meaning that the autarky constraints admit no generation of surplus either.

A slight strengthening of the analysis shows that s, the underlying activity vector, may be stuck at the observed value. Recall that prices, π, fulfilling

$$\pi\left(V_0^{\mathrm{T}} - U_0\right) = 0,$$

were found by minimizing $\mu \geqq 0$, subject to $\pi\left(V_0^{\mathrm{T}} - U_0\right) = \mu e^{\mathrm{T}}\left(V_0^{\mathrm{T}} - U_0\right)$. Note that $e^{\mathrm{T}}\left(V_0^{\mathrm{T}} - U_0\right)$ is the value-added vector, and hence is positive. If we allow μ to go into the negatives, and suppose it will do so, we then find prices π fulfilling $\pi\left(V_0^{\mathrm{T}} - U_0\right) < 0$. By homogeneity, there exists $t \geqq 0$ such that the negativity becomes as strong as you like, e.g. $t\left(V_0^{\mathrm{T}} - U_0\right) \leqq -e^{\mathrm{T}}$. Multiply through by any $s > 0$ fulfilling $\left(V^{\mathrm{T}} - U_0\right)s \geqq 0$ (obtained under autarky):

$$-e^{\mathrm{T}}s \geqq t\left(V_0^{\mathrm{T}} - U_0\right)s \geqq 0.$$

That is, the sum of components of s is negative or zero. Since $s \geqq 0$, it must be zero. In the context of the export promotion program, the replacement of s by $s-e$ yields that not only is the solution value stuck at the observed level, but also the underlying activities ($s = e$), when μ goes into the negatives.

The investigation of the optimality of $s = e$ in the *free trade* program is similar to the export promotion program analysis. The commodity constraints are restricted to non-tradables. The system continues to imply the inequality, $p\left(V_0^{\mathrm{T}} - U_0\right)s \leqq p\left(V_0^{\mathrm{T}} - U_0\right)e$, if and only if there exists $(t\ w\ r\ \sigma) \geqq 0$ as above, with t restricted, however, to non-tradables (for $t_i = 0$ for i tradable). By the same derivation, the question is whether there exist tariffs $t_j \geqq 0$, j non-tradable, such that

$$(p + t)\left(V_0^{\mathrm{T}} - U_0\right) = 0.$$

This is a system of equalities, one for each sector. One can hope to find a price solution only if the number of degrees of freedom (the dimension of t or the number of non-tradables) is at least the number of sectors. The number of non-tradables (eleven, see Table 1) is too small for this purpose. Since the existence of prices fulfilling the equality was shown to be necessary and sufficient for the optimality of the observed levels of activities, it follows that a free trade improvement always is feasible.

To which sectors the comparative advantages of the economy, in terms of commodities, can be ascribed is an open issue. A natural guess is to pick the primary producers of the commodities with comparative advantages. However, a number of complications arise. What if there is no clear-cut primary producer? If it exists, what if its other outputs perform badly in the sense of having a high competitive domestic price? A more direct investigation of the issue would be to compare the solution of the primal program with the observed levels of activity, e. Thus, a high activity level would signal a comparative advantage. This approach is also troublesome because, as we have noted before, levels of activity may be driven by the intermediate demand of other sectors through the trade regime constraints, rather than contributions to the objective function.

The unambiguous ascription of comparative advantages to sectors seems possible only if the trade constraints apply to sectors instead of commodities. For example, if sectors are permitted to compensate some commodity imports by exports of commodities belonging to the same sector, then the trade constraints would be $S(V_0^T - U_0)s \geqq Sz$, where S is an aggregation matrix of dimension: no. of sectors × no. of commodities. Although this assumption is implicit in traditional input–output analysis, it ignores the non-tradability of certain commodities, be they within or across sectors.

We now turn to the results. Recall that $s = e$ solves the export promotion program if $\mu^* = 0$ solves the linear program associated with $\pi(V_0^T - U_0) = 0$. This happens to be the case for the Canadian use and make tables, $(U_0 - V_0)$. We can therefore conclude that the observed levels of activity solve the export promotion program. Any increase in activity would violate a commodity import constraint. Thus, the 1980 Canadian economy cannot boost or maintain its net exports in all commodities simultaneously. In this sense, the economy is truly open. As a corollary, the import substitution program for the 1980 Canadian economy admits no generation of surplus.

Recall also that if μ goes into the negatives when allowed, then $s = e$ and $s = 0$ are the only solutions to the export promotion and import substitution programs, respectively. Also this happens to be the case for the Canadian use and make tables, (U_0, V_0). In essence, we have shown that the 1980 Canadian economy is incapable of supporting non-negative final demand. In other words, it is not self-reliant. The demonstration was through our competitive price test. It should be mentioned again that this result is obtained in the rigid context of an activity model with fixed input and output coefficients.

The results of the free trade program are reported in Tables 4 and 5. Recall from section 2 that $(V_0^T - U_0)e = f_0 + g_0$ is observed final demand, comprising net exports, g_0, and domestic final demand, f_0. In the solution, the final demand becomes $(V_0^T, U_0)s = f_0 + g$, with g the optimum net exports obtained at activity levels, s. Net exports (g_0 and g, respectively) are reported in Table 4 and the activity levels (vector s) in Table 5. The activity levels of three sectors are significantly boosted, with the remaining activity levels suppressed or slightly increased (particularly

Table 4: Free Trade and Commodities.

Commodity	Actual net exports	Optimum net exports[a]	Tariffs
1. Grains	3,764.2	445.8	0.00
2. Live animals	169.0	−688.7	0.00
3. Other agricultural products	−287.8	−9,708.0	0.00
4. Forestry products	10.1	−147.7	0.00
5. Fish landings	55.0	−47.1	0.00
6. Hunting & trapping products	−3.2	−0.1	0.00
7. Iron ores & concentrates	879.3	**9,967.3**	0.00
8. Other metal, ores & concentrates	−3,014.7	**34,073.9**	0.00
9. Coal	−328.4	**4,507.0**	0.00
10. Crude mineral oils	−4,974.2	**60,483.0**	0.00
11. Natural gas	3,775.6	**34,922.4**	0.00
12. Non-metallic minerals	733.3	**10,119.0**	0.00
13. Services incidental to mining	0.0	11,867.3	0.00
14. Meal products	292.5	−6,413.3	0.00
15. Dairy products	73.8	−3,611.6	0.00
16. Fish products	−320.3	−1,530.1	0.00
17. Fruits & vegetables preparations	−401.6	−2,023.3	0.00
18. Feeds	42.1	−290.5	0.00
19. Flour, wheat, meal & other cereals	−29.7	−340.8	0.00
20. Breakfast cereal & bakery prod.	4.7	−1,949.3	0.00
21. Sugar	3.3	−314.2	0.00
22. Misc. food products	−512.2	−2,857.7	0.00
23. Soft drinks	−10.7	−972.0	0.00
24. Alcohol beverages	22.8	−1,989.3	0.00
25. Tobacco processed unmanufactured	26.0	**2,161.8**	0.00
26. Cigarettes & tobacco mfg.	−15.7	**25,436.4**	0.00
27. Tires & tubes	−170.0	−170.0	0.00
28. Other rubber products	−199.0	−3,795.7	0.00
29. Plastic fabricated products	−435.6	−1,850.9	0.00
30. Leather & leather products	−449.0	−1,164.5	0.00
31. Yarns & man made fibres	−329.9	−40.9	0.00
32, Fabrics	−781.7	−346.9	0.00
33. Other textile products	−316.0	−1,744.4	0.00
34. Hosiery & knitted wear	−347.7	−1,275.4	0.00
35. Clothing & accessories	−456.1	−3,844.1	0.00
36. Lumber & timber	3,090.7	−1,082.9	0.00
37. Veneer & plywood	109.6	−607.2	0.00
38. Other wood fabricated materials	367.7	−2,173.1	0.00
39. Furniture & fixtures	−90.5	−2,379.7	0.00
40. Pulp	3,570.9	−94.7	0.00
41. Newspaper & other paper stock	3,975.9	−2,250.0	0.00
42. Paper products	−328.4	−5,710.0	0.00
43. Printing & publishing	−583.5	−91.3	0.00
44. Advertising, print media	0.0	0.0	1.35

(*Continued*)

Table 4: (*Continued*)

Commodity	Actual net exports	Optimum net exports[a]	Tariffs
45. Iron & steel products	417.0	−22,216.3	0.00
46. Aluminum products	−424.4	−3,477.6	0.00
47. Copper & copper alloy products	903.4	−1,027.4	0.00
48. Nickel products	1,038.9	−417.3	0.00
49. Other non-ferrous metal products	999.3	−133.7	0.00
50 Boilers, tanks & plates	−24.1	−944.4	0.00
51. Fabricated structural metal products	147.6	−3,355.7	0.00
52. Other metal fabricated products	−1,678.0	−7,535.1	0.00
53. Agricultural machinery	−1,208.5	**29,392.5**	0.00
54. Other industrial machinery	−5,535.0	**76,465.1**	0.00
55. Motor vehicles	923.9	−4,653.4	0.00
56. Motor vehicle parts	3,795.4	−4,966.7	0.00
57. Other transport equipment	89.6	−2,650.5	0.00
58. Appliances & receivers, household	−1,465.9	706.8	0.00
59. Other electrical products	−1,692.7	4,830.2	0.00
60. Cement & concrete products	94.7	−2,276.3	0.00
61. Other non-metallic mineral products	637.9	−3,094.6	0.00
62. Gasoline & fuel oil	326.2	−10,903.6	0.00
63. Other petroleum & coal products	1,271.00	5,701.4	0.00
64. Industrial chemicals	−2,038.5	3,299.5	0.00
65. Fertilizers	−64.1	5,367.9	0.00
66. Pharmaceuticals	−300.5	−1,128.3	0.00
67. Other chemical products	−1,157.9	−5,170.0	0.00
68. Scientific equipment	−1,806.6	−3,215.7	0.00
69. Other manufactured products	−295.7	2,718.9	0.00
70. Residential construction	0.0	6,035.2	0.00
71. Non-residential construction	0.0	12,278.2	0.00
72. Repair construction	0.0	0.0	6.25
73. Pipeline transportation	153.6	−758.8	0.00
74. Transportation & storage	610.2	23,732.9	0.00
75. Radio & television broadcasting	−10.1	−1,717.6	0.00
76. Telephone & telegraph	−48.7	−6,729.1	0.00
77. Postal services	14.8	−1,405.3	0.00
78. Electric power	807.5	−1,145.5	0.00
79. Other utilities	0.0	0.0	8.36
80. Wholesale margins	2,170.6	780.0	0.00
81. Retail margins	0.0	0.0	1.91
82. Inputed rent owner-occupied dwelling	0.0	0.0	0.36
83. Other finance, insurances real estate	−753.9	−29,065.6	0.00
84. Business services	1,205.1	−2,298.0	0.00
85. Education services	32.6	299.9	0.00
86. Health services	−16.5	2,144.8	0.00
87. Amusement & recreation services	150.3	827.8	0.00
88. Accomodation & food services	0.0	4,014.8	0.00
89. Other personal & misc. services	−90.9	3,053.7	0.00

(*Continued*)

Table 4: (*Continued*)

Commodity	Actual net exports	Optimum net exports[a]	Tariffs
90. Transportation margins	3,413.0	6,271.0	0.00
91. Supplies for office, lab. & cafeteria	0.0	0.0	1.84
92. Travel, advertising & promotion	0.0	0.0	2.57
Increase as % of GDP	0.0	55.6	
Wage rale ($/hour)			13.7
Rental rate			14.2%

[a]Exports are in millions of dollars. Bold figures indicate comparative advantages. Bold indexes indicate non-tradable commodities.

Table 5: Free Trade and Sectors.

Sector	Activity level[a] (actual = 1)
1. Agricultural & related services	0.00
2. Fishing & trapping	0.00
3. Logging and forestry	0.00
4. Mining, quarrying & oil wells	**6.28**
5. Food	0.00
6. Beverage	0.00
7. Tobacco products	**29.10**
8. Plastic products	0.00
9. Rubber & leather products	0.00
10. Textile & clothing	0.00
11. Wood	0.00
12. Furniture and fixtures	0.00
13. Paper & allied products	0.00
14. Printing, publishing & allied	1.34
15. Primary metals	0.00
16. Fabricated metal products	0.00
17. Machinery	**27.58**
18. Transportation equipment	0.00
19. Electrical and electronic products	0.00
20. Non-metallic mineral products	0.00
21. Refined petroleum & coal	0.00
22. Chemical & chemical products	0.00
23. Other manufacturing	0.00
24. Construction	1.42
25. Transportation & communication	0.00
26. Electric power and gas	0.90
27. Wholesale & retail trade	1.01
28. Finance, insurance and real estate	1.00
29. Community, business, personal services	1.34

[a]Bold figures are explained in Table 4.

services) to meet intermediate demand requirements of non-tradable commodities. Likewise, Table 4 shows that some net exports are boosted and these items correspond to the three very active sectors. The comparative advantages are thus considered to reside in *mining, quarrying & oil wells, tobacco*, and *machinery*. The contributions to optimum net exports are 154,073 by mining, quarrying & oil wells (or 54%), 27,598 by tobacco (or 10%), and 105,858 by machinery (or 37%). (The figures are millions of dollars. The percentages do not add up precisely due to rounding.) From the viewpoint of factor endowments and technology, the Canadian economy is resource-oriented. The mining, quarrying & oil wells sector is extremely capital-intensive and the residual labor-intensive mix of factor endowments is fully employed by two more sectors. Qualitatively, the outcome confirms the aggregated version of the model. In the traditional input–output model (section 6), the comparative advantages were in mining, quarrying & oil wells (all trade regimes), plus tobacco (free trade regime) or machinery (export promotion and import substitution regimes). Machinery is now also an exporting sector in the free trade scenario, resurrecting the Ricardian theorem (see the last section). Note also that the surplus of some non-tradables (commodities 13, 70, 71 and 88) are increased, even though they are not valued in the objective function. This is because they are by-products of some sectoral activities. Excluding these increases, net exports increase by 41.5% of GDP, comprising ten commodities (Table 4). Of these optimum net exports, only four commodities show net exports in actuality (Table 4), suggesting the serious international misspecialization of the Canadian economy. The other two components of inefficiency, namely X-inefficiency and allocalive inefficiency, are degenerate in the rectangular model, since the constraints needed to identify them would make the linear program get stuck at the observed levels of activities and net outputs, as we have analyzed above.

Tariffs are ascribed to non-tradable commodities only (of which there are seven), but not the ones that are sufficiently produced as by-products (commodities 13, 70, 71 and 88). There is a dual relationship between tariffs (Table 4) and activities (Table 5). By the theory of linear programming, the number of active variables is essentially equal to the number of binding constraints where the latter are signaled by positive shadow prices. If more variables are active, they are collinear in terms of the utilization rates of resources and other constrained entities. Now from Table 4, we see that the number of positive shadow prices is nine. In fact, binding are seven commodity non-tradability constraints and both factor input constraints. Table 5 shows that nine sectors are active indeed. The low activity levels fulfill the final demand for non-tradables. Three sectors operate at a high activity level: mining, quarrying & oil wells, tobacco, and machinery. These three sectors exhaust the factor inputs and contribute heavily to net exports (Table 4). Mining is capital-intensive, while the other two, tobacco and machinery, are labor-intensive. There are two labor-intensive sectors active, as they also take care of non-tradability constraints, particularly on travel, advertising & promotion (commodity 92).

8. Conclusion

The maximization of foreign earnings, subject to material balance and factor input constraints, constitutes a linear program. The variables in the program are sectoral output levels, both gross and net. If the latter are positive in the solution, they indicate sectors that contribute to net exports under conditions of free trade. Thus, the primal program detects the comparative advantage of the economy. As is well known, the Lagrange multipliers of the constraints can be considered shadow prices and are interrelated by the dual program. The constraints of the dual program are essentially the value equations of input–output analysis. The neoclassical ingredient of profit maximization thus embeds the determination of value in the quantity system. Prices and quantities are determined simultaneously, yielding marginal productivities of factor inputs and comparative advantages of sectors.

The Canadian economy is not self-reliant. It is not possible to increase the net export of any commodity without calling forth some additional import requirements. This result does not hinge on import coefficients. In fact, all imports are endogenous to the model. The only distinction is between tradable and non-tradable commodities. Although fixed commodity proportions are properly specified in a commodity-by-sector framework, it turns out that this hypothesis is so restrictive that it admits no efficiency decomposition of gains to free trade. Input–output analysis is no different from other methodologies. When the assumptions are pushed to the limit, input–output is nipped in the bud.

Traditional input–output analysis circumvents these complications. Commodities are aggregated and sectoral outputs are purified in the construction of the matrix. Detailed commodity constraints are no longer binding and sectors can freely neutralize each others' net outputs. From a methodological viewpoint, the latter two aspects can be considered sources of substitution which free the use make model from being stuck at observed or even zero levels of activities. However, the underlying hypotheses are extreme. Aggregation implicitly assumes perfect substitution, albeit within classes of commodities. Purification assumes, also implicitly, the possibility of negative sectoral activity levels. The difference between the use-make and the traditional models can be ascribed to aggregation. Purification does not alter the results further. The choice between the by-product and commodity technology models [in the square case of equal commodities and sectors, Kop Jansen and ten Raa (1990)] is immaterial for the Canadian economy.

The Lagrange multipliers associated with the material balance constraints are shadow prices that include tariffs. Zero values of the latter signal comparative advantages. In a model with 29 sectors and 92 commodities, we have located the comparative advantage of the 1980 Canadian economy in mining, quarrying & oil wells, tobacco, and machinery. The optimum exploitation of the Canadian resources would boost these sectors and increase GDP by 41.5%. A traditional version of the model with the commodities aggregated into the sectors permits a decomposition analysis and a verification of the Ricardian theorem, notwithstanding theoretical rejections. The main problem is the international misdirection of the Canadian economy. The patterns of optimum and actual commodity net exports are very different. No wonder severe adjustment problems have emerged in the face of the free trade agreement with the United States.

Acknowledgements

A Royal Netherlands Academy of Sciences senior fellowship, a Canadian Government research award and ACSN conference participation support provided to the first author, fellowships from the Fonds pour la Formation de Chercheurs et I'Aide a la Recherche, Quebec and from the Centre National de la Recherche Scientifique, France to the second author, and observations by Chiang Dang, Peter Hanel, Pieter Kop Jansen, Franz Palm, Pierre Pestieau, anonymous referees and editor Konrad Stahl are gratefully acknowledged.

This paper was refereed under the editorial control of Konrad Stahl and John Quigley.

References

Dorfman, R., P.A. Samuelson and R.M. Solow (1958) *Linear Programming and Economic Analysis* (McGraw-Hill, New York).

Drabicki, J.Z. and A. Takayama (1979) An antinomy in the theory of comparative advantage, *Journal of International Economics*, 9, pp. 211–223.

Kop Jansen, P. and T. ten Raa (1990) The choice of model in the construction of input–output coefficients matrices, *International Economic Review*, 31(1), pp. 213–227.

Leontief, W. (1953) Domestic production and foreign trade: The American capital position re-examined, *Proceedings of the American Philosophical Society*, 97(4), pp. 332–349.

Leontief, W. (1979) *Input–Output Economics* (Oxford University Press, New York).

von Neumann, J. (1945) A model of general economic equilibrium, *Review of Economic Studies*, 13, pp. 1–9.

ten Raa, Th. (1994) On the methodology of input–output analysis, *Regional Science and Urban Economics*, 24, pp. 3–25.

ten Raa, Th. and P. Mohnen (1991) Domestic efficiency and bilateral trade gains, with an application to Canada and Europe, CERP Cahier de recherche 70.

Rockafellar, T. (1970) *Convex Analysis* (Princeton University Press, Princeton, NJ).

Schrijver, A. (1986) *Theory of Linear and Integer Programming* (John Wiley & Sons, Chichester).

Statistics Canada (1987) System of national accounts the input– output structure of the Canadian economy 1961–1981 (Minister of Supply and Services Canada, Ottawa).

Statistics Canada (1990a) Input–output division. Person-hours 1961–1989, unpublished.

Statistics Canada (1990b) Input–output division. Current and constant price capital stock for 1980, unpublished.

Williams, J.R. (1978) *The Canadian-United States tariff and Canadian industry: A multi-sectoral analysis* (University of Toronto Press, Toronto).

Woodland, A.D. (1982) *International Trade and Resource Allocation* (North-Holland, Amsterdam).

Appendix

We present the data base in this appendix. The use and make tables are directly available from Statistics Canada (1987). For the sources and constructions of the sectoral labor flows, the total labor force, the capital stocks and the capacity utilization rates, we refer to ten Raa and Mohnen (1991). Non-business activities, mostly government services, are treated as exogenous. The labor pertaining to those activities are netted out from the employment and total labor force figures. The use and make tables, and capital stock data relate to business activities only. The total labor force figure has been converted from persons to person-hours using the average number of person-hours a year per person for the entire economy. The final demand vector is obtained residually by the subtraction of the new totals of the use and make tables to neutralize errors of measurement. Domestic final demand is obtained by subtracting from final demand the domestic exports plus re-exports minus imports, contained in the final demand table of Statistics Canada (1987). All data are expressed in millions of 1980 Canadian dollars, or in thousands of person-hours. For the traditional model, we put the capital coefficient for sector 8 at 0, in lieu of a small negative number. The sector and commodity aggregations are presented in Table 1. We are constrained by a 29 sectoral classification because of the capital statistics.

Those commodities, printed in bold in Table 1, for which neither imports nor exports were reported in the 1980 final demand table, are declared as non-tradables. The number of non-tradable commodities is eleven. The only sectors that are declared as non-tradable are sector 24 (construction), all commodities of which are non-tradable as, well as sectors 14 (printing, publishing & allied) and 28 (finance, insurance & real estate), each of which comprises a non-traded commodity and a non-exported affiliate.

We have to allocate sectoral stock K_i to products v_{ij} and to aggregate over i to get the stock available for commodity j. The vector of sectoral stocks may be divided into utilized stocks and excess stocks,

$$K_0 = K_0\hat{c} + K_0(l - \hat{c}).$$

Utilized stocks are allocated to commodities by applying capital coefficients, $k = K_0\hat{c}V_0^{-\mathrm{T}}$, to gross commodity outputs, one at a lime, $\widehat{V_0^{\mathrm{T}}e}$:

$$K_0\hat{c}V_0^{-\mathrm{T}}\widehat{V_0^{\mathrm{T}}e}.$$

Under-utilized stocks per dollar of sectoral outputs (obtained by division by $\widehat{Ve}$) are allocated to commodities in proportion to outputs (V),

$$K_0(I - \hat{c})\widehat{Ve}^{-1}V.$$

In sum, the row vector of capital stocks per commodity is defined by the following expression,

$$K^c = K_0[\hat{c}V_0^{\mathrm{T}}\widehat{V_0^{\mathrm{T}}e} + (I - \hat{c})\widehat{Ve}^{-1}V].$$

As a check, note that the total stock is preserved:

$$K^c e = K_0[\hat{c}V_0^{-\mathrm{T}}V_0^{\mathrm{T}}e + (I - \hat{c})\widehat{Ve}^{-1}Ve] = K_0[\hat{c}e + (I - \hat{c})e] = K_0 e.$$

Chapter 11

The Substitution Theorem

Thijs ten Raa

Abstract: The substitution theorem states that an economy with many commodities, but only one factor input (say labor), will not substitute inputs (commodities or labor) when final demand changes. This Note drops the assumption that all activities require some labor input and constructs the dominant technology.

JEL classification: C67; D20

1. Introduction

The substitution theorem states that an economy with many commodities, but only one factor input (say labor), will not substitute inputs (commodities or labor) when final demand changes. For an obvious reason, it is also called the nonsubstitution theorem. The most general formulation is by Johansen (1972) who shows that an assemblage of input coefficients vectors (one for each commodity) which is supported by a competitive price system is capable of generating any feasible net output vector. In other words, an assemblage of activities, breaking even under a price system which renders all other activities unprofitable, fulfills the production of any bill of final demand. Johansen's analysis has two shortcomings. First, the pertinent assemblage of input coefficients must be identified *a priori* in order to verify the support by competitive prices. Second, he assumes that all activities

*Received June 28, 1993; Revised April 4, 1994.

require some labor input. The purpose of this Note is to present a general and self-contained formulation of the substitution theorem and to provide a rigorous and constructive proof. It should be mentioned, however, that unlike Johansen, I do not address the case of joint production. Section 2 presents the economy. Section 3 states and proves the theorem. Section 4 discusses the improvements.

2. The Model

There are n commodities and N labor units. There are m activities. An activity comprises an $n+1$-dimensional input vector and an n-dimensional output vector. Following the System of National Accounts Convention of the U.N. (1967), the output vectors are organized as the rows of an $m \times n$-dimensional make Table $\mathbf{V}$, while the input vectors are organized as the columns of an $n \times m$-dimensional use table $\mathbf{U}$ and of the $1 \times m$-dimensional labor employment row vector L. The economy is the quadruple ($\mathbf{V}$, $\mathbf{U}$, L, N). There is no joint production. Each commodity is produced by some activity. Formally, the make table is pure: $\mathbf{V}$ is *pure* if rows are unit vectors and columns are nonzero. As $\mathbf{V}$ is pure, it must have at least as many rows as there are columns: $m \geq n$. Only when the number of activities exceeds the number of commodities is there scope for substitution; m may even go off to infinity. $\mathbf{U}$, L, and N are *nonnegative*. An assemblage of activities, one for each commodity, is a technology. Formally, a technology is a table of the same dimension as $\mathbf{V}$, obtained by the suppression of all, but one element, in each column: $\mathbf{V}^*$ is a *technology* if columns are unit vectors and $v^*_{ij} = 1$ only if $v_{ij} = 1$. Note that the input *coefficients* of a technology are given by $\mathbf{U}\mathbf{V}^*$ and $L\mathbf{V}^*$. The former is $n \times n$ dimensional and the latter $1 \times n$ dimensional. [They are denoted by a and b in Johansen (1972).] Note also that $\mathbf{V}^\top\mathbf{V}^* = \mathbf{I}$ (the $n \times n$-dimensional identity matrix) for any technology $\mathbf{V}^*$ of a make Table $\mathbf{V}$.

An *activity vector* is a nonnegative m-dimensional vector s. An activity vector is feasible if $Ls \leq N$. A commodity vector y is feasible if $y \leq (\mathbf{V}^\top - \mathbf{U})s$ for a feasible activity vector. A commodity vector y is feasible *by means of technology* $\mathbf{V}^*$ if it is feasible and the activity vector is of the form $s = \mathbf{V}^*x$. Note that x must be a commodity vector and that $\mathbf{V}^*$ selects one activity for each commodity, setting the level equal to the quantity and setting all nonselected activity levels to zero.

Our analysis of the economy is via the production possibility frontier. Thus, for every commodity vector, a, determine the expansion factor, c, such that commodity vector ac is still feasible:

$$\max_{s,c}\ c \text{ subject to } ac \leq (\mathbf{V}^{\top} - \mathbf{U})s, \quad Ls \leq N, \quad s \geq 0.$$

Call the solution $c(a)$. Its graph is the *production possibility frontier*. I will make only one assumption, namely that the frontier point exists and is positive for some positive commodity vector. Formally, there exists an $a_0 > 0$ such that $c(a_0) > 0$ but is finite. The inequality sign applied to vectors is supposed to hold for all components.

There are two exceptions to the fulfillment of this assumption. One exception is an economy that can produce no net output. The other exception is an economy that can produce infinite amounts of all commodities. Note that exceptional economies are not interesting. They can produce either nothing or anything. In neither case is there an economic problem. (Examples of exceptional economies are given by $N = 0$ and $L = 0$, respectively.)

It is possible, albeit not very interesting, to push the assumption back to the data of the economy ($\mathbf{V}$, $\mathbf{U}$, L, N). The assumption is basically fulfilled if some positive commodity vector a_0 is feasible, but any sustaining activity vector requires a labor input bounded away from zero. (For some $a_0 > 0$, $a_0 \leq (\mathbf{V}^{\top} - \mathbf{U})s$, $Ls \leq N$, $s \geq 0$. Moreover, $(\mathbf{V}^{\top} - \mathbf{U})s \geq a_0$ implies that $Ls \geq \varepsilon$ for some $\varepsilon > 0$.) The first part is equivalent to nonnegativity of the Leontief inverse of the commodity coefficients of some technology plus positivity of the labor force. The second part is equivalent to nonzeroness of the product of the labor coefficients of a technology and the Leontief inverse. For technologies with a connected matrix of input coefficients, it is necessary and sufficient that the row vector of labor coefficients has a positive component.

3. The Theorem

The substitution theorem claims that the entire production possibility frontier is attainable through one technology. The proof constructs the technology.

Substitution Theorem. *Let an economy comprise a pure make table,* **V**, *a nonnegative use table,* **U**, *a nonnegative employment row vector, L, and a nonnegative labor force, N, such that some positive commodity vector,* a_0, *has a positive and finite frontier point,* $c(a_0)$. *Then there exists a technology,* $\mathbf{V}^*$, *such that any nonnegative feasible commodity vector is feasible by means of* $\mathbf{V}^*$.

Proof. Let activity vector $s(a_0)$ sustain $c(a_0)$. Then $\mathbf{V}^\top s(a_0) > 0$ by the first constraint and the assumption. Hence we may define $\mathbf{A} = \mathbf{U}\widehat{s(a_0)}\mathbf{V}\,\widehat{\mathbf{V}^\top s(a_0)}^{-1}$ where $\widehat{\ }$ diagonalizes a vector into a matrix. Denote the vector with all entries equal to one by e. Since $\mathbf{A}\mathbf{V}^\top s(a_0) = \mathbf{U}\widehat{s(a_0)}\mathbf{V}e = \mathbf{U}\widehat{s(a_0)}e = \mathbf{U}s(a_0) \leq \mathbf{V}^\top s(a_0) - a_0 c(a_0) < \mathbf{V}^\top s(a_0)$, a positive vector, the Leontief inverse, $\sum_{k=0}^{\alpha} \mathbf{A}^k$, converges (Minc 1988). Hence $p = e^\top \sum_{k=0}^{x} \mathbf{A}^k$ exists. Among all activities, i producing $(s_i(a_0) > 0)$ commodity $j(v_{ij} = 1)$, let $i(j)$ minimize costs, $pu._j$.[$i(j)$ exists because $\mathbf{V}^\top s(a_0)$ is positive.] Then $pu._j \geq pu._{i(j)}$ whenever $v_{ij} = 1$ and $s_i(a_0) > 0$ $a_{.j}$ is defined as a weighted average of such $u_{.j}$. Hence also $pa._j \geq pu._{i(j)}$ or $p\mathbf{A} \geq p\mathbf{U}\mathbf{V}^*$ where $\mathbf{V}^*$ is the technology defined by $v_{ij}^* = 1$ for $i = i(j)$ and zero otherwise. Since p is positive, the Leontief inverse of $\mathbf{U}\mathbf{V}^*$, $\sum_{k=0}^{\infty} (\mathbf{U}\mathbf{V}^*)^k$, converges *a fortiori*. Let $y \geq 0$ be feasible. Define $x = \sum_{k=0}^{\infty} (\mathbf{U}\mathbf{V}^*)^k y$ and $s = \mathbf{V}^*\mathbf{x}$. Then $(\mathbf{V}^\top - \mathbf{U})s = (\mathbf{V}^\top\mathbf{V}^* - \mathbf{U}\mathbf{V}^*)\sum_{k=0}^{\infty} (\mathbf{U}\mathbf{V}^*)^k y = (I - \mathbf{U}\mathbf{V}^*)\sum_{k=0}^{\infty} (\mathbf{U}\mathbf{V}^*)^k\, y = y$, since $\mathbf{V}^*$ is a technology of **V**. It remains to prove that $Ls \leq N$. This will be done by the theory of linear programming (Schrijver 1986). The dual of the production possibility frontier program reads $\min_{p,w,\sigma \geq 0} wN$, subject to $p(\mathbf{V}^\top - \mathbf{U}) = wL - \sigma, pa = 1$. Let $p(a_0)$, $w(a_0)$, $\sigma(a_0)$ solve when the commodity vector is a_0. Then $p(a_0)yc(y) \leq c(a_0)$. (This is trivial for $p(a_0)y = 0$. Otherwise $p(a_0)/p(a_0)y$, $w(a_0)/p(a_0)y$, and $\sigma(a_0)/p(a_0)y$ are feasible for the dual program associated with commodity y and, therefore, the inequality in $c(a_0)/p(a_0)y = w(a_0)N/p(a_0)y \geq w(y)N = c(y)$ obtains; the equalities reflect the main theorem of linear programming.) Now $w(a_0)Ls = w(a_0)LV^*x = [p(a_0)(V^\top - U) + \sigma(a_0)])V^*x = p(a_0)y + 0 \leq p(a_0)yc(y) \leq c(a_0) = w(a_0)N$, by definition of s, the dual constraint, the definition of x plus the phenomenon of complementary slackness ($s_{i(j)}(a_0) > 0$ hence $\sigma_{i(j)}(a_0) = 0$), feasibility of y (hence $c(y) \geq 1$), the derived inequality, and the main theorem of linear programming, respectively. The last equality yields positivity of $w(a_0)$. Division yields $Ls \leq N$. □

4. Discussion

The present formulation of the substitution theorem is general. The only assumption made is that the production possibility frontier admits a point. As noted in Section 2, the economy ceases to be interesting when the assumption is not fulfilled. The proof of the theorem is constructive and proceeds in two stages. In the first stage, attention is confined to an ensemble of activities that sustains the frontier point. The Leontief inverse of the weighted input coefficients table is evaluated. In the second stage, a further selection of activities is made on the basis of costs. The costs are *not* evaluated at the competitive prices (the shadow prices associated with the linear program that defines the frontier or, alternatively, the total labor costs using the Leontief inverse). As a matter of fact, any activity in the ensemble of the first stage would just break even at the competitive prices which, therefore, are of little help. The costs are therefore evaluated at a price vector that yields positive value added. (In fact, value added was chosen to be one for each sector and the price vector was obtained by applying the Leontief inverse.) The cost-minimizing activities, one for each commodity, constitute the dominant technology.

Johansen (1972), however, identifies a technology on the basis of the competitive price system alone. In other words, he investigates a technology $\mathbf{V}^*$ with a positive price vector $p^* = p\mathbf{UV}^* + L\mathbf{V}^* \leq p^*\mathbf{UV}^{**} + L\mathbf{V}^{**}$ for all other technologies $\mathbf{V}^{**}$. Any technology selected from the first stage of our construction would qualify, but the claim that it would sustain all feasible net output is false. Johansen [1, p. 388] notes that $\mathbf{V}^*$ with supporting p^* exists if the technologies form a closed set and one of them can produce positive net output. A counterexample is the single-commodity economy with $u_i = 1 - 1/i$ and $l_i = 1/i^2$. It is crucial to have positive value added. Johansen (1972, p. 384) assumes that all activities require some labor input and claims that this assumption could be dispensed with, but at the cost of some unrewarding complications. Some positivity of labor input must be assumed however. (In the counterexample, technologies are progressively better and have a perfect limit, $u^* = 1$ and $l^* = 0$, but the latter is not feasible for positive net output.)

The contribution of this Note is twofold. First, the dominant technology has been constructed. Second, the assumption of positive labor input has been limited to the macroeconomic requirement that some net output must have positive labor input.

References

Johansen, L. (1972) Simple and general nonsubstitution theorems for input output models. *Journal of Economic Theory*, 5, pp. 383–394.
Minc, H. (1988) Nonnegative Matrices. New York: Wiley.
Schrijver, A. (1986) Theory of Linear and Integer Programming. New York: Wiley.
U.N. Statistical Commission (1967) Proposals for the revision of SNA, 1952. Document E/CN3/356.

Chapter 12

Bródy's Capital

Thijs ten Raa

1. Introduction

The dynamic input–output (I–O) model reads (Leontief 1970)

$$x = Ax + B\dot{x} + y. \tag{12.1}$$

The left-hand side features the state variable of the economy, the vector of sectoral capacities, as measured by the output levels. The right-hand side lists the material inputs, investment and household demand, respectively. The structure of the economy is given by two matrices of technical coefficients. A is the matrix of input flow coefficients and B is the matrix of input stock coefficients. Input flows, for example electricity, are fully consumed, but input stocks, like housing, carry over. Material inputs are, therefore, proportional to the output levels, but investment is proportional to the new capacity, $\dot{x}$, where the dot denotes the time derivative. Output x and household demand y are functions of time, but the technical coefficients are constant in the absence of structural change. Implicit in the dynamic I–O model is the assumption that productive activity is instantaneous. If you have the commodity vectors $a_{.1}$ and $b_{.1}$ (the first columns of technical coefficients matrices A and B), then you get instantaneously the commodity vectors e_1 and $b_{.1}$, where e_1 is the first unit vector, representing the output flow, and $b_{.1}$ is the carry-over stock. In ten Raa (1986a), I have dropped this assumption, redefining an input flow coefficient as a time profile on the past; see Chapter 11. Thus, to produce one unit of output 1 at time zero, you need inputs $\alpha_{.1}(s)$ at times $s, s \leq 0$. The matrix of input flow coefficients, α, is a function on the past. It is convenient to work with generalized functions. The dynamic I–O model with instantaneous production is recouped by $\alpha = A\delta$, where δ is the Dirac function (unit mass in the origin).

A time profile of inputs or outputs that is not concentrated in the origin implies that commodities are tied up in the productive activity. Such commodities constitute capital. The distributed inputs (α) represent working capital. In ten Raa (1986b), the analysis is applied to the input stock coefficients, modelling Polish investment lead times by distributing matrix B over the past; see Chapter 12. In a letter, András Bródy wrote to the author:

> Thank you for sending your interesting new paper with computations for the Polish economy. I have to confess I am less enthusiastic about it than I have been with your former papers.
>
> I rather expected you to forge ahead and to drop the notion of a capital matrix, B, altogether. You had a distributed input-point output model, already indicating that the inclusion of stocks can be dispensed with. If you generalize to a distributed input-distributed output model, then our traditional approach becomes truly obsolete. Why don't you do it? It is within your reach.

In this chapter, I attempt to take up Bródy's challenge. In other words, let me address the question under which circumstances the dynamic I–O model describes a distributed input-distributed output economy without a preconceived distinction between input flows and stocks.

2. The Structure of an Economy

I maintain the state variable of the economy, x, the vector of sectoral capacities. A unit capacity in sector 1 at time zero requires inputs $\alpha_{.1}(s)$ at times $s, s \leq 0$, and yields outputs $\beta_{.1}(s)$ at times $s, s \geq 0$. Organizing the sectoral input and output time profiles in a pair of matrix valued (generalized) functions of time, the *structure of the economy* is (α, β). Input and output coefficients α and β are defined as the past and the future, respectively. All commodities are the output of some productive activity. Account for stocks: the capacity of sector 1 at time $t, x_1(t)$, contributes $\beta_{.1}(s)x_1(t)$ to the economy's commodity stock at time $t + s, s \geq 0$. By changing the time variable, the capacity of sector 1 at time $t - s$ contributes $\beta_{.1}(s)x_1(t - s)$ to the stock at time $t, s \geq 0$. Summing up all contributions of the past $(s \geq 0)$ by all sectors, we obtain the commodity stock at time t, $\int_0^\infty \beta(s)x(t - s)\mathrm{d}s$. This is *capital*. Since β is confined to the non-negatives, the domain of integration may just as well be extended to the real time. Thus we obtain the convolution product of β and x, $\beta * x$, at time t. Capital is thus given by the convolution product of the output coefficients, β, and the sectoral capacities, x. The units of capacity are arbitrary, just like the activity levels of von Neumann (1945). Any rescaling is offset by the output coefficients, and the measure of capital is invariant; it is determined by the physical units of the commodities.

Capital at time t can be allocated to future capacity utilization, $x(t - s)$, where $s \leq 0$. In fact, $x(t - s)$ requires commodities $\alpha(s)(t - s)$ at time $t, s \leq 0$. The total allocation of capital at time t to future production amounts $\int_{-\infty}^0 \alpha(s)x(t - s)\mathrm{d}s$ or $\alpha * x$ valued at time t.

The residual capital constitutes the household stock of commodities, $Y(t)$. Consequently,

$$\int_0^\infty \beta(s)x(t - s)\mathrm{d}s = \int_{-\infty}^0 \alpha(s)x(t - s)\mathrm{d}s + Y(t) \qquad (12.2)$$

or, in short

$$(\beta - \alpha) * x = Y. \qquad (12.3)$$

This is the distributed input-distributed output model of the economy. The purpose of this chapter is to determine the structure of the economy for which the dynamic I–O model, (12.1), is submitted by the distributed model with no preconceived flow-stock distribution (12.3).

3. The Material Balance

If the total mass of the net output coefficients, $\int(\beta - \alpha)$, is an M-matrix (Minc 1988), then any non-negative stock of household commodities can be sustained by non-negative capacities. However, interesting economics is in terms of flows rather than stocks. The material balance is usually defined in flows, see equation (12.1) for example. The transition to flow is by the differentiation of equation (12.2) with respect to time. Differentiating the left-hand side (capital), we obtain

$$\begin{aligned}\frac{\mathrm{d}}{\mathrm{d}t}\int_0^{\infty}\beta(s)x(t-s)\mathrm{d}s &= \int_0^{\infty}\beta(s)\frac{\mathrm{d}}{\mathrm{d}t}x(t-s)\mathrm{d}s\\ &= -\int_0^{\infty}\beta(s)\frac{\mathrm{d}}{\mathrm{d}s}x(t-s)\mathrm{d}s\\ &= -\beta(s)x(t-s)|_0^{\infty}+\int_0^{\infty}\frac{\mathrm{d}}{\mathrm{d}s}\beta(s)x(t-s)\mathrm{d}s\\ &= \beta(0)x(t)+\int_0^{\infty}\dot{\beta}(s)x(t-s)\mathrm{d}s \qquad (12.4)\end{aligned}$$

where $\dot{\beta}$ is the reduction of output of the capacity units, that is *depreciation*. It takes negative values. Differentiating the first term on the right-hand side of equation (12.2), we get $\int_0^{\infty}\alpha(s)\dot{x}(t-s)\mathrm{d}s$. Lastly, we have $\dot{Y}$, the additions to the household stock of commodities, a commodity flow vector. Thus (12.2) can be rewritten as

$$\beta(0)x(t) = -\int_0^{\infty}\dot{\beta}(s)x(t-s)\mathrm{d}s + \int_0^{-\infty}\alpha(s)\dot{x}(t-s)\mathrm{d}s + \dot{Y}(t) \qquad (12.5)$$

This is the material balance of the economy. It is a rewrite of the simple distributed input-distributed output model (12.3). No assumptions have been made. On the left-hand side, we have the instantaneous rates of the output of current sectoral capacities. On the right-hand side, we have, first, replacement investment, second investment in new capacity, and third additions to the household stock.

4. The Subsumption of Dynamic Input–Output

Replacement investment, $-\int_0^{\infty}\dot{\beta}(s)x(t-s)\mathrm{d}s$, equals the amount of depreciation of capacity s time units old, $-\dot{\beta}(s)$, times the level of capacity at that time, $x(t-s)$, summed over ages s. Thus, to determine replacement investment, one must know the life pattern of output, β, and the past distribution of capacity, x. In dynamic I–O analysis, one makes the simplifying assumption that one must know only the current stock of capital.

The latter is given by the convolution product of β and x valued at time t (see second section of 'The structure of an economy'). Now it is well-known that replacement investment is independent of the age structure of capital (x) if and only if the life pattern (β) is given by the exponential decay function and independent of the sector of installation.

Assumption 1. $\beta_{ij}(s) = \beta_{ij}(0)e^{-\rho_i s}$

Then depreciation is, in absolute value,

$$-\dot{\beta} = \rho\beta \tag{12.6}$$

where ρ is the diagonal matrix with elements ρ_i. Under Assumption 1, replacement investment is $\rho\int_0^\infty \beta(s)x(t-s)\mathrm{d}s$, the direct product of the matrix of depreciation rates and the stock of capital.

As a matter of fact, the dynamic I–O model incorporates replacement investment in the material inputs term, Ax. This requires a second step. Replacement investment must not only be proportional to the current stock of capital (irrespective its age structure), but the latter, on its turn, must be proportional to the current level of capacity. In general, the amount of capital allocated to production depends on the entire path of future capacities, through the convolution product with the input time profile, α (see second section of 'The structure of an economy'). When is only the current level of capacity relevant? Well, if production takes no time, but is instantaneous:

Assumption 2. $\alpha(s) = \alpha(0)\delta(s)$

Here δ is the Dirac function, the unit mass in the origin. In the 'Introduction', it was noted that this assumption reduces my distributed input model to the traditional one. Thus, what remains crucial now is the distribution of output. Now let us trace the implication of the assumptions on the structure of the economy on the material balance. Substituting Assumption 1's consequence (12.6) and Assumption 2 into balance equation (12.5), we obtain

$$\beta(0)x(t) = \rho\int_0^\infty \beta(s)x(t-s)\mathrm{d}s + \alpha(0)\dot{x}(t) + \dot{Y}(t). \tag{12.7}$$

Now replace the capital term by the expression given in equation (12.2) and substitute Assumption 2. Then equation (12.7) becomes

$$\beta(0)x(t) = \rho\alpha(0)x(t) + \alpha(0)\dot{x}(t) + \rho Y(t) + \dot{Y}(t). \tag{12.8}$$

This, then, is the material balance equation under Assumptions 1 and 2. It coincides with the dynamic I–O model, provided secondary products are absent: $\beta(0) = I$, the identity matrix. Note the household demand comprises household stock replacement investment as well as additions to the stock. It is interesting to relate the dynamic I–O coefficients matrices to the structure of the distributed input-distributed output economy:

$$A = \rho\alpha(0), \quad B = \alpha(0) \tag{12.9}$$

Consequently,

$$A = \rho B \tag{12.10}$$

That is, the dynamic I–O model is consistent with a distributed input-distributed output model of the economy if the flow coefficients are *proportional* to the stock coefficients, where the proportions are the rates of depreciation. This relationship between circulating and fixed capital was first noted by Bródy (1974).

I do not wish to subscribe to this relationship as an absolute requirement on technical coefficients matrices. However, an important corollary to the analysis is that if equation (12.10) fails, then the dynamic I–O model, (12.1), is misspecified. The simplifying assumptions made on the structure of the economy will not be valid and one must resort to the general formulation of the material balance: (12.3) (in stocks) or (12.5) (in flows).

5. Conclusion

In this chapter, I have attempted to carry out András Bródy's program to dispense with the distinction between flows and stocks in dynamic I–O analysis by modelling the time profiles of the input and output components of the structure of an economy. The traditional model is retrieved when capital decays exponentially and production is instantaneous. However, the flow and the stock coefficients must be consistent with Bródy's capital equation. If this is not the case, the model should be replaced by the distributed input-distributed output material balance equation derived in this chapter.

References

Bródy, A. (1974) *Production, Prices and Planning* (North-Holland, Amsterdam).
Leontief, W. (1970) The dynamic inverse. In: A. P. Carter and A. Bródy (eds.), *Contributions to Input–Output Analysis* (North-Holland, Amsterdam), pp. 17–46.
Minc, H. (1988) *Nonnegative Matrices* (Wiley, New York).
ten Raa, Th. (1986a) Dynamic input–output analysis with distributed activities, *The Review of Economics and Statistics*, 68(2), pp. 300–310.
ten Raa, Th. (1986b) Applied dynamic input–output with distributed activities, *European Economic Review*, 30(4), pp. 805–831.
von Neumann, J. (1945) A model of general economic equilibrium, *The Review of Economic Studies*, 13, pp. 1–9.

Part IV

Dynamic Input–Output Analysis

Chapter 13

Dynamic Input–Output Analysis with Distributed Activities

Thijs ten Raa

Abstract: This paper offers a new approach to economic models in which activities take time. Departing from a standard economic model (Leontief's dynamic input–output model), we recast the activities from ordinary vectors into temporal distributions. In doing so, we preserve the formal structure and simplicity of the standard model. This is the secret of the power of our approach which asserts itself in the resolution of some open dynamic input–output problems. In particular, we are able to solve models with singular capital structures (i.e. singular derivatives coefficients matrices), unbalanced growth and different time profiles of investment or other production activities.

De cost gaet voor de baet uyt.
(The cost goes before the benefit.)

Temporally distributed activities are important. De Galan (1980, p. 217) ascribes labor market failure to, among other things, the sluggishness of certain adjustments which results from the fact that activities such as education take time. Furthermore, if one neglects the time used up

Received for publication February 23, 1984. Revision accepted for publication August 6, 1985.

in the production process, then one will generate too high growth rates as most dynamic economic models actually do. Yet little work has been done on modeling with distributed economic activities. Exceptions are input–output analysis with transit and production lags by Bródy (1965), or with investment lead times by Gladyshevskii and Belous (1978), Johansen (1978), and Zhuravlev (1982). But these studies are in the realm of balanced growth in which the structure of the problem is the same as in static input–output; Zhuravlev comes closest to our work with the inclusion of turnpike results.

Temporally distributed activities will be considered single elements in a distribution space and be subjected to the calculus of distributions, which yields simple expressions for seemingly complicated equations involving lags and so on, and solutions to the distributed input–output models. It enables us to resolve open dynamic input–output problems, such as the solution of equations with singular capital structures and the analysis of economies with different time profiles of investment or other production activities under conditions of unbalanced growth. It should be mentioned that the same approach is relevant for regional economic models as that of Leontief *et al.* (1977). Then economic activities are modeled as spatial distributions. This topic is the subject of ten Raa (1984). Similarly, our analysis of distributed activities may serve as a model for capital of circulation and the complete economic system as outlined by Foley (1982).

The organization of the present paper is as follows. Section 1 identifies the economic subjects of this study and develops the central theme: input–output profiles are considered single elements in a distribution space, a concept that is defined in the appendix. Section 2 analyzes the static input–output model with possibly continuously distributed activities. Section 3 widens the scope to the case of balanced growth. Section 4 handles a pure dynamic model with a possibly singular capital structure. Section 5 solves the traditional dynamic input–output model. By synthesis of the treatment of continuity (Section 2) and invertibility (Section 4), Section 6 analyzes the distributed dynamic input–output model. Section 7 concludes the paper.

1. Productive Capital

Productive capital is divided into circulating capital and fixed capital (Marx 1974, p. 158). Circulating capital is absorbed in production and consists of flows of goods. Fixed capital must merely be present when production takes place and consists of stocks of goods. Circulating and fixed capital are represented by, respectively, the input–output flow coefficients matrix A and the input–output stock coefficients matrix B, both of Leontief.

Circulating capital (A) is fluid, but it can be like water or like syrup. Some circulating capital, such as electricity, is absorbed immediately, but other circulating capital, such as minerals, must be treated during some time. Electricity is (super) fluid capital; minerals are working capital. (Super) fluid capital is, by definition, processed instantaneously; working capital is defined to be capital in the pipeline.

The same distinction can be made with regard to fixed capital (B). Some fixed capital, such as a stapler, is ready for immediate use, but other fixed capital, such as a transport container, must be present some time in advance. A stapler is instant capital; the container is advanced capital. Instant capital is fixed capital which can produce instantaneously, while advanced capital must be installed in advance, all by definition.

A good starting point for the incorporation of the production times in the circulating and fixed capital matrices A and B is Marx (1974, p. 239). For example, if input i's production time in sector j equals τ_{ij}, then we can write interindustry demand for i at time 0 as $\sum_j a_{ij}x_j(\tau_{ij})$ where $x(t)$ is the output vector at time t.

In general, the ith input requirement for one unit of sector jth output is represented by an input profile on the past. We shall now introduce a powerful point of view. Giving up the idea of a_{ij}, being some number altogether, we redefine an *input–output coefficient* as a non-negative distribution on the non-positive time axis. The width of its support (τ_{ij}) reflects the production time. This set-up obviously applies to capital stock coefficients as well. Then the width of the support of the distribution reflects the investment lead time.

2. Static Input–Output Analysis

An input–output flow coefficient a_{ij} is a *non-negative* distribution with *non-positive support*, where $i, j = 1, \ldots, n$ represent the sectors of the economy. The future and current flow requirements exercised by sector j — with *output* distribution x_j — on sector i at time t sum up to, heuristically,

$$\int_{s=-\infty}^{0} a_{ij}(s)x_j(t-s)ds,$$

abstracting from technical change. Summing over j, which may be done under the integral sign, we obtain interindustry demand for i at time t:

$$\int_{s=-\infty}^{0} \sum_{j=1}^{n} a_{ij}(s)x_j(t-s)ds.$$

The material balance for good i at time t between output and interindustry demand plus *final demand* z_i reads

$$x_i(t) = \int_{s=-\infty}^{0} \sum_{j=1}^{n} a_{ij}(s)x_j(t-s)ds + z_i(t).$$

Letting x, z and A denote the output and final demand vectors, and the input–output flow coefficients matrix,

$$x(t) = \int_{s=-\infty}^{0} A(s)x(t-s)ds + z(t).$$

Invoking the notation for the convolution product (appendix), we obtain

$$x = A^{*}x + z. \tag{1}$$

Formulation (1) is free of integrability requirements. It holds for x and z n-dimensional vector distributions and A an $n \times n$-dimensional matrix distribution (non-negative and with non-positive support) over time in the sense of Schwartz (1957). The purpose of this section is to solve the *Leontief planning problem* of finding output x fulfilling (1), given final demand z.

Our input–output distribution a_{ij} is essentially the outgrowth of the temporal disaggregation of a traditional input–output coefficient. Thus, summing over time, we capture the traditional coefficient, now denoted $\int a_{ij}$. This expression is shorthand for $\langle a_{ij}, 1\rangle$ (where $\int$ generalizes the Lebesgue-Stieltjes integral). We see that the traditional input–output matrix corresponds to $\int A$. This matrix is defined component-wise. Therefore, the well-known conditions for the producibility of final demand now apply to $\int A$:

Assumption. Non-negative matrix $\int A$ fulfills the Hawkins-Simon (1949) conditions.

There are some well-known equivalent conditions. One is the condition that the *spectral radius is less than one*:

$$\rho\left(\int A\right) < 1. \tag{2}$$

The other is the *convergence* of the power expansion of the inverse of $I - \int A$:

$$\sum_{0}^{\infty}\left(\int A\right)^{k} < \infty. \tag{3}$$

We wish to derive that $\sum_0^\infty A^{*k}$ itself converges ($A^{*2} = A^*A$ and so on) and is a continuous functional. For then, it is the *inverse distribution* of $I\delta - A$ (where δ is the Dirac distribution or unit point mass at the origin denned in the appendix). The latter is the operator in our equation (1) which consequently can be solved. Essentially, standard input–output results are confirmed for the more general case of distributed inputs.

Proposition 1. *Let the above assumption be fulfilled. Then $\sum_0^\infty A^{*k}$ exists and is continuous. And for every z which is non-negative and agrees with a bounded function near infinity, there is a solution x to* (1) *which is similar.*

Proof. See the appendix. □

Remarks. The assumed boundedness can be relaxed to hold just almost surely.

Example. A typical fully distributed input–output flow coefficient is $A(t) = \frac{1}{4}e^t\check{H}(t)$. Here, $\check{H}$ is the *Heaviside function on the negative reals*, defined by $\check{H}(t) = 1$ for $t < 0$ and zero elsewhere. The assumption is fulfilled as the total mass of A is $\frac{1}{4}$. Now let us calculate $\sum_0^\infty A_0^{*k}$. For $t < 0$,

$$\begin{aligned} A^{*2}(t) &= \int_t^0 A(s)A(t-s)ds \\ &= \frac{1}{16}\int_t^0 e^s e^{t-s} ds = \frac{1}{16}e^t(-t). \end{aligned}$$

And so on, for $t < 0$,

$$A^{*k}(t) = \frac{1}{4^k} e^t (-t)^{k-1} \Big/ (k-1)!$$
$$= \frac{1}{4} e^t \left(-\frac{1}{4} t\right)^{k-1} \Big/ (k-1)!.$$

In sum, for $t < 0$,

$$\sum_0^\infty A^{*k}(t) = \delta + \sum_0^\infty A^{*k+1}(t)$$
$$= \delta + \sum_0^\infty \frac{1}{4} e^t \left(-\frac{1}{4} t\right)^K \Big/ k!$$
$$= \delta + \frac{1}{4} e^t e^{\frac{1}{4}t} = \delta + \frac{1}{4} e^{\frac{3}{4}t}.$$

For $t \geq 0$, $A^{*k}(t) = 0$. Thus the inverse operator is $\delta + \frac{1}{4} e^{\frac{3}{4}(\cdot)} \check{H}$.

3. Balanced Growth

An input stock coefficient b_{ij} is also a *non-negative* distribution with *non-positive support*. The future and current capacity expansion of sector j demands, heuristically,

$$\int_{s=-\infty}^{0} b_{ij}(s) \dot{x}_j(t-s) ds$$

of i at time t, where the dot denotes differentiation (see the appendix). These *investment* terms are separated from final demand. The material balance for good i at time t becomes

$$x_i(t) = \int_{s=-\infty}^{0} \sum_{j=1}^{n} [a_{ij}(s) x_j(t-s)$$
$$+ b_{ij}(s) \dot{x}_j(t-s)] ds + z_i(t)$$

or

$$x = A^* x + B^* \dot{x} + z \tag{4}$$

which is free of integrability requirements. The purpose of this paper is to solve the Leontief planning problem for equation (4).

The remainder of this section is confined to the case of *balanced growth*:

$$z(t) = z(0)e^{gt}$$

and also

$$x(t) = x(0)e^{gt}.$$

Proposition 2. *Let the assumption of Section 2 be fulfilled. Consider balanced growth. Then there is a maximum growth rate $g^* > 0$ such that the following holds. For every z with $z(0)$ non-negative and $0 \leq g < g^*$, there is a solution x to* (4) *with similar $x(0)$ and g.*

Proof. See the appendix. □

4. Pure Dynamics

In dynamic input–output analysis, as well as control theory, it is assumed that the matrix of coefficients of the first (vector) derivative is invertible. This practice constitutes a problem which manifests itself most pointedly in equation (4) of the last section if we neglect the nonderivative term and concentrate the derivative coefficients in the origin by putting $A = 0$ and $B = B_0\delta$, B_0 an ordinary but possibly singular matrix. Then equation (4) becomes

$$x = B_0\dot{x} + z. \tag{5}$$

The standard technique is to write $\dot{x} = B_0^{-1}x - B_0^{-1}z$ and to proceed as usual. However, as Bródy (1974, p. 137) notes:

> Yet the presence of the matrix $[B_0^{-1}]$ alerts us to further theoretical problems. First, B_0 itself can be singular in practice. If, say, two sectors have the same capital structure, then B_o, having two columns equal, will be singular, and if the capital structures are very similar, B_0 will be severely ill-conditioned. Furthermore, $[B_0^{-1}]$, if it exists at all, will have the economically meaningful growth rate, λ, as its eigenvalue of minimal modulus. Actual computation, then, will be dominated by other eigenvalues, and therefore be clumsy and inexact.

Another source of trouble is that some goods need no fixed capital or only to a minor extent. In such a case, B_0 has zero or almost zero rows and, therefore, is singular or "severely ill-conditioned."

We shall overcome the singularity shortcoming of dynamic input–output analysis and control theory by deriving a more general solution to equation (5) which does not hinge on the invertibility of B_0. In other words, B_0's with zero eigenvalues must be facilitated. We shall proceed gradually and first admit only zero eigenvalues with a *complete* system of eigenvectors, that is, zero eigenvalues with a number of eigenvectors equal to the multiplicity of the zero eigenvalues. For then the role of B_0^{-1} can be played by a generalized inverse reminiscent of the one of Rao (1974), that is, any A_0 satisfying $B_0A_0B_0 = B_0$. The *form* of the generalized inverse is chosen such that equation (5) *can be solved* explicitly which will be done after the presentation and discussion of the definition. Surprisingly, Moore-Penrose generalized inverses do not work, in spite of suggestions in the literature. For example, Kendrick (1972) and Livesey (1973, 1976) make a number of full rank assumptions that implicitly rule out conditions such as capital structure similarity across sectors.

Definition. Let B_0 be a square matrix of which the zero eigenvalue has a complete system of eigenvectors. A generalized inverse of B_0 is a square matrix B_0^- such that $B_0^-B_0^2 = B_0$.

Justification. Bring B_0 on *triangular form*

$$T\begin{pmatrix} J_1 & 0 \\ 0 & J_2 \end{pmatrix}T^{-1}$$

such that the *zero* eigenvalues are precisely arranged in the diagonal of J_1. J_1 and J_2 are upper triangular and all nonzero eigenvalues are displayed on the diagonal of J_2. T is the base transformation matrix. By the nature of B_0, J_1 may be assumed zero. This can be seen by taking the Jordan canonical form of B_0 which fulfills the described conditions on J_1 and J_2. Since the diagonal of upper triangular J_2 never vanishes, this matrix is invertible. The generalized inverse is now

$$B_0^- = T\begin{pmatrix} K & 0 \\ L & J_2^{-1} \end{pmatrix}T^{-1}$$

with K and L arbitrary matrices of appropriate size. This is easily verified:

$$B_0^- B_0^2 = T \begin{pmatrix} K & 0 \\ L & J_2^{-1} \end{pmatrix} T^{-1} T \begin{pmatrix} 0 & 0 \\ 0 & J_2^2 \end{pmatrix} T^{-1}$$
$$= T \begin{pmatrix} 0 & 0 \\ 0 & J_2 \end{pmatrix} T^{-1} = B_0.$$

Thus, the generalized inverse of B_0 exists, but is not unique. The justification is rounded off by the next example which shows that B_0^- generalizes the inverse.

Examples. (1) B_0 regular. Then $B_0^- = B_0^{-1}$. (2) B_0 zero. Then B_0^- is arbitrary. (3) $B_0 = \begin{pmatrix} 1 & 1 \\ 0 & 0 \end{pmatrix}$. Then the Rao inverse defined in the introduction of this section is $\begin{pmatrix} a & b \\ 1-a & c \end{pmatrix}$. The Moore-Penrose inverse is obtained by putting $a = \frac{1}{2}$ and $b = c = 0$. Our B_0^- is obtained by putting $a = 1$. (4) $B_0 = \begin{pmatrix} 0 & 1 \\ 0 & 0 \end{pmatrix}$. Then $B_0^2 = 0$ and B_0^- is undefined. Indeed, B_0 does not fulfill the assumption: zero is the only eigenvalue, but there is no complete system of eigenvectors.

Equation (5) is now rewritten such that solving it amounts to inverting a distribution: $(I\delta - B_0\dot{\delta})^* x = z$. The next proposition inverts the operator. The solution features the *Heaviside function on the negatives* $\check{H}$ which was defined by $\check{H}(t) = 1$ for $t < 0$ and zero elsewhere (Section 2, the example).

Proposition 3. *Let B_0 be a square matrix whose zero eigenvalue has a complete system of eigenvectors. Then*

$$(I\delta - B_0\dot{\delta})^{*-1} = \check{H} \exp(B_0^- t) B_0^{-2} B_0 + \delta(I - B_0^- B_0).$$

Proof. See the appendix. □

Examples. (1) B_0 regular. Then $B_0^- = B_0^{-1}$. Hence the inverse operator becomes $\check{H} \exp(B_0^- t) B_0^{-1}$. (2) B_0 zero. Then the inverse operator is $0 + \delta(I - 0) = \delta I$, as should be. (3) $B_0 = \begin{pmatrix} 1 & 1 \\ 0 & 0 \end{pmatrix}$. Then we may choose $B_0^- = I$. Hence the inverse operator becomes $\check{H} e^t \begin{pmatrix} 1 & 1 \\ 0 & 0 \end{pmatrix} + \delta \begin{pmatrix} 0 & -1 \\ 0 & 1 \end{pmatrix}$.

Remarks. (1) In example 3, the arbitrary

$$B_0^- = \begin{pmatrix} 1 & b \\ 0 & c \end{pmatrix}.$$

But in the inverse operator,

$$\exp(B_0^- t)B_0^{-2}B_0 = \sum_0^\infty \frac{t^k}{k!}B_0^{-(k+2)}B_0$$

$$= \sum_0^\infty \frac{t^k}{k!}B_0^{-(k+1)}\begin{pmatrix}1 & 1\\ 0 & 0\end{pmatrix}$$

$$= \sum_0^\infty \frac{t^k}{k!}\begin{pmatrix}1 & 1\\ 0 & 0\end{pmatrix}$$

and

$$B_0^- B_0 = \begin{pmatrix}1 & 1\\ 0 & 0\end{pmatrix},$$

i.e. the arbitrariness in B_0^- is immaterial in the sense that a and b do not show up in the inverse operator. In fact, it is easy to show that the inverse operator is unique. (2) The inverse in example 3 has a negative component. This means that there is *disinvestment*, in fact, of good 1 in sector 2. For further discussion, see Leontief (1970).

Next, we admit zero eigenvalues with an incomplete system of eigenvalues. B_0 can now be any square matrix. This complete generality has a price, however. It is no longer possible to express the inverse operator in sole terms of B_0. We now have to invoke its triangular form factors J_1, J_2 and T.

Proposition 4. *Let $B_0 = T\left(\begin{smallmatrix}J_1 & 0\\ 0 & J_2\end{smallmatrix}\right)$ be the triangular form with diag J_1 zero and diag J_2 never vanishing. Then*

$$(I\delta - B_0\delta)^{*-1} = T\begin{pmatrix}\sum_0^{n-1} \overset{(k)}{\delta} J_1^k & 0\\ 0 & \check{H}\exp(J_2^{-1}t)J_2^{-1}\end{pmatrix}T^{-1},$$

where $\overset{(k)}{\delta}$ is the kth derivative of δ, $k = 0, \ldots, n$, and n is the size of B_0 or the number of sectors in the economy.

Proof. See the appendix. □

Example. $B_0 = \left(\begin{smallmatrix} 0 & 1 \\ 0 & 0 \end{smallmatrix}\right)$. Then $J_1 = B_0$, $J_2 = \emptyset$ and $T = I$. Hence the inverse becomes

$$\sum_0^1 \overset{(k)}{\delta} B_0^k = \delta I + \dot{\delta} B_0 = \begin{pmatrix} \delta & \dot{\delta} \\ 0 & \delta \end{pmatrix}.$$

5. Traditional Dynamics

In traditional input–output, production is instantaneous. The coefficients are concentrated in the origin: $A = A_0\delta$ and $B = B_0\delta$ with A_0 and B_0 matrices and δ the Dirac distribution (see the appendix). Equation (4) of Section 2 reduces to the familiar dynamic input–output equation,

$$x = A_0 x + B_0 \dot{x} + z. \tag{6}$$

Although equation (6) is standard, its Leontief planning problem has not been solved yet, due to the B_0 singularity problems discussed in the last section. The next proposition does it. Recall that the Leontief planning problem was defined in Section 2 as that of finding output x given final demand z. The connection with initial value problems will be discussed in Section 6.

Proposition 5. *Let the assumption of Section 2 be fulfilled, i.e. A_0 fulfills the Hawkins-Simon* (1949) *conditions. Let B_0's zero eigenvalues have a complete system of eigenvectors. Then for every z, the solution to equation* (6) *is*

$$x = \{\check{H} \exp[B_0^-(I - A_0)t]\}^* B_0^-(I - A_0)$$
$$\times B_0^- B_0 \sum_0^\infty A_0^k z + (I - B_0^- B_0) \sum_0^\infty A_0^k z.$$

Proof. See the appendix. □

Remarks. (1) z may not grow too fast, for then x would become infinite. Formally, z must fulfill the convolution condition of Schwartz (1961). In fact, z must be tempered by a growth rate which is less than g^* of Proposition 2. (2) The assumption on B_0 can be dropped. Then the solution is modified by applying Proposition 4 instead of 3 in the derivation. (3) In the special case that B_0 is invertible, the solution reduces to

$$x = \check{H} \exp[B_0^{-}(I - A_0)t]^* B_0^{-1} z.$$

This agrees with the literature, e.g. Bródy (1974, p. 136). (4) A discrete time formulation and solution to the problem yields Leontief's (1970) "Dynamic Inverse." The relation between the formulations, such as the bias involved, is discussed in ten Raa (1986).

6. Distributed Dynamics

Last, but not least, we shall solve the Leontief planning problem for the full equation with distributed input–output coefficients of Section 3, reproduced here for convenience:

$$x = A^* x + B^* \dot{x} + z. \tag{4}$$

The technique will be factorization. The matrix distributions will be split into parts which are concentrated in the origin and parts away from the origin. The first parts will be subjected to Proposition 4, the latter to a standard device of the theory of distributions. The procedure works provided that there is an intermediate time span over which the coefficients matrices are regular. Therefore, it is assumed that on some open interval $(\epsilon, 0)$, however small, A agrees with an integrable function and B with an absolutely continuous function. (This means that for all positive γ, there is a positive Δ such that

$$\sum_{k=1}^{m} \|B(t_k) - B(s_k)\| < \gamma$$

for every finite system of pairwise disjoint subintervals (s_k, t_k) of $(\epsilon, 0)$ with total length $\Sigma_{k=1}^{m}(t_k - s_k)$ less than Δ.) The assumption is met in applied econometrics where A and B have finite supports. We now have

Proposition 6. *Let the assumption of Section 2 be fulfilled. On some interval $(\epsilon, 0)$, let A be integrable and B absolutely continuous. Then for every z, the solution x to the above equation is the convolution product of a*

locally integrable function, a multiple of the Dirac distribution and a distribution with support in the negatives, all with z. The expression for x is specified in the proof.

Proof. See the appendix. □

Remarks. (1) Remark 1 of Section 5 applies. (2) A discrete time formulation and solution to the problem is presented in ten Raa (1986) who also comments on the length of the industrial reporting period, as compared to the time between the purchase of input and the production of output in terms of the significance of distributed versus traditional input–output.

Example. Consider a simple economy with a fixed capital good 1 and a circulating capital good 2. For simplicity, let each sector require only one kind of capital. To keep the example interesting, let each sector require the capital of the other. The circulating capital consumption by sector 1 is 1/3 per unit of output, exponentially distributed. One unit of fixed capital is needed per unit of output in sector 2. Formally,

$$A(t) = \begin{pmatrix} 0 & 0 \\ 1 & 0 \end{pmatrix} \frac{1}{3} e^{t} \check{H}(t) \tag{7}$$

and

$$B = \begin{pmatrix} 0 & 1 \\ 0 & 0 \end{pmatrix} \delta.$$

A straightforward application of Proposition 6 in the appendix shows that the solution to the Leontief planning problem for final demand z is given by the output path

$$x(t) = \begin{pmatrix} \frac{3}{4} z_1(t) + \frac{3}{4} \dot{z}_2(t) - \frac{3}{16} z_2(t) + \frac{3}{16} \int_{-\infty}^{0} e^{\frac{3}{4}s} \\ \times z_1(t-s)ds + \frac{9}{64} \int_{-\infty}^{0} e^{\frac{3}{4}s} z_2(t-s)ds \\ \frac{3}{4} z_2(t) + \frac{1}{4} \int_{-\infty}^{0} e^{\frac{3}{4}s} z_1(t-s)ds + \frac{3}{16} \int_{-\infty}^{0} e^{\frac{3}{4}s} z_2(t-s)ds \end{pmatrix}. \tag{8}$$

Note that current and future values of final demand, z, determine output, x. Capital requirements are met by the appropriate past production levels, as indicated by the same formula for x. Should one desire a particular level of output and capital stock at, say, time zero, then the formula implicitly determines all feasible future paths of final demand, z, and their sustaining output paths, x. The selection of such a path of final demand z requires a behavioral rule or plan, and goes beyond the scope of the present article. For an interesting discussion of this issue, I refer to Leontief (1963).

7. Conclusion

The new approach to economic models with temporally distributed activities, exemplified by distributed input–output analysis, consists of four steps. First, the standard, nondistributed economic model (Leontief's dynamic input–output model) is taken as the point of departure. Second, activities are reinterpreted as temporal distributions. Third, the ordinary product is replaced by the convolution product. Fourth, the consequent model is subjected to the calculus of distributions.

The approach offers a unifying and extending framework for the dynamic inverse of Leontief (1970) and also Bródy (1974), and for the distributed lag studies of Bródy (1965), Gladyshevskii and Belous (1978), Johansen (1978), and Zhuravlev (1982).

The application of the theory of distributions of Schwartz (1957) is novel and promising for economic science. This paper features the following results:

1. Solutions to dynamic economic models with singular capital structures.
2. Unbalanced growth solutions to the traditional dynamic input–output model.
3. Analysis of the dynamic input–output model with distributed activities.

Acknowledgements

I owe Wassily Leontief much for his help throughout the study. I would like to thank Erik Thomas whom I consulted for the analysis. Andras Bródy, Duncan Foley, and the late Leif Johansen kindly commented on the first draft. I am grateful to Teun Kloek, Rick van der Ploeg, Albert Verbeek and Ton Vorst for suggestions on the generalized inverse of the capital matrix. Harm Bart provided some useful references. The paper was presented at the fourth IFAC/IFORS Conference on the Modelling and Control of National Economies, Washington, D.C., June 17–19, 1983, and at the Econometric Society Winter 1985 meetings, New York City. Travel support by the Netherlands Organization for the Advancement of Pure Research (Z.W.O.) is gratefully acknowledged.

References

Bródy, A. (1965) The model of expanding reproduction, *Applications of Mathematics to Economics* (Budapest: Akadémiai Kiadó), pp. 61–63.

—— (1974) *Proportions, Prices and Planning* (Budapest: Akadémiai, Kiadó and Amsterdam: North-Holland Publishing Company).

Foley, D.K. (1982) Accumulation, realization, and crisis, *Journal of Economic Theory*, 30(2), pp. 300–319.

Galan, C. de (1980) Gediflerentieerde Loonvorming, *Economisch Statistische Berichten*, 65, pp. 214–218.

Gel'fand, I.M. and G.E. Shilov (1967) *Generalized Functions* (New York: Academic Press).

Gladyshevskii, A.I. and G.K. Belous (1978) Microeconomic calculations of distributed lags in capital construction, *Matekon*, 14(3), pp. 58–79.

Hawkins, D. and H.A. Simon (1949) Some conditions of macro-economic stability, *Econometrica*, 17, pp. 245–248.

Johansen, L. (1978) On the theory of dynamic input–output models with different time profiles of capital construction and finite life-time of capital equipment, *Journal of Economic Theory*, 19(2), pp. 513–533.

Kendrick, D. (1972) On the Leontief dynamic inverse, *Quarterly Journal of Economics*, 86, pp. 693–696.

Leontief, W. (1963) When should history be written backwards? *The Economic History Review*, Second Series, 16(1), pp. 1–8.

—— (1970) The dynamic inverse, in *Contributions to Input–Output Analysis*, Carter A.P. and A. Bródy (eds.) (Amsterdam: North-Holland Publishing Company), pp. 17–46.

Leontief, W., A.P. Carter and P.A. Petri (1977) *The Future of the World Economy*.(New York: Oxford University Press).

Lighthill, M.J. (1964) *Introduction to Fourier Analysis and Generalized Functions* (Cambridge: Cambridge University Press).

Livesey, D.A. (1973) The singularity problem in the dynamic input–output model, *International Journal System Science* 4, pp. 437–440.

—— (1976) A minimal realization of the Leontief dynamic input–output model, in *Advances in Input–Output Analysis*, Polenske, K.R. and J. Skolka (eds.) (Cambridge, MA: Ballinger Publishing Company), pp. 527–541.

Marx, K. (1974) *Capital 2: The Process of Circulation of Capital* (New York: International Publishers).

ten Raa, Th. (1984) The distribution approach to spatial economics, *Journal of Regional Science*, 24(1), pp. 105–117.
—— (1986) Applied dynamic input–output with distributed activities, *European Economic Review*.
Rao, C.R. (1974) *Linear Statistical Inference and Its Applications* (New York: John Wiley & Sons).
Schwartz, L. (1957) *Théorie des Distributions* (Paris: Hermann).
—— (1961) Méthodes Mathématiques pour les Sciences Physiques (Paris: Hermann).
Zhuravlev, S.N. (1982) On solutions to a dynamic input–output model with the maximization of consumption as the criterion, *Matekon*, 18(3), pp. 50–64.

Appendix

Distributions for Economists

Having reconsidered input–output coefficients, now being non-negative distributions on the non-positive time axis, it may be helpful to the non-mathematical reader to give a precise account of the concepts involved. Non-negative distributions are essentially measures (Schwartz, 1957). Unsigned distributions are generalizations that cover basically all linear operators. So let us first recapitulate the concept of a measure and then generalize. Throughout this paper, time will be the underlying space.

A measure associates amounts of mass with subsets of the time axis. Thus, a measure can be viewed as a mapping from indicator functions to the reals. The indicator functions are "test" functions representing subsets of time. A measure is no arbitrary mapping defined on the test space of indicator functions, but must be non-negative and additive, meaning that the measure of the sum of indicator functions that is still an indicator function equals the sum of the measures. It is possible to extend measures to the test space of continuous and bounded functions: First, the measure of a multiple of an indicator function is defined as the multiple of the measure of the indicator function itself. Second, the measure of a step function is the sum of the measures of the steps. And third, the measure of a continuous and bounded function is defined by a limit process of step functions. By the non-negativity and additivity assumptions, a measure is a non-negative linear operator on the test space of continuous and bounded functions.

A prime example is the *Dirac* measure, δ, that represents the unit point mass at the origin. Being a measure, it is defined by the value it associates with an *indicator function*, 1_I. Here, I is a subset of the time axis and 1_I is defined by $1_I(t) = 1$ if $t \in I$ and $1_I(t) = 0$ if $t \notin I$. The value δ associates with 1_I could be denoted $\delta(1_I)$. However, since the argument itself is a function here, $\langle \delta, 1_I \rangle$ is a more common notation. Measure δ is defined by $\langle \delta, 1_I \rangle = 1_I(0)$. In other words, if I contains the origin, then $\langle \delta, 1_I \rangle = 1 - I$ embodies one unit of mass — but if I does not contain the origin, then $\langle \delta, 1_I \rangle = 0 - I$ embodies no mass. The extension of δ to a continuous and bounded function, ϕ, is straightforward: $\langle \delta, \phi \rangle = \phi(0)$.

Measures have been defined on the wide class of continuous and bounded functions. A distribution is a generalization of a measure. In other words, there are more distributions than measures. This is obtained by defining distributions on a narrower class of test functions. At first sight, this procedure seems paradoxical, but it is right. By requiring that operators are defined *only* on a smaller set of functions, one admits more of them, in other words, generalizes. Distributions are defined on the *test space* of infinitely differentiable functions with compact support. (The support of a function is defined as the closure of the set of points where the function is nonzero.) The test space is endowed with a natural topology that corresponds with a uniform convergence of all derivatives. A *distribution* is formally defined as a continuous linear mapping from this test space to the reals (or sometimes the complex numbers).

Since measures are defined a fortiori on the narrow test space of infinitely differentiable functions with compact supports, they are distributions. Distributions also generalize locally integrable functions f. For such an f, one can define the distribution T_f by $\langle T_f, \phi \rangle = \int f(t)\phi(t)dt$. A first manifestation of the flexibility of distributions is the possibility to define their *derivatives* no matter what. The definition of the derivative of a distribution T, $\dot{T}$, should generalize the derivative of, say, a continuously differentiable function, f. In other words, we want $\dot{T}_f = T_{\dot{f}}$. Now $T_{\dot{f}}$ is defined by

$$\langle T_{\dot{f}}, \phi \rangle = \int \dot{f}(t)\phi(t)dt = -\int f(t)\dot{\phi}(t)dt = -\langle T_f, \dot{\phi} \rangle.$$

(The integration by parts produced no residual term as ϕ has compact support.) This motivates the following definition of $\dot{T}$: $\langle \dot{T}, \phi \rangle \doteq -\langle T, \dot{\phi} \rangle$.

The *convolution product* of two continuous functions, f and g, with compact supports, is defined by

$$(f^* g)(t) = \int f(s)g(t-s)ds.$$

The definition of the convolution product of a distribution, T, and a test function, ϕ, should generalize; in other words, we want

$$T_f^*\phi = f^*\phi = \int f(s)\phi(t-s)ds = \langle T_f, \phi(t-\cdot)\rangle.$$

This motivates the definition of $T^*\phi$ as an infinitely differentiable function by

$$(T^*\phi)(t) = \langle T, \phi(t-\cdot)\rangle.$$

The definition of the convolution product can be generalized further to apply to two distributions, provided that a certain condition is fulfilled (Schwartz 1961, p. 123). Elementary facts are $\delta^*T = T$ (in other words, δ is the unit element) and $\dot{S}^*T = S^*\dot{T}$. It is easy to check this for $T = T_\phi$. Then

$$(\delta^*\phi)(t) = \langle \delta, \phi(t-\cdot)\rangle = \phi(t-0) = \phi(t),$$

while

$$\begin{aligned}(\dot{S}^*\phi)(t) &= \langle \dot{S}, \phi(t-\cdot)\rangle = -\langle S, [\phi(t-\cdot)]\rangle \\ &= -\langle S, \dot{\phi}(t-\cdot)\cdot(-1)\rangle = \langle S, \dot{\phi}(t-\cdot)\rangle \\ &= (S^*\dot{\phi})(t).\end{aligned}$$

Distributions even generalize operations such as differentiation. The convolution product of $\dot{\delta}$ and any distribution T yields $\dot{\delta}^*T = \delta^*\dot{T} = \dot{T}$. This device will take care of the investment term in the dynamic input–output equation. $\dot{\delta}$ is a distribution, but not a measure (which must be non-negative). This is why distributions are more convenient tools for dynamic input–output than measures. Moreover, in some cases, distributions along with the convolution product form an algebra and equations can be solved by finding inverse distributions. This observation is the clue to the resolution of distributed input–output problems.

Before starting the main analysis, let me disclaim any rigor or comprehensiveness in this mathematical section. A referee suggested a better introduction, namely Lighthill (1964), as well as a more advanced and encyclopedic treatment: Gel'fand and Shilov (1967).

Proof of Proposition 1. To demonstrate existence of $\Sigma_0^\infty A^{*k}$ and its continuity in test functions, ϕ, we estimate, using nonnegativity,

$$\left\langle \sum_0^\infty A^{*k}, \phi \right\rangle \leq \left\langle \sum_0^\infty A^{*k}, \|\phi\|_\infty \right\rangle = \left\langle \sum_0^\infty A^{*k}, 1 \right\rangle \|\phi\|_\infty$$

$$= \int \left(\sum_0^\infty A^{*k} \right) \|\phi\|_\infty = \sum_0^\infty \left(\int A \right)^k \|\phi\|_\infty \qquad (9)$$

where the last equality rests on the fact $\int (A^{*k}) = (\int A)^k$. (This fact will be established for $k = 2$, the further cases going by induction. The (i, j)th element of the left-hand side matrix equals

$$\left[\int (A^{*2}) \right]_{ij} = \int \left[(A^{*2})_{ij} \right] = \langle (A^{*2})_{ij}, 1 \rangle$$

$$= \left\langle \sum_m a_{im} * a_{mj}, 1 \right\rangle$$

$$= \sum_m \langle a_{im}, \langle a_{mj}, 1 \rangle \rangle = \sum_m \left\langle a_{im}, \int a_{mj} \right\rangle$$

$$= \sum_m \langle a_{im}, 1 \rangle \int a_{mj} = \sum_m \int a_{im} \int a_{mj}$$

$$= \left(\int A \int A \right)_{ij} = \left[\left(\int A \right)^2 \right]_{ij},$$

the (i, j)th element of the right-hand side.)

By the convergence consequence, (3), of the assumption, the right-hand side of (9) is finite. Consequently, the distribution on the left-hand side, $\sum_0^\infty A^{*k}$ exists and is continuous in ϕ. To demonstrate the second part of the proposition, consider a distribution z which is non-negative and near infinity agrees with a bounded function. Then $z = z' + z''$ with z' non-negative and agreeing with a bounded function, and with z'' non-negative and support bounded from above. We shall show that, first,

$$x' = \left(\sum_0^\infty A^{*k} \right) * z'$$

is non-negative and agrees with a bounded function, and second,

$$x'' = \left(\sum_0^\infty A^{*k}\right) * z''$$

is a bounded (i.e. finite total mass) non-negative distribution with support bounded from above. Since $x = x' + x''$, this is enough. Non-negativity is obvious. To demonstrate the boundedness of x', choose non-negative locally integrable functions A_m that approximate $\sum_0^\infty A^{*k}$ from below and define $x_m = A_m^* z'$. Then, by non-negativity, $x_m \uparrow x'$, and defining $\| \|_\infty$ of a vector or matrix component wise as a vector or matrix of the same order,

$$\begin{aligned}
\|x_m\|_\infty &\le \|A_m\|_1 \|z'\|_\infty = \langle A_m, 1\rangle \|z'\|_\infty \\
&\le \left\langle \sum_0^\infty A^{*k}, 1 \right\rangle \|z'\|_\infty = \int \left(\sum_0^\infty A^{*k}\right) \|z'\|_\infty \\
&= \sum_0^\infty \left(\int A\right)^k \|z'\|_\infty
\end{aligned}$$

by the first part of the proof, (9). By the assumption and the principle of monotone convergence, x_m converges in the $\|\cdot\|_\infty$-norm. In fact, $\|x_m\|_\infty \uparrow \|x\|_\infty$ for our $x_m \uparrow x$. Taking the limit in our inequality, we obtain $\|x\|_\infty \le \sum_0^\infty (\int A)^k \|z'\|_\infty$. x'' is as desired since the supports of both $\sum_0^\infty A^{*k}$ and z'' are bounded from above so that these distributions fulfill the convolution condition of Schwartz (1961) and their convolution also has support bounded from above. □

Proof of Proposition 2. Substituting the balanced growth expressions, equation (4) becomes

$$x(0)e^{gt} = (A + Bg) * x(0)e^{gt} + z(0)e^{gt}$$

or, by the definition of the convolution product (see the first section of this appendix),

$$x(0)e^{gt} = \langle A + Bg,\ x(0)e^{g(t-\cdot)}\rangle + z(0)e^{gt}$$

or, by the linearity of distribution $A + Bg$,

$$x(0)e^{gt} = e^{gt}\langle (A + Bg)e^{-g(\cdot)},\quad x(0)\rangle + z(0)e^{gt}.$$

Dividing through we obtain

$$x(0) = A(g) * x(0) + z(0) \tag{10}$$

with

$$A(g) = (A + Bg)e^{-g(\cdot)}. \tag{11}$$

Equation (11) shows that for $g \geq 0$, $A(g)$ is a non-negative distribution. It has nonpositive support. Thus $A(g)$ is an input–output matrix distribution. By the nonpositivity of the support, $\int A(g)$ is an increasing function of g. By a standard result on non-negative matrices, spectral radius $\rho[\int A(g)]$ is a continuous function of g. By spectral radius consequence (2) of the assumption, $\rho[\int A(0)] < 1$. Ruling out the trivial case $A = B = 0$ (for which $g^* = \infty$ fulfills the proposition), $\rho[\int A(\infty)] = \infty$. By the intermediate value theorem, there is a $g^* > 0$ such that $\rho[\int A(g^*)] = 1$. It follows that for $0 \leq g < g^*$, $\rho[\int A(g)] < 1$. By (2), $A(g)$ fulfills the Hawkins-Simon conditions and we may subject it to Proposition 1. Hence for every $z(0)$ which is non-negative, there is a non-negative solution to equation (10). The solution can be taken constant and denoted $x(0)$. It remains to justify that g^* is the maximum growth rate. This rests on the fact that for $g = g^*$, $\rho[\int A(g)] = 1$, which implies, by the theory of non-negative matrices, that the condition — for every non-negative $z(0)$, there is a solution $x(0)$ of

$$x(0) = \left[\int A(g)\right] x(0) + z(0) = A(g) * x(0) + z(0)$$

— is violated. Consequently, in the statement of the proposition, g has to be strictly less than g^* indeed and any higher critical growth rate would invalidate the proposition. □

Proof of Proposition 3. To prove that the expression in the statement of the Proposition is truly the inverse distribution, we multiply through by the operator, $I\delta - B_0\dot{\delta}$, to check that it yields the unit distribution, δI. Thus,

$$\begin{aligned}
&\left[\check{H} \exp(B_0^- t) B_0^{-2} B_0 + \delta(I - B_0^- B_0)\right]^* (I\delta - B_0\dot{\delta}) \\
&= \check{H} \exp(B_0^- t) B_0^{-2} B_0 + \delta(I - B_0^- B_0) \\
&\quad - [\check{H} \exp(B_0^- t)]^* B_0^{-2} B_0^2 - (I - B_0^- B_0) B_0 \dot{\delta} \\
&= \check{H} \exp(B_0^- t) B_0^{-2} B_0 + \delta(I - B_0^- B_0)
\end{aligned}$$

$$
\begin{aligned}
&-\check{H}\exp(B_0^- t)B_0^{-3}B_0^2 + \delta B_0^{-2}B_0^2 - (B_0 - B_0^- B_0^2)\dot{\delta} \\
&= \check{H}\exp(B_0^- t)B_0^{-2}(B_0 - B_0^- B_0^2) \\
&\quad + \delta[I - B_0^-(B_0 - B_0^- B_0^2)] - (B_0 - B_0^- B_0^2)\dot{\delta}
\end{aligned}
$$

which equals δI for $B_0 - B_0^- B_0^2 = 0$. □

Proof of Proposition 4. The left-hand side of the statement of the Proposition equals

$$
\begin{aligned}
(I\delta - B_0\dot{\delta})^{*-1} &= \left(I\delta - T\begin{pmatrix} J_1 & 0 \\ 0 & J_2 \end{pmatrix} T^{-1}\dot{\delta}\right)^{*-1} \\
&= \left[T\left(I\delta - \begin{pmatrix} J_1 & 0 \\ 0 & J_2 \end{pmatrix}\dot{\delta}\right)T^{-1}\right]^{*-1} \\
&= T\begin{pmatrix} I_1\delta - J_1\dot{\delta} & 0 \\ 0 & I_2\delta - J_2\dot{\delta} \end{pmatrix}^{*-1} T^{-1} \\
&= T\begin{pmatrix} (I_1\delta - J_1\dot{\delta})^{*-1} & 0 \\ 0 & (I_2\delta - J_2\dot{\delta})^{*-1} \end{pmatrix} T^{-1}.
\end{aligned}
$$

Since the diagonal of upper triangular J_2 never vanishes, this matrix is regular, and by Proposition 3 (example 1),

$$
(I_2\delta - J_2\dot{\delta})^{*-1} = \check{H}\exp(J_2^{-1}t)J_2^{-1}.
$$

Since the diagonal of upper triangular J_1, is zero, the nth power of this matrix is zero, and therefore,

$$
\begin{aligned}
\sum_0^{n-1} \overset{(k)}{\delta} J_1^{k*}(I_1\delta - J_1\dot{\delta}) &= \sum_0^{n-1} \overset{(k)}{\delta} J_1^k - \sum_0^{n-1} \overset{(k+1)}{\delta} J_1^{k+1} \\
&= \overset{(0)}{\delta} J_1^0 - \overset{(n)}{\delta} J_1^n = \delta I_1
\end{aligned}
$$

or

$$
(I_1\delta - J_1\dot{\delta})^{*-1} = \sum_0^{n-1} \overset{(k)}{\delta} J_1^k.
$$

The substitution of the two derived inverses yields the right-hand side of the statement of the Proposition. □

Proof of Proposition 5. The proof is organized as follows. First, we rewrite equation (6) such that on the left-hand side, an operator applies to unknown x, and on the right-hand side there is a known z. Then we find the inverse of the operator. Convoluting through with the inverse, the left-hand side becomes x and the right-hand side the convolution product of the inverse and z. This is the solution. Simplification finishes the proof. We differentiate (6) by parts (see the first section of this appendix) which, incidentally, makes the treatment of circulating and fixed capital uniform:

$$[(I - A_0)\delta - B_0\dot{\delta}]^* x = z.$$

We factorize the operator:

$$(I - A_0)\delta - B_0\dot{\delta} = (I - A_0)[I\delta - (I - A_0)^{-1}B_0\dot{\delta}].$$

Here, we used the Hawkins-Simon conditions. These also yield that the B_0 property carries over to $(I - A_0)^{-1}B_0$. Proposition 3 inverts the operator:

$$\begin{aligned}
&[I\delta - (I - A_0)^{-1}B_0\dot{\delta}]^{*-1}(I - A_0)^{-1} \\
&\quad = \{\check{H}\exp[[(I - A_0)^{-1}B_0]^{-}t][(I - A_0)^{-1}B_0]^{-2}(I - A_0)^{-1}B_0 \\
&\qquad + \delta(I - [(I - A_0)^{-1}B_0]^{-}(I - A_0)^{-1}B_0)\}(I - A_0)^{-1}
\end{aligned}$$

where $[(I - A_0)^{-1}B_0]^{-}$ is the generalized inverse of $(I - A_0)^{-1}B_0$ which can also be written $B_0^{-}(I - A_0)$, by which the inverse operator becomes

$$[\check{H}\exp[B_0^{-}(I - A_0)t]B_0^{-}(I - A_0)B_0^{-}B_0 + \delta(I - B_0^{-}B_0)]\sum_0^{\infty} A_0^k.$$

Convoluting with the right-hand side, z, we obtain the solution,

$$\begin{aligned}
x &= \{\check{H}\exp[B_0^{-}(I - A_0)t]B_0^{-}(I - A_0)B_0^{-}B_0 + \delta(I - B_0^{-}B_0)\}\sum_0^{\infty} A_0^{k*} z \\
&= \left\{\check{H}\exp[B_0^{-}(I - A_0)t]B_0^{-}(I - A_0)t]B_0^{-}B_0 \sum_0^{\infty} A_0^k\right\} * z
\end{aligned}$$

$$+\,\delta(I - B_0^- B)\sum_0^\infty A_0^{k*} z$$

$$= \{\check{H}\exp[B_0^-(I - A_0)t]\} * B_0^-(I - A_0)B_0^- B_0 \sum_0^\infty A_0^k z$$

$$+\,(I - B_0^- B)\sum_0^\infty A_0^k z. \qquad \square$$

Proof of Proposition 6. The organization of the proof is just like the previous one. Thus, refer to the first paragraph of the proof of Proposition 5. By the assumption that A is integrable on $(\epsilon, 0)$, $A = A_0\delta + A_1 + A_2$ with A_0 a matrix, A_1 a locally summable function on $(-\infty, 0)$, and A_2's support in $(-\infty, \epsilon)$ for some negative ϵ. Here, we use the fact that a non-negative distribution concentrated in the origin must be a multiple of the Dirac distribution according to Schwartz (1957).

Similarly, $B = B_0\delta + B_1 + B_2$ with B_0 a matrix, B_1, absolutely continuous, and B_2's support in (∞, ϵ). Through differentiation by parts (see the first section of this appendix), the equation becomes

$$(I\delta - A - \dot{B}) * x = z. \tag{12}$$

By substitution, the operator in (12) becomes

$$I\delta - A - \dot{B} = C_0 - C_1 - C_2 \tag{13}$$

with

$$C_0 = (I - A_0)\delta - B_0\dot{\delta} \tag{14}$$

the traditional dynamic input–output operator,

$$C_1 = A_1 + \dot{B}_1 \tag{15}$$

a locally integrable function on $(\infty, 0)$, and

$$C_2 = A_2 + \dot{B}_2 \tag{16}$$

whose support is in $(-\infty, \epsilon)$. We factorize the operator, (13):

$$C_0 - C_1 - C_2 = C_0^*(I\delta - C_0^{*-1} * C_1 - C_0^{*-1} * C_2). \tag{17}$$

Here

$$C_0^{*-1} = \{\check{H} \exp[B_0^-(I - A_0)t]B_0^-(I - A_0)B_0^-B_0 + \delta(I - B_0^-B_0)\} \sum_0^\infty A_0^k \tag{18}$$

(or a straightforward modification) by equation (14) and Proposition 5 (remark 2); A_0 fulfills the Hawkins-Simon conditions by the assumption of section III and the fact $0 \leq A_0\delta \leq A$. In further factorizing, the operator, (17), becomes

$$C_0^*(I\delta - C_0^{*-1} * C_1) * [I\delta - (I\delta - C_0^{*-1} * C_1)^{*-1} * C_0^{*-1} * C_2]. \tag{19}$$

This makes sense and is invertible provided that the factors

$$I\delta - C_0^{*-1} * C_1$$

and

$$I\delta - (I\delta - C_0^{*-1} * C_1)^{*-1} * C_0^{*-1} * C_2$$

are invertible. By equation (18), C_0^{*-1} is the sum of an infinitely differentiate function on $(-\infty, 0)$ and a multiple of the Dirac distribution. Consequently, its convolution product, with C_1 which is locally summable by (14), exists and is a locally summable function on $(-\infty, 0)$. By Schwartz (1961, p. 143) $I\delta - C_0^{*-1} * C_1$, has an inverse which is the sum of the Dirac distribution and a locally integrable function C_1^- on $(-\infty, 0)$. The last factor of equation (19) now is

$$I\delta - (I\delta + C_1^-) * C_0^{*-1} * C_2,$$

where the remainder has support in $(-\infty, \epsilon)$ by virtue of C_2 as specified in (16). Consequently, this factor has a power expansion inverse which is the sum of the Dirac distribution and a distribution C_2^- with support in $(-\infty, \epsilon)$. Thus the inverse of (19) becomes

$$(I\delta + C_2^-) * (I\delta + C_1^-) * C_0^{*-1}$$

with C_0^{*-1}, C_1^- and C_2^- given by (18) and the above text. Convoluting through this distribution with z yields the specific expression for x. To determine the nature of this solution, recall that C_0^{*-1} is, by (18), the sum of an infinitely differentiable function on $(-\infty, 0)$ and a multiple of the Dirac distribution, C_1^- is a locally integrable function on $(-\infty, 0)$, and C_2^- is a distribution with support in $(-\infty, \epsilon)$. Let us summarize this symbolically as

$$C_0^{*-1} \in C_-^\infty + D_0', \quad C_1^- \in L_{\text{loc},-}^1,$$

and

$$C_2 \in D'_{(-\infty,\epsilon)}.$$

It follows that the inverse belongs to

$$(D_0' + D'_{(-\infty,\epsilon)}) * (D_0' + L_{\text{loc},-}^1) * (C_-^\infty + D_0').$$

This space can be written out as

$$D'_- * C_-^\infty + (D_0' + D'_{(-\infty,\epsilon)}) * \left(D_0' + L_{\text{loc},-}^1\right)$$

or

$$C_-^\infty + (D_0' + L_{\text{loc},-}^1) + D'_{(-\infty,\epsilon)} * (D_0' + L_{\text{loc},-}^1)$$

which is simply

$$L_{\text{loc},-}^1 + D_0' + D'_{(-\infty,\epsilon)}. \qquad \square$$

Example. Consider the full input–output equation, (4), with A and B given by equation (7) of Section 6. Then, in the proof of Proposition 6,

$$A = A_0\delta + A_1 + A_2 = 0 + \begin{pmatrix} 0 & 0 \\ 1 & 0 \end{pmatrix} 1/3e^{(\cdot)}\check{H} + 0$$

and

$$B = B_0\delta + B_1 + B_2 = \begin{pmatrix} 0 & 1 \\ 0 & 0 \end{pmatrix} \delta + 0 + 0.$$

so that equations (14), (15) and (16) reduce to

$$C_0 = I\delta - \begin{pmatrix} 0 & 1 \\ 0 & 0 \end{pmatrix} \dot{\delta},$$

$$C_1 = \begin{pmatrix} 0 & 0 \\ 1 & 0 \end{pmatrix} \frac{1}{3} e^{(\cdot)}\check{H},$$

$$C_2 = 0.$$

Consequently, the operator, (19), reduces to

$$\left[I\delta - \begin{pmatrix} 0 & 1 \\ 0 & 0 \end{pmatrix} \dot{\delta}\right] * \left[I\delta - C_0^{*-1} * \begin{pmatrix} 0 & 0 \\ 1 & 0 \end{pmatrix} \frac{1}{3} e^{(\cdot)} \check{H}\right]. \qquad (19')$$

The second factor of this operator, (19′), becomes by the example to Proposition 4,

$$\begin{aligned} I\delta - \begin{pmatrix} \delta & \dot{\delta} \\ 0 & \delta \end{pmatrix} * \begin{pmatrix} 0 & 0 \\ 1 & 0 \end{pmatrix} \frac{1}{3} e^{(\cdot)} \check{H} &= I\delta - \frac{1}{3} \begin{pmatrix} \dot{\delta} & 0 \\ \delta & 0 \end{pmatrix} * e^{(\cdot)} \check{H} \\ &= I\delta - \frac{1}{3} \begin{pmatrix} e^{(\cdot)} \check{H} - \delta & 0 \\ e^{(\cdot)} \check{H} & 0 \end{pmatrix} \\ &= \begin{pmatrix} \frac{4}{3}\delta - \frac{1}{3} e^{(\cdot)} \check{H} & 0 \\ -\frac{1}{3} e^{(\cdot)} \check{H} & \delta \end{pmatrix}. \end{aligned} \qquad (20)$$

The inverse of this second factor, (20), is

$$\begin{aligned} &\begin{pmatrix} \left[\frac{4}{3}\delta - \frac{1}{3} e^{(\cdot)} \check{H}\right]^{*-1} & 0 \\ \frac{1}{3} e^{(\cdot)} \check{H} * \left[\frac{4}{3}\delta - \frac{1}{3} e^{(\cdot)} \check{H}\right]^{*-1} & \delta \end{pmatrix} = \begin{pmatrix} \frac{3}{4}\left[\delta - \frac{1}{4} e^{(\cdot)} \check{H}\right]^{*-1} & 0 \\ \frac{1}{4} e^{(\cdot)} \check{H} * \left[\delta - \frac{1}{4} e^{(\cdot)} \check{H}\right]^{*-1} & \delta \end{pmatrix} \\ &\qquad = \begin{pmatrix} \frac{3}{4}\left[\delta + \frac{1}{4} e^{\frac{3}{4}(\cdot)} \check{H}\right] & 0 \\ \frac{1}{4} e^{(\cdot)} \check{H} * \left[\delta + \frac{1}{4} e^{\frac{3}{4}(\cdot)} \check{H}\right] & \delta \end{pmatrix} \\ &\qquad = \begin{pmatrix} \frac{3}{4}\delta + \frac{3}{16} e^{\frac{3}{4}(\cdot)} \check{H} & 0 \\ \frac{1}{4} e^{\frac{3}{4}(\cdot)} \check{H} & \delta \end{pmatrix}, \end{aligned}$$

by the example to Proposition 1 and the easily verifiable elementary fact, $e^{(\cdot)}\check{H} * e^{\frac{3}{4}(\cdot)}\check{H} = 4e^{\frac{3}{4}(\cdot)}\check{H} - 4e^{(\cdot)}\check{H}$. Convoluting through with the inverse of the first factor of (19′) which is given by the example to Proposition 4, we obtain the inverse operator related to equation (19′),

$$\begin{pmatrix} \frac{3}{4}\delta + \frac{3}{16}e^{\frac{3}{4}(\cdot)}\check{H} & 0 \\ \frac{1}{4}e^{\frac{3}{4}(\cdot)}\check{H} & \delta \end{pmatrix} * \begin{pmatrix} \delta & \dot{\delta} \\ 0 & \delta \end{pmatrix}$$

$$= \begin{pmatrix} \frac{3}{4}\delta + \frac{3}{16}e^{\frac{3}{4}(\cdot)}\check{H} & \left[\frac{3}{4}\delta + \frac{3}{16}e^{\frac{3}{4}(\cdot)}\check{H}\right] * \dot{\delta} \\ \frac{1}{4}e^{\frac{3}{4}(\cdot)}\check{H} & \left[\frac{1}{4}e^{\frac{3}{4}(\cdot)}\check{H}\right] * \dot{\delta} + \delta \end{pmatrix}$$

$$= \begin{pmatrix} \frac{3}{4}\delta + \frac{3}{16}e^{\frac{3}{4}(\cdot)}\check{H} & \frac{3}{4}\dot{\delta} + \frac{9}{64}e^{\frac{3}{4}(\cdot)}\check{H} - \frac{3}{16}\delta \\ \frac{1}{4}e^{\frac{3}{4}(\cdot)}\check{H} & \frac{3}{16}e^{\frac{3}{4}(\cdot)}\check{H} - \frac{1}{4}\delta + \delta \end{pmatrix}$$

$$\times \begin{pmatrix} \frac{3}{4}\delta & \frac{3}{4}\dot{\delta} - \frac{3}{16}\delta \\ 0 & \frac{3}{4}\delta \end{pmatrix} + \begin{pmatrix} \frac{3}{16} & \frac{9}{64} \\ \frac{1}{4} & \frac{3}{16} \end{pmatrix} e^{\frac{3}{4}(\cdot)}\check{H}.$$

Convoluting through this distribution with z yields the specific expression for x, (8), posted in the example to Proposition 6 in Section 6. □

Chapter 14

Applied Dynamic Input–Output with Distributed Activities

Thijs ten Raa

Abstract: This paper implements dynamic input–output analysis with distributed activities. For this purpose, the input–output equation is formulated and solved in discrete time. Existing dynamic input–output models are shown to be instances. The fully distributed input–output model is applied to analyze the dynamic structure of the Polish economy. The effects of investment distributions are expressed by a comparison with conventional, non-distributed input–output results.

1. Introduction

The analysis of distributed activities like capital construction is greatly facilitated by defining the flow and stock coefficients matrices of the economy, A and B, as *distributions* on the past in the sense of ten Raa (1986). For example, $A(-s)$ represents the direct unit requirements s time units prior to the delivery of output. In this paper, for a comparison with other dynamic input–output studies, we want to allow for technical change. Then the whole

Received September 1984, final version received June 1985.

input profile, A, depends on time, say of delivery, which we will denote by a subscript. Thus, $A_t(-s)$ are the direct unit requirements s time units prior to delivery time t, that is at time $t - s$. The stock coefficients distribution, B, is made time-dependent in the same way.

Following Leontief (1970), $B_{t+1}(0)$ are the direct and immediate unit investment requirements at time t for new capacity usable the year after. Moreover, this capacity also requires investment quantities of $B_{t+1}(-s)$ s time units prior to t, at least in our model which mimics the distribution of investment over time. Note that we doggedly follow Leontief's (1970) convention of indexing technology not by the final year of production of particular capital goods, but rather the year in which they are first put to use.

A_t and B_{t+1}, thus defined, constitute the general input–output model presented and solved in Section 2. The model that comes closest is in Kigyóssy-Schmidt and Schwarz (1983) who consider distributed investment only and solve implicitly by presenting an algorithm. Sections 3–5 show how existing dynamic input–output models with explicit solutions fall out as special cases. Computational aspects are dealt with in Section 6. Section 7 discusses choice of time unit issues such as the bias involved. Section 8 applies the model to analyze the dynamic structure of the Polish economy. Section 9 concludes with a call for further data collection.

2. The Material Balance Equation and its Solution

The material balance between output $x(t)$ and final demand $z(t)$ reads (ten Raa 1986)

$$x(t) = \sum_{s=0}^{\infty} A_{t+s}(-s)x(t+s) + \sum_{s=0}^{\infty} B_{t+s+1}(-s)[x(t+s+1) - x(t+s)] + z(t). \quad (1)$$

Here, we have chosen a sufficiently small unit of time such that the derivative $\dot{x}(t)$ may be approximated by $x(t+1) - x(t)$. A later section will dwell on this. To ease the notation, define

$$\begin{aligned} G_t(0) &= I - A_t(0) + B_{t+1}(0) \quad \text{and for } s = 1, 2, 3, \ldots, \\ G_t(s) &= -A_{t+s}(-s) + B_{t+s+1}(-s) - B_{t+s}(-s+1). \end{aligned} \quad (2)$$

Then the material balance, (1), reduces to

$$\sum_{s=0}^{\infty} G_t(s)x(t+s) = z(t), \tag{3}$$

or

$$\begin{bmatrix} \ddots & & & & & \\ & G_0(0) & G_0(1) & G_0(2) & \cdots & \\ & & G_1(0) & G_1(1) & G_1(2) & \cdots \\ & 0 & & G_2(0) & G_2(1) & G_2(2) \cdots \\ & & & \ddots & & \end{bmatrix} \begin{bmatrix} \vdots \\ x(0) \\ x(1) \\ x(2) \\ \vdots \end{bmatrix} = \begin{bmatrix} \vdots \\ z(0) \\ z(1) \\ z(2) \\ \vdots \end{bmatrix}. \tag{4}$$

The supermatrix that appears here is a generalization of the structural matrix of Leontief (1970) that underlies his dynamic inverse. The presence of production times greater than one and of investment lead times disrupts the familiar bidiagonal structure. However, since these lags are non-negative, the structure is still triangular. This enables us to find the inverse of the general structural matrix. [Singularity problems are taken care of in ten Raa (1986).] The inverse will be triangular and its diagonal entries will be the inverses of the respective ones on the diagonal of the super G-matrix, like in

$$\begin{bmatrix} \ddots & & & & \\ & G_0(0)^{-1} D_0(1) \cdots D_0(v) \cdots & & & \\ & \ddots & & \ddots & \\ & & G_t(0)^{-1} D_t(1) \cdots D_t(v) \cdots & & \\ & & \ddots & & \end{bmatrix}. \tag{5}$$

There remain to be determined the off-diagonal matrices $D_t(v)$, $t = \ldots, 0, 1, 2, \ldots$ and $v = 1, 2, \ldots$.

Proposition 1. *$D_t(v) = \sum R_t(s_1) \cdots R_{t+s_1+\cdots+s_{l-1}}(s_l) G_{t+v}(0)^{-1}$, where $R_t(s) = -G_t(0)^{-1} G_t(s)$ and the summation is over all $(s_1, \ldots, s_l)$ with each component in $\{1, \ldots, v\}$ and the sum of the components equal to v.*

Proof. See the appendix. □

It follows that

$$x(t) = G_t(0)^{-1}z(t) + \sum_{v=1}^{\infty} D_t(v)z(t+v), \tag{6}$$

with $D_t(v)$ given by Proposition 1. This completes the formulation and solution of the general discrete input–output equation.

Before we turn to specializations of the model in the next sections, we address two interrelated issues raised by the referee: (i) the accounting for existing capacities, and (ii) the investment requirements solution to a mere increase in final demand.

Existing capacities are accounted for only in so far as they are currently needed for plan fulfillment. For example, imagine an economy with final demand from time zero on that lasts for some extended period. Then, after an initial period of capital construction, the stock of capital is transferred from year to year. The investment term, the second one on the right-hand side of (1), is zero as there are no output changes in the intermediate period. Capital stock that is given in excess of minimum plan fulfillment requirements, due to an 'initial endowment' or, more historically, to overinvestment, is not accounted for explicitly. To remedy the model, one proceeds as follows. To account for overinvestment, final demand is widened as to include excess capacity additions. Or should one desire a particular level of output and capital stock at some 'initial' point of time, then solution (6) implicitly determines all feasible future paths of final demand, z, and sustaining output paths, x. The selection of such a path of final demand, z, is a matter of plan. The restriction of investment requirements to those called for by mere increases of final demand is indeed an alternative way to deal with existing capacities. Luckily, the model need not be respecified for this purpose. Since the model is linear in an abstract mathematical sense, the change in requirements associated with alternative values of final demand equals the requirements for the increase. In other words, the linearity insures that changes are governed by the same Eq. (1) and solution (6). The unit requirements which will be evaluated in Section 8 can thus be interpreted as deviations from an overall development of the economy that results from unit changes in the final demand such as an export program increase of one unit. In particular, the negative values reported that there are reductions in output levels facilitated by the disinvestment of capital constructed for the program. The disinvested quantities are absorbed by the rest of the economy in its production of the established final demand quantities.

3. No Technical Change

In this case, the coefficients matrix distributions, A and B, do not depend on time and their subscripts can be suppressed. Consequently, the subscripts of the structural matrix (2) drop out too:

$$G_t(s) = G(s) \tag{7}$$

and the solution, (6), becomes

$$x(t) = G(0)^{-1}z(t) + \sum_{v=1}^{\infty} D(v)z(t+v), \tag{8}$$

with

$$D(v) = \sum R(s_1)\cdots R(s_l)G(0)^{-1}, \tag{9}$$

where $R(s) = -G^{-1}(0)G(s)$ and the summation is over all $(s_1, \ldots, s_t)$ with each component in $\{1, \ldots, v\}$ and the sum of the components equal to v. This case will be relevant for our application to the Polish economy below.

4. Unitary Lags

In Nikaidô's (1962) lagged model, all production times are unity while fixed capital is absent. Formally, structural matrix (2) becomes

$$G_t(0) = I, \quad G_t(1) = -A_{t+1}(-1), \quad G_t(2) = G_t(3) = \cdots = 0. \tag{10}$$

Hence, in Proposition 1, $R_t(s) = 0$ for $s \geqq 2$, and, therefore, the summation in $D_t(v)$ is over $(1, \ldots, 1)$ with v components and over that only. Thus

$$\begin{aligned} D_t(v) &= R_t(1)\cdots R_{t+v-1}(1)G_{t+v}(0)^{-1} = [-G_t(1)]\cdots[-G_{t+v-1}(1)] \\ &= A_{t+1}(-1)\cdots A_{t+v}(-1) \end{aligned}$$

and

$$x(t) = z(t) + \sum_{v=1}^{\infty} A_{t+1}(-1)\cdots A_{t+v}(-1)z(t+v).$$

So far, the model is more general than Nikaidô's that assumes technical change away. Then A's subscripts may be dropped and one obtains

$$x(t) = \sum_{v=0}^{\infty} A(-1)^v z(t+v). \tag{12}$$

This agrees with the particular solution of Proposition 3 of Nikaidô (1962).

5. Instantaneous Production

In Leontief's (1970) dynamic model, there are neither production times nor investment lead times. Formally, structural matrix (2) becomes

$$\begin{aligned} G_t(0) &= I - A_t(0) + B_{t+1}(0), \\ G_t(1) &= -B_{t+1}(0), \\ G_t(2) &= G_t(3) = \cdots = 0. \end{aligned} \tag{13}$$

As in Section 4, the solution matrix of Proposition 1 can be specialized as follows:

$$\begin{aligned} D_t(v) &= R_t(1) \cdots R_{t+v-1}(1) G_{t+v}(0)^{-1} \\ &= R_t(1) \cdots R_{t+v-1}(1)[I - A_{t+v-1}(0) + B_{t+v-1}(0)]^{-1}, \end{aligned}$$

with

$$R_t(1) = -G_t(0)^{-1} G_t(1) = [I - A_t(0) + B_{t+1}(0)]^{-1} B_{t+1}(0).$$

This agrees with the typical element of Leontief's (1970) dynamic inverse. Recalling our general solution (6), we now obtain

$$\begin{aligned} x(t) = G_t(0)^{-1} z(t) + \sum_{v=1}^{\infty} D_t(v) z(t+v) &= [I - A_t(0) + B_{t+1}(0)]^{-1} z(t) \\ &+ \sum_{v=1}^{\infty} [I - A_t(0) + B_{t+1}(0)]^{-1}(0) \cdots [I - A_{t+v-1}(0) + B_{t+v}(0)]^{-1} \\ &\times B_{t+v}(0)[I - A_{t+v}(0) + B_{t+v+1}(0)]^{-1} z(t+v). \end{aligned} \tag{14}$$

Note that when $z(t) = 0$ for $t \neq$ some s, the solution reduces to

$$\begin{aligned} x(t) &= [I - A_t(0) + B_{t+1}(0)]^{-1}z(t) \\ &\quad + [I - A_t(0) + B_{t+1}(0)]^{-1}B_{t+1}(0) \\ &\quad \cdots [I - A_{s-1}(0) + B_s(0)]^{-1}B_s(0) \\ &\quad \times [I - A_s(0) + B_{s+1}(0)]^{-1}z(s) \end{aligned} \tag{15}$$

with the second term eliminated when $t \geqq s$. When a technical change is absent, the solution is further simplified to

$$\begin{aligned} x(t) &= [I - A(0) + B(0)]^{-1}z(t) \\ &\quad + \{[I - A(0) + B(0)]^{-1}B(0)\}^{s-t}[I - A(0) + B(0)]^{-1}z(s) \end{aligned} \tag{16}$$

with the second term eliminated when $t \geqq s$.

6. Computational Aspects

In general, the greatest lag, be it production time or investment lead time, is important. Recall that the lagged technical coefficients are collected in matrix $G_t(s)$ of (2), where s denotes the lag. Thus the general lag can be represented by

$$\sigma = \sup_{s,t}\{s \mid G_t(s) \neq 0\}. \tag{17}$$

The implication for the computational buildup of a typical element of the general solution, that is $D_t(v)$ of Proposition 1, is as follows:

Proposition 2. *$D_t(v)$ of Proposition 1 consists of one term if $\sigma = 1$. Otherwise, writing $v = s\sigma + k$ ($s = 0, 1, \ldots$ and $k = 1, \ldots, \sigma$), $D_t(v) = D_t(s\sigma + k)$ consists of $2^{k-s-1}\sum_{j=0}^{s}(-1)^j[((s-j)\sigma_j + k) + ((s-j)\sigma_{j-1} + k - 1)]2^{(s-j)(\sigma+1)}$ terms. Each term in $D_t(v)$ is the product of at most $n \times n$-matrices where n is the number of vectors.*

Proof. See the appendix. □

The unknown itself, output $x(t)$, is an infinite expansion of $D_t(v)$'s, as given by (6). The convergence of the series can be analyzed in the same manner as the dynamic inverse of Leontief (1970). Furthermore, eigensolutions of the homogeneous equation may arise just as in Nikaidô (1962). But basically our equation is a discretization of the distribution equation in ten Raa (1986) which has been analyzed in detail. This discretization error involved will be discussed now.

7. Time Unit

The time unit was chosen sufficiently small to facilitate the discretization of the material balance equation. Since this choice is clearly not unique, it is desirable to know the impact of variation of the time unit.

The model of instantaneous production of Section 5, that is Leontief's (1970) dynamic inverse, reveals the essence of the problem as it contains a single lag — representing investment requirements. Thus we consider the discrete input–output equation,

$$x_\tau(t) = A(0)x_\tau(t) + B_\tau(0)[x_\tau(t+\tau) - x_\tau(t)] + z(t), \tag{18}$$

where the subscript, τ, as well as same τ in the capacity term, refers to the unit of time in the following sense. To study the variation of the time unit, we must measure the unit with some objective yardstick which is fixed once and for all. Say this measurement is in years, then τ is the chosen time unit expressed in years and x_τ is the implied output rate, measured against the objective yardstick, that is quantity per year, for comparison with other x_τ's under the variation of τ. As is well known, the choice of time unit affects the capital matrix, unlike the flow matrix. B's subscript refers to this, not to technical change which is neglected in this section as it constitutes an independent problem.

The benchmark for our comparisons is the limiting case of the continuous input–output equation,

$$x(t) = A(0)x(t) + B(0)\dot{x}(t) + z(t). \tag{19}$$

The first equation (18), is a direct discretization of (19), provided that

$$B_\tau(0) = B(0)/\tau. \tag{20}$$

This is true indeed, as the dimensional argument of Leontief (1970) demonstrates.

As Wassily Leontief told me, the choice of the time unit is an aggregation issue. All output produced during a period of length τ by a sector is lumped together. This observation suggests a framework for the determination of the impact of the choice of the time unit, τ. We define the *bias distribution* as $x_\tau - x$. The total bias, or shortly *bias*, is defined as the bias distribution summed over time, interpreting x_τ as a step function. Note that we allow negative and positive parts of the bias distribution to cancel out. A zero (total) bias need not imply that the bias distribution vanishes everywhere on the time axis. It merely implies that the *total requirements* x_τ, summed over time, are equal in the discrete and the continuous cases.

By the linearity and absence of technical change, it suffices to determine the bias distribution associated with $z(t) = 0$ for $t \neq$ some s and $z_j(s)\tau^{-1}\delta_{i,j}$, where $j = 1, \ldots, n$ and $\delta_{i,j}$ is the Kronecker symbol, for $i = 1, \ldots, n$, the number of sectors. (In the continuous case, τ^{-1} is replaced by its limit, δ_s, the Dirac distribution concentrated at s.) In other words, we consider the n unit final demand vectors at time s as all having one quantity equal to one and the other quantities zero. By linearity, these final demand vectors can be handled simultaneously through the formal substitution of the matrix $\tau^{-1}I$ for $z(s)$ in the Eqs. (18) and (19). In the first discrete case, we thus obtain a *matrix* of output vectors $x_\tau(t)$, say $X_\tau(t)$. Similarly, the second continuous case will produce a *matrix* $X(t)$ of output vectors $x(t)$. The issue is to determine $X_\tau - X$ which summarizes the n elementary bias distributions, and its sum over time which summarizes the biases. The first proposition presents explicit expressions for X_τ and X. The second proposition concerns the bias itself.

Proposition 3. *Assume that $B(0)$ is invertible. Then*

$$X_\tau(t) = \{I + B(0)^{-1}[I - A(0)]\tau\}^{(t-s-\tau)/\tau} B(0)^{-1}$$

and $X(t) = \exp\{B(0)^{-1}[I - A(0)](t - s)\}B(0)^{-1}$, *both for $t \leqq s$ and both zero otherwise.*

Proof. See the appendix. □

Remarks 14.1. The assumption is inessential. If necessary, one can use the generalized inverse and decomposition device of ten Raa (1986). Moreover, ultimately we want the bias. The result will extend to singular $B(0)$ by the perturbation of such a matrix and a limiting argument.

Proposition 4. *The choice of the time unit is asymptotically pointwise unbiased in the sense that the bias distributions, $X_\tau - X$, tend to zero for vanishing τ. The total requirements, summed over time, of both X_τ and X equal $[I - A(0)]^{-1}$ so that, a fortiori, the biases are zero for all sectors and time units.*

Apparently, the time unit and even the capital matrix may be chosen arbitrarily as far as the total requirements, summed over time, are concerned. The choice merely affects the time scheduling of the required output levels, not their total amounts. Thus, we expect our study to be relevant for the timing of production which, of course, is not surprising in the context of a theory of distributed input–output. When the time unit is large, the economy need not produce capital shortly before the delivery of the final goods, but can even disinvest already; investment must be at an early stage. On the other hand, an economy with a small time unit can, relatively speaking, postpone investment.

It does not follow that the choice of the time unit and the capital matrix is immaterial for output matters other than timing. The capability to postpone investment required for a given bill of final goods is a positive one, not from a subjective time preference point of view, but in an objective sense. The capability to postpone adds growth potential. Thus, while the time unit is immaterial for the total requirements of a *given* bill of final goods, it does affect the class of admissible bills of final goods, that is the potence of the economy. The choice of a large time unit is biased in that it reduces the maximum growth rate.

Proposition 5. *The maximum growth rate, say g_τ, is inversely related to the time unit, τ.*

Proof. See the appendix. □

This section is completed with more philosophical musings on time. While the last proposition suggests that discretization yields a downward bias of the estimated maximum growth rate, it may also be that if the true world is discrete, and neat, continuous modelling will produce an upward bias. So far, the proposition bears on model selection. But there is more to it, as can be seen by considering two economies, one relatively continuous, with a small time unit, the other relatively discrete, with a large unit. Then the first economy is superior in that it can sustain higher growth rates. Thus, with a view to enhancing the potence of an economy, it makes sense to smooth investment. The improvement rests on the possibility of fine-tuning the productive capacity to the instantaneous output requirements. This should not be confused with the betterment of performance which can be strived for by the direct reduction of delays. The mere metering with a finer time unit has a more modest impact than the speeding up of production which severely affects the structure of the economy as we shall see in the next section.

8. The Dynamic Structure of the Polish Economy

The fully distributed input–output model (1), and its solution, (6) or (8), are now evaluated for the case of Poland, using input–output data of 1969. The purpose is to determine the direct and indirect requirements of the 1969 Polish final demand components. The requirements will be distributed over time, extending into the preceding years. The distributions will be presented in the form of plots.

Abstracting from technical change, central plans can be rationally drawn by the superposition of the requirements distributions, weighted by final demand target values. The 'total mass' of the distributions must be consistent with resource availability, while their time patterns dictate the scheduling of production in agreement with technical lags and interindustry links. In this first exercise, the economy is divided into 15 sectors only: (1) Fuel and Energy, (2) Metallurgy, (3) Machinery and Electrical Equipment, (4) Chemicals, (5) Stone, Clay and Glass Products, (6) Wood and Paper Products, (7) Textiles, Leather and Clothing, (8) Food Products, (9) Unspecified Manufactured Products, (10) Construction, (11) Agriculture, (12) Forestry, (13) Transport and Communication, (14) Trade, (15) Other Material Services. Following Czerwiński, Jurek, Panek and Sledziński (1980), the flow matrix, A, is instantaneous, while the stock matrix, B, is distributed over four years. $A(0)$, $B(0)$, $B(-1)$, $B(-2)$, and $B(-3)$, as defined in the introduction of the paper, are taken from the Central Statistical Office (1971) and Czerwinski, Guzik, Jurek, Panek, Runka and Sledziński (1982), respectively. To make this article self-contained, the matrices are reproduced in Table 1. The (i,j)th entry of $A(0)$ is the amount

Table 1: Flow Coefficient Matrix *A(0)* and Stock Matrix Distribution *B*.

A(0)	0.2470	0.1249	0.0224	0.0895	0.1051	0.0289	0.0129	0.0145	0.0192	0.0273	0.0139	0.0118	0.1137	0.0177	0.0678
	0.0062	0.6023	0.1887	0.0187	0.0400	0.0066	0.0012	0.0024	0.0100	0.0584	0.0011	0.0026	0.0100	0.0021	0.0349
	0.0590	0.0491	0.2933	0.0359	0.0666	0.0126	0.0147	0.0148	0.0393	0.1231	0.0159	0.0345	0.0894	0.0215	0.1579
	0.0171	0.0122	0.0433	0.2681	0.0300	0.0932	0.0904	0.0072	0.0288	0.0269	0.0374	0.0122	0.0213	0.0088	0.0380
	0.0119	0.0239	0.0095	0.0156	0.1189	0.0075	0.0007	0.0079	0.0036	0.1290	0.0011	0.0113	0.0071	0.0059	0.0355
	0.0177	0.0028	0.0154	0.0234	0.0380	0.2133	0.0087	0.0016	0.0300	0.0103	0.0007	0.0262	0.0082	0.0206	0.0366
	0.0112	0.0045	0.0109	0.0431	0.0182	0.0367	0.3604	0.0049	0.0242	0.0115	0.0328	0.0064	0.0118	0.0247	0.0137
	0.0005	0.0004	0.0009	0.0277	0.0011	0.0022	0.0160	0.1882	0.2973	0.0003	0.0143	0.0084	0.0017	0.0144	0.0002
	0.0008	0.0012	0.0048	0.0052	0.0033	0.0310	0.0080	0.0069	0.1707	0.0033	0.0283	0.0012	0.0029	0.0094	0.0248
	0.0259	0.0092	0.0036	0.0040	0.0128	0.0038	0.0021	0.0034	0.0038	0.0257	0.0062	0.0247	0.0064	0.0134	0.0217
	0.0001	0.0001	0.0001	0.0057	0.0007	0.0018	0.0651	0.3634	0.1355	0.0013	0.4482	0.0108	0.0026	0.0163	0.0119
	0.0001	0.0009	0.0003	0.0175	0.0019	0.1817	0.0005	0.0009	0.0007	0.0037	0.0002	0.0200	0.0006	0.0001	0.0002
	0.0631	0.0182	0.0177	0.0273	0.0790	0.0300	0.0097	0.0228	0.0249	0.0902	0.0007	0.1115	0.0481	0.1223	0.0164
	0.0049	0.0169	0.0117	0.0109	0.0114	0.0138	0.0050	0.0649	0.0199	0.0173	0.0151	0.0044	0.0179	0.0071	0.0135
	0.0015	0.0009	0.0021	0.0013	0.0035	0.0010	0.0008	0.0016	0.0021	0.0007	0.0248	0.0032	0.0056	0.0039	0.0111
B(0)	0.0000	0.0000	0.0000	0.0000	0.0000	0.0000	0.0000	0.0000	0.0000	0.0000	0.0000	0.0000	0.0000	0.0000	0.0000
	0.0000	0.0000	0.0000	0.0000	0.0000	0.0000	0.0000	0.0000	0.0000	0.0000	0.0000	0.0000	0.0000	0.0000	0.0000
	0.2542	0.1763	0.1537	0.4777	0.4219	0.4365	0.2359	0.1650	0.0995	0.4024	0.4474	0.6972	0.1892	0.2089	0.8083
	0.0000	0.0000	0.0000	0.0000	0.0000	0.0000	0.0000	0.0000	0.0000	0.0000	0.0000	0.0000	0.0000	0.0000	0.0000
	0.0000	0.0000	0.0000	0.0000	0.0000	0.0000	0.0000	0.0000	0.0000	0.0000	0.0000	0.0000	0.0000	0.0000	0.0000
	0.0005	0.0003	0.0006	0.0014	0.0022	0.0016	0.0006	0.0010	0.0004	0.0005	0.0114	0.0138	0.0112	0.0020	0.0044
	0.0000	0.0000	0.0000	0.0000	0.0000	0.0000	0.0000	0.0000	0.0000	0.0000	0.0000	0.0000	0.0000	0.0000	0.0000
	0.0000	0.0000	0.0000	0.0000	0.0000	0.0000	0.0000	0.0000	0.0000	0.0000	0.0000	0.0000	0.0000	0.0000	0.0000
	0.0000	0.0000	0.0000	0.0000	0.0000	0.0000	0.0000	0.0000	0.0000	0.0000	0.0000	0.0000	0.0000	0.0000	0.0000
	0.2469	0.1353	0.0456	0.1228	0.2228	0.0949	0.0291	0.0398	0.0248	0.0075	0.3117	0.4359	0.0000	0.0980	0.9537
	0.0000	0.0000	0.0000	0.0000	0.0000	0.0000	0.0000	0.0000	0.0000	0.0000	0.0079	0.0000	0.0000	0.0000	0.0000
	0.0000	0.0000	0.0000	0.0000	0.0000	0.0000	0.0000	0.0000	0.0000	0.0000	0.0000	0.0000	0.0000	0.0000	0.0000
	0.0006	0.0007	0.0004	0.0026	0.0016	0.0012	0.0005	0.0004	0.0003	0.0009	0.0021	0.0022	0.0018	0.0021	0.0018
	0.0050	0.0035	0.0030	0.0086	0.0079	0.0092	0.0046	0.0030	0.0019	0.0089	0.0091	0.0140	0.0233	0.0037	0.0097
	0.0000	0.0000	0.0000	0.0000	0.0000	0.0000	0.0000	0.0000	0.0000	0.0000	0.0000	0.0000	0.0000	0.0000	0.0000

(Continued)

Table 1: (*Continued*)

$B(-1)$	0.0000	0.0000	0.0000	0.0000	0.0000	0.0000	0.0000	0.0000	0.0000	0.0000	0.0000	0.0000	0.0000	0.0000	0.0000
	0.0000	0.0000	0.0000	0.0000	0.0000	0.0000	0.0000	0.0000	0.0000	0.0000	0.0000	0.0000	0.0000	0.0000	0.0000
	0.1963	0.1651	0.0998	0.0989	0.2993	0.3282	0.0740	0.1034	0.0571	0.0451	0.2132	0.4969	0.6475	0.0673	0.6961
	0.0000	0.0000	0.0000	0.0000	0.0000	0.0000	0.0000	0.0000	0.0000	0.0000	0.0000	0.0000	0.0000	0.0000	0.0000
	0.0000	0.0000	0.0000	0.0000	0.0000	0.0000	0.0000	0.0000	0.0000	0.0000	0.0000	0.0000	0.0000	0.0000	0.0000
	0.0004	0.0003	0.0004	0.0003	0.0015	0.0012	0.0002	0.0006	0.0002	0.0001	0.0054	0.0098	0.0061	0.0006	0.0037
	0.0000	0.0000	0.0000	0.0000	0.0000	0.0000	0.0000	0.0000	0.0000	0.0000	0.0000	0.0000	0.0000	0.0000	0.0000
	0.0000	0.0000	0.0000	0.0000	0.0000	0.0000	0.0000	0.0000	0.0000	0.0000	0.0000	0.0000	0.0000	0.0000	0.0000
	0.0000	0.0000	0.0000	0.0000	0.0000	0.0000	0.0000	0.0000	0.0000	0.0000	0.0000	0.0000	0.0000	0.0000	0.0000
	0.9274	0.5108	0.1680	0.4518	0.8278	0.3636	0.1091	0.1523	0.0885	0.1840	0.9802	0.9826	0.7613	0.4583	0.8213
	0.0000	0.0000	0.0000	0.0000	0.0000	0.0000	0.0000	0.0000	0.0000	0.0000	0.0000	0.0000	0.0000	0.0000	0.0000
	0.0000	0.0000	0.0000	0.0000	0.0000	0.0000	0.0000	0.0000	0.0000	0.0000	0.0000	0.0000	0.0000	0.0000	0.0000
	0.0005	0.0006	0.0002	0.0005	0.0011	0.0009	0.0002	0.0003	0.0002	0.0000	0.0010	0.0016	0.0010	0.0007	0.0016
	0.0038	0.0032	0.0020	0.0018	0.0056	0.0069	0.0015	0.0019	0.0011	0.0011	0.0044	0.0100	0.0127	0.0012	0.0084
	0.0000	0.0000	0.0000	0.0000	0.0000	0.0000	0.0000	0.0000	0.0000	0.0000	0.0000	0.0000	0.0000	0.0000	0.0000
$B(-2)$	0.0000	0.0000	0.0000	0.0000	0.0000	0.0000	0.0000	0.0000	0.0000	0.0000	0.0000	0.0000	0.0000	0.0000	0.0000
	0.0000	0.0000	0.0000	0.0000	0.0000	0.0000	0.0000	0.0000	0.0000	0.0000	0.0000	0.0000	0.0000	0.0000	0.0000
	0.1516	0.1546	0.0422	0.0204	0.2123	0.0000	0.0231	0.0000	0.0000	0.0000	0.0000	0.3543	0.3527	0.0000	0.0000
	0.0000	0.0000	0.0000	0.0000	0.0000	0.0000	0.0000	0.0000	0.0000	0.0000	0.0000	0.0000	0.0000	0.0000	0.0000
	0.0000	0.0000	0.0000	0.0000	0.0000	0.0000	0.0000	0.0000	0.0000	0.0000	0.0000	0.0000	0.0000	0.0000	0.0000
	0.0003	0.0003	0.0003	0.0001	0.0011	0.0000	0.0001	0.0000	0.0000	0.0000	0.0000	0.0070	0.0033	0.0000	0.0000
	0.0000	0.0000	0.0000	0.0000	0.0000	0.0000	0.0000	0.0000	0.0000	0.0000	0.0000	0.0000	0.0000	0.0000	0.0000
	0.0000	0.0000	0.0000	0.0000	0.0000	0.0000	0.0000	0.0000	0.0000	0.0000	0.0000	0.0000	0.0000	0.0000	0.0000
	0.0000	0.0000	0.0000	0.0000	0.0000	0.0000	0.0000	0.0000	0.0000	0.0000	0.0000	0.0000	0.0000	0.0000	0.0000
	0.2760	0.1537	0.0493	0.1325	0.2512	0.1110	0.0326	0.0465	0.0251	0.0000	0.0000	0.5205	0.3136	0.0000	0.0000
	0.0000	0.0000	0.0000	0.0000	0.0000	0.0000	0.0000	0.0000	0.0000	0.0000	0.0000	0.0000	0.0000	0.0000	0.0000
	0.0000	0.0000	0.0000	0.0000	0.0000	0.0000	0.0000	0.0000	0.0000	0.0000	0.0000	0.0000	0.0000	0.0000	0.0000
	0.0004	0.0006	0.0001	0.0001	0.0008	0.0000	0.0000	0.0000	0.0000	0.0000	0.0000	0.0011	0.0005	0.0000	0.0000
	0.0030	0.0030	0.0013	0.0004	0.0040	0.0000	0.0004	0.0000	0.0000	0.0000	0.0000	0.0071	0.0069	0.0000	0.0000
	0.0000	0.0000	0.0000	0.0000	0.0000	0.0000	0.0000	0.0000	0.0000	0.0000	0.0000	0.0000	0.0000	0.0000	0.0000

(*Continued*)

Table 1: (Continued)

$B(-3)$	0.0000	0.0000	0.0000	0.0000	0.0000	0.0000	0.0000	0.0000	0.0000	0.0000	0.0000	0.0000	0.0000
	0.0000	0.0000	0.0000	0.0000	0.0000	0.0000	0.0000	0.0000	0.0000	0.0000	0.0000	0.0000	0.0000
	0.1171	0.0000	0.0000	0.0000	0.0000	0.0000	0.0000	0.0000	0.0000	0.0000	0.0000	0.0000	0.0000
	0.0000	0.0000	0.0000	0.0000	0.0000	0.0000	0.0000	0.0000	0.0000	0.0000	0.0000	0.0000	0.0000
	0.0000	0.0000	0.0000	0.0000	0.0000	0.0000	0.0000	0.0000	0.0000	0.0000	0.0000	0.0000	0.0000
	0.0002	0.0000	0.0002	0.0000	0.0000	0.0000	0.0000	0.0000	0.0000	0.0000	0.0000	0.0000	0.0000
	0.0000	0.0000	0.0000	0.0000	0.0000	0.0000	0.0000	0.0000	0.0000	0.0000	0.0000	0.0000	0.0000
	0.0000	0.0000	0.0000	0.0000	0.0000	0.0000	0.0000	0.0000	0.0000	0.0000	0.0000	0.0000	0.0000
	0.0000	0.0000	0.0000	0.0000	0.0000	0.0000	0.0000	0.0000	0.0000	0.0000	0.0000	0.0000	0.0000
	0.0049	0.0027	0.0008	0.0020	0.0045	0.0018	0.0005	0.0007	0.0004	0.0000	0.0000	0.0000	0.0000
	0.0000	0.0000	0.0000	0.0000	0.0000	0.0000	0.0000	0.0000	0.0000	0.0000	0.0000	0.0000	0.0000
	0.0000	0.0000	0.0000	0.0000	0.0000	0.0000	0.0000	0.0000	0.0000	0.0000	0.0000	0.0000	0.0000
	0.0003	0.0000	0.0001	0.0000	0.0000	0.0000	0.0000	0.0000	0.0000	0.0000	0.0000	0.0000	0.0000
	0.0023	0.0000	0.0008	0.0000	0.0000	0.0000	0.0000	0.0000	0.0000	0.0000	0.0000	0.0000	0.0000
	0.0000	0.0000	0.0000	0.0000	0.0000	0.0000	0.0000	0.0000	0.0000	0.0000	0.0000	0.0000	0.0000

of flow i needed per unit of j. The (i,j)th entry of say $B(-2)$ is the quantity of i to be invested in sector j, two years prior to a unit of capacity expansion. Since the model is linear, it suffices to consider the 15 unit final demand vectors, $z(0)$, with one component unity and the others zero. For each final demand vector, we have computed the sectoral total requirements distributions, summed up by vectors $x(t), t = 0, -1, -2, \ldots$, not by the direct evaluation of solution (6), but by going through its derivation, that is the proof of Proposition 1. Since there are 15 sectors, the output consists of $15 \times 15 = 275$ unit requirement plots. To save space, we have selected ten plots, representing the requirements of the two typical investment sectors, (3) (Machinery and Electrical Equipment) and (10) (Construction), for the five typical final demand sectors, (3), (7), (8), (11) and (14). Sectors were classified on the basis of 1969 investment/- and consumption/output ratios. Figure 1 displays the investment sector requirements for final demand sector (3), Fig. 2 for sector (7), Fig. 3 for sector (8), Fig. 4 for sector (11), and Fig. 5 for final demand sector (14). Throughout the paper, final demand excludes investment which is endogenized in our model.

Let us explain one plot in detail. Figure 1 shows the output requirements of sector (10) (Construction) for the final delivery of one unit of good 3 (Machinery and Electrical Equipment) in zlotys per zlotys. (The continuous graph is relevant, the dashed one will be explained below.) Thus, if it is decided to increase exports of Machinery and Electrical Equipment at some future year, say 1990, the Fig. 1 presents the required change in Construction. The level of construction must be adjusted practically six years in advance, that is 1984, to observe investment lead times and interindustry balances. Negative adjustment values, notably in the year prior to final delivery, represent output reduction quantities which are compensated by Construction stock releases in the Machinery and Electrical Equipment or its supply sectors. This familiar disinvestment emerges in the context of interrupted demand, here as well as in Leontief (1970). We have found additional disinvestment three years before final delivery. This is a consequence of the temporal distribution of capital construction. In the absence of future demand, initial capital layers are released at intermediate stages of production.

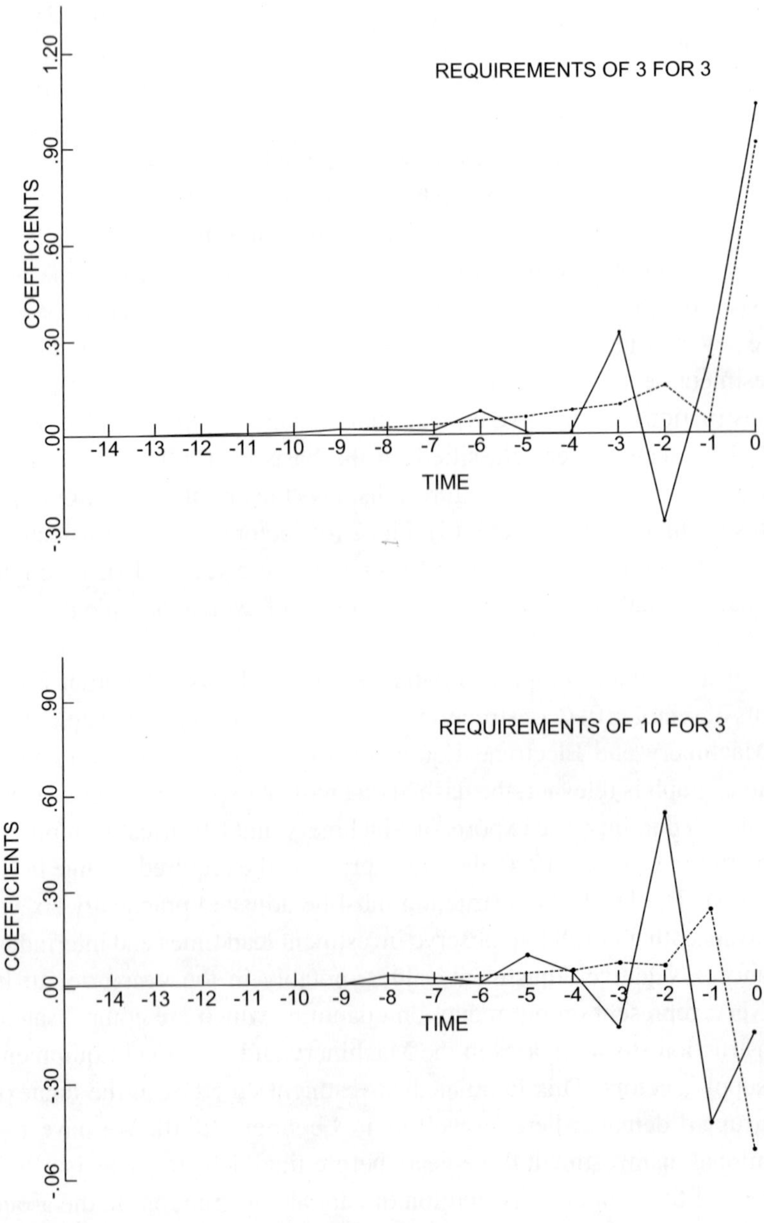
REQUIREMENTS OF 3 FOR 3
COEFFICIENTS
1.20
.90
.60
.30
.00
-.30
-14 -13 -12 -11 -10 -9 -8 -7 -6 -5 -4 -3 -2 -1 0
TIME
REQUIREMENTS OF 10 FOR 3
COEFFICIENTS
.90
.60
.30
.00
-.30
-.06
-14 -13 -12 -11 -10 -9 -8 -7 -6 -5 -4 -3 -2 -1 0
TIME

Fig. 1:

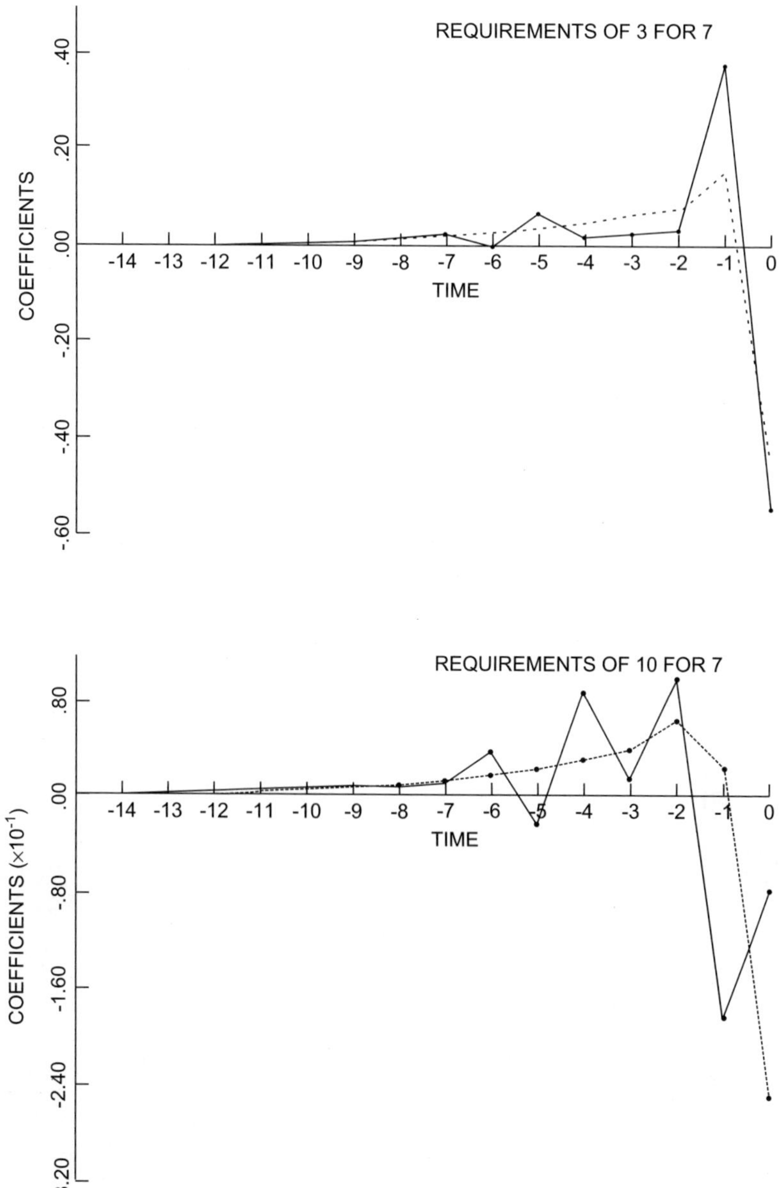
REQUIREMENTS OF 3 FOR 7
COEFFICIENTS
.40
.20
.00
-.20
-.40
-.60
-14 -13 -12 -11 -10 -9 -8 -7 -6 -5 -4 -3 -2 -1 0
TIME
REQUIREMENTS OF 10 FOR 7
COEFFICIENTS (×10⁻¹)
.80
.00
-.80
-1.60
-2.40
-3.20
-14 -13 -12 -11 -10 -9 -8 -7 -6 -5 -4 -3 -2 -1 0
TIME

Fig. 2:

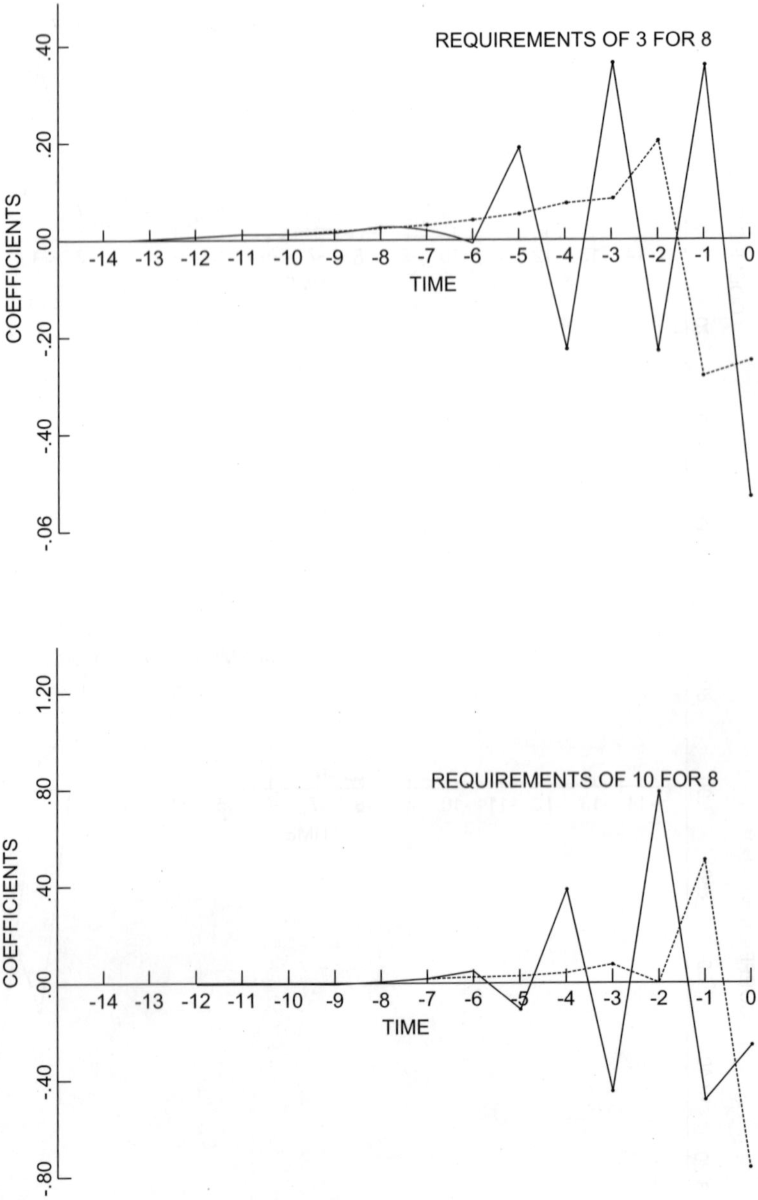
REQUIREMENTS OF 3 FOR 8
COEFFICIENTS
.40
.20
.00
-.20
-.40
-.06
-14 -13 -12 -11 -10 -9 -8 -7 -6 -5 -4 -3 -2 -1 0
TIME
REQUIREMENTS OF 10 FOR 8
COEFFICIENTS
1.20
.80
.40
.00
-.40
-.80
-14 -13 -12 -11 -10 -9 -8 -7 -6 -5 -4 -3 -2 -1 0
TIME

Fig. 3:

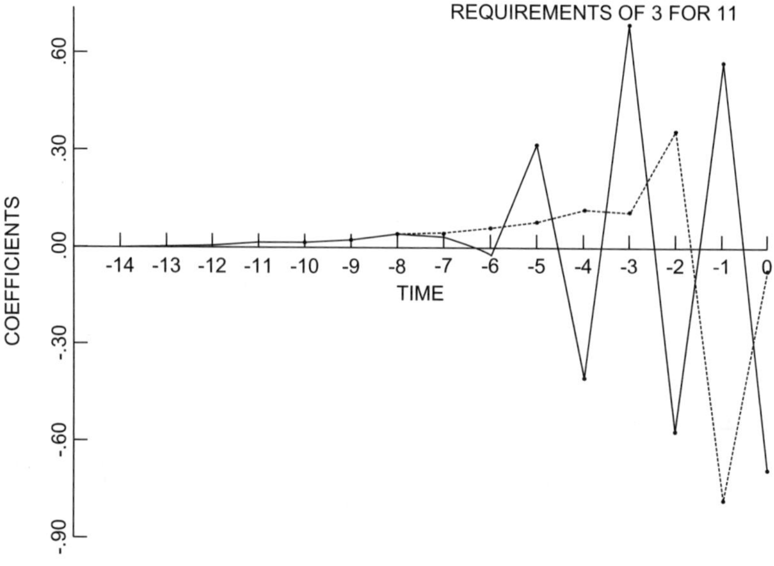
REQUIREMENTS OF 3 FOR 11
COEFFICIENTS
.60
.30
.00
-.30
-.60
-.90
-14 -13 -12 -11 -10 -9 -8 -7 -6 -5 -4 -3 -2 -1 0
TIME

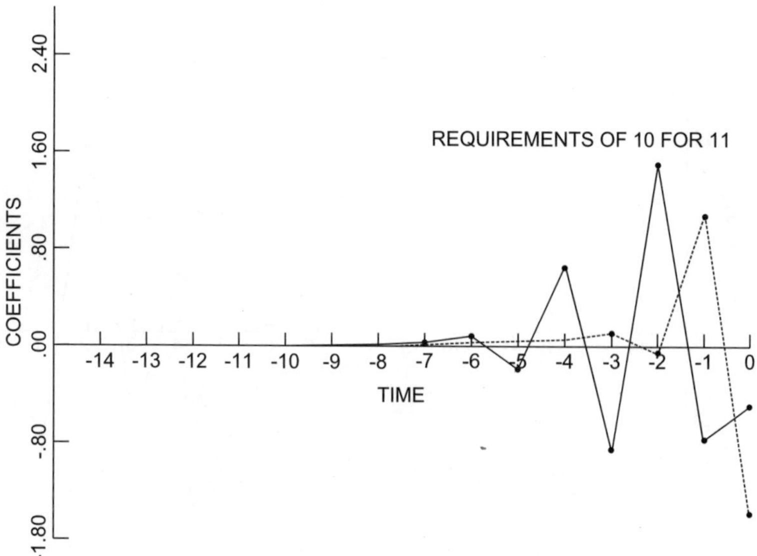
REQUIREMENTS OF 10 FOR 11
COEFFICIENTS
2.40
1.60
.80
.00
-.80
-1.80
-14 -13 -12 -11 -10 -9 -8 -7 -6 -5 -4 -3 -2 -1 0
TIME

Fig. 4:

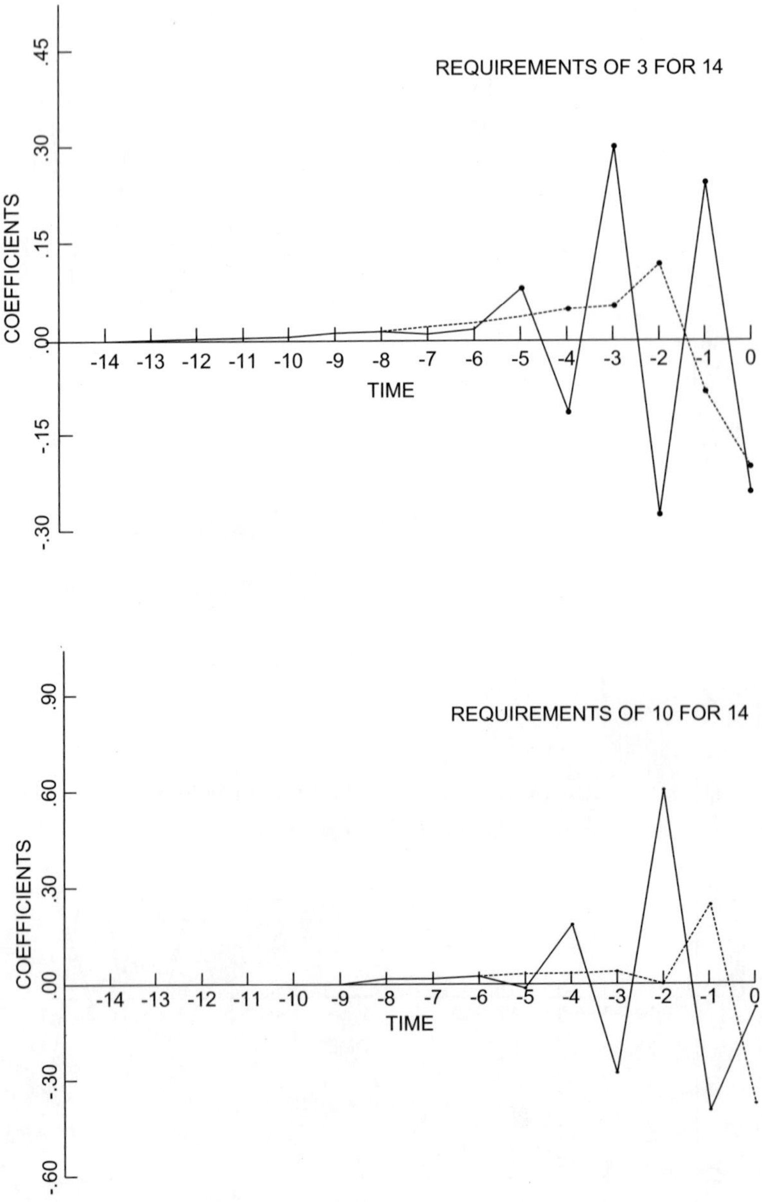
REQUIREMENTS OF 3 FOR 14
COEFFICIENTS
.45
.30
.15
.00
-.15
-.30
-14 -13 -12 -11 -10 -9 -8 -7 -6 -5 -4 -3 -2 -1 0
TIME
REQUIREMENTS OF 10 FOR 14
COEFFICIENTS
.90
.60
.30
.00
-.30
-.60
-14 -13 -12 -11 -10 -9 -8 -7 -6 -5 -4 -3 -2 -1 0
TIME

Fig. 5:

Disinvestments make a cyclical pattern of direct and indirect requirements, even though the investment coefficients themselves are smoothly distributed. This is caused by the interindustry interplay of the investment distributions. Especially Construction [sector (10)] undergoes wild cycles in the fulfillment of final demand components. These business cycles are purely technical, independent of investor behaviour. Their existence restrains the power of the price system to clear markets on the basis of current supply and demand conditions, and calls for some conscious timing of sectoral activities in the course of plan fulfillment.

While Figs. 1–5 display the requirements of Machinery and Electrical Equipment (sector 3) for various separate sectors of final demand, they can be combined to obtain the total Machinery and Electrical Equipment requirements for the 1969 final demand vector. Each plot is blown up by a factor equal to the receiving final demand component and then they are added. The results are displayed in Figs. 6–13 for all productive sectors and, in particular, in Fig. 7 for sector (3).

The noted fluctuations at the sector-to-sector level do not wash out when the requirement distributions are aggregated by final demand sectors. To fulfill aggregated final demand of 1969, Construction (sector 10) started around 1960 in the absence of productive capacities left over from before the 1969 final demand fulfillment, as depicted in Fig. 10. The cyclical path demonstrates that the price system problems with market clearance do not cancel out at the economy level. Their persistence underscores the need for some planning, although two problems must be acknowledged. The referee rightly noted that planning is difficult in the sense that business cycles in the final demand have to be forecasted and that it may be a recipe worse than the cure. Planning in centrally planned economies such as Poland until now managed to create a strong investment cycle: investment boom in the starting years and investment stagnation at the end of the five-year periods. The intelligent use of the distributed dynamic inverse of this article may muffle the cycle, but, due to the first complication, not to the extent of complete elimination.

The investment–disinvestment accelerator effects are dramatic in sectors (3), (10) and (13), typical capital industries, but also present in sectors (1), (2), (5) and (12), which are typical intermediate goods producers. (See Figs. 7, 10 and 12, and Figs. 6, 8 and 11, respectively.) Total

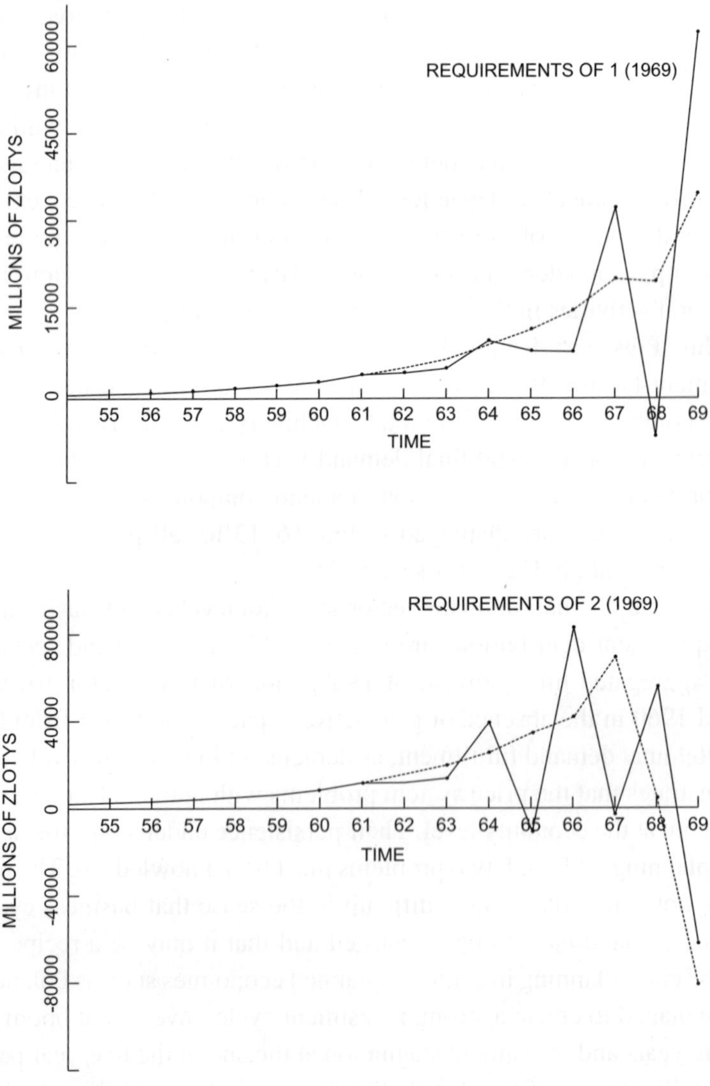

Fig. 6:

requirement distributions tell a better story about the role of sectors in the economy than the direct input–output coefficients. On the other end of the spectrum, we have the typical final consumption sectors (8) (Food Products), (7) (Textiles, Leather and Clothing), and (11) (Agriculture)

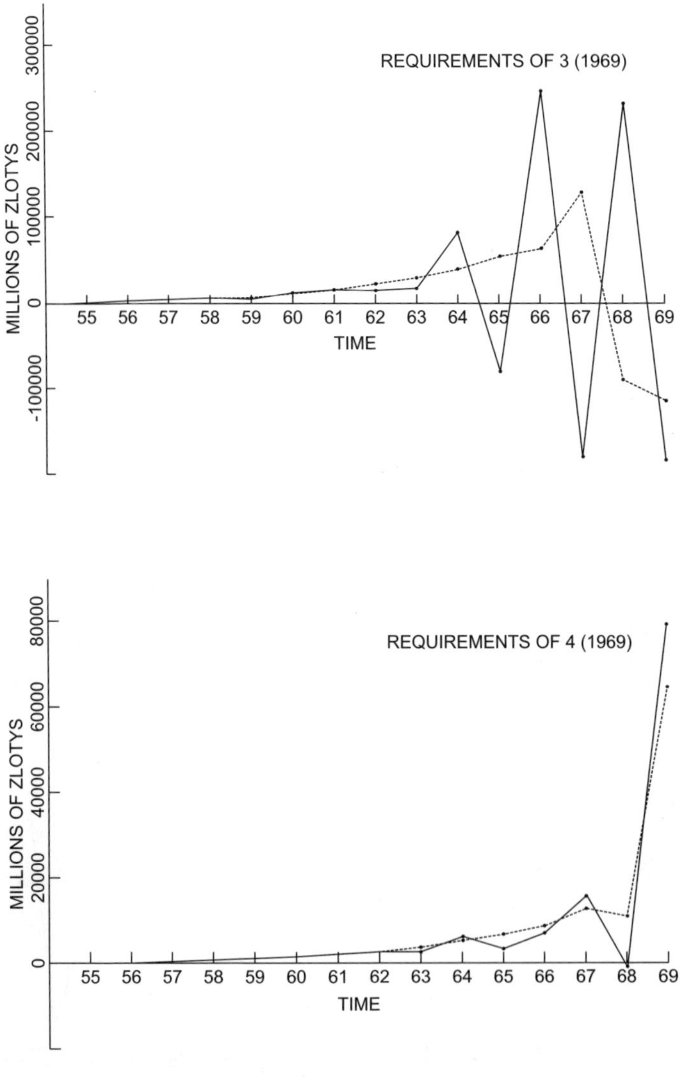

Fig. 7:

which can postpone production practically till the year of final delivery, even when the direct and indirect requirements are taken into account. (See Figs. 9 and 11.)

When the final demand of 1969 is appropriately embedded in a sequence of similar vectors for the surrounding years, the cycles of the magnitude in the discussed 1969 requirements figures wash out in summing up to the

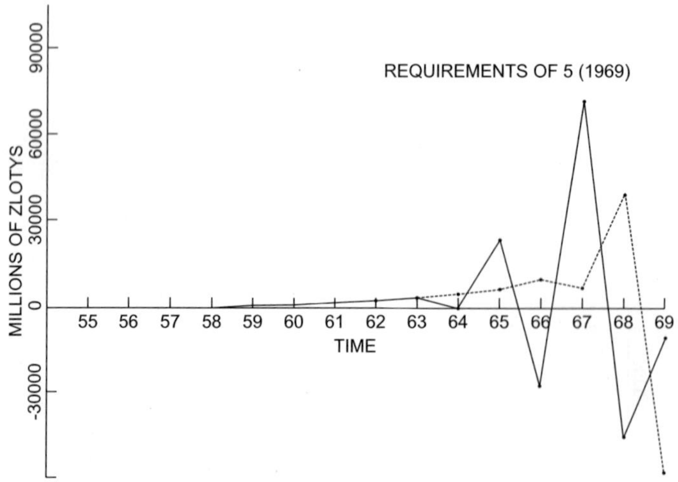

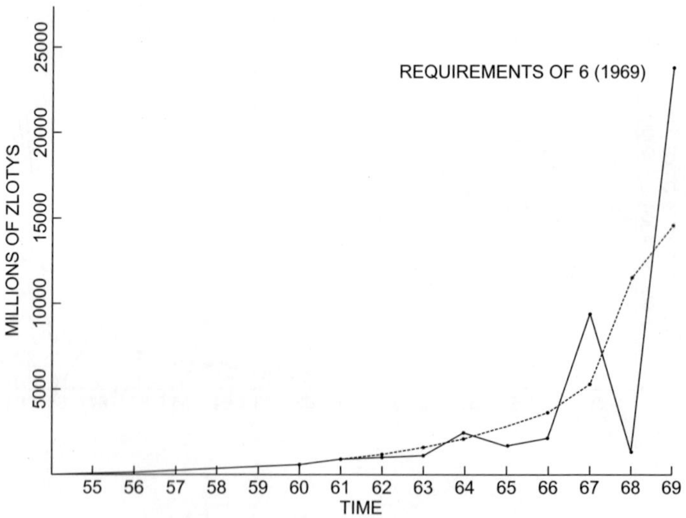

Fig. 8:

overall development of the economy. The *increases* of final demand produce cycles of smaller order. These minor cycles, as argued in Section 2, have the same shape as the ones discussed so far. Thus, the irregularities in the sectoral pattern of the final demand increases generate oscillations about the

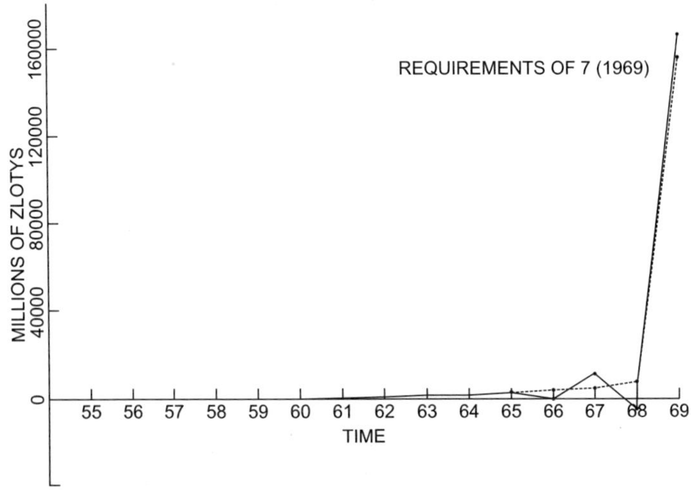

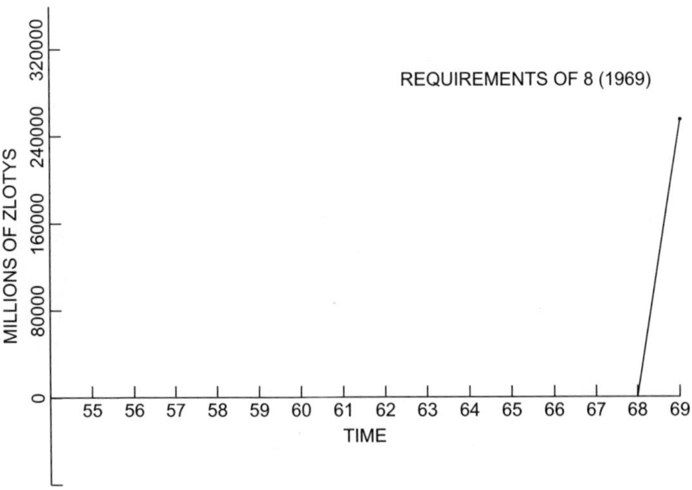

Fig. 9:

overall development of the economy. The referee has correctly conjectured that even these oscillations could very well be smoothed out by the structure of the irregularities of the final demand increases since the latter include inventory investments caused by delays in the fulfillment of investment

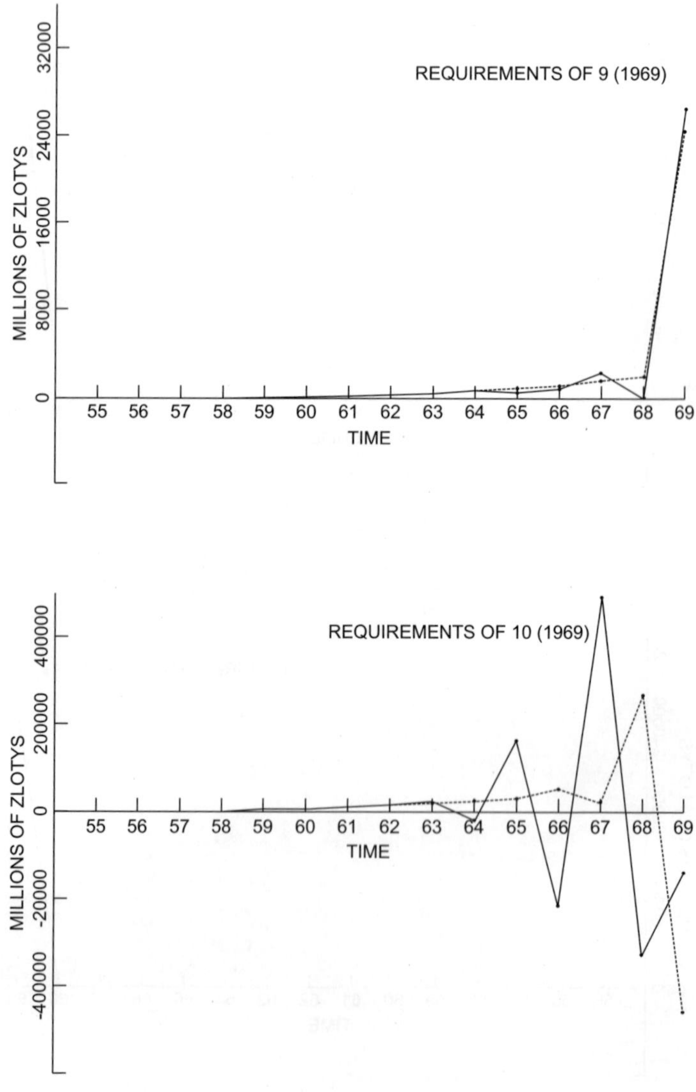

Fig. 10:

plans. It should be mentioned though that this smoothing-out is no virtue. Efficient planning of sectoral outputs entails variations that precisely match the exogenous increases of final demand. Smoothing, especially through

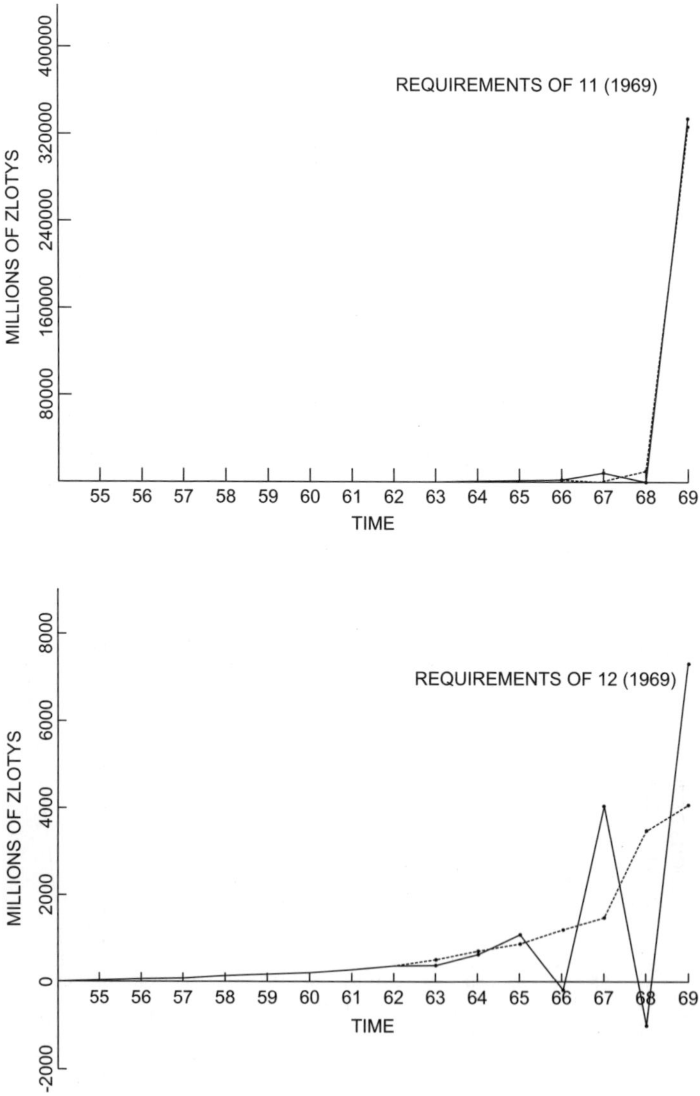

Fig. 11:

filling final demand with inventory investment, is a form of overinvestment that keeps the economy beyond its true production possibilities.

While the analysis of the distributed structure of the economy is appealing both theoretically and empirically, it remains to be seen if the

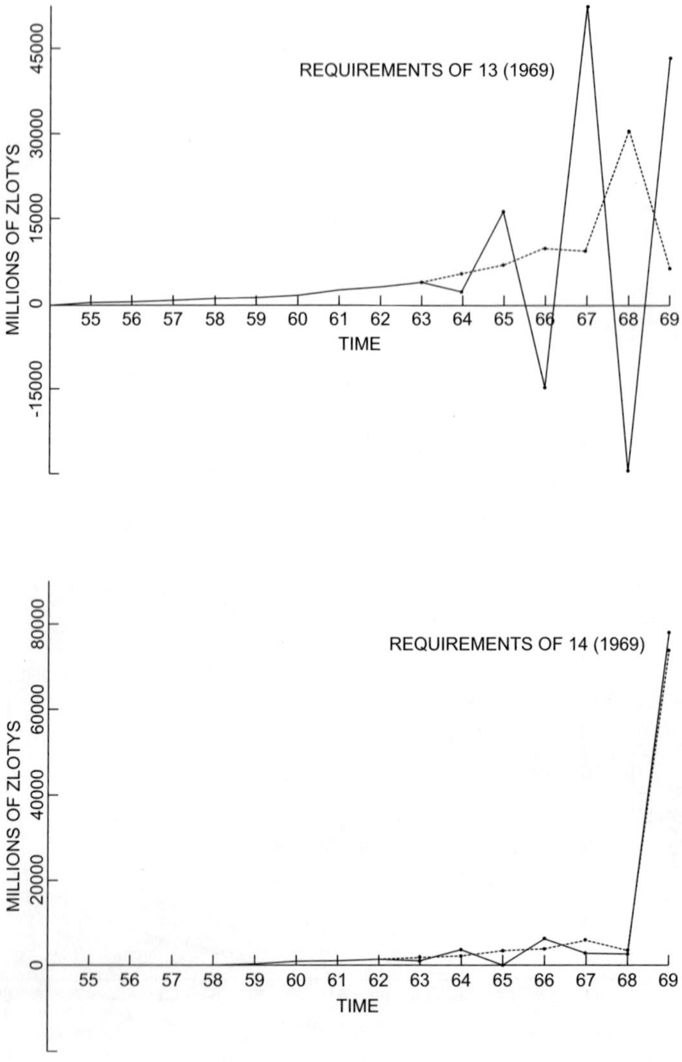

Fig. 12:

whole exercise is worthwhile on pure pragmatic grounds. In other words, do the results deviate significantly from the classical input–output analysis, without distributed activities? For comparison, we have performed all the computations for the non-distributed case too with $B(-1)$, $B(-2)$, and $B(-3)$ suppressed and $B(0)$ equal to the standard capital matrix of

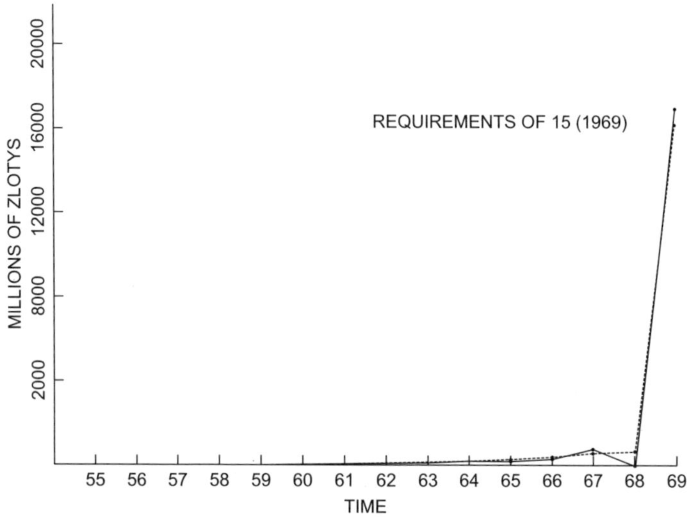

Fig. 13:

Czerwiński *et al.* (1980). This matrix is reproduced in Table 2. It should be mentioned that the nondistributed matrix is not obtained by the simple aggregation of the distribution ones, but is a little bigger. If one neglects lags, then inputs are divided by current rather than future outputs or rates of change. But since current rates are relatively small, at least for a growing economy, the nondistributed coefficients must be relatively big. The classical input–output results are indicated by the dashed graphs in Figs. 1–13. The comparison shows that investment distributions are responsible for great differences which, however, can be qualified. A careful inspection reveals that the requirements based on distribution activities (the continuous graphs) fluctuate around the classical requirements (the dashed graphs). The differences fluctuate quite evenly in the sense that over- and undershootings are balanced. This finding confirms Proposition 4 by which the total requirements, summed over time, are independent of the investment distribution B. [It is easy to see that Proposition 4 extends to stock coefficients, B, with finite total mass by the partial differentiation and Neumann series arguments of ten Raa (1986).]

An indirect test of distributed versus classical input–output is possible by looking at the typical final consumption sectors (8), (7), and (11). Since

Table 2: Investment Matrix $\bar{B}$.

Supplier sector	Recipient sector: Fuel and energy	Metallurgy	Machinery and electrical equipment	Chemicals	Stone, clay and glass products	Wood and paper products	Textiles, leather clothing	Food products	Unspecified manufactured products	Construction	Agriculture	Forestry	Transport and communication	Trade	Other material services
Fuel and energy	0	0	0	0	0	0	0	0	0	0	0	0	0	0	0
Metallurgy	0	0	0	0	0	0	0	0	0	0	0	0	0	0	0
Machinery and electrical equipment	0.7877	0.5289	0.3963	0.6108	0.9855	0.7820	0.3421	0.2740	0.1641	0.4511	0.6714	1.5710	2.2991	0.2811	1.6165
Chemicals	0	0	0	0	0	0	0	0	0	0	0	0	0	0	0
Stone, clay and glass products	0	0	0	0	0	0	0	0	0	0	0	0	0	0	0
Wood and paper products	0.015	0.0009	0.0016	0.0018	0.0051	0.0028	0.0009	0.0016	0.0007	0.0006	0.0171	0.0310	0.0217	0.0027	0.0087
Textiles, leather and clothing	0	0	0	0	0	0	0	0	0	0	0	0	0	0	0
Food products	0	0	0	0	0	0	0	0	0	0	0	0	0	0	0

(Continued)

Table 2: (*Continued*)

Supplier sector	Recipient sector														
	Fuel and energy	Metallurgy	Machinery and electrical equipment	Chemicals	Stone, clay and glass products	Wood and paper products	Textiles, leather clothing	Food products	Unspecified manufactured products	Construction	Agriculture	Forestry	Transport and communication	Trade	Other material services
Unspecified manufactured products	0	0	0	0	0	0	0	0	0	0	0	0	0	0	0
Construction	1.5688	0.8594	0.2899	0.7802	1.4131	0.6029	0.1846	0.2526	0.1573	0.2078	1.3411	1.9796	1.1872	0.5890	1.9074
Agriculture	0	0	0	0	0	0	0	0	0	0	0.0118	0	0	0	0
Forestry	0	0	0	0	0	0	0	0	0	0	0	0	0	0	0
Transport and communication	0.0019	0.0021	0.0010	0.0033	0.0037	0.0021	0.0008	0.0007	0.0005	0.0010	0.0032	0.0050	0.0036	0.0029	0.0037
Trade	0.0155	0.0104	0.0078	0.0110	0.0185	0.0164	0.0067	0.0050	0.0032	0.0088	0.0137	0.0315	0.0450	0.0050	0.0194
Other material services	0	0	0	0	0	0	0	0	0	0	0	0	0	0	0

their total requirements do not extend into the past (see Fig. 3), future final demand does not add to the 1969 requirements which consequently must closely agree with actual output of those sectors in 1969. This is true of our results, but less so of the classical, nondistributed ones. For example, 1969 Food Products (sector 8) and Textiles, Leather and Clothing (sector 7) produced 256,986 and 168,639 millions zlotys of output, respectively, which is closely approximated by our results (257,500 and 166,260), but less so by classical input–output (255,600 and 156,900).

The other sectors, capital industries and intermediate goods producers, show more significant absolute requirements differences when investment lead times are taken into account. Thus, distributed input–output merits attention and is especially useful for the proper time scheduling of production.

9. Conclusion

The theory of dynamic input–output analysis with distributed activities lends itself to discretization and then generalizes existing dynamic input–output models by facilitating stock and flow input profiles without preempting empirical applications. Direct and indirect requirements for the Polish final demand vector of 1969 based on investment distributions fluctuate dramatically around classical results that ignore the time structure of production. The generalized inverse that summarizes the requirements is a central planning tool for proper time scheduling of production.

The results are sensitive with respect to the distributions of economic activities. Direct information on production and investment lead times at the level of input–output data collection is called for, especially since present research suggests that statistical inference is a poor substitute due to the presence of multicollinearities.

Acknowledgement

The assistance of Henk Gravesteijn was crucial. Zbigniew Czerwiński and Jan Pakulski kindly supplied Polish input–output information. René de Koster detected some errors in the first draft. An anonymous referee provided useful comments. The support of the Netherlands Organization for the Advancement of Pure Research (Z.W.O.) is gratefully acknowledged.

References

Bernstein, L. (1971) *The Jacobi–Perron–Algorithm: Its Theory and Application* (Springer Lecture Notes in Mathematics 207).

Bródy, A. (1965) *The Model of Expanding Reproduction, Applications of Mathematics to Economics* (Akademiai Kiado, Budapest) pp. 61–63.

Bródy, A. (1974) *Proportions, Prices and Planning* (Akademiai Kiadò, Budapest and North-Holland, Amsterdam).

Central Statistical Office (1971) *Statistical Year Book* (Warsaw), pp. 142–143.

Czerwiński, Z., W. Jurek, E. Panek and W. Sledzinski (1980) On the application of the dynamic Leontief model in planning, *Oeconomica Polona*, 4, pp. 469–487.

Czerwiński, Z., B. Guzik, W. Jurek, E. Panek, H. Runka and W. Sledzinski (1982) *Modelling and Planning for Growth of the National Economy* (Polish Scientific Publishers, Warsaw), pp. 148 and 162–163.

Gladyshevskii, A.I. and G.K. Belous (1978) Microeconomic calculations of distributed lags in capital construction, *Matekon*, 14, pp. 58–79.

Johansen, L. On the theory of dynamic input–output models with different time profiles of capital construction and finite life-time of capital equipment, *Journal of Economic Theory*, 19, pp. 513–533.

Kigyóssy-Schmidt, E. and R. Schwarz (1983) *Nichtmaterielle leistungen* (Akademie, Berlin).

Leontief, W. (1970) *The Dynamic Inverse*, in: A.P. Carter and A. Bródy, eds., Contributions to input–output analysis (North-Holland, Amsterdam-London), pp. 17–46.

Nikaidó, H. (1962) Some dynamic phenomena in the Leontief model of reversely lagged type, *Review of Economic Studies*, 29, pp. 313–323.

ten Raa, Th. (1986) Dynamic input–output analysis with distributed activities, *Review of Economics and Statistics*, 68, forthcoming.

Appendix

Proof of Proposition 1. Multiply the tth row ($t \geqq 0$) of the original matrix with the $(t+v)$th column ($v > 0$) of the inverse. This yields

$$G_t(0)D_t(v) + \cdots + G_t(v-1)D_{t+v-1}(1) + G_t(v)G_{t+v}(0)^{-1} = 0$$

or

$$D_t(v) = \sum_{s=1}^{v-1} R_t(s)D_{t+s}(v-s) - G_t(0)^{-1}G_t(v)G_{t+v}(0)^{-1}.$$

This is a diophantine equation for $D_t(v)$ with different weights for the predecessors; the solution is presented in the statement of Proposition 1 and will now be derived by induction on v.

For $v = 1$, the summation index consists of 1 and the proposition reads

$$D_t(1) = R_t(1)G_{t+1}(0)^{-1}$$

which is true by the established expression for $D_t(v)$ and the definition of $R_t(1)$.

Now suppose the proposition is valid for $1, \ldots, v-1$. Then the established expression for $D_t(v)$ becomes

$$D_t(v) = \sum_{s=1}^{v-1} R_t(s) \sum R_{t+s}(s_1) \cdots R_{t+s+s_1+\cdots+s_{l-1}}(s_l)G_{t+v}(0)^{-1}$$
$$- G_t(0)G_t(v)G_{t+v}(0)^{-1},$$

where the $\sum$-summation is over all $(s_1, \ldots, s_l)$ with each component in $\{1, \ldots, v-s\}$ and their sum equal to $v-s$. We have to prove that this expression coincides with that in the statement of Proposition 1 and shall do so by showing that any term in one expression shows up in the other. Since in each expression, the summation indices — $(s, s_1, \ldots, s_l)$ with $s_1, \ldots, s_l$ in $\{1, \ldots, v-s\}$ summing up to $v-s$ and s in $\{1, \ldots, v-1\}$ plus the element 0 (representing the separate term $-G_t(0)^{-1}G_t(v)G_{t+v}(0)^{-1}$) over here and $(s_1, \ldots, s_l)$ with $s_1, \ldots, s_l$ in $\{1, \ldots, v\}$ summing up to v in the statement of the proposition — assume different values, the double counting of terms is avoided.

First, take the derived expression. The separate term, $-G_t(0)^{-1}$ $G_t(v)G_{t+v}(0)^{-1}$, shows up in the statement of the proposition when $l = 1$ by the definition of $R_t(v)$. Now pick any other term:

$$R_t(s)R_{t+s}(s_1) \cdots R_{t+s+s_1+\cdots+s_{l-1}}(s_l)G_{t+v}(0)^{-1}$$

with

$$s_1, \ldots, s_l \quad \text{in } \{1, \ldots, v-s\}$$

summing up to $v-s$ and s in $\{l, \ldots, v-1\}$ summing up to v. Consequently, the term shows up in the statement of the proposition.

Next, take the expression in the statement of Proposition 1. When $l = 1$, then $s_l = v$ and the term equals the separate term $-G_t(0)^{-1}G_t(v)G_{t+v}(0)^{-1}$. Otherwise, $l \geqq 2$ and the term equals $R_t(s_1) \cdots R_{t+s_1+\cdots+s_{l-1}}(s_l)G_{t+v}(0)^{-1}$ with $s_1, \ldots, s_l \geqq 1$ summing up to v. Consequently, $s_2, \ldots, s_l$ are in

$\{1,\ldots,v-s_1\}$ and sum up to $v-s_1$ while s_1 is in $\{1,\ldots,v-1\}$. Consequently, the term shows up in the derived expression. □

Proof of Proposition 2. Recall from the proof of Proposition 1 that

$$D_t(v) = \sum_{s=1}^{v-1} R_t(s)D_{t+s}(v-s) - G_t(0)^{-1}G_t(v)G_{t-v}(0)^{-1}$$
$$= \sum_{s=1}^{v} R_t(s)D_{t+s}(v-s)$$

with $D_t(0) = G_t(0)^{-1}$. In fact, since

$$R_t(s) = -G_t(0)^{-1}G_t(s), D_t(v) = \sum_{s=1}^{\sigma} R_t(s)D_{t+s}(v-s).$$

Here the number of terms is independent of t and can be denoted $\#_v^{(\sigma)}$. By the last equation, $\#_v^{(\sigma)} = \sum_{s=1}^{\sigma} \#_{v-s}^{(\sigma)}$. For $v < 0$, $\#_v^{(\sigma)} = 0$, and $\#_0^{(\sigma)} = 1$.

It follows that $\#_v^{(\sigma)}$ are the generalized Fibonacci numbers of dimensions σ. If $\sigma = 1$, the solution is obviously $\#_v^{(1)} = 1 (v \geqq 1)$. Otherwise, for $\sigma \geqq 2$, the solution is due to Bernstein (1971, p. 141): $\#_{s\sigma+k}^{(\sigma)} = 2^{k-s-1}\sum_{j=0}^{s}(-1)^j [((s-j)\sigma_j + k) + ((s-j)\sigma_{j-1} + k - 1)]^{2(s-j)(\sigma+1)}$ ($s = 0, 1, \ldots$ and $k = 1, \ldots, \sigma$). By Proposition 1, each term in $D_t(v)$ is the product of at most v $n \times n$-matrices where n is the number of sectors. □

Proof of Proposition 3. Equation (15) implies $X_\tau(t)$ values for $\tau = 1$. This motivates the change of variables $t' = t/\tau$ and $X'_\tau(t') = X_\tau(\tau t')$. Then $X'_\tau(t') = X_\tau(t)$ and by (18) and (20),

$$[I - A(0)X'_\tau(t')] = [I - A(0)]X_\tau(t)$$
$$= B_\tau(0)[X_\tau(t+\tau) - X_\tau(t)] + \tau^{-1}I\delta_{s,t}$$
$$= \tau^{-1}B(0)[X'_\tau(t'+1) - X'_\tau(t')] + \tau^{-1}I\delta_{s/\tau,t'}.$$

This is Leontief's (1970) dynamic equation with capital matrix $\tau^{-1}B(0)$. Substituting this for $B(0)$ in (16), we obtain

$$X'_\tau(t') = \{[I - A(0) + \tau^{-1}B(0)]^{-1}\tau^{-1}B(0)\}^{s/\tau - t'}[I - A(0) + \tau^{-1}B(0)]^{-1}\tau^{-1},$$

for $t \leqq s$ and zero otherwise.

It follows that

$$\begin{aligned}X_\tau(t) &= \{[I - A(0) + \tau^{-1}B(0)]^{-1}\tau^{-1}B(0)\}^{s/\tau - t/\tau}\\ &\quad\times[I - A(0) + \tau^{-1}B(0)]^{-1}\tau^{-1}\\ &= \{[I - A(0) + \tau^{-1}B(0)]^{-1}\tau^{-1}B(0)\}^{(s-t)/\tau+1}B(0)^{-1}\\ &= \{B(0)^{-1}\tau[I - A(0) + \tau^{-1}B(0)]\}^{-(s-t)/\tau-1}B(0)^{-1}\\ &= \{I + B(0)^{-1}[I - A(0)\tau]\}^{(t-s-\tau)/\tau}B(0)^{-1},\end{aligned}$$

for $t \leqq s$ and zero otherwise.

By Remark 3 of Section 8 of ten Raa (1986),

$$\begin{aligned}X(t) &= \check{H}\exp\{B(0)^{-1}[I - A(0)]t\} * B(0)^{-1}\delta_s\\ &= \check{H}(t-s)\exp\{B(0)^{-1}[I - A(0)](t-s)\}B(0)^{-1}\\ &= \exp\{B(0)^{-1}[I - A(0)](t-s)\}B(0)^{-1},\end{aligned}$$

for $t \leqq s$ and zero otherwise. □

Proof of Proposition 4. $X_\tau - X$ tends to zero for vanishing τ if, roughly speaking, $\log X_\tau$ tends to $\log X$ or, more precisely and using Proposition 3, $\frac{t-s-\tau}{\tau}\log\{I + B(0)^{-1}[I - A(0)]\tau\}$ tends to $B(0)^{-1}[I - A(0)](t-s)$, which is clearly true. Here $\log\{\cdot\}$ is defined for τ sufficiently small by the usual Taylor series.

By Proposition 3, the total requirements, X_τ, summed up over time

$$\begin{aligned}\sum_{t/\tau=-\infty}^{s/\tau} X_\tau(t) &= \sum_{t/\tau=-\infty}^{s/\tau}\{I + B(0)^{-1}[I - A(0)]\tau\}^{(t-s)/\tau-1}\\ &\quad\times\{I + B(0)^{-1}[I - A(0)]\tau - I\}[I - A(0)]^{-1}\\ &= \left\{\sum_{t/\tau=-\infty}^{s/\tau}\{I + B(0)^{-1}[I - A(0)]\tau\}^{(t-s)/\tau}\right.\\ &\quad\left.-\sum_{t/\tau=-\infty}^{s/\tau}\{I + B(0)^{-1}[I - A(0)]\tau\}^{(t-s)/\tau-1}\right\}[I - A(0)]^{-1}\end{aligned}$$

$$= \{I + B(0)^{-1}[I - A(0)]\tau\}^{(s-s)/\tau}[I - A(0)]^{-1}$$
$$= [I - A(0)]^{-1}.$$

By Proposition 3, the total requirements, X, summed up over time to

$$\int_{-\infty}^{s} X(t)\mathrm{d}t = \int_{-\infty}^{s} e^{B(0)^{-1}[I-A(0)](t-s)}B(0)^{-1}\mathrm{d}t$$
$$= e^{B(0)^{-1}[I-A(0)](t-s)}[I - A(0)]^{-1}|_{-\infty}^{s}$$
$$= e^{0}[I - A(0)]^{-1} - 0$$
$$= [I - A(0)]^{-1}. \qquad \square$$

Proof of Proposition 5. Maximum growth is obtained when all surplus is invested. Then the input–output equations become homogeneous and the determination of the growth rates is an eigenvalue problem. See Bródy (1965, 1974). Thus consider $x_\tau(t) = e^{g_\tau t}x_\tau(0)$ for the discrete input–output equation and $x(t) = e^{gt}x(0)$ for the continuous one. The substitution in homogeneized (18) yields using (20), $[I - A(0)]x_\tau(0) = \tau^{-1}B(0)(e^{g_\tau \tau} - 1)x_\tau(0)$ and in homogeneized (19), $[I - A(0)]x(0) = B(0)gx(0)$. Consequently $\tau^{-1}(e^{g_\tau \tau} - 1) = g$.

By a Taylor expansion, we see that $g_\tau \uparrow g$ for $\tau \downarrow 0$. This proves that the maximum growth rate, g_τ, is inversely related to the time unit, τ.

Chapter 15

Working Capital in an Input–Output Model

Thijs ten Raa, Debesh Chakraborty and Tuhin Das

Abstract: Working capital is capital in the pipeline of the production process. Little has been done to formalize the concept of working capital in an input–output framework. The objective of the paper is to provide an input–output model of working capital and to assess its empirical value. In Section 1, a brief discussion on capital is presented. In Section 2, we develop the theoretical framework of the analysis. Section 3 deals with the empirical work, and Section 4 concludes the paper.

1. Capital

The distribution of economic activity over time manifests itself in the form of capital. Such distributions are of great variety and, as a result, capital assumes all sorts of forms. Our discussion of capital will follow Marx and give a systematic account of the classification in Volume II of *Capital*. The presentation will be geared towards an analysis of economies and temporally distributed input–output relationships.

Capital has different connotations. To the man in the street, it is a *store of value*, like money. But economists claim it to be the means of production and as such a *physical good.* Marx used the term in a broad sense which captures both elements. The man in the street's capital corresponds with Marx's capital of circulation (to be distinguished below from circulating capital), while the economist's capital corresponds with Marx's productive capital. We refer to Marx (1974, p. 192) and take up the two kinds in turn.

Capital of circulation consists of commodity-capital and money-capital, denoted C and M, respectively, by Marx (1974, pp. 26 and 36). Capital of circulation is in part the dual of productive capital, in the sense that monetary relations can be obtained by the transposition of the physical relations, as has been shown by Brody (1974) and others. For this reason, we confine ourselves to a treatment of productive capital. Thus we position ourselves in the classical tradition of attributing no real role to finance. It should be admitted that in this way we do no justice to the pecularities of the circuits of money-capital and commodity-capital. However, it is possible to treat capital of circulation in the same way as productive capital. This is clear from the symmetry in Foley (1982) and others. Thus our treatment of productive capital may serve as a model for capital of circulation and the complete economic system.

Marx (1974, p. 218) divides *productive capital* into variable capital and constant capital. Here variable capital adds value in production and consists of labor services and, in Marx's view, nothing but labor services. Constant capital transmits value and consists of all other necessary means of production: flows and stocks of physical goods. The classification is most useful for the theories of value and exploitation. An alternative classification is obtained when the objects are rearranged. Then productive capital is divided into circulating capital and fixed capital following Marx (1974, p. 158). Circulating capital is absorbed in production and consists of flows of goods. Fixed capital must merely be present when production takes place and consists of stocks of goods. This classification is appropriate for our analysis of the production process: circulating and fixed capital are represented by Leontief's input–output flow coefficients matrix, A, and the input–output stock coefficients matrix, B, respectively.

Circulating capital (A) is fluid. However, it can be like water or like syrup. Some circulating capital, such as electricity, is absorbed immediately, but other circulating capital, such as minerals, must be treated for some time. Electricity is (super)fluid capital, while minerals are working capital. (Super)fluid capital, by definition, is processed instantaneously, while working capital is defined to be capital in the pipeline,

The same distinction can be made with regard to fixed capital (B). Some fixed capital, such as a stapler, is ready for immediate use, but other fixed capital, such as a transport container, must be present some time in advance. A stapler is instant capital, the container is advanced capital. Instant capital is fixed capital which can be put to use instantaneously, while advanced capital must be installed in advance, all by definition.

Leontief's A, B-model of circulating and fixed capital is a great advance which facilitates quantitative analysis. His model, however, does not take into account the fact that production takes *time*. In Leontief's world, production is instantaneous. But the time feature is crucial in economic planning, however, as any manager or planner will readily confirm: The faster production takes place, the higher the growth rate. One of Marx's outstanding contributions is that he pays a great deal of attention to the time element in production: a good starting point for the incorporation of the production times in the circulating and fixed capital matrices A and B is Marx (1974, p. 239). For example, if input i's production time in sector j equals τ_{ij}, then we can write interindustry demand for i at time 0 as

$$\sum_j a_{ij} x_j(\tau_{ij})$$

where $x(t)$ is the output vector at time t. This set-up is still unnecessarily restrictive as it assumes that, for the production of one unit of output, sector j must absorb a_{ij} units of input i exactly τ_{ij} time units prior to the delivery of output and no input at other times, a situation depicted schematically in Figure 1.

In reality, input will also be required at other times prior to the delivery of output. The situation can be, for example, as in Figure 2.

In general, the ith input requirement for one unit of sector jth output is represented by an input profile on the past. We shall now introduce a powerful point of view. Giving up the idea of a_{ij} being some number altogether, we redefine an input–output coefficient as a non-negative and bounded distribution on the non-positive time axis. (The boundedness merely means

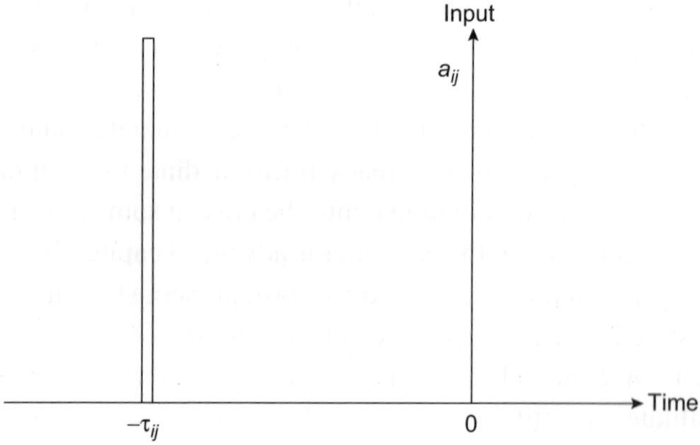

Fig. 1:

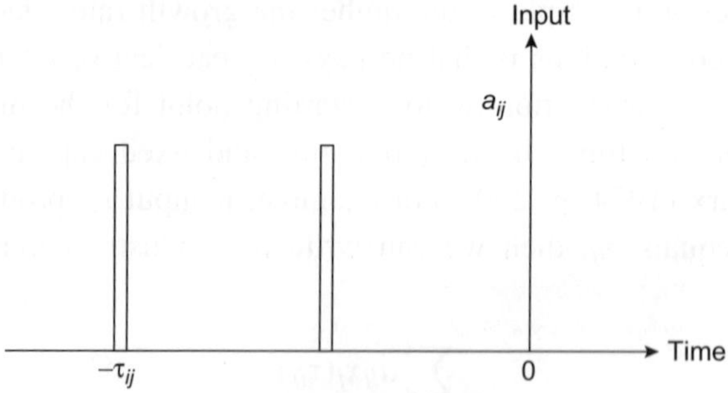

Fig. 2:

that the total input requirement, i.e. aggregated over time, is finite.) The whole profile in Figures 1 or 2 is considered to be the input–output coefficient. The width of its support (τ_{ij}) reflects the production time. This set-up obviously applies to capital stock coefficients as well. Then the width of the support of the distribution reflects the investment lead time.

We have modelled the time aspect of productive capital, be it circulating or fixed. The same can be done for capital of circulation. Then a good starting point for the incorporation of the so-called circulation time is Marx (1974, pp. 248–49). If we add up the production time, investment lead time and circulation time, we obtain the turnover time of capital, a centre-piece in the theory of Marx (1974, p. 155). The many forms of capital encountered

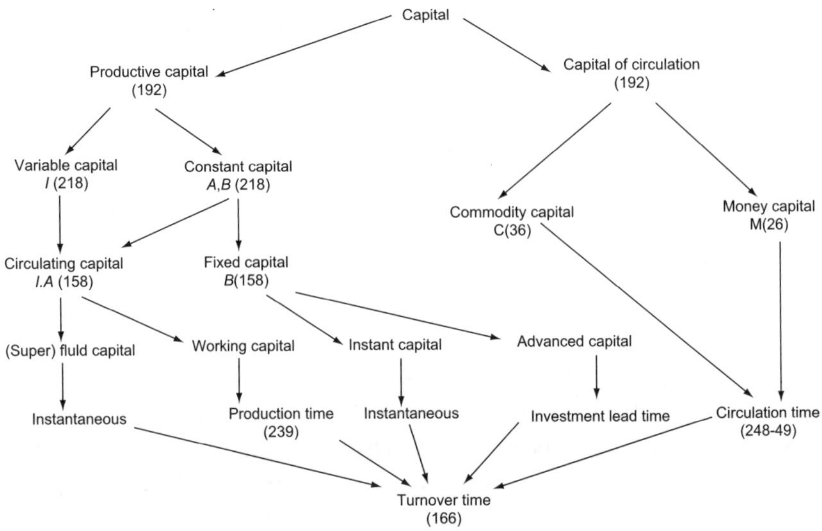

Fig. 3:

so far are displayed in Figure 3, where numbers refer to pages in Marx (1974). l, A and B represent Leontief's labor, flows and stock coefficients, respectively. C and M are Marx' own notation for commodity-capital and money-capital which are still open for Leontief like quantitative exploration.

2. The Model

This section models an economy in which any circulating capital in any sector is working capital with a single production time, and any fixed capital in any sector has to be advanced by a single investment lead time. Allowing for technical change, $a_{ij}(t)$ and $\tau_{ij}(t)$ denote the amount of and the production time for input i entering sector j at time t, and $b_{ij}(t)$ and $\sigma_{ij}(t)$ denote the amount of and the investment lead time for capital good i installed in sector j at time t (see Figure 1). The material balance for good i at time t now becomes

$$x_i(t) - \sum_{j=1}^{n}[a_{ij}(t)x_j(t + \tau_{ij}(t))] + b_{ij}(t)\dot{x}[t + \sigma_{ij}(t)] = y_i(t), \quad i = 1, \ldots, n$$

where x is the output vector, as before, and y is the final demand vector. Next, choose the time unit so small that, first, all $\tau_{ij}(t)$ and $\sigma_{ij}(t)$ become integers, and second, $x(t)$ can be approximated by $x(t+1)-x(t)$. Then we may limit our attention to integer values of t. For comparison with related studies below, we also neglect the past. Then

$$1x_i(t) - \sum_{j=1}^{n}[a_{ij}(t)x_j(t+\tau_{ij}(t)) - b_{ij}(t)x_j(t+\sigma_{ij}(t))$$
$$+ b_{ij}(t)x_j(t+\sigma_{ij}(t)+1)] = y_i(t), \quad i = 1,\ldots,n,\ t = 0,1,2,\ldots$$

Observe that any coefficient is multiplied by a quantity valued at a non-negative time lag further into the future. All coefficients, including the ones, are sorted out by the respective lags. These lags are contained in the set of $s = 0,1,2,\ldots$ $G_s(t)$ is defined as the $n \times n$-matrix which contains all $-a_{ij}(t)$ such that $\tau_{ij}(t) = s$, all $b_{ij}(t)$ such that $\sigma_{ij}(t) = s$, and all $-b_{ij}$ such that $\sigma_{ij}(t)+1 = s$. The locations of these coefficients are dictated by their subscripts. In addition, the one coefficient of $x_i(t)$ enters the ith diagonal element of $G_0(t)$. If no coefficient enters a $G_s(t)$ element, then this element is set at zero. (Formally, $G_s(t)$ is defined as follows. Its (i,j)th element equals

$$\delta_{i,j}\delta_{0,s} - a_{ij}(t)\delta_{\tau ij(t),s} + b_{ij}(t)\delta_{\sigma ij(t),s} - b_{ij}(t)\delta_{\sigma ij(t)+1,s}$$

where $\delta_{i,j}$ is the Kronecker symbol which is one for $i+j$ and zero otherwise.) The material balances can now be summarized as

$$\sum_{s=0}^{\infty} G_s(t)x(t+s) = y(t), \quad t = 0,1,2,\ldots$$

which casts it in the mould of ten Raa (1986), where the equation is solved for output levels.

3. Estimation

In principle, the classical technique of measuring all plans and stocks at each time is sufficient to determine the flow coefficients $a_{ij}(t)$ and the stock coefficient $b_{ij}(t)$, and to deduce the associated lags $\tau_{ij}(t)$ and $\sigma_{ij}(t)$. However, there are three complications. First, it is hard to know for which output, an observed input is required: current output, next period's output, or some future output? In fact, in a stationary economy, this is impossible. On the other hand, it is also irrelevant, provided that the economy remains stationary. Similar observations hold for intermediately regular economies. The most favorable environment for the determination of lags is a highly irregular economy with a constant structure. Then one has many linearly independent observations for a few lagged coefficients. The second complication is that the structure itself may vary. The observed input–output ratio variation need no longer be the unique manifestation of the lag structure through a varying bill of final goods. It can also reflect technical change, pure and simple. Thirdly, a general complication is that the determination of the coefficients and the lags through inference requires massive data collection.

In view of these limitations, better results will be obtained by the circulation of a questionnaire in which coefficients and lags are asked directly from the production managers. Since these data are technical it may be good to collect them at the source.

Of course, it may prove impossible to collect all these data, especially the lags. However, inference can be done with a Canadian time series of input–output tables for the period 1961–71 (Statistics Canada 1979). We follow the static model, since we have the current transaction tables.

The Canadian tables adhere to the United Nations (1967) Systems of National Accounts which comprise an input or 'use' table $U = (u_{ij})$ of commodities i consumed by industries j and an output or 'make' table $V = (v_{jk})$ of industries j producing commodities k. The aim now is to derive an industry-by-industry transactions matrix, To this end, we need an industry-by-industry input–output coefficients matrix and an industry output vector. The multiplication of the two yields the desired industry-by-industry transactions matrix.

The derivation of the industry-by-industry input–output coefficients matrix is standard. One defines a commodity-by-industry coefficients matrix $B = U\widehat{Ve}^{-1}$, where e is the vector with all entries unity, and an industry-by-commodity market share matrix $D = V\widehat{V'e}^{-1}$. The industry-by-industry input–output coefficients matrix is DB. The industry output vector is Ve. It follows that the transactions matrix is

$$Z = DBVe = V\widehat{V'e}^{-1}U.$$

The static model can be written as

$$x(t) = Z(t)e + y(t)$$

with industry demand Z defined by

$$z_{ij}(t) = a_{ij}x_j(t + \tau_{ij}).$$

In the remainder of this section, we fix the transaction, ij, so that the subscripts can be deleted. Our problem is to estimate a and τ simultaneously. We use an empirical regularity. The stability of input–output proportions over time suggests that a geometrical average should be considered with a multiplicative error. In other words, approximate $x(t + \tau)$ by the geometric mean of $x(t)$ and $x(t + 1)$:

$$x(t + \tau) = x(t)^{1-\tau}x(t + 1)^{\tau}.$$

Then we obtain

$$\log z(t) = \log a + (1 - \tau) \log x(t) + \tau \log x(t + l).$$

This cannot be subjected directly to ordinary least squares estimation, as coefficients are $(1 - \tau)$, as well as τ. A rewrite does the trick:

$$\log \frac{z(t)}{x(t)} = \log a + \tau \log \frac{x(t + 1)}{x(t)}$$

Tacking on a multiplicative lognormally distributed error term to $z(t) = ax(t + \tau)$ can easily be shown to yield a normally distributed error term attached to the present equation. Thus we obtain an ordinary regression of (the log of) the conventional Leontief input–output coefficients on (the log of) the growth rate, with coefficient τ and constant term (log) a. It should be noted that dividing through by $x(t)$ affects neither the deterministic nature of the explanatory variables nor the stochastic nature of the variable to be explained. In other words, the ordinary least squares assumption is maintained.

Note that statistically, a and τ are separated out. Confidence intervals for τ and $\log a$ (hence a) can be obtained immediately, since they coincide with the coefficient and the constant term, respectively, in the regression equation. The estimates, along with 95% confidence intervals, are reported in Tables 1 and 2. Coefficients are multiplied by a factor of 100, so that

Table 1: Estimated Values of τ.

	Agriculture	Forestry	Fishing and hunting	Mines and quarries
Agriculture	0.55 (−0.29, 1.40)	2.80 (−3.13, 8.73)	−2.77 (−8.11, 2.58)	−5.99 (−22.1, 10.1)
Forestry	−0.36 (−2.73, 2.00)	0.83 (−2.11, 3.76)	0.53 (−1.00, 2.05)	8.62 (−9.62, 26.9)
Fishing and hunting	1.39 (−0.35, 3.13)	−0.14 (−5.56, 5.29)	2.07 (−0.97, 5.10)	−1.45 (−6.35, 3.44)
Mines and quarries	−0.83 (−3.34, 1.67)	−1.66 (−3.60, 0.28)	0.31 (−3.50, 4.12)	−0.67 (−5.67, 4.12)
Manufacturing	0.36 (−0.48, 1.19)	0.34 (−1.58, 2.26)	0.22 (−0.86, 1.30)	0.22 (−2.76, 3.20)
Construction	−0.48 (−14.4, 13.4)	−0,12 (−17.6, 17.4)	−1.09 (−16.0, 13.8)	−4.99 (−46.7, 36.7)
Transport and storage	0.46 (−0.33, 1.24)	−1.12 (−3.58, 1.33)	0.47 (0.16, 0.79)	0.44 (−2.41, 3.28)
Communication	0.67 (−0.01, 1.34)	0.45 (−0.49, 1.39)	−0.22 (−1.61, 1.17)	1.11 (−0.10, 2.32)
Utilities	−0.21 (−1.13, 0.71)	−2.25 (−10.2, 5.73)	0.19 (−1.47, 1.85)	0.62 (−0.69, 1.92)
Wholesale trade	0.49 (−0.29, 1.27)	−0.04 (−0.57, 0.48)	−0.07 (−1.12, 0.98)	0.65 (−0.94, 2.24)
Retail trade	0.56 (−0.11, 1.23)	−0.36 (−1.19, 0.47)	−1.71 (−8.27, 4.85)	0.11 (−2.19, 2.41)
Finance	−0.28 (−0.92, 0.36)	−0.04 (−1.15, 1.08)	0.13 (−1.19, 1.44)	0.46 (−1.01, 1.94)
Services	0.46 (−0.09, 1.01)	−0.45 (−1.00, 0.10)	0.99 (−0.50, 2.48)	0.48 (−0.94, 1.91)
Transport margins	0.09 (−0.95, 1.12)	0.52 (−0.35, 1.39)	0.03 (−0.75, 0.81)	−0.18 (−1.87, 1.50)
Office supplies	−0.57 (−1.95, 0.81)	−0.03 (−1.41, 1.36)	0.93 (−0.71, 2.56)	−0.94 (−4.73, 2.84)
Travel and advtg.		0.01 (0.00, 0.01)		1.03 (−0.87, 2.93)

(*Continued*)

Table 1: (*Continued*)

	Manufacturing	Construction	Transport and storage	Communication
Agriculture	2.54 (0.84, 4.34)	−0.16 (−3.33, 3.00)	−4.29 (−8.40, −0.18)	−17.2 (−61.0, 26.5)
Forestry	1.89 (−0.10, 3.89)	−0.22 (−5.62, 5.19)	12.9 (1.96, 23.8)	43.7 (−3.74, 91.0)
Fishing and hunting	1.24 (−0.47, 2.95)	0.10 (−6,85, 7.06)	−12.8 (−21.8, −3.84)	−21.0 (−32.4, −9.62)
Mines and quarries	1.41 (0.64, 2.19)	−2.09 (−4.75, 0.57)	−2.01 (−6.35, 2.33)	11.8 (1.90, 21.7)
Manufacturing	−0.84 (−1.44, −0.25)	0.06 (−0.22, 0.35)	2.05 (−2.03, 6.13)	5.14 (−17.0, 27.3)
Construction	−9.05 (−46.9, 28.8)	4.20 (−15.8, 24.2)	−22.6 (−74.1, 28.9)	−21.9 (−175, 131)
Transport and storage	−0.44 (−1.88, 1.00)	−0.40 (−4.56, 3.75)	−2.40 (−5.17, 0.37)	7.29 (−6.20, 20.8)
Communication	−0.96 (−2.34, 0.43)	−0.12 (−3.96, 3.72)	−1.62 (−3.42, 0.19)	0.24 (−4.14, 4.63)
Utilities	−0.43 (−1.15, 0.29)	0.10 (−0.77, 0.97)	−0.19 (−1.19, 0.81)	−11.7 (−23.3, −0.14)
Wholesale trade	−0.86 (−1.76, 0.03)	0.65 (0.17, 1.13)	1.00 (1.39, 3.39)	2.62 (−5.67, 10.9)
Retail trade	1.40 (−0.38, 3.18)	0,37 (0.09, 0.64)	−0.93 (−1.82, −0.04)	−15.8 (−44.9, 15.4)
Finance	0.04 (−0.93, 1.01)	0.69 (−2.31, 3.68)	−3.19 (−5.27, −1.11)	8.80 (0.80, 16.8)
Services	−2.02 (−3.79, −0.26)	−1.30 (−4.47, 1.88)	−3.54 (−5.94, −1.14)	−1.03 (−6.05, 3.98)
Transport margins	0.49 (0.06, 0.93)	−0.05 (−0.78, 0.67)	−0.17 (−1.47, 1.13)	−1.57 (−6.37, 3.23)
Office supplies	−0.47 (1.66, 0.72)	1.04 (−2.20, 4.26)	2.19 (0.07, 4.46)	11.3 (−4.86, 27.5)
Travel and advtg.	1.38 (−0.04, 2.79)	0.40 (−0.93, 1.72)	−0.07 (−1.37, 1.22)	7.19 (2.50, 11.9)

(*Continued*)

Table 1: (*Continued*)

	Utilities	Wholesale trade	Retail trade	Finance
Agriculture	−7.10 (−24.2, 10.0)	1.18 (−2.40, 4.75)	−0.13 (−10.4, 10.1)	−1.42 (−37.3, 34.5)
Forestry	3.66 (−4.68, 12.0)	8.52 (−3.75, 20.8)	2.42 (−3.44, 8.28)	−0.13 (−6.60, 6.34)
Fishing and hunting	−0.35 (−18.2, 17.5)	−0.21 (−6.12, 5.69)	−7.16 (−19.1, 4.83)	3.48 (−19.8, 26.8)
Mines and quarries	−2.15 (−24.3, 20.0)	−0.53 (−3.56, 2.49)	0.63 (−3.57, 4.83)	1.16 (−4.31, 6.64)
Manufacturing	20.4 (−1.42, 42.2)	0.88 (−0.52, 2.29)	1.73 (−1.43, 4.89)	29.4 (−26.1, 84.8)
Construction	−76.8 (−136, −17.5)	−1.09 (−20.2, 18.0)	−13.5 (−61.7, 34.7)	−51.1 (−159, 57.1)
Transport and storage	−2.97 (−15.3, 9.39)	1.14 (−1.01, 3.29)	0.33 (−1.86, 2.52)	3.90 (−8.91, 16.7)
Communication	0.12 (−4.12, 4.35)	0.21 (−0.48, 0.90)	2.08 (−2.18, 6.35)	1.42 (−8.47, 11.3)
Utilities	2.08 (−3.32, 7.47)	0.67 (−0.77, 2.11)	1.55 (−2.71, 5.81)	2.03 (−10.6, 14.7)
Wholesale trade	−0.46 (−11.0, 10.1)	1.13 (−0.81, 3.07)	1.80 (−4.92, 8.51)	2.89 (−4.46, 10.2)
Retail trade	0.15 (−6.54, 6.84)	1.51 (−1.46, 4.47)	0.46 (−3.69, 4.61)	1.64 (−2.35, 5.63)
Finance	0.43 (−10.2, 11.0)	1.23 (0.20, 2.26)	0.60 (−0.68, 1.88)	0.02 (−2.42, 2.47)
Services	0.65 (−4.81, 0.11)	0.26 (−1.25, 1.76)	−0.13 (−2.13, 1.87)	0.57 (−5.72, 6.86)
Transport margins	−1.67 (−24.2, 20.6)	0.64 (−0.12, 1.40)	0.18 (−2.19, 2.56)	0.66 (−4.12, 5.44)
Office supplies	−3.39 (−16.0, 9.26)	0.73 (−1.54, 3.01)	3.50 (−1.66, 8.66)	1.57 (−9.75, 12.9)
Travel and advtg.	0.87 (−7.73, 9.46)	0.84 (−1.52, 3.21)	0.01 (−1.90, 1.92)	0.79 (−0.85, 2.44)

(*Continued*)

Table 1: *(Continued)*

	Services	Transport margins	Office supplies	Travel and advtg.
Agriculture	−1.59 (−3.80, 0.62)		2.36 (0.37, 4.34)	
Forestry	−1.33 (−2.88, 0.22)	10.3 (−11.9, 32.5)	2.89 (1.22, 4.56)	6.23 (−1.32, 13.8)
Fishing and hunting	0.12 (−4.01, 4.25)		1.48 (−1.18, 4.14)	−2.95 (−10.9, 5.00)
Mines and quarries	3.62 (−3.27, 10.5)		−4.39 (−9.22, 0.45)	−2.66 (−8.18, 2.86)
Manufacturing	−0.80 (−1.87, 0.28)	−13.0 (−28.5, 2.51)	−0.10 (−0.51, 0.30)	0.28 (−0.40, 0.97)
Construction	6.83 (−16.0, 29.7)		−8.15 (−20.0, 3.73)	−1.28 (−6.57, 4.01)
Transport and storage	0.29 (−1.75, 2.34)	−0.01 (−0.05, 0.02)	0.67 (−1.11, 2.45)	−2.60 (−4.42, −0.79)
Communication	1.27 (−0.30, 2.84)		−0.91 (−2.81, 0.98)	0.86 (−1.16, 2.88)
Utilities	1.11 (−3.54, 5.77)		−0.77 (−3.19, 1.66)	2.04 (0.42, 3.65)
Wholesale trade	0.46 (−0.40, 1.31)		0.12 (−0.54, 0.77)	−0.31 (−1.95, 1.21)
Retail trade	−0.09 (−1.15, 0.97)	2.59 (−4.40, 9.58)	0.34 (0.02, 0.64)	1.03 (0.08, 1.98)
Finance	0.69 (−0.73, 2.11)		−3.63 (−6.31, −0.97)	−4.35 (−12.3, 3.56)
Services	−0.39 (−2.07, 1.28)		0.71 (−0.15, 1.57)	1.03 (−0.05, 2.11)
Transport margins	−0.02 (−1.53, 1.49)		−0.42 (−1.30, 0.46)	−0.66 (−2.29, 0.97)
Office supplies	0.02 (−2.51, 2.55)			
Travel and advtg.	0.82 (−1.05, 2.70)			

Table 2: Estimated Values of A (Times 100).

	Agriculture	Forestry	Fishing and hunting	Mines and quarries
Agriculture	4.19 (3.88, 4.50)	0.31 (0.22, 0.40)	0.00 (0.00, 0.00)	0.00 (−0.00, 0.01)
Forestry	0.01 (0.01, 0.02)	6.91 (5.89, 7.94)	0.01 (0.01, 0.01)	0.00 (−0.00, 0.01)
Fishing and hunting	0.00 (0.00, 0.00)	0.00 (0.00, 0.00)	1.25 (0.96, 1.54)	0.00 (0.00, 0.00)
Mines and quarries	0.36 (0.28, 0.44)	0.10 (0.09, 0.11)	0.56 (0.40, 0.72)	3.93 (2.69, 5.18)
Manufacturing	20.3 (18.8, 21.8)	4.95 (4.47, 5.43)	22.6 (20.7, 24.4)	5.67 (4.55, 6.78)
Construction	1.27 (−0.28, 2.82)	1.22 (0.14, 2.30)	0.28 (−0.04, 0.60)	1.66 (−2.91, 6.23)
Transport and storage	0.35 (0.33, 0.38)	10.2 (8.98, 11.5)	1.29 (1.26, 1.32)	1.02 (0.83, 1.21)
Communication	0.30 (0.28, 0.32)	0.33 (0.32, 0.35)	0.31 (0.27, 0.34)	0.31 (0.28, 0.33)
Utilities	0.95 (0.89, 1.04)	0.16 (0.09, 0.22)	0.13 (0.11, 0.15)	2.01 (1.84, 2.19)
Wholesale trade	2.24 (2.08, 2.39)	0.86 (0.84, 0.88)	2.06 (1.89, 2.22)	0.80 (0.72, 0.89)
Retail trade	0.67 (0.63, 0.71)	0.52 (0.50, 0.54)	0.71 (0.35, 1.06)	0.21 (0.18, 0.24)
Finance	3.78 (3.57, 4.00)	8.04 (7.59, 8.49)	1.13 (1.02, 1.24)	7.38 (6.66, 8.10)
Services	0.25 (0.24, 0.26)	2.33 (2.26, 2.39)	0.76 (0.67, 0.84)	2.34 (2.12, 2.57)
Transport margins	1.78 (1.61, 1.94)	0.25 (0.24, 0.26)	1.05 (0.99, 1.11)	0.46 (0.41, 0.51)
Office supplies	4.43 (3.89, 4.97)	12.6 (11.7, 13.5)	1.47 (1.28, 1.65)	7.78 (5.83, 9.73)
Travel and advtg.		0.57 (0.48, 0.67)		0.53 (0.47, 0.60)

(*Continued*)

Table 2: (*Continued*)

	Manufacturing	Construction	Transport and storage	Communication
Agriculture	4.98 (4.41, 5.55)	0.06 (0.05, 0.07)	0.02 (0.02, 0.03)	0.00 (−0.01, 0.01)
Forestry	1.98 (1.72, 2.24)	0.07 (0.05, 0.10)	0.01 (0.00, 0.02)	0.00 (−0.00, 0.00)
Fishing and hunting	0.31 (0.27, 0.34)	0.00 (0.00, 0.00)	0.00 (0.00, 0.01)	0.00 (0.00, 0.00)
Mines and quarries	5.51 (5.23, 5.78)	1.54 (1.31, 1.77)	0.29 (0.21, 0.38)	0.01 (0.00, 0.01)
Manufacturing	34.5 (32.3, 36.7)	41.1 (40.5, 41.8)	7.16 (5.19, 9.13)	2.47 (−1.59, 6.52)
Construction	0.60 (−0.89, 2.08)	0.06 (−0.01, 0.13)	8.20 (−20.3, 36.7)	8.98 (−92.9, 111)
Transport and storage	0.85 (0.77, 0.93)	0.86 (0.66, 1.06)	9.19 (7.47, 10.9)	2.73 (−0.00, 5.47)
Communication	0.62 (0.57, 0.68)	0.36 (0.28, 0.43)	1.33 (1.17, 1.50)	2.44 (1.65, 3.23)
Utilities	1.06 (1.01, 1.11)	0.06 (0.06, 0.06)	0.48 (0.45, 0.52)	0.60 (0.09, 1.11)
Wholesale trade	2.23 (2.10, 2.36)	4.34 (4.22, 4.45)	1.35 (1.13, 1.57)	0.21 (0.08, 0.34)
Retail trade	0.24 (0.21, 0.26)	0.90 (0.88, 0.91)	0.98 (0.92, 1.04)	2.89 (−3.35, 9.13)
Finance	1.25 (1.17, 1.33)	1.15 (0.96, 1.35)	2.62 (2.25, 2.99)	0.90 (0.37, 1.43)
Services	1.10 (0.97, 1.22)	3.49 (2.88, 4.11)	2.13 (1.78, 2.47)	2.56 (1.61, 3.51)
Transport margins	2.08 (2.02, 2.14)	2.36 (2.26, 2.45)	0.40 (0.36, 0.43)	0.08 (0.05, 0.11)
Office supplies	3.01 (2.77, 3.24)	1.79 (1.47, 2.11)	4.00 (3.39, 4.62)	0.99 (−0.20, 2.17)
Travel and advtg.	2.26 (2.05, 2.47)	0.41 (0.38, 0.43)	0.98 (0.90, 1.07)	0.53 (0.35, 0.72)

(*Continued*)

Table 2: (*Continued*)

	Utilities	Wholesale trade	Retail trade	Finance
Agriculture	0.00 (−0.00, 0.00)	0.10 (0.08, 0.14)	3.94 (2.06, 5.23)	0.00 (−0.00, 0.01)
Forestry	0.00 (0.00, 0.00)	0.01 (0.00, 0.01)	0.01 (0.01, 0.01)	0.00 (0.00, 0.00)
Fishing and hunting	0.00 (−0.00, 0.00)	0.00 (0.00, 0.00)	0.00 (0.00, 0.00)	0.00 (0.00, 0.00)
Mines and quarries	3.26 (−1.78, 8.30)	0.10 (0.08, 0.12)	0.20 (0.16, 0.23)	0.08 (0.06, 0.09)
Manufacturing	0.35 (−0.18, 0.88)	4.26 (3.84, 4.68)	3.47 (2.96, 3.98)	0.18 (−0.28, 0.64)
Construction	4.41 (−13.85, 22.67)	0.19 (−0.01, 0.45)	0.89 (−1.10, 2.87)	46.1 (−184, 276)
Transport and storage	0.34 (0.05, 0.63)	3.26 (2.76, 3.75)	1.09 (0.98, 1.20)	0.07 (0.03, 0.11)
Communication	0.35 (0.25, 0.46)	2.08 (1.98, 2.18)	2.07 (1.66, 2.49)	1.31 (0.71, 1.90)
Utilities	1.63 (1.02, 2.24)	0.62 (0.56, 0.69)	1.72 (1.37, 2.05)	0.41 (0.17, 0.66)
Wholesale trade	0.37 (0.10, 0.64)	0.96 (0.83, 1.10)	0.42 (0.29, 0.56)	0.07 (0.05, 0.10)
Retail trade	0.15 (0.08, 0.23)	0.39 (0.31, 0.47)	0.30 (0.24, 0.36)	0.10 (0.08, 0.12)
Finance	2.00 (0.52, 3.48)	4.47 (4.14, 4.79)	6.85 (6.44, 7.26)	6.03 (5.35, 6.71)
Services	0.74 (0.46, 1.03)	2.24 (2.00, 2.47)	1.15 (1.04, 1.25)	1.61 (1.14, 2.08)
Transport margins	0.53 (−0.30, 1.37)	0.22 (0.21, 0.23)	0.21 (0.19, 0.23)	0.01 (0.01, 0.02)
Office supplies	1.59 (0.19, 2.99)	4.18 (3.51, 4.85)	4.35 (3.30, 5.39)	2.77 (1.32, 4.22)
Travel and advtg.	0.39 (0.16, 0.64)	5.44 (4.53, 6.35)	3.12 (2.85, 3.40)	1.93 (1.79, 2.08)

(*Continued*)

Table 2: **(*Continued*)**

	Services	Transport margins	Office supplies	Travel and advtg.
Agriculture	0.95 (0.83, 1.08)		0.67 (0.57, 0.77)	
Forestry	0.01 (0.01, 0.01)	0.07 (−0.04, 0.19)	0.05 (0.04, 0.06)	0.08 (0.05, 0.11)
Fishing and hunting	0.11 (0.09, 0.14)		0.02 (0.02, 0.03)	0.00 (0.00, 0.00)
Mines and quarries	0.09 (0.05, 0.13)		0.33 (0.21, 0.45)	0.08 (0.06, 0.11)
Manufacturing	13.0 (12.2, 13.9)	0.09 (−0.01, 0.19)	60.5 (58.7, 62.4)	33.2 (32.0, 34.3)
Construction	0.21 (−0.08, 0.50)		0.23 (0.02, 0.44)	0.19 (0.14, 0.24)
Transport and storage	0.32 (0.28, 0.36)	99.6 (99.4, 99.9)	0.14 (0.12, 0.16)	16.3 (14.8, 17.9)
Communication	1.57 (1.43, 1.72)		0.16 (0.14, 0.18)	7.58 (6.78, 8.37)
Utilities	0.63 (0.45, 0.80)		0.06 (0.05, 0.07)	0.07 (0.06, 0.07)
Wholesale trade	1.04 (0.99, 1.10)		8.99 (8.54, 9.44)	2.43 (2.23, 2.64)
Retail trade	1.23 (1.10, 1.35)	0.16 (0.08, 0.24)	5.89 (5.75, 6.03)	4.45 (4.23, 4.67)
Finance	4.61 (4.22, 5.00)		0.09 (0.07, 0.11)	0.14 (0.08, 0.20)
Services	3.33 (3.00, 3.67)		10.2 (9.58, 10.9)	23.9 (22.5, 25.2)
Transport margins	0.44 (0.40, 0.48)		2.80 (2.61, 2.99)	0.63 (0.57, 0.68)
Office supplies	6.16 (5.24, 7.09)			
Travel and advtg.	2.33 (2.07, 2.59)			

the unit is cents per dollar. The separation property is a nice by-product of the multiplicative stochastic structure of our input–output model. It does not hold for additive errors which we tried initially, but which seem less appropriate from an input–output perspective. In other words, theoretical purity and statistical convenience go together in this analysis. For those who believe less in beauty, the alternative stochastic specifications can be nested in a model of heteroscedasticity of esteemable degree and thus be tested. See Judge, Hill, Griffiths, Lütkepohl and Lee (1982, Sections 14.4 and 14.5).

4. Conclusion

Table 1 displays an interesting picture of the times material inputs spent in the production process, that is of working capital. The confidence intervals are disturbingly wide, though. Basically, there is too little information in the data. In the extreme case of no departure from balanced growth, the lags cannot be identified at all, as is easily illustrated. The last equation reduces to

$$\log \frac{z(t)}{x(t)} = \log a + \tau \log \frac{e^{g} x(t)}{x(t)} = \log a e^{g\tau}$$

where g is the growth rate. One can estimate $ae^{g\tau}$, but a and τ cannot be identified. The standard procedure is, of course, to fix $\tau = 0$ and to estimate a by contemporary division of flows. This is observationally equivalent to a sluggish economy with smaller coefficients. In our data set, the situation is not this bad, but a scatter diagram exposes the problem. In Figure 4, we have plotted

$$\log \frac{z(t)}{x(t)}$$

against the growth rate of agriculture for the agricultural and manufacturing inputs, respectively. The slopes estimate the lags. It is clear that the slopes are poorly determined.

We conclude that our input–output model lends itself to a sound statistical analysis of working capital, but that the data contain too little information. We need either observations of more irregular economies, or direct information about time spent in the pipeline of production. This conclusion holds *a fortiori* for more complicated production functions and, therefore, casts some doubt on the precision of results on time to build studies such as Kydland and Prescott (1982).

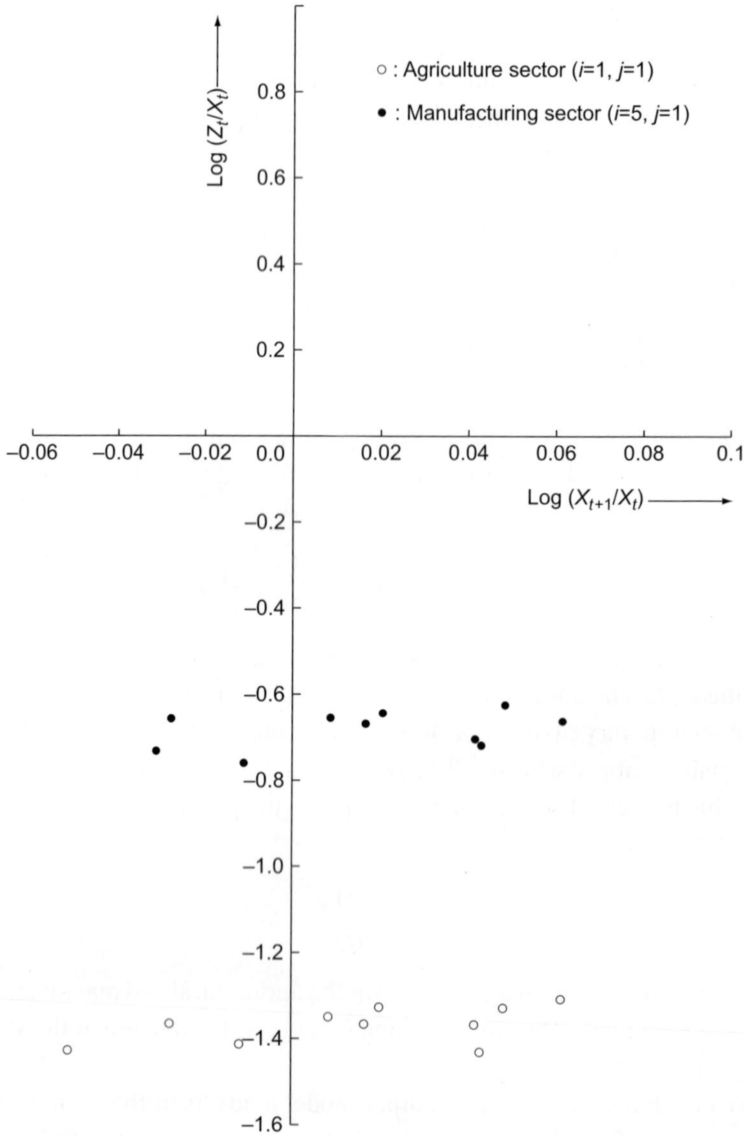
○ : Agriculture sector (i=1, j=1)
● : Manufacturing sector (i=5, j=1)
Log (Z_t/X_t)
Log (X_{t+1}/X_t)
0.8
0.6
0.4
0.2
0.0
−0.2
−0.4
−0.6
−0.8
−1.0
−1.2
−1.4
−1.6
−0.06
−0.04
−0.02
0.02
0.04
0.06
0.08
0.1

Fig. 4:

Acknowledgments

The research of the first author has been made possible by a senior fellowship of the Royal Netherlands Academy of Arts and Sciences. Teun Kloek kindly discussed the subject matter with us. Henk Gravesteijn kindly did some preliminary investigations.

References

Brody, A. (1974) *Proportions, Prices and Planning* (Budapest, Akademiai Kiado, and Amsterdam–London, North Holland Publishing Company).

Foley, D.K. (1982) Accumulation, realization, and crisis, *Journal of Economic Theory*, 30(2), pp. 300–319.

Judge, G.G., R.C. Hill, W. Griffiths, H. Lütkepohl and T.-C. Lee (1982) *Introduction to the Theory and Practice of Econometrics* (New York, John Wiley & Sons).

Kydland, F.E. and E.C. Prescott (1982) Time to build and aggregate fluctuations, *Econometrica*, 50(6), pp. 1345–1370.

Leontief, W. (1970) The Dynamic Inverse, In Carter, A.P. and A. Brody (eds.), *Contributions to Input-Output Analysis* (Amsterdam-London, North Holland Publishing Company), pp. 17–46.

Marx, K. (1974) *Capital II: The Process of Circulation of Capital* (New York, International Publishers).

Nikaido, H. (1962) Some dynamic phenomena in the Leontief model of reversely lagged type, *Review of Economic Studies*, 29, pp. 313–23.

Statistics Canada (1979) *The Input-Output Structure of the Canadian Economy in Constant Prices*, pp. 1961–1974.

ten Raa, Th. (1986) Applied dynamic input-output with distributed activities, *European Economic Review*, 30(4), pp. 805–31.

UN Statistical Commission (1967) *Proposals for the Revision of SNA, 1952* (Document E/CN.3/356).

Part V

Stochastic Input–Output Analysis

Chapter 16

Primary Versus Secondary Production Techniques in U.S. Manufacturing

Joe Mattey and Thijs ten Raa

Abstract: In this paper, we analyze the determinants of material inputs into individual production activities as a function of their outputs. We use observations on a large cross-section of U.S. manufacturing plants from the Census of Manufactures, including those that make goods primary to other industries, to study differences in production techniques. We find that in most cases, material requirements do not depend on whether goods are made as primary products or as secondary products. We thus elucidate support for the commodity technology model as a useful working hypothesis.

1. Introduction

In multi-sectoral modelling, it is customary to use an input–output core for the intermediate input requirements. In this paper, we shed some light on the soundness of this strategy by analyzing the determinants of material inputs in individual manufacturing plants as a function of their outputs. The basic data refer to no less than 96,515 plants, 71 separate inputs and 370 outputs.

The immediate relevance of our study pertains to Stone's 1961 commodity technology model. Stone distinguishes between activities and commodities, and his commodity technology model postulates input–output relations between the commodities, irrespective of the pattern of activities at the producing units. In this context, activities can be represented as alternative linear combinations of the elementary multiple-input/single-output processes used to make commodities.

In national accounting and input–output analysis, researchers usually rely on data which aggregates the activities of individual producing units to a sectoral level. The commodity technology coefficients must be inferred from a use table (with dimensions commodity by sector) and a make table (with dimensions sector by commodity). Assuming that there are the same number of sectors as activities and commodities, the input–output coefficients are exactly identified and obtained by multiplication of the use table and the (transposed) inverse of the make table. In this paper, however, we steer closer to Stone's framework by letting activities represent the behavior of individual plants. The wealth of plant data can be used for various tests of the commodity technology model (although a single comprehensive, system-wide test is not feasible). As it turns out, our results elucidate a great deal of support for the commodity technology model as a useful working hypothesis.

Our findings about material inputs also address one part of a more general issue, whether differences in factor intensities tend to reflect patterns of specialization, or the co-existence of alternative techniques to produce outputs. For example, the traditional Hecksher-Ohlin trade-theory explanation of labor- vs. capital-intensive modes of production is that economies favor relatively abundant factor inputs. Equilibrium differences in factor intensities are explained by patterns of specialization in final goods and services. Per commodity, the co-existence of multiple techniques is not admitted.

In practice, patterns of specialization seldom conform to the sharp implications of such theory; specialization is not complete. To prevent such obvious contradictions, applied trade models often posit differences between seemingly identical commodities, either in terms of their price or perceived quality.[1] Alternatively, trade models following the Ricardian tradition consider differences of technologies as exogenous and exploit them to determine comparative advantages. The co-existence of multiple techniques is taken as given, without explanation. Similar issues arise with respect to materials usage, which is the main interest here.

Distinguishing between the alternative explanations of existing patterns of factor intensity — specialization or differences in production techniques — also confronts us at the level of measurement. Inputs are not reported by product or activity separately; the micro reporting units generally are conglomerates of production activities, establishments or legal forms of organization such as corporations. Moreover, applied studies generally use even more aggregative data. The traditional approach to aggregation is to classify reporting units into sectors, $j = 1, \ldots, n$ and to label the commodities primarily associated with these sectors accordingly. In national accounts, the inputs of all commodities to sector j are listed in column vector $v_{.j}$, and the make of all commodities by sector j is given in the row vector $v_{j.}$ (U.N., 1993). Many of the off-diagonal elements of the corresponding make matrix V are non-zero. In considering perturbations of the patterns of production of final goods — changes in row vectors of the make matrix, a modeler needs to decide whether analysis can proceed on an element-by-element basis; alternatively, if this form of separability cannot be imposed, one must specify the nature of joint production.

Typically, jointness in production is ignored, and modelers adopt the commodity-technology assumption that the requirements for intermediates depend just on the commodity being made, not on what else is being produced at the same location.[2] To apply the commodity technology

[1]For example, a wide range of posited differences between seemingly identical commodities appears in the models used to study the effects of North American free trade agreements. The early work of Wonnacott and Wonnacott (1967) assumed that the violation of the law of one price could explain the existing patterns of specialization; they argued that because of substantial tariff and non-tariff trade barriers between the U.S. and Canada, Canadian manufacturers attempted to take advantage of economies of scale through product diversification. More recently, Hamilton and Whalley (1985), among others, explain patterns of specialization by following Armington (1969) in assuming that the demand for a good depends on its country of origin. Alternatively, Brown and Stern (1989) allow for monopolistic competition created by firm-specific product differentiation, such as that established by brand-name advertising.

[2]For example, in the applied general-equilibrium model Lopez-de-Silanes, Markusen and Rutherford (1992) use to study the effect of a North American Free Trade Agreement on the motor vehicle industry, the intermediate input requirements of motor vehicle producers are assumed to just depend on whether

assumption, one assumes that a technical coefficient a_{ij} represents the requirements for commodity i per unit of commodity j. Summing across the outputs v_{jk} of sector j of commodities k, the overall requirements for the i-th input are $\Sigma_k a_{ik} v_{jk}$. Equating observed inputs, u_{ij}, to requirements yields, given obvious matrix notation, $AV' = U$, where the superscript denotes transposition. If the matrices are square (the number of commodities equals the number of sectors), this equation can be solved for the commodity-specific input-coefficients A. Distinguishing between specialization and differences in production techniques as explanations for factor intensity is important to applied general equilibrium modeling; if the commodity technology assumption is invalid and techniques do differ, the predicted patterns of use will diverge from actual patterns.

With aggregated data, the ability to test the commodity technology assumption is limited. In fact, if the information on patterns of use and make are restricted to a single point in time, both the commodity technology assumption and the theoretically inferior alternatives critiqued by Kop Jansen and ten Raa (1990) will fit the base-year data exactly, leaving no over-identifying restrictions to be tested.

In this paper, we provide a stochastic framework for the measurement of production techniques, a framework that tests the commodity technology assumption and alternatives that allow for significant jointness of production. Instead of aggregating the reporting units — manufacturing plants — into sectors, we analyze the plant-level data. The micro data give us extensive variation in product mix and intermediate use; by simply regressing plant input on the whole vector of plant outputs, we investigate whether differences in factor intensities reflect patterns of specialization or the co-existence of alternative techniques to produce output. In terms of the above notation, we calculate the coefficients per material input for all products simultaneously; i.e. the estimation of input-coefficients is row by row, using the i-th row of the above equation, $u_{i.} = a_{i.}V'$.

they are making finished goods or parts (of two varieties), not on whether the production of finished vehicles and parts occurs jointly. More generally, the Social Accounting Matrices (SAMs) used to calibrate applied general equilibrium models (Reinert, Roland-Holist and Shiells, 1993) adopt this "commodity technology" assumption; see Pyatt (1993) for an explication of why the validity of the commodity technology assumption is critical in this context.

In summary, we offer three contributions to the literature. First, we improve upon the traditional procedure of measuring technical coefficients from sectoral aggregates by allowing aggregation principles to be determined by the micro data. Second, by using raw data (reports from 96,515 U.S. manufacturing plants) we have a sound statistical basis for quantifying the accuracy of technical coefficient estimates; this lets us, for example, evaluate the so-called problem of negatives associated with the solution to the aggregate equation $AV' = U$. Last, but not least, we test for the co-existence of differing production techniques.

2. Data and Estimation Methods

To avoid the trap that variation of input intensities reflects specialization rather than a technical phenomenon, the definition of products must be disaggregated enough to render insignificant the concept of further specialization. We attempt to achieve product homogeneity by following the detailed U.S. benchmark input–output (I/O) table commodity classification system and the Census product code extensions of the U.S. Standard Industrial Classification (SIC) system. Specifically, each I/O sector is associated with a group of SIC industries, and each I/O commodity is associated with a list of Census products. For now, Census products are assumed to be homogeneous if they belong to the same I/O commodity category. This assumption seems modest, since there are hundreds of I/O commodities, and we do not aggregate them.

For each I/O commodity, producers are classified into two sets. For one set of producers, the make of the product is considered primary output because these producers are regarded as members of the corresponding I/O sector, and for the other set of producers, it is considered secondary output. This dichotomy of producers is known because the manufacturing industrial classification system has assigned producers to sectors on the basis of identifying their dominant products, and in the U.S. I/O system, there is exactly one primary manufactured product for each I/O manufacturing sector.

Under the commodity technology assumption, this dichotomy in primary production — the make of the product characteristic to the sector — and secondary production — the make of products characteristic to other sectors — has no special significance. However, we adopt the primary-secondary dichotomy in order to give our test of the commodity technology assumption power against likely alternatives. In other words, we assume that if a multiplicity of techniques really does exist, then the choice of techniques is likely to be highly correlated with the primary/secondary split.

For each material input, the observations are the consuming plants. Mattey (1993) analyzed patterns of intermediate use for the subset of pure plants with no secondary production (Table 1, line 8) to focus on the role of data truncation and errors of measurement in the problem of negative coefficients. Since we are interested in possible differences in techniques, we also include the producers of secondary products (Table 1, line 9). About 10 percent of the manufacturing plants report some secondary production, but because these manufacturers tend to be larger than average, about 46 percent of overall materials use occurs in plants with some secondary production. When secondary production is

Table 1: Coverage of Specified Materials Use in the 1982 Census of Manufacturers.

	Number of Plants	%	Amount of Materials[a]	%
1. Total manufacturing	348,385	100	990,060	100
2. Nonreporters	251,870	72	149,881	15
3. Not required	135,042	39	29,168	3
4. Noncompliance[b]	116,828	34	120,713	12
5. Reporters	96,515	28	840,179	85
6. Materials n.e.c[c]			180,094	18
7. Specified materials			660,085	67
Memo:				
8. Pure plants reporting[d]	62,757	18	384,554	39
9. Other plants reporting	33,758	10	455,624	46

[a]Millions of dollars of materials purchased and consumed. Excludes materials produced and consumed.

[b]For plants in industries asked to report specified materials use, includes non-administrative-record plants with materials use explicitly coded as n.s.k. and plants with only a positive balancing record in the detailed materials records.

[c]Also includes some unknown amount of materials of the types specified by kind but not reported under specified materials because the amount consumed was less than a censoring threshold, typically 10,000 dollars.

[d]Pure plants make only primary products (I/O basis). Miscellaneous receipts are excluded from our calculation of this degree of specialization, but less than half of a pure plant's total receipts are allowed to come from miscellaneous activities.

present in a plant, it tends to comprise a significant portion of a plant's activities; about 11 percent of all manufacturing output is secondary production.[3]

With regard to the decision of how many materials to study, we chose to focus on the 71 commodities used significantly as intermediates in manufacturing.[4] For each of these 71 commodities (i), the null hypothesis of a commodity technology relation is represented in equations of the following form:

$$u_{im} = a_{i1}v_{m1} + a_{i2} + v_{m2} + \cdots + a_{i370}v_{m370}. \tag{1}$$

Here, u_{im} is the use of material (i) by a manufacturing plant (m). There are 370 manufacturing products in the I/O system and the make of each of these products by the plant is denoted by the variables v_{m1} through v_{m370}. The unknown commodity technology coefficients a_{i1} through a_{i370} do not depend on the manufacturing plant or its industry affiliation. Thus, for estimating the unknown coefficients for use of material (i), we can stack the observations for all reporting plants in all manufacturing industries into an equation:

$$\mathbf{u}_i = a_{i1}\mathbf{v}_1 + a_{i2}\mathbf{v}_2 + \cdots + a_{i370}\mathbf{v}_{370}, \tag{2}$$

where $\mathbf{u}_i$ and $\mathbf{v}_1$ through $\mathbf{v}_{370}$ are now vectors with components representing the use or make entries for unique manufacturing plants.[5] Data are available for the 96,515 manufacturing plants that report some specified materials use in 1982 (Table 1). Thus, in principle, the vectors in equation (2) have 96,515 elements.

[3]The benchmark make table for 1982 from the U.S. I/O accounts indicates that 11 percent of manufacturing output is secondary production.

[4]Specifically, we restrict the analysis to those 71 materials for which the median pure-plant commodity technology coefficient was at least 5 percent in at least one industry. The scrap commodity and non-comparable imports meet this 5 percent requirement but are excluded because of their heterogeneity. Five other materials also meet this 5 percent requirement, but are excluded, because their use is so broad-based (more than 100 industries report some use) that our econometric approach is intractable; the excluded materials with broad-based reporting are paperboard containers and boxes, plastics materials and resins, miscellaneous plastics products, blast furnace and steel mill products, and rolled or drawn aluminum products.

[5]The column-vector $\mathbf{u}_i$ of equation (2) is specified by the corresponding row of the use matrix U, and $\mathbf{v}_1$ through $\mathbf{v}_{370}$ are specified by the columns of the make matrix V.

However, not all plants in all industries are asked about the use of every type of material, so no particular material input regression has this many observations.[6]

To illustrate the scope of the dataset with regard to types of materials, Table 2 lists the sectors in which the materials under study are produced as

Table 2: List of Sectors Producing Materials Under Study.

Material-producing Sector	Sector Description	Material-producing Sector	Sector Description
	Agricultural Materials		
1	Dairy farm products	9	Tobacco
2	Poultry and eggs	10	Fruits
3	Meat animals	12	Vegetables
5	Cotton	13	Sugar crops
6	Food grains	15	Oil bearing crops
7	Feed grains	19	Commercial fishing
	Mining Materials		
23	Copper ore mining	28	Sand and gravel mining
26	Crude petroleum and natural gas	29	Clay, ceramic, and refractory minerals mining
27	Dimension, crushed and broken stone mining	30	Nonmetallic mineral services and misc. minerals
	Food and Tobacco Materials		
91	Meat packing plants	120	Chewing gum
97	Condensed and evaporated milk	122	Malt
99	Fluid milk	124	Distilled liquor, except brandy
108	Flour and other grain mill products	126	Flavoring extracts and syrups, n.e.c.
117	Sugar	128	Soybean oil mills
119	Chocolate and cocoa products	139	Tobacco stemming and redrying
	Textile, Wood and Paper Materials		
140	Broadwoven fabric mills and fabric finishing	196	Pulp mills
142	Yarn mills and finishing of textiles n.e.c.	197	Paper mills, except building paper
169	Logging camps and contractors	198	Paperboard mills
170	Sawmills and planing mills	202	Paper coating and glazing
175	Veneer and plywood	217	Blank books and looseleaf binders

(*Continued*)

[6]We implicitly assume that all plants making a particular product combination use the same production techniques. Another possibility is that some plants use inferior production techniques. If such plants could be identified, it would be interesting to eliminate them from the sample and to just estimate the techniques which define an efficient frontier. However, data limitations prevent us from identifying the relative efficiency of plants. In particular, the Census includes estimates of total output, total labor costs, and total materials costs for each plant, but capital costs and expenditures on purchased business services are not separately identified.

Table 2: (*Continued*)

Material-producing Sector	Sector Description	Material-producing Sector	Sector Description
	Chemical, Plastics and Petroleum Materials		
224	Industrial inorganic and organic chemicals	237	Organic fibers, noncellulosic
225	Nitrogenous and phosphatic fertilizers	243	Paints and allied products
229	Adhesives and sealants	244	Petroleum refining
233	Chemical preparations, n.e.c.	249	Tires and inner tubes
235	Synthetic rubber	255	Leather tanning and finishing
	Stone, Clay and Glass Materials		
264	Glass and glass products	266	Cement, hydraulic
265	Glass containers	285	Minerals, ground or treated
	Metal Materials		
298	Primary copper	304	Copper rolling and drawing
299	Primary lead	307	Nonferrous wire drawing and insulating
300	Primary zinc	312	Metal cans
301	Primary aluminum	331	Hardware, n.e.c.
302	Primary nonferrous metals, n.e.c.	334	Miscellaneous fabricated wire products
	Equipment Components and Parts		
340	Internal combustion engines	412	Motor vehicles and car bodies
377	Refrigeration and heating equipment	413	Motor vehicle parts
	Miscellaneous Materials and Parts		
436	Jewelers' materials	443	Pens and mechanical pencils

Notes: The sector code ranges from 1 to 537, corresponding to the sequence of sectors in the benchmark U.S. I/O accounts for 1977. The 370 manufacturing sectors in this system are in the 85-454 range of codes.

primary products. The analysis covers a wide range of materials. We study the use of particular agricultural materials such as dairy farm products. We also analyze the available reports on the use of mining materials such as copper ores, processed foods such as packed meat, and various textiles, wood, and paper materials. There are several chemicals, plastics and petroleum materials. We also study the use of manufactured materials such as stone, clay and glass and metals. Only a few equipment components and parts are included in the dataset.

To illustrate the scope of the dataset with regard to the identity of the users of the materials, Table 3 lists the industry availability of reports on specified materials use of selected commodities. The use of dairy farm products is reported by plants in five manufacturing industries, those which produce butter, cheese, condensed milk, ice cream, and fluid milk. The plants in these five industries make a variety of products, including those

Table 3: Availability of Reports on Specified Materials Use for Selected Commodities by Sector.

Sector Reporting Use	Sector Description	Sector Reporting Use	Sector Description
	Use of Dairy Farm Products (1)		
95	Creamery butter	98	Ice cream and frozen desserts
96	Cheese	99	Fluid milk
97	Condensed and evaporated milk		
	Use of Copper Ores (23)		
224	Industrial inorganic and organic chemicals	298	Primary copper
	Use of Meat Packing Plant Products (91)		
91	Meat packing plants	132	Shortening and cooking oils
92	Sausages and other prepared meats	238	Drugs
101	Canned specialties	244	Petroleum refining
102	Canned fruits and vegetables	245	Lubricating oils and greases
107	Frozen specialties	255	Leather tanning and finishing
115	Bread, cake and related products	256	Boot and shoe cut stock
116	Cookies and crackers		
	Use of Logging Camp Products (169)		
170	Sawmills and planing mills	180	Particleboard
171	Hardwood dimension mills	181	Wood products n.e.c.
172	Special product sawmills	182	Wood containers
173	Millwork	196	Pulp mills
175	Veneer and plywood	197	Pulp mills
178	Wood preserving	198	Paperboard mills
179	Wood pallets and skids	201	Building paper and board mills
	Use of Synthetic Rubber (235)		
229	Adhesives and sealants	256	Boot and shoe cut stock
249	Tires and inner tubes	283	Asbestos products
250	Rubber and plastics footwear	284	Gaskets, packing and sealing devices
252	Fabricated rubber n.e.c.	307	Nonferrous wire drawing
254	Rubber and plastics hose	451	Hard surface floor coverings
	Use of Primary Lead (299)		
289	Blast furnaces and steel mills	306	Nonferrous rolling and drawing n.e.c.
291	Steel wire and related products	312	Metal cans
299	Primary lead	313	Metal barrels, drums and pails
303	Secondary nonferrous metals	405	Storage batteries
304	Copper rolling and drawing		
	Use of Refrigeration and Heating Equipment (377)		
375	Automatic merchandising machines	410	Truck and bus bodies
376	Commercial laundry equipment	411	Truck trailers
377	Refrigeration and heating equip.	412	Motor vehicle and car bodies
379	Service industry machines n.e.c.	421	Travel trailers and campers
389	Household refrigerators	423	Motor homes

(Continued)

Table 3: (*Continued*)

Sector Reporting	Use Sector Description	Sector Reporting	Use Sector Description
	Use of Synthetic Rubber (235)		
229	Adhesives and sealants	256	Boot and shoe cut stock
249	Tires and inner tubes	283	Asbestos products
250	Rubber and plastics footwear	284	Gaskets, packing and sealing devices.
252	Fabricated rubber n.e.c.	307	Nonferrous wire drawing
254	Rubber and plastics hose	451	Hard surface floor coverings
	Use of Primary Lead (299)		
289	Blast furnaces and steel mills	306	Nonferrous rolling and drawing n.e.c.
291	Steel wire and related products	312	Metal cans
299	Primary lead	313	Metal barrels, drums and pails
303	Secondary nonferrous metals	405	Storage batteries
304	Copper rolling and drawing		
	Use of Refrigeration and Heating Equipment (377)		
375	Automatic merchandising machines	410	Truck and bus bodies
376	Commercial laundry equipment	411	Truck trailers
377	Refrigeration and heating equip.	412	Motor vehicle and car bodies
379	Service industry machines n.e.c.	421	Travel trailers and campers
389	Household refrigerators	423	Motor homes

Note: The I/O sector codes of the materials are shown in parentheses.

primary to 25 other industries, which are as diverse as cereal breakfast foods and manufactured ice. Correspondingly, for this first material, indexed by the subscript $i = 1$, equation (2) has a vector of observed dairy products use as the left-hand-side variable, and there are 30 right-hand-side variables describing the product composition of these plants, five for the primary products and 25 for the secondary products. The commodity technology equations (2) explaining the use of copper ores, meat packing plant products, or other materials have a similar form: observations on use of the materials by plants in several industries are explained by the wide-ranging product composition of these plants.

3. Primary vs. Secondary Production Techniques

In fact, the most natural division of plants to test for differences in technical coefficients is between primary and secondary producers. So, in the estimation, we focus on a subset of material-product combinations for which it is possible to estimate requirements for make as a primary product, a^p, separately from the requirements for make as a secondary product, a^s. Our regression equations are a less restrictive form of equation (2):

$$\mathbf{u}_i = a_{i1}^p \mathbf{v}_1^p + \cdots + a_{i370}^p \mathbf{v}_{370}^p + a_{i1}^s \mathbf{v}_1^s + \cdots + a_{i370}^s \mathbf{v}_{370}^s, \qquad (3)$$

where the superscripts p and s on $\mathbf{v}_1$ through $\mathbf{v}_{370}$ now index primary and secondary production of the specific commodities indexed 1 through 370. This dichotomy is useful for investigating whether multiple production techniques are present. If techniques do differ substantially across manufacturing plants, it is likely that the distribution of techniques will be correlated with the product mix.

Table 4 summarizes the distribution of regression summary statistics. Estimates are computed from 71 separate OLS regressions, one regression for each of the materials.[7] The goodness-of-fit tends to be quite high; only about 5 percent of the regressions explain less than 50 percent of the variation in materials use, and most of the regressions explain more than 80 percent of the variation.

Table 4: Distribution of Regression Summary Statistics for Use of 71 Specific Materials by Manufacturers with Use Dependent on Make as Primary or Secondary Product.

Quantile of Statistic	Fit and Scope of the Regression		
	Goodness of Fit	Number of Products	Number of Plants
0	0.38	5	27
5	0.50	10	75
10	0.53	28	98
25	0.66	46	373
50	0.80	84	934
75	0.89	129	1,816
90	0.97	154	3,239
95	0.98	170	4,585
100	0.99	205	6,360

Notes: There are 1,073 observations on the statistics in the columns, one observation per material-product combination with reports of specified materials use available from manufacturing plants; material-product combinations with too few reports to identify both the primary- and secondary-production requirements parameters are excluded. The regression statistics in each column are sorted separately. Thus, for example, the smallest goodness-of-fit is 38 percent, but this does not necessarily arise in the regression with the fewest products (5).

[7] In Tables 4 and 5, each regression statistic is sorted relative to the same statistics from other regressions. Thus, for example, the smallest goodness-of-fit is 38 percent, but this lowest R^2 does not necessarily arise in the regression with the fewest products (5).

The number of products of material users ranges from a low of five products in the regression explaining the use of sugar to a high of 205 products in the regression explaining the use of rolled or drawn copper. Most regressions reflect the make of 84 or more products. There are at least 27 manufacturing plant observations in each regression. Most regressions attempt to explain the use by more than 934 manufacturing plants of a specific material. The high numbers of observations facilitates the estimation and testing of technologies and their differences.

As shown in Table 5, the estimates of requirements for make as a primary product generally are in the expected range from zero to one, with less than 5 percent clearly negative and statistically significant at the 5 percent significance level. The estimates of requirements for make as a secondary product are a bit more imprecise and wide-ranging. A bit more than 5 percent of the estimates are significantly negative, suggesting that there are a few secondary production techniques that use fewer of these specified materials than the use in primary production. Also, about 4.5 percent of the estimated requirements for secondary production exceed one, whereas very few of the estimated requirements for primary production exceed this upper threshold.

Table 5: Distribution of Regression Results for Use of 71 Specific Materials by Manufacturers with Use Dependent on Make as Primary or Secondary Product.

Quantile of Statistic	Make as a				T-statistic for Difference
	Primary Product		Secondary Product		
	a^p	*t*-Statistic	a^s	*t*-Statistic	
0	−1.17	−5.00	−305.81	−18.38	−12.39
5	0.00	0.05	−0.38	−2.25	−3.22
10	0.00	0.05	−0.21	−1.04	−1.44
25	0.01	0.43	−0.03	−0.17	−0.37
50	0.02	1.55	0.02	0.13	0.04
75	0.09	6.33	0.13	0.91	0.57
90	0.23	16.75	0.43	2.85	2.07
95	0.37	29.05	0.90	5.79	3.32
100	232.48	348.89	29.85	46.81	19.98

Notes: There are 1,073 observations on the statistics in the columns, one observation per material-product combination with reports of specified materials use available from manufacturing plants; material product combinations with too few reports to identify both the primary- and secondary-production requirements parameters are excluded. The regression statistics in each column are sorted separately.

To more fully quantify the extent to which secondary production techniques really do tend to differ, we also have computed the difference between the parameter estimates and scaled the difference by its conventional standard error. This *t*-statistic for the difference between primary and secondary production requirements is significantly negative in about 7 percent of the cases and is significantly positive in another 10 percent of the cases (final column of Table 5). In all, there is no evidence of a significant difference between primary and secondary production techniques in about 83 percent of the 1,073 material-product combinations we tested. Thus, in the vast majority of cases, the results support the common assumption that material requirements for a product are not dependent on whether this production is the modal activity of a manufacturing plant.

The conclusion that techniques are mostly uniform across primary and secondary production is strengthened when the cases of different techniques are examined more closely. The 17 percent of the cases where material–product coefficients are different will be broken down into three, roughly equal subgroups. In one-third of these cases, the differences can be ascribed to possibly improper aggregation in the original tests. In a second third, the further examination is inconclusive due to insufficient reporting of the data needed for additional tests. Only in the remaining third, that is 6 percent of all the material–product combinations, do differences in primary and secondary production techniques withstand the tests with alternative specifications and, therefore, can be said to be indigenous. This share is low enough to be ascribed to measurement error. In other words, with regard to materials use, the neoclassical assumption that a single, most efficient technique is chosen for making each product appears to be a good one for most U.S. manufacturing products.

In examining in more detail the material–product combinations which appear to have different proportions in primary vs. secondary production, we note that the following specification issues could cause false rejections of the homogeneity test.

3.1. *Underlying Product Diversity*

Sometimes products are classified as primary to the same sector on the basis of similarities in the customer market, rather than similarities in production

(Triplett 1992). An example is the pet food sector, whose primary products include both "dog and cat food" — which contains significant amounts of beef and fish — and "other pet food" — which contains significant amounts of grains and seed for feeding pets such as birds. Pet food plants which make secondary products tend to have different underlying primary product mixes from pet food plants which make only primary products; for example, a tuna packing plant is likely to can goods for both household and pet consumption, and the former counts as a secondary product in the pet food sector. Bird seed packagers likely do not make secondary products for household consumption. Too much aggregation in this pet food primary product group could lead us to infer that the technical coefficients differ across primary and secondary producers, when really they only differ because of product diversity within the primary product group. In principle, further disaggregation can be used to identify this source of technical difference.

To identify cases in which the apparent difference in primary and secondary production techniques is explained by product heterogeneity among the products classified as primary to the same sector, we modify equation (3) by further disaggregating the explanatory variables that gave rise to the finding of heterogeneity in techniques. If the significant differences between primary and secondary production techniques get resolved by further disaggregation, we count the case as an instance explained by product diversity among primary products. As shown in Table 6, about two-thirds of the cases can be tested for underlying product diversity. Of these, 53 material product combinations no longer reject the test of homogeneity between primary and secondary production techniques. In other words, in 28 percent of the cases where we originally found an apparent difference, primary and secondary production techniques did look similar at a more disaggregate product level; this 28 percent of the differences between techniques is ascribed to underlying product diversity.

3.2. *Use of Similar Delivered Materials*

In this case, too little aggregation of materials could create differences in technical coefficients that really only reflect the use of close substitute materials which, for most purposes, could just as well have been counted as a single material in the original analysis. For example, there are separate

Table 6: Summary of Classification of Apparent Differences Between Primary and Secondary Production Techniques.

Explanation Code	Description	Number of Cases	Percent of Cases
	Total apparent differences	190	100
A	Underlying product diversity		
	Not testable	64	34
	Testable	126	66
	No rejection	53	28
	Still reject	73	38
B	Use of similar delivered materials		
	Not testable	152	80
	Testable	38	20
	No rejection	16	8
	Still reject	22	12
C	Use of produced-and-consumed materials		
	Not testable	148	78
	Testable	42	22
	No rejection	23	12
	Still reject	19	10
Memo:			
A, B, C	Any of the explanations		
	Not testable	54	28
	Testable under at least one	136	72
	No rejection under at least one	70	37
	Still reject under all tested	66	35

Source: Calculations by the authors by the method described in the text.

sectors for the primary production of fluid milk and of condensed or evaporated milk, so these items are counted as separate materials, even though the ultimate requirements on dairy farms from the use of the materials is similar.

To identify cases in which the apparent differences in techniques can be explained by very close substitutability of the materials, we aggregate close substitute materials and re-do the test at the more aggregate levels.[8] As shown in the second grouping of rows in Table 6, some use of similar delivered materials is reported by only enough respondents to apply this test to 20 percent of the cases. Of these, 16 cases, or 8 percent of the total 190

[8]Again, we rely on the SIC as an indicator of substitutability. Specifically, materials use at the 6-digit materials code level is aggregated to a 3-digit level.

rejections, no longer indicate a difference between primary and secondary production techniques.

3.3. *Use of Produced-and-Consumed Materials*

The use of produced-and-consumed materials is relatively common in industries such as meat-packing. Under-reporting of materials use arises if the analysis is restricted to purchased materials, which is the conventional format of the data. To investigate the extent to which the omission of produced-and-consumed materials has introduced the appearance of heterogeneity, we also have estimated equation (3) under the broader definition of materials, that include self-supplied inputs.[9]

As shown in the third group of rows in Table 6, some use of produced and consumed materials is reported by enough respondents to test this explanation for about 22 percent of the cases. Of these, 23 cases no longer reject the test of similarity. In other words, about 12 percent of all of the initial rejections can be resolved by the incorporation of the use of produced-and-consumed materials. Many of these are cases in which requirements for delivered materials are lower for secondary producers. Apparently, there is some tendency for the simultaneous production and consumption of materials to occur in conjunction with secondary production.

To summarize these results, underlying product diversity explains 28 percent of the original 190 findings of heterogeneity. The use of close substitute materials explains 8 percent, and the use of produced-and-consumed materials explains 12 percent of the original findings of heterogeneity. A bit over one-third (37 percent) of the differences are explained (eliminating the double-counting that could arise because more than one explanation could be applicable). In 35 percent of the cases, the rejection of the *t-test* is still there under all tested explanations. The remainder of 28 percent is not testable.[10]

---

[9]The dependent and independent variables in equation (3) are measured in dollars, but the data on produced-and-consumed materials is available only in physical units. To aggregate across delivered and produced-and-consumed materials, we value the produced-and-consumed materials at the average price of the plant-specific delivered materials of the same kind.

[10]For product diversity, the explanation is not testable if there are not enough plants that report the make of the more disaggregate products; such additional detail must be available for both primary and secondary producers, but often the secondary producers specialize in a single product class. For the use of close substitute materials, the explanation is not testable if the questionnaires on materials use do not

4. Sensitivity to Scale Effects

Our main results, shown in Table 5, are from estimating equation (3) by ordinary least squares (OLS) and testing the restriction that materials use requirements do not depend on whether products are made as primary products or as secondary products. The statistical properties of these coefficient estimators and tests depend both on the distribution of the explanatory variables — make as a primary or secondary product — and on the distribution of the implicit error term in equation (3). In this section, we discuss the sensitivity of these statistical properties to scale effects, the presence of very large and very small (in terms of output) plants in the sample, and the possibility that the model should exhibit dependence on plant size.

The presence of both large and small plants in the sample contributes to the ability of the regressions to achieve a high goodness of fit (Table 4). However, we do not use the goodness of fit measures for any inferences about economic structure, and this wide size distribution does not, in and of itself, bias our OLS coefficient estimators or test statistics. Scale effects are potentially important for our statistical inferences only if these scale effects have contaminated the implicit error term in equation (3).

One possibility is that the standard deviation of the error term for equation (3) is directly proportional to a measure of plant size; in other words, there could be size-related heteroskedasticity of the first degree. To help us be specific in discussing this, note that the m-th row of equation (3) corresponds to the observation on the m-th manufacturing plant and can be written as

$$u_{im} = \sum_{k=1}^{370} (a_{ik}^{p} v_{mk}^{p} + a_{ik}^{s} v_{mk}^{s}) + \varepsilon_{im}, \qquad (3')$$

where ε_{im} is the implicit error term. Using the plant's level of primary production, v_{mj}^{p}, as a convenient measure of plant size, this type of size-related heteroskedasticity is a proportional relationship between the standard deviation of ε_{im} and v_{mj}^{p}. In this case, OLS estimators of the coefficients in equation (3′) remain unbiased, but OLS is not an efficient (minimum

ask about close substitutes (other materials in the 3-digit class) in both the industry where production is primary and the industries where production is secondary. For the use of own-produced materials, the explanation is not testable unless such activity is reported by both primary and secondary producers.

variance) estimator. A weighted least squares procedure, using the v^p_{mj} as weights, would be more efficient. Also, heteroskedasticity would render invalid the conventionally-calculated OLS standard errors, biasing the test statistics, whereas the conventional standard errors and test statistics from the weighted least squares regression would be correct.

The estimation of equation (3′) by such a weighted least squares procedure likely would be preferable to our OLS estimation of equation (3) and would be equivalent to estimating the following transformed equation by OLS[11]:

$$\frac{u_{im}}{v^p_{mj}} = \sum_{k=1}^{370} \left(a^p_{ik} \frac{v^p_{mk}}{v^p_{mj}} + a^s_{ik} \frac{v^s_{mk}}{v^p_{mj}} \right) + \frac{\varepsilon_{im}}{v^p_{mj}}, \qquad (3'')$$

Whether or not size-related heteroskedasticity is present and to what degree is an empirical matter which cannot be ascertained at this time.[12] However, the econometric theory in this area is well-known and indicates that the OLS standard errors from the untransformed regression (3) generally will understate the true degree of estimation error which would be revealed by estimating (3″).[13] Tests based on (3) instead of (3″) of the equality of material requirements for primary and secondary production would be biased toward rejection. We found little evidence of differences with a test which might be biased toward finding evidence of frequent differences. Accordingly, the possible presence of such size-related heteroskedasticity reinforces our main conclusions.[14]

---

[11]We thank an anonymous referee for suggesting tests based on equations like (3″) to avoid possible problems with scale effects.

[12]Our research affiliation with the Census Bureau has expired, and we no longer have access to the confidential Census data used in our original empirical work. Furthermore, this dataset is so rich — as many as 71 inputs and 370 outputs could be reported for each of 96,515 manufacturing plants — that exploring alternative forms for the regression would be quite burdensome computationally.

[13]See, for example, Theil (1971), p. 248.

[14]We conducted some Monte Carlo experiments to simulate how size-related heteroskedasticity could have affected our results. In particular, we generated random data on the use of materials and the make of primary and secondary products by one hundred hypothetical manufacturing plants, supposing that 20 percent of these were large plants with output levels which averaged ten times that of the small plants. We split the plants into two industries and allowed for the make of one additional secondary product, with eighty percent of production, on average, devoted to primary production. In one set of experiments, there was no size-related heteroskedasticity, and in the other set of experiments, the standard deviation of the error term was proportional to the plant's level of primary production. We generated the artificial

The recognition of another possible scale-related misspecification — the omission of an intercept from equation (3″) — also works to strengthen the support for our main conclusions. Allowing for overhead materials requirements in this form that allows for economies of scale would introduce in the model another parameter that would be capable of absorbing any originally-estimated differences in technical coefficients between primary and secondary producers. The commodity technology model does not allow for such economies of scale, and we did not find many estimated differences; so such richer parameterizations appear unneeded for evaluating the commodity technology model.

5. Conclusion

This paper lends support to the commodity technology model of material input use. Material input requirements can be reasonably well-approximated without considering joint production. Using raw data reports from almost 100,000 U.S. manufacturing plants, technical coefficients have been estimated and tested. The problem of negative coefficients in the presence of secondary production appeared to be significant in only about 5 percent of the material-product combinations. Moreover, after further testing, we find that in only about 6 percent of the cases (which is 35 percent of the initial rejections), the difference between primary and secondary coefficients withstands further scrutiny. In other words, generally, we find that material requirements do not depend on whether the goods are made as primary products or as secondary products. Within U.S. manufacturing sectors, differences in material input factor intensities tend to reflect patterns

data 1000 times for each of the 100 plants, and calculated the regressions and tests corresponding to both equation (3) and equation (3″).

As expected, in the set of experiments without size-related heteroskedasticity and a true null hypothesis of no difference in requirements between primary and secondary production, the rejection frequencies for the 5 percent significance level hypothesis tests based on (3) were close to their theoretical values; no difference was detected in 4.4 percent of the 1000 cases for the tests based on (3). In the set of experiments with size-related heteroskedasticity, the tests based on (3) rejected much too often; 41.5 percent of the 1000 cases showed a false rejection. In contrast, the rejection frequency of the tests based on (3") was relatively insensitive to the presence of size-related heteroskedasticity. These Monte Carlo experiments illustrate that tests based on (3″) are superior in the sense that they are robust to the possible heteroskedasticity. However, the Monte Carlo experiments also illustrate that our main conclusion that there is little apparent difference between material requirements for primary and secondary production is reinforced by the possibility of bias in the tests based on equation (3).

of product specialization, not the co-existence of alternative techniques to produce output.

Acknowledgements

We thank an anonymous referee and participants at numerous seminars for helpful comments. The bulk of this research was completed while Mattey was a Research Associate at the Center for Economic Studies (CES), U.S. Bureau of the Census, for the Board of Governors of the Federal Reserve System. The paper presents the authors' own views, not those of the Census Bureau or the Federal Reserve System.

References

Armington, P. (1969) The Geographic Pattern of Trade and the Effects of Price Changes, International Monetary Fund Staff Papers.

Brown, D.K. and R.M. Stern (1989) Computable General Equilibrium Estimates of the Gains from U.S.-Canadian Trade Liberalization, in Greenaway, D., Hyciak, T. and Thornton, R.J. (eds.), *Economic Aspects of Regional Trading Arrangements*. New York: University Press.

Hamilton, R. and J. Whalley (1985) Geographically discriminatory trade arrangements, *Review of Economics and Statistics*, 446–455.

Kop Jansen, P. and Th. ten Raa (1990) The choice of model in the construction of input-output coefficients matrices, *International Economic Review*, 31(1), 213–227.

Lopez-de-Silanes, F., J.R. Markusen and T.F. Rutherford (1992) Complementarily and Increasing Returns in Intermediate Inputs: A Theoretical and Applied General-Equilibrium Analysis, NBER Working Paper No. 4179.

Mattey, J.P. (1993) Evidence on IO Technology Assumptions from the LRD, U.S. Bureau of the Census Center for Economic Studies Discussion Paper 93-8.

Pyatt, G. (1993) Modelling Commodity Balances, paper presented as the Richard Stone Memorial Lecture at the Tenth International Conference on Input Output Techniques, Seville, Spain.

Reinert, K.A., D.W. Roland-Holist and C.R. Shiells (1993) Social accounts and the structure of the North American economy, *Economic Systems Research*, 5(3), 295–326.

Stone, R. (1961) *Input-Output and National Accounts*, OECD, Paris.

Thiel, H. (1971) *Principles of Econometrics*. New York: John Wiley & Sons.

Triplett, J.E. (1992) Perspectives on the SIC: Conceptual Issues in Economic Classification, manuscript, Bureau of Economic Analysis, U.S. Department of Commerce.

United Nations (1993) A System of National Accounts.

Wonnacott, R.J. and P. Wonnacott (1967) *Free Trade Between the United States and Canada: The Potential Economic Effects*. Cambridge, MA: Harvard University Press.

Doms, M. E. and J. B. Jensen (1998) [illegible] in the [illegible] Economic [illegible]

[illegible] (1996) [illegible]

Chapter 17

Stochastic Analysis of Input–Output Multipliers on the Basis of Use and Make Tables

Thijs ten Raa and José Manuel Rueda-Cantuche

Abstract: Although technical coefficients are estimated on the basis of flow data (use and make matrices), they are rarely treated as random variables. If this is done, an error term is added to the coefficients, rather than derived from the distribution of the data. Even so, the calculation of multipliers, by means of the Leontief inverse, is difficult. Due to the nonlinearity of this operation, the multiplier estimates are biased. By going back to the flow data, this paper provides unbiased and consistent employment and output multipliers estimates for the Andalusian economy. Rectangular use and make matrices are accommodated, and problems associated with the construction and estimation of technical coefficients and the Leontief inverse are circumvented.

1. Introduction

The prime use of input and output accounts is the estimation of multiplier effects, such as the employment and output effects of increases in alternative final demand components. The multipliers are "given" by the

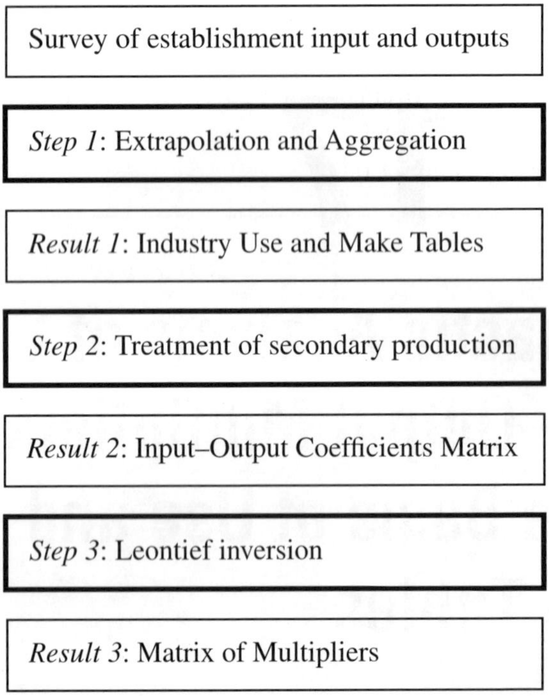

Fig. 1: From Establishment Data to Input–Output Multipliers.

Leontief inverse of the matrix of input–output coefficients. The practice of interrelating accounts and input–output multipliers can be decomposed into three steps, see Figure 1.

Step 1 consists of filling data gaps, imputing values to non-observed establishments, and summation over firms within industries. These operations are straightforward and produce the so-called use and make tables, U and V, which display the commodity inputs and outputs of the industries. The off-diagonal elements of the make table are the so-called secondary products, which must be treated one way or another in Step 2. The System of National Accounts (U.N. 1993) advocates the so-called commodity technology, which involves the inversion of the make table. Anyway, the result is a matrix of input–output coefficients, A. The third and last step is Leontief inversion, $(I-A)^{-1} = I+A+A^2+\ldots$. In multiplier analysis, the first term represents the direct effect, the second term the direct input requirement, and the third and further terms the indirect input requirements.

The literature is as piecemeal as Figure 1 suggests. The theory of input–output coefficients addresses Step 2 and analyzes alternative models for their construction. Results are partial and problems persist, such as the problem of negative coefficients. Basically, input–output coefficients measure inputs per units of outputs and the division by outputs involves the inversion of the make table, a complicated, nonlinear operation. The stochastic input–output literature focuses on Step 3, analyzing the transmission of errors under Leontief inversion. Here, the problem is also a nonlinearity, but not one associated with the presence of secondary products. In fact, the problem is already there in a one-sector economy, where matrix A, reduces to a scalar a. Because the Leontief inverse, $(I - a)^{-1} = 1+a+a^2+\ldots$, is a convex function of input–output coefficient a, Young's Theorem yields that the expectation of the Leontief inverse exceeds the Leontief inverse of the expectation of the input–output coefficient. Since the latter constitutes the standard Leontief inverse, it follows that the standard Leontief inverse underestimates its true value. Simonovits (1975) and Kop Jansen (1994) extend this result, albeit under rather restrictive assumptions, such as the independence of technical coefficients. Dietzenbacher (1995) and Roland-Holst (1989) find more overestimation than underestimation.

In this paper, we make two, interrelated contributions to the literature. First, we derive information on the precision of multipliers not from stochastic assumptions on the input–output coefficients, but from the variability of the underlying input and output statistics across establishments. In other words, we go back to square 1 in Figure 1. Second, we integrate the steps of Figure 1 by reducing the formulas for multipliers to the establishment use and make tables. To our delight, the nonlinearities which plague the construction of input–output coefficients and the transmission of errors in the Leontief inverse neutralize each other. In this way, we are able to present consistent linear unbiased estimates of multipliers. We contrast our results with the official ones of the Institute of Statistics of Andalusia (IEA).

2. From Data to Coefficients and From Coefficients to Multipliers

Modern input–output accounting distinguishes commodities $i = 1, \ldots, n$ and activities $j = 1, \ldots, m$. (We have traced this approach to Edmonston 1952.) At the most disaggregated level, an activity represents a plant. Plant

j uses inputs (both factor services and commodities) to make products (commodities). For reasons of national accounting, it is customary to list the inputs in the j-th column of *use* matrix $U = (u_{ij})$, but the outputs in the j-th row of *make* matrix $V = (v_{ji})$. The requirements of input i by industry j are proportional to its products v_{jk}. If we assume that the proportions, a_{ik}, are independent of the industry, (the so-called commodity technology assumption), we obtain for the technical coefficients:

$$u_{ij} = \sum_{k=1}^{n} a_{ik} v_{jk} \quad \text{for all } i = 1, \ldots, n \text{ and } j = 1, \ldots, m. \tag{1}$$

According to Konijn and Steenge (1995), an input–output matrix A has to fulfill the commodity technology assumption to achieve full consistency with the fundamentals of input–output analysis. Kop Jansen and ten Raa (1990) arrived at the same conclusion on axiomatic grounds. Moreover, Avonds (2005) demonstrated that the product technology assumption need not break the economic circuit, as de Mesnard (2004) argued.

If there are more activities than commodities ($m > n$), the system of equations (1) is overdetermined; an error term must be attached, and the input–output coefficients become regression coefficients. Several studies have attempted to estimate technical coefficients from econometric models with cross-section data on firms' inputs and outputs. Miernyk (1970) quantifies the level of uncertainty in measured technical coefficients. Mattey and ten Raa (1997) support the commodity technology hypothesis for United States manufacturing.

In the literature on stochastic input–output analysis, technical coefficients are the point of departure for the analysis of the probabilistic properties of the Leontief inverse, $B = (I - A)^{-1}$. Kop Jansen (1994) reviews how stochastics affect the multipliers, i.e. the distributional properties of the Leontief inverse. Young's Theorem extends (assuming independence and symmetry) and the expected value of the Leontief inverse is underestimated by the Leontief inverse of the expected value of the A-matrix. This bias of the standard Leontief inverse will be revealed by our results. For purists, the situation is as follows. Denote the true value of the input–output matrix by α and of its Leontief inverse by β. Denote the estimate of α by A and of β by B. The standard estimator of β is $B = (I - A)^{-1}$. The expectation of B is $\mathrm{E}(B) = \beta + \text{bias}$. Denote the estimator we will develop in the next section by $\boldsymbol{B}$. Since it will be unbiased, $\mathrm{E}(\boldsymbol{B}) = \beta$. It follows that the bias of the standard Leontief inverse is $\mathrm{E}(B) - \mathrm{E}(\boldsymbol{B})$. We will estimate this bias by $B - \boldsymbol{B}$. If the assumptions of the extension of Young's Theorem are valid, we expect $B < \boldsymbol{B}$, or that standard multipliers *under*estimate our estimates of the true values.

An output multiplier is given by the total value of production needed to satisfy a euro's worth of a particular component of final demand and an multiplier measures the associated number of workers. We will adopt the commodity technology hypothesis for intermediate and labor inputs. Use and make transactions exclude imports, and are valued at basic prices. Net commodity taxes and non-deductible Value Added Tax (VAT) are excluded, as are trade and transport margins. The latter are assigned to the trade and transport services industry. The measurement in basic prices accommodates the treatment of net exports as part of final demand.

Employment multipliers are derived from labor coefficients. Commodity technology labor coefficients are determined by the following expression:

$$L = lV^{\mathrm{T}}, \tag{2}$$

where L represents a row vector of labor employment (of order m), l is the row vector of labor coefficients and V^{T} the transposed make matrix. Inflation by the Leontief inverse yields the employment multipliers (λ):

$$\lambda = l(I - A)^{-1}. \tag{3}$$

Multipliers (3) measure the employment generated by a monetary unit expended on alternative commodities. It is no workers per worker figure, but a kind of return-on-investment measure.

In traditional input–output analysis, all matrices are square ($m = n$) and equations (1) and (2) imply the well-known commodity technology coefficients $A = U(V^{\mathrm{T}})^{-1}$ and $l = L(V^{\mathrm{T}})^{-1}$ (Kop Jansen and ten Raa, 1990). In this case, the employment multipliers (3) reduce to:

$$\begin{aligned}\lambda &= L(V^{\mathrm{T}})^{-1}[I - U(V^{\mathrm{T}})^{-1}]^{-1} = L\{[I - U(V^{\mathrm{T}})^{-1}]V^{\mathrm{T}}\}^{-1} \\ &= L(V^{\mathrm{T}} - U)^{-1}.\end{aligned} \tag{4}$$

or

$$L = \lambda(V^{\mathrm{T}} - U). \tag{5}$$

If there are more activities than commodities ($m > n$), the system of equation (5) is overdetermined, an error term must be attached, and the employment multipliers become regression coefficients:

$$L = \lambda(V^{\mathrm{T}} - U) + \varepsilon, \tag{6}$$

In (6), L is a row vector of order m with labor employment; λ is a row vector of order n with employment multipliers; V is a make matrix of order $m \times n$; U is a use matrix of order $n \times m$; and ε is a row vector of independently normally random disturbance errors with zero mean and constant variance, with order m. Notice that m is the number of establishments or observations, and that net outputs by commodities would therefore constitute the independent variables of the resulting model. The estimation of employment multipliers becomes a matter of multiple linear regression analysis, with linear, unbiased and consistent multipliers estimates. In section 3, we estimate (6) for the Andalusian economy in the year 1995.

Output multipliers, μ, are given by the column totals of the Leontief inverse:

$$\mu = e(I - A)^{-1} \tag{7}$$

The only difference with equation (4) is the replacement of the row vector of labor coefficients l by the unit vector $e = (1 \cdots 1)$. In standard input–output analysis, the output multipliers (7) are represented by:

$$\mu = e[I - U(V^{\mathrm{T}})^{-1}]^{-1} = eV^{\mathrm{T}}(V^{\mathrm{T}} - U)^{-1} \tag{8}$$

or

$$eV^{\mathrm{T}} = \mu(V^{\mathrm{T}} - U). \tag{9}$$

Analogous to the system of equations (5), the output multipliers become regression coefficients when there are more activities than commodities ($m > n$). That is, net outputs would be considered again as exogeneous variables.

$$eV^{\mathrm{T}} = \mu(V^{\mathrm{T}} - U) + \varepsilon, \tag{10}$$

In (10), eV^{T} is a row vector of total outputs of establishments (of order m) and μ, a row vector of output multipliers (of order n), having V, U and ε the same meaning as for employment multipliers. In the next section, equation (10) will also be estimated for the Andalusian economy in 1995.

Both for the employment and the output multipliers, the huge sample size justifies our normality assumption by the Central Limit Theorem.

3. Results

The sample used by the IEA (1999) to construct published use and make tables covered nearly 45% of total regional outputs and more than a third of total employment. The IEA completed the initial survey-based information on industries' disaggregated turnovers and purchases with other statistical sources from the National Statistical Institute (INE), the Central Balance Sheet Office and public institutions (health services, government budget data, education, agriculture, etc.) to achieve such a large sample coverage. However, while most observations were establishments, some industries data had to be consolidated into single observations (see Table 1) being the final sample size of our analysis equal to 18,084 observations.

The official input–output table (IEA 1999) was compiled using the commodity technology model as a first estimation. Next, changes were made manually depending on the resulting negatives and their possible causes, i.e. errors in use and make tables, the heterogeneity of the industry classification and vertical integration, where sometimes the industry technology assumption was preferable. Nevertheless, for comparison purposes, the published input–output based multipliers shown in Table 1 were not constructed on the basis of the official A matrix, but on a pure product technology basis. This means that equations (3) and (7) were computed using published use and make tables and $A = U(V^{\mathrm{T}})^{-1}$.

3.1. *Employment Multipliers*

The employment multipliers estimates are presented in Table 1. For comparison, the second column displays the employment multipliers based on published use and make matrices under the commodity technology assumption.

The model has been estimated for 87 commodities by means of ordinary least squares. The resulting R-squared is 0.9948, which is quite satisfactory. Due to the presence of certain forms of unknown heteroskedasticity, the White estimate (White 1980) of the covariance matrix of estimated

Table 1: Employment Multipliers (number of workers per 600,000 Euros).

	Description	Sample Size	Estimated Multiplier	Leontief Inverse Multiplier	p Value	Lower Bound	Upper Bound	Industry Share* (%)	Commodity Share** (%)
1	Fruit and vegetables	1	23.9	24.1	0	23.3	24.6	3.0	0.2
2	Olive and vine	1	21	21.2	0	20.5	21.5	5.1	0.1
3	Other agriculture and related services	1	14.6	14.8	0	14.2	15.1	2.9	15.9
4	Livestock and hunting	1	21.1	21.3	0	20.7	21.5	1.4	10.2
5	Forestry and related services	1	30	30.3	0	29.5	30.5	6.0	7.7
6	Fish and fishing products	173	11	18.3	0	9.7	12.4	24.7	0.0
7	Coal mining	4	7.2	13.7	0	5	9.3	3.6	0.0
10	Metallic minerals	7	7	8.8	0	4.2	9.8	28.2	0.0
11	Non-metallic and non-energetic minerals	1	11	10.9	0	10.1	12	3.4	2.2
12	Meat and meat products	239	6.4	9.8	0.0001	3.2	9.7	8.0	2.4
13	Canned and preserved fish, fruit and vegetables	148	15	17.5	0	12.1	17.9	3.8	12.5
14	Fats and oils	252	3.4	14.5	0	2.2	4.7	3.7	1.0
15	Milk and dairy products	34	11.5	11.6	0	6.5	16.4	5.6	21.7
16	Grain mills, bakery, sugar mills, etc	469	4.6	15.6	0	2.7	6.5	3.3	4.0
17	Miscellaneous food products	139	6	6.8	0.001	2.4	9.5	12.6	4.8
18	Wine and alcoholic beverages	105	7.7	11.7	0	6.2	9.3	7.8	0.9
19	Beer and soft drinks	23	5.5	7.2	0	4.7	6.3	0.7	3.3
20	Tobacco products	3	5.4	7	0.0478	0.1	10.7	0.0	0.0
21	Textile mill products	1	10.6	10.5	0	10.2	11	4.1	1.4
22	Clothing products	483	4.4	18.4	0.0186	0.7	8	1.4	0.2
23	Leather tanning, leather products and footwear	135	7.2	18.5	0.0013	2.8	11.5	2.9	0.5
24	Cork and wood products	299	8	22.6	0.0413	0.3	15.7	2.8	1.0
25	Paper and allied products	51	3.6	7.1	0	2	5.1	2.5	2.3
26	Printing, publishing and editing services	447	33.9	10.7	0.0868	−4.9	72.7	28.2	1.7
27	Petroleum refining products	9	2	1.6	0	1.5	2.6	2.9	0.5
28	Basic chemical products	52	2.2	5.1	0.0079	0.6	3.7	2.2	7.2
29	Other chemical products	96	5	8.7	0.0185	0.8	9.2	15.4	3.6
30	Rubber and plastic products	122	3.3	9.1	0.0001	1.6	4.9	3.2	2.4
31	Cement, lime and allied products	200	4.3	10.2	0.0018	1.6	7	2.1	1.1
32	Ceramics, clay, bricks and other products for building	126	11.7	17.7	0	8.6	14.7	1.5	2.6
33	Stone and glass products	282	7.1	15.5	0	5.2	9.1	1.2	1.4

(Continued)

Table 1: *(Continued)*

	Description	Sample Size	Estimated Multiplier	Leontief Inverse Multiplier	p Value	Lower Bound	Upper Bound	Industry Share* (%)	Commodity Share** (%)
34	Primary metal products	58	0.8	2.3	0.005	0.2	1.3	2.1	0.2
35	Fabricated metal products	1,087	6.6	15.6	0.0001	3.3	9.9	1.2	3.6
36	Machinery and mechanic equipment	1	14.1	14	0	13.4	14.8	4.2	1.9
37	Computers and office equipment	1	5.5	5.9	0	4.7	6.3	0.2	5.0
38	Electrical and electronic machinery	88	3.6	8.6	0.0166	0.7	6.6	0.8	3.1
39	Electronic materials, radio and television equipment	1	7.7	7.5	0	6.9	8.5	3.1	0.0
40	Professional and scientific instruments	60	3.6	9.2	0.0664	−0.2	7.4	1.1	1.8
41	Motor vehicles transportation equipment	45	11.3	8.6	0	6.4	16.2	1.4	0.4
42	Naval transportation and repairing services	65	2.3	15.4	0.1319	−0.7	5.4	2.3	0.2
43	Miscellaneous transportation equipment	22	1.5	10.5	0.2899	−1.2	4.2	2.6	0.2
44	Furniture	601	9.7	23.1	0.0017	3.7	15.8	0.5	2.7
45	Miscellaneous manufactured products	1	14.6	14.6	0	13.9	15 3	1.6	1.5
46	Recycling products	1	9.8	11 1	0	8	11.5	0.0	0.0
47	Electricity and irrigation services	51	2.8	3.4	0	2.6	2.9	1.8	0.6
48	Gas and water steam and irrigation services	1	3.5	3.8	0	2.1	5	1.1	0.2
49	Water and sewerage services	67	10.8	11.8	0	8.1	13.5	6.5	18.2
50	Construction	1,136	7	12.2	0	5.2	8.7	1.8	3.4
51	Preparing, installation and finishing construction services	1	18.3	18.4	0	17.7	18.8	9.4	4.1
52	Petrol and motor vehicles trade services	380	18.1	17.6	0.1137	−4.3	40.4	14.8	0.0
53	Repair motor vehicles services	1	15.9	16.3	0	15.5	16.3	2.0	6.4
54	Wholesale trade	4,535	3.4	12.4	0.3184	−3.3	10.2	1.2	3.9
55	Retail trade and repair domestic and personal effects	4,113	42.9	22.1	0.1186	−11	96.8	4.5	0.6
56	Hotel services	20	19.4	14.1	0	12.8	26	26.3	3.3
57	Bar and restaurant services	352	31.1	18.8	0	23.2	39.1	1.2	7.5
58	Railway transportation services	1	10.6	11.1	0	9.9	11.2	2.6	0.0
59	Other earthbound transportation services	1	17	17.1	0	16.1	17.8	1.7	15.6
60	Sea and river transportation services	2	7.2	13.7	0	5	9.4	0.0	0.0
61	Air transportation services	1	8.4	7.6	0	4.7	12.1	19.9	0.0
62	Allied transportation services	142	8.1	13.6	0.0007	3.4	12.8	4.4	3.2

(Continued)

Table 1: (*Continued*)

	Description	Sample Size	Estimated Multiplier	Leontief Inverse Multiplier	p Value	Lower Bound	Upper Bound	Industry Share* (%)	Commodity Share** (%)
63	Post and communication services	205	5.2	10.4	0	4.7	5.8	1.1	5.2
64	Finances	1	8.7	9.1	0	7.9	9.5	0.0	0.0
65	Insurance	1	12.1	15.9	0	10.3	13.9	0.0	0.0
66	Allied financial services	1	6.4	15.4	0.0021	2.3	10.5	0.1	0.7
67	Real estate	1	2.1	2	0	1.6	2.6	0.9	4.7
68	Machinery and equipment rental	9	8.8	11	0.0001	4.5	13.2	3.0	2.1
69	Computer services	84	15.1	12.7	0.3185	−14.6	44.9	12.8	40.3
70	Research and development	1	20.1	19.9	0	19.5	20.6	0.0	0.0
71	Accounting and law activity services	235	72	18.1	0.106	−15.3	159.3	12.8	19.9
72	Engineering and architectural technical services	31	23.2	16.5	0.0203	3.6	42.8	0.5	8.9
73	Marketing services	8	1.5	21.5	0.3509	−1.7	4.7	3.2	81.9
74	Security services	48	23.5	31.6	0.0004	10.5	36.4	1.6	16.7
75	Cleaning services	1	32.7	32.1	0	31.6	33.7	1.4	0.3
76	Other business services	1	4.3	19.7	0.7309	−20.3	29	42.7	41.5
77	Public administration	1	19	18.6	0	18.2	19.8	7.6	0.0
78	Public education services	2	18.3	17.5	0	17.4	19.2	0.2	0.0
79	Private education services	150	31.8	28.1	0	29.8	33.8	10.5	1.2
80	Public medical and hospital services	1	16.6	16.8	0	16.4	16.8	0.0	0.0
81	Private medical and hospital services	4	4.9	7.6	0.0008	2	7.8	0.3	0.1
82	Public social services	1	25.6	25.7	0	25.4	25.9	0.0	0.0
83	Private social services	1	40.2	40.6	0	39.2	41.2	2.8	1.5
84	Public drainage and sewerage services	15	23.8	16.5	0	20.5	27.1	1.7	36.4
85	Social services	1	22.2	18.8	0	14.2	30.2	25.8	0.0
86	Cinema, video, radio and television services	1	29.1	5.9	0	25.2	33	44.0	3.6
87	Other amusement, cultural, sport and recreation services	538	9.6	12.4	0	84	10.9	35.3	4.1
88	Personal services	1	31.9	32.6	0	31.6	32.3	0.4	4.0
89	Household employers services	1	116.2	116.2	0	116.2	116.2	0.0	0.0

Source: Own elaboration and IEA (1999).
*Secondary product share of industry outputs.
**Secondary product share of commodity outputs.

coefficients was used to provide consistent and robust standard errors. We find that problems of autocorrelation and multicollinearity do not plague our analysis. Only 12 out of the 7482 (87 × 86) possible off-diagonal elements of a correlations matrix with 87 different explanatory variables were higher than 0.5, with only one higher than 0.75. Eventually, 76 estimated multipliers are significant at a 95% confidence level. All remaining estimators are assumed to be zero (no impact) at the same confidence level, since the null hypothesis is accepted in each one of the cases. Negative values of multipliers are insignificant.

Three major contributions are provided by the results presented in Table 1:

(a) In most cases, published data-based employment multipliers *over* estimate the true values. Indeed, 57 out of 87 commodities have lower employment multipliers than those calculated with the published use and make matrices. On the other hand, 19 commodities have higher employment multipliers. Our findings contradict the underestimation of the Leontief inverse found in Simonovits' (1975), or rather its restrictive assumptions, such as the independence of technical coefficients, and firm up the conclusions of Dietzenbacher (1995) and Roland-Holst (1989).

(b) Input–output estimates are unbiased and consistent, providing confidence intervals for employment multipliers. These intervals may be seen as a measure of the true estimates of the accuracy of multipliers. About 56% of the published based input–output multipliers values are included.

(c) The estimated bias of employment multipliers is generally positively related with secondary production. Commodities which are the primary output of industries with sizeable secondary production and commodities of which a large share is produced as secondary output have employment multipliers with a larger estimated bias, as measured by the difference between the published data based and our estimated employment multipliers. Estimated multipliers not significant at a 95% confidence level are set at zero, and therefore the estimated bias equals the official data-based multiplier.

The Spearman's rank correlation between estimated and official data-based multipliers is 0.65. Additionally, four out of the six most prominent rank reversals are insignificant at a 95% confidence level, i.e. other business services have large proportions of secondary activities (42.74%) and their primary products are produced elsewhere in sizeable amounts (41.45%), and nearly 82% of marketing services are produced by other industries. Also, just one out of the seven commodities with the highest estimated bias (in absolute values) are significant at a 5% significance level, i.e. cinema, video, radio and television services, where the secondary activities of the corresponding industry represent almost 44% of their total production.

From a theoretical view, when some industries with no secondary activities produce commodities for which other industries provide sizeable amounts, it is reasonable to assume that the technologies used by the rest of the economy for making such commodities should not match that of the industries for which they are primary products (the latter industries' technology can be considered as commodities technology since no secondary products are involved). This could explain the sizeable estimated bias of marketing services, computer services and public drainage and sewerage services.

On the contrary, when some commodities are produced by a single industry with large proportions of secondary outputs, it is reasonable to assume that these primary commodities are not produced according to a commodity technology hypothesis if the estimated bias is sizeable. Such are the cases of cinema, video, radio and television services and printing, publishing and editing services.

3.2. *Output Multipliers*

Maintaining the number of observations of the last section, the output multipliers are as presented in Table 2.

The proposed model has been estimated for 87 commodities by means of ordinary least squares and, as before, with quite satisfactory goodness of fit (R-squared equal to 0.9993). The White (1980) estimated covariance matrix of estimated regression coefficients was used to obtain consistent standard errors. The model is free from serial correlation and multicollinearity issues. This time, 84 estimated multipliers are significant at a 5% significance level.

Table 2: Output Multipliers.

	Description	Estimated Multiplier	Leontief Inverse Multiplier	p Value	Lower Bound	Upper Bound
1	Fruit and vegetables	1.266	1.323	0	1.3	1.3
2	Olive and vine	1.142	1.179	0	1.1	1.2
3	Other agriculture and related services	1.226	1.264	0	1.2	1.2
4	Livestock and hunting	1.325	1.357	0	1.3	1.3
5	Forestry and related services	1.224	1.262	0	1.2	1.2
6	Fish and fishing products	1.163	1.23	0	1.0	1.3
7	Coal mining	0.724	1.799	0.0325	0.1	1.4
10	Metallic minerals	1.337	1.365	0	1.3	1.4
11	Non-metallic and non-energetic minerals	1.523	1.562	0	1.5	1.6
12	Meat and meat products	1.447	1.664	0	1.2	1.7
13	Canned and preserved fish, fruit and vegetables	1.755	1.872	0	1.6	2.0
14	Fats and oils	1.439	1.949	0	1.3	1.5
15	Milk and dairy products	1.654	1.603	0	1.4	1.9
16	Grain mills, bakery, sugar mills, etc	1.201	1.534	0	1.1	1.3
17	Miscellaneous food products	1.3	1.402	0	1.1	1.5
18	Wine and alcoholic beverages	1.433	1.696	0	1.3	1.5
19	Beer and soft drinks	1.309	1.417	0	1.2	1.4
20	Tobacco products	1.117	1.159	0	1.0	1.3
21	Textile mill products	1.273	1.289	0	1.3	1.3
22	Clothing products	1.165	1 336	0	1.0	1 4
23	Leather tanning, leather products and footwear	1.177	1.366	0	1.1	1.3
24	Cork and wood products	0.679	1.431	0.0069	0.2	1.2
25	Paper and allied products	1.117	1.314	0	1.0	1.2
26	Printing, publishing and editing services	0.507	1.243	0.1699	−0.2	1.2
27	Petroleum refining products	1.271	1.245	0	1.2	1.3
28	Basic chemical products	1.206	1.621	0	1.0	1.4
29	Other chemical products	1.031	1.287	0	1.0	1.1
30	Rubber and plastic products	0.921	1.29	0	0.8	1.1
31	Cement, lime and allied products	1.183	1.739	0	1.0	1.4
32	Ceramics, clay, bricks and other products for building	1.182	1.415	0	1.1	1.3
33	Stone and glass products	1.299	1.546	0	1.2	1.4
34	Primary metal products	1.058	1.2	0	1.0	1.1
35	Fabricated metal products	1.04	1.272	0	0.9	1.2
36	Machinery and mechanic equipment	1.266	1.284	0	1.2	1.3
37	Computers and office equipment	1.296	1.352	0	1.3	1.3
38	Electrical and electronic machinery	1.045	1.156	0	1.0	1.1
39	Electronic materials, radio and television equipment	1.17	1.202	0	1.2	1.2
40	Professional and scientific instruments	1.043	1.155	0	1.0	1.1

(*Continued*)

Table 2: (*Continued*)

	Description	Estimated Multiplier	Leontief Inverse Multiplier	p Value	Lower Bound	Upper Bound
41	Motor vehicles transportation equipment	1.318	1.243	0	1.1	1.5
42	Naval transportation and repairing services	1.024	1.502	0	1.0	1.0
43	Miscellaneous transportation equipment	1.032	1.232	0	1.0	1.1
44	Furniture	1.21	1.464	0	1.1	1.4
45	Miscellaneous manufactured products	1.34	1.367	0	1.3	1.4
46	Recycling products	1.346	1.493	0	1.2	1.5
47	Electricity and irrigation services	1.072	1.434	0	1.1	1.1
48	Gas and water steam and irrigation services	1.05	1.147	0	0.9	1.2
49	Water and sewerage services	1.293	1.448	0	1.1	1.5
50	Construction	1.353	1.67	0	1.2	1.5
51	Preparing, installation and finishing construction services	1.352	1.374	0	1.3	1.4
52	Petrol and motor vehicles trade services	−0.168	1.295	0.5752	−0.8	0.4
53	Repair motor vehicles services	1.197	1.232	0	1.2	1.2
54	Wholesale trade	0.593	1.253	0	0.3	0.8
55	Retail trade and repair domestic and personal effects	0.917	1.391	0	0.8	1.0
56	Hotel services	1.264	1.329	0	1.1	1.4
57	Bar and restaurant services	1.355	1.523	0	1.2	1.5
58	Railway transportation services	1.22	1.252	0	1.2	1.2
59	Other earthbound transportation services	1.422	1.465	0	1.4	1.4
60	Sea and river transportation services	1.876	2.256	0	1.7	2.0
61	Air transportation services	1.321	1.304	0	1.2	1.5
62	Allied transportation services	1.106	1.607	0	1.0	1.2
63	Post and communication services	1.069	1.145	0	1.1	1.1
64	Finances	1.183	1.193	0	1.2	1.2
65	Insurance	1.711	1.74	0	1.7	1.8
66	Allied financial services	1.421	1.431	0	1.3	1.5
67	Real estate	1.082	1.088	0	1.1	1.1
68	Machinery and equipment rental	1.151	1.236	0	1.1	1.3
69	Computer services	1.597	1.231	0.0001	0.8	2.4
70	Research and development	1.076	1.086	0	1.0	1.1
71	Accounting and law activity services	2.465	1.477	0.069	−0.2	5.1
72	Engineering and architectural technical services	1.156	1.409	0	0.8	1.5
73	Marketing services	1.046	1.68	0	0.9	1.2
74	Security services	1.227	1.094	0	0.8	1.7
75	Cleaning services	1.104	1.11	0	1.1	1.1
76	Other business services	1.002	1.427	0.03	0.1	1.9
77	Public administration	1.309	1.317	0	1.3	1.3
78	Public education services	1.027	1.051	0	1.0	1.0
79	Private education services	1.193	1.284	0	1.1	1.2

(*Continued*)

Table 2: (*Continued*)

	Description	Estimated Multiplier	Leontief Inverse Multiplier	p Value	Lower Bound	Upper Bound
80	Public medical and hospital services	1.13	1.142	0	1.1	1.1
81	Private medical and hospital services	1.214	1.208	0	1.2	1.3
82	Public social services	1.178	1.195	0	1.2	1.2
83	Private social services	1.471	1.524	0	1.4	1.5
84	Public drainage and sewerage services	1.165	1.346	0	1.1	1.2
85	Social services	2.136	2.124	0	1.9	2.4
86	Cinema, video, radio and television services	2.097	1.411	0	1.9	2.3
87	Other amusement, cultural, sport and recreation services	1.689	1.457	0	1.7	1.7
88	Personal services	1.385	1.443	0	1.4	1.4
89	Household employers services	1	1	0	1.0	1.0

Source: Own elaboration and IEA (1999).

The same as in employment multipliers holds for nonsignificant estimates and negative values.

The output multipliers results presented above provide similar employment multipliers contributions. These are:

(a) Mostly, official data-based output multipliers are *over*estimated and not underestimated. It is remarkable that 73 out of 87 commodities have lower output multipliers than published data-based multipliers, whilst 11 commodities have higher output multipliers. Again, most of the output multipliers obtained by using published data are overestimated and not underestimated, confirming Dietzenbacher (1995) and Roland-Holst (1989).

(b) Unbiasedness and consistency of estimated input–output multipliers, jointly with derived confidence intervals. In this case, 34.5% of published data-based multipliers are included within them.

(c) Once more, the estimated bias of output multipliers has a positive relationship with secondary production. The Spearman's rank correlation between official data based and estimated multipliers is 0.51. Moreover, we find that the three products with highest estimated bias correspond exactly with the three isolated insignificant commodities at a 95% confidence level, i.e. accounting and law activity services

(12.8% of secondary productions and 19.9% of services produced elsewhere), printing, publishing and editing services (28.2% of secondary outputs) and petrol and motor vehicles trade services (14.8% of secondary activities).

It is surprising that the output multipliers are more accurate than the employment multipliers. With only three exceptions, the p-values in Table 2 are smaller than the corresponding ones in Tabel 1.

Some macrochecks have been carried out in order to test the robustness and coherence of the results by using equations (5) and (9) with our estimated input–output multipliers and the published net outputs matrix. Consequently, the estimated total employment requirements reach 1,871,800 people, which is only 2.38% higher than the official value (1,828,400); furthermore, the estimated total outputs, which yield €105,799 million, is just 3.65% higher than published total productions (€102,070 million).

4. Conclusions

Technical coefficients are the subject of two disjoint bodies of literature. The construction of technical coefficients is linked to flow data (use and make matrices), but stochastics are imposed on the coefficients when multipliers are calculated, by means of the Leontief inverse. Due the nonlinearity of this operation, the multiplier estimates are biased as it is generally argued that the Leontief inverse underestimates input–output multipliers.

In this paper, we let the flow data tell the stochastics and take them all the way to confidence intervals for multipliers. We focus on the use and make matrices, instead of the A-matrix, to obtain unbiased and consistent multipliers estimates. Our output and employment multipliers are normally distributed and do not suffer from over- or underestimation. Our results for the Andalusian economy indicate that the Leontief inverse is not underestimated but overestimated in most of the cases.

Statistical offices combine use and make flow data (including the inversion of the make matrix) to construct input–output coefficients, and economists invert the Leontief matrix to determine the output and cost multipliers of the economy. The construction and the inversion are nonlinear operations with complicated errors transmission and have been studied in relative isolation. This paper shows, however, that an integrated analysis, from the use and make data directly to the multipliers, provides simple, unbiased and consistent estimates.

Acknowledgements

This paper was written when J. M. Rueda Cantuche was a visiting fellow at CentER, Tilburg University, supported by a grant of Pablo de Olavide University. Thanks are due to M. Asensio (Institute of Statistics of Andalusia) and Dr. A. Titos (University of Cordoba) for technical support. We are grateful to three anonymous referees and editor Bart van Ark for criticisms and suggestions which led to significant improvements of the paper.

References

Avonds, L. (2005) Belgian Input–Output Tables: State of the Art, working paper, Federal Planbureau, Brussels, Belgium.

de Mesnard, L. (2004) Understanding the shortcomings of commodity-based technology in input–output models: an economic-circuit approach, *Journal of Regional Science*, 44, pp. 125–141.

Dietzenbacher, E. (1995) On the bias of multiplier estimates, *Journal of Regional Science*, 35, pp. 377–390.

Edmonston, J.H. (1952) A treatment of multiple-process industries, *Quarterly Journal of Economics*, 66, pp. 557–571.

EUROSTAT (1996) *Sistema Europeo de Cuentas SEC-1995*. Oficina de Publicaciones Oficiales de las Comunidades Europeas, Luxemburgo.

IEA (Institute of Statistics of Andalusia) (1999) *Sistema de Cuentas Económicas de Andalucía. Marco Input–Output 1995 (MIOAN95)* Seville, Spain.

Konijn, P.J.A. and A.E. Steenge (1995) Compilation of input–output data from the national accounts, *Economic Systems Research*, 7, pp. 31–45.

Kop Jansen, P.S.M. (1994) Analysis of multipliers in stochastic input–output models, *Regional Science and Urban Economics*, 24, pp. 55–74.

Kop Jansen, P.S.M. and Th. ten Raa (1990) The choice of model in the construction of input–output coefficients matrices, *International Economic Review*, 31, pp. 213–227.

Mattey, J.P. and Th. ten Raa (1997) Primary versus secondary production techniques in US manufacturing, *Review of Income and Wealth*, 43, pp. 449–464.

Miernyk, W.H. *et al.* (1970) *Simulating regional economic development*. DC Heath, Lexington.

Roland-Holst, D.W., "Bias and Stability of Multiplier Estimates," *Review of Economics and Statistics*, 71, pp. 718–721, 1989.

Simonovits, A. (1975) A note on the underestimation and overestimation of the Leontief inverse, *Econometrica*, 43, pp. 493–498.
United Nations (1993) *Revised System of National Accounts*, Studies in Methods, Series F, No. 2, Rev. 4.
Viet, V.Q. (1994) Practices in input–output table compilation, *Regional Science and Urban Economics*, 24, pp. 27–54.
White, H. (1980) A heteroscedasticity-consistent covariance matrix estimator and a direct test for heterocedasticity, *Econometrica*, 48, pp. 817–838.

Appendix: Data

The Andalusian Input–Output Framework 1995 (MIOAN95) is one of the first Spanish input–output tables based on the new European System of Accounts (ESA-95) published by EUROSTAT (1996). The IEA provided the cross-section inputs and outputs establishment data. These data were used for the elaboration of the Input–Output Andalusian Framework 1995 (IEA, 1999).

IEA publishes two use tables, which differ by valuation. One is valued at purchasers' prices and the other at basic prices, which is the same as the former, but excluding trade and transport margins and net commodity taxes; see Viet (1994, p.28). (Trade and transport margins are simply reallocated from the commodities where they are included, at purchasers' values, to the use matrix rows of trade and transport services). The make table is published exclusively at basic prices. The United Nations System of National Accounts (SNA) recommends basic values; the production costs of good and services are measured before they are conveyed to the market for consumption so that the effects of tax and subsidy policies, as well as differences in types of economic transactions, are isolated.

IEA transforms use data at purchasers' prices into basic prices, as described below. The use and make tables at basic prices are balanced to obtain the final official accounts for the Input–Output framework.

Since all input and output data provided by IEA were valued at purchasers' prices and at basic prices, respectively, we subtracted trade and transport margins, and also net commodity taxes, from establishment inputs in order to have the same valuation (basic prices) for inputs and outputs, and to estimate equations (6) and (9). As detailed below, we applied the same formula, formalized here for the first time, as IEA used for the elaboration of the use matrix at basic prices, and assumed equality of margins and net commodity taxes between establishments in industry j, which consume some commodity k. We will focus now on the procedure.

According to the ESA-95, the intermediate uses at basic values are equal to the intermediate uses at purchasers' prices minus trade and transport margins and minus net commodity taxes. Let u_{kj}^b and u_{kj}^p be the total inputs of commodity k by industry j (excluding imports) at basic and at purchasers' prices, respectively. Then, we can write:

$$u_{kj}^b = u_{kj}^p - T_{kj}^d - T_{kj} - N_{kj} - H_{kj}, \tag{11}$$

where, for each use of commodity k by industry j, T_{kj}^d and T_{kj} are the total amount of trade and transport margins, respectively, N_{kj} is the total amount of net commodity taxes (excluding non-deductible VAT) and H_{kj} is the total amount of non-deductible VAT.

We will assume that the trade margins are proportional to the use data at purchasers' prices. The proportions are defined by:

$$T_{kj}^d = t_{kj}^d u_{kj}^p, \quad 0 < t_{kj}^d < 1. \tag{12}$$

Next, we will assume that net commodity taxes (excluding non-deductible VAT) and transport margins are proportional to the use data at basic prices:

$$N_{kj} = n_{kj} u_{kj}^b, \quad 0 < n_{kj} < 1; \tag{13}$$

$$T_{kj} = t_{kj} u_{kj}^b, \quad 0 < t_{kj} < 1. \tag{14}$$

With respect to VAT, the hypothesis is as follows:

$$H_{kj} = h_{kj}\left(\frac{u_{kj}^p}{1 + h_{kj}}\right), \quad 0 < h_{kj} < 1. \tag{15}$$

Then, by substituting (12), (13), (14) and (15) in (11), we obtain:

$$u_{kj}^b = u_{kj}^p\left(\frac{1 - t_{kj}^d - \frac{h_{kj}}{1+h_{kj}}}{1 + t_{kj} + n_{kj}}\right). \tag{16}$$

Yet this formula would be used to transform use data from basic values to purchasers' values when dealing with industries but not with establishments.

However, our purpose is to estimate the unknown u^b_{kji}, that is, the total use of commodity k by an establishment i from industry j at basic prices. Then since survey available data is based on establishments of a particular industry and not on products, we denote u^p_{kji} and u^b_{kji} as purchasers' and basic prices use data, respectively. Based on (16), our objective would be to apply the following formula for each establishment, i:

$$u^b_{kji} = u^p_{kji}\left(\frac{1 - t^d_{kji} - \frac{h_{kji}}{1+h_{kji}}}{1 + t_{kji} + n_{kji}}\right). \tag{17}$$

A problem arises when available information does not enable us to value establishment-specific t^d_{kji}, h_{kji}, t_{kji} and n_{kji}. In this case, we will assume the equality of margins and net commodity taxes across firms in industry j, which consumes some commodity k. We consequently use (17) with:

$$\begin{aligned} t^d_{kji} &= t^d_{kj} && \text{for all } i,\\ t_{kji} &= t_{kj} && \text{for all } i,\\ n_{kji} &= n_{kj} && \text{for all } i,\\ h_{kji} &= h_{kj} && \text{for all } i, \end{aligned}$$

so that the formula becomes:

$$u^b_{kji} = u^p_{kji}\left(\frac{1 - t^d_{kj} - \frac{h_{kj}}{1+h_{kj}}}{1 + t_{kj} + n_{kj}}\right). \tag{18}$$

Once trade and transport margins, and net commodity taxes, have been subtracted from use flow data, the last step would be to reallocate the subtracted total trade and domestic transport margins to trade and transport industries, respectively. This was done with the help and technical support of IEA.

Part VI

Performance Analysis

Chapter 18

A Neoclassical Analysis of TFP Using Input–Output Prices

Thijs ten Raa

Abstract: Input–output analysis and neoclassical economics do not seem to mix. Neoclassical economists consider input–output analysis a futile exercise in central planning or at least resent the separation between the quantity and value systems. Conversely, input–output economists resent marginal analysis without an understanding of the underlying structure of the economy. In this paper, I turn the perceptions upside down by analyzing productivity. I ground the concept in the orthodox neoclassical general equilibrium framework. Then I introduce a linear specification and use input–output analysis to derive a measure of total factor productivity without using value shares of factor inputs. In other words, input–output analysis has the potential to explain prices which neoclassical growth accountants take at face value.

1. Introduction

During one of our very last discussions, Wassily Leontief asked me: "What are you doing these days?" I replied that I am reconciling input–output analysis and neoclassical economics. He leant back, thought, looked me straight into the eyes, and said "Should be easy."

Yet input–output analysis and neoclassical economics seem hard to mix. The resentment between the two schools of economics is a two-way affair.

Neoclassical economists consider input–output analysis a futile exercise in central planning. The relationship between the delivery of a bill of final goods and its requirements in terms of gross output and factor inputs is considered mechanical, with no or little attention paid to the role of the price mechanism in the choice of techniques (Leontief 1941). True, input–output analysis is used to relate prices to factor costs, but here too, the analysis is considered mechanical as input–output coefficients are presumed to be fixed. To make things worse, the quantity and value analyses are perceived to be disjunct with no interaction between supply and demand.

Conversely, input–output economists consider neoclassical economics a futile exercise in marginal analysis that fails to grasp the underlying structure of the economy. Firms supply up to the point that marginal revenue equals marginal cost and set the price accordingly. But does not marginal cost depend on all prices in the system, including the one of the product under consideration? And if the answer is yes, should we not take into account the interindustry relations, i.e. apply input–output analysis?

Many, including myself, have been held captive by these perceptions. Yet they are misleading. Instead of criticizing the critiques, a meta-analysis which is doomed to have little input, I provide some shock therapy, that puts the perceptions upside down, by analyzing a concrete issue, namely productivity measurement. Why productivity? Well, the standard, neoclassical measure of productivity growth, the so-called Solow residual between output growth and input growth employs market values of labor and capital to compute a weighted average of their input growth rates. Now it can be shown that the Solow residual is equal to a weighted average of the growth rates of the real wage and the real rental rate of capital. (In other words, total factor productivity growth is the sum of labor productivity growth and capital productivity growth.) By taking the wage rate and rental rate at market values in computing the Solow residual, neoclassical economists accept at face value what they are supposed to measure.

In this paper, I adopt the methodological position of neoclassical economics, by which productivity is defined as the marginal contribution of factors inputs, but apply input–output analysis to determine its value. The analysis is framed in the orthodox general equilibrium model, which subsequently will be specified to accommodate growth accounting. I will recover the neoclassical formulas, such as the Solow residual, but the structure of the economy will be exploited to determine the values.

2. Earlier Work

My first attempt to reconcile input–output and neoclassical economics is in the sequel papers: ten Raa (1994), and ten Raa and Mohnen (1994). We maximized the value of final demand at world prices. The final demand for non-tradable commodities was simply fixed at the observed level. In short, we expanded final demand for tradable commodities, but not for non-tradable commodities. The model lacks a utility foundation. We rectified this in ten Raa (1995) and Mohnen *et al.* (1997), where we maximized the level of the entire domestic final demand vector, given its proportions. In ten Raa and Mohnen (2002), we investigated not only the frontier of the economy, but also the fluctuations of the observed economy about its frontier. All the aforementioned papers are about small, open economies with exogenous prices for the tradable commodities. The main contribution of this paper is that it lays out the theory for a closed economy. In other words, we make the step from partial to general equilibrium analysis.

Subsidiary, I now present the theory from an orthodox mathematical economic perspective, say Debreu (1959). First and foremost, the two "practical" approaches of input–output analysis and growth accounting are clearly embedded in a unifying framework. Second, the general equilibrium framework endogenizes the value shares used in growth accounting exercises (such as Jorgenson and Griliches 1967). Third, the exposition makes Debreu's framework accessible to applied economists.

3. Growth Accounting

There are two sources of growth. The first is that economies produce more output, simply because they use more input, such as labor. Of course, this is a mere size effect; there is no increase in the standard of living. The second source of growth is more interesting. Economies produce more output per unit of input because of technological progress. The classical exposition of these two sources of growth is Solow (1957). He demonstrates that the residual between output and input growth measures the second source of growth, that is the shift of the production possibility frontier. In his analysis, Solow makes two assumptions. First, the production function is macro-economic, hence transforming labor and capital into a single output. Second, the economy must be perfectly competitive, so that factor inputs are priced according to their marginal productivities. By the first assumption, the output has a well-defined growth rate. The input growth rate, however, must be some weighted average of the labor growth and capital growth rates; the appropriate weights are shown to be the value shares of labor and capital in national income. The two assumptions are quite restrictive. The use of a single output requires the aggregation of commodities and makes it difficult to compare sectors in terms of productivity performance. The notion of perfect competition is a far cry from most observed economies.

I will show how growth accounting can be freed from these assumptions. Basically, I will work in a multi-dimensional commodity model and calculate productivities without using observed value shares. The analysis is self-contained and serves as a nice refresher of mathematical economics. The main concepts of this branch of economics are equilibrium, efficiency, and the welfare theorems that interrelate equilibrium and efficiency. I will review all this in the next section. To make the theory operational, I will then consider the linear case of the model, with constant returns to scale and nonsubstitutability in both production and household consumption. Efficiency is then the outcome of a linear program and the Lagrange multipliers of the factor input constraints measure their productivities. Summing over endowments, I obtain total factor productivity. The analysis is shown to be consistent with the aforementioned Solow residual. Moreover, input–output analysis will enable us to reduce total factor productivities growth rates to sectoral productivity and thus to pinpoint the strong and the weak sectors.

4. Equilibrium and Efficiency

Denote the number of commodities in an economy by integer n. The commodity space is the n-dimensional Euclidian space, $\mathbb{R}^n$. A commodity bundle is a point in this space, say $\mathbf{y} \in \mathbb{R}^n$. Negative components represent inputs and positive components outputs. For example, in a Robinson

Crusoe economy, where (labor) time is transformed into food, $(1, -1)'$ is the bundle representing 1 hour of work and a metric ounce of food. A prime is used to indicate transposition. Denote the collection of all technically feasible commodity bundles by Y. Y is a subset of $\mathbb{R}^n$. It represents the production possibilities of the economy. I make two assumptions on Y. First, Y is convex. This means that if $\mathbf{y}$ and $\mathbf{z}$ belong to Y, then so does $\lambda\mathbf{y}+(1-\lambda)\mathbf{z}$ for any λ between 0 and 1. Although the assumption is always made in the general equilibrium analysis, it is not innocent. It rules out increasing returns to scale. Second, Y is compact. In the context of our Euclidian commodity space, this means that Y is bounded and closed. In the literature, this assumption, namely the boundedness, is relaxed, but at the expense of uninteresting complications.

In a perfectly competitive economy, producers pick the production plan that maximizes profit given the prices. Denote the commodity prices by vector $\mathbf{p}$ and let a prime denote transposition. The profit of any production plan $\mathbf{y}$ is then given by $\mathbf{p}'\mathbf{y}$ since inputs have negative signs in $\mathbf{y}$. $\mathbf{p}'\mathbf{y}$ is the inner product of $\mathbf{p}$ and $\mathbf{y}$: $\sum_{i=1}^{n} p_i y_i$. Here, the positive terms represent revenue and the negative terms cost. Now maximize $\mathbf{p}'\mathbf{y}$ by choosing $\mathbf{y}$. The solution will depend on $\mathbf{p}$ and, therefore, is denoted $\mathbf{y}(\mathbf{p})$. Formally,

$$\mathbf{y}(\mathbf{p}) = \operatorname*{argmax}_{\mathbf{y}\in Y} \mathbf{p}'\mathbf{y}.$$

Given $\mathbf{p}$, producers "supply" $\mathbf{y}(\mathbf{p})$. Strictly speaking, only the positive components represent supply, while the negative components represents business demand, as for labor. I define **supply** as the mapping $\mathbf{y}(\cdot)$. This constitutes one side of equilibrium analysis.

Turning to consumers. For simplicity, I assume there is only one utility function, u, so consumers have the same preferences. For a commodity bundle $\mathbf{y}$, the real number $u(\mathbf{y})$ represents the utility it yields to the consumers. Utility is essentially ordinal. Comparing commodity bundles $\mathbf{y}$ and $\mathbf{z}$, what matters is if $u(\mathbf{y}) > u(\mathbf{z})$, $u(\mathbf{y}) < u(\mathbf{z})$, or $u(\mathbf{y}) = u(\mathbf{z})$, but the absolute difference between the utility levels is immaterial. In fact, the entire analysis will be unaffected by a monotonic transformation of the utility function. I make three assumptions on u. First, u is continuous. This is an innocent, technical assumption, that can be shown to be implied by the other assumptions, using a monotonic transformation. The second assumption is that u is increasing. This means that more is preferred. Third, u is quasi-concave. This is defined by the condition that the preferred set, $\{\mathbf{y} \mid u(\mathbf{y}) \geq \text{constant}\}$ is convex. It means that consumers prefer convex combinations.

In a perfectly competitive economy, consumers pick the commodity bundle that maximizes utility subject to the budget constraint and given the prices. What is the budget constraint? For a moment, ignore dividends, so that all income stems from labor. In the framework of Robinson Crusoe's economy, the question is when $\mathbf{y} = (-h, f)'$ is financially feasible. (Here h is hours worked and f is amount of food.) If p_2 is the price of good and p_1 the price of labor time, then the answer is $p_2 f \leq p_1 h$, which can be written briefly as $\mathbf{p}'\mathbf{y} \leq 0$. The budget constraint is basically zero, because the commodity bundle has a negative component that generates (labor) income. In a private enterprise economy, profit, $\mathbf{p}'\mathbf{y}(\mathbf{p})$, supplements the budget constraint and consumers solve the following optimization problem

$$\max_{\mathbf{y}} u(\mathbf{y}) \text{ subject to } \mathbf{p}'\mathbf{y} \leq \mathbf{p}'\mathbf{y}(\mathbf{p}).$$

The commodity bundle that comes out of this is what consumers "demand." (The positive components represent demand, the negative components household supply, as of labor.) I define **demand** as the mapping from prices $\mathbf{p}$ to the commodity bundle that solves the consumers' problem.

Now we have all the building bricks and can proceed to define the main concepts of mathematical economics, namely equilibrium and efficiency. Conceptually, they are very different. Equilibrium requires a price system; it is defined by the equality between demand and supply. Since the latter are both mappings from prices to commodity bundles, **equilibrium** is defined formally as a price vector, $\mathbf{p}^*$, such that supply and demand assume a common value. Equilibrium is a positive concept, to describe what actually happens in market economies, without saying it is good or bad. Statements on the performance of an economy, however, are normative and require no price mechanism. Suppose we want to compare a centrally planned economy to a decentralized market economy. The centrally planned economy may have no price system at all. Still we want to evaluate which one performs better. This is a matter of utility. We say one economy is better than another if it attains a higher utility level for the consumers. An economy is efficient if it obtains the maximum utility level that is technologically feasible. Since utility is defined on commodity bundles, **efficiency** is defined formally by a commodity bundle, $\mathbf{y}^*$, such that utility is maximized over Y:

$$\mathbf{y}^* = \operatorname*{argmax}_{\mathbf{y}\in Y} u(\mathbf{y}).$$

Notice the conceptual difference between equilibrium and efficiency. The former is given by a price vector, the latter by a commodity bundle. An equilibrium equates supply and demand, but makes no statement on the level of utility. Efficiency promotes utility, but requires no price system.

Although the concepts are very different, there is a deep, close relationship for perfectly competitive economies. By definition, an economy is perfectly competitive if no producer or consumer can manipulate the prices, but considers them as given. It can be claimed that the commodity bundle generated by the equilibrium price vector is efficient. In short, an equilibrium is efficient. This statement is called the **first welfare theorem**. I also claim that an efficient commodity bundle can be generated by an equilibrium price vector. In short, an efficient allocation is an equilibrium. This statement is called the **second welfare theorem**. The two welfare theorems are deep and must be proved.

The proof of the first welfare theorem is relatively easy. We must show that an equilibrium, say $\mathbf{p}^*$, generates an efficient allocation, $\mathbf{y}(\mathbf{p}^*)$. The proof is by contradiction. Suppose $\mathbf{y}(\mathbf{p}^*)$ is not efficient. By the definition of efficiency, there exists $\mathbf{y} \in Y$ such that $u(\mathbf{y}) > u(\mathbf{y}(\mathbf{p}^*))$. By the definition of demand, it must be that y is too expensive: $\mathbf{p}^{*\prime}\mathbf{y} > \mathbf{p}^{*\prime}\mathbf{y}(\mathbf{p}^*)$. By the definition of supply, it must be that $\mathbf{y}$ is not feasible: $\mathbf{y} \notin Y$. This contradicts the definition of $\mathbf{y}$. The supposition that $\mathbf{y}(\mathbf{p}^*)$ is not efficient is therefore not tenable. This completes the proof that an equilibrium is efficient.

The proof of the second welfare theorem proceeds as follows. Let $\mathbf{y}^*$ be efficient, hence maximize $u(\mathbf{y})$ over Y. Then we must construct an equilibrium price system that generates it. Consider the feasible set, Y, and the preferred set, $\{\mathbf{y} \in \mathbb{R}^n \mid u(\mathbf{y}) > u(\mathbf{y}^*)\}$. By the efficiency of $\mathbf{y}^*$, the sets do not intersect. By the assumptions on production and utility, the two sets are convex. Now we invoke Minkowski's separating hyperplane theorem, by which two convex sets that do not intersect can be separated by a hyperplane.

(See, for example, Rockafellar 1970). Hence there exists a row vector, say $\mathbf{p}^*$, such that

$$\mathbf{p}^{*\prime}\mathbf{y}_1 > \mathbf{p}^{*\prime}\mathbf{y}_2$$

holds for all $\mathbf{y}_1 \in \{\mathbf{y} \in \mathbb{R}^n \mid u(\mathbf{y}) > u(\mathbf{y}^*)|\}$ and $\mathbf{y}_2 \in Y$. I claim $\mathbf{p}^*$ is an equilibrium. For this, we must show that given $\mathbf{p}^*$, $\mathbf{y}^*$ is supplied and demanded. First, consider supply. Since utility is increasing, the above inequality yields for any $\varepsilon > \mathbf{0}$ (in $\mathbb{R}^n$)

$$\mathbf{p}^{*\prime}(\mathbf{y}^* + \varepsilon) > \mathbf{p}^{*\prime}\mathbf{y}, \quad \mathbf{y} \in Y.$$

Hence $\mathbf{p}^{*\prime}\mathbf{y}^* \geq \mathbf{p}^{*\prime}\mathbf{y}$, hence $\mathbf{y}^*$ maximizes profit and therefore, is supplied: $\mathbf{y}^* = \mathbf{y}(\mathbf{p}^*)$. Next consider demand. If $\mathbf{y}$ is superior to $\mathbf{y}^*$, $u(\mathbf{y}) > u(\mathbf{y}^*)$, then it is out of the budget, $\mathbf{p}^{*\prime}\mathbf{y} > \mathbf{p}^{*\prime}\mathbf{y}^* = \mathbf{p}^{*\prime}\mathbf{y}(\mathbf{p}^*)$. Hence, $\mathbf{y}^*$ maximizes utility subject to the budget constraint and therefore, is demanded. This completes the proof that an efficient allocation is an equilibrium.

So far, I have remained silent about existence. Does an equilibrium exist? The usual analysis to find an intersection point of supply and demand is by means of a so-called fixed point theorem. This is difficult. We make a shortcut. It is easy to see that an efficient allocation exists. All we have to do is to maximize utility, u over the feasible set, Y. Since u, is continuous and Y is compact, a maximum exists, say $\mathbf{y}^*$. By the second welfare theorem, it is an equilibrium, say $\mathbf{p}^*$. Hence an equilibrium exists.

In the literature, all sorts of variations on the above analysis are found. More commodities, more products, more consumers, you name it. The basic structure, however, remains the same. Equilibrium is defined by the equality of supply and demand, efficiency by the impossibility to raise the utility level further, and the two are related by the first and second welfare theorem, provided convexity assumptions hold and agents are price takers. Then competitive prices can be analyzed by studying the efficiency problem, where utility is maximized over the feasible set. For example, the well-known statement that competitive economies reward factor inputs according to their productivities can be demonstrated. This will be done in the next section for linear economies.

5. Efficiency and Productivity

The model of the last section is quite general, at least in terms of functional forms. I now add the flesh and blood of linear economics, including input–output analysis. Let there be m activities. Denote an $m \times n$-dimensional matrix of outputs by $\mathbf{V}$ and an $n \times m$-dimensional matrix of inputs by $\mathbf{U}$. Add an m-dimensional vector of capital inputs, $\mathbf{k} \geq \mathbf{0}$, and similarly for labor, $\mathbf{l} \geq \mathbf{0}$. Assume every activity requires positive factor input (k_i and l_i not both zero). Let the economy be endowed with a capital stock k and labor force l. Let

$$Y = \{\mathbf{y} \in \mathbb{R}^n \mid \mathbf{y} \leq (\mathbf{V}' - \mathbf{U})\mathbf{s}, \quad \mathbf{k}'\mathbf{s} \leq k,\ \mathbf{l}'\mathbf{s} \leq l, \mathbf{s} \geq \mathbf{0}\}$$

where $\mathbf{s} \in \mathbb{R}^m$ is the vector listing m activity levels. Then Y is an example of a production possibility set as we defined it in Section 3. Y is the intersection of a number of half-spaces, which is obviously convex. The assumption that every activity requires factor input ensures that Y is compact.

The modelling of household consumption is similar. Denote an n-dimensional vector of consumption coefficients by $\mathbf{a} > \mathbf{0}$. Then for $\mathbf{y} \geq \mathbf{0}$,

$$u(\mathbf{y}) = \min y_i/a_i$$

is the Leontief utility function. (I choose this utility function, because it enables us to substitute observed consumption values in the Total Factor Productivity growth expression of the next section.) Basically, consumers want their bundle in the proportions of $\mathbf{a}$, say $c\mathbf{a}$, where c is a scalar. It is easy to see that

$$u(\mathbf{y}) = \max_{c\mathbf{a} \leq \mathbf{y}} c.$$

Proof. First, we prove $u(\mathbf{y}) \geq \max_{c\mathbf{a}\leq\mathbf{y}} c$. For all $\mathbf{y} \geq c\mathbf{a}$, $u(\mathbf{y}) \geq u(c\mathbf{a}) = c$. Hence also $u(\mathbf{y}) \geq \max_{c\mathbf{a}\leq\mathbf{y}} c$. Next, we prove the converse. At least one constraint in $\max_{c\mathbf{a}\leq\mathbf{y}} c$ is binding: $a_j c^* = y_j$ for some j, where c^* is the constrained maximum. Now $u(\mathbf{y}) = \min y_i/a_i \leq y_j/a_j = c^* = \max_{c\mathbf{a}\leq\mathbf{y}} c$. This completes the proof. □

We have production and utility, so we can set up the efficiency problem,

$$\max_{\mathbf{y}\in Y} u(\mathbf{y}).$$

Using the alternative formulation of the utility function, we can rewrite the efficiency problem as

$$\max_{\mathbf{s},\mathbf{y},c} c \text{ subject to } c\mathbf{a} \leq \mathbf{y} \quad \text{and} \quad \mathbf{y} \in Y.$$

Notice that both the objective and the constraints are linear in the variables. The efficiency problem of a linear economy is a linear program. The linear program can be simplified slightly by eliminating one of the variables, $\mathbf{y}$:

$$\max_{\mathbf{s},c} c \text{ subject to } c\mathbf{a} \leq (\mathbf{V}' - \mathbf{U})\mathbf{s}, \quad \mathbf{k}'\mathbf{s} \leq k, \;\; \mathbf{l}'\mathbf{s} \leq l, \;\; \mathbf{s} \geq \mathbf{0}.$$

This linear program maximizes the level of final consumption subject to the material balance, the capital and labor constraints, and a nonnegativity constraint. Another, succinct formulation of the linear program, is

$$\max\,(\mathbf{0}'\;1)\begin{pmatrix}\mathbf{s}\\ c\end{pmatrix} \text{ subject to } \begin{bmatrix}\mathbf{U}-\mathbf{V}' & \mathbf{a}\\ \mathbf{k}' & 0\\ \mathbf{l}' & 0\\ -\mathbf{I} & \mathbf{0}\end{bmatrix}\begin{bmatrix}\mathbf{s}\\ c\end{bmatrix} \leq \begin{bmatrix}\mathbf{0}\\ k\\ l\\ \mathbf{0}\end{bmatrix}.$$

In general, when we $\max f(\mathbf{x})$ subject to $g(\mathbf{x}) \leq b$, the first order conditions are $\mathbf{f}' = \lambda\mathbf{g}'$, $\lambda \geq 0$. Here $\mathbf{f}'$ is the (row) vector of partial derivatives $\partial f/\partial x_i$ of f. If g is scalar valued, $\mathbf{g}'$ is also the row vector of partial derivatives $\partial g/\partial x_i$. If the constraints are given by $G(\mathbf{x}) \leq \mathbf{b}$, with G vector valued, the first order conditions are $\mathbf{f}' = \boldsymbol{\lambda}'\mathbf{G}$, $\boldsymbol{\lambda} \geq \mathbf{0}$, where $\mathbf{G}$ is the Jacobian matrix of partial derivatives (i.e. element g_{ij} of matrix $\mathbf{G}$ equals $\partial g_i(\mathbf{x})/\partial x_j$).

The first order conditions reflect the tangency of the isoquants of the objective and constraint functions. In the picture, f and g grow in the same direction (the North-East), hence $\lambda \geq 0$. If λ were negative, then f and g would grow in opposite directions and one could simply increase f by wandering into the feasible region (g would be reduced). λ is called the Lagrange multiplier. Because $\mathbf{f}' = \lambda\mathbf{g}'$, and $g(\mathbf{x}) \leq b$, λ measures the rate of change of the objective function with respect to the constraint. If b is relaxed by one unit, then f goes up by λ units. If G is vector-valued, then each constraint has a Lagrange multiplier and $\boldsymbol{\lambda}$ is a vector of Lagrange multipliers.

In our linear program, $f\binom{\mathbf{s}}{c} = (\mathbf{0}'\ 1)\binom{\mathbf{s}}{c}$ and $\mathbf{f}' = (\mathbf{0}'\ 1)$. Also,

$$G\begin{pmatrix}\mathbf{s}\\ c\end{pmatrix} = \begin{bmatrix}\mathbf{U}-\mathbf{V}' & \mathbf{a}\\ \mathbf{k}' & 0\\ \mathbf{l}' & 0\\ -\mathbf{I} & \mathbf{0}\end{bmatrix}\begin{pmatrix}\mathbf{s}\\ c\end{pmatrix} \quad \text{and} \quad \mathbf{G} = \begin{bmatrix}\mathbf{U}-\mathbf{V}' & \mathbf{a}\\ \mathbf{k}' & 0\\ \mathbf{l}' & 0\\ -\mathbf{I} & \mathbf{0}\end{bmatrix}.$$

The constraints are the material balance, the capital constraint, the labor constraint, and the nonnegativity constraint. It is customary to denote the Lagrange multipliers by $\mathbf{p}$, r, w, and $\boldsymbol{\sigma}$, respectively. The first order conditions, $\mathbf{f}' = \boldsymbol{\lambda}'\mathbf{G}$, $\boldsymbol{\lambda} \geq \mathbf{0}$ read

$$(\mathbf{0}'\ 1) = (\mathbf{p}',\ r,\ w,\ \boldsymbol{\sigma}')\begin{bmatrix}\mathbf{U}-\mathbf{V}' & \mathbf{a}\\ \mathbf{k}' & 0\\ \mathbf{l}' & 0\\ -\mathbf{I} & \mathbf{0}\end{bmatrix}, \quad (\mathbf{p}',\ r,\ w,\ \boldsymbol{\sigma}') \geq \mathbf{0}'.$$

The second component, $\mathbf{p}'\mathbf{a} = 1$, is a price normalization condition. The first component, $\mathbf{0}' = \mathbf{p}'(\mathbf{U} - \mathbf{V}') + r\mathbf{k}' + w\mathbf{l}' - \boldsymbol{\sigma}'$, can be rewritten as $\mathbf{p}'(\mathbf{V}' - \mathbf{U}) = r\mathbf{k}' + w\mathbf{l}' - \boldsymbol{\sigma}$, $\boldsymbol{\sigma} \geq \mathbf{0}$, or

$$\mathbf{p}'(\mathbf{V}' - \mathbf{U}) \leq r\mathbf{k}' + w\mathbf{l}'.$$

On the left-hand side, we find value-added, and on the right-hand side, factor costs, for the respective activities.

$\mathbf{p}$, r and w are the perfectly competitive equilibrium prices. I am going to demonstrate this by means of the so-called phenomenon of complementary slackness. Let me explain this phenomenon in terms of $\max f(\mathbf{x})$, subject to $G(\mathbf{x}) \leq \mathbf{b}$. The first order conditions are $\mathbf{f}' = \boldsymbol{\lambda}'\mathbf{G}$, $\boldsymbol{\lambda} \geq \mathbf{0}$. The phenomenon says that if a constraint is non-binding, $g_i(\mathbf{x}) < b_i$, then the Lagrange multiplier is zero, $\lambda_i = 0$. Hence g_i plays no role in the first order condition. The phenomenon also says, that if a Lagrange multiplier is strictly positive, $\lambda_i > 0$, then the constraint is binding, $g_i(\mathbf{x}) = b_i$. A nice way to write the phenomenon of complementary slackness is

$$\boldsymbol{\lambda}'[G(\mathbf{x}) - \mathbf{b}] = 0.$$

The left-hand side is the inner product of two nonnegative vectors. It is zero if and only if each term of the inner product is zero: $\lambda_i[g_i(\mathbf{x}) - b_i] = 0$.

This, indeed, is a short way of writing $g_i(\mathbf{x}) < b_i \Rightarrow \lambda_i = 0$ and $\lambda_i > 0 \Rightarrow g_i(\mathbf{x}) = b_i$.

Now I explain why the Lagrange multipliers are competitive prices. Suppose that for some activity, value added is strictly less than factor costs. Then $\sigma_i > 0$. By the phenomenon of complementary slackness, $s_i = 0$. Hence the price system is such that negative profits signal activities that are inactive in the coefficient allocation. If the economy would have this price system and producers are profit maximizers, they would undertake precisely those activities which we want them to do. Notice that profits would be zero: The unprofitable activities are inactive, and value added is everywhere less than or equal to factor costs.

There is another interesting consequence of the phenomenon of complementary slackness, namely the identity between national product and national income. If G is linear, $G(\mathbf{x}) = \mathbf{G}\mathbf{x}$ and the last equation becomes

$$\boldsymbol{\lambda}'\mathbf{G}\mathbf{x} = \boldsymbol{\lambda}b.$$

By the first order condition, $\mathbf{f}' = \boldsymbol{\lambda}'\mathbf{G}$,

$$\mathbf{f}'\mathbf{x} = \boldsymbol{\lambda}b.$$

If f is also linear, this reads

$$f(\mathbf{x}) = \boldsymbol{\lambda}b.$$

In our linear program,

$$(\mathbf{0}'\ 1)\begin{pmatrix}\mathbf{s}\\ c\end{pmatrix} = (\mathbf{p}',\ r,\ w,\ \boldsymbol{\sigma}')\begin{bmatrix}\mathbf{0}\\ k\\ l\\ \mathbf{0}\end{bmatrix}$$

or

$$c = rk + wl.$$

This is the famous macro-economic identity of the national product and national income. It confirms that Lagrange multipliers measure the rate of change of the objective function (consumption level c) with respect to the constraints (capital k and labor l). If the stock of capital is increased by a unit, then the contribution to the objective is r. Hence r measures the productivity of capital. Similarly, w measures the productivity of labor. r and w need not be the observed prices of capital and labor, but are the Lagrange multipliers of the efficiency program, also called shadow prices. For perfectly competitive economies, however, there is agreement.

6. Total Factor Productivity

Capital productivity is r and labor productivity is w, where r and w are the shadow prices of the linear program that maximizes consumption subject to the material balance, the capital constraint, the labor constraint, and the nonnegativity constraint. Now let time evolve. Everything changes, not only the output levels, but also the technical coefficients and the consumption coefficients. The linear program changes. r and w change. Hence, there is capital productivity growth, $\dot{r} = dr/dt$, and labor productivity growth, $\dot{w} = dw/dt$. All this is per unit of capital or labor. Total capital productivity growth is $\dot{r}k$ and total labor productivity growth is $\dot{w}l$. Normalizing by the level, we obtain the nominal total factor productivity growth rate, $(\dot{r}k + \dot{w}l)/(rk+wl)$. To obtain it in real terms, we must subtract the price increase of the consumption bundle, $\dot{p}a$. The (real) **total factor productivity growth rate** is

$$TFP = (\dot{r}k + \dot{w}l)/(rk + wl) - \dot{p}a.$$

Here k and l are the factor constraints and r and w their Lagrange multipliers; a is the vector of consumption coefficients. Although this productivity growth concept is grounded in the theory of mathematical programming (where Lagrange multipliers measure productivities of constraints), there is perfect consistency with the traditional Solow residual. Recall the macroeconomic identity of the national product and national income, $c = rk+wl$, dividing though by the identity itself, we obtain total differentiation yields $\dot{r}k + \dot{w}l = \dot{c} - r\dot{k} - w\dot{l}$ and the division by the identity itself leads to

$$TFP = \dot{c}/c - \dot{p}a - r\dot{k}/(rk + wl) - w\dot{l}/(rk + wl).$$

If we use shorthand $\hat{c} = \dot{c}/c$ for a relative growth rate, we obtain

$$TFP = \hat{c} - \dot{p}a - \alpha_k\hat{k} - \alpha_l\hat{l}$$

where $\alpha_k = rk/(rk + wl)$, the competitive value share of capital, and $\alpha_l = wl/(rk + wl)$, the competitive value share of labor. The right-hand side of the last equation is precisely the Solow residual. Notice, however, that the competitive value shares are not necessarily the observed ones. For noncompetitive economies, they must be calculated by means of the linear program of Section 4; for an application, see ten Raa and Mohnen (2000).

7. Input–Output Analysis of Total Factor Productivity

By definition, positive TFP-growth means that output grows at a faster rate than input and therefore, the output/input ratio or standard of living goes up. In this section, I will explain the phenomenon in terms of technical change at the sectoral level.

The linear program selects activities to produce the required net output of the economy. In continuous time, we may consider infinitesimal changes and the pattern of activities that are actually used is locally constant (except in degenerate points where the linear program has multiple solutions). In this section, we ignore the activities that are not used. Hence, the activity vector **s** is and remains positive.

From the last section, the Solow residual is

$$TFP = \dot{c}/c - \dot{p}a - r\dot{k}/(rk + wl) - w\dot{l}/(rk + wl) = (\dot{c} - \dot{p}ac - r\dot{k} - w\dot{l})/c.$$

We are going to express c, k and l in terms of $\mathbf{s}$. By the complementary slackness between $c\mathbf{a} \leq (\mathbf{V}' - \mathbf{U})\mathbf{s}$ and $\mathbf{p} \geq \mathbf{0}$, we have $c\mathbf{p}'\mathbf{a} = \mathbf{p}'(\mathbf{V}' - \mathbf{U})\mathbf{s}$, or using the price normalization condition,

$$c = \mathbf{p}'(\mathbf{V}' - \mathbf{U})\mathbf{s}.$$

Assume that capital and labor have positive productivity. Then, also by complementary slackness,

$$k = \mathbf{k}'\mathbf{s}, \quad l = \mathbf{l}'\mathbf{s}.$$

Substitution yields

$$TFP = \{[\mathbf{p}'(\mathbf{V}' - \mathbf{U})]^{\cdot} - r\dot{\mathbf{k}}' - w\dot{\mathbf{l}}'\}\mathbf{s}/c - \dot{p}a + [\mathbf{p}'(\mathbf{V}' - \mathbf{U}) - r\mathbf{k}' - w\mathbf{l}']\dot{\mathbf{s}}/c.$$

Since $\mathbf{s}$ remains positive, by complementary slackness, $\mathbf{p}'(\mathbf{V}'-\mathbf{U}) = r\mathbf{k}' - w\mathbf{l}'$, and the second term vanishes. It is customary to define TFP-growth of sector i as output growth minus input growth, normalized by output:

$$TFP_i = \frac{[\mathbf{p}'(\mathbf{V}'-\mathbf{U})^{\cdot}]_i - r\dot{k}_i - w\dot{l}_i}{(\mathbf{p}'\mathbf{V}')_i}.$$

It then follows that

$$\begin{aligned} TFP &= \sum_i (\mathbf{p}'\mathbf{V}')_i TFP_i s_i/c + [\dot{\mathbf{p}}'(\mathbf{V}'-\mathbf{U})\mathbf{s} - \dot{p}ac]/c \\ &= \sum_i d_i TFP_i \end{aligned}$$

where $d_i = (\mathbf{p}'\mathbf{V}')_i s_i / \mathbf{p}'(\mathbf{V}'-\mathbf{U})\mathbf{s}$ and the remainder vanishes because of the material balance, assumed to be binding. These weights d_i are called Domar weights and sum to the gross/net output ratio of the economy, which is greater then one.

To see the reduction of TFP-growth as reductions of input–output coefficients in the traditional sense, consider the case where sectors produce single outputs. Then

$$TFP_i = \left(p_i\dot{v}_{ij(i)} - \sum_j p_j\dot{u}_{ji} - r\dot{k}_i - w\dot{l}_i\right)/(p_i v_{j(i)}).$$

In this case, input coefficients are defined by $a_{ji} = u_{ji}/v_{ij(i)}$, $\kappa_i = k_i/v_{ij(i)}$ and $\mu_i = l_i/v_{ij(i)}$. Substitution yields

$$\begin{aligned} TFP_i = \Bigg[& p_i\dot{v}_{ij(i)} - \sum_j p_j(a_{ji}v_{ij(i)})^{\cdot} - r(\kappa_i v_{ij(i)})^{\cdot} \\ & - w(\mu_i v_{ij(i)})^{\cdot}\Bigg]/(p_{j(i)}v_{ij(i)}). \end{aligned}$$

By complementary slackness, $p_i v_{ij(i)} = \sum_j p_j a_{ji} v_{ij(i)} - r\kappa_i v_{ij(i)} - w\mu_i v_{ij(i)}$ and we obtain

$$TFP_i = \left(-\sum_j p_j\dot{a}_{ji} - r\dot{\kappa}_i - w\dot{\mu}_i\right)/p_{j(i)},$$

that is sectoral cost reductions. With obvious matrix notation,

$$TFP = -\sum_i d_i(\mathbf{p}'\dot{\mathbf{a}}_i - r\dot{\kappa} - w\dot{\mu})/p_{j(i)}$$

is reduced to a reduction in input–output coefficients. If there is only one sector producing each commodity, then $j(i) = i$. If sectors produce multiple outputs, then the result basically holds, but input–output coefficients are no longer obtained by simple scalar divisions.

8. Conclusion

For perfectly competitive economies, there is an intimate relationship between efficiency and equilibrium. The marginal productivities of capital and labor that are the Lagrange multipliers to the efficiency program coincide with perfectly competitive equilibrium prices. For such economies, one can measure TFP-growth by means of the Solow residual, using the observed value share of the factor inputs. Most economies, however, are not perfectly competitive. Then, to measure productivities, one must find the shadow prices of the factor inputs by solving a linear program. In this paper, I proposed the linear program that maximizes Leontief utility subject to resource constraints. We thus obtained a Solow residual measure for TFP without assuming that the economy is on its frontier. The flip side of the coin is that the numerical values we use in the residual reflect shadow prices, instead of observed prices. The data required for the determination of TFP are input–output coefficients and constraints on capital and labor. These data capture the structure of the economy and are real rather than nominal. Our measure of TFP-growth, firmly grounded in the theory of mathematical programming, admits a decomposition in sectoral contributions, allowing us to pinpoint the strong and the weak sectors of the economy.

We have freed neoclassical growth accounting from its use of market values of factor inputs in the evaluation of the Solow residual and therefore, some circularity in its methodology. Perhaps surprisingly, we accomplished this by using the input–output analysis to determine the values of factor inputs. Input–output analysis and neoclassical economics can be used fruitfully to fill gaps in each other. Contrary to perception, the gap in input–output analysis is not the interaction between prices and quantities, but the concept of marginal productivity, and the gap in neoclassical economics is not the structure of the economy, but the determination of value shares of factor inputs.

References

Debreu, G. (1959) *Theory of Value* (New Haven, CT, Yale University Press).

Jorgenson, D. and Z. Griliches (1967) The explanation of productivity change, *Review of Economic Studies*, 34, pp. 308–350.

Leontief, W. (1941) *The Structure of the American Economy, 1919–1929* (Cambridge, Harvard University Press).

Mohnen, P., Th. ten Raa and G. Bourque (1997) Mesures de la croissance de la productivité dans un cadre d'équilibre général: L'é conomie du Québec entre 1978 et 1984, *Canadian Journal of Economics*, 30, pp. 295–307.

ten Raa, Th. (1994) On the methodology of input–output analysis, *Regional Science and Urban Economics*, 24, pp. 3–25.

ten Raa, Th. (1995) *Linear Analysis of Competitive Economies* (New York, Harvester Wheatsheaf).

ten Raa, Th. and P. Mohnen (1994) Neoclassical input–output analysis, *Regional Science and Urban Economics*, 24, pp. 135–158.

ten Raa, Th. and P. Mohnen (2002) Neoclassical growth accounting and frontier analysis: a synthesis, *Journal of Productivity Analysis*, 18, pp. 111–128.

Rockafellar, R.T. (1970) *Convex Analysis* (Princeton, NJ, Princeton University Press).

Solow, R.M. (1957) Technical change and the aggregate production function, *Review of Economics and Statistics*, 39, pp. 312–320.

Chapter 19

Neoclassical Growth Accounting and Frontier Analysis: A Synthesis

Thijs ten Raa and Pierre Mohnen

Abstract: The standard measure of productivity growth is the Solow residual. Its evaluation requires data on factor input shares or prices. Since these prices are presumed to match factor productivities, the standard procedure amounts to accepting at face value what is supposed to be measured. In this paper, we determine total factor productivity growth without recourse to data on factor input prices. Factor productivities are defined as Lagrange multipliers to the program that maximizes the level of domestic final demand. The consequent measure of total factor productivity is shown to encompass not only the Solow residual, but also the efficiency change of the frontier analysis and the hitherto slippery terms-of-trade effect. Using input–output tables from 1962 to 1991, we show that the source of Canadian productivity growth has shifted from technical change to terms-of-trade effects.

JEL classification: O47

1. Introduction

In this paper, we synthesize two strands of productivity analysis, namely neoclassical growth accounting and a frontier approach, known as data envelopment analysis (DEA).[1] In either branch of literature, productivity is essentially the output-input ratio and therefore, productivity growth is the residual between output growth and input growth. The difficulty is to implement these concepts when there is more than one output or input. Neoclassical analysis weights them by value shares, a procedure that has been justified for competitive economies by Solow (1957). In such economies, inputs are rewarded according to their marginal productivities and outputs according to their marginal revenues. Therefore, the residual measures the shift of the production function. The DEA analysis considers the output and input proportions observable in activities (representing various economies and/or various years) and determines for instance how much more output could be produced if the inputs were processed by an optimal combination of all observed activities.

Although each approach tracks changes in the output-input ratio of an economy, the constructions are quite distinct. Neoclassical growth accounting attributes productivity growth to the inputs, say labor and capital. Indeed, Jorgenson and Griliches (1967) have shown that the total factor productivity (TFP-) growth residual equals the growth of the real factor rewards, summed over endowments. In this sense, the residual truly represents total factor productivity growth indeed. The frontier approach decomposes productivity growth in a movement of the economy towards the frontier and a shift of the latter. Productivity growth is efficiency change plus technical change. The alternative decompositions inherit the advantages and disadvantages of their respective methodologies. Neoclassical growth accounting imputes productivity growth to factors, but cannot distinguish a movement towards the frontier and a movement of the frontier. This is the contribution of the frontier approach, which, however, is not capable of imputing value to factor inputs.

The two approaches differ not only in methodology, but also in focus. The overwhelming majority of empirical studies of economic growth (whether "old" or "new" growth papers) are based on the Solow model or some variant of it. Alternatively, the overwhelming majority of DEA papers deal with micro issues. In fact, the technique is used primarily for

[1] In the frontier literature, there is a distinction between deterministic and stochastic frontiers. The former are obtained by linear programming methods such as DEA; the latter are estimated by econometric methods. See Coelli *et al.* (1998).

benchmarking within firms or industries (e.g., the burgeoning use of DEA in financial service industries). Our paper breaks the common ground by applying all the tools to a national economy with a multitude of sectors. The issue is macro-growth, but the model is more micro in flavor. Basically, we will decompose productivity growth into frontier productivity growth and efficiency change. DEA practitioners restrict the first term to technical efficiency, but we take into account allocative efficiency. The frontier is obtained not by some best practice, but by efficient allocation of resources across sectors. Neoclassical growth accountants overlook the efficiency change term.

Some practitioners of both approaches are aware of each others' work and sometimes report correlations between the alternative productivity measures (Perelman 1995). What is missing, however, is a theoretical framework that encompasses the two approaches. This is the purpose of our paper. We reproduce the neoclassical TFP growth formulas, but in a framework that is DEA in spirit. Unlike Färe, Grosskopf, Lovell and Zhang (1994), we do not determine an economy's frontier by benchmarking on other economies, but by reallocating resources domestically so as to maximize the level of domestic final demand (that is excluding net exports), given input and output proportions and subject to a set of feasibility constraints. The shadow prices of the factor constraints measure the individual factor productivities. Our model is a general equilibrium activity analysis model with multiple inputs and outputs, and intermediate inputs, where the frontier is determined by an economic criterion and not a mechanical expansion factor. A first attempt to model intermediate inputs was made by Färe and Grosskopf (1996).

Our starting point is the Solow residual between output and input growth. We derive the equality of the Solow residual with the growth rates of the factor productivities by differentiating not the national income identity, but the related formula of the main theorem of linear programming applied to the aforementioned frontier program. By the same token, we capture the movement towards the frontier, or efficiency change, in addition to the standard Domar decomposition of TFP, involving technical change at the sectoral levels. A further contribution is the identification of the terms-of-trade effect in productivity analysis. It is well-known that an improvement in the terms of trade is equivalent to technical progress, but the treatment of this effect has been ad hoc so far. For example, Diewert and Morrison (1986) classify commodities a priori as exports or imports. In our frontier program, net exports are appropriately endogenous.

We model trade by inclusion of a constraint on net imports. For balanced trade, the value of net imports, assessed at world prices, must be nonpositive. The model will select resource extensive commodities for exports and resource intensive commodities for imports, all relative to the world prices. If the price of an export item goes up, the net imports constraint is less tight and potential output is increased, in the same way as in response to an input coefficient reduction. This is the terms-of-trade effect. The economic system that maps factor inputs into domestic final demand has two components: production and trade. The contributions to TFP-growth in the primal representation are given by the sectoral Solow residuals and the terms-of-trade effect, respectively, which can be considered shift effects. On top of this, we must accommodate the empirical fact that trade is not always balanced. The economy may run a deficit, which we enter on the right hand side of our net imports constraint. This modification, however minor, adds a conventional input aspect to trade. We do not endogenize the year-to-year deficit of the economy, but, given the value of the deficit, the commodity composition of the trade vector will be determined along with the efficient allocation of resources. This is the input effect of debt which emerges in the dual decomposition of TFP, alongside the factor input productivities. The terms-of-trade effect will be an important source of growth, but the deficit effect will prove insignificant in the empirical part of this study.

Although we reproduce the formulas of neoclassical growth accounting and frontier analysis in a consistent way, there are some subtle differences. Compared to traditional growth accounting, the input value shares that enter our Solow residual are no longer the observed ones, but those based on the shadow prices of the frontier program. In perfectly competitive economies, where inputs are rewarded according to their marginal productivities and outputs according to their marginal revenues, it is perfectly legitimate to use the observed value shares in aggregating inputs or outputs. But observed economies are not perfectly competitive and are not even on their production possibility frontiers. Hence, the Solow residual, based on observed value shares, does not only isolate technical change, but also captures variations of the economy about the competitive benchmark, such as changes in market power, returns to scale, disequilibrium in factor holdings, and suboptimal capacity utilization. The possibility of disequilibrium in factor holdings has preoccupied economists for a long time. In the early studies, the capital stock was corrected for variations in estimated capacity utilization or variations in electricity use to remove the effect of cyclical fluctuations from productivity growth. Berndt and Fuss (1986) proposed an alternative measure of capacity utilization, casted in terms of prices, rather than quantities. The degree of capacity utilization was measured and interpreted as the gap between observed and shadow prices (those at which the observed quantities would be optimal). There was an obvious link to be made with the q-theory of investment (Hayashi, 1982) that predicted the capital stock to be optimal when the ratio of the market price to the purchase price of capital is equal to unity at the marginal. If capital is only one quasi-fixed input and if the marginal q equals the average q, the shadow price of capital could be measured by the market value. Morrison (1986) generalized the disequilibrium analysis to multiple inputs and recommended the estimation of shadow prices for total factor productivity measurement.

The shadow prices can be estimated using a temporary equilibrium model with some quasi fixed factors. Caves, Christensen and Swanson (1981) estimated the shadow prices without specifying the source of disequilibrium in factor holdings. Alternatively, it is possible to estimate the shadow prices by specifying the source of inefficiencies in factor holdings or output supplies. The input demands, as well as the output supplies, may not be at their optimal values with respect to the observed prices because of adjustment costs, regulatory constraints, uncertainty, non-maximizing behavior, or imperfect competition. The gap between the observed and the shadow prices may be due to marginal adjustment costs (e.g., Morrison, 1988), regulatory distortions (Sickles, Good and Johnson 1986), the value of the option to invest (Dixit and Pindyck 1994), price-mark-ups related to demand elasticities (Bernstein and Mohnen 1991). The Solow residual has been corrected for such departures from perfect competition, estimating mark-ups over marginal cost, scale elasticities and shadow prices, and modifying the formula for the residual (Morrisson, 1988; Hall, 1990). The econometric literature is in the realm of partial equilibrium analysis.

We however, endogenize commodity and factor prices by finding the frontier of the economy subject to its fundamentals, namely endowments, technology, and preferences. This general equilibrium approach goes back to Debreu (1959) who pursued it in a microeconomic model. Our model is at a medium level of disaggregation, but could conceivably be disaggregated further. Endowments are represented by the labor force, the accumulated stocks of capital and the trade deficit. They constrain the economy-wide allocation, but not the sectors in isolation. Technology is given by the combined inputs and outputs of the various sectors of the economy. Preferences are represented by the commodity proportions of domestic final demand.[2]

The paper is organized as follows. In the next section, we set up an activity analysis model to determine an economy's frontier. Then we define TFP-growth in the spirit of Solow (1957) and decompose it into frontier productivity growth and efficiency change. In Section 3, frontier productivity growth is further decomposed into technical change and a terms-of-trade effect. In Section 4, we measure TFP-growth and its various components for the Canadian economy over the period 1962–1991. Section 5 concludes and the data are described in an appendix.

2. TFP-Growth as the Sum of Frontier Productivity Growth and Efficiency Change

Figure 1 explains our model for an open economy with two commodities. Net output is given by vector y. Trade moves it to the domestic final consumption vector, f. (Domestic final demand is consumption plus investment, but not net exports. Note that commodity 1 is exported and commodity 2 imported.) Trade is a means to align domestic final consumption with the preferences. Assuming a Leontief welfare function, the optimum output is attained by expanding vector f in its own direction, up to fc, where c is the expansion vector. In Figure 1, this is achieved by three things. Production y is pushed to the production possibility frontier (the curved line), reallocated in favor of output 2, yielding point y^*, and the pattern of trade is changed (exporting commodity 2 and importing commodity 1). The frontier of domestic final consumption, fc, is attained by the elimination of slack and

[2]This is in the spirit of Mohnen, ten Raa and Bourque (1997) who, however, stay in the realm of neoclassical growth accounting and therefore, do not capture efficiency changes nor the terms-of-trade effect.

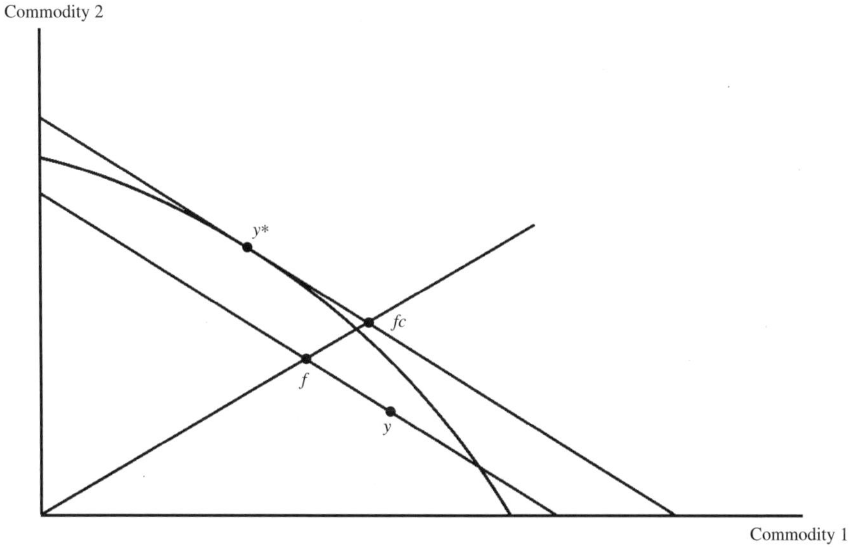

Fig. 1: The production possibility frontier with actual and optimal net outputs (y and y^*, respectively) and domestic final demands (f and fc, respectively). The straight lines are budget lines in world trade.

the reallocation of resources across sectors. Expansion vector c is a negative measure for efficiency. If $c = 1$, the economy is already at its optimum. If $c = 1.1$, the economy's potential is 10% more than actual performance.

Now consider the next period. For simplicity, assume that the factor inputs remain fixed. Any improvement, or TFP, shows an increase in domestic final demand, f. One extreme case is a movement from f to fc in Figure 1, without any structural change in the production possibility frontier or the terms of trade (the slope of the straight lines). Then all TFP is ascribed to efficiency change. Another extreme case is where f stays put, but the production possibility frontier moves out. Then the new fc would be greater. The increase in c signals a negative efficiency change which, however, is offset by the positive technical change.

We consider an open economy endowed with labor N, capital M (decomposed into various types) and an allowable trade deficit D. The economy is subdivided into a number of sectors, each producing a vector of commodities. Part of the commodities are used as intermediate inputs and the rest flows to final demand (either domestic final demand or exports). The frontier of the economy is defined as the maximal expansion of its vector of final demand f, keeping the relative composition of that vector as fixed. The composition reflects preferences. The frontier of the economy can be reached by an optimal allocation of inputs (primary and intermediate) and production across sectors, and by an optimal trade of commodity with the rest of the world.

The *frontier* of the economy is defined by the primal program,

$$\max_{s,c,g} e^{\mathsf{T}} fc \text{ subject to}$$

$$\begin{aligned} (V^{\mathsf{T}} - U)s &\geq fc + Jg =: F \\ Ks &\leq M \\ Ls &\leq N \\ -\pi g &\leq -\pi g^t =: D \\ s &\geq 0. \end{aligned} \tag{1}$$

The variables (s, c, g) and parameters (all other) are the following [with dimensions in brackets]

s activity vector [# of sectors]
c level of domestic final demand [scalar]
g vector of net exports [# of tradeable commodities]
e unit vector of all components one
T transposition symbol
f domestic final demand [# of commodities]
V make table [# of sectors by # of commodities]
U use table [# of commodities by # of sectors]
J 0-1 matrix placing tradeables [# of commodities by of tradeables]
F final demand [# of commodities]
K capital stock matrix [# of capital types by # of sectors]
M capital endowment [# of capital types]
L labor employment row vector [# of sectors]
N labor force [scalar][3]
π U.S. relative price row vector [# of tradeables]
g^t vector of net exports observed at time t [# of tradeables]
D observed trade deficit [scalar].

[3]Labor could also be decomposed into various types, but we have not done so in the empirical part.

We discuss the objective and the constraints, respectively, and then list all the variables and parameters. The objective is the expansion of the level of domestic find demand, c. Domestic final demand comprises consumption and investment. Investment is merely a means to advance consumption, albeit in the future. We include it in the objective function to account for future consumption. In fact, Weitzman (1976) shows that for competitive economies, domestic final demand measures the present discounted value of consumption.[4]

Preserving the proportions of domestic final demand, f, we expand its level by letting the economy produce fc, where scalar c is the expansion factor. $c = 1$ is feasible (as it reflects the status quo), but $c > 1$ represents a movement towards the frontier of the economy. The model maximizes c. This is equivalent to the maximization $e^{\mathsf{T}}fc$, where e is the unit vector (with all entries equal to one), T the transposition sign, and f the given domestic final demand vector. It is important to understand that f is not a variable, but an exogenous vector. The positive multiplicative factor in the objective, $e^{\mathsf{T}}f$, will control the nominal price level.

The preservation of domestic final demand in finding the frontier of the economy in each year amounts to imposing a Leontief preference structure (fixed consumption pattern). It should be noted that the ray output expansion typical in multi-output DEA (the Farrell (1957) measure of efficiency) implicitly assumes fixed output proportions. It should also be noted that the Leontief specification of production and preferences that we adopt admits a great deal of substitutability as trade is free and therefore, acts as a valve for factor imbalances between endowments and factor contents of domestic final demands. The economy may even mimic a Cobb-Douglas behavior, as demonstrated in ten Raa (1995). The main reason we opt for the Leontief specification is that the productivities associated with program (1) (in the sense of Lagrange multipliers) combine to TFP expressions which have exactly the same form as the ones in growth accounting. The imposition of fixed proportions ensures that optimal, frontier proportions are the same as the observed ones, while level differences (between the optimum and actual allocations) are a wash in productivity growth analysis. If we

[4]In principle, our methodology could accommodate endogenous investment and the determination of the intertemporal production possibility frontier as in Hulten (1979), but we have not pursued this approach.

would have used a different production function, then the frontier allocation of the economy would feature different input–output proportions than the observed ones and there is no hope that measures for technical change look like the familiar ones of growth accounting.

The first constraint of the linear program (1) is the material balance: net output must cover domestic final demand plus net exports. Then follow the capital and labor constraints.[5] The next-to-last constraint is the trade balance: net imports valued at world prices may not exceed the existing trade deficit. Finally, sector activity levels must be nonnegative.

The linear program basically reallocates activity so as to maximize the level of domestic final demand. Final demand also includes net exports, but they are considered not an end, but a means to fulfill the objective of the economy.[6] This endogenization of trade explains the role of the terms-of-trade in TFP analysis, as we shall see in Section 3.

The theory of mathematical programming teaches us that the Lagrange multipliers corresponding to the constraints of the primal program measure the competitive values or marginal products of the constraining entities (the commodities and factors) at the optimum. We will use the Lagrange multipliers in defining productivity growth. They are p (a row vector of commodity prices), r (a row vector of capital productivities), w (a scalar for labor productivity), and ε (a scalar for the purchasing power parity). They are determined by the dual program associated with (1),

$$\min_{p,r,w,\varepsilon\geq 0} \; rM + wN + \varepsilon D \text{ subject to}$$

$$\begin{aligned} p(V^{\top} - U) &\leq rK + wL \\ pf &= e^{\top} f \\ pJ &= \varepsilon\pi. \end{aligned} \tag{2}$$

Factor costs are minimized, subject to price constraints.[7] The first dual constraint defines competitive shadow prices of the commodities. Value

[5]Actually, there is also non-business capital and labor, proportional to the activity level of the non-business sector, that is c. We have included their levels in the capital and labor constraints and their factor rewards in the coefficient of c in the objective function. For reasons of clarity in the exposition, we have not indicated these additional terms related to the non-business sector in (1).

[6]We make no distinction between competitive and non-competitive imports. (Non-competitive imports are indicated by zeros in the make table.)

[7]Since the commodity constraint in the primal program has zero bound, p does not show up in the objective function of the dual program. For details of the derivation, see, for example, ten Raa (1995).

added must be less than or equal to factor costs in each sector. (If it is less than factor costs, the sector will be inactive according to the phenomenon of complementary slackness.) The second dual constraint normalizes the prices.[8] Our commodities are measured in base-year prices and hence observed prices are one. The optimal competitive prices from the linear program will be slightly off, but we maintain the overall price level. The third and last dual constraint aligns the prices of the tradeable commodities with their opportunity costs: the relative U.S. prices. In free trade, the law of one price must hold (in the absence of transaction costs and imperfect information).

Following Solow (1957), we define total factor productivity growth as the residual between the final demand growth and aggregate-input growth, where each of them is a weighted average of component growth rates and the weights are competitive value shares. The growth rate of domestic final demand for commodity i is $\hat{f}_i = \dot{f}_i/f_i$, where $\dot{}$ denotes the time derivative. The competitive value shares are $p_i f_i/(\Sigma p_i f_i) = p_i f_i/(pf)$. Hence overall output growth amounts to

$$\Sigma[p_i f_i/(pf)]\hat{f}_i = \Sigma p_i \dot{f}_i/(pf) = p\dot{f}/(pf). \tag{3}$$

Inputs are aggregated in the same vein. The growth rate of labor is $\hat{N}$ and its competitive value share is $\beta = wN/(rM + wN + \varepsilon D)$. Likewise, denote the competitive value shares of capital by α (a row vector) and of the trade deficit by γ (a scalar). Then overall input growth can be written as

$$\alpha\hat{M} + \beta\hat{N} + \gamma\hat{D} \tag{4}$$

where each of the terms can be rewritten in time derivatives as we have done for outputs. For example, $\beta\hat{N} = [wN/(rM + wN + \varepsilon D)]\hat{N} = w\dot{N}/(rM + wN + \varepsilon D)$. *Total factor productivity growth* is the residual between (1) and (2):

$$\begin{aligned} TFP &= p\dot{f}/(pf) - (\alpha\hat{M} + \beta\hat{N} + \gamma\hat{D}) \\ &= p\dot{f}/(pf) - (r\dot{M} + w\dot{N} + \varepsilon\dot{D})/(rM + wN + \varepsilon D). \end{aligned} \tag{5}$$

[8]Remember from footnote 4 that there are two more constraint terms featuring c, namely non-business capital and labor. To preserve the price normalization, we have also included in the objective function of the primal program, (1), the base-year expenditure on non-business capital and labor which also shows up on the right-hand side of the second dual constraint.

In the growth accounting literature, it is customary to assume that the economy is perfectly competitive. Unfortunately, this assumption is seldom fulfilled. Observed prices are not perfectly competitive and the economy need not be on its frontier. Also notice that p is not a device to convert nominal values into real values, but the endogenous price vector that sustains the optimal allocation of resources in the linear program.

In the spirit of Nishimizu and Page (1982) and further frontier analysis, such as DEA, for example Färe *et al.* (1994), we will decompose TFP in a shift of the frontier and a movement towards the frontier:

$$TFP = FP + EC \tag{6}$$

where FP if frontier productivity growth and EC is efficiency change. We will now define each of them.

By the theory of Lagrange multipliers, real shadow prices measure the marginal products of the factors at the optimum. Hence, *frontier productivity growth* is the growth rates of the shadow prices of the factors (weighted by relative factor costs) minus the growth rate of the commodity prices.[9]

$$FP = (\dot{r}M + \dot{w}N + \dot{\varepsilon}D)/(rM + wN + \varepsilon D) - \dot{p}f/(pf) \tag{7}$$

Frontier productivity growth so defined corresponds to the dual expression of TFP-growth for perfectly competitive economies elaborated by Jorgenson and Griliches (1967). It imputes productivity growth to factor inputs, which is beyond the scope of standard frontier analysis. The latter, however, is capable of accounting for efficiency change. Inefficiency is measured by the degree to which the economy can be expanded towards its frontier, c. A reduction in c signals an efficiency gain and therefore, *efficiency change* is defined by

$$EC = -\hat{c}(= -\dot{c}/c) \tag{8}$$

We must now demonstrate that frontier productivity growth and efficiency change sum to total factor productivity growth. In other words, we must prove equation (6), given definitions (5), (7) and (8). Now, by the main theorem of linear programming, (1) and (2) have equal solution values, or,

[9] Since prices are normalized at unity by the second dual constraint, see (2); the price correction term is a sheer compositional effect. If the composition of domestic final demand, f, is constant, then pf is also constant, by (2), and it follows that $p(f)^{\cdot} = \dot{p}f$ is zero. Otherwise the price correction term corrects marginal factor productivity growth rates for an inflationary effect, which does not reflect a change in the price level (since everything is already specified in real prices), but only a compositional effect.

substituting the price normalization constraint of (2),

$$pfc = rM + wN + \varepsilon D. \tag{9}$$

The left hand side is the value of optimal domestic final demand and the right hand side is factor income. Thus, (9) is essentially the macro-economic identity of the national product and income. Differentiating totally, we obtain by the product rule

$$\dot{p}fc + pfc + pf\dot{c} = \dot{r}M + rM + \dot{w}N + w\dot{N} + \dot{\varepsilon}D + \varepsilon\dot{D} \tag{10}$$

or, rearranging terms,

$$p\dot{f}c - r\dot{M} - w\dot{N} - \varepsilon\dot{D} = \dot{r}M + \dot{w}N + \dot{\varepsilon}D - \dot{p}fc - pf\dot{c} \tag{11}$$

Now divide the first term on the left hand side and the last two terms on the right hand side of (11) by the left hand side of (9). Notice that c cancels out everywhere, except in the last term on the right hand side. Divide the remaining three terms on either side of (11) by the right hand side of (9). Then we obtain

$$\begin{aligned} &p\dot{f}/(pf) - (r\dot{M} + w\dot{N} + \varepsilon\dot{D})/(rM + wN + \varepsilon D) \\ &\quad = (rM + \dot{w}N + \dot{\varepsilon}D)/(rM + wN + \varepsilon D) - \dot{p}f/(pf) - \dot{c}/c \end{aligned} \tag{12}$$

By definitions (5), (7) and (8), (12) reduces to (6). The noted cancellation of the expansion factor except in one term, enabled us to separate the efficiency change term from the frontier productivity growth term.

3. Frontier Productivity Growth Decomposition Into Technical Change and the Terms-of-Trade Effect

In the previous section, we decomposed *TFP* into frontier productivity growth and efficiency change. This section provides the further decomposition of frontier productivity growth into technical change and the terms-of-trade effect. The latter is not an add-on, but emerges naturally from our linear programming model of TFP. It should not come as a surprise that terms-of-trade and sectoral technical changes arise simultaneously. The trade sector is like a production sector, with multiple inputs (namely exports) and outputs (namely imports). Like all sectors, productivity goes up when more output (import) is obtained per input (export), in other words, when the terms of trade improve. The specification of the function that maps inputs into outputs is different. In production, we have the Leontief function. In trade, we have the balance of payments, which is a linear function. From a formal point of view, the functions feature perfect complementarity and perfect substitutability, respectively, where the marginal rate of substitution is given by the terms of trade. The structures of production and trade (input–output proportions and terms of trade) may shift and thus cause TFP-growth. These are the Solow residual and the terms-of-trade effect, which we will spell out in this section. As always, TFP-growth accrues to factor income additions, to capital, labor, and debt supply, though the latter is typically very small and even zero when payments are balanced.

Our point of departure is *TFP* as defined in (5). Focus on the numerator of (5), by multiplying with the denominator, or (9). Then we obtain the following *TFP* numereator,

$$\dot{pfc} - r\dot{M} - w\dot{N} - \varepsilon\dot{D}. \tag{13}$$

By definition of F, see (1), the first term is $p\dot{F} - pJ\dot{g} - pf\dot{c}$. If the factor constraints are binding, then $M = Ks$, $N = Ls$ and $\varepsilon\dot{D} = -\varepsilon\pi\dot{g} - \varepsilon\dot{\pi}g$. The second subterm of the first term, $-pJ\dot{g}$, cancels against the first subterm of the last term, $-\varepsilon\pi\dot{g}$, (because of the third constraint of (2)) and (13) reduces to

$$[p\dot{F} - r(Ks)^{\cdot} - w(Ls)^{\cdot}] + \varepsilon\dot{\pi}g - pf\dot{c}. \tag{14}$$

Dividing by the denominator of *TFP*, or (9), we reobtain *TFP*, but now in the following three-way form[10]:

$$TFP = SR + TT + EC \tag{15}$$

where *SR* is the **Solow residual**,

$$SR = [p\dot{F} - r(Ks)^{\cdot} - w(Ls)^{\cdot}]/(rM + wN + \varepsilon D) \tag{16}$$

[10]If the factor constraints are not binding, a fourth term accounts for slack changes. Notice that all components, including the Solow residual, account for the value of trade balance in the numerator. This minor departure from the standard expression in the literature (including Mohnen, ten Raa and Bourque, 1997) is a consequence of our unifying framework that encompasses terms-of-trade effects.

TT is the **terms-of-trade effect**,

$$TT = \varepsilon\dot{\pi}g/(rM + wN + \varepsilon D) \tag{17}$$

and EC is the efficiency change, defined earlier in (8). A comparison of TFP decompositions (15) and (6) reveals that we have effectively decomposed the structural change term, frontier productivity growth FP, into the technical change and terms-of-trade effects,

$$FP = SR + TT. \tag{18}$$

In discrete time, the expressions involving differentials are approximated using the identity $x_t y_t - x_{t-1}y_{t-1} = \hat{x}\overline{x_t y_t} + \hat{y}\overline{x_t y_t}$, where discrete time $\hat{x}_t = (x_t - x_{t-1})/\bar{x}_t$ and $\bar{x}_t = (x_t + x_{t-1})/2$, and similarly for $\hat{y}_t$ and $\bar{y}_t$.

4. Application to the Canadian Economy

To illustrate our methodology, we examine productivity growth in the Canadian economy during the period from 1962 to 1991 at the medium level of disaggregation, which comprises 50 industries and 94 commodities. The linear program was solved for each year from 1962 to 1991 yielding the optimal activity levels and shadow prices for the TFP-expressions.

Table 1 contains the shadow prices of labor (in 1986$/hour), the three types of capital (building, equipment and infrastructure), and the trade deficit (the latter four are in 1986$/1986$, that is rates of return) from 1962 to 1991. Labor was worth at the margin $16.13 in 1986 prices in 1962. Its productivity followed an increasing trend until 1982 and then a bumpy road ending at $46.13 in 1991. The rate of return on buildings followed a downward trend, dropping to zero in 1982, sharply rebounding in 1984, and then dropping again to reach zero from 1988 onwards. In other words, there were excess buildings in 1982 and in 1988–1991. Equipment was not fully utilized until 1983 and again in 1988, 1990 and 1991. Comparing the evolutions of their shadow prices, labor seems to be a substitute to building and equipment. Infrastructure had an increasing rate of return until 1974, much greater than the other two types of capital, and then a declining productivity until the end of our period. On average, over the 1962–1991 period, a dollar increase in the trade deficit allowed a 64-cents increase in final

Table 1: Factor Productivities (Shadow Prices).

Year	Labor	Buildings	Equipment	Infrastructure	Trade deficit
1962	16.13	0.32	0.00	0.20	0.71
1963	16.50	0.33	0.00	0.19	0.71
1964	17.46	0.26	0.00	0.22	0.69
1965	17.86	0.28	0.00	0.18	0.69
1966	18.28	0.28	0.00	0.18	0.69
1967	19.31	0.20	0.00	0.18	0.68
1968	20.38	0.21	0.00	0.17	0.67
1969	20.91	0.17	0.00	0.18	0.67
1970	20.40	0.19	0.00	0.23	0.68
1971	21.78	0.14	0.00	0.24	0.66
1972	22.44	0.08	0.00	0.28	0.66
1973	22.96	0.05	0.00	0.32	0.65
1974	23.24	0.01	0.00	0.47	0.61
1975	22.70	0.05	0.00	0.45	0.64
1976	23.61	0.12	0.00	0.37	0.64
1977	24.52	0.08	0.00	0.34	0.65
1978	24.83	0.07	0.00	0.31	0.65
1979	24.85	0.06	0.00	0.32	0.65
1980	24.60	0.07	0.00	0.28	0.66
1981	24.31	0.10	0.01	0.25	0.69
1982	29.66	0.00	0.00	0.18	0.57
1983	12.07	0.62	0.83	0.15	0.82
1984	12.22	0.49	1.03	0.11	0.81
1985	23.11	0.24	0.22	0.16	0.73
1986	20.09	0.18	0.83	0.05	0.72
1987	20.76	0.11	0.99	0.03	0.70
1988	44.11	0.00	0.00	0.01	0.31
1989	22.41	0.00	1.21	0.00	0.63
1990	44.33	0.00	0.00	0.01	0.32
1991	46.13	0.00	0.00	0.01	0.29

Note: Labor productivity is in 1986$ per hour. The shadow prices of capital (buildings, equipment and infrastructure) and the trade deficit are rates of return.

demand.[11] Its shadow price was pretty stable until 1981 and more volatile and somewhat lower after 1981.

Table 2 shows the decomposition of TFP-growth into a shift of the frontier (frontier productivity growth *FP*) and a movement towards the frontier (efficiency change *EC*). The healthy TFP-growth in the 1962–1974 period reflects frontier productivity growth. The frontier slowed down, in

[11]Final demand does not increase by the full dollar because of the need to produce locally nontradeable commodities for a given commodity composition of final demand.

Table 2: Frontier Productivity Growth (*FP*) and Efficiency Change (*EC*) (Equations (4) and (8), Annualized Percentages).

	1962–1974	1974–1981	1981–1991
FP	2.4	−0.8	3.6
EC	−0.6	0.9	−3.7
TFP	1.8	0.1	−0.1

fact contracted, in the period 1974–1981, but this was compensated by efficiency change, yielding a tiny TFP-growth rate. The 1981–1991 period showed no recovery, but an interesting reversal of the components. The frontier moved out, but this effect was nullified by a detoriation in efficiency change. The economy became healthy, but there were severe adjustment problems. The shift of the frontier displays the well-known pattern of the golden 1960s, the slowdown in the 1970s, and the structural recovery of the 1980s.[12]

Table 3 accounts for frontier productivity growth by factor input. The bulk of FP-growth is attributed to labor, next to nothing to the trade deficit, and the remainder to capital. In the first period, FP and labor productivity both grew by 2.4%. The 0.2% capital productivity growth is distributed very unevenly over the three types of capital, with infrastructure picking

Table 3: Frontier Productivity Growth (*FP*) by Factor Input (Equation (7), Annualized Percentages).

	1962–1974	1974–1981	1981–1991
Buildings	−0.9	0.4	−0.3
Equipment	0.0	0.1	0.3
Infrastructure	1.1	−1.5	−1.2
Capital, total	0.2	−1.0	−1.1
Labor	2.4	0.5	5.0
Deficit	−0.0	0.0	−0.1
Price	−0.2	−0.3	−0.2
FP	2.4	−0.8	3.6

[12]According to Bergeron, Fauvel and Paquet (1995), Canada hit a recession from January 1975 to March 1975, from May 1980 to June 1980, from August 1981 to November 1982, and from April 1990 to March 1991. We chose the breakpoints before the slump years 1975 and 1982 to compare productivity performances as much as possible over comparable phases of the business cycles.

up by 1.0%, equipment none, and buildings plummeting by 0.8%. The slowdown in the second period is ascribed to both labor (dropping to 0.4% a year) and capital (turning −1.2% a year). As in the first period, infrastructure was decisive, explaining all of the negative productivity growth in the second period. The successful FP-growth in the last period was again a labor story. Labor productivity grew at a dramatic 4.8% a year, offsetting a reduction in capital productivity growth of 1.1% a year. Again, the latter was determined by the productivity of infrastructure. The price correction term reflecting a change in final demand composition played a minor role. Demand has always tended to shift towards commodities requiring scarce resources, decreasing, but not by much, the positive effects of individual factor productivities on frontier productivity growth.

While Table 3 shows the composition of FP-growth by factor input, Table 4 decomposes it into the two sources of frontier shift, namely technical change and the terms-of-trade effect. In the first period, the bulk of FP-growth (2.4%) was caused by technical change (the Solow residual at shadow prices is 1.7%). The FP-slowdown in the second period was also ascribed to a downturn in technology. The recovery in the last period, however, was due not only to a Solow residual (at shadow prices) increase of one percent, but above all to an improvement in the terms-of-trade effect from 0.5 to 3.8% annually. It might look strange to have some negative Solow residuals, albeit at shadow prices. How can technology regress? There are at least two serious explanations. First, technical progress does not show in the statistics right away. This is the argument raised by David (1990) to explain the productivity paradox. It takes time to absorb new information technology and to use it to its maximal efficiency, just as it took time to adjust to electricity at the beginning of the century. Second, the negative

Table 4: Frontier Productivity Growth (*FP*) by Solow Residual and Terms-of-Trade Effect (Equations (15)–(17), Annualized Percentages).

	1962–1974	1974–1981	1981–1991
SR	1.7	−1.3	−0.3
TT	0.7	0.5	3.8
FP	2.4	−0.8	3.6
SR at observed prices and activity levels	1.4	0.5	0.2

productivity growth is due to infrastructure, where the benefit might show up in the long run, and not in the short run because of adjustment costs.

It is interesting to contrast our measure of technical change (Table 4, line 1) with the traditional Solow residual, which we have added to Table 4. The main distinction of our productivity measures is the endogeneity of value shares. Prices are marginal productivities and quantities reflect frontier allocations. The Solow residual is a Domar weighted average of sectoral productivity growth rates, see Equation (18), but our Domar weights are different, say from Wolff (1985), by the use of competitive activity levels for sectors and supporting prices for commodities and factor inputs. Table 4 reveals quite dramatic differences. The observed price-based Solow residual is fairly unbiased in the period 1962–1974, but overstates the role of technical change in the periods 1974–1981 and 1981–1991. The terms-of-trade effect was far more important in explaining total factor productivity growth, particularly in the 1980s.

The intended contribution of this paper is to demonstrate that, at least in principle, productivity can be measured without recourse to factor shares or prices. The main reason for this disclaimer is that our model is fairly macro-economic in nature, featuring only one type of labor and three types of capital, with perfect mobility across sectors. More detailed specifications would affect the shadow prices and hence measured TFP. For example, if some type of capital is sector-specific, then its constraint separates, and each sector yields its own rate of return.

5. Conclusion

Standard measures of TFP-growth hinge on the use of value shares, hence of factor input prices. Since the latter are presumed to match factor productivities, the standard procedure amounts to accepting at face value what is supposed to be measured. In this paper, we have demonstrated that factor productivities can be determined as the Lagrange multipliers to a program that maximizes the level of domestic final demand. The consequent measure of total factor productivity growth encompasses not only the Solow residual, but also the terms-of-trade and the efficiency change effects.

We have applied our new measure of TFP-growth to the Canadian economy in the period from 1962 to 1991. Canadian TFP grew by 1.8% yearly in the 1960s, dropped in the 1970s to 0.1% and stayed put in the 1980s. The healthy TFP-growth in the 1960s reflects an outward shift of the frontier. The frontier then contracted in the 1970s, but this was offset by efficiency change. The 1980s shows a reversal of the two components. The frontier moved again, but efficiency change was negative, reflecting adjustment problems. The shift of the frontier tells the story of the golden 1960s, the slowdown of the 1970s, and the structural recovery of the 1980s. It appears that the bulk of this movement in frontier productivity can be attributed to labor productivity growth. We also find the infrastructure component of the capital stock is the key driving force of capital productivity. The healthy factor productivity growth in the 1960s and the slowdown in the 1970s were both caused by technical change, but the recovery in the 1980s was due almost wholly to an improvement in the terms of trade.

The Solow residual measures the shift of the production possibility frontier of an economy that is presumed to be on its frontier. In this paper, we have shown that when this assumption is not valid, the frontier can be traced using input–output statistics. The Lagrange multipliers to the program that determines potential GDP measure the factor productivities. The expansion factor of the program is an inverse measure of the efficiency of the economy. By the main theorem of linear programming, factor productivity growth and efficiency change sum to TFP-growth. The significance of this paper to applied researchers is that it demonstrates how to combine neoclassical growth accounting and frontier analysis, in order to account for technical change and efficiency change in TFP. The latter refers not only to "catching up" with best practice, but also to the broader notion of optimal allocation across sectors, including with respect to trade.

Acknowledgements

We thank Nathalie Viennot and Sofiane Ghali for their dedicated research assistance and René Durand, Jean-Pierre Maynard, Ronald Rioux and Bart van Ark for their precious cooperation in constructing the data. We thank editor Catherine Morrison and a referee for incisive suggestions. We acknowledge the financial support of the Social Sciences and Humanities

Research Council of Canada (SSHRC), CentER, the Netherlands Foundation for the Advancement of Research (NWO), and the Association for Canadian Studies in the Netherlands.

References

Bergeron, L., Y. Fauvel and A. Paquet (1995) L'indicateur synthétique avancé de l'économie canadienne selon la méthode de Stock et Watson, mimeo, Centre de recherche sur l'emploi et des fluctuations économiques, UQAM.

Berndt, E. and M. Fuss (1986) Productivity Measurement with Adjustments for Variations in Capacity Utilization, and Other Forms of Temporary Equilibrium, *Journal of Econometrics* 33, pp. 7–29.

Bernstein, J.I. and P. Mohnen (1991) Price Cost Margins, Exports and Productivity Growth: With an Application to Canadian Industries, *Canadian Journal of Economics* 24, pp. 638–659.

Carter, A.P. (1970) *Structural Change in the American Economy*, Harvard University Press, Cambridge, MA.

Caves, D.W., L.R. Christensen and J.A. Swanson (1981) Productivity Growth, Scale Economies, and Capacity Utilization in U.S. Railroads, 1955–1974," *American Economic Review* 71, pp. 994–1002.

Coelli, T., D.S.P. Rao and G. Battese (1998) *An Introduction to Efficiency and Productivity Analysis*, Kluwer Academic Publishers, Boston.

David, P. (1990) The Dynamo and the Computer, *American Economic Review*, Papers and Proceedings, 80(2), pp. 355–361.

Debreu, G. (1959) *Theory of Value.* New Haven, CT: Yale University Press.

Diewert, W.E. and C. Morrison (1996) Adjusting Output and Productivity Indexes for Changes in the Terms of Trade, *Economic Journal*, 96, pp. 659–679.

de Jong, G. (1996) Canada's Postwar Manufacturing Performance: A Comparison with the United States, Research Memorandum, Groningen Growth and Development Center, GD-32.

Dixit, A. and R. Pindyck (1994) *Investment under Uncertainty.* Princeton: Princeton University Press.

Färe, R., S. Grosskopf, C.A.K. Lovell and Z. Zhang (1994) Productivity Growth, Technical Progress and Efficiency Changes in Industrialised Countries, *American Economic Review*, 84, pp. 66–83.

Färe, R. and S. Grosskopf (1996) Productivity and Intermediate Products: A Frontier Approach, *Economics Letters*, 50, pp. 65–70.

Farrell, M. (1957) The Measurement of Productive Efficiency, *Journal of the Royal Statistical Society*, Series A, General, 120(3), pp. 253–282.

Hall, R. (1990) Invariance Properties of Solow's Residual, in *Growth/Productivity/Employment*, P. Diamond ed., MIT Press, Cambridge, MA, pp. 71–112.

Hayashi, F. (1982) Tobin's Marginal q and Average q: A Neoclassical Interpretation, *Econometrica* 50, pp. 213–224.

Hulten, C.R. (1978) Growth Accounting with Intermediate Inputs, *Review of Economic Studies* 45(3), pp. 511–518.

Hulten, C.R. (1979) On the Importance of Productivity Change, *American Economic Review*, 65, pp. 956–965.

Johnson, J. (1994) Une base de données KLEMS décrivant la structure des entrées de l'industrie canadienne, Statistique Canada, Division des Entrées-Sorties, Cahier Technique #73F.

Jorgenson, D. and Z. Griliches (1967) The Explanation of Productivity Change, *Review of Economic Studies*, 34(3), pp. 308–350.

Lichtenberg, F.R. and Z. Griliches (1989) Errors of Measurement in Output Deflators, *Journal of Business and Economic Statistics*, pp. 1–9.

Mohnen P., Th. ten Raa and G. Bourque (1997) Mesures de la croissance de la productivité dans un cadre d'équilibre général: L'économie du Québec entre 1978 et 1984', *Canadian Journal of Economics*, 30(2), pp. 295–307.

Morrison, C. (1986) Productivity Measurement with Non-Static Expectations and Varying Capacity Utilization: An Integrated Approach, *Journal of Econometrics* 33, pp. 51–74.

Morrison, C. (1988) Quasi-fixed inputs in U.S. and Japanese manufacturing: A Generalized Leontief Restricted Cost Function Approach, *Review of Economics and Statistics*, 70(2), pp. 275–287.

Nishimizu, M. and J.M. Page Jr. (1982) Total Factor Productivity Growth, Technological Progress and Technical Efficiency Change: Dimensions of Productivity Change in Yugoslavia, 1965–1978, *Economic Journal*, 92, pp. 920–936.

Perelman, S. (1995) R&D, Technological Progress and Efficiency Change in Industrial Activities, *Review of Income and Wealth*, 41(3), pp. 349–366.

Sickles, R., D. Good and R. Johnson (1986) Allocative Distortions and the Regulatory Transition of the U.S. Airline Industry, *Journal of Econometrics* 33(1/2), pp. 143–163.

Siegel, D. (1994) Errors in Output Deflators Revisited: Unit Values and the PPI, *Economic Inquiry* 32(1), pp. 11–32.

Solow R. (1957) Technical Change and the Aggregate Production Function, *Review of Economics and Statistics*, 39(3), pp. 312–320.

ten Raa, Th. (1995) *Linear Analysis of Competitive Economies* . LSE Handbooks in Economics, Prentice Hall-Harvester Wheatsheaf, Hemel Hempstead.

Weitzman, W. (1976) On the Welfare Significance of National Product in a Dynamic Economy, *Quarterly Journal of Economics*, 90, pp. 156–162.

Wolff, E. (1985) Industrial Composition, Interindustry Effects, and the U.S. Productivity Slowdown, *Review of Economics and Statistics*, 67, pp. 268–277.

Appendix: Data

The constant price input–output tables obtained from Statistics Canada are expressed in 1961 prices from 1962 to 1971, in 1971 prices from 1971 to 1981, in 1981 prices from 1981 to 1986, and in 1986 prices from 1986 to 1991. All tables have been converted to 1986 prices using the chain rule.

For reasons of confidentiality, the tables contain missing cells, which we have filled using the following procedure. The vertical and horizontal sums in the make and use tables are compared with the reported line and column totals, which do contain the missing values. We select the rows and columns where the two figures differ by more than 5% from the reported totals, or where the difference exceeds $250 million. We then fill holes or adjust cells on a case-by-case basis filling in priority the intersections of the selected rows and columns, using the information on the input or output structure from other years, and making sure the new computed totals do not exceed the reported ones.

There are three capital types, namely buildings, equipment, and infrastructure.[13] The gross capital stock, hours worked and labor earnings are from the KLEMS database of Statistics Canada, described in Johnson (1994). In particular, corrections have been made to include in labor the earnings of the self-employed, and to separate business and non-business labor and capital. The total labor force figures are taken from Cansim (D767870) and converted into hours using the number of weekly hours worked in manufacturing (where it is the highest). Out of the 50 industries, no labor nor capital stock data exist for sectors 39, 40, 48, 49, 50, and no capital stock data for industry 46. The capital stock for industry 46 has been constructed using the capital/labor ratio of industry 47 (both industries producing predominantly the same commodity).

The international commodity prices are approximated by the U.S. prices, given that 70% of Canada's trade is with the United States. We have used the U.S. producer prices from the U.S. Bureau of Labor Statistics, Office of Employment Projection. The 169 commodity classification has been bridged to Statistics Canada's 94 commodity classification. As the debt constraint in (1) is given in Canadian dollars, we convert U.S. prices to Canadian equivalents. We have used, whenever available, unit value ratios,

[13]Statistics Canada calls them "building constructions," "equipment" and "engineering constructions." Alternatively, we could have modeled capital as being sector-specific, the so-called putty-clay model. We prefer the present hypothesis of sectoral mobility of capital within each group for three reasons. First, to let the economy expand, we would have needed capacity utilization rates which are badly measured and unavailable for a number of service sectors. Second, to relieve a numerical collinearity problem, we would have to relieve the capital constraint on the non-business sector. Third, the combination of 11 non-tradeables and sector-specific capacity expansion limits is too stringent. It would lead to a high shadow price on construction commodities and zero shadow prices almost anywhere else.

(UVRs, which are industry specific) computed and kindly provided to us by Gjalt de Jong (1996). The UVRs are computed using Canadian quantities valued at U.S. prices. For the other commodities, we have used the purchasing power parities (PPP) computed by the OECD (which are based on final demand categories). The UVRs establish international price linkages for 1987, the PPPs for 1990 in terms of Canadian dollars per U.S. dollar. We hence need two more transformations. First, U.S. dollars are converted to Canadian dollars using the exchange rates taken from Cansim (series 0926/133400). Second, since the input–output data are in 1986 prices, we need the linkage for 1986, which is computed by using the respective countries' commodity deflators: the producer price index for the U.S. (see above) and the total commodity deflator from the make table (except for commodities 27, 93 and 94, for which we use the import deflator from the final demand table) for Canada. Finally, international commodity prices are divided by a Canadian final demand weighted average of international commodity prices to express them in real terms.

The absence of trade in the input–output tables for most of the sample period renders the following commodities: non-tradeable, services incidental to mining, residential construction, non-residential construction, repair construction, retail margins, imputed rent from owner occupied dwellings, accommodation & food services, supplies for office, laboratories & cafeterias, and travel, advertising & promotion.

We do not claim that the data were measured without error. Particularly UVRs can be imprecise, according to Lichtenberg and Griliches (1989) and Siegel (1994). For a sensitivity analysis, we refer to ten Raa (1995).

The structure of some non-tradeability constraints implies the equality of the activity levels of "construction" and final demand, "owner-occupied dwellings" and final demand, and "printing and publishing" and "travel, advertising and promotion." We have forced the activity level of industry 39 (government royalties on natural resources, which essentially pertains to oil drigging in Alberta) to follow industry 5 (crude petroleum and natural gas) to ensure there are no such royalities without oil drigging. A more detailed documentation of the data and their construction is available from the authors upon request.

Chapter 20

Competition and Performance: The Different Roles of Capital and Labor

Thijs ten Raa and Pierre Mohnen

Abstract: Neoclassical economists argue that competition promotes efficiency, but Schumpeter argues that it is monopoly rents that help entrepreneurs to invest in R&D. We investigate the overall effect of competition on TFP-growth. We use rent, defined as the factor reward above its perfectly competitive value, as a negative measure of competition. Our main finding is that performance is positively associated with rents on capital, but not with rents on labor. Neoclassical economists and Schumpeter may both be right, but the mechanisms differ.

Keywords: Competition; Rent; TFP; Schumpeter hypothesis.

JEL classification: L16; O41; C67

1. Introduction

Is competition good for performance? Yes, say neoclassical economists, arguing that it eliminates slack and hence promotes static efficiency. No, say Schumpeter and others, pointing out that monopoly rents induce entrepreneurs to invest in R&D and thus promote dynamic efficiency. The mechanisms alluded to are quite different, and the overall effect of competition becomes an empirical issue. Nickell (1996) finds some support for the view that competition improves performance, but the evidence is not overwhelming. Aghion *et al.* (2001, 2002) and Boone (2001) argue that the relationship between competition and innovation is non-monotonic. Griffith (2001) finds that product market competition improves performance in principal-agent type firms. We will review the argument in some detail and then pitch our approach.

If a market is more competitive, the stakes of sweeping it by winning an innovation contest are greater, as the scope is wider. On a product-by-product basis, however, margins are lower in a more competitive market. Aghion *et al.* (2001) combine the two countervailing effects in a single model, where industries are duopolies engaged in price (Bertrand) competition. 'Competition' is measured by the elasticity of substitution between the duopolists' products. A higher degree of substitutability boosts the reward to an innovation winner among leveled firms (the neoclassical effect), but reduces the (marginal) reward to non-leveled firms (the Schumpeterian effect). A level field will become less leveled and the new equilibrium is less congenial for innovation; followers face low rents to gain when demand is more elastic, while leaders do not distance themselves further as technological knowledge is assumed to spill over anyway after a single period. Industries become less leveled and the rent dissipation effect overtakes the contest effect. Competition and innovation have an inverted U relationship as a result. In a Hotelling-style example of three vendors, Boone finds a U relationship and notes that "basically anything can happen," but Aghion *et al.* (2002) find empirical support for the inverted U relationship between competition and innovation.

Since Aghion *et al.* (2001, 2002) measure competition by means of the elasticity of substitution, both the neoclassical and the Schumpeterian effects are channelled through the product markets. This is also the market studied by Griffith? who suggests, however, that agency costs play a role in the scope for performance. We want to analyze the role of factor markets. Do neoclassical economists not argue that competition is good because it keeps managers sharp? And does Schumpeter not argue that monopoly profits are good because they fund R&D? Labor and capital may play conflicting roles in terms of the relationship between competition and performance. This conflict may explain why there is no simple relationship between the two.

Rather than relating rents to elasticities of demand in a neoclassical model of price competition, we decompose rents into factor components in a classical input–output framework and investigate whether the opposing effects of competition operate through different markets. A natural thought seems to be that competition in the labor market may be good, but competition in the capital market may be bad, both in terms of performance. In other words, neoclassical and Schumpeterian economists may both be right, but rather than combining the opposing effects in some nonlinear relationship, we point to different factor markets. The potential policy conclusions would be vastly different. The aforementioned literature may suggest an optimal level of product market competition at best. We say at best, because competition is modeled as a shift in consumers' preferences (more substitutability) and firms are assumed to (Bertrand) price compete throughout. In this paper, however, departures from competition are modeled directly as rents and factor markets are targeted.

What do we mean by competition and performance? The measurement of performance is relatively straightforward. Solow (1957) has demonstrated for perfectly competitive economies that the shift of the production possibility frontier, which is the ultimate determinant of the standard of living, is measured by total factor productivity growth (TFP). TFP is also the relevant measure for the standard of living in non- or less competitive economies, where it measures not only the shift of the frontier, but also the change in efficiency (Nishimizu and Page 1982). In short, we let performance be measured by TFP.

The measurement of competition is trickier. The industrial organization literature provides a number of indices. Perhaps concentration indices are the most popular ones, but we will not employ them. We believe that industries with a low number of firms may well be competitive. In the tradition of Lerner (1934), we measure market power more directly by the extent that price has been raised over cost (i.e. by rent). Indeed, Nickell finds that rent is the most important determinant in the assessment of the influence of competition on performance, but rent is hard to measure. Nickell takes the difference between the rates of return on company capital and treasury bonds and admits this merely measures capital rent, and even as such is only a rough proxy; neoclassical economists point out that competition stamps out labor rent.

In the spirit of Nickell, we take rent as the (negative) measure of competition and define it by the difference between actual and perfectly competitive rewards. Actual rewards are given by value-added and perfectly competitive rewards by factor costs at shadow prices. To determine the latter, we need a general equilibrium model, which may have been the main obstacle in assessing the role of competition in the performance of an economy. We do so by analyzing Canadian input–output data over the period 1962–1991. Rent and TFP are determined at a level of aggregation that is more macro- than micro-economic.

Section 2 presents the model we employ to determine competitive valuations. Then, in Section 3, we define rent and impute it to capital and labor. Section 4 investigates the relationship between competition and performance (as measured by rent and TFP, respectively).

2. The Productivity Model

Both competition and performance are related to productivity. For performance, the connection to productivity is straightforward, as it is measured by TFP, the growth of (total factor) productivity. The connection between competition and rent is slightly more indirect. Competition is (negatively) measured by rent. Rent is the difference between actual and perfectly competitive rewards where the latter are essentially marginal productivities.

The standard approach to productivity is the neoclassical TFP analysis, where output and input components are combined into indices using value shares as weights. The acceptance of value shares at face value is equivalent to taking factor rewards for granted, and this procedure has been justified for perfectly competitive economies (Solow 1957; Jorgenson and Griliches 1967). We, however, are interested in the difference between observed and competitive rewards and therefore, cannot apply the standard procedure, but must derive productivities from the real input and output data of the economy.

We follow Nishimizu and Page in letting total factor productivity growth be the composition of a shift of the best-practice frontier (true technological progress) and a change in technical efficiency, and in using linear programming techniques to identify the frontier and the resulting level of efficiency. Nishimizu and Page use sectoral panel data to estimate a time-shifting translog production frontier for every sector and sectoral levels of technical efficiency in each period, but ignore the input balance constraints. We estimate instead a general equilibrium model with different sectoral levels of activity in each period and an overall level of technical efficiency for the whole economy in each period.

Our model is input–output in spirit, but we admit different numbers of industries and of commodities, as in activity analysis. Industries transform factor inputs and intermediate inputs into outputs, and the net output commodity vector feeds domestic final demand and net exports. The marginal productivities of the factor inputs are the shadow prices associated with the factor constraints of the program that maximizes welfare. Now if we assume that producers use Leontief technologies and end-users of the commodities have Leontief preferences, then the formulas governing these shadow prices are perfectly consistent with neoclassical growth accounting and moreover, capture the efficiency change effect of frontier analysis; see ten Raa and Mohnen (2002).

The model maximizes the level of domestic final demand, given its commodity proportions and subject to material balances, factor constraints, and balance of payments:

$\max_{s,c,g} e^{\mathrm{T}} fc$ subject to

$$\begin{aligned} (V^{\mathrm{T}} - U)s &\geq fc + Jg =: F \\ Ks &\leq M \\ Ls &\leq N \\ -\pi g &\leq -\pi g^{t} =: D \\ s &\geq 0. \end{aligned} \tag{1}$$

The variables (s, c, g) and parameters (all other) are the following [with dimensions in brackets]:

- s activity vector [# of industries]
- c level of domestic final demand [scalar]
- g vector of net exports [# of tradable commodities]
- e unit vector with all components equal to one
- T transposition symbol
- f domestic final demand [# of commodities]
- V make table [# of industries by # of commodities]
- U use table [# of commodities by # of industries]

J 0-1 matrix placing tradable [# of commodities by # of tradables]
F potential final demand [# of commodities]
K capital stock matrix [# of capital types by # of industries]
M capital endowment [# of capital types]
L labor employment row vector [# of industries]
N labor force [scalar]
π U.S. relative price row vector [# of tradable]
g^t vector of net exports observed at time t [# of tradable]
D observed trade deficit [scalar].

In (1), the observed allocation corresponds to $s = e$ and $c = 1$. This is feasible. The optimal value of expansion factor c will be greater than one. It measures the ratio of potential to actual domestic absorption. Domestic absorption is GDP except net exports; it is also called domestic GDP. We denote the shadow prices associated with the constraints of program (1) by p (a row vector of commodity prices), r (a row vector of capital productivities), w (a scalar for labor productivity), ε (a scalar for the purchasing power parity), and σ (a row vector of slacks for the sectors). Then the dual program reads

$$\min_{p,r,w,\sigma \geq 0} rM + wN + \varepsilon D \text{ subject to}$$

$$\begin{aligned} p(V^{\mathrm{T}} - U) &= rK + wL - \sigma \\ pf &= e^{\mathrm{T}} f \\ pJ &= \varepsilon \pi. \end{aligned} \tag{2}$$

The first dual constraint equates value added to factor costs for active industries (which have zero slack according to the theory of linear programming), all at shadow prices. The second dual constraint normalizes the level of commodity prices by the multiplicative constant we entered in the objective function of (1). The third dual constraint aligns the prices of the tradable commodities with the terms of trade.

The primal (1) and dual (2) programs have equal value by the main theorem of linear programming. In view of the price normalization constraint of (2) the identity reads

$$pfc = rM + wN + \varepsilon D \tag{3}$$

The *level* of total factor productivity is given by the ratio of actual output to optimally weighted factor input, $e^{\mathrm{T}} f/(rM + wN + \varepsilon D)$. According to equation (3), the level of total factor productivity is $1/c$, which is essentially Debreu's coefficient of resource allocation (ten Raa 2003). *Total factor productivity growth* is the rate of growth of the level of total factor productivity at *fixed* price weights[1]:

$$TFP = p\dot{f}/pf - (rM + wN + \varepsilon D\dot{)}/(rM + wN + \varepsilon D). \tag{4}$$

Total factor productivity growth has been shown to be the sum of the Solow residual,

$$SR = [p\dot{F} - r(Ks\dot{)} - w(Ls\dot{)}]/(rM + wN + \varepsilon D), \tag{5}$$

the terms-of-trade effect,

$$TT = \varepsilon\dot{\pi}g/(rM + wN + \varepsilon D), \tag{6}$$

and the efficiency change,

$$EC = -\dot{c}/c, \tag{7}$$

in ten Raa and Mohnen. The Solow residual is a Domar weighted average of industry Solow residuals (Mohnen and ten Raa 2000):

$$SR_i = [p(V^{\mathrm{T}} - U\dot{)}_{.i} - r\dot{K}_i - w\dot{L}_i]/pV_{i.} \tag{8}$$

with weights

$$pV_i s_i/(pfc). \tag{9}$$

The industry Solow residuals measure the dynamic performance of the economy. The static performance is measured by the efficiency change. The latter, see formula (8), measures the growth rate of the actual/potential GDP ratio because c measures the ratio of potential to actual domestic GDP. Here, efficiency change is driven by reallocations of the factor inputs, capital and labor, between industries. It could be imputed to the industries following ten Raa (2003), but these efficiency changes would still measure inter-industry allocative gains rather than intra-industry catching up with best practices. Input–output analysis implicitly identifies technical coefficients with observed input–output proportions. Sectoral productivity growth rates,

---

[1] *Warning*: We use *TFP* for TFP growth. No symbol is needed for the level of TFP. As usual, a dot denotes differentiation with respect to time.

see (8), capture technical change, intra-firm efficiency changes and inter-firm allocative efficiency changes (ten Raa 2005). It would be interesting to make this further decomposition, but that requires access to and use of the establishment data underlying the use and make tables.

3. Rent

In a broad sense, rent comprises all payments made to factor inputs for the provision of their services. The owner of a building collects rent from the businesses that use the space, and a worker receives compensation for the labor provided. This broad concept of rent includes not only the opportunity costs of the services, but also the bonuses that reflect distortions such as market power. The narrow concept of rent, however, is limited to these bonuses and therefore, consists of the excess payments over and above the opportunity cost. It is the latter concept of rent that we use to measure departures from competition.

The first dual constraint of (2) is the value relationship between value-added and factor costs when prices are competitive. It has its counterpart for observed prices, which we denote by p°, r°, and w° for commodities, capital and labor, respectively, where the superscript indicates 'observed.' Thus,

$$p^\circ(V^{\mathrm{T}} - U) = r^\circ K + w^\circ L + \sigma^\circ. \tag{10}$$

Here, σ° is defined residually and represents profits.[2]

We define *Rent* as the difference between observed value-added, given by row vector $p^\circ(V^{\mathrm{T}} - U)$, and competitive value-added, given by row vector $v = p(V^{\mathrm{T}} - U)$. The row vector of differences defines rent by sector. We can impute rent (in each sector) to the factor suppliers. Subtracting the first dual equation in program (2) from equation (10), we obtain

$$Rent = (r^\circ - r)K + (w^\circ - w)L + (\sigma^\circ + \sigma). \tag{11}$$

[2]Given that the make matrix V is in producer prices and the use matrix U (and the final demand vector F) is in consumer prices, there is a discrepancy due to various types of margins. The Canadian input–output tables contain a separate table of 7 types of margins. We have assimilated the margins to final demand, which is computed residually from the U, V and net trade (g) data. The margins are most likely included in our residual measure of observed capital rents, obtained by subtracting observed labor payments from observed value added.

In words, rent is the sum of capitalists' rent, workers' rent, and excess profits. Often capitalists' rent and excess profits are pooled to define *K-rent*, $(r^\circ - r)K + (\sigma^\circ + \sigma)$. Similarly denoting workers' rent $(w^\circ - w)L$ by *L-rent*, equation (11) is consolidated as follows:

$$Rent = K\text{-}rent + L\text{-}rent. \tag{12}$$

Notice that each term in equation (12) is a row vector of industry rents. The consolidation of profits into capital rent is apt for economies where profits accrue to shareholders rather than workers (i.e. capitalism). All the rent terms represent excess payments, over and above competitive values, so that rent is a negative measure for competitiveness. This is in the spirit of Nickell, who captures capital rent by putting $r =$ treasury bills rates and $\sigma = 0$, and who misses labor rent. We fill the gaps by letting our general equilibrium model determine the shadow prices.

Although we are able to dissociate capital from labor rents, we admit that we face some aggregation problems. There are more than three types of capital: often software, hardware, telecommunication equipment and inventories are measured as separate pieces of the aggregate capital stock, and the separation of R&D from value-added is presently under discussion in statistical offices. There is certainly more than one type of labor. Actually, data on labor by type of occupation exist for Canada, but not for the whole period that we are analyzing.[3] Therefore we have not separated out labor into different types. Given the different compositions by type of labor and capital across industries, our assumption of uniform competitive factor payments across sectors is certainly debatable, and we will do this in the next section.

4. Competition and Performance

The standard approach to measuring the impact of competition on performance is to regress the Solow residual (representing performance) on rent

[3]Canadian data on skill levels, based on the national occupational classification (NOC) or the standard occupational classification, exist continuously only from 1980 onwards. Gera *et al.* (2001) have used those data and constructed two sets of four skill levels (based on occupations, however, and not on qualifications) using the NOC classification and a skill classification proposed by Baumol and Wolff (1989) and updated by Wolff (2006). We have preferred to work with a longer dataset spanning 30 years without distinguishing labor by type of skills.

(representing the departure from competition):

$$SR_{it} = \alpha + \beta Rent_{it-1} + \varepsilon_{it},$$
$$\varepsilon_{it} = \mu_i + \lambda_t + \nu_{it}; \quad i = 1, \ldots, 45, \ t = 1963, \ldots, 1991. \qquad (13)$$

A positive role of competition would be signaled by a negative value of β. Coefficient α represents technological progress. The *data* underlying our panel of growth rates for 45 Canadian sectors and 29 time periods are described in the Appendix. In order to control for industry-specific and time-specific effects on productivity, we model a two-way error component model:μ_i represents the sector effect and is distributed i.i.d. with mean zero and standard deviation σ_μ; λ_t represents the time effect, distributed i.i.d. with mean zero and standard deviation σ_t; and ν_{it} is the idiosyncratic effect, distributed i.i.d. with mean zero and standard deviation σ_ν. A generalized least-squares estimation produces consistent estimates if there is no correlation between the composite error term and the rent. If $\sigma_\mu = \sigma_\nu = 0$, we have a fixed sectoral and time effects model. In equation (13), we have instrumented rent by its one-period lagged value to avoid a possible simultaneity bias.[4]

We have first tested to see whether we cannot pool the data. The Chow test rejects the pooling of different industries (a test statistic of 1.56 above the tabulated value of a $\chi^2_{44,1303}$). When, however, we allow for different βs over time or over time and sectors, we cannot reject homogeneity ($0.50 < \chi^2_{28,1303}$ and $1.16 < \chi^2_{72,1303}$, respectively). Next, we have estimated equation (13) using sector, time and sector/time dummies (i.e. exploiting respectively deviations from the industry means, from the year means, and the double deviations from time and industry means). We have estimated the model once using total rent, and once with rent split into labor and capital components. Since labor and capital rents may influence performance in different ways, it is interesting to investigate their separate effects. The results are tabulated in Table 1. In all cases, we reject the absence of sector-specific or time-specific fixed effects. We see that the effect of total rents on TFP is always positive, although in the most preferred specification (with time and industry dummies), it is significant only at 6.7%

[4]It should be mentioned that the causality between rent and TFP may also flow the other way. Rents may be the result of ex-post successful innovations. By inverting the lag structure, one could try to identify the direction of causality.

Table 1: Within Regression of TFP on Rents. (Percentage Points Increases per Billion Canadian Dollars, *p*-Values in Parentheses).

Regressors	1	2	3	4	5	6	7	8
	Standard: Total rent				Separate labor and capital rents			
Total rent	0.023 (0.154)	0.037 (0.166)	0.026 (0.091)	0.047 (0.067)	—	—	—	—
Labor rent	—	—	—	—	0.0161 (0.406)	0.059 (0.065)	−0.051 (0.786)	−0.003 (0.920)
Capital rent	—	—	—	—	0.028 (0.114)	0.024 (0.399)	0.052 (0.004)	0.084 (0.004)
Dummies	None	Industry	Time	Both	None	Industry	Time	Both
SSR	2.02191	1.79794	1.84367	1.61900	2.02119	1.79566	1.83093	1.61009
df	1303	1259	1275	1231	1302	1258	1274	1230
F-test		3.28**	4.10**	3.60**		3.30**	4.38**	3.67**

Note: The dependent variable is the industry Solow residual; SSR is the sum of squared residuals; df is degrees of freedom; the F-test tests the joint significance of the dummy coefficients; ** indicates significance at the 5% level.

level of confidence. Splitting rents, we find that the labor components are generally insignificant and that the capital components consistently have positive effects, significant at the 5% level as soon as we control for time effects.

The interesting result is thus that rents in the hands of capital, but not rents in the hands of labor, yield higher TFP. The estimates indicate the need to control for time-specific effects (although the test of pooling reveals no heterogeneity over time). Remember that the sectoral TFP figures are obtained jointly by the resolution of pairs of linear programs. By the general equilibrium property, year-specific shocks are transmitted to all sectors. Thus we have good reasons to believe that time effects are important indeed.

In Table 2, we estimate a random effects specification of heterogeneity for the model with both types of factor rents. The sector and year error components have standard deviations that are significantly different from zero. According to the Hausman test, there is no correlation between the factor rents and the error terms, except when sector effects are not controlled for. We therefore prefer the random effects estimates, since under that hypothesis, they are more efficient. Labor rent is never significant. Capital rent, however, boosts TFP. A billion dollar increase in capital rents,

Table 2: One-way and Two-way Random Effects Regression of TFP on Rents (percentage points increases per billion Canadian dollars) (*p*-values in parentheses, except where indicated).

	One-way	One-way	Two-way
Labor rent	0.037	0.000	0.007
	(0.152)	(0.998)	(0.795)
Capital rent	0.025	0.058	0.057
	(0.288)	(0.009)	(0.016)
σ_μ	0.0112	—	0.0111
	(0.0017)*		(0.0016)*
σ_t	—	0.0108	0.0111
		(0.0018)*	(0.0018)*
Hausman test of exogeneity of rents	2.64	7.83	4.09
	(0.267)	(0.020)	(0.129)

**Note*: Standard errors in parentheses. The dependent variable is the industry Solow residual.

which corresponds on average to roughly 30% of the total capital rents per sector, increases sectoral TFP growth by 0.06%. The magnitude of the lack of competition effect is not tremendous, but the sign agrees with the Schumpeterian perspective.

The conflict between neoclassical and Schumpeterian economists on the role of competition has never been resolved by the evidence. Our disaggregation of rent into capital and labor components throws some dim light on the issue. Both Schumpeter and the neoclassical economists may be right, but their mechanisms are channeled through different markets, namely the capital and labor markets, respectively. On hindsight, this should not come as a surprise. Schumpeter's argument, that departures from competition may yield positive contributions to dynamic efficiency, was built on the role of R&D, particularly the way it is financed. The neoclassical argument, that competition is good, has been built on the insight that it eliminates slack, particularly managerial laziness. Upon closer inspection, the arguments point at different factor markets and may both apply. We obtain evidence in favor of a Schumpeterian effect that operates through the capital market, but no evidence of a neoclassical effect that would operate through the labor market. At this juncture, we wish to recall that our data set does not allow for differences in labor quality. A referee's hunch is that sectors with a preponderance of high quality labor would exhibit higher TFP. Because labor 'rent' is high in these sectors when not corrected for quality, correcting for

Table 3: Effects of net R&D Expenditures on Rents. Fixed and Random Effects Models, With Sector and/or Time as Sources of Heterogeneity (*p*-values in parentheses, except where otherwise indicated).

	Sector heterogeneity		Time heterogeneity		Sector and time heterogeneities	
	Fixed effects	Random effects	Fixed effects	Random effects	Fixed effects	Random effects
Labor rent	−0.319 (0.568)	−0.279 (0.614)	1.190 (0.049)	0.994 (0.096)	0.238 (0.671)	0.148 (0.787)
Capital rent	1.336 (0.008)	1.308 (0.009)	−0.067 (0.907)	0.182 (0.747)	0.641 (0.211)	0.764 (0.125)
σ_μ	—	104.177 (11.141)*	—	—	—	103.72 (11.08)*
σ_t	—	—	—	17.42 (4.87)*	—	22.42 (3.54)*
Hausman test		1.030 (0.598)		7.46 (0.024)+		2.18 (0.340)+

Notes: The dependent variable is the industry Solow residual. ∗: Standard errors in parentheses. +: The Hausman test of exogeneity of rents is not very reliable as it is based on a non-positive definite difference in the variance-covariance matrices of the respective estimates.

quality will lead to a more negative coefficient of labor rent on TFP, resurrecting the neoclassical effect.[5]

In Table 3, we double-check the hypothesis of a Schumpeterian effect from capital rent on productivity, knowing that there is a large consensus that R&D earns a positive rate of return and hence has a positive effect on TFP. We regress by ordinary least squares the pooled data of R&D stock on capital rent and labor rent, again lagged by one period. We present the estimates of both the fixed effects and the random effects models, with one and two sources of heterogeneity. The Hausman test is only reliable for the sector heterogeneity, where it accepts the exogeneity of the regressors with respect to the error terms. In any case, the fixed and random effects estimates tell the same story. When we control for the greatest source of heterogeneity (sectoral effects), the capital rent is positively correlated with the R&D

[5]The issue of disentangling capital rents from higher return requirements is also difficult. For example, in cyclical sensitive sectors, one would expect a higher return to capital, and not call this rent. Also, in sectors where large intangible investments are made (media, pharma), high rents may just reflect measurement error in capital services. Luckily, any systematic, non-time varying effect of these will be soaked up by the fixed effects.

expenditures, as hypothesized by Schumpeter, but not with labor rent. When we control for time effects, surprisingly, it is labor rent that is positively correlated with R&D expenditures, whereas capital rent is not significant. The deviations over the time of R&D expenditures with respect to industry means is positively correlated with deviations in capital rents from industry means. The sectoral deviations with respect to yearly means across all sectors seem to be correlated with the same kind of deviations in labor rents. The story could still be consistent with a neoclassical view, in the sense that excess labor rent stimulates attempts to reduce cost through process R&D. (This interpretation would require additional verification. We do not at this stage have R&D split into process and product R&D.) If we control for both sources of heterogeneity, no factor rent is significant, although at the margin (if we accept a 12.5% level of confidence), we would accept the Schumpeter hypothesis.

5. Conclusion

We have investigated the influence of competition on performance. Performance is measured by Solow residuals derived from a general equilibrium model that maximizes the standard of living. The factor rewards are shadow prices, which are not necessarily equal to the observed rewards. In fact, the difference is rent, which we take as the (negative) measure of competition.

The weak evidence we have found can be summarized as follows. Total rent exerts a positive influence on productivity performance, and it is significant at the 7% level, even if we control for business cycle and technological opportunity effects by using time and sector dummies. Capital rents dominate the total effect. When capital and labor rents enter the equation separately, labor rents become insignificant, but capital rents continue to have a strong positive sign. Schumpeter and the neoclassical economists may both be right, but their mechanisms are channeled through different factor markets, namely the capital and labor markets, respectively. Indeed, the use of rent as a source of funding for R&D applies to capital, and the argument that rent yields slack pertains to labor. The Schumpeter hypothesis is also backed by R&D regressions on capital rent.

If capital rent is positive for performance, the policy issue emerges of how to promote technological progress without skewing the income distribution too much. An intelligent policy suggestion would be to reallocate the Schumpeterian advantages of capital rents to workers by providing them with stock options. This practice is spreading in the Western world and may indeed reconcile the different roles of capital and labor competition in performance.

Acknowledgements

We gratefully acknowledge Duncan Foley's suggestion to consider including efficiency in our measure of performance. We thank two anonymous referees for their insightful comments. The second author thanks CentER for its hospitality.

References

Aghion, P., C. Harris, P. Howitt and J. Vickers (2001) Competition, imitation and growth with step-by-step innovation. *Review of Economic Studies* 68, pp. 467–92.

Aghion, P., N. Bloom, R. Blundell, R. Griffith and P. Howitt (2002) Competition and innovation: An inverted-U relationship. NBER Working Paper 9269.

Baumol, W. and E. Wolff (1989) Sources of postwar growth of information activity in the United States. In Osberg, L., Wolff, E. and Baumol, W. (Eds.). The information economy: The implications of unbalanced growth. Halifax: Institute for Research on Public Policy, 17–46.

Boone, J. (2001) Intensity of competition and the incentive to innovate. *International Journal of Industrial Organization* 19, pp. 705–726.

de Jong, G. (1996) Canada's postwar manufacturing performance: A comparison with the United States. Groningen Growth and Development Center Research Memorandum GD-32.

Gera, S., W. Gu and Z. Lin (2001) Technology and the demand for skills: An industry-level analysis. *Canadian Journal of Economics* 34, pp. 132–148.

Griffith, R. (2001) Product market competition, efficiency and agency costs: An empirical analysis. The Institute for Fiscal Studies WP01/12.

Johnson, J. (1997) A KLEMS database: Describing the input structure of Canadian industry. Statistics Canada Aggregate Productivity Measures 15–204^{E}, pp. 19–32.

Jorgenson, D. and Z. Griliches (1967) The explanation of productivity change. *Review of Economic Studies* 34, pp. 308–350.

Lerner, A. (1934) The concept of monopoly and the measurement of monopoly power. *Review of Economic Studies* 1, pp. 157–175.

Mohnen, P. and Th. ten Raa (2000) A general equilibrium analysis of the evolution of Canadian service productivity. *Structural Change and Economic Dynamics* 11, pp. 491–506.

Nickell, S. (1996) Competition and corporate performance. *Journal of Political Economy* 104, pp. 724–746.
Nishimizu, M. and J.M. Page Jr. (1982) Total factor productivity growth, technological progress and technical efficiency change: Dimensions of productivity change in Yugoslavia, 1965–78. *Economic Journal* 92, pp. 920–936.
Solow, R. (1957) Technical change and the aggregate production function. *Review of Economics and Statistics* 39, pp. 312–320.
Statistics Canada (2005) CANSIM Time Series Data Base — Data Usage Charge.
Statistics Canada (2006) Industrial Research and Development, Catalogue, pp. 88–202.
ten Raa, Th. (2003) Debreu's coefficient of resource utilization, the Solow residual, and TFP: The connection by Leontief preferences. CentER Discussion Paper 111.
ten Raa, Th. (2005) Aggregation of productivity indices: The allocative efficiency correction. *Journal of Productivity Analysis* 24, pp. 203–209.
ten Raa, Th. and P. Mohnen (2002) Neoclassical growth accounting and frontier analysis: A synthesis. *Journal of Productivity Analysis* 18, pp. 111–128.
Wolff, E. (2006) The growth of information workers in the U.S. economy: The role of technological change, computerization, and structural change. *Economic Systems Research* 18, pp. 221–55.

Appendix: Data

The constant price input–output tables obtained from Statistics Canada are expressed in 1961 prices from 1962 to 1971, in 1971 prices from 1971 to 1981, in 1981 prices from 1981 to 1986, and in 1986 prices from 1986 to 1991. All tables have been converted to 1986 prices using the chain rule. For reasons of confidentiality, the tables contain missing cells, which we have filled using the following procedure. The vertical and horizontal sums in the make and use tables are compared with the reported line and column totals, which do contain the missing values. We select the rows and columns where the two figures differ by more than 5% from the reported totals, or where the difference exceeds \$250 million. We then fill holes or adjust cells on a case-by-case basis filling in priority the intersections of the selected rows and columns, using the information on the input or output structure from other years and making sure the new computed totals do not exceed the reported ones.

Statistics Canada reconfigures mixed income data uniquely, distinguishing net income unincorporated business and other operating surplus. Moreover, to assign even more accurately income to the different factor input categories, we employ additional factor input data. There are three capital types, namely buildings, equipment, and infrastructure.[6] The gross capital stock, hours worked and labor earnings are from the KLEMS database of Statistics Canada, described in Johnson (1997). In particular, corrections have been made to include in labor the earnings of the self-employed and to separate business and non-business labor and capital. This approach solves the problem of allocating mixed income (sole proprietor's income that should be classified as labor income). The total labor force figures are taken from Statistics Canada's (2005) CANSIM (series D767870) and converted in hours using the number of weekly hours worked in manufacturing (where it is the highest). Out of the 50 industries, neither labor nor capital stock data exist for sectors 39, 40, 48, 49, 50; these sectors have been deleted from our panel of growth rates. The missing capital stock for industry 46 has been constructed using the capital/labor ratio of industry 47 (both industries producing predominantly the same commodity). R&D expenditures are provided by Statistics Canada (2006) Science, Innovation and Electronic Commerce Division and are expressed in 1986 prices.

The international commodity prices are approximated by the U.S. prices, given that 70% of Canada's trade is with the United States. We have used the U.S. producer prices from the U.S. Bureau of Labor Statistics, Office of Employment Projection. The 169-commodity classification has been bridged to Statistics Canada's 94-commodity classification. As the debt constraint in (1) is given in Canadian dollars, we convert U.S. prices to Canadian equivalents. We have used, whenever available, unit value ratios (UVRs, which are industry specific), computed and kindly provided to us by Gjalt de Jong (1996). The UVRs are computed using Canadian quantities valued at U.S. prices. For the other commodities, we have used the purchasing power parities (PPP) computed by the OECD (which are based on final demand categories). The UVRs establish international price linkages for 1987, the PPPs for 1990 in terms of Canadian dollars per U.S. dollar.

[6] Statistics Canada calls them "building constructions," "equipment" and "engineering constructions." Alternatively we could have modeled capital as being sector-specific, the so-called putty-clay model. We prefer the present hypothesis of mobility of each type of capital across sectors for three reasons. First, to let the economy expand, we would have needed capacity utilization rates, which are badly measured and unavailable for a number of service sectors. Second, to relieve a numerical collinearity problem, we would have to relieve the capital constraint on the non-business sector. Third, the combination of 11 non-tradable and sector-specific capacity expansion limits is too stringent. It would lead to a high shadow price on construction commodities and zero shadow prices almost everywhere else.

We hence need two more transformations. First, U.S. dollars are converted to Canadian dollars using the exchange rates taken from Statistics Canada's (2005) CANSIM (series 0926/133400). Second, since the input–output data are in 1986 prices, we need the linkage for 1986, which is computed by using the respective countries' commodity deflators: the producer price index for the U.S. (see above) and the total commodity deflator from the make table (except for commodities 27, 93 and 94, for which we use the import deflator from the final demand table) for Canada. Finally, international commodity prices are divided by a Canadian final demand weighted average of international commodity prices to express them in real terms.

The following commodities are considered non-tradable: services incidental to mining, residential construction, non-residential construction, repair construction, retail margins, imputed rent from owner occupied dwellings, accommodation and food services, supplies for office, laboratories and cafeterias, and travel, advertising and promotion, for which no trade shows up in the input–output tables for most of the sample period.

The structure of some non-tradability constraints implies the equality of the activity levels of "construction" and final demand, "owner-occupied dwellings" and final demand, and "printing and publishing" and "travel, advertising and promotion." We have forced the activity level of industry 39 (government royalties on natural resources, which essentially pertains to oil rigging in Alberta) to follow industry 5 (crude petroleum and natural gas) to ensure there are no such royalties without oil rigging. A more detailed documentation of the data and their construction is available from the authors upon request.

Part VII

The Canadian Economy

Chapter 21

A General Equilibrium Analysis of the Evolution of Canadian Service Productivity

Pierre Mohnen and Thijs ten Raa

Abstract: Can the slowdown in total factor productivity that we have experienced since the mid-seventies be ascribed to the increasing importance of services, or do we instead observe an improvement of productivity in the service sectors by way of learning-by-doing or specialization? We feel that such questions are best answered within a general equilibrium analysis of the whole economy, i.e. a structural view of the whole economy. We maximize the level of domestic consumption subject to commodity balances and endowment constraints. The Lagrange multipliers associated with the endowment constraints measure the marginal productivities of labor and capital. We declare these shadow prices to be the factor productivities. The main empirical contribution of this paper is a reexamination of the services paradox. In Canada, the sluggish productivity in services is limited to finance, insurance and real estate, and to business and personal services. Any attempt to resolve the services paradox may focus on these two sectors. Transportation, trade, and to a lesser extent communication, are progressive sectors.

1. Introduction

Services have long ago relegated manufacturing to second rank in the importance of an economy's total activity. It is often argued that services suffer from the Baumol disease. More and more resources are devoted to services, where productivity gains are limited. The whole economy thus drifts to a lower productivity performance, unless the growth of services is offset by input savings in manufacturing. Oulton (1997) shows how resource shifts to service sectors with sluggish productivity may increase aggregate productivity if it concerns intermediate (business) rather than final (personal) services. Can the slowdown in total factor productivity (TFP) that we have experienced since the mid-seventies be ascribed to the increasing importance of services, or has this drag been offset by big savings of other inputs in manufacturing? Have services suffered from the Baumol disease at all, or do we instead observe an improvement of productivity in the services sectors by way of learning-by-doing or specialization? We feel that such questions are best answered within a general equilibrium analysis of the whole economy, i.e. a structural view of the whole economy. Our approach does not belong to the class of general equilibrium models, which model supply and demand functions, and aim at finding prices which sustain observed data as equilibrium outcomes. Our position is to start from the fundamentals of the economy to establish the production frontier and its shift over time, and to compute competitive prices which sustain that frontier. We do not capture the variations of the economy about its frontier in this paper. The full theory of fundamentals based productivity measurement is presented in ten Raa and Mohnen (2000). Also, in this paper, we focus on the service sectors and assume that capital is sector-specific and not differentiated by type.

The fundamentals are the usual ones — endowments, technology and preferences. Endowments are represented by a labor force and stocks of capital. Technology is given by the combined inputs and outputs of the sectors of the economy. Preferences are reflected by the pattern of domestic final demand. All the information can be extracted from input and output tables in real terms, that is constant prices. The productivities are determined as follows. We maximize the level of domestic consumption subject to commodity balances and endowment constraints. Now, as is known from the theory of mathematical programming, the Lagrange multipliers associated with the endowment constraints measure the marginal productivities of labor and capital: the consumption increments per units of additional labor or capital. In economics, these Lagrange multipliers are shadow prices that would reign under idealized conditions of perfect competition. We declare these shadow prices to be the factor productivities.

The paper is organized as follows. Factor productivities and TFP are defined by means of a linear program in the next section. In section 3, we present the data of the Canadian economy from 1962 to 1991. In section 4, we present our results. The last section concludes.

2. Productivities

We find the economy's frontier by the maximization of the level of domestic final demand, which excludes trade by definition. Exports and imports are endogenous, controlled by the balance of payments. We make no distinction between competitive and non-competitive imports. (The latter are indicated by zeros in the make table.) Domestic final demand comprises consumption and investment. Investment is merely a means to advance consumption, albeit in the future. We include it in the objective function to account for future consumption. In fact, Weitzman (1976) shows that for competitive economies, domestic final demand measures the present discounted value of future consumption.

Productivity growth will be defined as the measure of the shift of the frontier. Suppose an economy with only two commodities. Instead of comparing observations of the economy in subsequent periods (represented by

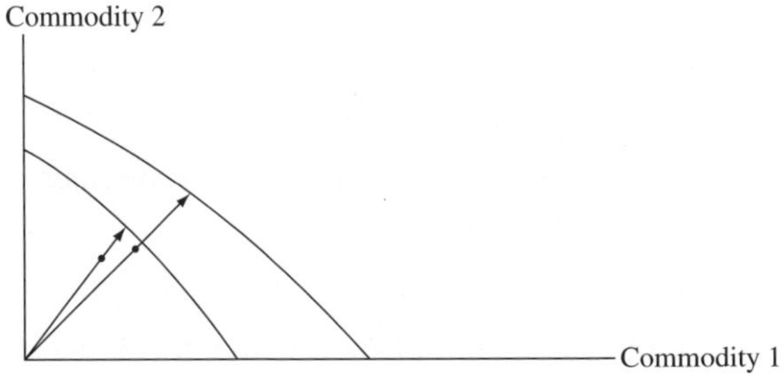

Fig. 1:

the dots in Fig. 1), we will compare the projections on the respective frontiers (the arrows).

The frontier of the economy in a particular year is determined by the resolution of a linear program. The primal program reads

$$\max_{s,\gamma,g} (e^\top f + w^0 l)\gamma$$
$$(V^\top - U)s \geq fc + Jg =: F$$
$$c_j K_j s_j \leq K_j$$
$$Ls + l\gamma \leq N$$
$$-\pi g \leq -\pi g^t =: D$$
$$s \geq 0$$

where

s activity vector [# of sectors]
γ level of domestic final demand [scalar]
g vector of net exports [# of tradeable commodities]
e unit vector of all components one
$\top$ transposition symbol
f domestic final demand [# of commodities]
w^0 base year price for non-business labor [scalar]
l non-business labor employment [scalar]
V make table [# of sectors by # of commodities]
U use table [# of commodities by # of sectors]
J 0-1 matrix placing tradeables [# of commodities by # of tradeables]
F final demand [# of commodities]
c_j capacity utilization rate of sector j [scalar between 0 and 1]
K_j capital stock of sector j [scalar]
L labor employment row vector [# of sectors]
N labor force [scalar]
π U.S. row price vector [# of tradeables]
g^t vector of net exports observed at time t [# of tradeables]
D observed trade deficit [scalar].

The linear program determines the activity levels of the various sectors of the economy (s), the expansion of final demand (y), and the net export vector (g) that together maximize the expansion of final demand. Those are the endogenous variables of the primal. The expression in front of γ

in the objective function only serves to normalize the commodity prices which sustain the optimal solution (essentially around unity, as we shall see when we interpret the dual program). The production structure of the economy is given by the net output matrix ($V^{\top} - U$), the capital stock used in each sector (c_jK_j), and the labor used in each business sector (L_j) and in the non-business sector (l). The structure of preferences is given by the domestic final demand vector f. The capital, labor and allowed trade deficit endowments of the economy are given by the available capital stock in each sector (K_j), the total labor force N, and the observed trade deficit D. The competitive world prices are given by sector π. Labor is supposed to be mobile across sectors, but capital is sector-specific. The sum of net imports for tradeable commodities valued at world prices may not exceed the observed trade deficit.

The program thus activates to a certain extent the various sectors of the economy, thereby producing a certain amount of all commodities, which is given by the observed sectoral production vectors blown up by the respective optimal activity levels (s_j). Likewise, the observed domestic final demand vector for all commodities is multiplied by the expansion factor of domestic final demand. If the activity levels were unity, we would reproduce the observed resource allocation in the economy. The first constraint of the linear program forces production for each commodity to be sufficient to accommodate domestic final demand and the optimal net exports (in case of tradeable commodities). The second set of constraints simply limits the activity levels of all sectors to be smaller than the inverse of the sector capacity utilization rates. The labor constraint stipulates that the sum of the labor used in all sectors may not exceed the available labor force. Labor is perfectly mobile across sectors in the economy, but totally immobile across countries. The last constraint, before the positivity constraint of sectoral activity levels, puts a limit to total net imports.

It should be noted that we do not set up the problem in terms of input–output coefficients, because of rectangular input–output tables, but in terms of given sectoral production and total demand structures. If we had a square input–output matrix, we could write the first commodity balance constraint, the first constraint of the primal, as $[I - A]x \geq fc + Jg$, where A is the matrix of input–output coefficients and x is the vector of sectoral gross output. The role of x is played by s and the role of A by the pair (U, V).

Productivities are not measured using market prices, but are determined by the dual program, which, as is well-known, solves for the Lagrange multipliers of the primal program. The latter measure the marginal products of the objective value with respect to the constraining entities, unlike observed factor rewards with all their distortions. The dual program reads, ˆ denoting a diagonal matrix,

$$\begin{aligned} &\min_{p,r,w,\varepsilon\geq 0} rK + wN + \varepsilon D \\ &p(V^{\top} - U) \leq r\hat{c}\hat{K} + wL \\ &pf + wl = e^{\top}f + w^0 l \\ &pJ = \varepsilon\pi. \end{aligned}$$

The endogenous variables in the dual program are shadow prices: p of commodities, r of capital (# of sectors), w of labor and ε of foreign debt (the exchange rate). Since the commodity constraint in the primal program has a zero bound, p does not show up in the objective function of the dual program. The commodity prices p are normalized by the second dual constraint, essentially about unity. They are not deflations that convert nominal values into real values, but a price vector that sustains the optimal allocation of resources in the linear program.

We now introduce the concept of productivity growth. Since labor productivity is the Lagrange multiplier or shadow price associated with the labor constraint, w, labor productivity growth is the growth of w, $\dot{w} = dw/dt$. Similarly, r is the vector of marginal productivities for each sectoral capital stock and ε the marginal productivity of the trade deficit.[1] TFP-growth is obtained by summing all factor productivity growth figures over endowments, $\dot{r}K + \dot{w}N + \dot{\varepsilon}D$, and normalizing by the level of productivity, $rK + wN + \varepsilon D$. Formally,

Definition. TFP-growth $= (\dot{r}K + \dot{w}N + \dot{\varepsilon}D)/(rK + wN + \varepsilon D)$.

Remark. Replacement of (f, l) by $(\lambda f, \lambda l)$ in the primal program with $\lambda > 0$ yields solution $(s, \gamma/\lambda, g)$. The value of the objective function is not affected. By the main theorem of linear programming, $rK + wN + \varepsilon D$ is not either. In

[1] In fact, there is also a non-business capital stock. Its value enters the objective function. In principle, its level constrains the expansion of domestic final demand. In practice, the capital constraint in the non-business sector is never binding at reasonable rates of capacity utilization, and hence its shadow price is zero. For notational simplicity, we have not included the non-business capital stock in the formulation of the program.

fact, the productivities are unaffected, as is, by extension, TFP-growth. The replacement does affect the commodity prices, as to preserve the identity between national product and national income, which we present next.

This straightforward definition of TFP-growth is now related to the commonly used Solow residual. By the main theorem of linear programming, substituting the price normalization equation, we obtain the macro-economic identity of national product and income (apart from the net exports on either side):

$$pf\gamma + wl\gamma = rK + wN + \varepsilon D.$$

By total differentiation:

$$\text{TFP-growth} = [(pf\gamma + wl\gamma)^{\cdot} - r\dot{K} - w\dot{N} - \varepsilon\dot{D}]/(pf\gamma + wl\gamma).$$

To establish the link with the Solow residual, focus on the numerator, substituting the assumed binding labor and balance of payment constraints:

$$(pF - pJg + wl\gamma)^{\cdot} - r\dot{K} - w(Ls + l\gamma)^{\cdot} + \varepsilon(\pi g)^{\cdot}.$$

Differentiating products, rearranging terms, and using the second dual constraint and the definition of F presented in the primal program

$$\begin{aligned} &p\dot{F} - r\dot{K} - w(Ls)^{\cdot} - pJ\dot{g} + \varepsilon(\pi g)^{\cdot} + \dot{p}(F - Jg) + (wl\gamma)^{\cdot} - w(l\gamma)^{\cdot} \\ &\quad = p\dot{F} - r\dot{K} - w(Ls)^{\cdot} + \varepsilon\dot{\pi}g + \dot{p}f\gamma + \dot{w}l\gamma. \end{aligned}$$

Now normalize again, dividing by $rK + wN + \varepsilon D$. Then the first term yields the technical change effect or *Solow residual*. It corresponds to the traditional Solow residual, except that here it is evaluated at shadow commodity prices and optimal sectoral activity levels. The second term, with the numerator $\varepsilon\dot{\pi}g$, is the *terms-of-trade effect*. Proportional changes in π are offset by a change in ε. Only relative international price changes matter. The last two terms are the *preference-shift effect*. By the remark, $pf + wl$ may be held constant, so that the preference-shift effect reads $-(p\dot{f} + w\dot{l})\gamma$. If demand (f, l) shifts to commodities with low opportunity costs, it is relatively easy to satisfy domestic final demand and TFP gets a boost. The terms-of-trade and preference-shift effects disappear when there is only one commodity and no non-business labor. Under these circumstances, π is unity and p also by the second dual constraint, hence their derivatives vanish. In other words, in a macro-economic setting, TFP-growth reduces to the Solow residual. It should be mentioned, however, that a tiny difference remains in the denominators. We divide by $pf\gamma + wl\gamma = pF - pJg + wl\gamma = pF - \varepsilon\pi g + wl\gamma = pF + \varepsilon D + wl\gamma$. In other words, we account for the deficit and non-business labor income.

Remarks

1. The TFP measure used in Mohnen, ten Raa and Bourque (1997) is confined to the Solow residual without the terms-of-trade and preference-shift effects. There is also a slight normalization difference. In this paper, we normalize with respect to $rK + wN + \varepsilon D = pf\gamma + wl\gamma$, whereas Mohnen, ten Raa and Bourque (1997) normalize with respect to $pF = pf\gamma + pJg$.
2. In discrete time, the differentials are approximated using the identity $x_t y_t - x_{t-1} y_{t-1} = \tilde{x}_t \overline{x_t y_t} + \tilde{y}_t \overline{x_t y_t}$, where $\tilde{x}_t = (x_t - x_{t-1})/\overline{x_t}$ and $\overline{x_t} = (x_t + x_{t-1})/2$, and similarly for $\tilde{y}_t$ and $\overline{y_t}$.
3. By Domar's aggregation, we can decompose the aggregate Solow residual into sectoral and group-sectoral Solow residuals. Let j index the sectors, i the commodities, and k the sector groups. Define the Solow residual of group-sector k as:

$$SR_k = \frac{\sum_{j\in k}\sum_i p_i (s_j v_{ji})^{\cdot}}{\sum_{j\in k}\sum_i p_i v_{ji} s_j} - \frac{\sum_{j\in k}\sum_i p_i (s_j u_{ij})^{\cdot}}{\sum_{j\in k}\sum_i p_i v_{ji} s_j} - \frac{\sum_{j\in k} w (s_j L_j)^{\cdot}}{\sum_{j\in k}\sum_i p_i v_{ji} s_j} - \frac{\sum_{j\in k} r_j \dot{K}_j}{\sum_{j\in k}\sum_i p_i v_{ji} s_j}.$$

Notice that if $k = j$, we get the Solow residual for sector j. Also notice that it is defined with respect to the available factor inputs rather than the utilized factor inputs. It can be shown that our aggregate Solow residual (SR) expression can be written as a Domar weighted average of sectoral Solow residuals (with weights adding to more than unity, see e.g. ten Raa 1995):

$$SR = \frac{\sum_k \sum_{j\in k}\sum_i p_i v_{ji} s_j}{\sum_i p_i F_i} SR_k.$$

In continuous time, this is exact. In discrete time, one must involve full employment of labor at the frontier point. Otherwise a slack change term emerges that cannot be allocated to the sectors. With capital, there is no such complication, since we assume it is sector-specific.

3. Data

We use the input–output tables of the Canadian economy from 1962 to 1991 at the medium level of disaggregation, which has 50 industries and 94 commodities.

The constant price input–output tables have been obtained from Statistics Canada in 1961 prices from 1962 to 1971, in 1971 prices from 1971 to 1981, in 1981 prices from 1981 to 1986, and in 1986 prices from 1986 to 1991. All tables have been converted to 1986 prices using the chain rule. For reasons of confidentiality, the tables contain missing cells, which we have filled using the following procedure. The vertical and horizontal sums in the make and use tables are compared with the reported line and column totals, which do contain the missing values. We select the rows and columns where the two figures differ by more than 5% from the reported totals, or where the difference exceeds $250 million. We then fill holes or adjust cells on a case-by-case basis, filling in priority the intersections of the selected rows and columns, using the information on the input or output structure from other years, and making sure the new computed totals do not exceed the reported ones.

The gross capital stock, hours worked and labor earnings data are from the KLEMS dataset of Statistics Canada, described in Johnson (1994). In particular, corrections have been made to include in labor the earnings of the self-employed, and to separate business and non-business labor and capital. The total labor force figures are taken from Cansim (D767870) and converted in hours using the number of weekly hours worked in manufacturing (where it is the highest). Out of the 50 industries, no labor nor capital stock data exist for sectors 39, 40, 48, 49, 50, and no capital stock data for industry 46.

The sectoral capacity utilization rates have been provided by the National Wealth and Capital Stock Division of Statistics Canada. They have been constructed using the Hodrick-Preston filter. For agriculture and fishing, we use the utilization rate for food. For all the missing service sectors, that is other than construction, pipeline transportation, and power and gas distribution, we use the rate for total non-farm goods (excluding energy) producing industries, the most encompassing capacity utilization rate available. The capacity constraints on construction has been lifted as it can be supplemented by U.S. capacity, as suggested on the Service Sector Productivity and the Productivity Paradox pre-conference.

The international commodity prices are approximated by the U.S. prices, given that 70% of Canada's trade is with the United States. We have used the U.S. producer prices from the U.S. Bureau of Labor Statistics, Office of Employment Projection. They are made relative prices using final demand shares to define the price level. The 169 commodity classification has been bridged to Statistics Canada's 94 commodity classification. To convert U.S. prices to Canadian equivalents, we have used, whenever available, unit value ratios, (UVRs, which are industry specific) computed and kindly provided to us by Gjalt de Jong (1996). The UVRs are computed using Canadian quantities valued at U.S. prices. For the other commodities, we have used the purchasing power parities computed by the OECD (which are based on final demand categories). The UVRs establish international price linkages for 1987, the PPPs for 1990 in terms of Canadian dollars per U.S. dollar. We hence need two more transformations. First, U.S. dollars are converted to Canadian dollars using the exchange rates taken from Cansim (series 0926/B3400). Second, since the input–output data are in 1986 prices, we need the linkage for 1986, which is computed by using the respective countries' commodity deflators: the producer price index for the U.S. (see above) and the total commodity deflator from the make table (except for commodities 27, 93 and 94, for which we use the import deflator from the final demand table) for Canada.

Commodities 13, 44, 70, 71, 72, 79, 81, 82, 88, 91 and 92 are considered as nontradeable, for which no trade shows up in the input–output tables for most of the sample period. For computational reasons and similar output composition, we have aggregated the nontradeable commodities 70–72 (residential, non-residential and repair construction). Due to the absence of labor,capital stock and intermediate inputs for industry 39 (government royalties on natural resources), it has been aggregated with industry 5 (crude petroleum and natural gas). In the end, we are thus left with 49 industries and 92 commodities, which are listed in Tables 1 and 2. A more detailed documentation of the data and their construction is available from the authors upon request.

Table 1: List of Commodities.

1. Grains	47. Copper & copper alloy products
2. Live animals	48. Nickel products
3. Other agricultural products	49. Other non-ferrous metal products
4. Forestry products	50. Boilers, tanks & plates
5. Fish landings	51. Fabricated structural metal products
6. Hunting & trapping products	52. Other metal fabricated products
7. Iron ores & concentrates	53. Agricultural machinery
8. Other metal. ores & concentrates	54. Other industrial machinery
9. Coal	55. Motor vehicles
10. Crude mineral oils	56. Motor vehicle parts
11. Natural gas	57. Other transport equipment
12. Non-metallic minerals	58. Appliances & receivers, household
13. Services incidental to mining	59. Other electrical products
14. Meat products	60. Cement & concrete products
15. Dairy products	61. Other non-metallic mineral products
16. Fish products	62. Gasoline & fuel oil
17. Fruits & vegetables preparations	63. Other petroleum & coal products
18. Feeds	64. Industrial chemicals
19. Flour, wheat, meal & other cereals	65. Fertilizers
20. Breakfast cereal & bakery prod.	66. Pharmaceuticals
21. Sugar	67. Other chemical products
22. Misc. food products	68. Scientific equipment
23. Soft drinks	69. Other manufactured products
24. Alcoholic beverages	**70.** Construction
25. Tobacco processed unmanufactured	71. Pipeline transportation
26. Cigarettes & tobacco mfg.	72. Transportation & storage
27. Tires & tubes	73. Radio & television broadcasting
28. Other rubber products	74. Telephone & telegraph
29. Plastic fabricated products	75. Postal services
30. Leather & leather products	76. Electric power
31. Yarns & man made fibres	**77.** Other utilities
32. Fabrics	78. Wholesale margins
33. Other textile products	**79.** Retail margins
34. Hosiery & knitted wear	**80.** Imputed rent owner ocpd. dwel.
35. Clothing & accessories	81. Other finance, insurance, real estate
36. Lumber & timber	82. Business services
37. Veneer & plywood	83. Education services
38. Other wood fabricated materials	84. Health services
39. Furniture & fixtures	85. Amusement & recreation services
40. Pulp	**86.** Accommodation & food services
41. Newsprint & other paper stock	87. Other personal & misc. services
42. Paper products	88. Transportation margins
43. Printing & publishing	**89.** Supplies for office, lab. & cafetaria
44. Advertising, print media	**90.** Travel, advertising & promotion
45. Iron & steel products	91. Non-competing imports
46. Aluminum products	92. Unallocated import & exports

Note: The nine bold indexes indicate nontradeable commodities. The commodities correspond to the M-classification of the Canadian input–output tables, except for the aggregation of the original commodities 70–72.

Table 2: List of Industries.

1. Agricultural & related services industries	25. Non-metallic mineral products industries
2. Fishing & trapping industries	26. Refined petroleum & coal products
3. Logging and forestry industries	27. Chemical & chemical products industries
4. Mining industries	28. Other manufacturing industries
5. Crude petroleum, natural gas, govermt's royalties on natural resources	29. Construction industries
	30. Transportation industries
6. Quarry & sand pit industries	31. Pipeline transport industries
7. Service related to mineral extraction	32. Storage & warehousing industries
8. Food industries	33. Communication industries
9. Beverage industries	34. Other utility industries
10. Tobacco products industries	35. Wholesale trade industries
11. Rubber products industries	36. Retail trade industries
12. Plastic products industries	37. Finance & real estate industries
13. Leather & allied products industries	38. Insurance
14. Primary textile & textile products industries	39. Owner occupied dwellings
15. Clothing industries	40. Business service industries
16. Wood industries	41. Educational service industries
17. Furniture and fixtures industries	42. Health service industry
18. Paper & allied products industries	43. Accommodation & food service industries
19. Printing, publishing & allied industries	44. Amusement & recreational services
20. Primary metal industries	45. Personal & household service industries
21. Fabricated metal products industries	46. Other service industries
22. Machinery industries	47. Operating, off., cafet. & lab. sup.
23. Transportation equipment industries	48. Travel, advertising & promotion
24. Electrical & electronic products	49. Transportation margins

Note: The industries correspond to the M-classification of the Canadian input–output tables, except for the aggregation of the original industries 5 and 39. The industries are defined according to the 1980 Standard Industrial Classification.

4. Results

Perhaps it is most illuminating to discuss the temporally aggregated results first. In Table 3, we have productivity growth figures obtained using endogenous weights, i.e. evaluated at the shadow prices and optimal activity levels of the linear program. Table 3, under the heading TFP decomposition, shows a 1.26% annual TFP-growth rate over the 1962–74 period. We chose the period breakpoints before the slump years 1975 and 1982 to compare productivity performances over comparable phases of the business cycle.[2]

[2]A referee suggested that this comparability renders the correction for utilization rates irrelevant. However, the inclusion of utilization rates ensures that capital constraints are not binding in the actual, observed allocation, and therefore, avoids the possibility that there is excess labor, with zero labor productivity.

Table 3: Average Annual Growth Rates and TFP Decomposition at Shadow Prices and Optimal Activity Levels (in percentages).

	1962–1974	1974–1981	1981–1991
Solow residual			
Primary sector	−0.42	−7.46	1.46
Manufacturing	0.57	−0.22	−1.11
Construction	−0.19	−1.11	0.00
Transportation	2.60	−0.04	0.38
Communication	1.85	−0.96	−0.21
Trade	1.13	−0.04	0.29
FIRE	−2.49	−1.89	−3.81
B&P services	0.32	−2.50	−2.01
TFP decomposition			
Solow residual	1.09	−1.59	−0.67
Terms of trade	0.22	−0.14	−0.08
Preference shift	−0.04	0.10	0.02
TFP-growth	1.26	−1.63	−0.72
Marginal productivity growth contributions			
Labor	−1.68	4.19	−0.73
Capital	3.17	−6.28	−0.02
Trade deficit	−0.21	0.49	0.05
TFP-growth	1.28	−1.59	−0.70

Canada hit recessions from January to March 1975, from May to June 1980, from August 1981 to November 1982, and from April 1990 to March 1991, according to Bergeron, Fauvel and Paquet (1995). Over the next business cycle (1974–81), TFP-growth fell to −1.63%. It recovered to −0.72% per annum in the 1980's (1981–91). The preference-shift effect was nearly zero in the first and last periods and positive in the middle period, when consumers apparently switched their patterns of demand towards commodity bundles with lower contents of expensive factors. The technical change effect explains the lion's share of TFP-growth: the Solow residual fell far below zero after 1974, but then recovered in the 80s. The terms of trade effect played a minor role and followed a similar pattern as technical change. At the optimal terms of trade and trade balance, relative world prices moved so as to increase our purchasing power before 1970 and to decrease it afterwards. The three effects add up to TFP-growth.

From its definition, TFP-growth can also be decomposed into its constituent marginal productivity growth rates. We then get a second accounting identity. The numbers, at the bottom of Table 3, are slightly different because of rounding. We see that the contribution of labor productivity declined on average by 1.68% per year in 1962–74 and by 0.73% per year in 1981–91. During the turbulent period of the oil shocks (1974–81), it actually increased on average by a strong 4.19% per annum. Capital productivity growth followed the same pattern as TFP-growth, reflecting the predominant value of capital in the value of output. The contribution of the productivity of the trade deficit, i.e. the increased consumption permitted by a marginal increase in the allowed deficit was small throughout.

The primary sector very much determines the aggregate evolution in Canadian productivity. It was mostly struck by the slowdown in the 70s, but also led the recovery in the 80s. Manufacturing and construction are average sectors, following the economy-wide Solow residual. Of the remaining service sectors, the first three are surprisingly healthy. Transportation, trade, and to a lesser extent communication, all perform above the economy-wide average. Last and least, FIRE and B&P services drag the economy.

Table 4 lists the annual productivity growth figures, giving a more precise timing of the up- and downturns of productivity growth. As is well-known and also very apparent here, TFP-growth fluctuates a lot. The primary sector, manufacturing and construction feature as many negative as positive Solow residuals over time. Transportation, communication and trade report predominantly solid positive Solow residuals, confirming their status as progressive sectors. Last and least, FIRE and B&P services have a negative performance. It is interesting that shadow price-based Solow residuals fluctuate to the extent that not a single year reported economy-wide positive values.

We have checked the sensitivity of our results to the use of net instead of gross capital stocks. The solutions to the linear programs are unaffected, so are the optimal shadow wage rates. The only difference is in the shadow prices of capital, which adjust to the new capital stock measures so as to yield zero profit conditions. It is like a scaling problem. All that matters in our model for the expansion to the efficiency frontier are the rates of capacity utilization. The choice of measurement for the capital stocks would only matter if capital from various sectors was substitutable. TFP-growth rates differ because the marginal productivities of capital differ. But both qualitatively and quantitatively, the results are rather similar.

Table 4: Solow Residual at Shadow Prices and Optimal Activity Levels (in percentages).

Period	Primary sector (1–7)	Manufacturing (8–28)	Construction (29)	Transportation (30–32)	Communication (33–34)	Trade (35–36)	FIRE (37–39)	B&P Services* (40–49)
1962–1963	−0.84	0.66	−0.03	5.18	0.45	1.07	−2.91	0.91
1963–1964	0.38	1.56	2.64	4.98	1.74	3.34	−1.99	0.55
1964–1965	2.75	1.16	−0.30	2.08	2.12	2.10	−3.15	−0.17
1965–1966	−0.16	0.23	−1.23	3.31	2.23	3.03	−1.82	0.48
1966–1967	−2.10	−0.89	0.67	0.20	2.09	1.52	−3.96	0.04
1967–1968	0.66	1.33	1.30	1.80	2.64	0.63	1.81	−1.24
1968–1969	−0.50	1.19	−0.90	4.59	0.15	1.48	−3.79	0.34
1969–1970	−0.21	−2.27	0.22	4.45	1.66	1.63	0.00	−0.91
1970–1971	−5.30	0.65	1.04	−0.01	2.94	0.01	−4.68	0.80
1971–1972	2.13	1.93	−0.95	1.44	7.32	−1.32	−5.38	0.68
1972–1973	7.56	1.42	−8.30	2.63	−2.93	1.09	0.14	1.65
1973–1974	−9.41	−0.11	3.53	0.54	1.78	−1.06	−4.12	0.75
1974–1975	−13.00	−3.32	5.25	−2.85	−0.88	1.70	−3.46	−2.04
1975–1976	−7.36	1.98	3.80	0.56	0.75	3.05	−0.94	1.14
1976–1977	−4.64	0.31	1.69	2.66	0.63	−1.31	−1.25	−3.84
1977–1978	−3.79	0.51	−3.59	2.03	−5.93	0.42	−2.41	−1.99
1978–1979	0.77	−0.58	−5.42	4.07	−0.78	−1.66	0.34	−6.71

(*Continued*)

Table 4: (*Continued*)

Period	Primary sector (1–7)	Manufacturing (8–28)	Construction (29)	Transportation (30–32)	Communication (33–34)	Trade (35–36)	FIRE (37–39)	B&P Services* (40–49)
1979–1980	2.75	−1.20	−11.65	−4.83	0.85	−2.53	−3.26	−3.52
1980–1981	−26.92	0.74	2.12	−1.94	−1.39	0.08	−2.22	−0.56
1981–1982	−3.11	−4.45	7.80	−3.19	−7.19	−0.30	−6.33	−0.51
1982–1983	0.81	1.52	−0.13	4.14	0.09	3.41	−3.59	−3.87
1983–1984	2.15	2.25	−4.21	5.56	0.74	1.32	−0.46	−2.23
1984–1985	−0.53	−2.28	1.49	0.49	1.43	2.41	−0.81	3.04
1985–1986	−1.45	−1.02	0.03	0.22	−0.94	1.16	−3.05	−1.71
1986–1987	2.12	−0.76	−2.57	1.76	7.51	1.60	−5.72	−4.09
1987–1988	3.31	−0.54	−0.86	0.00	−0.88	0.19	−3.88	−1.49
1988–1989	−5.52	−1.71	8.08	−0.31	2.85	−0.73	−2.93	−2.56
1989–1990	9.03	−1.73	−4.87	−1.26	−3.13	−3.19	−6.79	−5.18
1990–1991	7.75	−2.40	−4.71	−3.48	−2.60	−2.95	−4.48	−1.55

Note:* In parentheses, industry aggregations from Table 2. FIRE denotes finance, insurenace and real estate. B&P services denotes business and personal services.

5. Conclusions and Qualifications

Annual TFP growth was positive on average over the 1962–74 period. It dropped quite sharply during the 1974–81 interval and recovered, but not to the levels of the golden sixties, after 1982. This finding confirms conventional wisdom. Our productivity figures show greater fluctuations than what is usually reported, because they are extracted endogenously from a linear program with corner solutions. Of course, our methodology differs from conventional productivity analysis in one major respect. We compute in some sense social productivities, i.e. marginal valuations of inputs in terms of attainable total domestic consumption and not in terms of attainable individual sectoral production. We take the whole economy into account globally, with its interdependencies and mutual constraints, to derive the efficient production frontier and define productivity growth as the outward shift of that efficiency frontier rather than changes in observed input–output ratios.

Our model offers some explanation to productivity growth. Some inputs can earn high returns if they are in short supply. TFP-growth is nothing but a reflection of the evolution of marginal valuations of primary factor inputs. The modeling of existing constraints is very crucial in our approach. Another key role in our analysis is played by the levels of capacity utilization. Their construction is still controversial. No estimates are available for services. Proper measures of output and capacity utilization for services are problematic, but we urge Statistics Canada to devote resources to construct such measures. Our analysis would also be enriched if we could have data on sectoral use and total availability of labor disaggregated by level of qualification and of sectoral utilization and availability of capital disaggregated by type of capital. It would allow us to get a more precise picture of scarcities in the Canadian economy. By construction, the vintage structure of capital does not matter. To relax this assumption, we would need to make investment endogenous and switch to a dynamic model, which would lead to Hulten's (1979) notion of a dynamic residual.

We must also admit that our assessment of productivity growth in services might be biased because of improper price measurements. New products and services or improved quality of existing ones are seldom measured in national accounts statistics. This problem is especially acute in services where output and prices are harder to measure than for manufacturing goods. The bias may show up in various places in the productivity formulas (see Oulton (1997) for a related discussion). First, the optimal solution of the linear program which determines the frontier of the economy may differ if the underlying input and output quantities are different. For example, if a given commodity is actually larger than measured because of quality improvement (say computers), and if it is used heavily as an intermediate input in a sector with a high potential of being assigned a high activity level at the optimal solution of the linear program (e.g. because it has a low rate of capacity utilization and requires few other inputs), it may well happen that either the final demand can expand less or that the main sector producing that commodity must expand more. The shadow prices underlying the optimal solution may therefore change as well (different bottlenecks may show up) and hence the measured productivity figures will differ. Second, assuming for the sake of argument that the optimal solutions do not change, it can readily be seen from the TFP-growth decomposition that the Solow residual will increase if final demand increases, i.e. that the TFP-growth is underestimated, if growth in observed final demand is underestimated. It is unclear what the final bias in our sectoral TFP figure will be.

Despite these words of caution about the interpretation of our results, our analysis reveals some interesting insights into the productivity of Canadian services. The main empirical contribution of this paper is a qualification of sluggish service productivities and the consequent services paradox. In Canada, poor productivity in the services is limited to finance, insurance and real estate, and business and personal services. Any attempt to resolve the services paradox may focus on those two sectors. Transportation, trade, and to a lesser extent communication, are progressive service sectors.

Acknowledgements

We thank Nathalie Viennot and Sofiane Ghali for their dedicated research assistance and Rene Durand, Jean-Pierre Maynard, Ronald Rioux and Bart van Ark for their precious cooperation in constructing the data. We are grateful to Carl Sonnen and other participants of the Service Sector Productivity and the Productivity Paradox conference, Ottawa, April 1997, for their helpful comments. We are also greateful to Michael Landesmann and other participants of the Technical Change, Growth and International Trade conference, Eindhoven, October 1999, for their helpful comments. We acknowledge the financial support of the Social Sciences and Humanities Research Council of Canada, CentER, the Netherlands Foundation for the Advancement of Research (NWO), and the Association for Canadian Studies in the Netherlands.

References

Bergeron, L., Y. Fauvel and A. Paquet (1995) L'indicateur synthétique avancé de l'économie canadienne selon la méthode de Stock et Watson, mimeo, Centre de recherche de l'emploi et des fluctuations économiques, UQAM.

de Jong, G. (1996) Canada's Postwar Manufacturing Performance: A Comparison with the United States, Research Memorandum, Groningen Growth and Development Center, GD-32.

Hall, R. (1990) Invariance Properties of Solow's Residual, in *Growth/Productivity/-Employment*, P. Diamond (ed.), pp. 71–112, MIT Press, Cambridge, MA.

Hulten, C.R. (1979) On the Importance of Productivity Change, *American Economic Review*, 65, 956–965.

Johnson, J. (1994) Une base de données KLEMS décrivant la structure des entrées de l'industrie canadienne, Statistique Canada, Division des Entrées-Sorties, Cahier Technique #73F.

Mohnen, P., Th. ten Raa and G. Bourque (1997) Measures de la croissance de la productivité dans un cadre d'équilibre général: L'économie du Québec entre 1978 et 1984, *Canadian Journal of Economics*, 30(2), pp. 295–307.

Oulton, N. (1997) Total factor productivity growth and the role of externalities, *National Institute Economic Review*, 161(3), pp. 99–111.

Solow R. (1957) Technical change and the aggregate production function, *Review of Economics and Statistics*, 39(3), pp. 312–320.

ten Raa, Th. (1995) *Linear Analysis of Competitive Economies*, LSE Handbooks in Economics, Harvester Wheatsheaf, New York.

ten Raa, Th. and P. Mohnen, Neoclassical Growth Accounting and Frontier Analysis: A Synthesis, Center Discussion Paper.

Weitzman, W. (1976) On the welfare significance of national product in a dynamic economy, *Quarterly Journal of Economics*, 90, pp. 156–162.

Chapter 22

Productivity Trends and Employment Across Industries in Canada

Pierre Mohnen and Thijs ten Raa

1. Introduction

In a famous article of 1967, William Baumol predicted that services would price themselves out of the market, given their lower productivity growth and the consequent rise of their relative price, compared to non-service goods. Twenty years later, we observe that measured productivity growth in services is indeed relatively low, but that at the same time, the modern economy is based less on manufacturing and more on service. Economic activity has substantially shifted away from manufacturing towards services, as it had moved from the primary sector to manufacturing in the first half of the last century. How to reconcile these observations?

In this chapter, we examine the apparent paradox in the light of the Canadian experience. We first look at the facts. In the next section, we trace productivity trends and employment shifts for the Canadian economy over the period 1962–91. Second, we review a list of potential explanations.

Labor productivity growth provides only a partial picture of productivity performance since it ignores the role of capital accumulation, so we look at total factor productivity (TFP) growth. In the third section, we distinguish between value added and final demand. Their macro identity breaks down at the sectoral level and this has implications on the issue. Value added might be more concentrated in services than before, reflecting a crowding out of services from manufacturing, and yet final demand composition has barely changed. We then examine shifts in final demand composition at both the commodity and final demand category levels. In the fourth section, we explore the hypothesis that Canadian services may have gained a comparative advantage in international trade. Last, but not least, production and final demand for services may have gained ground as a result of technical change. The verdict on the latter mechanism is provided in the fifth section. We conclude in the sixth section by summarizing the results of our analysis of the Canadian experience.

2. Labor Employment and Productivity

To assess the extent to which economic activity has shifted towards services and to examine the sluggishness of productivity in services, we use the input–output (I–O) data of the Canadian economy at the medium level of aggregation (50 sectors and 92 commodities) and the KLEMS database (Johnson 1994; Statistics Canada, various issues). We report results for ten groups of sectors: the primary sector, manufacturing, construction, transportation, communication, wholesale trade, retail trade, FIRE (finance, insurance and real estate), business services and personal services.[1] We compare three periods, the 1960s, 1970s and 1980s, which are not exactly decades, but cover the periods 1962–74, 1975–81 and 1982–91. The two years separating the periods are slump years. This choice enables us to compare productivity and employment as much as possible over comparable phases of the business cycles. Table 1 reveals the changing pattern of labor employment by sector. The big losers are the primary sector and

[1] Sectors 41–50 were allocated to business or to personal services according to their ratio of shipments to domestic intermediate and final demand. Business services are characterized by a preponderance of deliveries to intermediate domestic demand.

Table 1: Labor Distribution (sectoral shares in percent).

Groups of sectors	1960s	1970s	1980s	60–80s
Primary	15.4	11.8	9.8	−5.6
Manufacturing	27.7	24.4	21.6	−6.1
Construction	9.8	9.3	8.6	−1.2
Transportation	6.4	6.3	5.8	−0.6
Communication	3.1	3.6	3.5	0.4
Wholesale trade	5.7	6.2	7.0	1.3
Retail trade	14.3	15.2	14.9	0.6
FIRE	5.0	6.3	7.0	2.0
Business services	4.2	6.8	9.6	5.4
Personal services	8.4	10.1	12.2	3.8
Total economy	100	100	100	0

Notes: 1. The 1960s correspond to the 1962–74 period, the 1970s to 1975–81 and the 1980s to 1982–91.
2. At the M-level of disaggregation, primary regroups sectors 1–7 and 39, manufacturing 8–28, construction 29, transportation 30–32, communications 33–34, wholesale trade 35, retail trade 36, FIRE 37, 38 and 40, business services 41, 47–50 and personal services 42–46.

manufacturing. Their combined employment share has dwindled by 11.7 percentage points. Employment in services has gone up, except for construction and transportation. The big winners are business and personal services with a surge in total employment share of 9.2 percentage points.

The shift of employment towards the services can to some extent reflect the stagnant productivity in services. The story is usually cast in terms of labor productivity. Table 2 shows real value added per unit of labor for the ten groups of sectors and the three time periods. Value added is the value of the net output vector of commodities for a group of sectors. The figures are in 1986 $C(Canadian) per hour worked. Table 2 reveals the Baumol disease. The top five groups of sectors, the 'nuts-and-bolts' chamber of the Canadian economy, all show dramatic increases in real value added per hour from the 1960s to the 1980s, ranging from 47 per cent (in construction) to 103 per cent (in communication). The bottom five groups of sectors, the 'soft' chamber of the economy (wholesale and retail trade, FIRE, and business and personal services), depict increases in real value added per hour below the total economy's average over the same period, with personal services trailing at 3 per cent. At the M-level of aggregation, labor productivity growth is thus negatively correlated with employment growth. Services,

Table 2: Value Added/Labor (1986 $C per hour).

Groups of sectors	1960s	1970s	1980s	60–80s (%)
Primary	15.66	19.32	23.96	+53
Manufacturing	17.37	22.63	26.47	+52
Construction	17.60	21.90	25.83	+47
Transportation	15.42	19.11	23.11	+50
Communication	26.52	39.81	53.87	+103
Wholesale trade	16.32	19.01	22.32	+37
Retail trade	10.62	11.86	12.82	+21
FIRE	58.52	64.08	70.30	+20
Business services	13.28	14.95	16.23	+22
Personal services	15.72	17.86	16.27	+3
Total economy	17.92	22.30	25.41	+42

Note: See Table 1 for the definition of periods and sectors.

Table 3: Capital–Labor Ratios (1986 $C per hour).

Groups of sectors	1960s	1970s	1980s	60–80s (%)
Primary	55.81	93.36	128.99	+131
Manufacturing	31.75	43.48	58.41	+84
Construction	5.71	7.90	11.41	+100
Transportation	106.54	107.00	121.90	+14
Communication	253.51	309.64	424.04	+67
Wholesale trade	12.33	11.92	11.76	−5
Retail trade	9.01	8.94	9.85	+9
FIRE	35.45	52.52	86.17	+143
Business services	13.41	10.60	15.42	+15
Personal services	22.65	22.39	26.57	+17
Total economy	38.69	48.62	61.26	+58

Note: See Table 1 for the definition of periods and sectors.

except for construction and communication, display the greatest growth in employment, but also the lowest growth in labor productivity.

Now, we know that labor productivity is not the ideal way to measure productivity since it relates output only to the labor input. A stagnant labor productivity is not a problem if labor substitutes for capital and the factor savings are just on another input. Table 3 reports the capital-labor ratios, also in 1986 $C per person-hour. All sectors but wholesale trade have increased their capital intensity.

The question is whether the 'soft' part of the economy has done so at a lower pace and thereby compensated for its poorer labor productivity performance. The answer is 'yes' for retail trade and for business and personal services, but 'no' for FIRE. Because of the relative capital savings in at least four of these five sectors, the Baumol disease may be less severe if we measure the performance of sectors in terms of TFP, instead of labor productivity. It can be shown that, under constant returns to scale, TFP growth is equal to labor productivity growth minus the growth in the capital–labor ratio multiplied by the cost share of capital.

Table 4 reports annualized TFP growth rates for our ten groups of sectors over the three periods. The Canadian economy was healthy in all periods. In fact, the aggregate Solow residual, that is, the Domar weighted averages of the sectoral Solow residuals are 1.41, 0.47 and 0.17, respectively for the three periods. Notice the pervasive TFP slowdown between the 1960s and the 1980s, except for the primary sector, which went through a tremendous recovery in the 1980s. It is interesting to see that, with the exception of personal services, the weak services sectors that we have identified so far did not perform worse than manufacturing. In fact, Canadian manufacturing TFP growth declined throughout the three periods. It even became negative in the 1980s. Personal services match this downward trend, but wholesale and retail trade, business services and FIRE outperformed manufacturing. As we suspected, the Baumol disease is more localized when measured in terms of TFP growth. It mainly applies to personal services. Now that we have clarified the symptom, let us turn to some of the possible explanations.

Table 4: TFP-Growth Rates (annualized percentages).

Groups of sectors	1960s	1970s	1980s	60–80s
Primary	−0.83	−2.11	1.10	+1.93
Manufacturing	0.94	0.16	−0.20	−1.14
Construction	−0.17	1.92	−0.39	−0.22
Transportation	2.82	0.08	1.03	−1.79
Communication	3.91	1.50	0.64	−3.27
Wholesale trade	2.04	1.39	0.98	−1.06
Retail trade	1.58	−0.16	0.81	−0.77
FIRE	1.09	1.31	0.40	−0.69
Business services	0.48	0.62	−0.12	−0.60
Personal services	−0.12	−1.02	−1.87	−1.75
Total economy	1.41	0.47	0.17	−1.24

Note: See Table 1 for the definition of periods and sectors.

3. Value Added Versus Final Demand

Perhaps the clue in understanding the persistence of services is the presence of intermediate inputs. Most economic models treat sectors as production units that map factor inputs, labor and capital, into 'output'. The summation of these 'outputs' over the sectors yields national product. In such a framework, national product and income are equal, not only in the aggregate, but also sector by sector. The presence of intermediate inputs preserves the macro-identity between national product and national income, but invalidates it at the sectoral level. The contributions of services to the national product and national income differ.

To obtain a concise understanding of the issue, let $(u_{ij})_{i=1,\ldots,n;j=1,\ldots,m}$ be the use table, where n is the number of commodities and m the number of sectors. Here, u_{ij} is the amount of commodity i used by sector j. Similarly, let $(v_{ij})_{j=1,\ldots,m;i=1,\ldots,n}$ be the make table, where v_{ji} is sector j's output of commodity i. The use and make tables are the heart of the System of National Accounts. Subtracting the use table from the transposed make table, one obtains the net output table, where the typical element is $(w_{ij})_{i=1,\ldots,n;j=1,\ldots,m} = (v_{ji} - u_{ij})_{i=1,\ldots,n;j=1,\ldots,m}$. The dimension is commodity by sector. Column totals yield value added by sector, while row totals yield final demand by commodity. Total value added equals total final demand, as the sum of the column totals must be equal to the sum of the row totals. This is the identity between national income and national product, but there is no need for an equality between any column total and any row total. In particular, the contributions of the services to value added and final demand may differ. This is particularly true of the business services. Although value added is high (a large column total), final demand may be negligible (a small row total). Many sectors outsource their service activities to the business service sector. As a result, much activity is carried out in the business service sector, creating value added. However, this sector does not produce many commodities for final demand. As said, most studies measure the contribution of services in terms of value added, so it is of interest to contrast the latter with the contribution of services to final demand. Tables 5 and 6 show the shares of services in value added and in final demand, respectively.

Table 5 confirms the growing importance of services as sources of earning. The primary sector and manufacturing saw their shares of real

Table 5: Real Value Added Distribution (sectoral shares, 1986 $C in percent).

Groups of sectors	1960s	1970s	1980s	60–80s
Primary	13.1	10.2	9.2	−3.9
Manufacturing	26.8	24.7	22.4	−4.4
Construction	9.6	9.1	8.7	−0.9
Transportation	5.6	5.4	5.2	−0.4
Communication	4.7	6.5	7.4	+2.7
Wholesale trade	5.2	5.3	6.2	+1.0
Retail trade	8.5	8.1	7.5	−1.0
FIRE	16.2	18.1	19.4	+3.2
Business services	3.1	4.6	6.2	+3.1
Personal services	7.3	8.0	7.8	+0.5
Total economy	100	100	100	0

Note: The 1960s correspond to the 1962–74 period, the 1970s to 1974–81 and the 1980s to 1981–91. For the groups of sectors, see Table 1.

Table 6: Final Demand Distribution (commodity shares, 1986 $C in percent).

Groups of commodities	1960s	1970s	1980s	60–80s
Primary	2.7	1.6	3.1	+0.4
Manufacturing	29.9	27.8	24.1	−5.8
Construction	19.5	18.6	16.7	−2.8
Transportation	2.5	2.4	2.3	−0.2
Communication	2.5	3.5	4.1	+1.6
Wholesale trade	3.4	4.0	5.0	+1.6
Retail trade	8.4	8.7	8.5	+0.1
FIRE	15.5	16.9	18.7	+3.2
Business services	5.4	5.7	6.7	+1.3
Personal services	10.2	10.9	10.7	+0.5
Total economy	100	100	100	0

Notes: At the M-level of disaggregation, primary corresponds to commodities 1–13 and 93–94, manufacturing to 14–69, construction to 70–72, transportation to 73–74, communication to 75–79, wholesale trade to 80, retail trade 81, FIRE to 82–83, business services to 84, part of 89, 90–92 and personal services 85–88, part of 89. For the definition of periods, see Table 1.

value added substantially and continuously decline. Between the 1960s and the 1980s, roughly 8.3 per cent of real value added moved from agriculture and manufacturing towards the services. A continuous, but less severe relative loss of activity, also took place in construction, transportation and retail trade. Whereas personal services saw their relative value added share increase only slightly, all other services, in particular FIRE and business services, became much more important in relative terms.

Table 6 shows the final demand shares for the commodity groups roughly corresponding to our ten groups of sectors. The correspondence is not exact, as sectors may be active in more than one line of product, but it is sufficiently close for comparison. The pattern is basically the same as for value added, that is manufacturing shrinks and services expand. The shift of final demand towards services amounts to 5.3 per cent, which is three percentage points less than the shift of value added. So indeed, the rise of the services in terms of commodities is not as dramatic as in terms of value added. Among the services, construction, transportation, retail trade and personal services are the weakest growth performers. The increase in final demand for services is less pronounced when expressed in terms of the categories of final demand.

In Table 7, consumption can be split into goods, housing and other services. Housing and other services together explain 3.6 percentage points of the shift in final demand towards services. Investment and government expenditures are not broken down into goods and services, which could in part explain the lower increase in services when analysed in terms of categories of final demand. If we compare our results with those reported by Joe Mattey (2001, ch. 5), the apparent shift towards services in final demand is even less pronounced in the USA than in Canada.

However modest, it remains a fascinating challenge to explain the increase of the real share of services in final demand. As a first step towards solving the mystery of increasing demand for services, we must distinguish between domestic final demand and net exports. Table 8 shows the domestic final demand share for the ten commodity groupings. Compared to Table 6,

Table 7: Final Demand Distribution by Categories of Final Demand (category shares, 1986 $C in percent).

Categories of final demand	1960s	1970s	1980s	60–80s
Goods	40.6	38.9	35.5	−5.1
Housing	11.3	12.3	14.1	2.8
Services other than housing	17.8	17.9	18.6	0.8
Investment	27.8	28.2	26.8	−1.0
Government	5.0	6.6	7.5	+2.5
Net trade	−2.4	−3.9	−2.5	−0.1

Notes: At the M-level of disaggregation, goods correspond to final demand categories 1–9, housing to 10, services other than housing to 11 and 13, investment to 14–23, government to 27 and 28, and net trade to 12, 24–26. For the definition of periods, see Table 1.

Table 8: Domestic Final Demand Distribution (commodity shares, 1986 $C in percent).

Groups of commodities	1960s	1970s	1980s	60–80s
Primary	2.3	2.3	2.2	−0.1
Manufacturing	32.9	31.3	28.6	−4.3
Construction	19.1	17.6	16.2	−2.9
Transportation	1.9	1.9	2.0	+0.1
Communication	2.4	3.1	3.8	+1.4
Wholesale trade	2.7	3.2	4.0	+1.3
Retail trade	8.2	8.3	8.2	0
FIRE	15.5	16.5	18.7	+3.2
Business services	5.1	5.5	5.8	+0.7
Personal services	10.0	10.4	10.5	+0.5
Total economy	100	100	100	0

Note: For the definition of commodities and periods, see Table 6.

it includes all final demand categories but net exports. The shift from the primary and secondary sectors of activity towards services is down to 4.4 per cent only. This further reduction prompts us to explore the possibility that the Baumol disease in Canada has been countered by a shift in comparative advantage towards services.

4. A Shift in Comparative Advantage?

Canada is a small, open economy. The output of services is determined not only by preference and technology, but also by the terms of trade. In other words, even when productivity developments are relatively unfavorable to services and when shifts in the preferences of consumers are insufficient to counter this trend, the output of services may still be strong if the Canadian comparative advantage has shifted towards the production of services.

It is not easy to determine the comparative advantage of a national economy. The standard approach is to compare costs across countries, but there are two problems with this line of analysis. First, the observed costs reflect not only technology, but also market distortions, such as monopoly power, tariffs and rents resulting from barriers to entry or to trade. Second, the abundance of factor inputs co-determines the comparative advantage. Ricardian technology and Heckscher-Ohlin factor abundance effects are equally crucial in the determination of comparative advantage

(Trefler 1995). Learner and Levinsohn (1995) note that the empirical testing of comparative advantage along the lines of the Heekscher-Ohlin-Vanek theory of the factor content of trade, requires independent data on endowments, technology and trade, but that one ingredient, usually technology, is missing in applied work. Instead, we have analyzed the optimal allocation of activity across sectors for the Canadian economy, given real I–O data describing the structure of domestic absorption and technology, data on factor availabilities from Statistics Canada KLEM's database, and finally proxies for world prices.

Formally, we maximize the level of domestic final demand (given the observed proportions across commodities), subject to the material balance, the labor, capital and the balance of payment constraints. The latter constraint is evaluated at world prices. We equate the world prices with the US prices, given that Canada is a small and open economy, and that most of Canadian trade is with the USA. The maximization of the level of domestic final absorption subject to the aforementioned constraints constitutes a linear program. The shadow prices of the tradable commodities can be shown to be proportional to the US prices. The shadow prices of the factor inputs measure their productivities. The shadow prices of the non-tradable commodities are equal to their costs. The primal variables, the activity levels of the sectors, reveal the comparative advantages. They signal which sectors would expand or contract under perfectly competitive conditions and free trade. We have run the linear program for every year in the 1962–91 period. A shift of comparative advantage is indicated by (dis)activation of sectors. A fuller presentation of the model is contained in ten Raa and Mohnen (1998); see Chapter 19.

The pattern of comparative advantage is surprisingly stable, even at the medium level of aggregation comprising 50 sectors. Crude petroleum or pipeline transport enjoys a comparative advantage for all years but one. The industry of fabricated metal products enjoys a comparative advantage through 1988. Tobacco products and printing and publishing do so from 1981 onwards. All these primary and manufacturing sectors share the comparative advantage with essentially one service sector each year: first FIRE (the 1962–72 period), then health services (the 1973-80 period, except for 1976, when it is amusement and recreational services), and lastly travel, advertising and promotion (the 1981–91 period), accompanied by accommodation and food services through 1988. There is no shift from the primary sectors and manufacturing towards services. We can therefore conclude that international trade cannot explain the persistence of Canadian activity in services.

5. Technological Change

Another potential explanation for the shift of value added and final demand towards the service sectors is technological change. First, new products appear at a much faster rate than before and at affordable prices: videos, CD-ROMS, laser discs, cellular phones, roller-blades, notebooks, scanners and so on. Second, with these new products, entirely new services emerge. Think of video stores, computer stores, cybercafes, internet server providers, software companies, internet search companies, central alarm systems, new telecommunication companies and so on. Third, information and communication technologies (ICT) have changed the way of doing business. Many tasks along the product value chain are now outsourced: advertising, programming, after-sales service and so on. New business units specialize in these tasks, which partially explains the rise in value added in business services. Because of the pressure of competition and innovation in business services, companies specialize in their core activities and tend to outsource secondary activities, which they used to perform in-house. Even households switch from non-business services to market services. Time is devoted to earn money and letting the personal services sector perform part of the household chores, such as housekeeping, babysitting, financial planning and so on. Fourth, new products and services often carry higher value added, because of customer snobbishness, low competition at the beginning of the product life-cycle, product differentiation, tied-in sales, high income elasticities and low substitution possibilities. Demand for old, but especially for new services have a higher income elasticity than demand for traditional manufactured goods. Competition shifts value creation from the manufacturing stages towards the various stages of servicing, for example providing life-time service plans, product-life insurance contracts, purchase on credit options, car-leasing instead of car-selling. There might also be a saturation effect for manufactured goods, whereas demand for services can be boundless. For example, a household's demand for cars is pretty dry after owning two or three cars, but demand for health services, leisure, or travel can increase by much more than a factor of two or three. Fifth, some companies producing manufactured goods have diversified into offering new services connected with their manufactured product. The service arm of the company may have grown so much that the whole company becomes classified into services.[2]

To give some substance to the hypothesis of technological change, we examine in Table 9 the sectoral evolution of R&D stocks. Those stocks represent not yet obsolete stocks of knowledge accumulated from past R&D expenditures. Although R&D is only an input in the generation of technological change, it is one of the most revealing indicators of innovation. Table 9 shows that the proportion of total R&D stock residing in manufacturing has dropped sharply from 91.1 per cent in the 1960s to 75.2 per cent in the 1980s. Manufacturing still remains the sector where most R&D is done, but services are rapidly gaining ground, especially in communication and in business and personal services. Since, as a first approximation, we can assume that the efficiency of converting R&D into new products is the same in all industries, differential growth in R&D stocks across sectors implies differential growth in economic activity across sectors.

Table 9: R&D Stock Distribution (sectoral shares, 1986 $C in percent).

Groups of sectors	1960s	1970s	1980s	60–80s
Primary	4.6	5.9	5.3	+0.7
Manufacturing	91.1	84.3	75.2	−15.9
Construction	0.1	0.1	0.2	+0.1
Transportation	0.6	1.2	0.8	+0.2
Communication	1.8	5.0	7.2	+5.4
Wholesale trade	0.1	0.2	0.8	+0.7
Retail trade	0.1	0.2	0.8	+0.7
FIRE	0.4	0.7	2.3	+1.9
Business services	0.6	1.2	3.8	+3.2
Personal services	0.6	1.2	3.8	+3.2
Total economy	100	100	100	0

Note: For the definition of sectors and periods, see Table 1.

[2]For more documentation on some of these dimensions of technological change and their impact on productivity and activity in services, see Neef (1998), Coyle (1999) and Shapiro and Varian (1999).

6. Conclusion

In the period spanning the three decades from 1961 to 1992, the Canadian service sectors accounted for an ever greater share of employment in the economy, even though their productivity growth was lower than in the primary sector and in manufacturing. To reconcile this apparent contradiction with the so-called Baumol disease, which predicts a decline in the share of services given their relative poor productivity performance and ensuing rising relative price, we have explored four potential explanations. First, the incorporation of capital in productivity analysis makes the disease less acute. Indeed, over this period, annualized TFP-growth rates were not worse in the two most expanding service sectors (FIRE and business services) than in manufacturing. Second, the proper accounting of intermediate inputs drives a wedge between the income and product shares of the services, rendering them less buoyant in terms of product share: for all service sectors combined, the real value-added share rose by 8.3 percentage points, whereas the commodity output share rose by only 5.3 percentage points. Third, limitation to domestic final demand shares makes the role of services even more modest: an increase of only 4.4 percentage points. Fourth, and related to this, we found no validity to the argument that a shift in comparative advantage towards services may have countered the decline of services due to their higher relative prices. In short, Canadian services suffer little from the Baumol disease when capital is taken into account. However, their share of domestic final demand does not keep pace with their employment and value-added shares. Yet the service shares of domestic final demand do rise and this remains a puzzle to be explained. One explanation could be a shift of innovation towards services and, related to this, a shift of consumer preferences towards these new services. If R&D figures are anything to go by, they tend to bolster this explanation.

One final remark is in order. The very figures of labor productivity or TFP in services might be seriously mismeasured. Services are hard to measure, and for some of them, accurate estimates of output are not even available. Moreover, in the presence of technological change, quality improvements in services and the prices of entirely new services are even harder to measure correctly. It is very likely that services are undervalued, as their output is often measured by their cost of production, given the lack of reliable price data and a proper definition of what services are actually supposed to measure. Hence it may well be that there is no real Baumol disease in services, as prices are rising by less and TFP by more than what is actually measured in the official statistics.

Acknowledgements

We thank the participants of the Amsterdam conference and an anonymous referee for helpful comments.

References

Baumol, W. (1967) Macroeconomics of unbalanced growth: The anatomy of urban crisis, *American Economic Review*, 57, pp. 415–426.

Coyle, D. (1999) *The Weightless World* (MIT Press, Cambridge).

Johnson, J. (1994) Une base de donnees KLEMS decrivant Ia structure des entrees de l'industrie canadienne Statistique Canada, Division des Entrees-Sorties, Cahier Technique #73F.

Learner, E.E. and J. Levinsohn (1995) International trade theory: The evidence. In: G. Grossman and K. Rogoff (eds.), *Handbook of International Economics*, Vol. III (North-Holland, Amsterdam).

Mattey, J. (2001) Will the new information economy cure the cost disease in the US? In: ten Raa Th. and R. Schettkat (eds.), *The Growth of Service Industries, The Paradox of Exploding Costs and Persistent Demand* (Edward Elgar Publishing, Aldershot), chapter 5.

Neef, D. (ed.) (1998) *The Knowledge Economy* (Butterworth-Heinemann, Boston).

Shapiro, C. and H. Varian (1999) *Information Rules* (Harvard Business School Press, Boston).

Statistics Canada (various issues), System of National Accounts — The Input–Output Structure of the Canadian Economy, Minister of Supply and Services, Ottawa.

ten Raa, Th. and P. Mohnen (1998) Sources of productivity growth: technology, terms of trade, and preference shifts, Center discussion paper #98105.

Trefler, D. (1995) The case of missing trade and other mysteries, *American Economic Review*, 85, pp. 1029–1045.

Chapter 23

The Location of Comparative Advantages on the Basis of Fundamentals Only

Thijs ten Raa and Pierre Mohnen

Abstract: We propose a new way to locate the comparative advantages of two economies linked by international trade. We construct a competitive benchmark based only on the fundamentals of the two economies: endowments, preferences and technologies. The direction of trade is endogenously determined by a linear program with an input–output core. The factor contents of that trade are compared with factor endowments to test the Heckscher–Ohlin model in the presence of different technologies and preferences. We can also evaluate the gains of free bilateral trade. The model is applied to a customs union between Europe and Canada. The Heckscher–Ohlin factor abundance specialization hypothesis is supported by the data.

Keywords: Comparative advantage; gains to free trade.

1. Introduction

One of the basic issues in trade theory is the determination of the sources of comparative advantage and hence of trade between countries. The early

Received February 1999; revised August 2000.

theories stressed one aspect at a time (such as differences in technology in the Ricardian model and differences in endowments in the Heckscher–Ohlin model). They neutralized the other possible sources of relative domestic price differences in order to prove their argument in the simple way. That is what theory should do.

A number of studies have tried to test the various theories (see the survey by Learner and Levinsohn 1995). The tests often reject the Heckscher–Ohlin-Vanek (HOV) model. Two problems are encountered in those studies. Either they do not use independent data on trade, endowments and technologies, in which case the test is largely invalidated, or they are counterfactual by assuming common technologies and/or preferences, in which case it comes as no surprise that the HOV model is rejected. Bowen *et al.* (1987) and Trefler (1993, 1995) find empirical support but for a modified HOV model where technology and/or preferences are allowed to depart from those prevailing in the United States. Davis *et al.* (1997) show, on Japanese regional data, that geographical differences in direct factor requirements may be sufficient to restore the HOV predictions on the factor content of trade.

We go a step further by allowing country-specific endowments, preferences and technologies, the fundamentals of the economy according to neoclassical theory. We need no reference country for technology, as in Bowen *et al.* (1987), Trefler (1993, 1995) and Davis *et al.* (1997). Numerous distortions, such as monopoly power, externalities, tariffs and other impediments, drive a wedge between the hypothetical and observed patterns of trade. Rather than trying to get a handle on these departures from perfect competition, we give up all the information contained in the trade statistics and return to the fundamentals. On the basis of those, we construct a competitive benchmark by solving a linear program and use it to locate the comparative advantages and the gains from free trade. All patterns of specialization are admitted and, therefore, we do not make the international trade theoretic assumption of a common cone of diversification. To test the Heckscher–Ohlin model, we do not confront the observed factor contents of net trade and those predicted by the theory, but we check whether endowments alone determine the factor movements of free trade; that is, the endogenous trade within the model, controlling for taste and technology.

For illustration, we take two economies, Europe and Canada in 1980, keeping trade with the rest of the world fixed. The choice of the two economies is entirely opportunistic, suggested by data availability. The model is a general equilibrium version of ten Raa and Chakraborty (1991). Since it is based on the fundamentals, with all prices endogenous, the incorporation of the rest of the world as a third economy (or family of economies) would now be a straightforward extension.

From a theoretical point of view, our contribution is modest as it merely implements ideas that have been around quite some time. A reference is the theoretical introduction of Ginsburgh and Waelbroeck (1981, pp. 30–31) where they consider the maximization of consumption subject to commodity and factor input constraints. In the empirical part, however, Ginsburgh and Waelbroeck (1981, p. 176) note that such a model could not be handled with available means. We carry out the program they suggested. No statistics or constructs beyond the fundamentals of the economies are used. In particular, we employ no price statistics. Nor do we admit artifical limitations on the direction of trade. The model provides a truly general equilibrium determination of the commodity pattern of trade.

The paper is organized as follows. Section 2, we present the model used to set up the competitive benchmark. In Section 3, we determine the comparative advantages of the two economies and compare the factor contents of net bilateral trade with the factor endowments. In Section 4, we compute the magnitude of gains to free bilateral trade. In Section 5, we relate details of our model to the literature. We conclude by summarizing the main features of our model and the results in Section 6.

2. Locating Comparative Advantages

We set up a single neoclassical model of international trade with fixed domestic endowments, with tradeable and non-tradeable commodities, used for intermediate or final consumption, and with Leontief functions for the technologies and preferences, i.e. with fixed input coefficients and fixed proportions of final consumption and investment in each economy. The efficient allocation of resources is obtained by maximizing the level of domestic final demand (including consumption and investment) in one economy, subject to a given proportion of final consumption in the two economies. We position the latter to be such that the outcomes preserve the actual bilateral balance of payments. We will find this balanced, efficient allocation by scanning the final consumption frontier for the two economies. Thus, let c denote the level of final consumption in Europe and c^* the same for Canada. Star superscripts represent Canadian items. We scan the (c, c^*)-frontier with the Canadian-European final consumption ratio, γ, by putting $c^* = \gamma c$. For every ratio γ, a linear program will determine the maximum level of final consumption, c, subject to material balance and endowment constraints.[1] Apart from c itself, the variables are the vectors of gross outputs, $\mathbf{x}$ for Europe and $\mathbf{x}^*$ for Canada. The linear program is

$$\max_{\mathbf{x},\mathbf{x}^*,c\geq 0} \mathbf{e}^\top \mathbf{y}c + \mathbf{e}^\top \mathbf{y}^*\gamma c \tag{1}$$

subject to the following constraints. For tradeable commodities:

$$(\mathbf{I} - \mathbf{A})\mathbf{x} + (\mathbf{I} - \mathbf{A}^*)\mathbf{x}^* \geq (\mathbf{y} + \mathbf{y}^*\gamma)c + \mathbf{z} + \mathbf{z}^* \tag{2}$$

for non-tradeable commodities:

$$(\mathbf{I} - \mathbf{A})\mathbf{x} \geq \mathbf{y}c, (\mathbf{I} - \mathbf{A}^*)\mathbf{x}^* \geq \mathbf{y}^*\gamma c \tag{3}$$

and for factor inputs:

$$\mathbf{k}^\top \mathbf{x} \leq K, 1^\top \mathbf{x} \leq L, (\mathbf{k}^*)^\top \mathbf{x}^* \leq K^*, (1^*)^\top \mathbf{x}^* \leq L^* \tag{4}$$

The expression 'for (non)tradeable commodities' restricts the announced vector in equality to the respective components.[2] In the objective function, $\mathbf{e}^\top = (1 \cdots 1)$. The program features the following European parameters:

$\mathbf{y}$ = domestic final demand vector (including consumption and investment, excluding trade)
$\mathbf{z}$ = net exports vector (except for bilateral trade)
$\mathbf{A}$ = commodity input coefficients matrix
$\mathbf{k}$ = capital input coefficients row vector
1 = labor input coefficients row vector
K = capital stock
L = labor force.

[1]The location of comparative advantages in a system of more than two economies would involve a vector scanner, γ, and a fixed point alogrithm to find the value such that the consequent vector of national surpluses for all economies but one is mapped into the observed surpluses. (Walras' law would take care of the remaining economy.)

[2]Tradeable commodities are those for which Statistics Canada (1983) reports data of foreign trade.

The Canadian variables are denoted with a star superscript. Variable c acts as an expansion factor. The solution is not affected by the monotonic transformation of the objective function. For normalization of the supporting price system, we have included a positive constant in the objective function. For every value of the final consumption ratio, $\gamma = c^*/c$, denote the optimum (European) consumption level by $c(\gamma)$ and the outputs in the two countries by $\mathbf{x}(\gamma)$ and $\mathbf{x}^*(\gamma)$, respectively. For low values of γ, Canadian consumption is unimportant and the bulk of net output is exported to Europe. Similarly, the trade balance shows a European surplus for high values of γ. For tradeable commodities, European *net exports* to Canada are given by the vector:

$$(\mathbf{I} - \mathbf{A})\mathbf{x}(\gamma) - \mathbf{y}c(\gamma) - \mathbf{z} \tag{5}$$

In a general equilibrium framework like the above, the supporting competive prices are given by the shadow prices of the linear program. Denote those for tradeable commodities by $\mathbf{p}(\gamma)$. By the dual constraint associated with the c-coefficients in equations (2) and (3), the value of final consumption, $\mathbf{y} + \mathbf{y}^*\gamma$, under the shadow prices, is equal to its nominal value, the coefficient in (1). In other words, the coefficient in the objective function has been selected such that only relative prices change. This is the normalization rule. By the dual constraint associated with the $\mathbf{x}$-coefficients in (2) to (4), European profits are non-positive. Similarly, by the dual constraint associated with the $\mathbf{x}^*$-coefficients in equations (2) to (4), Canadian profits are non-positive. Sectors with negative profits are inactive by the phenomenon of complementary slackness.

The European surplus on the bilateral trade account is equal to the (inner) product of $\mathbf{p}(\gamma)$ and (5) and will be denoted by $s(\gamma)$. For γ low, $s(\gamma)$ is negative, and for γ high, $s(\gamma)$ is positive. For some intermediate value, $s(\gamma)$ will match the observed surplus on the bilateral trade account,

$$s^0 = \mathbf{e}^\top(\mathbf{x}^0 - \mathbf{A}\mathbf{x}^0 - \mathbf{z}) \tag{6}$$

where $\mathbf{x}^0$ is the observed value of gross output vector $\mathbf{x}$. We find the intermediate value of γ by the Newton algorithm,

$$\gamma_{n+1} = \frac{[s(\gamma_n) - s^0]\gamma_{n-1} - [s(\gamma_{n-1}) - s^0]\gamma_n}{s(\gamma_n) - s(\gamma_{n-1})} \tag{7}$$

with initial values $\gamma_0 = 0$ and $\gamma_1 = 1$. The limit of process (7) solves $s(\gamma) = s^0$ and is, therefore, the general equilibrium value of the Canadian-European final consumption expansion ratio, $\gamma = c^*/c$. For this value, the linear program determines the levels, $c(\gamma)$ and $c^*(\gamma)$, the allocations, $\mathbf{x}(\gamma)$ and $\mathbf{x}^*(\gamma)$ and the bilateral trade vector, (5).

The sign pattern of bilateral trade locates the comparative advantages of the two economies. Notice that this is accomplished solely on the basis of parameters for Europe and similar parameters for Canada. The parameters represent *taste* ($\mathbf{y}$), *technology* ($\mathbf{A}$, $\mathbf{k}$ and 1) and *endowments* (K and L), and fix the rest of the world ($\mathbf{z}$). In other words, we have located the comparative advantages on the basis of the fundamentals of the economies, without recourse to exogenous prices. All prices are endogenous. Prices of the tradeable commodities $\mathbf{p}(\gamma)$ are shadow prices associated with constraint (2). The prices of the non-tradeable commodities, associated with constraints (3), and those of the factor inputs, associated with constraints (4), are specific to the individual economies.

By comparing the expansion of final demand under the autarky and free trade scenarios, we can assess the gains of free trade. By letting consumption and input proportions represent taste and technology, we make a short-cut. Strictly speaking, technology is a blue-book of techniques and the choice of techniques depends on the relative prices. The observed input–output coefficients reflect the techniques prevailing under the observed prices. Now, if the prices change to the general equilibrium values, the choice of technique and hence the input–output coefficients may be different. An induced change of techniques within the technology blue-book thus prompts further reallocations of endowments and gains to specialization. The same holds for consumption: taste is a blue-book of consumption coefficients and the latter may adjust. By restricting the blue-book of technology and consumption to a single page for each economy, our model ignores the further reallocations and therefore, the results will be conservative. Since the point of this paper is to demonstrate how endogenous patterns of productive activity create significant gains to free trade, it suffices to do so in the context of the narrow Leontief framework that underlies the above model.

3. Canadian Advantages Compared with Europe

If bilateral trade were completely free and the national economies were perfectly competitive, the free trade pattern of Table 1 would emerge, if we ignore the ramifications of the trade with the rest of the world. The first two columns of the table contrast the actual and the optimum trade figures (Statistics Canada, 1983 and equation (5)). By construction, the observed European trade deficit with Canada is the same.[3] The second column reveals that the Canadian comparative advantage *vis-à-vis* Europe, given that the trade with the rest of the world rests in *minerals, machines*, and *clothing & footwear*.

The resulting comparative advantage contrasts with observed trade (first column of Table 1). In reality, Canada exports chiefly minerals, metal products, consumption goods, and other manufactures, and imports machines, transportation equipment, and clothing & footwear. The endogenous comparative advantages may also conflict with intuition. For example, agricultural exports are not taken up by Canada, but by Europe. To some extent, this is due to model limitations: land is not modeled as a separate factor and the rest of the world is not included. However, we also note

Table 1: Observed, Free and Superfree Exports Minus Imports From Europe to Canada (millions ECU).

		Observed exports minus imports		Free exports minus imports		Superfree exports minus imports	
1	Agriculture	30	−174	6,405	−0	9,413	−0
2–4	Minerals	196	−1,394	4,178	−65,734	6,830	−0
5	Chemical products	315	−433	2,161	−0	6,099	−0
6	Metal products	265	−804	14,294	−0	8,648	−0
7–8	Machines	915	−337	6,828	−12,222	6,483	−5,163
9	Transportation equipment	598	−162	11,081	−0	10,534	−0
10–12	Consumption goods	316	−799	21,964	−0	21,557	−0
13–15	Clothing & footwear	270	−125	9,864	−22,373	4,920	−97,040
16–18	Other manufactures	263	−1,718	20,776	−0	24,491	−0
Total		3,168	−5,946	97,551	−100,329	99,425	−102,203

Note: For sector aggregation, see Table A-1 in Appendix A. Observed exports and imports are at observed prices and (super) free exports and imports are at endogenous prices.

[3]In fact, algorithm (7) stopped after only six iterations and the difference between the computed and actual deficits was only 24 ECU, an incredibly small fraction of the deficit.

that Canada has only a slight edge in agricultural value added per worker (10 110 versus 8884 ECU per worker), whereas agricultural value added per unit of capital is the same in the two economies. Because of the scarcity of Canadian capital, it does not pay to exploit the mild Canadian technological edge in this sector. It will, however, when access to technology is free, as we shall see at the end of this section.

Bilateral trade liberalization would multiply the volume of trade and let the small economy (Canada) specialize in only a few sectors. Note, however, that these sectors continue to feature two-way trade under perfectly competitive conditions. This is due to product differentiation. For example, in minerals, the (dominant) Canadian export is in mining, but it is countered by European exports in petroleum & natural gas and non-metallic minerals. Similarly, Canadian exports of machines are countered by European exports of electrical goods. And in clothing and footwear, Canada picks up the footwear.

The revelation of product differentiation in the phenomenon of two-way trade is limited by the level of disaggregation. In our model, where we want to determine comparative advantages on the basis of the fundamentals of the economies, we choose the most disaggregated classification of products that we could reconcile with the Eurostat and Statistics Canada production units (see Table A.1 in Appendix A). In this approach, footwear is footwear, be it European or Canadian. At this level of aggregation, there is no two-way trade, because according to the logic of the model, each economy specializes in what it is best at. Seminar participants have suggested that Italian footwear is different from Canadian and that, therefore, trade should be two-way even at the disaggregated level. We admit that this is true, but in our opinion, the only correct way of modeling this is to disaggregate the data. Our view deviates from the dominant one in the literature where product differentiation is imposed by taking into account the origin of commodities (the so-called Armington assumption, Harris 1984, and Srinivasan and Whalley 1986). Such an imposition of two-way trade may be a practical device to obtain a good fit, but it is useless for the location of comparative advantages, particularly when they are not assumed to be revealed by the international trade statistics.

Let us give some idea of the relative importance of the determinants of comparative advantage. As is common in the literature, we will focus on the role of endowments by holding technology and taste constant across the economies. This is implemented in the neoclassical fashion by assuming free access to each other's technology and similarly, by introducing substitutability between the mean consumption vectors in either economy. The modification yields a model of free trade between economies with free access to technology in production and consumption. This so-called superfree model is presented in Appendix B and the consequent pattern of superfree trade is reported in the last column of Table 1. The Canadian comparative advantages in machines and clothing & footwear persist when technology differences in production and consumption are eliminated, but the minerals production is picked up by Europe. The initial conclusion is, therefore, that the Canadian comparative advantage is determined by endowments (for machines and clothing & footwear) and technology (for minerals). A qualification of the technology determinant seems in order. It turns out that Europe adopts the Canadian technology to produce minerals. The Canadian input coefficients are relatively small in this sector. Note, however, that our model does not account for natural resources separately. The Canadian abundance or quality of the ores is reflected in the level of the input coefficients. The superfree scenario, by moving this technology to Europe, sort of endows Europe with the Canadian edge in minerals. This peculiar role of input coefficients in minerals is known. Carter (1970) showed that it is the only sector where input–output developments indicate technical regress and that the underlying problem is not a deterioration of knowledge, but a reduction of the quality of the unaccounted resource. As long as the Canadian edge in mineral production is a reflection of the abundance of natural resources, the transfer of Canadian technology to Europe would not be supportable by a more detailed model. We therefore speculate that a fuller model, accounting for natural resources as a third endowment in addition to capital and labor, would ascribe the Canadian comparative advantage in minerals to the natural resource endowment, rather than technology. We are thus inclined to conclude that the Canadian comparative advantage is determined by endowments.

Now let us shift attention from the product nature of trade to the factor contents. Are differences in European and Canadian factor endowment proportions leveled out by trade? We have calculated the factor contents embodied in the net trade vectors (actual, free, and superfree),

Table 2: Capital-Labor Ratios (ECU per worker).

		Europe	Canada
Endowments		96,096	38,101
Endowments plus net imports:	Observed	96,060	37,730
	Free	96,404	36,802
	Superfree	94,334	55,501

see Table 2. The technique is due to Leontief (1953), but now the pattern of the comparative advantage revealing trade is endogenous.

The first line of Table 2 shows the capital/labor endowments ratios of the two economies. (These figures are obtained by simple divisions of the data at the bottom of Table A-2 in Appendix A. Europe is endowed with relatively much capital. The second and third lines of Table 2 show agreement between the effects of observed and free trade. We focus on trade augmented endowment ratios rather than exports and imports factor intensities to make the analysis Learner (1980) proof. The capital-labor ratio in the big economy, Europe, is not affected. The capital-labor ratio of Canada deteriorates further. Obviously, the Heckscher–Ohlin theorem does not work here. There are numerous reasons for this, as pointed out by Batra and Casas (1973), Deardorff (1984), and Bowen *et al.* (1987). Perhaps the most important one is that the theorem assumes free access to technology and common preferences. Now these conditions are precisely the ones of the superfree trade scenario. Hence the last line of Table 2 is a more appropriate test of the Heckscher–Ohlin theorem. The results show that with common access to technology and consumption patterns, free trade would indeed level out factor intensity differences.

That factor abundance theory is reflected in net exports between Europe and Canada is not a trivial result. In our high-dimensional model (with more commodities than factors), the Heckscher–Ohlin theorem need not hold. Factor prices are not equalized in the solution to our linear program. In the superfree trade model, the difference in relative factor prices may induce the two economies to select different techniques of production and different consumption patterns, and hence the direction of trade may be the result of relative factor abundance, but also of differential production and consumption input coefficients. Yet, a dominant technique is adopted for each output (except for one non-tradeable commodity, where two techniques coexist), and the Canadian consumption pattern is preferred in both countries. Differences in input structures (in production and consumption) are neutralized and trade is driven by differences in endowments.

At the suggestion of a referee, we have included results on the production structures in the free and superfree trade scenarios. Table 3 shows the sign patterns of the solution in either scenario. Since Canada is small compared with Europe, Europe must produce nearly everything. Leather and footwear is the only activity that can be taken up wholy by Canada, in the free trade scenario, where the two economies stick to their own techniques of production. Canada is also active in mining and machines. Turning to the superfree trade scenario, the pattern of specialization changes to electrical good and textiles and clothing for Canada, with the latter being the inactive sector in Europe. The shift to the neoclassical paradigm of free access to technology has dramatic ramifications and in particular, explains the differences in factor contents we encountered in Table 2. It is particularly noteworthy that Canadian technology is superior in the majority of sectors, including agriculture. In ten sectors, Europe adopts it, while Canada employs no European technology.

Table 3: Activities Sustaining the Free and SuperFree Trade Scenarios, Tradeables only (E = Europe, C = Canada, E^* = Europe Using Canadian technology).

Sector	Free trade	Superfree trade
1. Agriculture	E	E^*
2. Mining	E, C	E^*
3. Petroleum & natural gas	E	E
4. Non-metallic minerals	E	E^*
5. Chemical products	E	E^*
6. Metal products	E	E^*
7. Machines	E, C	E^*
8. Electrical goods	E	E^*, C
9. Transportation equipment	E	E
10. Food	E	E^*
11. Beverages	E	E
12. Tobacoo products	E	E
13. Textiles & clothing	E	C
14. Leather and footwear	C	E^*
15. Rubber & printing	E	E
16. Wood products	E	E
17. Paper & printing	E	E^*
18. Other manufactures	E	E

4. Gains to Free Trade

The solutions to equations (l)–(4) and (7) yield $\gamma = c^*/c$ and c. The consequent expansion factors for European and Canadian final consumption are

$$c = 1.075 \quad \text{and} \quad c^* = 1.40 \tag{8}$$

respectively. Perfect competition and free bilateral trade would hence boost the European and Canadian economies by 7.5% and 40%, respectively. The difference reflects the relative importance of bilateral trade to the two economies. Gains accrue to both. Parts of the efficiency gains, however, are obtained by the elimination of the domestic waste of resources from misallocation and the less than full utilization of resources. To isolate the gains to free trade, we must determine the domestic efficiency gains that the program can achieve without departing from the observed bilateral trade vector.

The domestic expansion factor for Europe, given the full net exports vector, $\bar{\mathbf{z}}$, is obtained by

$$\max_{\mathbf{x},d\geq 0} \mathbf{e}^\top \mathbf{y}d \quad \text{subject to} \tag{9}$$

$$(\mathbf{I} - \mathbf{A})\mathbf{x} \geq \mathbf{y}d + \bar{\mathbf{z}} \tag{10}$$

$$\mathbf{k}^\top \mathbf{x} \leq K, \quad \mathbf{l}^\top \mathbf{x} \leq L \tag{11}$$

In star superscript, this would be the domestic expansion factor program for Canada. The consequent allocations of production and consumption are feasible with respect to the free trade program, (1)–(4), with $\gamma = d^*/d$, for the following reason. The domestic material balances, (10), and the same but starred for Canada, sum to (2) and (3) because the bilateral net exports cancel out. The solutions to (9)–(11) and its Canadian version are

$$d = 1.073 \quad \text{and} \quad d^* = 1.18 \tag{12}$$

The bulk of the European efficiency gain can thus be ascribed to the elimination of domestic waste of capital and labor. A comparison of results in (8) and (12) shows that Europe would gain only 0.2% in free trade with Canada. This underscores the insignificance of the Canadian economy to Europe. For Canada, however, the picture is different. Half of the efficiency gain of 40%, in fact 22%, can be ascribed to free trade with Europe, as seen by subtraction of the second figures of (8) and (12).

5. Discussion of the Model

Linear programming yields a high degree of specialization. This is merely a reflection of the dimensionality of the issue. A key test for the factor-endowments approach is whether it can accommodate reality in a context simple enough (i.e. of low enough dimensionality) to be theoretically tractable. Indeed, a distinctive feature of our attempt is to determine the disaggregated pattern of comparative advantage on the basis of only *a few* fundamentals, namely the primitives suggested by neoclassical theory. Consequently, we face many more goods than factors and specialization is natural. Contrary to what Krueger (1984, p. 545) suggests, this property does not depend on the input–output assumption of fixed coefficients. As a matter of fact, input substitutability would widen the scope for specialization. To avoid the latter, one must resort to brute force.[4]

As it is well-known, estimates of inefficiencies of trade restrictions are modest when the patterns of trade are taken for granted. Within a framework of goods that agrees with the observed outputs, exports, and imports, the welfare losses are given by the Harberger triangles. The size of a triangle is half the base times the height and the two are related to each other by the elasticity of demand. In short, the welfare losses are quadratic in either the price or the quantity distortion, hence small. Romer (1994) shows that gains to free trade are of a higher order if the list of goods that defines the framework of an economy is endogenous, namely the outcome of profit maximization involving fixed costs. Free trade would lengthen the list and create new areas of consumer surplus. We have shown that one does not have to go as far as Romer, questioning the observed categories of goods, to suggest high welfare stakes of free trade. It suffices to endogenize the direction of trade in order to show the existence of efficiency gains of a higher order than the ones implied by Harberger calculations.

All market imperfections and departures from the simple perfectly competitive model are ignored when the benchmark is calculated. Some departures from the competitive benchmark cannot be separated from the fundamentals, but are grounded in the physical structure of the economies,

[4]In linear programming, artificial constraints are used (e.g. trade and activity restrictions as in Williams, 1978). In a neoclassical study, Diewert and Morrison (1986) assume a form of jointness of output which is conditioned by the pattern of trade and preserves it. Chipman and Tian (1992) also bar trade reversals.

particularly product differentiation and scale economies. Harris (1984) builds a real trade general equilibrium model to assess trade liberalization effects. This purpose, as well as the requirement that some historical data set is produced as an equilibrium, infringe on the 'pureness' of the model.[5]

In our opinion, product differentiation is an aggregation phenomenon. If products are differentiated, they constitute different commodities and the efficient pattern of trade must be determined at the most disaggregated level. Aggregating back to the level of differentiated products, intra-industry trade emerges. Cross-hauling actually represents different commodity components at the more detailed level of classification. Scale economies are a more intrinsic phenomenon. Since the related monopoly power is *a priori* excluded from our model, as noted above, only the scale-induced changes in technical coefficients could be relevant for the detection of comparative advantages. This effect is ignored in this study. Its inclusion would reinforce the gains to free trade. In fact, it is interesting to note that we can explain significant gains to free trade without using scale economies. In principle, scale economies might change the locational pattern of comparative advantages, but we do not expect them to be that high.

Our methodology differs from Bowen *et al.* (1987), Trefler (1993, 1995) and Davis *et al.* (1997) in the following sense. An exact equation is 'net exports equals net output minus domestic consumption'. In the cited papers, the terms on the right-hand side of the equation are replaced by theoretical constructs, namely a linear function of endowment and a share of world net

[5]The theoretical requirement that supply and demand are derived from the fundamentals of the economy is sacrificed by installing CES-'muffles' (make 'Armington') at four interfaces of supply and demand (Harris 1984, pp. 1020, 1022 and 1026). 'Muffles' limit substitutability between commodities which differ by origin. These components are combined in a non-additive formula that is minimized to determine their shares. For example, to determine exports (E for domestic and E^* for all other countries exports), CES-muffle $[\beta E^{-\lambda} + (1-\beta)E^{*-\lambda}]^{-1/\lambda}$ is supposed to be 'produced' at minimum cost. Exports are thus 'determined' as a smooth function of domestic and foreign prices. A Cobb–Douglas version of the muffle divides intermediate demand between domestic supply and imports. One might think of goods and services supplied by different countries or industries as being differentiated not only in transportation costs, but also in terms of intrinsic product characteristics. When the purpose of study is the location of comparative advantage, however, the procedure is unnecessary and unwanted. From an econometric perspective, the evidence is no longer indirect (estimates of muffle parameters β and λ), but direct (observations of endowments, technology, and preferences). A second, related difference is that we are not plagued by the need to manipulate price formation. Harris averages Chamberlanian prices with the more oligopolistic ones of Eastman-Stijkolt. Deardorff (1986) shows that this element introduces a theoretical inconsistency, but is necessary to get effects of tariff reductions.

output. The authors then test whether the net exports predicted by the modified Heckscher–Ohlin model are close to the observed net exports. They introduce an error term in what should be an accounting identity and they check the magnitude and variation of the error term. Instead, we use actual data on endowments, input–output coefficients and consumption patterns and we check whether, were there free trade, countries would specialize according to factor abundance. In other words, we preserve the accounting identity and check if free competition would let the economies pick the same techniques and consumption pattern and then trade on the basis of factor abundance.

Ideally, the rest of the world is to be included as the third economy. Our method of detecting comparative advantages would remain perfectly valid. The detected comparative advantages from a bilateral trade model might differ from those obtained from a multilateral model, when we make stringent assumptions. We could, for instance, assume that the rest of the world has the same technologies as those in Europe and Canada and factor allocations similar to those in Europe. Canada, the smallest country, would continue to specialize in the same two activities that make abundant use of the factors it is comparatively better endowed with. Such assumptions are not more unrealistic than those of separability or extreme symmetry made by Helpman (1984) and Ethier (1984) to predict trade from factor endowments.

6. Conclusions

We locate the comparative advantages of two economies linked by international trade by computing a competitive benchmark on the basis of fundamentals only. No assumption is made about prices, and the direction of the trade is endogenously determined. We use independent and country-specific data on the three fundamentals: endowments, preferences and technologies. Instead of testing whether the Heckscher–Ohlin-Vanek model fits observed trade data, we ignore actual trade and derive it from the competitive benchmark. The factor contents of that trade are compared with factor endowments to test the Hecksch–Ohlin model in the presence of different technologies and preferences. The gains to free bilateral trade can also be computed.

The observed allocation is well within the frontier. The difference between observed and optimal allocations can be ascribed to domestic inefficiencies and to gains to free trade. The Canadian comparative advantage *vis-à-vis* Europe is in minerals, machines and clothing & footwear. The gains to free trade would be 0.2% for Europe and 22% for Canada. The pattern of comparative advantage persists when we allow for free access to technology and consumption coefficients and therefore, it can be ascribed to the endowments. This free access would alter, however, the movement of factor contents, in agreement with the Heckscher–Ohlin theorem.

Acknowledgements

A Royal Netherlands Academy of Sciences senior fellowship, research awards from the Canadian Government and the Fondation de I'Universite du Quebec a Montreal to the first author, an FCAR grant and CentER support to the second author, and a SSHRC grant to both authors, are gratefully acknowledged. We thank Ronald Rioux of Statistics Canada and Carlos Meira of Eurostat for providing unpublished data and good support, and Wilfred Ethier, seminar participants and a referee for stimulating comments and suggestions.

References

Bank of Canada (1983) *Bank of Canada Review*, December issue.

Batra, R.N. and F.R. Casas (1973) Intermediate products and the pure theory of international trade: A neo-Heckscher–Ohlin framework, *American Economic Review*, pp. 297–311.

Bowen, H., E.E. Learner and L. Sveikauskas (1987) Multicountry, multifactor tests of the factor abundance theory, *American Economic Review*, 77, pp. 791–809.

Carter, A.P. (1970) *Structural Change in the American Economy* (Cambridge, Harvard University Press).

Chipman, J.S. and G. Tian (1992) A general equilibrium intertemporal model of an open economy, *Economic Theory*, 2, pp. 215–246.

Commission of the European Communities (1984) *Economic Paper* 31.

Davis, D., D. Weinstein, S. Bradford and K. Shinpo (1997) Using international and Japanese regional data to determine when the factor abundance theory of trade works, *American Economic Review*, 87, pp. 421–446.

Deardorff, A.V. (1984) Testing trade theories and predicting trade flows, in: Jones, R.W. and P.B. Kenen (eds.), *Handbook of International Economics*, Vol. I (Amsterdam, North-Holland).

Deardorff, A.V. (1986) Comments, in: Srinivasan, T.N. and Whalley J. (eds.), *General Equilibrium Trade Policy Modeling* (Cambridge, MIT Press).

Diewert, W.E. and C.J. Morrison (1986) Adjusting output and productivity indexes for changes in the terms of trade, *Economic Journal*, 96, pp. 659–679.

Ethier, W.J. (1984) Higher dimensional issues in trade theory, in: Jones, R.W. and P.E. Kenen (eds.) *Handbook of International Economics* Vol. I (Amsterdam, North-Holland).

Eurostat (1976) *Methodology of the Community Input–Output Tables 1970–75*, Vol. 1 (Luxembourg, Statistical Office of the European Communities).

Eurostat (1985) *Employment and Unemployment* (Luxembourg, Statistical Office of the European Communities).

Eurostat (1986) *National Accounts ESA-Input–Output Tables 1980*, Theme 2, Series C (Luxembourg, Statistical Office of the European Communities).

Eurostat (1989) Input–output section. The input–output table of Europe 1980, unpublished.

Eurostat (1990a) Fixed capital stock data, unpublished.

Eurostat (1990b) Input–output section. Total employment Belgium 1980 I/O Tables, unpublished.

Ginsburgh, V.A. and J.L. Waelbroeck (1981) *Activity Analysis and General Equilibrium Modelling* (Amsterdam, North-Holland).

Government of Canada (1984) Regional industrial expansion, Rate of capacity utilization, unpublished.

Harris, R. (1984) Applied general equilibrium analysis of small open economies with scale economies and imperfect competition, *American Economic Review*, 74, pp. 1016–1032.

Helpman, E. (1984) Increasing returns, imperfect markets, and trade theory, in: Jones, R.W. and P.E. Kenen (eds.), *Handbook of International Economics*, Vol. I (Amsterdam, North-Holland).

IMF (1985) *International Financial Statistics*, supplement on exchange rates 9 (Washington DC, International Monetary Fund).

Kop Jansen, P. and T. ten Raa (1990) The choice of model in the construction of input–output coefficients matrices, *International Economic Review*, 31, pp. 213–227.

Krueger, A.O. (1984) Trade policies in developing countries, in: Jones, R.W. and P.B. Kenen (eds.), *Handbook of International Economics*, Vol. 1 (Amsterdam, North-Holland).

Learner, E.E. (1980) The Leontief paradox, reconsidered, *Journal of Political Economy*, 88, pp. 495–503.

Learner, E.E. and J. Levinsohn (1995) International trade theory: The evidence, in: Grossman, G. and K. Rogoff (eds.), *Handbook of International Economics*, Vol. III (Amsterdam, North-Holland).

Leontief, W. (1953) Domestic production and foreign trade: The American capital position re-examined, *Proceedings of the American Philosophical Society*, 97, pp. 332–349.

Romer, P. (1994) New goods, old theory, and the welfare costs of trade restrictions, *Journal of Development Economics*, 43, pp. 5–38.

Srinivasan, T.N. and J. Whalley (1986) *General Equilibrium Trade Policy Modeling* (Cambridge, MIT Press).

Statistics Canada (1983) External trade division, *Trade of Canada, Imports by Countries, Exports by Countries* (Ottawa, Minister of Supply and Services Canada).

Statistics Canada (1987) *System of National Accounts — The Input–Output Structure of the Canadian Economy 1961–1981* (Ottawa, Minister of Supply and Services Canada).

Statistics Canada (1989) *Household Surveys Division, Historical Labour Force Statistics-actual Data, Seasonal Factors, Seasonally Adjusted Data* (Ottawa, Minister of Supply and Services Canada).

Statistics Canada (1990a) Input–output division. Current and constant price capital stock for 1980, unpublished.

Statistics Canada (1990b) Input–output division. Persons-hours 1961–89, unpublished.

ten Raa, Th. and D. Chakraborty (1991) Indian comparative advantage vis-á-vis Europe as revealed by linear programming of the two economies, *Economic Systems Research*, 3, pp. 111–150.

ten Raa, Th. and P. Mohnen (1997) The location of comparative advantages on the basis of fundamentals only, CIRANO discussion paper 97s–07.

Trefler, D. (1993) International factor price differences: Leontief was right!, *Journal of Political Economy*, 101, pp. 961–987.

Trefler, D. (1995) The case of missing trade and other mysteries, *American Economic Review*, 85, pp. 1029–1046.

Williams, J.R. (1978) *The Canadian–United States Tariffland Canadian Industry: A Multi-sectoral Analysis* (Toronto, University of Toronto Press).

Appendix A: Data

The European database comprises Denmark, the Federal Republic of Germany, France, Belgium, the Netherlands, Italy and the United Kingdom. The transactions matrix and final demand tables are from Eurostat (1989), the capital stock data from Eurostat (1990a) and the employment figures from Eurostat (1986). The capacity utilization rate is the EC manufacturing rate from the Commission of the European Communities (1984). The labor force figure is from Eurostat (1985). Non-market services in Europe, which correspond to non-business activities in Canada, are treated as exogenous. The labor and capital requirements from these sectors are substracted from the total labor and capital availabilities, and their intermediate input requirements are added to exogenous final demand.

The Canadian database, involving one country only, is straightforward. The use and make tables are directly available from Statistics Canada (1987). They relate to business activities only. Sectoral capital stock and labor employment data were kindly released to us by Statistics Canada (1990a and 1990b). The capital utilization rates are from Government of Canada (1984), and from Bank of Canada (1983) for the construction sector. The commodity input coefficients matrix is given by $\mathbf{A} = \mathbf{U}\mathbf{V}^{-\top}$ (see Kop Jansen and ten Raa, 1990; superscript $-\top$ denotes the composition of transposition and inversion, two commuting operations), where **U** is the commodity by sector input matrix (use table) and **V** is the sector by commodity output matrix (make table). The capital and labor input coefficients row vectors are obtained in the same way by the postmultiplication of the row vector of sectoral utilized capital stocks and of the row vector of sectoral labor employments with $\mathbf{V}^{-\top}$.

Eurostat (1976, p. 162–167) uses 44 sectors in the input–output classification and 25 sectors in the capital accounts. Statistics Canada (1987, 1990b) uses 50 industries and 92 commodities in the M-level input–output classification and 29 industries in the capital accounts. In either economy, the labor accounts follow basically the input–output classifications, but slightly more aggregated. The so-called R-44 and M-level classifications have been aggregated into a common base of 26 sectors. The sectors are listed 1 to 26 throughout this study. These codes and the names we have assigned to the sectors are listed in the first column of Table A-1. The second column shows how they can be obtained by aggregating the R-44 sectors. The third column relates them to the European capital sector classification. The fourth and fifth columns show how the sectors can be obtained by aggregating the M-level industries and commodities, respectively. The sixth column relates them to the Canadian capital sector/ classification.

Table A-2 lists the sectoral and labor and capital inputs and their overall availability. The total labor force figures are taken from Eurostat (1985) and Statistics Canada (1989). The exchange rate used to convert Canadian dollars to ECU is from IMF (1985). More detailed information on the construction of the dataset (harmonization aggregation, disaggregation and handling of missing data) can be found in the appendix of ten Raa and Mohnen (1997).

Appendix B: The Superfree Trade Model

The superfree trade model is obtained by the following modification of linear program (1)–(4).

$$\max_{\mathbf{x},\tilde{\mathbf{x}},\mathbf{x}^*,\tilde{\mathbf{x}}^*,c,\tilde{c},c^*\geq 0} \mathbf{e}^\top\mathbf{y}(c+\tilde{c})+\mathbf{e}^\top\mathbf{y}^*\gamma(c+\tilde{c}) \tag{B-1}$$

Table A-1: Classification of Sectors and European and Canadian (Dis)aggregations.

Present study 26 sectors	R-44 44 sectors	EC capital 25 sectors	M-level 50 industries	M-level 92 commodities	Canadian capital 29 industries
1 Agriculture	010	1	1, 2, 3	1, 2, 3, 4, 5, 6	1, 2, 3
2 Mining	030, 050, 110, 130	2, 5	4, 7	7, 8, 9, 13	4
3 Petroleum & Natural Gas	070	2	5, 26	10, 11, 62, 63	4, 21
4 Non-metallic Minerals	150	6	6, 25	12, 60, 61	4, 20
5 Chemical Products	170	7	27	64, 65, 66, 67	22
6 Metal Products	190	8	20, 21	45, 46, 47, 48, 49, 50, 51, 52	15, 16
7 Machines	210, 230	9, 10	22	53, 54	17
8 Electrical Goods	250	11	24	58, 59	19
9 Transportation Equipment	270, 290	12	23	55, 56, 57	18
10 Food	310, 330, 350	13	8	14, 15, 16, 17, 18, 19, 20, 21, 22	5
11 Beverages	370	13	9	23, 24	6
12 Tobacco Products	390	13	10	25, 26	7
13 Textiles & Clothing	410	14	14, 15	31, 32, 33, 34, 35	10
14 Leather & Footwear	430	14	13	30	9
15 Rubber & Plastic	490	16	11, 12	27, 28, 29	8, 9
16 Wood Products	450	17	16, 17	36, 37, 38, 39	11, 12
17 Paper & Printing	470	15	18, 19	40, 41, 42, 43, 44	13, 14
18 Other Manufactures	510	17	28	68, 69	23
19 Construction	530	19	29	70, 71, 72	24
20 Wholesale & Retail	510	20	35, 36	80, 81	28
21 Lodging & Catering	590	23	44	88	30
22 Transportation	610, 630, 650	24, 25, 26	30, 31, 32, 50	73, 74, 90	25
23 Communication	670	27	33	75, 76, 77	25
24 Utilities	090	2	34	78, 79	27
25 Finance	690, 730	28	37, 38, 39, 40	82, 83	29
26 Service	790, 550, 710, 750, 770	20, 29	41, 42, 43, 45, 46, 47, 48, 49	84, 85, 86, 87, 89, 91, 92	30

Note: R-44 sectors 810, 850, 890 and 930 and EC capital sector 22 pertain to non-market services, which are excluded from sector 26 and modeled as exogenous in the present study.

subject to the following constraints. For tradeable commodities:

$$(\mathbf{I}-\mathbf{A})\mathbf{x}+(\mathbf{I}-\mathbf{A}^*)\tilde{\mathbf{x}}+(\mathbf{I}-\mathbf{A}^*)\mathbf{x}^*+(\mathbf{I}-\mathbf{A})\tilde{\mathbf{x}}^*$$
$$\geq \mathbf{y}c+\frac{\mathbf{e}^\top\mathbf{y}}{\mathbf{e}^\top\mathbf{y}^*}\mathbf{y}^*\tilde{c}+\mathbf{y}^*c^*+\frac{\mathbf{e}^\top\mathbf{y}^*}{\mathbf{e}^\top\mathbf{y}}\mathbf{y}\tilde{c}^*+\mathbf{z}+\mathbf{z}^* \qquad \text{(B-2)}$$

Table A-2: Capital and Labor, 1980.

	Europe		Canada	
Sector	Utilized gross stock (millions ECU)	Employment (1000 persons)	Utilized gross stock (millions dollars)	Employment (persons)
1	255,339	7,278	47,127	735,518
2	131,252	2,006	19,355	118,192
3	335,647	199	35,010	62,383
4	70,347	1,539	4,912	64,444
5	141,435	1,729	13,642	87,284
6	65,256	2,806	20,016	305,501
7	89,933	3,859	1,793	98,423
8	59,177	2,901	2,531	141,608
9	94,758	2,957	5,823	195,028
10	115,891	2,502	7,749	204,892
11	12,127	370	2,868	33,323
12	3,116	107	453	7,622
13	55,449	2,960	4,677	182,166
14	15,655	1,015	764	27,410
15	37,657	1,109	1,642	62,642
16	26,868	1,553	5,635	177,202
17	58,342	1,870	21,977	245,841
18	8,980	504	1,028	68,201
19	90,170	8,265	5,605	726,220
20	333,574	141,616	20,120	1,713,967
21	65,645	3,368	9,276	433,900
22	94,553	5,887	53,712	499,772
23	160,684	1,806	35,659	210,192
24	116,174	978	91,924	94,176
25	253,540	7,045	25,892	522,077
26	246,610	187,388	33,309	1,003,204
Total	8,159,849	97,512	471,499	8,021,276
Force	10,049,079	104,573	563,382	9,450,655
			Exchange rate	1.5646 $/ECU
			Total stock	360,081 millons ECU

with $\tilde{c}^*$ determined by

$$c^* + \tilde{c}^* = \gamma(c + \tilde{c}) \tag{B-3}$$

for non-tradeable commodities:

$$(\mathbf{I} - \mathbf{A})\mathbf{x} + (\mathbf{I} - \mathbf{A}^*)\tilde{\mathbf{x}} \geq \mathbf{y}c + \frac{\mathbf{e}^\top \mathbf{y}}{\mathbf{e}^\top \mathbf{y}^*}\mathbf{y}^*\tilde{c} \tag{B-4}$$

$$(\mathbf{I} - \mathbf{A}^*)\mathbf{x}^* + (\mathbf{I} - \mathbf{A})\tilde{\mathbf{x}}^* \geq \mathbf{y}^*c^* + \frac{\mathbf{e}^\top \mathbf{y}^*}{\mathbf{e}^\top \mathbf{y}}\mathbf{y}\tilde{c}^*$$

and for factor inputs:

$$\mathbf{k}^\top \mathbf{x} + (\mathbf{k}^*)^\top \tilde{\mathbf{x}} \leq K, \quad \mathbf{l}^\top \mathbf{x} + (\mathbf{l}^*)^\top \tilde{\mathbf{x}} \leq L, \tag{B-5}$$
$$(\mathbf{k}^*)^\top \mathbf{x}^* + \mathbf{k}^\top \tilde{\mathbf{x}}^* \leq K^*, \quad (\mathbf{l}^*)^\top \mathbf{x}^* + \mathbf{l}^\top \tilde{\mathbf{x}}^* \leq L^*,$$

European net output $(\mathbf{I} - \mathbf{A})\mathbf{x}$ has been augmented with $(\mathbf{I} - \mathbf{A}^*)\tilde{\mathbf{x}}$, the net output in Europe using Canadian technology. Any European gross output component is generated by European or Canadian technologies with activity levels x_i, and $\tilde{x}_i$, respectively. The same kind of substitutability is introduced in the consumption section. European consumers are assumed to be indifferent between European final consumption, y, and Canadian final consumption scaled up to the European level $(\mathbf{e}^\top \mathbf{y}/\mathbf{e}^\top \mathbf{y}^*)\mathbf{y}^*$. These alternative life style vectors are multiplied by the consumption expansion factors, c and $\tilde{c}$, respectively. Finally, the premultiplication by the unit row vector yields the European terms in the objective function, (B-1). The Canadian terms are analogous, $\mathbf{e}^\top \mathbf{y}^*(c^* + \tilde{c}^*)$. We force them to trace the European consumption level by means of constraint (B-3).

Part VIII

Asian Economies

Chapter 24

Competitive Pressures on China: Income Inequality and Migration

Thijs ten Raa and Haoran Pan

Abstract: How would perfect competition affect the distribution of income in China? To answer this question, we integrate the two main streams of income distribution theory, namely the functional and the personal income approaches. First, using a general equilibrium model of China comprising 30 sectors and 27 provinces, marginal productivities are used as competitive commodity prices and factor rewards. Second, the rewards are imputed to households using their compositions in terms of persons and factor endowment entitlements. The ensuing distribution is contrasted with the status quo. Less skilled labor would stand to lose and, therefore, inequality would mount. Skilled workers, managers and technicians would move from Western and Central China to Eastern China. These flows would be more than offset by a flow of unskilled labor from Eastern China to Central China. Our finding that Eastern China has too many unskilled workers, relative to the competitive benchmark, suggests that the Harris-Todaro mechanism operates in China. Competition would change the predominant nature of inequality from the rural-urban divide to differences between the social classes. Moreover, the existing negative relationship between development and inequality would evaporate.

Keywords: Competition; Income inequality; Migration; Development; China.

JEL classification: D13; D33; O15; O18; J61; R11; R23; O53

1. Introduction

There are two strands in the theory and measurement of income distribution. Economists focus on the *functional* distribution of income, using the concept of factor productivity. Their standard model features a macroeconomic production function that maps factor inputs, such as labor and capital, into national income. The factors are rewarded according to their marginal products. Scarce factors fetch a high price. Inequality issues are implicit. Basically, when labor is abundant, relative to capital, the wage rate will be low and therefore, inequality is expected to be high. In the other "camp," statisticians focus on the *personal* distribution of income, with the emphasis on the measurement of income and inequality. They consider personal income as given and analyze it directly, without the need of a production function.

In this paper, however, we are not only interested in the actual distribution of income in an economy that becomes more market-oriented, but also in the distribution that would ensue under the benchmark of perfect competition. This issue suggests a two-step program. In the first step, we find the marginal productivities of the factor inputs, since they determine the factor incomes under perfect competition. In the second step, we reset the factor components of household incomes and reevaluate the distribution of the latter. The first step requires a general equilibrium model to determine the shadow prices of the factor inputs, while the second step requires detailed statistical information to express the rewards of factor inputs, such as the different types of labor, in terms of personal and family incomes. This integration of the functional and personal income analytic approaches seems to be novel.

We extend the model of ten Raa and Mohnen (2001) to an economy of many regions; we refer to the references given there for a review of the applied general equilibrium literature. The model comprises 30 input–output sectors, grouped in agriculture, mining, manufacturing, construction and other services. The standard convexity assumptions are fulfilled, so that the welfare theorems hold and therefore, a scan of the interprovincial utility frontier and an evaluation of the balance of payments can be used to determine equilibrium (Negishi 1960). More precisely, we let each province generate a domestic final demand vector (with the observed commodity proportions, assuming Leontief preferences), but multiplied by a (provincial) expansion factor. We scan in each direction in the space of provincial expansion factors by maximizing domestic final demand subject to the national material balances for the tradable commodities, the provincial material balances for the nontradeable commodities, and the factor constraints for the various types of labor and capital. The shadow prices of the tradable commodities codetermine the provincial trade balances, which are used to adjust the relative weights of the provincial expansion factors, until a full balance of payments is achieved. We follow the usual assumption that agriculture, mining and manufacturing produce tradable commodities, and that construction and the other services produce nontradeable commodities.

China is perhaps the most dramatic example of a transition to a market economy. Not only is central planning replaced by entrepreneurship, trade liberalized, and millions of workers on the move, but what makes China particularly fascinating for a case study, is its starting point of egalitarianism. The opening up to free markets of a right-wing dictatorship, is interesting from the viewpoint of efficiency gains, which overwhelm distributional issues. In China, however, there are serious equity stakes.

China is thought to be more egalitarian than other developing countries and features less urban income inequality than rural income inequality. How will competition alter the picture? There will be winners and losers, both in terms of factor claims and in terms of regions and provinces. Income gradients will press people to migrate. This mechanism will take some steam off the inequality problem that surrounds free markets in China. Our main finding is that inequality would multiply under competition, but the predominant nature of inequality would change from the rural-urban divide to differences between the social classes.

We measure inequality by the so-called Theil index, which admits a decomposition of inequality in within-group inequalities and between-group inequality. Normally, there is one dimension of classification. Location, profession, or perhaps income itself, defines the subgroups. Our division of the population is three-way though, namely rural-urban, by province and by social class. There is a naughty methodological issue. We may, first, divide Chinese income in rural income and urban income and, second, break down further by province and social class, and then decompose inequality accordingly. Alternatively, we could first divide Chinese income in provincial incomes and then break down each in a rural and an urban component and further by social class. The problem is that the Theil decomposition is influenced by the order of classification. We shall present this slight theoretical problem formally and assess its magnitude.

The remainder of the paper is organized as follows. Section 2 discusses the general equilibrium model (an input–output model with a non-linear adjustment mechanism for the weights of the provinces) and its main outcomes (the competitive allocation, the shadow prices, and the implied migrations). Section 3 reviews the income inequality literature, extends inequality decompositions to multiple dimensions (rural-urban and regional), implements it for China, and investigates how the general equilibrium valuations alter the results. Section 4 draws conclusions. The details of the model are in Appendix 1. Appendices 2 and 3 describe the sources of the input–output data and the population/personal income statistics, respectively. The resulting population and income tables are reported in Appendices 4 and 5, where also a map of China can be found. Appendix 6 explains how the functional rewards (generated by the model) have been transformed to personal incomes.

2. The General Equilibrium Model

We extend the model of ten Raa and Mohnen (2001) to many regions, dividing China into 30 input–output sectors and 27 provinces.[1] Each province generates domestic final demand plus net exports, which are both 30-dimensional commodity vectors. The provincial net exports sum to the national net exports (in the sense of vectors), because inter-provincial deliveries cancel out. National net exports remain fixed in our analysis, so any efficiency gain is brought about by provincial specialization. However unrealistic, this conservative assumption steers the competitive allocation relatively close to the actual one. The introduction of a free world trade assumption would complicate the analysis — efficiency would have not only the domestic component captured in this paper, but also an international

[1]We miss Neimeng, Hainan, and Tibet because of input–output data problems. Fortunately, these are not populous provinces.

specialization component (ten Raa 1995) — and require even more data — the so-called Unit Value Ratios (ten Raa and Mohnen 2002). For similar reasons, we assume Leontief preferences, denoting the domestic final demand proportions of province i by vector f^i (obtained by scaling the provincial domestic final demand vector down to unity). The assumptions of the first and second welfare theorems are fulfilled, so we may determine the competitive allocation by maximizing the standard of living. The conflict of interest between provinces is handled using the equilibrium analytic technique of Negishi (1960).

We let each province generate a domestic final demand vector with the observed proportions (f^i), but multiplied by scalar d_iD where D represents the national domestic final use and d_i a provincial share. The provincial weights d_i will be determined by the balances of payments. For any vector of provincial weights, d, we maximize domestic final demand, D, preserving the commodity proportions in each province. More precisely, for any vector of provincial weights d, the linear program described in Appendix 1 maximizes D subject to the material balances and the factor constraints. The shadow prices to the constraints represent competitive commodity prices and factor rewards, respectively.

The determination of the provincial weights is as follows. For any vector of provincial weights d, the linear program determines provincial gross output vectors. The subtraction of the intermediate demands (as determined by the input–output matrix) and the domestic final demands ($f^i d_i D$) yields the competitive provincial net exports vectors. Valuation by competitive commodity prices yields the balance of payments of province i, for any vector of provincial weights d. We adjust the weights following Negishi (1960). If province i's balance of payments exceeds the balance of payments implied by the observed net exports vector, then the province under consideration exports too much and we give its domestic final demand share more weight by increasing the value of d_i, at the expense of the other provinces. In the limit, we obtain an optimal domestic final use that observes not only the consumption patterns in the provinces, but also their mutual balances of payments.

We thus find the optimum pattern of specialization between the provinces, along with the supporting shadow prices of the commodities and the factor inputs. The implementation of this program demands an enormous input–output database, comprising input statistics by sector and province for the commodities, capital, and labor, stock statistics by province for capital and labor, and a breakdown of the latter by skill. Appendix 2 outlines the data collection procedure. The data are made available by the authors upon request.

The factor inputs are capital plus four types of labor, namely technicians, managers, skilled and unskilled workers. This order is assumed to constitute a top-down hierarchy. In other words, technicians are capable of fulfilling any of the labor tasks, managers can do their own job, skilled or unskilled work, skilled workers can do their own job or perform unskilled work, and unskilled workers can only do their own job. We assume free labor mobility.

l_1^i is the row vector of technicians' employment coefficients in province i, l_2^i the same, but of managers, l_3^i of skilled labor, and l_4^i of unskilled labor. The vector of outputs by sector in province i, x^i, is *feasible* with respect to the labor forces N_1^i, N_2^i, N_3^i, and N_4^i, if

$$\sum l_1^i x^i \leq \sum N_1^i,$$

$$\sum (l_1^i + l_2^i) x^i \leq \sum (N_1^i + N_2^i),$$

$$\sum (l_1^i + l_2^i + l_3^i) x^i \leq \sum (N_1^i + N_2^i + N_3^i),$$

$$\sum (l_1^i + l_2^i + l_3^i + l_4^i) x^i \leq \sum (N_1^i + N_2^i + N_3^i + N_4^i).$$

All summations are over provinces, $i = 1, \ldots, 27$. The first inequality constrains the demand for technicians. The second constraint can be rewritten as

$$\sum l_2^i x^i \leq \sum N_2^i + \sum (N_1^i - l_1^i x^i).$$

This rewrite indicates that managerial demand is constrained by the sum of the labor force of managers and the number of redundant technicians. Similarly, the third constraint binds demand for skilled labor by the sum of the force of skilled workers and the numbers of technicians or managers for whom there are no jobs at the two top levels.

The four constraints pick up shadow prices as the model determines the optimum allocation. The shadow price of the fourth constraint is the base wage. The shadow price of the third constraint is the skill premium;

the shadow price of the second constraint is the managerial premium; and the shadow price of the first constraint is the technicians' premium. Technicians pick up shadow values from all four constraints and therefore, the competitive wage of a technician will be the sum of the base wage and all three premiums. If, for example, the first constraint is not binding, meaning that there is excess supply of technicians, then the wage of a technician will be the base wage, plus the skill and managerial premiums, while the technician's premium is zero. The hierarchy of labor tasks' fulfillment guarantees that wages will increase by skill (or at least not decrease). Table 1 shows the baseline (observed) figures and the competitive results, not only for labor, but also for capital.

Although actual labor rewards already increase by skill, competition would have some dramatic effects. The unskilled workers would receive a minimal wage of a mere sixth of the actual one. The next type of workers, skilled labor, would do no better. Managers would earn a hundred-fold compensation and on top of that technicians would earn a big bonus. Unskilled and even (lowly) skilled labor are abundant while the two top skills are very scarce. The shadow prices reveal the potential returns to higher education in China. Indeed, China now admits students to business schools and polytechnic institutes in great numbers. Investments in such schools should pay off handsomely.

Table 1: Observed and Competitive Factor Rewards (Yuan).

	Observed	Competitive
Base wage	150.62	25
Skilled wage	257.87	25
Managerial compensation	266.87	31756
Technician's salary	271.22	59361
Average Rent (%)	0.79	0.44
Central	0.66	0.22
Western	0.53	0.17
Eastern	0.98	0.59

Source: The observed wages are the October 1992 figures, Yearbook of Labor Statistics of China (1993), Table 7–13 "Increase Rate of Wages of 14 Cities' and Counties' Staff and Workers." The rent on capital is the sum of depreciation, net tax and profit (taken from the 1992 input–output tables, Dept. of National Economic Accounting, State Statistical Bureau of China, 1996) divided by the capital stock. The competitive rewards are our model results. Table 6 or the map in Appendix 4 shows the division of provinces in three regions.

The effects on capital rewards would be less dramatic. Table 1 shows that the rates of return would even decline. Since capital is assumed to be spatially immobile, the rates continue to vary by region.

Table 1 reveals that the comparative advantage of the Chinese economy rests in less skilled labor. If our assumption of fixed national exports were relaxed, the Chinese economy would export more skill-extensive commodities and import more skill-intensive commodities. As usual, international trade would be a valve for national scarcities and remove some of the competitive pressure on income distribution.

Table 2 shows how total income and inequality would shoot up under competition. (The Theil indices will be detailed in the next session.)

The first column of Table 1 indicates that Chinese domestic income is slightly over 80% of the level attainable under free labor mobility and efficient specialization.

Tables 1 and 2 reflect the so-called dual variables of the program that maximizes the standard of living in China. The underlying primal variables are the sectoral output levels by province and reveal the optimum pattern of specialization within China, see Table 3.

Agriculture remains active in a great number of provinces, but most other activities are best undertaken in specific provinces, except of course the ones producing non-tradable commodities, including the services.[2] Table 3 locates the comparative advantages of the Chinese provincial economies, revealing the threats and challenges they face.

The general equilibrium model reallocates economic activity as to maximize the standard of living in China and this affects the level and mix of labor demand by province. The new demand for labor requires immigration.

Table 2: China's Income and Theil Index.

	Income (Billion Yuan)	Theil Index
Observed	244	0.087
Competitive	300	0.758

[2]The efficient allocation of sectoral activities features specialization. Notice that we use an idealized concept of free interprovincial trade, neglecting trade frictions such as transportation costs over and above the ones captured in the intersectoral input–output statistics. The availability and incorporation of data on such frictions would generate a more diversified competitive allocation, including for agriculture.

Table 3: Sectoral Activity in Provinces.[3]

Sectors		Active Provinces
Agriculture	1	TJ, HB, SX, LN, JL, HLJ, JS, AH, FJ, JX, SD, HeN, HuB, HuN, GX, SC, YN, ShX, GS, QH
Coal mining & processing	2	SX, GZ
Petroleum & gas extraction	3	HLJ
Metal mining & processing	4	SH
Non-metals mining & processing	5	HB, FJ, NX
Food manufacturing	6	SH, GZ
Textile industry	7	HB, ZJ, XJ
Sewing & leather products	8	SH
Timer & furniture manufacturing	9	SH
Paper making & stationary goods	10	JS
Electrical power steaming	11	JS
Petroleum processing	12	JX
Coking gas & coal products	13	GZ
Chemical industry	14	JS, ZJ
Non-metals products	15	HB
Smelting & processing of metals	16	BJ, JS
Metal products	17	HB
Machinery & equipment manufacturing	18	GD
Transportation equipment manufacturing	19	TJ
Electric equipment & machinery	20	SD, GD
Electronics & telecommunications equipments	21	GD
Instrument & meters	22	HuN
Other manufacturing	23	AH
Construction	24	All
Transportation & telecommunications	25	All
Commerce	26	All
Social service	27	All
Culture, education & research	28	All
Banking & insurance	29	All
Public administration	30	All

We depict all labor motions in Table 4. Positive figures represent inflows of workers or immigration and negative figures denote outflows or emigration.

A clear pattern emerges from Table 4. Skilled workers, managers and technicians would move from Western and Central China to Eastern China. These flows would be more than offset by a flow of unskilled labor from

[3]The sectors producing non-tradable commodities are denoted in italics. See Table 6 for province codes.

Table 4: Labor Mobility in Competitive Markets (Thousands of workers).[4]

Region	Unskilled	Skilled	Managers	Technicians	Total
Eastern	−29211	10566	1521	4444	−12681
Central	43829	−20639	−1360	−3620	18210
Western	−1116	−3428	−161	−824	−5529
China	13501	−13501	0	0	0

Eastern China to Central China. Demand for unskilled labor would be so big in Central China that even some workers of the next rank ("skilled labor") would have to perform unskilled labor tasks. Western China would stand to lose all types of workers, if efficiency were to prevail.

Our finding that there are too many unskilled workers in Eastern China, relative to the competitive benchmark, suggests that the Harris and Todaro (1970) mechanism operates in China. The argument is that high wages in the cities attract workers beyond unemployment. The market failure underlying this distortion is wage rigidity. In view of the minimal competitive wages for the lowest types of labor, this wage rigidity has its virtue though.

Our investigation of the efficient reallocation of labor is extended to the dependants, to obtain people migration figures. Application of The dependency ratios are discussed in Appendix 3 and tabulated in Appendix 4. Application to the labor motions of Table 4 yields the net migration figures by region shown in Table 5.

Table 5: Population Migration in Competitive Markets (Thousands of persons).[5]

Region	Migration
Eastern	−22565
Central	31799
Western	−9939
China	0
Emigration	−32505
Immigration	31799
Numerical error	−705

[4]The figures are differences between competitive and observed labor employments. Hence they represent inflows of workers or immigration. Figures need not add due to rounding.

[5]Figures need not add due to rounding.

Across regions, the positive figures (denoting immigration) sum to the same total as the negative figures (denoting emigration). The figure is 33 million persons, suggesting that free markets would exercise limited migratory pressure between the three regions. There are numerous movements between provinces though.

For many decades, the Chinese government has conducted a special system of residence registration, the so-called "Hukou," but the economic reform has granted more freedom to labor markets. In recent years, tens of millions of farmers moved around the country in search for work. Wang *et al.* (1995) estimated that China counted 130 million surplus farmers and that the number will increase to 230 million in the next ten years.

Table 4, the last column, reveals that over 18 million workers would cross the borders between the regions. The inclusion of family members increases the figure to nearly 32 million; see Table 5. At the provincial level, there are many more migrations. In Eastern China, the provinces of Tianjin, Liaoning, Shanghai and Fujian would absorb 52 million migrants, while the other seven provinces would see 74.5 million emigrants leaving. The net figure for Eastern China is 22.5 million emigrants. In Central China, only the provinces Shanxi and Jiangxi would have emigrants, namely 1.3 million, and the other provinces would attract 33 million migrants, including 31.8 millions from Eastern and Western China. In Western China, 47.6 million migrants would leave the provinces Guizhou, Yunnan, Nixia and Xinjiang, while the other provinces would absorb only 37.7 million persons, with the remaining 10 millions leaving the West.[6]

3. Inequality

China is thought to be more egalitarian than other developing countries. The State Statistical Bureau found a Gini coefficient for China in 1979 of 0.33. Griffin *et al.* (1994) gave an estimate of 0.38 for China in 1988 and found this low in comparison to other Asian developing countries. Also, China was found to feature less urban income inequality than rural income inequality. Zhu and Wen (1990) found a Gini coefficient for rural areas

[6]Because Neimeng, Hainan and Tibet do not participate in the competitive market, their populations will remain constant in this research.

of 0.3 and Griffin *et al.* (1994) confirmed it to be 0.33, but only 0.23 for urban areas, all for the year 1988. Wang *et al.* (1995) found that the 1993 rural and urban Gini coefficients were 0.33 and 0.24, respectively. The rural inequality derives from farmers' non-production income, whereas staff and workers earn wages similar to the ones that prevail in urban areas, according to Griffin *et al.* (1994).

Wang *et al.* (1995) ascribed the rural-urban inequality gap to unbalanced development — with rural economic reform in the 1978–1985 period and urban economic reform in the 1985–1994 period — but few studies have explicit results on the relationship between inequality and development. Griffin *et al.* (1994) compared the rural incomes between all provinces and urban incomes between ten provinces (again for the year 1988), but were unable to ascribe provincial differences to the rural-urban gap. Wang *et al.* (1995) found a 2.58 : 1.16 : 1 ratio for rural income levels in Eastern, Central and Western China, respectively, and found that the Eastern provinces show great income variation, unlike the Central and Western provinces.[7] Similarly, a 2.13 : 0.89 : 1 ratio for urban income levels in the respective regions extended their finding, but their analysis was crude, featuring a "representative" province for each region. Yang (1992) and Wei (1992) calculated the relative mean deviations from per capita GNP in 1989 for the Eastern, Central and Western regions (and the constituent provinces) with findings similar to those of Wang *et al.* (1995).

Inequalities within provinces have been widely investigated. Zhu and Wen (1990) and Griffin *et al.* (1994) calculated all provincial Gini coefficients for rural income, but found no relationship between inequality and the level of economic development. For comparison, we include their results in Table 6.

Our own analysis is based on the *Theil index*. We believe that there is good reason to measure inequality in this way. Shorrocks (1980) examines the generalized entropy family of inequality indices, of which the Theil index is the main representative. A deep theorem of Shorrocks (1988) shows that subgroup consistency leads inexorably towards the generalized entropy family. An inequality measure is *subgroup consistent* if it fulfils an intuitive condition: a redistribution of income within any subgroup that increases

[7]See the map in Appendix 4 or Table 6 for the division of provinces.

Table 6: Income Inequalities in Rural China.

Province	Code	Rank by Next Column	1988 Per Capita Farmers' Income	1988 Gini Coefficient Griffin *et al.* (1994)	1988 Gini Coefficient Zhu and Wen (1990)	1992 Gini Coefficient This Study	1992 Theil Index This Study
Eastern							
Beijing	BJ	2	1063	0.305	0.233	0.271	0.0553
Tianjin	TJ	4	891	**0.394**	0.256	0.259	0.0521
Hebei	HB	13	547	0.293	0.289	0.228	0.0459
Liaoning	LN	7	700	0.330	0.300	0.254	0.0333
Shanghai	SH	1	1301	0.222	0.215	**0.312**	0.0323
Jiangsu	JS	6	797	0.383	0.299	0.282	0.0294
Zhejiang	ZJ	3	902	0.286	0.298	0.266	**0.0555**
Fujian	FJ	9	613	0.290	0.218	0.256	0.0245
Shandong	SD	10	584	0.285	0.267	0.225	0.0484
Guangdong	GD	5	809	0.306	0.305	0.249	0.0392
Central							
Shanxi	SX	23	439	0.320	0.275	0.240	0.0431
Neimeng	NM	15	500	0.339	0.293	0.245	0.0233
Jilin	JL	8	628	0.354	0.264	0.247	0.0184
Heilongjiang	HLJ	12	553	0.368	0.294	0.251	0.0157
Anhui	AH	20	486	0.249	0.207	0.238	0.0267
Jiangxi	JX	19	488	0.230	0.201	0.247	0.0280
Henan	HeN	27	401	0.299	0.250	0.238	0.0230
Hubei	HuB	16	498	0.231	0.229	0.242	0.0252
Hunan	HuN	14	515	0.255	0.212	0.242	0.0257
Western							
Guangxi	GX	25	424	0.291	0.279	0.234	0.0231
Hainan	HN	11	567	0.276	0.283	0.253	0.0267
Sichuan	SC	22	449	0.265	0.241	0.226	0.0276
Guizhou	GZ	28	398	0.295	0.234	0.234	0.0167
Yunnan	YN	24	428	0.287	0.259	0.236	0.0249
Tibet	TB	29	374		0.279	0.248	0.0181
Shaanxi	ShX	26	404	0.289	0.263	0.238	0.0275
Gansu	GS	30	340	0.263	0.248	0.230	0.0262
Qinghai	QH	18	493	0.313	**0.325**	0.251	0.0232
Ningxia	NX	21	473	0.273	0.315	0.237	0.0240
Xinjiang	XJ	17	497		0.323	0.243	0.0325

subgroup inequality, however defined, must increase overall inequality when all other incomes are preserved, according to the same definition. This monotonicity condition requires no additivity. Strictly speaking, subgroup consistency yields any monotonic transformation of a generalized entropy index, but this freedom is superficial; a weak adding-up requirement eliminates it, namely condition (19) of Shorrocks (1988).

Let the total income of a partitioned population be unity (so that 'incomes' are shares). The income of g-group member j is denoted y_{gj}, where $g = 1, \ldots, G$, the number of groups, and $j = 1, \ldots, N_g$, the size of group g. Denoting the total income of group g by Y_g, the Theil (1967) index of inequality can be written as

$$\sum_{g=1}^{G} Y_g \log \frac{Y_g}{N_g/N} + \sum_{g=1}^{G} Y_g \sum_{j=1}^{N_g} \frac{y_{gj}}{Y_g} \log \frac{y_{gj}/Y_g}{1/N_g}.$$

The first term is between-group inequality and the second term is average within-group inequality. The classical division is between rural and urban income ($g = 1$ and 2, respectively). Now refine each group in subgroups of sizes N_{gh}, where $h = 1, \ldots, H$, the common number of subgroups, think of provinces. Denoting individual incomes by y_{ghj}, $j = 1, \ldots, N_{gh}$, and subgroup incomes shares by Y_{gh}, inequality can be rewritten as

$$\sum_{g=1}^{G} Y_g \log \frac{Y_g}{N_g/N} + \sum_{g=1}^{G} Y_g \sum_{h=1}^{H} \frac{Y_{gh}}{Y_g} \log \frac{Y_{gh}/Y_g}{N_{gh}/N_g}$$
$$+ \sum_{g=1}^{G} Y_g \sum_{h=1}^{H} \frac{Y_{gh}}{Y_g} \sum_{j=1}^{N_{gh}} \frac{y_{ghj}}{Y_{gh}} \log \frac{y_{ghj}/Y_{gh}}{1/N_{gh}}.$$

The first term represents between-group inequality, the second term between-subgroup inequality, and the third term the average within-subgroup inequality. Now we decompose inequality in rural-urban inequality, provincial inequality, and social inequality. We face a nasty nesting issue. Had we divided China in provinces first and refined them in rural and urban areas, inequality would still be the sum of provincial inequality, rural-urban inequality, and social inequality, but the numbers could be different. Total inequality would still be the same, as would be the third terms, representing average within-subgroup or social inequality. The leading terms, representing rural-urban inequality and provincial inequality, would have the same sum, but the division might differ.

Let us discuss the data requirements of these inequality measures. We need personal incomes by (rural or urban) area, province, and social class, both for the observed economy and for the hypothetical, purely competitive economy. Appendix 3 describes our collection of the population and personal income statistics; for the respective tables, see Appendices 4 and 5. The incomes under perfect competition are derived from the factor input prices obtained in Section 2. We allocate these earnings to eight social classes, namely four types of labor (unskilled, skilled, managers, and technicians), the self-employed, the capitalists, the retirees, and, last but not least, the dependants. The imputation of labor income is straightforward, but the imputation of capital income is not. Moreover, factor incomes must be distributed to persons, taking into account family sizes. We assume that the population division between rural and urban remains constant in each province, because we have no bridge table between input–output sectors and the rural-urban classification.[8] The details of the transformation of the functional to the personal distribution of income are collected in Appendix 6.

The inequality measures in the literature (provincial Gini coefficients for rural income) are presented in Table 6, along with our own calculation for comparison. The first two columns give the province names and codes. The third and fourth columns display the levels and ranks of the provincial farmers' incomes. The fifth, sixth and seventh columns provide the Gini coefficients of Griffin *et al.* (1994), Zhu and Wen (1990), and this study, respectively. The eighth column provides the Theil indices of this study. It is noteworthy that all measures locate the most unequal distribution of income in different provinces (the bold figures). Income inequality measurement is no easy job!

In Table 7, the first column reproduces the rural income inequalities (from Table 6, last column) and the second column presents the urban inequalities. A weighted average of the two yields the inequality within areas, given in column 3. The inequality between the rural and urban economies is given in column 4. Columns 3 and 4 are reproduced as percentages of provincial inequality in columns 5 and 6, respectively, while the sum of respective elements is reported in column 7, the Theil index of any province. For example, in Beijing, the rural-urban divide contributes only 13% to inequality, but in Tibet, the share is 63%.

The discussion of the national Theil indices at the bottom of Table 7 is quite similar. The first column displays rural inequality. A weighted

[8]Rural China has many industries other than agriculture.

Table 7: Income Inequalities in the Observed Chinese Economy.

Province	Code	Rural In-Equality	Urban Inequality	Within Areas	Between Areas	Within Areas	Between Areas	Provincial Inequality
Eastern								
Beijing	BJ	0.0553	0.0328	0.0372	0.0058	87%	13%	0.0430
Tianjin	TJ	0.0521	0.0256	0.0321	0.0039	89%	11%	0.0360
Hebei	HB	0.0459	0.0327	0.0411	0.0342	55%	45%	0.0753
Liaoning	LN	0.0333	0.0401	0.0378	0.0187	67%	33%	0.0565
Shanghai	SH	0.0323	0.0209	0.0239	0.0062	79%	21%	0.0301
Jiangsu	JS	0.0294	0.0297	0.0295	0.0221	57%	43%	0.0516
Zhejiang	ZJ	0.0555	0.0515	0.0543	0.0005	99%	1%	0.0548
Fujian	FJ	0.0245	0.0905	0.0471	0.0189	71%	29%	0.0660
Shandong	SD	0.0484	0.0445	0.0472	0.0016	97%	3%	0.0488
Guangdong	GD	0.0392	0.0662	0.0512	0.0054	90%	10%	0.0566
Central								
Shanxi	SX	0.0431	0.0326	0.0379	0.0422	47%	53%	0.0801
Neimeng	NM	0.0233	0.0461	0.0357	0.0296	55%	45%	0.0653
Jilin	JL	0.0184	0.0455	0.0343	0.0235	59%	41%	0.0578
Heilongjiang	HLJ	0.0157	0.0436	0.0323	0.0114	74%	26%	0.0437
Anhui	AH	0.0267	0.0580	0.0379	0.0391	49%	51%	0.0770
Jiangxi	JX	0.0280	0.0585	0.0377	0.0160	70%	30%	0.0537
Henan	HeN	0.0230	0.0455	0.0303	0.0398	43%	57%	0.0701
Hubei	HuB	0.0252	0.0355	0.0297	0.0218	58%	42%	0.0515
Hunan	HuN	0.0257	0.0523	0.0346	0.0297	54%	46%	0.0643
Western								
Guangxi	GX	0.0231	0.0682	0.0371	0.0363	51%	49%	0.0734
Hainan	HN	0.0267	0.1082	0.0668	0.0648	51%	49%	0.1316
Shichuan	SC	0.0276	0.0467	0.0343	0.0257	57%	43%	0.0600
Guizhou	GZ	0.0167	0.0628	0.0323	0.0259	55%	45%	0.0582
Yunnan	YN	0.0249	0.0448	0.0316	0.0488	39%	61%	0.0804
Tibet	TB	0.0181	0.1045	0.0484	0.0821	37%	63%	0.1305
Shaanxi	ShX	0.0275	0.0393	0.0328	0.0587	36%	64%	0.0915
Gansu	GS	0.0262	0.0407	0.0334	0.0804	29%	71%	0.1138
Qinghai	QH	0.0232	0.0461	0.0365	0.0977	27%	73%	0.1342
Ningxia	NX	0.0240	0.0372	0.0312	0.0771	29%	71%	0.1083
Xinjiang	XJ	0.0325	0.0496	0.0424	0.0601	41%	59%	0.1025
Within provinces		0.0324	0.0455	0.0380	0.0284	57%	43%	0.0664
Between provinces		0.0243	0.0163	0.0208		100%	0%	0.0208
Theil's inequality		0.0567	0.0618	0.0588	0.0284	67%	33%	**0.0872**
Within provinces		57%	74%	65%	100%	44%		76%
Between provinces		43%	26%	35%	0%			24%

average of all the provincial Theil indices yields the inequality within the provinces, 0.0324. The inequality between the provinces is 0.0243. The two terms are reproduced as percentages at the bottom, and they sum to 0.0567, the Theil index for rural inequality in China. The explanations of urban inequality (column 2) and the weighted average of rural and urban inequality (within-area inequality, column 3) are similar. A weighted average of the rural-urban divides (column 4) yields the Theil index for this inequality, namely 0.0284.[9] Provincial inequality, be it rural, urban, or the divide, is given by the right-hand side column, column 7. Here, the weighted average yields a Theil index of 0.0664, which is well above the figures of the developed provinces, such as Beijing and Shanghai. Addition of the inequality between the provinces, 0.0208, yields the Theil index in bold on the right bottom of the table: 0.0872. This figure represents the *overall personal income inequality* in China for the year 1992. Once more, the two contributing terms are reproduced as percentages at the bottom (in columns 5 and 6).

Reading the row of Theil's inequality measure, overall personal income inequality (0.0872) is shown as the sum of rural-urban inequality (0.0284) and within-area inequality (0.0588), where the latter has been obtained by the vertical summation of the between-provinces (0.0208) and the within-province or social inequality (0.0380) measures. Reading the column of provincial inequality, overall personal income inequality (0.0872) is shown as the sum of the between-province inequality (0.0208) and the within-province inequality (0.0664) measures, where the latter has been obtained by horizontal summation of rural-urban inequality (0.0284) and within-area or social inequality (0.0380). Either way, overall inequality consists of 33% rural-urban inequality, 24% provincial inequality, and a remainder of 43% social inequality. How sensitive is the decomposition of inequality with respect to the naughty nesting issue? In the above analysis, we first divided between the rural and urban areas and then subdivided between provinces. If we reverse the order, the overall inequality would still be the same, 0.0872, but the rural-urban inequality would be only 28% (instead of 33%) and the provincial inequality 29% (instead of 24%); the residual social inequality would remain the same (43%), by construction. Roughly

[9]Notice that the variation of this statistic between provinces is meaningless; this is why Table 2 has an empty cell in column 4.

speaking, without any pretense to settle this methodological problem at the level of theory, it is safe to conclude that of Chinese inequality three/tenth is rural-urban, three/tenth provincial, and four/tenth social.

We now turn to the crucial question of what competition would do to inequality. Table 8 presents our findings as relative departures from the

Table 8: Inequality Changes from the Observed to the Competitive Economy.

Province	Code	Rural Inequality	Urban Inequality	Within Areas	Between Areas	Provincial Inequality
Eastern						
Beijing	BJ	5.95	8.05	7.23	5.12	6.94
Tianjin	TJ	9.50	14.33	11.77	12.33	11.83
Hebei	HB	4.24	17.85	10.90	0.85	6.34
Liaoning	LN	35.67	9.52	13.74	10.13	12.54
Shanghai	SH	19.06	17.13	16.62	4.92	14.21
Jiangsu	JS	20.74	13.23	16.42	3.49	10.88
Zhejiang	ZJ	8.71	8.95	8.62	118.40	9.62
Fujian	FJ	35.90	3.77	11.75	10.92	11.51
Shandong	SD	21.39	12.56	15.37	96.88	18.05
Guangdong	GD	7.15	7.00	8.26	9.93	8.42
Central						
Shanxi	SX	16.72	11.18	12.42	3.85	7.90
Neimeng	NM	1.00	1.00	1.00	1.00	1.00
Jilin	JL	55.56	5.44	11.54	9.28	10.62
Heilongjiang	HLJ	55.64	6.44	12.22	13.18	12.47
Anhui	AH	36.76	7.17	16.88	5.30	11.00
Jiangxi	JX	30.36	5.73	14.38	11.62	13.55
Henan	HeN	49.93	8.02	23.71	6.34	13.85
Hubei	HuB	44.22	10.77	19.58	11.52	16.17
Hunan	HuN	37.70	6.83	16.79	8.52	12.97
Western						
Guangxi	GX	41.60	4.16	14.83	7.83	11.37
Hainan	HN	1.00	1.00	1.00	1.00	1.00
Shichuan	SC	45.99	10.03	21.41	11.27	17.07
Guizhou	GZ	7.76	8.98	12.81	0.70	7.42
Yunnan	YN	20.90	3.94	8.89	4.86	6.44
Tibet	TB	1.00	1.00	1.00	1.00	1.00
Shaanxi	ShX	39.41	7.62	16.24	5.58	9.40
Gansu	GS	44.74	8.60	18.03	3.69	7.90
Qinghai	QH	37.12	5.34	13.28	1.69	4.84
Ningxia	NX	4.56	10.14	9.73	0.63	3.26
Xinjiang	XJ	4.97	8.06	7.72	0.44	3.45
Within provinces		19.23	9.14	12.57	6.28	9.88
Between provinces		8.94	3.24	4.90		4.90
Theil's inequality		14.82	7.59	9.86	6.28	**8.69**

empirical inequality statistics of Table 2 (ignoring the two columns with percentages, 5 and 6). For example, the first inequality figure of Table 7 (rural inequality in Beijing, 0.0553) is increased by a factor 5.95. The last ratio of Table 8 (in bold) is the most interesting one; overall inequality is increased by a factor of 8.69. The rural-urban inequality goes up by a relatively modest factor of 6.28. The inequality between provinces is increased by a factor of 4.90 and the inequality within provinces by a dramatic factor of 9.88. What accounts for this is the hefty increase in subgroup or social inequality by a factor of 7.52.

In short, *competition would breed inequality but the share of the rural-urban divide would diminish.*

The emergence of inequality should come as no surprise. The Chinese income distribution in the base year 1992 is egalitarian; Appendix 5 shows the small income differences between persons. In rural areas, the highest/lowest income ratio (representing the capitalists versus the unskilled) is only 15. In urban areas, it is still only 20. Each social class earns more in urban than in rural areas and urban mean income is about double the rural mean income. Shanghai and Guizhou are the richest and poorest provinces, respectively, but the mean income ratio is a modest 5.

The finding of the literature that China has less urban inequality than rural inequality is *not* confirmed. The rural and urban Theil indices are about the same (0.0567 and 0.0618, respectively, see Table 7). Within the two areas, inequality varies quite a bit, essentially by stage of development.[10] In the less and under-developed provinces, most inequality is in fact urban and indeed, in the developed Chinese provinces, there is less urban inequality than rural. One might say that the literature's finding pertains to developed China.

[10] In 1994, the Eastern provinces (see Table 6 for the classification) were home to 36.5% of China's population, but contributed 55.6% to national GDP. (The data are from the 1995 China Statistical Yearbook.) Per capita GDP for the east coast was 5720 Yuan. The Central provinces were home to 35.6% of China's population and contributed 27.6% to national GDP. Per capita GDP in the Central part was 2913 Yuan. The Western provinces were home to 27.9% of China's population, but contributed 16.8% to national GDP. Per capita GDP in the Western part was 260 Yuan. The Eastern, Central and Western parts are referred to as developed, less-developed and under-developed zones, respectively.

Under perfect competition, however, urban inequality would be less than rural inequality. (The expansion factors of rural and urban inequality are 14.82 and 7.59 according to Table 8, bottom line.)

So far, we have discussed the inequalities within rural and urban China. Now we turn to their differences. The literature stressed the difference between urban and regional income levels as a result of urban economic reform. We confirm this; the rural-urban divide is substantive (0.0284, that is 33% of overall inequality, 0.0872, see Table 2). Appendix 5 shows that urban income is more than double of rural income (all per person) and that all provinces except Zhejiang show higher levels of urban than of rural income.

The rural-urban divide would multiply under competition (by a factor 6.28), but at a lower rate than overall inequality (8.69, see also Table 8). Our analysis confirms the finding of the literature that Eastern China stands out in terms of income and that Central and Western China are not too far apart. The contribution of provincial variation to overall inequality is significant. Table 7 ascribed 24% to provincial inequality (0.0208 out of 0.0872). Competition would increase provincial inequality by a factor 4.90 (see Table 8), which is less than the rural-urban inequality increase (factor 6.28). *China's income inequality between provinces will be relatively modest when they fully reap their locational advantages under perfect competition.*

Contrary to Griffin *et al.* (1999), Table 6 reveals a negative relationship between income inequality and economic development. The figures in columns 3 and 4 of Table 7 indicate that income inequality between the social classes exceeds that between the rural and urban areas in all developed provinces, in six of the nine less developed provinces, and in four of the eleven least developed provinces. Rural-urban inequality and economic development are negatively-related, while rural-urban inequality correlates positively with overall inequality. Social inequality varies little with the level of development. Since under competition, the rural-urban divide would become relatively less important, this explains why the negative relationship between inequality and development would be dissolved. Inequality would be determined by differences in factor rewards that, at least for labor, would be independent of the province or the stage of development.

4. Conclusion

In this paper, we have presented an input–output model to reveal the potential of the Chinese economy, including the supporting shadow prices. The drawback of this approach is that a number of unrealistic assumptions have to be made. Commodities are classified in 30 categories, assuming perfect substitutability within categories and perfect complementarities between them, declaring each either perfectly tradable or not at all. A similar caveat applies to the classification of factor inputs. Trade with the rest of the world is not changed at all. Neither is technology. Subject to the limitations, the model indicates that perfect competition would restructure the Chinese economy severely along the following lines. If factor rewards would reflect provincial or national scarcities, the less skilled labor types would stand to lose and, therefore, inequality would mount. The flipside of this change is the potential for improvement of the average standard of living. Optimal specialization between provinces alone may add about 23% to the level of domestic final consumption in China. Skilled workers, managers and technicians would move from Western and Central China to Eastern China. These flows would be more than offset by a flow of unskilled labor from Eastern China to Central China. Our finding indicates that Eastern China accommodates too many unskilled workers, relative to the competitive benchmark, and thus suggests that the Harris-Todaro mechanism operates in China.

We have offered two three-way decompositions of Chinese income inequality in rural-urban, provincial, and social components, one pertaining to the observed data and the other to the income levels that would prevail under perfect competition. Competition would reduce the rural-urban divide (at least in relative terms) and dissolve the negative relationship between the level of development and income inequality. However, competition would skew factor rewards dramatically and thus create tension between the social classes. Compared to the competitive benchmark, Chinese policy is quite successful in checking inequality. As its economy is reorganized along competitive lines, skilled labor will prove scarce. It should be mentioned that this result is a consequence of our assumption of a fixed trade position and technology. Stimulating higher education and free world trade can alleviate the pressure.

References

Bacharach, M. (1970) *Biproportional Matrices and Input-Output Change* (Cambridge University Press).

Brooke, A. *et al.* (1998) GAMS: A User's Guide. GAMS Development Corporation. http://www.gams.com/docs/gams/GAMSUsersGuide.pdf.

Chu, Y. (1990) Research on income distribution among households during the period 1978–1988, *Planning Economic Research*, 3, pp. 14–24. (In Chinese).

Dept. of Agriculture, State Statistical Bureau of China (1993) *Rural Statistical Yearbook of China*, 1992 (China Statistical Publishing House, Beijing).

Dept. of Industry, State Statistical Bureau of China (1997) Data on the fixed capital and the fixed capital for production in 1992, unpublished.

Department of National Economic Accounting, State Statistical Bureau of China, (1996), *Input-output table of China*, 1992 (China Statistical Publishing House, Beijing).

Griffin, J., A.R. Keith and R.W. Zhao (1994) *The Distribution of Income in China* (China Social Science Press). (In Chinese)

Harris, J.R. and M.P. Todaro (1970) Migration, unemployment, and development: A two-sector analysis, *American Economic Review*, 60(2), pp. 126–142.

Li, C.M. (1990) On causes of recent difference in urban income, *Quantitative and Technical Economic Research*, 1, pp. 3–7. (In Chinese)

Luo, W.Z. (1989) An evaluation of current income distribution, *Consumption Economics*, 6, pp. 38–51. (In Chinese)

Negishi, T. (1960) Welfare economics and existence of an equilibrium for a competitive economy, *Metroeconomica*, 12, pp. 92–97.

Office of input-output survey, Provincial Statistical Bureaus (1995) Input-output Table by province, 1992, unpublished.

Office of input-output survey, State Statistical Bureau of China (1997) *Input-output Table of China, 1997* (China Statistical Publishing House).

Population Census Office of Provinces (1993) Tabulation on the 1990 population census by province, unpublished.

Population Census Office, China (1993) *Tabulation on the 1990 Population Census of China*, Vol. 2 (China Statistical Publishing House).

Shorrocks, A.F. (1980) The class of additively decomposable inequality measures, *Econometrica*, 48(3), pp. 613–625.

Shorrocks, A.F. (1988) Aggregation issues in inequality measurement, in W. Eichhorn (ed.), *Measurement in Economics* (Physica Verlag, Heidelberg).

State Statistical Bureau of China (1993) *China statistical yearbook, 1992* (China Statistical Publishing House, Beijing).

State Statistical Bureau of China (1994) *China Statistical Yearbook, 1993* (China Statistical Publishing House, Beijing).

State Statistical Bureau of China (1996) *China Statistical Yearbook, 1995* (China Statistical Publishing House, Beijing).

ten Raa, Th. and P. Mohnen (2001) The location of comparative advantages on the basis of fundamentals only, *Economics Systems Research*, 13(1), pp. 93–108.

ten Raa, Th. and P. Mohnen (2002) Neoclassical growth accounting and frontier analysis: A synthesis, *Journal of Productivity Analysis*, 18, pp. 11–128.
The Third National Industrial Census Office of China (1997) *The Data on the Third National Industrial Census of China in 1995, Volume of Regions* (China Statistical Publishing House, Beijing).
Theil, H. (1967) *Economics and Information Theory* (North-Holland).
Wang, C.Z. *et al.* (1995) *On Personal Income Distribution in China* (China Planning Press). (In Chinese)
Wei, H.K. (1992) On the situation of the income difference between regions in China, *Economic Research*, 4, pp. 61–65. (In Chinese)
Yang, W.M. (1992) Quantitative analysis on the income difference between regions, *Economic Research*, 4, pp. 70–74. (In Chinese)
Yang, Y.C. and Q.D. Shao (1989) Case analysis on urban household income, *Nankai Economic Research*, 6, pp. 14–17. (In Chinese)
Zhang, P. (1997) *Income Distribution During the Transition in China* (memo, Tilburg University, Tilburg, the Netherlands).
Zhao, R.W. (1992) Some special problems during economic transition in China, *Economic Research*, 3, pp. 53–63. (In Chinese)
Zhong, J.R. (1989) Quantitative analysis on the structure of household income distribution in China, *China's Economic Issues*, 2, pp. 7–14. (In Chinese)
Zhu, X.D. and J.M. Wen (1990) Study on the difference in farmer's income, *Statistical Research*, 4, pp. 48–53. (In Chinese)

Appendix 1. The General Equilibrium Model

We maximize scalar D, the overall value of national final uses, the sum of the values of final uses in all sectors and all provinces. The variables exogenous to the linear program are:

A^i a square matrix of intermediate input coefficients, 30 by 30, of province i
f^i a 30-dimensional column vector of the proportions of province i's final uses
e^i a 30-dimensional column vector of province i's net foreign exports
d^i the share of province i's overall final uses in domestic final uses.

The provincial shares d^i will be endogenized after the presentation of the linear program. At this stage, the endogenous variables are:

x^i a column vector of province i's 30 outputs (nonnegative)
D a scalar of overall domestic final uses.

The first constraints are the material balances:

$$\sum (I - A^i)x^i \geq \sum f^i d^i D + \sum e^i.$$

Notice that the material balances are pooled across provinces, meaning that the commodities are assumed to be tradable. There are a few exceptions. The commodities listed at the bottom of Table 3 in italics are *non-tradable*. For these components, the inequality must hold for each term *i separately*. The labor constraints have been described in Section 3. In addition, there are 27 capital constraints, presuming that capital is province-specific, but mobile between sectors:

$$\sum K^i x^i \leq M^i,$$

where K^i is a 30-dimensional row vector of fixed capital coefficients for province i and M^i is the stock of fixed capital in province i.

For each vector of provincial shares of domestic final demand, d, the linear program determines an optimal allocation of gross outputs and shadow prices. Denoting p as the shadow prices of commodities, the overall value of the net exports to the rest of China is for each province:

$$S^i(d) = p[(I - A^i)x^i - f^i d^i D - e^i], \quad i = 1, \ldots, 27.$$

Compare this to the observed balance of payments,

$$S_0^i(d) = (1 \ldots 1)[(I - A^i)x_0^i - f^i d_0^i D_0 - e^i], \quad i = 1, \ldots, 27.$$

The equilibrium provincial shares will be determined by the condition that the two expressions match. The combination of the linear program and the non-linear budget constraints constitutes the general equilibrium model. We solve the model by the method of the Mixed Complementarity Problem (MCP), which combines the linear programming with the Newton algorithm; see Brooke *et al.* (1998). MCP solves the model effectively if a solution to the model exists *and* the initial values are selected near the solution.

Appendix 2. The Input–Output Data

National and Provincial Input–Output Tables

Most Chinese provinces have produced square input–output tables in three versions, with 6, 33, and 118 commodities. We consolidate the 33 sectors table into one with 30 sectors by aggregating maintenance, repair and other industries, commerce and restaurants, and freight and passenger transports. The tables provide intermediate inputs, value added, domestic final use, some interprovincial and international trade, and gross outputs. To pinpoint the provincial final consumption vectors, we must determine their exports to not only the rest of the world, but also to the rest of China.

Now 12 provinces provide separate information on interprovincial and international trade. Their exports to the rest of China sum to 829,782 million Yuan, their imports to 898,960 million Yuan, hence their domestic net exports amount to −69,178 million Yuan. Net domestic exports in the 15 provinces without separate information on interprovincial and international trade must therefore be 69,178 million Yuan. We assume that the ratio of overall exports (829,782 million Yuan) to gross output (3,766,102 million Yuan) in the 12 provinces, which is 0.22, equals the ratio of overall import (58,596 million Yuan) to gross output (2,663,441 million Yuan) in the 15 provinces. Then overall import from the rest of China in the 15 provinces is 585,957 million Yuan (and the overall export is $585{,}957 + 69{,}178 = 655{,}135$ million Yuan). The overall export is allocated to the 30 sectors by their shares of net exports. The material balances then determine the imports from the rest of China.

The trade data need to be further separated in the 15 provinces. We calculate their shares in exports to the rest of China or the world and assume that these match the shares of exports to the rest of China. This procedure disaggregates exports to the rest of China by origin. The same procedure is applied to the imports from the rest of China.

Domestic trade in the 15 provinces is disaggregated by sector by means of the RAS method.[11] For 15 provinces, the exports are not

[11] For the RAS method, see Bacharach (1970).

separated between domestic and foreign. The provincial budget constraint (see Appendix 1) requires separation though. For this purpose, we have constructed a commodity by province table. Column 28, which is the sum of columns 1–27, shows the overall exports at the sectoral level, whereas row 31, which is the sum of rows 1–30, indicates the overall exports at the provincial level. Columns 1–28 and rows 1–31 are the original data, while column 29 and row 32 are the data estimated above. The former are the overall exports to the rest of China at the sectoral level; the latter are the overall exports to the rest of China at the provincial level. The data in columns 1–27 and rows 1–30 need to be adjusted such that the sum of columns 1–27 equals column 29, and the sum of rows 1–30 equals row 32 by the RAS method. The same procedure is also applied to the import from the rest of China. Once the exports to and the imports from the rest of China are separated, the exports to and the imports from the rest of the world can be obtained by extracting the exports to and the imports from the rest of China from the total mixture of exports and imports.

Capital Stocks

The State Statistical Bureau has made available to us the unpublished data on capital stocks in the year 1992 for 40 industrial sectors by province. We aggregate these data into 23 industrial sectors according to the sector classifications in the input–output table. The data for non-industrial sectors are estimated from the information on investment in the China Statistical Yearbook (1993).[12] Here, the classification is as follows: (1) agriculture, (2) industry, (3) geological prospecting, (4) construction, (5) transportation and telecommunications, (6) commerce, food services and storage, (7) real estate and public services, (8) health care, sports and social welfare, (9) education and culture, (10) scientific research, (11) banking and insurance, (12) administration, (13) others. Sectors (3)–(13) are simply aggregated into seven non-industrial sectors. We calculate the proportions of the investment

[12] See Tables 5–23 "Investment in Capital Construction by Sector of National Economy and Province in 1992" and 5–43 "Investment in Technical Updating and Transformation by Sector of National Economy and Province in 1992."

in industry to the investment in these non-industrial sectors and use these for the proportions of capital stocks. This determines the capital stocks in the non-industrial sectors. The data on the capital stocks in the agricultural sectors are obtained in a different way. The Rural Statistical Yearbook of China in 1993 provides data on the number of rural households by province and on the capital stocks per rural household.[13] The two sources are combined to derive the capital stocks in the agricultural sector by province.

Employment and Labor Resources

Information on employment and labor resources is obtained from the provincial *Population Census in 1990*. The original data in each province for employment and labor are broken down into 55 sectors and eight types of occupation; we aggregate them into 30 sectors and four types of occupations.

Appendix 3. Data on Population and Personal Income

The population data in terms of the eight social classes (unskilled worker, skilled worker, manager, technician, self-employed, capitalist, retiree and dependant), the rural and urban areas, and the provinces, are directly available from the China Population Census (1990), except for the number of capitalists and self-employed. The data for the labor classes (unskilled, skilled, manager and technician) are obtained from the China Population Census Vol. 2 (1990),[14] where there are eight occupations: technician, manager, staff, business, servant, farmer, worker and others. We aggregate staff, business and worker into the skilled class, and aggregate servant, farmer and others into the unskilled class. The data on retirees are available

[13]See Tables 4–3 "Rural Households and Population by Province in 1992" for the data on the number of rural households by province, and Tables 3–24 "Original Value of Fixed Assets for Production Per Rural Household by Province" for the information on capital stocks per rural household.

[14]Tables 6–15 "City Working Persons by Two Digits Classification of Occupation and Province", Tables 6–16 "Town Working Persons by Two Digits Classification of Occupation and Province", and Tables 6–17 "County Working Persons by Two Digits Classification of Occupation and Province" in the China Population Census Vol. 2 (1990). Among the three, the first two are for urban data, and the third is for rural data.

from the other three tables in the China Population Census Vol. 2 (1990).[15] The first two pertain to urban data and the third to rural data. The data on family-income dependants is obtained by subtracting the number of workers and retirees from the total population. Because the population census data are in the year 1990, they are updated to 1992 using the 1992 population figures from the Statistical Yearbook of China (1993).[16] The data on the number of capitalists and self-employed are collected separately from the China Labor Statistical Yearbook (1993).[17] Instead of presenting the data on capitalist and self-employed directly, the China Population Census (1990) has them included in the labor categories. Therefore, to make the data consistent, a number of workers corresponding to the number of capitalists and self-employed are subtracted from the labor categories. Neither the China Population Census (1990) nor the China Labor Statistical Yearbook (1993) provides information on the occupation of capitalists and the self-employed. It remains unclear how many of the capitalists and self-employed are either technicians, managers, skilled or unskilled. We simply assume that all the capitalists and self-employed come from the skilled class. The final data are presented in Appendix 4.

The first step to construct income data is the collection of data on urban wages. Normally, this wage includes two parts: the money wage and the social insurance and welfare funds. The China Labor Statistical Yearbook (1993) provides data on money wage by province and the data on the social insurance and welfare funds of staff and workers.[18] The urban

[15]Tables 6–28 "City Non-working Persons by Province", Tables 6–29 "Town Non-working Persons by Province", and Tables 6–30 "County Non-working Persons by Province" in the China Population Census Vol. 2 (1990).

[16]Tables 3–3 "Total Population, Birth Rate, Death Rate, and Natural Growth Rate of Population by Province, 1992" in the Statistical Yearbook of China (1993).

[17]Tables 6–3 "Urban Employment in Private Enterprises and Individual Households by Province" and Tables 6–4 "Rural Employment in Private Enterprises and Individual Households by Province" in the China Labor Statistical Yearbook (1993).

[18]In the China Labor Statistical Yearbook (1993), see Tables 1–65 "Number and Total Wage Bill of Staff and Workers by Province." The social insurance and welfare funds are presented in four other separate tables, Tables 9–20 "Composition of Total Social Insurance and Welfare Funds of Staff and Workers in State-owned Units by Province", Tables 9–31 "Composition of Total Social Insurance and Welfare Funds of Staff and Workers in Urban Collectively-owned Units by Province", Tables 9–34 "Composition of Total Social Insurance and Welfare Funds of Staff and Workers in Units of Other Ownership by Province", and Tables 9–36 "Composition of Total Social Insurance and Welfare Funds of Staff and Workers in Foreign Funded Enterprises by Province". The average of these tables is the total social insurance and welfare funds of staff and workers by province.

wages must be further separated by occupation, as Chinese information authorities usually collect the wage data by sector rather than occupation. A special survey in the Yearbook of Labor Statistics of China (1993) provides a section regarding occupational wages. According to this source, the skilled wage matches the average wage, the unskilled wage amounts 0.584 of the average wage, the manager's wage 1.035 of the average wage, and the technician's wage 1.052 times of the average wage.[19] Applying these ratios to all provinces, we can disaggregate the provincial urban wage data by occupation.

Most studies estimate that capitalist income could be ten-fold the wage of a skilled worker, and self-employed income four-fold.[20] In this research, we borrow the two ratios to determine capitalist and self-employed incomes in the urban areas.

The data on retired income in urban areas are directly available from the Yearbook of Labor Statistics of China (1993).[21]

Spreading income uniformly within families and using a constant ratio of dependants to primary income earners, we obtain dependants' income by dividing the average of the primary income earners' incomes over the dependency ratio.[22] The primary income earners have the same net income left (after sharing their primary income with the family).

---

[19] In the Yearbook of Labor Statistics of China (1993), Tables 7–13 "Increase Rate of Wages of 14 Cities' and Counties' Staff and Workers" gives the average wages by occupation in October, 1992 as follows: unskilled 150.62 Yuan, skilled 257.87 Yuan, technician 271.22 Yuan, and manager 266.87 Yuan. In other words, the technician's wage is 1.016 over the manager's wage, 1.052 over the skilled, and 1.8 over the unskilled. Since the average of the wages is 257.89 Yuan, it can be seen that the unskilled worker's wage equals 0.584 of the average, the skilled worker's wage equals the average, the manager's wage equals 1.035 of the average, and the technician's wage equals 1.052 of the average.

[20] See Zhong (1989), Yang and Shao (1989), Chu (1990), Li (1990), Luo (1989), and Zhao (1992).

[21] In the Yearbook of Labor Statistics of China (1993), there are four tables used: Tables 9–25 Composition of Total Social Insurance and Welfare Funds of Staff and Workers under Termination, Retirement and Resignation in State-owned Units by Province", Tables 9–32 "Composition of Total Social Insurance and Welfare Funds of Staff and Workers under Termination, Retirement and Resignation in Urban Collectively owned Units by Province", Tables 9–35 "Composition of Total Social Insurance and Welfare Funds of Staff and Workers under Termination, Retirement and Resignation in Units of Other Ownership by Province", and Tables 9–37 "Composition of Total Social Insurance and Welfare Funds of Staff and Workers under Termination, Retirement and Resignation in Foreign Funded Enterprises by Province". The weighted averages of the incomes in these tables are calculated to get the retired income in urban areas.

[22] We assume that retirees cannot afford dependants.

The Yearbook of Survey on Rural Households (1992) includes data on national rural households' income by education in the year 1991. We define the occupations of rural labor by education as follows: those with educational years fewer than six belong to the unskilled, those with 7–12 years belong to the skilled, and those having over 12 years belong to the manager and the technician. In this way, rural labor's income can be split by occupation, even though the data are national macro data rather than provincial data. The survey breaks down labor by education, but not in terms of income.[23] However, the survey has data on household income by labor education.[24] Using this information as a proxy for labor income by education, it can be derived that in rural areas the technicians' and managers' incomes are the same, namely 1.37 times the average, 1.34 times the skilled, and 1.59 times the unskilled labor wage.[25] (This estimate is consistent with the common recognition that in rural areas technicians and managers earn a high income, common to both, and that skilled and unskilled labor wages are low, also at a common level. Technicians and managers are paid urban wages, while the unskilled and skilled workers are residual claimants.) By applying these ratios to the provinces, we break down rural income by occupation or skill, as well as by province.

We estimate the income of rural capitalists and self-employed by assuming that rural capitalists and rural self-employed earn ten respectively four times the rural skilled wage, as we did for the urban incomes. Rural retirees receive the same income as urban retirees. The rural dependant income equals to the rural households' mean income, which is directly available from the China Statistical Yearbook (1993).[26] The final data are presented in Appendix 5.

---

[23]Tables 3–2 "Rural Labors' Quality by province" in the survey.

[24]Tables 2–5 "The Main Indicators of Rural Households by Labor's Education" in the survey.

[25]As a result, unskilled income is 611.67 Yuan, skilled 725.83 Yuan, and Manager's and Technician's 971.56 Yuan. The average income of rural households, moreover, is 708.55 Yuan in 1991. Assuming that technician and manager's incomes are equal, their income is 1.37 times more than the average, 1.34 times more than the skilled, and 1.59 more than the unskilled. The skilled income is 1.19 times more than the unskilled.

[26]Tables 8–23 "Net Income of Peasant Household Per Capita by Province" in China Statistical Yearbook (1993).

Appendix 4. 1992 Population in China[27]

Eastern	BJ	TJ	HB	LN	SH	JS	ZJ	FJ	SD	GD
Rural unskilled	866858	1107746	25642777	9326260	1053773	24566410	11576084	9612977	34129906	17959349
Rural skilled	407383	222743	42559	845708	1575239	6859832	3667196	1524030	52544	2010768
Rural manager	50628	26029	147691	130956	78436	574097	148838	80137	225585	129161
Rural technician	84921	53553	565004	376870	164136	998949	398194	363176	835486	412357
Rural self-employed	160865	95743	1653653	439673	104140	1101917	1456627	400015	2373151	1173421
Rural capitalist	599	6649	14784	6364	4389	6507	16911	7085	13390	27492
Rural retiree	33114	17375	273196	167245	148256	483125	178704	140144	341026	281656
Rural dependant	1323908	1270754	22353882	8333590	1410663	19620942	11713375	12378061	24584733	19272202
Rural population	2928276	2800592	50693546	19626666	4539032	54211779	29155929	24505625	62555821	41266406
Urban unskilled	823183	720507	1973178	2645268	584655	1927493	2503955	947115	6645257	4256586
Urban skilled	2460982	2156565	3419409	6220334	3298110	4975721	3870447	1654209	5251203	6199681
Urban manager	376242	191158	358758	696926	282544	636791	262927	130018	457677	471232
Urban technician	976299	594502	1024697	1597977	887702	1275515	915195	492557	1502633	1474986
Urban self-employed	117804	46516	183928	472894	79090	210288	283895	242530	296721	763701
Urban capitalist	15360	9342	6093	19782	11601	16385	17086	54533	16080	73095
Urban retiree	724366	510376	542809	1592882	1350286	1110513	655528	329770	731107	1049934
Urban dependant	2597535	2170440	4548201	7288136	2416981	4745513	4695051	2803633	8643502	9692481
Urban population	8091771	6399406	12057073	20534199	8910969	14898219	13204084	6654365	23544180	23981696
Dependency ratio	0.473	0.513	0.606	0.55	0.372	0.467	0.552	0.728	0.58	0.678
Total population	11020047	9199998	62750619	40160865	13450001	69109998	42360013	31159990	86100001	65248102

(Continued)

[27] See Table 6 for province codes.

(Continued)

Central	SX	NM	JL	HLJ	AH	JX	Hen	Hub	Hun
Rural unskilled	9270061	6707771	6975122	8178501	26467638	14856940	41049622	21130853	26863862
Rural skilled	557680	275091	320164	511357	914910	956758	1025825	902474	1195240
Rural manager	93304	61229	58740	108726	159854	112621	254606	151391	154599
Rural technician	338984	240144	241584	351239	547337	445507	993937	528277	602401
Rural self-employed	587676	193310	162505	152295	773824	590272	901166	654851	782226
Rural capitalist	11717	1662	1004	380	3019	3256	8231	1387	5846
Rural retiree	144714	60748	57175	165499	194696	202132	320295	168436	335698
Rural dependant	10197038	6510231	6803037	9307183	18869465	13998329	30558240	16221241	21429096
Rural population	21201174	14050186	14619331	18775180	47930743	31165815	75111922	39758910	51368968
Urban unskilled	1084208	1024358	1100966	1975755	1750715	1271044	2401093	2897862	2024164
Urban skilled	2376805	1954824	2854180	4361251	2680352	1875904	3497060	4361328	2801376
Urban manager	278229	201952	295529	524770	283010	193682	417715	438279	323793
Urban technician	729725	617411	858205	1240598	758248	592710	1074305	1288475	926929
Urban self-employed	154958	230212	336786	464219	409499	312093	368858	279548	367627
Urban capitalist	4615	4117	4778	9230	3326	3754	3943	4995	6902
Urban retiree	324393	346321	616772	982098	494470	384179	566840	785556	620861
Urban dependant	3635792	3640621	4633456	7746814	4029636	3330819	5168228	5985025	4229392
Urban population	8588725	8019816	10700672	17304735	10409256	7964185	13498042	16041068	11301044
Dependency ratio	0.734	0.831	0.764	0.811	0.632	0.719	0.62	0.595	0.598
Total population	29789899	22070002	25320003	36079915	58339999	39130000	88609964	55799978	62670012

(Continued)

(Continued)

Western	GX	HN	SC	GZ	YN	TB	Six	GS	QH	NX	XJ
Rural unskilled	19173645	2314405	53560310	14653369	17370544	894046	13474257	10219588	1651373	1719946	4781473
Rural skilled	147022	203049	1116132	160545	354377	43601	344610	59693	100307	29967	221014
Rural manager	90158	16845	172154	51317	84298	12863	74904	54628	14611	12556	48400
Rural technician	397080	78775	925725	237399	376764	49155	345036	198365	79054	48059	195241
Rural self-employed	545070	66887	1374038	196583	397675	14862	407374	264199	28951	48185	174221
Rural capitalist	3660	894	7410	4186	1394	1	4333	2280	361	469	1479
Rural retiree	121342	108280	543396	73417	162615	8249	124473	37435	13518	11665	125893
Rural dependant	16810368	2428165	30286707	11766952	13859138	994629	11942893	7213054	1515380	1732716	5123878
Rural population	37288345	5217300	87985872	27143768	32606805	2017406	26717880	18049242	3403555	3603563	10671599
Urban unskilled	889196	256836	5394754	1495736	1145500	33059	1023015	908238	112351	138315	538664
Urban skilled	1485203	282638	5281343	1142853	1309144	43655	1946758	1248429	323520	333784	1156415
Urban manager	191802	37609	426881	130045	132736	8748	233267	149210	37075	38742	145341
Urban technician	524734	125216	1702855	427361	499168	25424	708435	413525	106240	121541	431536
Urban self-employed	313935	91127	483389	186253	142059	25863	179326	105429	40952	27034	185482
Urban capitalist	8002	14529	7721	4664	1331	16	3030	2844	563	1376	2900
Urban retiree	325262	62107	1385758	257950	306219	10706	387123	194864	53891	56073	328993
Urban dependant	2773536	772638	7311433	2821369	2176994	115124	2851035	2068218	531853	549764	2349076
Urban population	6511670	1642700	21994134	6466231	5713151	262595	7331989	5090757	1206445	1266629	5138407
Dependency ratio	0.742	0.882	0.498	0.774	0.616	0.781	0.636	0.684	0.788	0.767	0.842
Total population	43800015	6860000	10998000	33609999	38319956	2280001	34049869	23139999	4610000	4870192	15810006

Fig. A-1: Location of Chinese provinces.

Note: The map is from *http://www.chinatour.com/map/a.htm.* Inner Mongolia is Neimeng. We have delineated the three regions of Eastern, Central and Western China. (They meet at the three-province point of Guangdong, Hunan and Guangxi.)

Appendix 5. 1992 Income in China[28]

Eastern	BJ	TJ	HB	LN	SH	JS	ZJ	FJ	SD	GD
Rural unskilled	1352	1126	587	856	1914	912	1169	846	691	1125
Rural skilled	1610	1340	698	1019	2279	1086	1392	1008	822	1339
Rural manager	2154	1793	934	1363	3050	1454	1862	1348	1100	1792
Rural technician	2154	1793	934	1363	3050	1454	1862	1348	1100	1792
Rural self-employed	6439	5362	2793	4076	9118	4346	5566	4030	3289	5358
Rural capitalist	16097	13404	6984	10189	22794	10865	13916	10076	8223	13394
Rural retiree	3128	2816	2878	2675	3416	2662	2858	2403	2635	3105
Rural dependant	1572	1309	682	995	2226	1061	1359	984	803	1308
Rural mean	1827	1429	720	1026	2433	1090	1524	998	853	1372
Urban unskilled	1562	1125	1039	1071	2071	1290	801	1029	672	1084
Urban skilled	2675	1927	1778	1834	3545	2208	1372	1762	1151	1856
Urban manager	2769	1994	1840	1898	3669	2285	1420	1824	1191	1921
Urban technician	2814	2027	1870	1930	3729	2323	1443	1854	1211	1953
Urban self-employed	10729	7716	7115	7320	14174	8830	5494	7032	4598	7418
Urban capitalist	26822	19289	17787	18299	35434	22074	13735	17580	11496	18546
Urban retiree	3128	2816	2878	2675	3416	2662	2858	2403	2635	3105
Urban dependant	2464	1776	1545	1618	3369	1993	1166	1502	916	1562
Urban mean	2719	1935	1718	1876	3539	2183	1375	1910	1031	1890
Overall mean	2482	1781	912	1461	3166	1326	1477	1193	901	1562
Central	**SX**	**NM**	**JL**	**HLJ**	**AH**	**JX**	**Hen**	**Hub**	**Hun**	
Rural unskilled	539	578	694	816	494	660	506	583	636	
Rural skilled	642	688	826	972	588	786	602	694	757	
Rural manager	859	921	1106	1300	786	1052	806	929	1012	
Rural technician	859	921	1106	1300	786	1052	806	929	1012	
Rural self-employed	2568	2753	3305	3887	2351	3146	2408	2777	3027	
Rural capitalist	6420	6881	8264	9718	5878	7864	6021	6943	7567	
Rural retiree	2602	2403	2399	2462	2290	2130	2439	2179	2391	
Rural dependant	627	672	807	949	574	768	588	678	739	
Rural mean	664	670	794	938	569	777	577	673	736	
Urban unskilled	964	814	863	851	838	825	922	787	990	
Urban skilled	1651	1394	1478	1457	1434	1413	1578	1348	1696	
Urban manager	1709	1443	1529	1508	1484	1462	1633	1395	1756	
Urban technician	1737	1466	1555	1532	1509	1486	1660	1418	1784	
Urban self-employed	6585	5564	5908	5822	5738	5664	6316	5388	6786	
Urban capitalist	16463	13910	14770	14556	14346	14161	15789	13470	16965	
Urban retiree	2602	2403	2399	2462	2290	2130	2439	2179	2391	
Urban dependant	1466	1195	1288	1260	1178	1157	1322	1150	1410	
Urban mean	1628	1406	1538	1488	1456	1426	1541	1295	1685	
Overall mean	942	937	1109	1201	727	909	724	852	907	

(*Continued*)

[28]See Table 6 for province codes.

(*Continued*)

Western	GX	HN	SC	GZ	YN	TB	Six	GS	QH	NX	XJ
Rural unskilled	630	725	545	435	531	714	481	421	519	508	636
Rural skilled	750	863	649	518	633	850	572	501	617	605	758
Rural manager	1003	1155	869	693	847	1137	766	670	826	810	1014
Rural technician	1003	1155	869	693	847	1137	766	670	826	810	1014
Rural self-employed	2998	3453	2597	2073	2531	3400	2290	2003	2470	2421	3031
Rural capitalist	7496	8632	6492	5181	6328	8499	5724	5007	6175	6052	7578
Rural retiree	2519	2279	2300	2394	2825	3956	2422	2905	3533	2741	2760
Rural dependant	732	843	634	506	618	830	559	489	603	591	740
Rural mean	723	862	624	487	610	820	559	481	597	587	762
Urban unskilled	1038	1382	821	642	1091	1734	972	1026	1301	1143	1253
Urban skilled	1778	2367	1405	1100	1868	2969	1663	1756	2228	1957	2145
Urban manager	1840	2450	1455	1139	1934	3072	1721	1818	2305	2026	2220
Urban technician	1870	2490	1478	1157	1965	3123	1750	1848	2343	2059	2256
Urban self-employed	7130	9467	5624	4403	7482	11894	6641	7033	8885	7831	8550
Urban capitalist	17825	23667	14060	11008	18704	29735	16604	17583	22213	19578	21375
Urban retiree	2519	2279	2300	2394	2825	3956	2422	2905	3533	2741	2760
Urban dependant	1460	2042	1135	861	1536	2159	1445	1488	1957	1756	1830
Urban mean	1866	2650	1332	1048	1791	3398	1660	1688	2328	1972	2200
Overall mean	893	1290	766	595	786	1117	796	746	1050	947	1230

Appendix 6. Transforming Competitive Functional Into Personal Incomes

Let IK_s^j denote capital income, where $j = 1, \ldots, 27$ represent provinces and $s = 1, \ldots, 30$ sectors. Let K and γ denote employed capital and rental rates. Capital income in the agricultural sector is

$$IK_a^j = K_1^j \gamma_1^j.$$

Capital income in the sectors of industry, construction, transports and communications, and commerce is

$$IK_b^j = \sum_{s=2}^{26} K_s^j \gamma_s^j.$$

Capital income in the sectors of public service, culture and education, finance and insurance, and administration is

$$IK_c^j = \sum_{s=27}^{30} K_s^j \gamma_s^j.$$

The model determines directly the unskilled wage rate and the wage premiums for the technicians, the managers, and the skilled.

In the agricultural sector, all capital belongs to farmers, who, however, are not capitalists. The rural capitalists hold their capital in sectors such as industry, commerce and construction. Capital income in the agricultural sector is distributed to all farmers who hold own capital, whereas the rural capitalists receive rent in non-agricultural sectors.

State and private capital exist mainly in the sectors of industry, commerce, and construction. Using the data on capital ownership in industrial sectors by province from The Third National Industrial Census of China in 1995, we calculate the proportions of private capital in total capital, and apply them to the data in 1992 to get the amounts of private capital in industrial sectors for 1992. Since the data on capital ownership in commerce and construction sectors are unavailable, we assume that the private share of total capital is the same as in the industrial sector. Public service, education and culture, finance and banking, and administration are dominated by state capital. We assume that the government collects all capital income in these sectors.

Not many people own capital, let alone rely on it for income. We simply assume that all private capital income accrues to the people who own significant amounts of capital, the capitalists. The capitalists' income is separated from total capital income, which includes both government and private capital incomes, according to the private/total capital ratio. The final step is to put $I^j = \alpha^j IK_b^j/N^j$ where α is the share of private capital income in total capital income, I the capitalists' average income, and N the number of capitalists, all indexed by province, j.

Chapter 25

Bilateral Trade between India and Bangladesh: A General Equilibrium Approach

Chandrima Sikdar, Thijs ten Raa, Pierre Mohnen and Debesh Chakraborty

Abstract: India and Bangladesh pursued policies of trade liberalization since the early 1990s. However, due to the differential speeds of opening up, Bangladesh's bilateral trade deficit with India widened substantially over the years. This aggravated the economic and the political tensions between the economies. It has been held that the promotion of free trade between the two economies may enhance trade and hence economic cooperation between them. Against this backdrop, the present chapter proposes a theoretical framework which provides a general equilibrium determination of the commodity pattern of trade and hence locates the comparative advantages of the economies. The empirical implementation of the model considers trade in 25 sectors comparable in the input–output tables of the economies. The study isolates the gains from free trade accruing to either economy. The chapter also explores the pattern of bilateral trade when each

An earlier version of the chapter has been presented at the Fifteenth International Input–Output Conference held at the Renmin University in Beijing, China, June 27-July 1, 2005.

economy produces goods by utilizing their own, as well as the other country's technology. The gains from this trading arrangement are also isolated.

Keywords: General equilibrium; comparative advantage; free trade; India–Bangladesh.

1. Introduction

Way back in 1947, Jawaharlal Nehru (Parthasarathi 1990) envisioned the great many advantages of political and economic cooperation among the countries of Asia. This spirit of Asian cooperation on a continental scale manifested in the functioning of the Association of South East Asian Nations (ASEAN) since 1967 and in the emergence of the South Asian Association for Regional Cooperation (SAARC) comprising the seven countries-Bangladesh, Bhutan, India, Maldives, Nepal, Pakistan, and Sri Lanka since 1985 as regional groupings of cooperation.

The most obvious measure of cooperation between the member states of any regional grouping is the level of trade taking place. Unfortunately however, the performance of the SAARC members on the trade front could hardly be termed as moderate when benchmarked with many other countries in Asia. In particular, the SAARC states were plagued with trade imbalances among themselves. This urged the member states to undertake a concrete step when a study on SAARC Trade, Manufactures and Services was commissioned at the Islamabad summit in 1998. An Inter-Governmental Group set up by the Colombo summit in 1991 to formulate and seek agreement on an institutional framework for trade liberalization among the members, finalized a draft agreement on SAARC Preferential Trading Agreement (SAPTA). Finally, the agreement on SAPTA was signed at the Dhaka summit in 1993. Thereafter, in December 1995, being ratified by the member states, it came into force with an attempt to integrate and strengthen the regional trade links in South Asia. The agreement on SAPTA aimed at track expansion among the members through exchanging concessions relating to tariffs, para-tariffs, nontariff measures and direct trade measures.

However, the ultimate aim of this region has not been to stop at preferential trading arrangements, but rather to take SAPTA towards a new vision of free flowing trade in the region under the arrangement of South Asian Free Trade Area (SAFTA). Accordingly, at the end of the 12th SAARC summit in

Islamabad, Pakistan, on January 6, 2004, the foreign ministers of the seven member states signed a framework pact on the Free Trade Area in the region, paving the way for the regional integration of the economies. As per the declarations of this summit, the South Asian Free Trade Area (SAFTA) treaty, which would come into force on January 1, 2006 would be fully implemented by December 31, 2015 (Poudel 2004). Accordingly, on January 1st, 2006, SAFTA came into force with the aim of reducing tariffs existing in the intraregional trade among the member countries of the SAARC. In particular, it has been laid down that the developing countries of the region — India and Pakistan — are to complete the implementation of the same by 2012, Sri Lanka by 2013 and the rest of the Least Developed Countries (LDCs) — Nepal, Bhutan, Bangladesh and Maldives — have to implement SAFTA by 2015. This emphasis given to free trade in the SAARC agenda led to several attempts to foster growth of bilateral trade between the two member countries of SAARC, namely, India and Bangladesh.

India and Bangladesh offer natural markets for each other's export products. In their mutual trade, they enjoy the advantages of reduced transaction costs and quicker delivery due to geographical proximity, common language and a heritage of common physical infrastructures. That is why soon after the launching of liberalization in Bangladesh in 1982, India's comparative advantage in the Bangladesh market started asserting itself and Indian exports registered unprecedented growth. The rate of growth of these bilateral exports of India to Bangladesh reached new dimensions, particularly since 1992–93. The total export of India to Bangladesh during 1985 was US$105.19 million. By 1990, it was US$305.07 million and very recently in 2004, this figure stood at US$1593.54 million. Thus, during the last two decades, India's exports to Bangladesh have gone up by more than 15 times. India tops the list of exporters to Bangladesh. India's share in the total import of Bangladesh was 3.6% in 1980, which rose to 9.37% in 1995 and in 2004 to 18.5%. On the other hand, Bangladesh's exports to India have also increased, but not at a commensurate rate. The total import of India from Bangladesh in 1985 was US$12.91 million. After a crest and fall, the import in 1995 was US$85.86 million and by 2004, this stood at US$58.76 million. For the last decade, India's share of imports from Bangladesh in its total imports remained less than 1%. Consequently, the trade gap between Bangladesh and India was staggering. In 1980, the gap was US$88 million, which increased to US$860.87 million in 2000 and by

2004, it stood at US$1534.78 million. In this span of 24 years, the rate of increase of Bangladesh's trade gap with India was enormous. India's share in the total trade gap of Bangladesh increased to as much as 55.7% in the year 2004 starting from a very small share of 4.84% in 1980.

Throughout the last one and a half decades, both India and Bangladesh have liberalized and opened up to global competition, yet both did so with differential speeds. Bangladesh in its own wisdom, and under the terms of the structural adjustment program (launched with the assistance of the International Monetary Fund and the World Bank and supported by other donors of the bilateral aid), very promptly and rapidly lowered its tariff and nontariff barriers, and moved much faster towards private-sector-led and market-driven economic policy reforms compared to India. This difference in economic policy regime of the two countries has enabled India to gain greater access to the markets of Bangladesh for its exports since the mid 1990s. This explains why Indian exports to Bangladesh for these years have grown at a rate of over 30% per annum, while the exporters from Bangladesh who sent their products to the Indian markets had to remain content with comparatively modest gains. As a consequence, Bangladesh's bilateral trade deficit with India widened substantially during the last 15 years.

Moreover, the existing bilateral trade pattern was such that it kept exports from Bangladesh at a much lower level, especially in the case of a few consumer goods such as shoes and other leather products, ready-made garments, textiles etc. This is explained by the prevalence of the relatively higher tariff and non-tariff barriers applicable to the import of consumer goods into India under its global trade policy. This has inevitably led to the ballooning of the official trade deficit of Bangladesh with India over the past few years (US$92.28 million in 1985 to US$1534.78 million in 2004). This growing bilateral trade deficit of Bangladesh has created and aggravated the economic and the political tensions between the economies.

Thus, in recent years, issues concerning India–Bangladesh bilateral trade have come to occupy an increasingly important place in the discourse on the evolving nature of economic relationship between these two neighbouring countries. Against this backdrop, it has been held by many at various levels of policymaking, in both a countries, that promotion of free trade between the two economies is imperative as this will go a long way in enhancing trade and hence economic cooperation between the two countries.

In recent times, contemporary researchers have shown considerable interest in promoting free trade in the world, including the SAARC region and also free bilateral trade among the SAARC's members. This concern has seen the development of a substantial volume of literature on this topic in recent years. However, very little work has been done regarding the bilateral trade relations between the two neighboring countries of India and Bangladesh. This chapter aims to provide a theoretical and empirical analysis of this bilateral trade between the two countries. For research that led to significant contributions in this area, see Sen (1972), Rahman (1997, 2000), Mukherjee (2000), Pohit and Taneja (2000), Pramanik (2000), Roy and Chakraborty (2000), Eusufzai (2001), Sobhan (2002) and Waheeduzzaman (2002).

Although these works relate to the promotion of bilateral trade between India and Bangladesh, none of them are based on theoretical model building that help to analyze the prospects and possibilities of trade between the two countries. Although such theoretical exercises have been attempted for few countries of the world, there does not exist one in the context of India and Bangladesh, to the best of the knowledge of the present researchers. In this context, a mention may be made of a preliminary work by Roy and Chakraborty (2000).

Roy and Chakraborty (2000) locate the comparative advantages of India vis-à-vis Bangladesh. In their chapter, they have developed three linear programming models, which maximize foreign earnings of India and Bangladesh at given world prices subject to material balance and factor endowments of the economies. This is in the same line of thought as ten Raa and Chakraborty's (1991). But although Roy *et al.* have made some humble attempts, yet a more comprehensive approach towards the analysis of the possibilities of bilateral trade between India and Bangladesh is still lacking. The present work aims at filling this gap by contributing to this area.

This chapter is organized as follows. The next section introduces the theoretical framework that describes the pattern of trade in a perfectly competitive world characterized by free bilateral trade. The third section states the data required for the empirical implementation of the theoretical model developed in the next section. The results of the model are discussed in the fourth section. The gains from free trade accruing to either country are presented in the fifth section. The sixth section extends the theoretical framework to explain the pattern of super free trade between India and

Bangladesh. The results of this model are discussed in the seventh section. The super free trade model points out the relative importance of the determinants of the pattern of comparative advantages, which is explained in the eighth section. The ninth section reports the gains accruing to either economy from such a super free trading arrangement. The chapter concludes with a summary of the theoretical models that it proposes along with the policy implications.

2. The Theoretical Framework

One of the basic issues in international trade theory is the determination of the sources of comparative advantages of nations and hence trade between nations. Ricardo (1817) came up with his theory of comparative advantage, which holds that it is the difference in technologies between countries that explains why a country trades with other countries. Later Heckscher–Ohlin (Heckscher 1919; Ohlin 1933) shows that comparative advantage is influenced by the interaction between the resources of nations (relative abundance) and the technology of production (relative intensity). An important corollary derivable from the Heckscher–Ohlin model is the famous factor price equalization theorem (Samuelson 1949). The corollary simply says that the international goods movement tends to act as a substitute for factor movements. The free movements of goods in international trade tend to equalize relative and absolute factor prices.

Based on this simple model of international factor price equalization, or what is more precisely termed as "integrated equilibrium" (Helpman and Krugman 1985), Vanek (1968) developed the concept of factor content of trade (Helpman 1984). A good traded internationally embodies fixed amounts of the services of the productive factors, independently of where it is produced. Hence trade can be conceived in two ways: (i) as the overt of exchange of goods, and (ii) as the international exchange of services of factors embodied in the goods traded. The traditional theories of international trade as developed by Ricardo, Heckscher–Ohlin and others conceived of trade in the former sense, while, Vanek's contribution (Davis and Weinstein 1997) was to recognize that we could equally think of trade as the international exchange of the services of factors embodied in the traded goods. Vanek's formulation of the problem allowed an extension of the logic of the Heckscher–Ohlin theory to settings in which the pattern of trade may be indeterminate but in which the net factor content of trade may nonetheless be determinate. This is the Heckscher–Ohlin–Vanek (HOV) model.

A number of studies in recent times have tried to test the various theories of trade mentioned above (Leamer and Levinsohn 1995). Most of these tests have rejected the HOV model. A problem with these studies is that independent data on trade, endowments and technologies are not used. This has resulted in the rejection of the Heckscher–Ohlin–Vanek model. Moreover, these studies often assume common technologies and preferences. However, Bowen *et al.* (1987) and Trefler (1993, 1995) gave empirical support for a modified HOV model where preferences and technology were allowed to be different from those prevailing in the United States. Davis *et al.* (1997) made use of the regional data for Japan and showed that geographical differences in direct factor requirements may be sufficient to restore the HOV predictions on the factor content of trade.

The model developed in this section of the chapter goes a step further by letting country-specific endowments, preferences and technologies, which are the fundamentals of an economy according to the neoclassical theory of trade, and on the basis of these fundamentals, a competitive benchmark is constructed by solving a linear program and this linear program is then used for locating the comparative advantages of the economies and assessing their gains from free trade. All patterns of specialization are admitted and therefore an international trade theoretic assumption of a common cone of diversification is not made. Thus, to check the Heckscher–Ohlin model, the observed factor contents of net trade, as well as those predicted by theory, is not confronted and the model checks whether the endowments alone determine factor movements of free trade; i.e. the endogenous trade within the model, controlling for taste and technology. This model is a general equilibrium version of ten Raa and Mohnen (2000).

Thus, the model that is set up with the purpose of locating the comparative advantages of the economy of India vis-à-vis that of Bangladesh in a perfectly competitive world with free bilateral trade is a neoclassical model of international trade. It begins with the assumption that each economy has fixed domestic endowments, with tradable and non-tradable commodities, which are used for intermediate as well as final consumption. Leontief functions are used to represent technologies and preferences i.e., there are fixed input coefficients and fixed proportions of final consumption and investment in each economy. The efficient allocation of resources is obtained by maximizing the level of domestic final demand (including consumption and investment) in one economy, subject to a given proportion of final consumption in the other. The novelty of this model lays in the fact that it proposes a new way to locate the comparative advantages of the two economies of the SAARC region linked by international trade. It constructs a competitive benchmark based only on the fundamentals of the two economies: endowments, preferences and technologies. No statistics or constructs beyond the fundamentals of the economies are used in the model. In particular, it employs no price statistics. Nor does it admit of any artificial limitations on the direction of trade. This model provides a truly general equilibrium determination of the commodity pattern of trade. In addition, one important point about the model which is worth noting is that although the model is worked out for the two economies of India and Bangladesh, and since it is based on fundamentals with all prices endogenous, the incorporation of rest of the world as a third economy would be a straightforward extension.

The model may be formally stated as follows. Let the scalar 'c' denote the level of final consumption in India and '$\bar{c}$' the same for Bangladesh, and let $\bar{c} = \gamma c$ i.e. 'γ' is Bangladesh–Indian final consumption ratio, γ being chosen such that the actual bilateral balance of payments is maintained.

The linear program is

$$\max_{\mathbf{x},\bar{\mathbf{x}},c} \mathbf{e}(\mathbf{y} + \bar{\mathbf{y}}\gamma)c$$

subject to

$$(\mathbf{I} - \mathbf{A})\mathbf{x} + (\mathbf{I} - \bar{\mathbf{A}})\bar{\mathbf{x}} \geq (\mathbf{y} + \gamma\bar{\mathbf{y}})c + \mathbf{z} + \bar{\mathbf{z}} \quad \text{for tradable commodities} \tag{1}$$

$$(\mathbf{I} - \mathbf{A})\mathbf{x} \geq \mathbf{y}c, (\mathbf{I} - \bar{\mathbf{A}})\bar{\mathbf{x}} \geq \gamma\bar{\mathbf{y}}c \quad \text{for non-tradable commodities} \tag{2}$$

$$\mathbf{kx} \leq K,\ \mathbf{lx} \leq L \quad \text{for factor inputs in India} \tag{3}$$

$$\bar{\mathbf{k}}\bar{\mathbf{x}} \leq \bar{K},\ \bar{\mathbf{l}}\bar{\mathbf{x}} \leq \bar{L} \quad \text{for factor inputs in Bangladesh} \tag{4}$$

where,

$\mathbf{e} = (1 \cdots 1)$
$\mathbf{y}, \bar{\mathbf{y}} =$ domestic demand vector (including consumption and investment, excluding trade) in India and Bangladesh, respectively.
$\mathbf{z}, \bar{\mathbf{z}} =$ net exports vector (except for bilateral trade) in India and Bangladesh, respectively.
$\mathbf{A}, \bar{\mathbf{A}} =$ input–output coefficients matrix in India and Bangladesh, respectively.
$\mathbf{K}, \bar{\mathbf{K}} =$ capital stock in India and Bangladesh, respectively.
$\mathbf{L}, \bar{\mathbf{L}} =$ labor force in India and Bangladesh, respectively.
$\mathbf{k}, \bar{\mathbf{k}} =$ capital input coefficients row vector in India and Bangladesh, respectively.
$\mathbf{l}, \bar{\mathbf{l}} =$ labor input coefficients row vector in India and Bangladesh, respectively.

For every value of the final consumption ratio γ, we denote the optimum (Indian) consumption level by $c(\gamma)$ and the outputs in the two countries by $\mathbf{x}(\gamma)$ and $\bar{\mathbf{x}}(\gamma)$, respectively. For low values of 'γ', consumption of Bangladesh is not important and the bulk of the net output is exported to India. Similarly, for high values of 'γ', the trade balance shows an Indian surplus.

For tradable commodities, Indian net exports to Bangladesh are given by the vector:

$$(\mathbf{I} - \mathbf{A})\mathbf{x}(\gamma) - \mathbf{y}\mathbf{c}(\gamma) - \mathbf{z}. \tag{5}$$

In a general equilibrium framework, the supporting competitive prices are given by the shadow prices of the linear program. Let us denote those for tradable commodities by $\mathbf{p}(\gamma)$. Indian surplus on bilateral trade account is equal to the product of $\mathbf{p}(\gamma)$ and equation (5) and is denoted by $s(\gamma)$.

For γ low, $s(\gamma)$ is negative, and for γ high, $s(\gamma)$ is positive. For some intermediate value, $s(\gamma)$ matches the observed surplus on the bilateral trade account,

$$s^0 = \mathbf{e}(\mathbf{x}^0 - \mathbf{A}\mathbf{x}^0 - \mathbf{y} - \mathbf{z}), \tag{6}$$

where $\mathbf{x}^0$ is the observed value of the gross output vector $\mathbf{x}$. We shall find the intermediate value of 'γ' by the Newton-Raphson algorithm,

$$\gamma_{n+1} = [\{s(\gamma_n) - s^0\}\gamma_{n-1} - \{s(\gamma_{n-1}) - s^0\}\gamma_n]/[s(\gamma_n) - s(\gamma_{n-1})], \qquad (7)$$

given initial values $\gamma_0 = 0$ and $\gamma_1 = 1$. The limit process in equation (7) solves $s(\gamma) = s^0$ and this gives the general equilibrium value of the Bangladesh-India final consumption expansion ratio, $\gamma = \bar{\mathbf{c}}/\mathbf{c}$

For this value, the linear program determines the levels, $c(\gamma)$ and $\bar{c}(\gamma)$, the allocations, $\mathbf{x}(\gamma)$ and $\bar{\mathbf{x}}(\gamma)$ and the bilateral trade vector in equation (5). The comparative advantages of the two economies are located on the basis of the sign pattern of the bilateral trade. This is done solely on the basis of the parameters or fundamentals of the two economies–taste $(\mathbf{y}, \bar{\mathbf{y}})$, technology $(\mathbf{A}, \bar{\mathbf{A}}; \mathbf{k}, \bar{\mathbf{k}}; \mathbf{l}, \bar{\mathbf{l}})$ and endowments ($K, \bar{K}$ and $L, \bar{L}$), and the rest of the world $(\mathbf{z}, \bar{\mathbf{z}})$ which is fixed. Thus, the model determines the comparative advantages of the two economies on the basis of their fundamentals only without recourse to any exogenous prices. In fact, all prices in the model — i.e. prices of tradables (shadow prices corresponding to constraint 1), prices of non-tradables (shadow prices corresponding to constraint 2), and factor prices (shadow prices corresponding to constraints 3 and 4) are endogenous.

A comparison of the expansion of final demand of the two economies under autarky and free trade scenarios enables one to find out the gains accruing from free trade to either economy. By making technology and taste represent input proportions and consumption respectively, we make a short cut. In a strict sense, technology is a blue book of techniques and the relative prices chosen decide the choice of technique. The observed input–output coefficients reflect the techniques prevailing in each economy under observed prices. Thus, if prices change to the general equilibrium values, then the choice of technique as also the input–output coefficients, may be different. Thus, any induced change of techniques within the technology blue book is likely to prompt further reallocations of endowments and gains to specialization. A similar analysis also holds for consumption. Taste is a blue book of consumption coefficients and these consumption coefficients may adjust. However, the model proposed in this section restricts the blue book of technology as also that of consumption to a single page for each economy and thereby ignores the further reallocations. Hence the results of this model are likely to be conservative to some extent. However, this may not be treated as a serious limitation of this model. This is because the purpose of this chapter is to primarily demonstrate how endogenous patterns of productive activity can create significant gains to free trade. Hence, ignoring such reallocations may well be allowed in the context of the Leontief framework that underlines the proposed model.

3. Data

The basis of the data of this study are the two Input–Output Tables of the Indian Economy for the 1991–92 year (Planning Commission, Government of India 1995) and of the economy of Bangladesh for the 1992–93 year (CIRDAP 1996). The Input–Output Table for the Indian economy consists of 60 sectors, while that of the economy of Bangladesh consists of 53 sectors. These two input–output tables have been aggregated into 25 sectors only in a way such that all sectors are common to India and Bangladesh. The sectors are: (1) Rice, (2) Wheat, (3) Jute, (4) Sugarcane, (5) Cotton, (6) Tea, (7) Other agriculture, (8) Livestock, (9) Fishing, (10) Forestry, (11) Beverages, (12) Jute textile, (13) Other textile, (14) Wood and wood products, (15) Paper and paper products, (16) Leather, (17) Chemicals, (18) Nonmetallic minerals, (19) Iron and steel, (20) Machinery, (21) Mining and miscellaneous manufacturing, (22) Communication and transport equipment, (23) Construction, (24) Electricity and gas, and (25) Services.

From the aggregated input–output table of each of the country, the input–output coefficient matrices have been computed ($\mathbf{A}$ for India and $\bar{\mathbf{A}}$ for Bangladesh). The sectoral labor coefficients ($\mathbf{l}, \bar{\mathbf{l}}$) for each sector of the economies have been computed from the sectoral employment and sectoral output data of the respective economies. The sectoral output data are available from the input–output table for each economy. For the economy of Bangladesh, the employment figures for all the required sectors are available for the 1992–93 year (CIRDAP 1996) and for the economy of India, the employment figures for majority of the sectors are available for the 1991–92 year from the economic tables (Census 1991). For some agricultural sectors like Rice, Wheat, Jute, Sugarcane and Cotton, the employment figures are obtained from website www.indiaagristat.com. Employment figures for Tea are obtained from the website www.teauction.com. To compute the sectoral capital coefficients ($\mathbf{k}, \bar{\mathbf{k}}$) for the economies, data on sectoral value added and wage rate for the different sectors were required. The figures for sectoral value added at factor cost ($\mathbf{v}$ and $\bar{\mathbf{v}}$) are available from the input–output tables of the respective economies. For the Indian economy, the data on wage rate is available (Ministry of Labor, Government of India 1995). For the economy of Bangladesh, we had the data on wage rates for all the sectors (CIRDAP 1996). Having thus obtained the data on sectoral capital coefficient, we used the degree of capacity utilization of each economy to obtain the total capital stock in each. The source of data on degree of capacity utilization for both economies is ten Raa and Chakraborty (1991). The source of data on total Labor force of both the economies is the World Development Report (1995).

4. Results and Discussion

In this section, we present the results of the above model. The results are shown in Tables 1 and 2. The gross output figures (Table 1) show the commodities which each of the economy would produce under perfect competition and free bilateral trade. Although the actual trade or observed trade figures show that both countries have positive outputs of all the 25 commodities mentioned in Table 1, but in a perfectly competitive world with free bilateral trade as postulated by the model presented in the second section, India produces all commodities other than Fishing. On the other hand, Bangladesh in a world of free trade characterized by perfect competition would specialize in the production of Rice, Fishing and Services and will obtain all the remaining 21 tradable commodities from India. However, both countries have positive outputs of Construction since it is assumed to be a non-tradable good. The respective comparative advantages of the two economies are located on the basis of the sign pattern of bilateral trade. The effect of perfect competition and free bilateral trade on the pattern of trade between India and Bangladesh would be as given in Table 2.

The figures in Table 2 reveal that in a competitive set-up with free bilateral trade as postulated by the model in the second section, India enjoys comparative advantages in almost all the commodities mentioned in Tables 1 and 2, except for Rice, Fishing and Services, which it finds suitable to import from her neighboring country, Bangladesh. However, India's observed trade figures suggest that she actually exports all goods

Table 1: Actual and Free Trade Gross Output Figures for India and Bangladesh (1992) in million US dollars.

Sectors	India		Bangladesh	
	Actual trade	Free trade	Actual trade	Free trade
1. Rice	14995.7	12973.8	4219.0	18817.7
2. Wheat	7877.4	13369.3	175.0	0
3. Jute	342.8	745.7	212.6	0
4. Sugarcane	3528.0	6180.3	216.8	0
5. Cotton	1835.5	2754.6	10.3	0
6. Tea	581.8	1238.1	114.4	0
7. Other Agricuture	33135.4	58549.2	1508.4	0
8. Livestock	18384.8	33985.3	2207.3	0
9. Fishing	2000.9	0	1687.7	6043.3
10. Forestry	3788.8	9749.5	2051.6	0
11. Beverages	20939.7	38132.1	1995.6	0
12. Jute textile	1223.6	2474.3	369.4	0
13. Other textile	27110.8	44589.6	2548.0	0
14. Wood and products	1901.6	3275.1	123.4	0
15. Paper and products	3491.3	4120.1	157.0	0
16. Leather	2482.4	3399.3	300.0	0
17. Chemicals	28190.3	55414.0	2807.5	0
18. Non-metallicminerals	4905.8	8331.3	20.8	0
19. Iron and steel	14996.2	30356.4	566.1	0
20. Machinery	16734.0	32910.1	150.6	0
21. Mining and miscellaneous manufacturing	17054.2	37019.2	2001.6	0
22. Communication and transport	13765.1	24351.0	73.9	0
23. Construction	28847.3	47248.4	3389.8	6810.2
24. Electricity and gas	11151.1	21589.6	1252.6	0
25. Services	128153.4	197251.3	13276.9	36407.6

barring Jute textile, Wood products and Leather. On the other hand, in a free trade set-up, Bangladesh's comparative advantage rests on Rice, Fishing and Services although her observed trade pattern, suggests that she is more competitive in producing Jute textile, Wood products and Leather. Thus, it is seen that the comparative advantages of the economies as obtained by solving the linear program are close to the observed pattern for most of the goods mentioned in Table 1. However, there also arise few contrasts of the free trade figures with the actual trade figures of the countries. As observed from the actual trade figures in Table 2, Rice is exported from India to Bangladesh. But the free trade figures suggest the same to be an item of export for the economy of Bangladesh. This seems to be justified to some

Table 2: Free Bilateral Trade from India to Bangladesh Contrasted With Actual Trade Figures (1992) in million US dollars.

Sectors	Actual exports of India to Bangladesh	Free net exports of India to Bangladesh
1. Rice	0.0	−10206.4
2. Wheat	0.0	353.7
3. Jute	0.0	39.0
4. Sugarcane	0	83.8
5. Cotton	101.5	6.2
6. Tea	0	369.8
7. Other Agricuture	51.1	1774.8
8. Livestock	0.5	4392.2
9. Fishing	0.0	−3458.1
10. Forestry	0.2	4622.5
11. Beverages	7.4	2855.5
12. Jute textile	−0.0	308.1
13. Other textile	147.6	2089.2
14. Wood and products	−3.1	80.2
15. Paper and products	1009.1	10.6
16. Leather	−3.7	336.1
17. Chemicals	25.9	4301.7
18. Non-metallic minerals	6.6	151.8
19. Iron and steel	12.6	1081.4
20. Machinery	33.6	924.1
21. Mining and miscellaneous manufacturing	98.9	3203.8
22. Communication and transport	10.2	412.6
23. Construction	0	0
24. Electricity and gas	0.0	2335.8
25. Services	0.0	−14570.1
Total	1498.6	1498.5

extent by the fact that Bangladesh has a significant edge in the value added per worker in this sector compared to India ($693.3 million versus $606.2 million per worker), whereas the value added per unit of capital in this sector is little different in the two countries. Thus, Bangladesh which happens to be a relatively labor-abundant country, adopts the production of this labor intensive good. The small figure of Indian exports of Other Agriculture to Bangladesh, as revealed by the actual or observed trade figures, in contrast to the free trade figures, can be explained in terms of the existence of a high tariff on Indian fruits and vegetables imposed by Bangladesh (at over 40% level) (Sobhan 2002). Similarly, such import restrictions are also applied to Livestock exported from India. Thus, with free trade, Livestock exported from India to Bangladesh will obviously record a manifold increase. This is, however, desirable in view of the fact that currently, 1.5 million Indian cattle per annum were informally imported into Bangladesh (Sobhan 2002). Such informal imports of cattle from India also provide hides and skins for manufacturing export-quality finished leather in Bangladesh's more modern slaughter houses and tanneries. This sizeable component of the informal trade clearly provides a strong basis for Bangladesh's revealed comparative advantage in exporting leather products not only to India (as revealed by the actual trade figures in Table 2), but also to the rest of the world. Thus, the removal of all trade restrictions and making trade between the two countries completely free would go a long way to reduce the incidence of informal trade with respect to cattle and livestock, and a possible consequence of this may be the comparative advantage of India in Leather production, rather than Bangladesh. However, goods like Jute textile, Wood products, etc feature as export items of Bangladesh in reality, but here, we see that these goods appear as export items for the economy of India. Similarly, for India also, the actual export figures are sometimes different from the competitive figures. For example, the observed trade figures show that India has been an exporter of Services, which comprises items like transport services, medical and educational services etc, to Bangladesh during the entire last decade. But free trade with Bangladesh, as postulated by the present model, ends up in Services being an export item for Bangladesh. As far as Tea is concerned, both the countries have proven expertise (as suggested by the observed output figures of the two countries in Table 1) and as such, there is no observed trade in Tea between the two countries. However, the free trade figure shows a flow of this good from India to Bangladesh. Thus, the pattern of comparative advantage resulting from the model often departs from the observed trade pattern. As explained, this contrast arises due to numerous distortions existing in the real world, which cause the private cost of production of a good to diverge from its social cost, in which case the free trade pattern does not confirm the observed pattern of trade. Examples of such distortions are monopoly power, externalities, tariffs and other impediments. The model assumes away all such market imperfections and departures from a simple perfectly competitive model.

However, there are some departures from the competitive benchmark that cannot be separated from the fundamentals, but are embedded in the physical structure of the economies. Particularly, worth mentioning are the phenomena of product differentiation and scale economies. Our model assumes away the possibility of two-way trade, which is the consequence of product differentiation existing in the real world. For instance, in Mining and Miscellaneous manufacturing, the dominant item of Bangladesh is the Ready-made garment, which is a major export item for the country. Thus, given free trade, Bangladesh is likely to export ready-made garments to India. But this, in turn, is likely to be countered by Indian exports of minerals to the country. This may end up in the export of Mining and Miscellaneous manufacturing from India to Bangladesh. Moreover, the quality of clothing accessories and footwear (included in Miscellaneous manufacturing) of Bangladesh is often different from the same product of Indian origin. Such differences in product quality are ignored in this model and any product considered here is taken to be the same in quality irrespective of its place of origin. However, since the purpose of this model is the determination of comparative advantages on the basis of the fundamentals of the economies, we selected the most disaggregated classification of products that we could reconcile given the available input–output tables of the two economies. As such, the possibility of product differentiation and hence two way trade is not considered in this model. As has already been pointed out, it is true that goods like clothing accessories (for instance zamdani sarees) being produced in Bangladesh are different from those being produced in India. Hence, even at this level of disaggregation, trade must be two-way. This is no doubt true, but in our opinion, the only correct way of modeling this is to go in for further disaggregation of the data. Our view deviates from the dominant view in literature, where product differentiation is imposed by taking into account the origin of commodities (the so-called Armington assumption, see Harris 1984; Srinivasan and Whalley 1986). The consideration of such two-way trade may be practical for obtaining a good approximation, but it is not necessary for the location of comparative advantages, particularly when they are not assumed to be revealed by international trade statistics.

As far as scale economies are concerned, such scale-induced changes in technical coefficients could be very much relevant for detecting comparative advantages of the economies, particularly, given the fact that monopoly power is a priori excluded from this model. However, the effect of such scale economies is ignored by the model. Its inclusion would reinforce the gains to free trade. But one would find it interesting to note that significant gains to free trade can be explained (the next section) with the help of this model even without the use of scale economies. However, the inclusion of scale economies might alter the locational pattern of comparative advantages, but they may not be very high.

Thus, the model developed in the second section of this chapter provides a new method for locating the comparative advantages of the economies of Bangladesh and India in a perfectly competitive world of free bilateral trade. Moreover, the model also enables one to probe into the related issue of gains from such free trade. This is discussed in the following section.

5. Gains From Free Trade

One can think of the gains from trade as consisting of two parts. First, the part depending on specialization in production, which is obtained by eliminating the domestic waste of resources due to misallocation and less than full utilization. Second the part depending on the possibility of exchange, which is attributed to free trade only. The solution to the linear programming model developed in the second section yields $\gamma = \bar{c}/c$ and c. The consequent expansion factors for final consumption in India and Bangladesh are

$$c = 1.643 \quad \text{and} \quad \bar{c} = 1.889 \tag{8}$$

Thus, free bilateral trade in a perfectly competitive world would fetch for the Indian economy a total gain of 64.3%, while for the economy of Bangladesh, the total gain would be 88.9%. Thus, both the economies gain from free bilateral trade, but the magnitude of gain is more for Bangladesh than for India. This shows bilateral trade is relatively more important for Bangladesh than for India.

It is now possible to isolate the gains from free trade only. For this, we have to solve yet another linear program, which will enable us to determine the domestic efficiency gains (gains by eliminating the domestic waste of resources due to misallocation and less than full utilization of resources) that the economies can achieve without having departed from the bilateral trade pattern, which was obtained by solving the previous linear program.

The linear program, which we now have to solve to find India's domestic expansion factor, is

$$\mathbf{Max\ ey}\,d, \tag{9}$$

subject to equation (3) and

$$(\mathbf{I} - \mathbf{A})\mathbf{x} \geq \mathbf{y}d + \mathbf{z}, \tag{10}$$

where d is the level of final consumption in India and $\mathbf{z}$ the full net exports vector of India. The solution to this linear program yields $d = 1.633$. In the same way (using overbars) we solve a linear program to obtain the domestic expansion factor for Bangladesh. From its solution, we obtain $\bar{d} = 1.372$. Hence, the efficiency gains of India due to the elimination of domestic waste of resources are 63.3% while those of Bangladesh are 37.2%.

Thus, from these results and those in equation (8), it follows that the total efficiency gains of India from bilateral free trade with Bangladesh are 64.3%, while similar gains for Bangladesh are as much as 88.9%. However, out of this 64.3% of Indian efficiency gains, as much as 63.3% is due to specialization in production. Such gains from specialization in production, obtained by eliminating domestic waste and misallocation of resources for Bangladesh, are only 37.2%. Hence, while for India only 1% of total gains can be ascribed to its free trade with Bangladesh, for Bangladesh, similar gains from the exchange are as high as 51.7%. Thus, while the extent of India's gains from free bilateral trade only with Bangladesh is just 1%, that of Bangladesh due to free bilateral trade with India is as large as 51.7%. The results are summarized in Table 3.

Therefore, to sum up, we may say that by solving a linear program, we have obtained the pattern of bilateral trade between India and Bangladesh in a world of free and perfectly competitive trade. The comparative advantages of the two economies are obtained from the sign pattern of the bilateral trade, and this is done solely on the basis of the parameters of the two economies — taste ($\mathbf{y}$ and $\mathbf{y}^*$), technology ($\mathbf{A}, \mathbf{A}^*, \mathbf{k}, \mathbf{k}^*, \mathbf{l}, \mathbf{l}^*$) and

Table 3: Gains From Free Trade Accruing to India and Bangladesh.

Countries	India	Bangladesh
Total Gains from trade	64.3%	88.9%
Gains by eliminating domestic waste of resources	63.3%	37.2%
Gains from free trade only	1.0%	51.7%

endowments (K, K^*, L, L^*), the rest of the world trade being fixed and represented by vector $\mathbf{z}$. Thus the comparative advantages of the two economies of India and Bangladesh are located absolutely on the basis of their fundamentals without recourse to exogenous prices. The resulting bilateral trade between the economies not only increases the volume of trade between them, but also enables both the countries to gain. In particular, Bangladesh, the relatively smaller economy, reaps significant gains.

Thus we have obtained the comparative advantages of the two economies on the basis of the fundamentals of an economy, namely, endowments, technology and preferences. However, the model developed in Section 1 of this chapter, which helps to locate the pattern of this comparative advantage between the two economies, does not shed any light on the relative importance of the determinants of comparative advantage. Following the conventions in literature, this can be done by holding technology and taste constant across the economies, in which case the role of endowment (the factor responsible for international trade between nations according to Hecksher–Ohlin) will get focused. This, in turn, can be implemented in a neo-classical fashion by assuming free access of each economy to the other's technology and that there is substitutability in the mean consumption vector of either economy. If the model in the second section is modified so as to include these new assumptions, then one comes up with a new trade model involving the economies of India and Bangladesh. This is the so-called super free trade model which is developed next.

6. Super Free Trade Model

The super free trade model of India and Bangladesh is set up by making certain modifications to the model developed in the second section. The model formed with such modifications is referred to as the *super free trade model* because here, the trading partners do not only freely trade with each other, but they are also endowed with the freedom to use each other's technology and to substitute its mean consumption vector with that of the other economy. The modifications in the original model, which bring out the super free trade model, are as follows:

First, the Indian net output $(\mathbf{I} - \mathbf{A})\mathbf{x}$ in equations (1) and (2) is replaced by $(\mathbf{I} - \mathbf{A})\mathbf{x} + (\mathbf{I} - \bar{\mathbf{A}})\chi$, so that any gross output component can be generated by applying activity $\mathbf{x}$ to the columns of the Indian input–output coefficient matrix $\mathbf{A}$ or by applying the activities χ to the columns of Bangladesh's input-output coefficient matrix $\bar{\mathbf{A}}$. Similarly, the net output vector of Bangladesh $(\mathbf{I} - \bar{\mathbf{A}})\bar{\mathbf{x}}$ is replaced by $(\mathbf{I} - \bar{\mathbf{A}})\bar{\mathbf{x}} + (\mathbf{I} - \mathbf{A})\bar{\chi}$.

Second, the Indian capital requirements are bounded according to $\mathbf{kx} + \bar{\mathbf{k}}\chi \le K$, instead of using $\mathbf{kx} \le \mathbf{K}$. Similarly, $\bar{\mathbf{k}}\bar{\mathbf{x}} \le \bar{K}$ is replaced by $\bar{\mathbf{k}}\bar{\mathbf{x}} + \mathbf{k}\bar{\chi} \le \bar{K}$ for Bangladesh. The same applies to the labour requirements, i.e. replace $\mathbf{lx} \le L$ by $\mathbf{lx} + \bar{\mathbf{l}}\chi \le L$ for India and replace $\bar{\mathbf{l}}\bar{\mathbf{x}} \le \bar{L}$ by $\bar{\mathbf{l}}\bar{\mathbf{x}} + \mathbf{l}\bar{\chi} \le \bar{L}$ for Bangladesh.

Third, the vector c is replaced by $c + c^*$. Indian consumers are now indifferent between Indian final consumption $\mathbf{y}$ and that of Bangladesh $(\mathbf{ey}/\mathbf{e}\bar{\mathbf{y}})\bar{\mathbf{y}}$, where the latter is scaled up to the Indian level. Similarly, people in Bangladesh are now indifferent between Bangladesh's final consumption $\bar{\mathbf{y}}$ and $(\mathbf{e}\bar{\mathbf{y}}/\mathbf{ey})\mathbf{y}$. Thus, $\mathbf{y}c$ and $\bar{\mathbf{y}}\bar{c} = \gamma\bar{\mathbf{y}}c$ in equation (1) are replaced by $[\mathbf{y}c + (\mathbf{ey}/\mathbf{e}\bar{\mathbf{y}})\bar{\mathbf{y}}c^*]$ and in equation (2) by $[\bar{\mathbf{y}}\bar{c} + (\mathbf{e}\bar{\mathbf{y}}/\mathbf{ey})\mathbf{y}\bar{c}^*]$. Finally, the scanning variable $\gamma = \bar{c}/c$ is now replaced by $\gamma = (\bar{c} + \bar{c}^*)/(c + c^*)$.

The super free trade model may thus be presented as follows.

$$\underset{\mathbf{x},\chi,\bar{\mathbf{x}},\bar{\chi},c,c^*,\bar{c},\bar{c}^*}{\text{Max}} \quad \mathbf{ey}(c + c^*) + \mathbf{e}\bar{\mathbf{y}}\gamma(c + c^*) \tag{11}$$

subject to

$$\begin{aligned}(\mathbf{I} - \mathbf{A})\mathbf{x} + (\mathbf{I} - \bar{\mathbf{A}})\chi + (\mathbf{I} - \bar{\mathbf{A}})\bar{\mathbf{x}} + (\mathbf{I} - \mathbf{A})\bar{\chi}& \\ \ge \mathbf{y}c + (\mathbf{ey}/\mathbf{e}\bar{\mathbf{y}})\bar{\mathbf{y}}c^* + \bar{\mathbf{y}}\bar{c} + (\mathbf{e}\bar{\mathbf{y}}/\mathbf{ey})\mathbf{y}\bar{\mathbf{c}}^* + \mathbf{z} + \bar{\mathbf{z}}&\end{aligned} \tag{12}$$

$$(\mathbf{I} - \mathbf{A})\mathbf{x} + (\mathbf{I} - \bar{\mathbf{A}})\chi \ge \mathbf{y}c + (\mathbf{ey}/\mathbf{e}\bar{\mathbf{y}})\bar{\mathbf{y}}c^* \tag{13a}$$

$$(\mathbf{I} - \bar{\mathbf{A}})\bar{\mathbf{x}} + (\mathbf{I} - \mathbf{A})\bar{\chi} \ge \bar{\mathbf{y}}\bar{c} + (\mathbf{e}\bar{\mathbf{y}}/\mathbf{ey})\mathbf{y}\bar{c}^* \tag{13b}$$

$$\mathbf{kx} + \bar{\mathbf{k}}\chi \le K, \mathbf{lx} + \bar{\mathbf{l}}\chi \le L \tag{14a}$$

$$\bar{\mathbf{k}}\bar{\mathbf{x}} + \mathbf{k}\bar{\chi} \le \bar{K}, \bar{\mathbf{l}}\bar{\mathbf{x}} + \mathbf{l}\bar{\chi} \le \bar{L} \tag{14b}$$

where equation (12) is for tradeable commodities, equations (13a) and (13b) for the nontradeable commodities in India and Bangladesh respectively, and equations (14a) and (14b) for the factor inputs in each country. Note that $\bar{c}^* = \gamma(c + \bar{c}) - c^*$.

The linear program presented here yields a model of so-called super free trade between India and Bangladesh with each economy having free access to each other's technology in production and consumption.

7. Results and Discussion

The gross output figures of the two economies of India and Bangladesh under a super free trading arrangement as postulated by the model developed in the last section is presented in Table 4, while the pattern of the super free trade between them is reported in Table 5. As noted from Table 4, India does

Table 4: Gross Output Figures of India to Bangladesh (1992) With Superfree Trade in million US dollars.

Sectors	Gross output of India		Gross output of Bangladesh	
	Using own technology	Using Bangladesh technology	Using own technology	Using Indian technology
1. Rice	0	68526.1	9690.8	0
2. Wheat	0	0	5163.1	0
3. Jute	0	0	445.0	0
4. Sugarcane	0	4050.8	0	0
5. Cotton	0	0	2152.5	0
6. Tea	0	2586.8	0	0
7. Other Agriculture	35925.0	0	0	0
8. Livestock	0	36386.4	0	0
9. Fishing	0	18985.2	9582.3	0
10. Forestry	35747.3	0	0	0
11. Beverages	44276.6	0	0	0
12. Jute textile	0	2278.9	0	0
13. Other textile	14436.6	26806.1	0	0
14. Wood and products	0	0	2947.4	0
15. Paper and products	0	0	0	2816.2
16. Leather	0	0	4076.6	0
17. Chemicals	90649.3	0	0	0
18. Non-metallic minerals	0	6257.5	0	0
19. Iron and steel	0	23670.1	0	0
20. Machinery	0	0	0	14084.5
21. Mining and miscellaneous manufacturing	0	0	58452.9	0
22. Communication and transport	5482.5	0	0	0
23. Construction	0	58744.1	5261.1	0
24. Electricity and gas	0	27934.4	0	0
25. Services	0	263691.2	0	0

Table 5: Super Free Net Exports of India to Bangladesh Contrasted With the Free Net Export Figures (1992) in million US dollars.

Sectors	Free net exports of India to Bangladesh	Net superfree exports of India to Bangladesh
1. Rice	−10206.4	−2313.9
2. Wheat	353.7	−5934.4
3. Jute	39.0	−340.3
4. Sugarcane	83.8	72.2
5. Cotton	6.2	−1881.3
6. Tea	169.8	221.2
7. Other Agriculture	1774.8	2228.3
8. Livestock	4592.2	6892.1
9. Fishing	−3458.1	−7083.0
10. Forestry	4622.5	11579.2
11. Beverages	2855.5	2991.0
12. Jute textile	308.1	420.9
13. Other textile	2089.2	2490.0
14. Wood and products	80.2	−1245.8
15. Paper and products	10.6	−1456.7
16. Leather	336.1	−3017.4
17. Chemicals	4301.7	18119.9
18. Non-metallic minerals	151.8	941.0
19. Iron and steel	1081.4	4934.0
20. Machinery	924.1	−10858.2
21. Mining and miscellaneous manufacturing	3203.8	−51538.9
22. Communication and transport	412.6	1320.3
23. Construction	0	0
24. Electricity and gas	2335.8	4522.3
25. Services	−14570.1	30435.6
Total	1498.5	1498.2

not produce Wheat, Jute, Cotton, Wood, Paper, Leather, Machinery, Mining and miscellaneous goods. Its trading partner, Bangladesh, on the other hand, produces all these goods and India finds it suitable to import these goods from there. Given the scope to use both its own as well as Bangladesh's technology to produce goods, India uses its own technology to produce goods like Other agriculture, Forest products, Beverages, Chemicals, Communication and transport equipment, while it uses the technology of Bangladesh to produce Rice, Sugarcane, Tea, Livestock, Fish, Jute textile, Non-metal mineral manufactures, Iron and steel, Construction (non-tradable), Electricity and gas and Services. However, for Other textile, India finds it best to make use of both the technologies.

Bangladesh, now being given free access to use Indian technology, uses it to produce only two goods, namely, Paper and paper products and Machinery. It uses its own technology to produce several other goods such as Rice, Wheat, Jute, Cotton, Fish, Wood and wood products, Leather, Mining and miscellaneous manufacturing and Construction (non-tradable). Under this arrangement of super free trade, Bangladesh does not produce Sugarcane, Tea, Other agriculture, Livestock, Forest products, Beverages, Jute textile, Other textile, Chemicals, Non-metal mineral manufactures, Iron and steel, Communication and transport equipment, Electricity and gas and Services. The country finds it profitable to obtain these goods by importing them from India, which produces all these goods either by using its own technology or the technology used by Bangladesh.

Thus, while India produces 16 out of the 24 tradable goods (Construction being non-tradable) considered in this empirical implementation of the super free trade model, Bangladesh produces ten of them. Together, they produce 26 tradable goods. Thus, there are two goods that both the countries are producing. These are Rice and Fish. However, for producing both these goods, both India and Bangladesh rely on the technology of Bangladesh, thereby revealing its superiority over the Indian technique of producing the same. Although there are such goods, which are produced by both the economies, the ultimate pattern of comparative advantage underlying this super free trade between India and Bangladesh is revealed by the sign of the net export vector. Table 5 shows this net export vector. This table also contains the figures to specify the trade flow under the free trade arrangement between the two economies so as to facilitate a comparison between the two different situations.

Table 5 reports that India now imports a larger number of goods from Bangladesh as compared to the free trade situation (discussed in the second section). It obtains from Bangladesh Rice, Wheat, Jute, Cotton, Fishing, Wood products, Paper and paper products, Leather, Machinery and Mining and miscellaneous manufacturings. Thus, although India produces both Rice and Fish using Bangladesh's technology, yet it also imports some of both these goods from Bangladesh. This indicates that the ultimate advantage in the production of these two goods rests with Bangladesh. As noted from Tables 4 and 5, India produces as much as US$68526.09 million worth of Rice and US$18985 million worth of Fish; yet its net imports of

Rice from Bangladesh is to the tune of US$2313.85 million and that of Fish is US$7083.03 million. This may be explained by the relatively higher demand of both these goods in this country compared to their supply. The supply of these goods depend on inputs like land, water which may be put to alternative use and hence additional quantities of these inputs cannot be brought in to increase the domestic supply of these goods within India. As such, although the country produces substantial amounts of both these goods, it has yet to depend on some imports of these from Bangladesh, which is endowed with a comparatively better ability to produce them (as is apparent from the super free trade pattern in Table 5).

8. Relative Importance of the Determinants of the Pattern of Comparative Advantage

The comparison of the super free trade figures with the free trade figures in Table 5 reveals that the comparative advantages of Bangladesh vis-à-vis India in the production of Rice and Fish persist when technology differences in production and consumption are eliminated. However, now with technology being the same across the two economies, Bangladesh gains comparative advantage in some additional goods. They are: Wheat, Jute, Cotton, Wood and wood products, Paper and paper products, Leather, Machinery, Mining and miscellaneous manufacturing. However, with such super free trading conditions prevailing, Bangladesh loses its comparative advantage to India in the production of Services, which it otherwise produces under a free trade set-up as postulated by the model developed in the second section of this chapter. India now enjoys advantage in the production and hence exports of this good to Bangladesh, which it otherwise imports in a free trade situation. This difference in the pattern of comparative advantage of the two economies in the two different trade situations leads one to a crucial inference. The comparative advantage of the economy of Bangladesh in the production of Rice and Fish is determined by endowments, while technology determines the economy's comparative advantage in the case of Services. Thus, it is the superior technology of the country in the production of Services that enables it to enjoy a comparative advantage in the production of this good. So the moment technology in production is equalized across the two countries, the country loses comparative advantage in the production of this good. Hence, given an opportunity to adopt the trading partner's technology, India is likely to adopt the superior technology that Bangladesh uses to produce Services.

An analysis along similar lines can be made to explain the changes observed in the pattern of trade flow from India to Bangladesh when the free trade conditions are replaced by super free trade conditions. As noted, India's production of Wheat, Jute, Cotton, Wood and wood products, Paper and paper products, Leather, Machinery, Mining and miscellaneous manufacturing is picked up by Bangladesh once the technology differences between the two economies are ironed out. However, as in a free trade arrangement, India continues to retain its comparative advantage in goods like Sugarcane, Tea, Other agriculture, Livestock, Forestry, Beverages, Jute textile, Other textile, Chemicals, Non-metallic minerals, Iron and steel, Communication and transport equipment and Electricity and gas. Hence India's comparative advantage in the former set of goods whose production are now picked up by Bangladesh is due to technology, while endowments are responsible for India's comparative advantage, in the goods in which the country retains its advantage, even when technology differences is leveled out. Hence, being endowed with the scope to adopt India's technology, Bangladesh picks up the production of the eight goods for which India's comparative advantage is solely due to its technology (Table 6).

In short, as Table 6 indicates, Bangladesh's comparative advantage in the production of Rice and Fish are due to the country's endowments while, in the case of India, the endowments of the country account for its comparative advantage in the production of as many as 13 goods, namely Sugarcane, Tea, Other agriculture, Livestock, Forestry, Beverages, Jute textile, Other textile, Chemicals, Non-metallic minerals, Iron and steel, Communication and transport equipment and Electricity and gas.

Therefore, given the opportunity to adopt a foreign technology, each country adopts the other country's technology for producing goods and uses it to its advantage. However, the question that arises is, does this change in the trade flow as a result of adopting new technology fetch any additional gains to the countries? The issue of gains in the case of super free trade between the two countries is discussed in the following section.

Table 6: Determinants of Comparative Advantages of India and Bangladesh.

	Sectors	Determinant of comparative advantage	
		India	Bangladesh
1.	Rice		Endowments
2.	Wheat	Technology	
3.	Jute	Technology	
4.	Sugarcane	Endowments	
5.	Cotton	Technology	
6.	Tea	Endowments	
7.	Other Agriculture	Endowments	
8.	Livestock	Endowments	
9.	Fishing		Endowments
10.	Forestry	Endowments	
11.	Beverages	Endowments	
12.	Jute textile	Endowments	
13.	Other textile	Endowments	
14.	Wood and products	Technology	
15.	Paper and products	Technology	
16.	Leather	Technology	
17.	Chemicals	Endowments	
18.	Non-metallic minerals	Endowments	
19.	Iron and steel	Endowments	
20.	Machinery	Technology	
21.	Mining and miscellaneous manufacturing	Technology	
22.	Communication and transport	Endowments	
23.	Construction		
24.	Electricity and gas	Endowments	
25.	Services		Technology

Note: Construction is non-tradable.

9. Gains From Super Free Trade

Gains accruing to either economy when technology differences in production and consumption are leveled out are reported in Table 7. It is noted that, given a chance, although Bangladesh adopts Indian technology to produce a host of goods and thereby reduces its dependence on India, as far gains from trade is concerned, Bangladesh loses a significant portion of its gains by adopting the Indian technique of production. While the extent of its gains from free trade with India (technology being specific to each economy) is as much as 51.7%, with technology differences between the economies being ruled out, the percentage of gains accruing to it come down to only 36.9%. However, India gains substantially from this trading

Table 7: Gains From Super Free Trade Accruing to India and Bangladesh Contrasted With Gains From Free Trade.

Countries	India		Bangladesh	
	Free trade	Super free trade	Free trade	Super free trade
Total Gains	64.3%	95.0%	88.9%	74.1%
Gains by eliminating domestic waste of resources	63.3%	63.3%	37.2%	37.2%
Gains from free trade only	1.0%	31.7	51.7%	36.9%

arrangement as compared to free trade. India's gains from super free trade with Bangladesh are recorded to be 31.7%, while the gains to it from free trade are only 1%.

Thus, when technology in production and consumption is assumed to be the same across the two countries of India and Bangladesh, Bangladesh loses a large part of its gain from trade while India makes substantial additional gains. This reduction in the gains of Bangladesh, however, may be explained by the fact that our model does not consider natural resources, climate etc as factors which can also influence the production of a good. Under super free trading arrangements with India, Bangladesh is found to produce goods such as Wheat and Cotton. The climatic condition suitable for the production of these goods is mostly found in the western part of India. Bangladesh, which lies on the eastern boundary of India, lacks the favorable climatic conditions required for the production of these goods. Thus, in so far as the Indian edge in Wheat or Cotton production is a reflection of the adequate climatic conditions prevailing in the country, the transfer of the Indian technology to Bangladesh to enable it to produce these goods are likely to lower Bangladesh's gains.

However, being the bigger trading partner, India experiences a larger increase in gains under super free trade than it reaps in a free trading arrangement with the other country. One factor that may explain this increase in gain to some extent is that bilateral free trade results in India losing its comparative advantage in the production of Services (in the production of which India is found to have comparative advantage according to the observed trade figures). However, with super free trade, India once again regains its advantage in this line of production. Besides, as suggested by the super free net trade figures (Table 5), India now imports Wood and Leather from Bangladesh. This is in conformity with the country's observed trade figures. In the case of bilateral free trade, both these were items of export for India. This may also serve to provide some sort of an explanation for the rise in the extent of India's gains once the country enters into a super free trading arrangement with Bangladesh. Thus, the super free trade model redistributes the gains from trade in favor of India rather than Bangladesh.

The above discussion indicates that the super free trade model of India and Bangladesh developed in the sixth section of this chapter serves a very useful purpose of isolating the determinants of comparative advantages of each economy. By holding technology in production and consumption constant across the two economies, the model enables one to separate out those goods in whose production an economy has a comparative advantage solely due to its technology, from those goods for which the comparative advantage is brought about by endowments of the economy. The model also highlights the role of international trade as a medium of transferring technology between nations. Here, the relatively less developed economy, Bangladesh, not only gains in terms of access to greater volume of goods and services by entering into free trade with its relatively developed partner, India, but it also gets an opportunity to use India's technology in quite a substantial number of cases. As obtained from Table 4, given free access to technology, Bangladesh is able to produce many more goods on its own than it could when technologies were different in the two economies under perfectly competitive free trade.

10. Summary and Conclusion

The emphasis given to free trade in the SAARC agenda led to several attempts to foster growth of bilateral trade between the two member countries of SAARC, namely India and Bangladesh. Moreover, in recent years, issues concerning bilateral trade between Bangladesh and India have received heightened interest and come under close scrutiny. This is because, during the last decade, while India's importance as a source of imports to Bangladesh registered a phenomenal increase, Bangladesh's role as an exporter to the Indian market has undergone further marginalization. As a result, Bangladesh's trade deficit with India has increased substantially. Such a state of affairs has given rise to concern both at the policy level, as well as at the level of public perception. Against this backdrop, this chapter attempts to study bilateral free trade between these two countries by constructing a competitive benchmark, based only on the fundamentals of the two economies: endowments, preferences and technologies. A linear program along with an input–output framework, helps to determine endogenously the direction of trade taking place between the countries. The chapter proposes a new way to locate the comparative advantages of the two economies linked by international trade. No statistics or constructs beyond the fundamentals of the economies are used in the model. In particular, it employs no price statistics. Nor does it admit of any artificial limitations on the direction of trade. This theoretical framework provides a truly general equilibrium determination of the commodity pattern of trade.

The gross output of commodities produced by each economy as obtained by solving the above model show that in a perfectly competitive world with free bilateral trade, India produces all commodities considered in the model other than Fishing. On the other hand, Bangladesh would specialize in the production of Rice, Fishing and Services and will obtain all the remaining 21 tradable commodities from India. However, both countries have positive outputs of Construction since it is assumed to be non-tradable. It is determined that India enjoys comparative advantage in almost all the commodities except Rice, Fishing and Services, which it finds suitable to import from her neighboring country, Bangladesh. On the other hand, in a free trade set-up, Bangladesh's comparative advantage rests in Rice, Fishing and Services. The extent of India's gains from such free bilateral trade with Bangladesh is just 1% while that of Bangladesh is as large as 51.7%. Thus, Bangladesh gains significantly from this bilateral trading arrangement with India.

The chapter also explores the possibility of either economy producing goods when not only is trade free between them, but also each economy has access to the other's technology. To show how this could be done, the chapter proposes the super free trade model of India and Bangladesh. The results of the model indicate that the comparative advantage of the economy of Bangladesh in the production of Rice and Fish is determined by endowments, while technology determines the economy's comparative advantage in the case of Services. Hence, given an opportunity to adopt the trading partner's technology, India is likely to adopt the superior technology that Bangladesh uses to produce Services. In the case of India, the endowments of the country accounts for its comparative advantage in the production of as many as 13 goods, namely Sugarcane, Tea, Other agriculture, Livestock, Forestry, Beverages, Jute textile, Other textile, Chemicals, Non-metallic minerals, Iron and steel, Communication and transport equipment, and Electricity and gas. On the other hand, technology determines the country's comparative advantage in the production of Wheat, Jute, Cotton, Wood and wood products, Paper and paper products, Leather, Machinery, Mining and miscellaneous manufacturings. Thus, this model demonstrates the relative importance of the determinants of the pattern of comparative advantage of the economies.

The chapter concludes on the note that, given the present global economic scenario, the formation of an Indo-Bangladesh free trade area seems to be a prospect. In particular, it notes that the ultimate aim of the SAARC region is to make way eventually for a free trade area in the region. Accordingly, SAFTA came into force on 1 January 2006 with the aim of reducing tariffs prevailing in the intra-trade within the SAARC region. This represents a 'historic' move of this region from 'preferential trade' to 'free trade'. Against this backdrop, a Free Trade Area (FTA) option, particularly between India and Bangladesh, needs to be looked at seriously by the governments of the both these countries. Such a free trade arrangement is likely to go a long way towards a deeper integration of the two South Asian countries, such as the freeing of trade in services, free flow of investment, trade facilitation, harmonization and mutual recognition of standards and coordination of macro-economic policies. In particular, it will fetch substantial gains for the economy of Bangladesh by improving its overall competitiveness through access to the marketing network, skill and technology of Indian manufacturers and trading partners. A similar suggestion has not only come up from various policy making levels in the two countries, but has also been put forward by various contemporary researchers in their writings. However, work based on theoretical model building that helps to analyze the viability of free bilateral trade between these two countries has not been attempted, to the best of the present researchers' knowledge. The present study thus makes a modest contribution to this area.

References

Bowen, H., E.E. Leamer and L. Sveikauskas (1987) Multicountry, multifactor tests of the factor abundance theory, *American Economic Review*, 77, pp. 791–809.

Census (1991) *Economic Tables* (Government of India, various volumes).

Centre on Integrated Rural Development for Asia and Pacific, Bangladesh (1996) Database for the General Equilibrium Model: *Input–Output and Related Tables for the Bangladesh Economy 1992–93 MAP, Working Paper Series No. 2.*

Davis, D., D. Weinstein, S. Bradford and K. Shinpo (1997) Using international and Japanese regional data to determine when the factor abundance theory of trade works, *American Economic Review*, 87, pp. 421–446.

Eusufzai, Z. (2001) *Liberalization in the Shadow of a Large Neighbour: A Case of Bangladesh-India Economic Relations* (Dhaka University Press).

Harris, R. (1984) Applied general equilibrium analysis of small open economies with scale economies and imperfect competition, *American Economic Review*, 74, pp. 1016–1032.

Heckscher, E.F. (1919) *'The Effect of Foreign Trade on the Distribution of Income' in Readings in the Theory of International Trade* (Clarendon Press, Oxford).

Helpman, E. (1984) The factor content of foreign trade, *Economic Journal*, 94, pp. 84–94.

Helpman, E. and P.R. Krugman (1985) *Market Structure and Foreign Trade* (Cambridge, MIT Press).

Leamer, E.E. and J. Levinsohn (1995) International trade theory: Evidence, in: G. Grossman and K. Rogoff (eds.), *Handbook of International Economics*, Vol. III, Amsterdam, North-Holland.

Ministry of Labour, Government of India (1995) *Indian Labour Year Book* (Labour Bureau).

Mukherjee, I.N. (2000) India's Trade and Investment linkages with Bangladesh: Identifying the Potential, *International Seminar on Indo-Bangladesh Relations — The New Millennium*, organized by Centre for Research in Indo-Bangladesh Relations, Kolkata and held at the Indian Institute of Chemical Engineers, Jadavpur University, Kolkata, December 7 & 8, 2000.

Ohlin, B. (1933) *Interregional and International Trade* (Cambridge, Mass, Harvard University Press).

Parthasarathi, G. (1990) *Economic Cooperation in the SAARC Region, Potential, Constraints and Policies* (Interest Publication, New Delhi).

Planning Commission, Government of India (1995) *A Technical Note to the Eighth Plan of India (1992–97).*

Pohit, S. and N. Taneja (2000) India's informal trade with Bangladesh and Nepal: A Qualitative Assessment, *Indian Council for Research on International Economic Relations, Working Paper No. 58*, July.

Poudel, K. (2004) *Coverstory*, Spotlight, Vol. 23, No. 24, January 9–15, 2004, nepalnews.com

Pramanik, B. (2000) A profile of Bangladesh foreign trade and prospect of Indo-Bangladesh economic cooperation, *International Seminar on Indo-Bangladesh Relations — The New Millennium*, organized by the Centre for Research in Indo-Bangladesh Relations,

Kolkata and held at the Indian Institute of Chemical Engineers, Jadavpur University, Kolkata, 7 and 8 December, 2000.

Rahman, M. (2000) Bangaldesh-India bilateral trade, an investigation into trade in services, paper prepared under *South Asia Network of Economic Research Institutes (SANEI) Study Programme*, August.

Rahman, S. (1997) Non-reciprocity in Bangladesh-India bilateral trade: A case for market access and domestic competitiveness, *Bangladesh Institute of International and Strategic Studies (BIISS) Journal*, 18, pp. 289–347.

Ricardo, D. (1817) "*On Foreign Trade*", *Principles of Political Economy and Taxation* (Paperback, 2004, Dover Publications, Barnes and Nobles).

Roy, C. and Chakraborty D. (2000) Location of comparative advantages in India and Bangladesh, *Journal of Applied Input–Output Analysis*, 6, pp. 17–35.

Samuelson, P. (1949) International trade and equalization of factor prices, *The Economic Journal*, 58, pp. 163–184.

Sen, S. (1972) Indo-Bangladesh trade: Problems and prospects, foreign trade/Bangladesh, *Economic and Political Weekly*, Vol. 7, No. 15.

Sobhan, R. (ed.) (2002) *Bangladesh-India Relations, Perspective from Civil Society Dialogues, Centre for Policy Dialogue* (The University Press limited, Dhaka, Bangladesh).

Srinivasan, T.N. and Whalley J. (1986) *General Equilibrium Trade Policy Modeling* (Cambridge, MIT Press).

ten Raa, Th. and D. Chakraborty (1991) Indian comparative advantage vis-a-vis Europe as revealed by linear programming of the two economies, *Economic Systems Research*, 3, pp. 111–150.

ten Raa, Th. and P. Mohnen (2001) The location of comparative advantages on the basis of fundamentals only, *Economic Systems Research*, 13, pp. 93–108.

Trefler, D. (1993) International factor pricing differences: Leontief was right! *Journal of Political Economy*, 101, pp. 961–987.

Trefler, D. (1995) The case of missing trade and other mysteries, *American Economic Review*, 85, pp. 1029–1046.

Vanek, J. (1968) *The Factor Proportions Theory: The N-Factor Case*, Kyklos, 21, pp. 749–756.

Waheeduzzaman, A.N.M. (2002) Facilitation of trade and investment among Bangladesh, India and Nepal: Sub-regional cooperation and competitiveness, in: Forrest E. Cookson and A.K.M. Shamsul Alam (eds.), *Towards Greater Sub-Regional Economic Cooperation: Limitations, Obstacles and Benefits* (University Press Limited, Dhaka).

World Bank (1995) *World Development Report* (New York, Oxford University Press).

Chapter 26

Competitive Pressure on the Indian Households: A General Equilibrium Approach

Thijs ten Raa and Amarendra Sahoo

Abstract: How would competitive pressure impact upon the income distribution and the poverty of household groups? We analyze the gains in efficiency and productivity due to competitive pressure, and its distributional effects using a general equilibrium input–output framework. The efficient utilization of the available resources, technical progress and free trade constitute our sources of growth. Welfare would increase under competition, but the income distribution would become more skewed. Rural household groups would stand to lose relative to the urban ones. Urban poverty would be reduced significantly more than rural. In fact, the agricultural worker would even suffer from an increase in poverty. The study shows that competitive pressure has a positive effect on efficiency, productivity and poverty, but an adverse effect on the income distribution in the Indian economy.

Keywords: Efficiency; productivity; applied general equilibrium; income distribution; poverty.

1. Introduction

After an economic crisis, India resorted to a major program of reform in 1991 to improve efficiency, productivity and global competitiveness. Macro- and microeconomic reforms were introduced in industrial, trade and financial policies (Bhagwati and Srinivasan 1993). The Indian economy seemed to be responsive to the reform measures undertaken during 1991–96; it featured globalization and liberalization. GDP grew more than 6.5% per annum during this period. However, reform commentators believe that India's agenda is still unfinished. Bajpai and Sachs (1997), Fischer (2002) and others advocate a greater momentum of reform, with more openness in trade, deregulation of industries, and agricultural and labor market reforms. It is expected that further reform will spur the economy to reallocate its resources efficiently and thus raise productivity. Once the economy operates at its frontier, competitive factor rewards would change the households' income and consumption and thus the welfare distribution. We analyze the consequences with the aid of a general equilibrium model built around a Social Accounting Matrix (SAM).

In the tradition of Kaldor (1956) and Kuznets (1955), Papanek and Kyn (1986) and Fields (1991), Cogneau and Guenard (2002) discussed the issue if growth creates or absorbs inequality. Economic growth creates employment opportunities and thus changes the income distribution. Indian industries were inefficient and hampered by pervasive government control. Although India has had an impressive record of growth since the late 1980s, it still faces massive poverty and inequality. Many studies, viz. Kawani and Subbarao (1990), Jain and Tendulkar (1990), Datt and Ravallion (1992), and Ravallion and Datt (1996), emphasized the influence of growth on poverty in India.

The Indian economy is still well within its production possibility frontier. The inefficiency can be measured by the degree to which the net output vector could be extended given the resource and technology constraints (ten Raa 1995). Despite many skeptical views on free trade versus growth (Rodriguez and Rodrik 1999; Rodrik 1999), there has been strong evidence that free trade enhances growth (Edwards 1992; Sachs and Warner 1995). Trade and development economists have exposited that in the absence of market failure and distortions, trade stimulates growth and improves welfare (Bhagwati 1994; Srinivasan and Bhagawati 1999). Competitive pressure can push the economy towards its production possibility set and trade can augment this set. Thus, the economy becomes not only productively efficient (on its production possibility frontier), but also allocatively efficient (on the utility possibility frontier) (Srinivasan and Bhagwati 1999).

Few studies have analyzed the sources of productivity growth in a general equilibrium framework. Ten Raa and Mohnen (2002) found a shift of the source of productivity growth from technical change to the terms of trade effect for the Canadian economy. Shestalova (2002) used a new technological measure to analyze the total factor productivity (TFP) performance of the three large trading economies endogenizing not only the domestic prices, but also the terms of trade. Ten Raa and Pan (2005) analyzed the personal income distribution using an inter-provincial model in the Chinese economy. We derive the sources of income for different household groups (or the ownership of factor endowments), and their expenditure patterns from the Indian SAM. As we confine our analysis to the income distribution of households at the national level, we adjust the weights attached to the household in the welfare function in Negishi (1960) style, comparing the computed propensities to consume to the observed ones, rather than the trade surpluses in the cited studies.

The rest of the paper is divided into five sections. The theoretical model is presented in the next section. The section after analyzes the basic data set. The fourth section briefly describes the analysis of poverty and inequality measures in our framework. Results and implications of the model are discussed in the fifth section, while the sixth section concludes the paper.

2. The Methodology

The benchmark data set describes the Indian economy for the fiscal year 1994–95. The model distinguishes 21 production sectors. Four rural and five urban household groups are classified by their main source of income. Households have a welfare function of the Leontief type, that is, the observed consumption bundles are presumed to be preferred by the household. We make the small country assumption, under which producers take the world prices of the commodities[1]. The pattern of trade will be endogenous, but the level of imports is controlled by the observed deficit on the balance of payment. Capital, labor, agricultural land and the deficit are considered to constitute the "endowments" of the economy. The model assumes that the competitive market allows labor to move freely among the sectors. However, we assume that capital and land are sector-specific.[2]

Each household group has a consumption demand vector, $f_h d_h D$, where D is the scalar of total consumption demand, f_h is the vector of consumption shares of the commodities and d_h represents the consumption weight attached to the household group. The model maximizes total final private consumption subject to the commodity, factor and trade deficit constraints, while preserving the compositions of the vectors of private consumption of the household groups. The other components of final demand government consumption and investment, are fixed in the model. The shadow prices are used to derive the competitive income of each household group. The implied competitive propensities to consume are matched to the observed ones, by adjusting the consumption weights given to the households. The allocations of activity and shadow prices that are finally obtained constitute the general equilibrium (Negishi 1960).

The SAM provides a consistent data framework for economy-wide models with detailed accounts for industries, categories of working persons, institutional sub-sectors, and various socio-economic household groups. The rows in the SAM state the receipts (or income) of the different accounts and the columns the expenditures (or costs). Table 1 gives a bird's eye view of the SAM we have used for our analysis. The input–output table is in the first cell. The first column also shows how factor endowments owned by the different household groups contribute to the production process (the value added cell). The second column shows the factor incomes returned, by ownership. The first row displays household consumption and the other component of final demand.

[1]India's share in world merchandise exports and imports in value terms have been only 1.1 percent and 1.4 percent respectively; its shares in world exports and imports of commercial services have been only 1.5 percent and 1.8 percent respectively (WTO 2005).

[2]In an economy like India, capital and land may not be mobile in the medium run. Most of the capital and land are highly specialized due to its inherent technology, product-specific, etc.

Table 1: A Schematic SAM

	Production account	Factors of production	Households	Government	Capital account	Rest of world	Total
Production account	I–O		Household consumption	Government consumption	Investment demand	Net exports	Total demand
Factors of production	Value added						Value added
Households		Factor income of households					Total household income
Government Account			Taxes				Government income
Capital account			Household savings	Government savings		Foreign savings	Total savings
Rest of world							
Total	Value of output	Value added	Total household expenditure	Total Govt. outlay	Total investment		

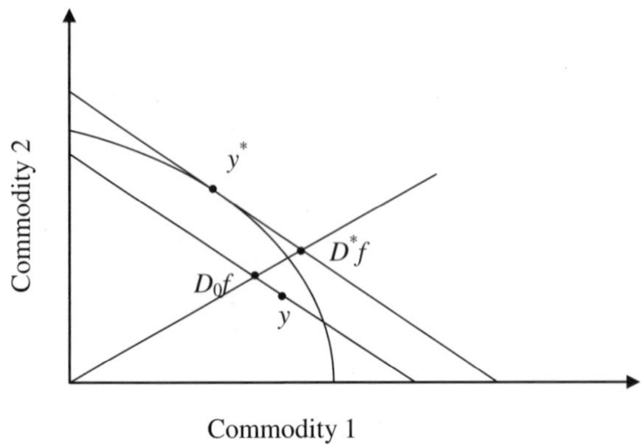

Fig. 1: Movement towards the frontier and efficiency.

The basic idea of the efficiency gain on the frontier can be illustrated graphically. This frontier can be reached by optimal allocations of factors of production across the sectors and by re-allocation of trade with the rest of the world (Figure 1). In Figure 1, y and D_0f denote the actual production and domestic final demand on the international trade budget line. As shown by ten Raa and Mohnen (2002), D_0f can be expanded to D^*f by producing y^* instead of y. Notice that the optimal pattern of trade is reversed in Figure 1. The following linear program determines the optimal allocation:

$$\max_{D,x,t} De \sum_{h=1}^{9} f_h d_h$$

subject to

$$x \geq Ax + \sum_{h=1}^{9} f_h d_h D + g + \begin{pmatrix} t \\ 0 \end{pmatrix}, \quad kx \leq K, \quad lx \leq L, \quad nx \leq N,$$

$$-\pi t \leq -\pi t^0, \quad x \geq 0.$$

Here the exogenous variables and parameters are the following:

f_h column vector of hth household's consumption share (21-dimensional)

d_h a scalar of share of consumption demand of each hth household in total consumption demand

e a unit row vector

A a 21×21-dimensional matrix of intermediate flow coefficients
g a 21-dimensional vector of fixed final demand comprising of government consumption demand, investment demand.
K a 21-dimension column vector of sector-specific capital stock
N total land endowment in the economy
L total labor endowment in the economy
k a diagonal matrix with sector-specific technical coefficients of capital
n a diagonal matrix with sector-specific technical coefficients of land
l row vector of technical coefficients of labor
π a 19-dimension row vector of terms of trade in dollar term.
t^0 a 19-dimensional vector of observed net exports

And the endogenous variables are:

x a 21-dimensional column vector of economy's output
D scalar of overall private consumption demand in the economy
t a 19-dimensional vector of net exports.

The primal problem expands the final private consumption demand (D) given the household groups weights, d_h. The weights will be adjusted as to equilibrate the model. The first constraint is the commodity constraint, i.e. the material balance, while the next three constraints are for capital, land and labor, respectively. The fourth constraint states that the net exports valued at world prices cannot conflict the existing trade deficit.

The dual problem reads:

$$\min_{P,r_1,r_2,w,\varepsilon} \quad r_1K + r_2N + wL - pg - \varepsilon\pi t^0$$

subject to

$$p \le pA + r_1k + r_2n + wl, \quad p\sum_{h=1}^{9} f_h d_h = e\sum_{h=1}^{9} f_h d_h, \quad p = \varepsilon\pi.$$

In the dual problem, the shadow prices p, r_1, r_2, w and ε are for output, capital, land, labor and purchasing power parity, respectively. The first dual constraint reflects that the factor cost of production exceeds value added. For active sectors, there is equality (ten Raa 1995). The second dual constraint takes care of the price normalization. The last constraint equalizes the prices of the tradeable sectors with their opportunity cost under the assumption of free trade.

The idea is to compute the propensity to consume at the competitive prices for each household group and to equalize relative propensities to consume with the observed ones. If the propensity to consume of the first household group turns out disproportionately high, its higher consumption demand signals that we have attributed too much welfare to this group in the social welfare function. We adjust the weight (downward in this case) and re-compute the optimal allocation given by linear program. Through an iteration process, we arrive at the optimum pattern of consumption and income for each household group. In a solution to the linear program, the households consume $pf_h d_h D$, whereas their incomes are $r_1\theta_K^h K + r_2\theta_N^h N + w\theta_L^h L$, given the household groups' ($h = 1,\ldots,9$) shares θ_K^h, θ_N^h and θ_L^h of the capital, land and labor endowments. The implied propensities to consume are $m_h^1(d) = (pf_h d_h D)/(r_1\theta_K^h K + r_2\theta_N^h N + w\theta_L^h L)$. The observed propensities to consume, $m_h^0(d)$, valued at competitive prices for current consumption are similar, but with the optimal consumption baskets $f_h d_h D$ replaced by the observed baskets. If a household category h has a low optimal propensity to consume, we rerun the linear program, giving it more weight in final consumption, d_h. There are eight such independent weights (one of the nine weights is determined by the adding-up condition) and the condition that nine household groups have equal optimal/observed ratios of the propensities to consume amounts to eight equations. In equilibrium, the optimal/observed ratios of the propensities to consume are the same for all household groups. Mathematically, the equilibrium is found as in ten Raa and Pan (2005).

3. Data

We use the SAM of Pradhan, Sahoo and Saluja (1999), with some adjustments. The intermediate flows in the SAM are based on the commodity-by-commodity matrix, which we have aggregated from the original 60 commodities down to 21. Households are classified according to their principal sources of income. There are four rural and five urban occupational household groups. The 1996 MIMAP-India Survey (NCAER 2000) provides the information on the factors of production, and the income and consumption distributions. Table 2 shows that the bulk of rural income derives from agriculture, while urban income stems nearly exclusively from the

Table 2: Sources of Income for Household Groups (in percentage).

Household categories	Agriculture	Non-agriculture	Total
All-India	32.14	67.86	100
Rural			
Self employed in agriculture	87.12	12.88	100
Self employed in non-agriculture	12.87	87.13	100
Agriculture wage earners	88.52	11.48	100
Non-agriculture wage earners	10.32	89.68	100
Other households	12.53	87.47	100
Total rural	55.66	44.34	100
Urban			
Agriculture households	74.91	25.09	100
Self employed in non-agriculture	0.95	99.05	100
Salaried earners	0.9	99.1	100
Non-agriculture wage earners	2.19	97.81	100
Other households	1.03	98.97	100
Total urban	2.46	97.54	100

Source: Pradhan and Roy (2003).

other activities. The rural agricultural households derive around 87% of their income from the agriculture. The other rural household groups derive between 87% and 89% of their income from non-agricultural activities.

Table 3 shows that the urban 'salaried class' (12% of the population) secures a big chunk of the wage bill (34%), whereas 'agriculture labor' (22% of the population) gets a meager part (17%). The small 'non-agriculture self-employed' household group (5.4% of the population) lays claim to the bulk of capital income (33%). The rural 'cultivator' household group also enjoys a great share of capital income (20%), but they are many (24% of the population). This group dominates agricultural land. Table 4 reveals that rural households have a rather uniform pattern of consumption, with the bulk spent on primary, mainly agricultural, goods. The vast majority of the urban households consume services.

The benchmark coefficients for the factor input are given in Table 5. The Annual Survey of Industry (ASI) (Government of India, 1994–95) gives information on the number of employees engaged in the different registered manufacturing industries and their total emoluments. We compute the average wage rate for each registered industry. Because of the difficulty in procuring information on unregistered industries, we apply the wage rates of the registered industries to the unregistered ones. The application of the

Table 3: Percentages of Income Across Household Groups by Sources.

Household	Population	Wage income	Capital income	Land rent	Total
Total	100	100	100	100	100
Rural					
Cultivator	24.22	13.36	20.46	78.49	23.92
Agriculture labor	22.08	16.85	0.46	0.56	9.97
Artisans	13.85	10.01	14.81	15.5	12.12
Other households	14.76	14.8	3.76	4.18	10.21
Urban					
Agriculture households	1.24	0.74	1.62	1.28	1.06
Non-agriculture self-employed	5.4	6.03	32.69	0	12.97
Salaried	12.19	34.34	14.26	0	24.04
Non-agriculture labor	2.81	2.96	3.54	0	2.74
Other households	3.44	0.9	8.4	0	2.96

Source: Calculated from the SAM for India, Pradhan *et al.* (1999).

Table 4: Composition of Household Expenditure.

Household	Primary	Secondary	Services	Total	Share in total spending
Rural					
Cultivator	41.16	26.10	32.74	100	0.12
Agriculture labor	47.17	25.71	27.11	100	0.06
Artisans	41.18	28.08	30.75	100	0.06
Other households	42.23	29.07	28.70	100	0.05
Urban					
Agriculture households	43.77	23.76	32.47	100	0.01
Non-agriculture self-employed	35.07	24.86	40.07	100	0.06
Salaried	24.63	31.36	44.00	100	0.11
Non-agriculture labor	44.37	25.32	30.31	100	0.02
Other households	19.08	27.46	53.46	100	0.02

Source: Calculated from the SAM for India, Pradhan *et al.* (1999).

wage rates to the SAM-based labor value added statistics yields estimates of the numbers of employees in the manufacturing industries. Unfortunately, ASI does not give information on agriculture sectors, mining and quarrying, construction and service sectors. Using the information on the numbers of main and marginal workers engaged in these activities given by the Government of India (1991), we compute the benchmark wage rate for these sectors. An unemployment rate of 6% is applied to get the labor

Table 5: Factor Prices and Coefficients Across the Sectors.

Sectors	Capital/ output	Labor/ output	Land/ output	Average wage*	Rent of capital*	Rent of land*
S1 Food grains	0.065	4.88	0.276	0.065	1.000	1.000
S2 Other agriculture	0.075	5.75	0.302	0.065	1.000	1.000
S3 Crude oil, natural gas	0.594	2.70		0.089	1.000	
S4 Other mining and quarrying	0.454	2.03		0.089	1.000	
S5 Food products, etc.	0.133	0.48		0.172	1.000	
S6 Textiles	0.117	0.63		0.262	1.000	
S7 Other traditional manufacturing.	0.162	0.58		0.289	1.000	
S8 Petroleum products	0.268	0.15		0.461	1.000	
S9 Finished petrochemicals	0.276	0.13		0.461	1.000	
S10 Fertilizer	0.230	0.20		0.365	1.000	
S11 Other chemicals	0.225	0.23		0.365	1.000	
S12 Non-metallic products	0.170	0.51		0.236	1.000	
S13 Basic metal industries	0.156	0.18		0.444	1.000	
S14 Metallic products	0.157	0.55		0.309	1.000	
S15 Capital goods	0.175	0.49		0.449	1.000	
S16 Other manufacturing	0.269	0.70		0.342	1.000	
S17 Construction	0.075	0.46		0.810	1.000	
S18 Electricity	0.277	0.30		0.383	1.000	
S19 Infrastructure service	0.377	0.80		0.311	1.000	
S20 Financial service	0.531	0.75		0.311	1.000	
S21 Other services	0.243	1.65		0.289	1.000	

Source: Calculated from the SAM for India, Pradhan *et al.* (1999).
*Wages are calculated from Annual Survey of India (various issues), Government of India (1991) and rent to capital and land are assumed to be one at observed level.

constraint in the model.[3] We assume that land is used in agriculture only and we assume it is fully utilized. We assume that capital and land rents are uniform across sectors. Table 6 shows the capacity utilization rates for different sectors, taken from different sources.

[3]The unemployment rate is the ratio of unemployed to the total labor force based on daily status. The source is National Sample Survey Organization, Report no. 409, "Employment and Unemployment in India, 1993–94: NSS Fiftieth Round," July 1993–June 1994, New Delhi, 1997.

Table 6: Capacity Utilization and Sources of Information.

Sectors		Capacity utilization (%)	Sources
S1	Food grains	81	Gupta *et al.* (2000) for irrigation
S2	Other agriculture	81	Gupta, *et al.* (2000) for irrigation
S3	Crude oil, natural gas	88	Indiainfoline.com (2003)
S4	Other mining and quarrying	85	Government of India (1996) for coal
S5	Food products, etc.	49	Government of India (1992a)
S6	Textiles	69	Government of India (1992a)
S7	Other traditional manufacturing	58	Government of India (2001)
S8	Petroleum products	88	Indiainfoline.com (2003)
S9	Finished petrochemicals	78	Government of India (2001)
S10	Fertilizer	90	Trivedi *et al.*.(1998)
S11	Other chemicals	78	Directories-today.com (2003)
S12	Non-metallic products	71	Government of India (1992b) for Cement industry
S13	Basic metal industries	78	Government of India (1992b) for aluminum industry
S14	Metal products	55	Government of India (2001)
S15	Capital goods	83	Government of India (2001)
S16	Other manufacturing	78	Government of India (2001)
S17	Construction	75	Indiainfoline.com (2003)
S18	Electricity	41	Economic Survey, 2000–2001,
S19	Infrastructure service	75	Indiainfoline.com (2003)
S20	Financial service	100	Authors' own assumption
S21	Other services	52	Govt. of India (1987)

4. Income Distribution and Poverty

This section of the study is based on Pradhan and Sahoo (2006). The measurement of poverty requires an estimation of the income distribution within the each group. The distribution will be used to evaluate the group poverty incidence. The implicit assumption is that, given the within-group variances, the intra-group distribution changes proportionally with the change in mean income. For the within-group distribution, we use a log-normal frequency distribution, $f(y) = \exp \frac{-[\log(y)-\mu]^2}{2\sigma}/(\sqrt{2\pi\sigma})$, parameterized by the log-mean μ and the standard deviation σ. The FGT poverty measure (Foster, Greer and Thorbecke 1984) is suitable for estimating group-wise poverty. It is defined by $P_\alpha^h = \frac{1}{n^h}\sum_{i=1}^{q^h}\left[\frac{z-y_i^h}{z}\right]^\alpha$, $h = 1,\ldots,9$, where n^h is the population size in household group h (i.e. occupational class), q^h the number of people below poverty line, z the poverty line[4] and y_i^h the income of the ith person in household group h. α is a measure of poverty aversion; the most commonly used values are 0, 1 and 2. P_0 is the 'head-count ratio measure', P_1 the 'poverty-gap measure' and P_2 the 'distributionally sensitive measure.' In this paper, we use only the head-count ratio of poverty measure; it is simply the fraction of households living below the poverty line.

When income distribution is given in the form of group data, the poverty measure requires a continuous income density functions, one for each household group, and the FGT poverty index can be expressed as $P_\alpha^h = \int_0^z \left(\frac{z-y}{z}\right)^\alpha f^h(y)dy \; h = 1, \ldots, 9$. By the assumption of the log-normal distribution and a transformation, the 'head-count ratio' becomes $P_0 = N\left(\frac{\log z - \mu}{\sigma}\right)$, where N is the standard normal distribution.

For each household group, we estimate μ and σ using the MIMAP-India household survey data (see Table 7). We estimate the observed level P_0 for household groups by applying information on income distribution from the SAM. However, this estimated observed poverty ratios at the observed

Table 7: Parameters of Lognormal Distribution.

Households	Log-mean (μ)	Standard deviation (σ)
Rural		
Cultivator	5.85	0.76
Agriculture labor	5.33	0.60
Artisan	5.55	0.79
Other household	5.93	0.72
Urban		
Farmer	5.41	1.05
Non-agricultural self-employed	6.36	0.89
Salaried class	6.68	0.76
Casual labor	5.54	0.82
Other household	6.47	1.35

Source: Pradhan and Roy (2003).

[4]Poverty lines for rural and urban are taken from NCAER (2000). The government of India (1993) estimated that the (nutritional) poverty line for Rural and Urban India for the 1973–74 year based on the pattern of consumption expenditures of households. NCAER (2000) revised the 1993–94 poverty lines by using the consumer price index number for agriculture labor and industrial workers for rural and urban areas respectively.

Table 8: Poverty Head-Count Ratio P_0 at Observed Period.

Households	Poverty (1994–95)	
	Estimated	Official*
Rural	0.3943	0.3979
Cultivator	0.3679	0.2946
Agriculture labor	0.5497	0.5675
Artisan	0.3586	0.4404
Other households	0.2041	0.2451
Urban	0.2837	0.2245
Farmer	0.7396	0.6179
Non-agricultural self-employed	0.3860	0.2389
Salaried class	0.1424	0.1038
Casual labor	0.6103	0.5910
Other household	0.2135	0.2912

*Pradhan and Roy (2003).

level could be different from that officially reported by Pradhan and Roy (2003) due to differences in assumption regarding distributions and other adjustments in the SAM (see Table 8). The optimum solutions of our general equilibrium model yields a set of new relative prices and mean income of household groups, which are used to calculate the changes in poverty line and mean income (μ) from the observed level. We measure inequality by the Gini coefficient.[5]

5. Results and Implications

The main objectives of the economic reforms in India have been to accelerate the growth of the economy by removing the distortions, domestic as well as trade, and to mitigate the poverty situation. Table 9 shows that since 1983, the rural poverty ratio has been higher than the urban. The poverty ratio has declined since the late 1980s.

If these policies of economic reform were realized to the fullest theoretical extent, the competitive pressure would twist the distribution of income. The Indian economy could expand by a factor of 1.42, indicating

[5]Our general equilibrium model provides the income for each group. If the log variances are known, then log means can be calculated from the following relationship $\mu = \ln(y) - \frac{1}{2}\sigma^2$, where y is the arithmetic mean income, σ^2 is log variance and μ is the log mean (Dervis, de Melo and Robinson 1984).

Table 9: Poverty Head-Count Ratio.

Year	Rural	Urban	Total
1973–74	56.4	49.0	54.9
1977–78	53.1	45.2	51.3
1983	45.7	40.8	44.5
1987–88	39.1	38.2	38.9
1993–94	37.3	32.4	36.0
1999–00	27.1	23.6	26.1
2007*	21.1	15.1	19.3

*Poverty projection for 2007.
Source: Government of India (2003).

that it operates at an efficiency level of 70%.[6] This would come with a great increase in the Gini coefficient from the observed 0.2739 to 0.3424. However, poverty (the head-count ratio P_0 defined in the previous section) would decline for the overall rural as well the overall urban households (see Table 10). The decline is quite significant for the urban household and marginal for the rural households.

Table 10: Household Consumption Weights, Income Inequality and Poverty Head-Count Ratio.

Households	Ratio of optimum to observed			Percentage change in poverty head-count
	Consumption weights	Income	Consumption	
Rural				**−0.62**
Cultivator	0.792	0.931	1.12	2.44
Rural agricultural labor	0.795	0.935	1.13	3.51
Artisan	1.072	1.261	1.52	−11.69
Rural other	0.881	1.036	1.25	−2.10
Urban				**−11.38**
Urban farmer	1.157	1.360	1.64	−17.39
Urban non agricultural self	1.458	1.714	2.07	−16.72
Urban salary	0.996	1.171	1.41	−5.57
Urban casual labor	1.196	1.406	1.70	−23.86
Urban other	1.513	1.779	2.15	−15.42
Gini coefficient	0.2739			0.3424
Expansion vector	1.00			1.42

[6]As $1/1.42 = 0.70$.

When the economy is allowed to be fully competitive, factors are fully utilized and the mobile factor, labor, is reallocated to the sectors with strong demand. The assumption of labor mobility gives rise to a single competitive wage rate. It is seen to be lower than the benchmark average wage (see Table 11). The rents of capital and land are determined by the interplay of demand and supply of each sector; and differ by industries. We observe that the demand for capital is stronger than that for labor and land. Land used in the 'other agriculture' sector is non-binding in the optimum, yielding a zero shadow price, while land used in the 'food grains' sector marginally gains in factor reward.

The rent of capital in all the industries other than the intensive-intensive primary sectors would increase, viz. agricultural sectors (S1 and S2), 'crude oil and natural gas' (S3) and, 'other mining and quarrying' (S4),

Table 11: Change in Output, Prices of Factors and Commodities.

Sectors		Ratio of optimum to benchmark				
		Factor prices			Prices	Output
		Labor	Land	Capital		
S1	Food grains	0.92	0.111		1.005	1.000
S2	Other agriculture	0.92	0.00		1.005	0.766
S3	Crude oil, natural gas	0.92		0.94	1.005	1.136
S4	Other mining and quarrying	0.92		1.04	1.005	1.176
S5	Food products, etc.	0.92		2.43	1.005	2.041
S6	Textiles	0.92		2.72	1.005	1.449
S7	Other traditional manufacturing	0.92		2.86	1.005	1.724
S8	Petroleum products	0.92		1.36	1.005	1.136
S9	Finished petrochemicals	0.92		1.56	1.005	1.282
S10	Fertilizer	0.92		1.45	1.005	1.111
S11	Other chemicals	0.92		1.70	1.005	1.282
S12	Non-metallic products	0.92		2.25	1.005	1.408
S13	Basic metal industries	0.92		2.06	1.005	1.282
S14	Metallic products	0.92		3.21	1.005	1.818
S15	Capital goods	0.92		2.36	1.005	1.205
S16	Other manufacturing	0.92		1.96	1.005	1.282
S17	Construction*	0.92			0.610	1.062
S18	Electricity*	0.92			0.527	1.362
S19	Infrastructure service	0.92		1.89	1.005	1.333
S20	Financial service	0.92		1.26	1.005	1.000
S21	Other services	0.92		4.10	1.005	1.923

*These are the nontradeable sectors.

and nontradeable sectors viz. 'construction' (S17) and 'electricity' (S18) (see Table 10). We observe that the agriculture sector has no comparative advantage. Agricultural output would not increase or drop (in the 'other agriculture' sector). Labor is thus released to the manufacturing and service sectors in which enjoy a strong comparative advantage. This observation is very close to that of Wood and Calandrino (2000). Labor is absorbed by the sectors with low capacity utilization rates.

As competitive factor prices of capital increase more than the other factors, we expect that household groups owning more capital stand to gain. Table 5 shows that among *rural* household groups, the 'cultivator' households own the most capital as well as land. Their income would decline though, because competitive land rent is low. The low competitive wage, and the near non-existent of capital and land rents in agricultural sectors, adversely affect the income of the rural 'agriculture labor' and 'cultivator' classes. Only the 'artisan' household group stands to gain. The worst affected household group in the economy is the rural 'agricultural labor', which has a very low share of capital and large labor endowment.

Urban household groups fare better under competition. The 'salaried class' with maximal labor endowment experiences the lowest gain in income, while the greatest gain is enjoyed by the 'non-agricultural self-employed' household group, which own capital (see Table 5 and 10). The wide income disparity between the rural and urban household groups gives rise to an increase in the Gini coefficient. Adverse income effects among most rural household groups explain the low gain in the rural poverty ratio. Only the 'artisan' household group shows a significant decline in poverty; the 'agricultural labor' suffers heavily from an increase in poverty ratio (see Table 10). The poverty ratio increases by around 19% for the rural 'agriculture labor' household group. As the ratio is already high for this group, (0.55 according to Table 8), the contribution is disastrous for this group. On the other hand, urban groups would enjoy a sharp decline in poverty.

6. Conclusion

The efficiency pursuit of the Indian economy comes at the cost of adverse income effects, particularly among the rural household groups. The income distribution would become more skewed. Households dependent on labor and land tend to suffer. The urban household groups attain a better welfare distribution, with a significant decline in the poverty headcount ratio. Not so for the rural household groups; the only rural household group, that stands to decline in poverty is the 'artisan'. The worst victim of competition is expected be the 'agricultural labor'. Similarly, among the urban household groups, the relative gain for 'salaried class' is low.

References

Bajpai, N. and J.D. Sachs (1997) India's economic reforms: some lessons from East Asia, *Journal of International Trade and Economic Development*, 6(2), pp. 135–164.

Bhagwati, J. and T.N. Srinivasan (1993) India's economic reform. Paper prepared for the Ministry of Finance, Government of India, Delhi.

Bhagwati, J. (1994) Free trade: Old and new challenges, *Economic Journal*, 104(423), pp. 231–246.

Cogneau, D. and C. Guenard (2002) Can relationship be found between inequality and growth. Documents de travail DIAL, in Dial-Paris Development Seminar, Paris.

Datt, G. and M. Ravallion (1992) Growth and redistribution components of changes in poverty measures: A decomposition analysis with applications to Brazil and India in the 1980s, *Journal of Development Economics*, 38, pp. 275–295.

Edwards, S. (1992) Trade orientation, distortions, and growth in developing countries, *Journal of Development Economics*, 39(1), pp. 31–57.

Fields, G.S. (1991) Growth and income distribution, in G. Psacharopoulos (eds.) *Essays on Poverty, Equity and Growth* (Oxford: Pergamon Press).

Fischer, S. (2002) Breaking out of the third world: India's economic imperative. A speech prepared for delivery at the India Today Conclave, New Delhi, January 22.

Foster, J.E., J. Greer and E. Thorbecke (1984) A class of decomposable poverty measures, *Econometrica*, 52(3), pp. 761–766.

Government of India (1991) Census of India. Ministry of Home Affair, New Delhi.

Government of India (1992a) All India census of small-scale industrial units 1987–88. Ministry of Small Scale Industries, New Delhi.

Government of India (1992b) India's eighth five-year plan: 1992–1997. Planning Commission, New Delhi.

Government of India (1993) *Report of the Expert Group on Estimates of Proportion and Number of Poor*. Planning Commission, New Delhi.

Government of India (1994–95) Annual Survey of Industries, Central Statistical Organisation, Department of Statistics, Ministry of Planning and Programme Implementation, New Delhi.

Government of India (1996) Public sector undertakings: A case for autonomy in pricing. Ministry of Personnel, Public Grievances and Pensions, New Delhi.

Government of India (2001a) *Hand Book of Industrial Policy and Statistics*. Office of Economic Advisor, Ministry of Commerce and Industry, New Delhi.

Government of India (2001b) *The Economic Survey 2000–2001*. Ministry of Finance, New Delhi.

Government of India (2003) *The Economic Survey 2002–2003*. Ministry of Finance, New Delhi.

Gupta, S.K., P.S. Minhas, S.K. Sondhi, N.K. Tyagi and J.S.P. Yadav (2000) Water resource management, in: J.S.P. Yadav and G.B. Sing (eds.) Proceedings Natural Resource Management for Agricultural Production in India, International Conference of Managing Natural Resources for the 21st Century, New Delhi.

http://www.directories-today.com, Industry overview on chemicals and petrochemicals, 2003.

http://www.Indiainfoline.com, Indiainfoline news letter on different sectors, 2003.

http://www.Indiainfoline.com (2003) Indiainfoline debate on construction and infrastructure, September 23.

Jain, L.R. and S.D. Tendulkar (1990) The role of growth and distribution in the observed change in headcount ratio measure of poverty: A decomposition exercise for India, *Indian Economic Review*, 25(2), pp. 165–205.

Kakwani, N. and K. Subarao (1990) Rural poverty and its alleviation in India, *Economic and Political Weekly*, 25, pp. A2–A16.

Kaldor, N. (1956) Alternative theories of distribution, *Reviews of Economic Studies*, 23(2), pp. 94–100.

Kuznets, S. (1955) Economic growth and income inequality, *American Economic Review*, 45(1), pp. 1–28.

NCAER (2000) MIMAP-India Survey Report. National Council of Applied Economic Research, Vol. 2, New Delhi.

Negishi, T. (1960) Welfare economics and existence of an equilibrium for a competitive economy, *Metrorconomica*, 12, pp. 92–97.

Pananek, G. and O. Kyn (1986) The effect on income distribution of development, the growth rate and economic strategy, *Journal of Development Economics*, 23, pp. 55–65.

Pradhan, B.K., A. Sahoo and M.R. Saluja (1999) A social accounting matrix for India, 1994–95, *Economic and Political Weekly*, 36(48), pp. 3378–3394.

Pradhan, B.K. and A. Sahoo (2003) Impact of trade liberalization on household welfare and poverty. MIMAP working paper, IDRC, Ottawa, Canada.

Ravallion, M. and G. Datt (1996) How important to India's poor in the sectoral composition of economic growth? *World Bank Economic Review*, 10(1), pp. 1–25.

Rodriguez, F. and D. Rodrik (1999) Trade policy and economic growth: A skeptic's guide to cross-national evidence. NBER Working paper No. W7081.

Rodrik, D. (1999) Making openness work: The new global economy and thee developing countries. The Overseas Development Council, Washington, D.C.

Sachs, J.D. and A. Warner (1995) Economics reforms and the process of global integration, *Brookings Paper on Economic Activity*, pp. 1–118.

Shestalova, V. (2002) Essays in productivity and efficiency. Doctoral dissertation, CentER, University of Tilburg, The Netherlands.

Srinivasan, T.N. and J. Bhagwati (1999) Outward-orientation and development: Are revisionists right? Center Discussion Paper No. 806, Economic Growth Center, Yale University.

ten Raa, Th. (1995) *Linear Anaylysis of Competitive Economics*, LSE Hand books in Economics (Prentice Hall-Harvester Wheatsheaf, Hempstead).

ten Raa, Th. and P. Mohnen (2002) Neoclassical growth accounting and frontier analysis: A synthesis, *Journal of Productivity Analysis*.

ten Raa, Th. (2004) A neoclassical analysis of TFP using input–output prices, in: E. Dietzenbacher and M. Lahr (eds.) *Wassily Leontief and Input–Output Economics* (Cambridge University Press), pp. 151–165.

ten Raa, Th. and H. Pan (2005) Competitive pressure on China: Income inequality, *Regional Science & Urban Economics*, 35, pp. 671–699.

Trivedi, A.N., J. Sathaye and M. Mukhopadhaya (1998) Energy efficiency and environmental management options in the Indian fertilizer Industry, ADB Technical Assistance Project (TA-2403-IND), Forest Knol, California.

Wood, A. and M. Calandrino (2000) When the other giant awakens: Trade and human resources in India. Institute of Development Studies, University of Sussex, England.

WTO (2005) World trade, prospects for 2005, Press releases, Press/401, 14th April.

Index